Pietro Bembo on Etna

The Ascent of a Venetian Humanist

GARETH D. WILLIAMS

OXFORD
UNIVERSITY PRESS

OXFORD
UNIVERSITY PRESS

Oxford University Press is a department of the University of Oxford. It furthers the University's objective of excellence in research, scholarship, and education by publishing worldwide. Oxford is a registered trade mark of Oxford University Press in the UK and certain other countries.

Published in the United States of America by Oxford University Press
198 Madison Avenue, New York, NY 10016, United States of America.

First issued as an Oxford University Press paperback, 2022

CIP data is on file at the Library of Congress
ISBN 978–0–19–027229–6 (hardback) | ISBN 978–0–19–760318–5 (paperback)

1 3 5 7 9 8 6 4 2

Paperback printed by LSC Communications, United States of America

For Claudia

Contents

List of Illustrations

Preface

This study aims to contribute what it can to modern scholarship on Pietro Bembo in general, and on his 1496 *De Aetna* in particular, by exploring the contextual background and the imaginative capacities that crucially shape his portrayal of his youthful ascent of the volcano in 1493. The Bembo presented in these pages offers much more than a one-dimensional account of the facts, sights, and findings of his climb. Far more important in this study is his eye for creative elaboration, or for transforming his literal experience on the mountain into a meditation on (i) his coming of age at a remove from the conventional career path expected of one of his station within the Venetian patriciate; (ii) the complex literary history of Greco-Roman treatments of the Etna theme; and (iii) the potential of the Etnean landscape to serve, via Bembo's artful manipulation of its symbolic properties, as a highly inventive mode of self-portraiture through figurative projection onto the natural canvas. Many debts have been incurred during the evolution of this study: for help and advice on many fronts I thank Michael Cole, Marco Fantuzzi, Andrew Feldherr, Charles Hope, Ermanno Malaspina, Silvia Montiglio, Roberto Nicosia, Laura Nuvoloni and Gareth Schmeling. Michael Reeve gave important encouragement at a moment when the project was taking embryonic shape. Three readers for Oxford University Press offered trenchant but invaluable criticisms of an earlier draft; in particular, Craig Kallendorf provided precious guidance for improvement on multiple fronts, and I have greatly benefitted from his advice. James Uden generously read the entire manuscript with his customary acumen and keen wit. So too did James Zetzel, who also made important interventions on many points of argument and scrutinized my translation of *De Aetna* with the greatest care: I gratefully acknowledge here more than two decades of fine friendship, wise counsel and many acts of kindness. I thank Leslie Safford for her excellent copy-editing; Prabhu Chinnasamy for managing the production process so efficiently; and John Veranes for his help in gaining permissions for the illustrations used in this book. But my greatest debt at Oxford University Press is to Stefan Vranka for his general encouragement of this project from its inception, for his patience and good humor as the chapters went through many stages of rewriting, and for his expertise in seeing the end-product through the press. I am also grateful to Columbia's Stanwood Cockey Lodge Foundation for a subvention toward the costs of production. I thank Joseph Solodow for his eagle eye in alerting me to some typographical errors that have been corrected in this paperback version. The dedication expresses my greatest debt of all.

Abbreviations

CIL	*Corpus Inscriptionum Latinarum*. 1853–. Berlin.
D-K	Diels, H. and Kranz, W. eds. 1952. *Die Fragmente der Vorsokratiker*. 3 vols. 6th ed. Berlin.
E-K	Edelstein, L. and Kidd, I. G. eds. 1989. *Posidonius, I: The Fragments*. 2nd ed. Cambridge Classical Texts and Commentaries 13. Cambridge.
FGrHist	Jacoby, F. ed. 1923–1958. *Die Fragmente der griechischen Historiker*. Leiden.
IG	*Inscriptiones Graecae*. 1873–. Berlin.
LS	Lewis, C. T. and Short, C. eds. 1879. *A Latin Dictionary*. Oxford.
LSJ	Liddell, H. G. and Scott, R. eds. 1968. Revised by Stuart Jones, H. and McKenzie, R. *A Greek-English Lexicon*. 9th ed. Oxford.
OLD	Glare, P. W. ed. 1968–1982. *Oxford Latin Dictionary*. Oxford.
RE	Pauly, A. F. von, ed. 1893–. Revised by Wissowa, G. et al. *Realencyclopädie der classischen Altertumswissenschaft*. Stuttgart.
Roscher	Roscher, W. H. ed. 1884–1937. *Ausführliches Lexikon der griechischen und römischen Mythologie*. Leipzig.
SVF	Arnim, H. von, ed. 1903–1924. *Stoicorum Veterum Fragmenta*. Leipzig.
TLL	*Thesaurus Linguae Latinae*. 1900–. Leipzig.

Introduction

ON MAY 4, 1492, Pietro Bembo (1470–1547), that flamboyant young Venetian patrician and future cardinal, at last set foot in the city of Messina after an arduous journey by land and sea from Venice.[1] He had traveled to Sicily with Angelo Gabriele, his friend from boyhood,[2] to study Greek under the distinguished Byzantine émigré scholar and teacher, Constantine Lascaris (1434–1501); after settling in Messina in 1466, Lascaris had been appointed in 1467 to a professorship at the Greek school attached to the Basilian monastery of San Salvatore in Messina. During his more than two-year stay in Sicily, Pietro briefly interrupted his studies to visit and climb Mount Etna and, after his return to Venice in the summer of 1494, he wrote of that adventure in the slender yet engaging work that is the focus of this study: his *De Aetna*. This was the first Latin text—or, more strictly, the first text entirely in Latin—to be published by the Aldine Press at Venice, appearing in February 1496 (1495 *more veneto*).[3] Set in the Bembo country retreat that was known as Noniano, outside Padua,[4] it is cast in the form of a dialogue between Pietro and his father, Bernardo (1433–1519), that distinguished humanist, diplomatist, and devoted servant of the Republic, who eagerly receives his son's account of his ascent. For convenience, a brief synopsis of the dialogue is offered at the end of this introduction, and the entire text is presented, with my own translation, at the end of this study. Within the dialogue Pietro enthusiastically broaches his Etna topic; that enthusiasm is further attested by Pietro's reaction to a letter that he received from Messina

1. The date is stated by Pietro himself: Travi (1987) 4 *Letter* 2, beginning *Messanam venimus ad quartum nonas Maias . . .*

2. For Angelo (1470–1533), Dal Borgo (1998).

3. I.e., February 1496 by the Julian calendar, but 1495 by Venetian fashion, the Venetian calendar year traditionally beginning on March 1. For the facing Latin translation already deployed in the 1495 Aldine edition of Lascaris' Ἐπιτομή, see Chapter 3 p. 132.

4. For Noniano, Chapter 6 p. 224 and then p. 311 and n.7.

many years later—a letter that just so happens to be dated to May 4, 1536, forty-four years to the day after the young Pietro first set foot in Messina on May 4, 1492.

This letter was written by the eminent Sicilian mathematician and astronomer of Greek descent, Francesco Maurolico (1494–1575).[5] Maurolico's father, Antonio, had studied under Lascaris as Pietro Bembo had done, and as Pietro may well recall:

> If you remember your Constantine Lascaris, under whom you once applied yourself to Greek learning here, most excellent Bembo, I believe that you have not forgotten us either. A fair number of our citizens mention that golden period, and now and again they show us the house in which you stayed, and they pay homage to it. What wonder if you were able to recall my father as well, Antonio Maurolico, a very close friend of Lascaris?[6]

As the letter proceeds, Maurolico laments what he portrays as the dearth of modern attention to the ancient mathematicians before he asserts his own efforts and achievements in the mathematical realm, including his authoring of a *Cosmographia* that he intends to dedicate to Pietro; he also possesses an astrolabe that, he writes, Pietro had once sent to Lascaris from Venice.[7] Beyond these initial allusions to Pietro's scientific interests, however, Maurolico then turns to describing the eruption of Etna that had occurred in late March 1536, some six weeks before he penned his letter; "for I know what great appetite you have for antiquities and for things of wonder." A lengthy account of the eruption and its effects follows before Maurolico abruptly closes the subject ("This is what I had to write about Etna") near the letter's end. In his reply of June 26, 1536, written in Padua,[8] Pietro expresses delight at Maurolico's letter:

> Don't imagine that any letter has reached me in this entire year that has caused me more pleasure than this one. For you've stirred, and brought back to my mind and senses with the sweetest recollection, my memory both of that time when I was in Messina to study Greek letters thoroughly, a time that was not only more pleasurable but certainly also more rewarding

5. First edited by Spezi (1862) 79–84 on the basis of Biblioteca Apostolica Vaticana Barb. lat. 2158 fols. 143*r*–146*v*; republished by Moscheo (1988a) 271–5 (cf. p. 351 no. 23 for wrong ascription to May 2, 1536, p. 507 no. 46 for right ascription to May 4). Further on Maurolico's relations with Bembo, Zaggia (2003) 1.189–94 with Cian (1897) 10–11 and 71 n.2.

6. For the Latin original, Spezi (1862) 79; Moscheo (1988a) 271–2.

7. Spezi (1862) 82; Moscheo (1988a) 273. For the astrolabe as evidence of Pietro's larger scientific interests, Grande (1905) 178 with Moscheo (1988b) 607–8, and cf. also my p. 274 and n.22.

8. Travi (1992) 649–50 *Letter* 1759, albeit wrongly dated by Travi 710 to April (not June) 26.

> than all the other times that I've lived through thereafter; and the memory also of Constantine Lascaris, that most excellent and venerable man, who trained me.[9]

As for Maurolico's account of the eruption,

> [d]id I not seem to myself, while reading your letter, actually to be watching that mountain vomiting forth streams of fire? So that, together with the pleasure of reading, I was affected almost by the same fear by which you say all the communities were terrified because of the sudden inundation. All told, not only did all the other matters [sc. on mathematics] about which you write bring me wonderful delight (for they're such that nothing could be more learned), but also that part of your missive that I mention [sc. about Etna]; [it brought me delight] I believe precisely because, when I visited the mountain during my stay there, I never saw anything in my life that I'm gladder to have seen. I also wrote a dialogue on that subject when I was very much a young man—a dialogue that is in fact in circulation (*Scripsi etiam de ea re Dialogum admodum adolescens, qui quidem circumfertur*). And so several factors have made that reading, pleasant as it is in itself, even more pleasurable by far.[10]

In stating that *De Aetna* is in circulation, Pietro surely refers here to the second edition of the work that was published in 1530,[11] along with three other Latin works of his, in the quarto edition of *Opuscula* produced at the Venetian press of Johannes Antonius da Sabio and brothers.[12] For now, however, his fond recollection in his letter to Maurolico of his youthful ascent of Etna sets the stage for my own approach to the vibrant and inventive meditation on the volcano—and on far more than the volcano per se—that is *De Aetna*. While Maurolico's letter of 1536 stirs Pietro's memory, *De Aetna* is itself an act of memory, and not just in the straightforward sense that it commemorates his youthful adventure on Etna. In its representation of the father-son relationship and of Pietro's youthful yearning for the life of lettered *otium* at a far remove from the Venetian civic *cursus honorum*, the dialogue memorializes a key tension point in the young Bembo's coming of age as one born

9. Travi (1992) 649 *Letter* 1759.9–15.

10. Travi (1992) 649 *Letter* 1759.22–32.

11. So "probabilmente" Mariano (1991) 443, referring also to allusions to the second edition elsewhere in his correspondence: see Travi (1992) 76 *Letter* 1012.17–19 (September 13, 1529) and 147 *Letter* 1105.1–2 (June 11, 1530, a missive to Lazaro Baisio accompanying a copy of the new edition).

12. Further on this edition, Chapter 5 p. 203.

to civic responsibilities in the Venetian patrician way: from this Venice-centered perspective, Pietro's devotion to his Greek studies under Lascaris in Sicily already represents a significant deviation from the patrician path of duty even before his spirit of independence is graphically expressed in *De Aetna* through his immersion in the Etnean wilderness.

Despite his many achievements in later life, my primary focus in the chapters that follow is on the earlier phase of Pietro's life and writings down to 1506. His early education readied him for the civic career expected of one of his station at Venice, but the political life had but limited appeal for him from a young age, drawn as he was far more strongly to the world of letters and learning. Despite this ambivalence toward the civic *cursus*, he dutifully ran for minor office on multiple occasions in the later 1490s and beyond, but without success. But he departed decisively from Venice in 1506 and soon settled into the courtly life at Urbino, where he remained until 1512;[13] the world of refined elegance, entertainment, and learning that opened to him in Urbino was in many ways an instantiation of the courtly aesthetic that he had already captured in his three-book vernacular dialogue, *Gli Asolani* (*The people of Asolo*), published in 1505. Yet for all the charms of *Gli Asolani*, Pietro is surely best known today for his codification of Italian orthography and grammar in his *Prose della volgar lingua* (*Discussions of the Vernacular Tongue*) of 1525, and hence for his role in establishing a standard vernacular language based on fourteenth-century Tuscan models, above all Dante, Petrarch, and Boccaccio; the long gestation of this work extended all the way back to his years in Urbino. Thereafter, in 1513, he was appointed secretary to the newly elected Pope Leo X (Giovanni de' Medici), and he spent the next years in Rome. His ailing health, however, and the financial straits that he faced after his father's death in 1519 led him back to the Veneto, and after Leo's death in 1521 he devoted himself to his literary pursuits in Padua. In 1530, at the invitation of the Venetian authorities, he was appointed historian of the Republic, and also librarian of St. Mark's Basilica, but late in life came a further calling when he was elevated to the cardinalate in 1539 by Pope Paul III. He died in 1547 after acquiring great fame as a scholar, a poet, a literary theorist, an art collector, a cardinal, and, above all, a remarkable, and remarkably well-connected, product of his Renaissance times. Such, in brief, were the life and achievements of Pietro Bembo, but central to this study are the formative years in which he struggled to reconcile his patrician obligation to serve the state with his calling to the literary life.

The relevance of *De Aetna* to this fuller story of Pietro's unease at the burden of patriciate expectation that weighed on him at Venice in the 1490s and beyond has

---

13. On these developments, and on the seminal importance of this turning point, Vagni (2010) with Kidwell (2004) 113–50.

been well documented in modern scholarship.[14] But the mode of "thick description" that is deployed in this study to contextualize *De Aetna* within the Venetian times and terms of its production is nevertheless designed to cast fresh light on the work by focusing in particular on three distinctive features of it that warrant new scrutiny—independent and separable features that nonetheless coalesce to form the harmoniously unified exercise in Classical reception, in print and typeface experimentation, and in symbolic projection that I claim for the 1496 *editio princeps* of *De Aetna*. These three features are (i) the stimulus that Pietro drew from the complex history of Mount Etna as treated in the Greco-Roman literary tradition from Pindar onward; (ii) the striking novelty of *De Aetna*'s status as the first Latin text produced at the nascent Aldine Press in Venice; and (iii) Pietro's ingenious deployment of Etna as a powerful, multivalent symbol that simultaneously reflects in different ways the diverse traits and tendencies of father and son, Pietro and Bernardo, in the course of their dialogical exchanges within *De Aetna*. To expand briefly on these three features:

(i) *De Aetna* and the Classical Tradition

For all Pietro's direct experience of Mount Etna, his dramatis persona within *De Aetna* defers to Bernardo when it comes to explaining the cause of Etna's fires:

PIETRO: Come on, then, father, explain to me rather what I'm after: where do these fires come from, and, once they've come into being, how do they keep going?

BERNARDO: . . . But since you now so want to hear me discuss the fires that I'd questioned you about previously, I'll set out what I think in just a few words . . .

§§32, 33

In his ensuing rationalization of the fires, Bernardo "normalizes" Etna by explaining its workings on principles of subterranean wind action and of ignition through contact with sulfur, an explanation that shows his easy familiarity with a range of Classical sources; prominent among them are Lucretius' account of Etna in *De rerum natura* 6.639–702, Seneca's *Natural Questions*, and the so-called *Aetna* poem of the later first century CE. As we shall see,[15] this bookish and borrowed discourse is set in tension with Pietro's far more lively, even life-threatening (cf. §27), engagement with the volcano; for now, however, Bernardo's disquisition serves usefully to distinguish two modes of appeal to the Classical tradition in *De Aetna*. The first

14. See esp. Floriani (1966); Dionisotti (1966b) 9–19 = Vela (2002) 23–32; Müller (2002); Finotti (2004), esp. 7–78.

15. Chapter 6, esp. pp. 252–68.

is determinedly "scientific" in orientation: even if traces of medieval speculation on the causes of Etna's eruptions are faintly discernible in Bernardo's discourse,[16] his reliance on Classical authority bears witness to the relative dearth of advances in the earth sciences in the Middle Ages, and to the poverty of any detailed record keeping about Etna's volcanic activity down to at least 1062.[17] Isolated exceptions aside,[18] "little is known about Etna's eruptions from *c.* A.D. 400 to 1329,"[19] "[a] true chronology of eruptions . . . can be reconstructed only from 1603 onward,"[20] and despite Pietro's claim that lava flows from an eruption "shortly before our time" (*paulo ante nostram aetatem*, §43) destroyed much of Catania, the volcano appears to have been relatively calm for almost a century before the eruption of 1536, except for its customary mild activity (as apparently witnessed by Pietro) at and near the summit.[21] In the absence of any consistently reliable reporting of volcanic events down to the sixteenth century, and given the hellish, theologically driven connotations of volcanic fire that persisted throughout the medieval era,[22] Bernardo expatiates on Etna's functioning in §§33–8 with the time-honored weightiness of Classical authority.

In contrast to this "scientific" mode of Classical appeal in *De Aetna*, however, the second mode of appropriation that concerns us still more centrally in this study takes its start from the many imaginative portrayals of Mount Etna that are strewn across the Classical tradition, especially in connection with the confinement of the monstrous Typhoeus or Enceladus beneath the volcano in the aftermath of the Gigantomachy.[23] Certainly, traces of post-Classical influence are detectable in Pietro's depiction of his climb in *De Aetna*, with Petrarch perhaps the clearest

16. See Chapter 6 pp. 253–4 on the pseudo-Aristotelian *De causis proprietatum elementorum* in particular.

17. See Tanguy (1981) 592 with Tanguy et al. (2007) 59.

18. See now Guidoboni and Ciuccarelli (2008) for textual evidence of a significant eruption (not recorded in previous historical catalogues) in 1224.

19. Chester et al. (2000) 187; for the 1329 event, Tanguy (1981) 593–4 and Tanguy et al. (2007) 78.

20. Tanguy et al. (2007) 59, with (pp. 76–9) Appendix 1 for a useful "Critical Review of Historically Dated Eruptions of Etna." For earlier listings see, e.g., Rodwell (1878) 79–113; Hyde (1916); Tanguy (1981); Romano and Sturiale (1982); Stothers and Rampino (1983) 6358–60 and 6366–7; Chester et al. (1985) 96–116; Chester et al. (2000), esp. 185–7; and Duncan et al. (2005). The ancient sources for Etna are usefully assembled in chronological order, along with volcanic occurrences elsewhere, in Panessa (1991) 1.155–245 ("Eruzioni e fenomeni vulcanici").

21. The words *paulo ante nostram aetatem* very possibly look back to eruptions in 1444, 1408, and perhaps even 1381; so Tanguy (1981) 596–7, rejecting any possible allusion in *De Aetna* to a major event in 1493 (Naselli [1934] 116) or so.

22. See Chapter 2 pp. 110–12.

23. For the separate traditions of Typhoeus and Enceladus under Etna, Chapter 1 p. 35 and n.32.

reference point.[24] Pietro's profound debt to the Classical tradition, however, is paraded through his allusions to Typhoeus and Enceladus (§31), to the Ovidian Pythagoras' coverage of Etna in his great speech in *Metamorphoses* 15 (§38), to the Hesiodic account of Typhoeus' demise in the *Theogony* (§39), to Virgil's visitation of Etna in *Aeneid* 3 (§43), and to Theocritus' love-struck Cyclops in *Idyll* 11 (§47). Of course, this network of evocations is the predictable accoutrement of an author who takes pains to reveal in this, apparently his first published work,[25] "an easy familiarity with a wide range of ancient authors, philosophical and poetic, a delicate mastery of the Ciceronian Style, and a sensitive (at times puckish) grasp of character portrayal through dialogue."[26] Beneath this veneer of surface allusion and quotation, however, the deeper distinctiveness that I claim for Pietro's procedure in *De Aetna* lies in his idiosyncratic deployment of what is presented in Chapter 1 as the Etna Idea. This Idea represents the totality of imaginative Classical elaborations of Etna, and even of related volcanic action in other locales such as Vesuvius and "Phlegraean" Campania—locales that came to be associated by attraction with the Etnean myth of the Gigantomachy, even though no monster, Typhoeus or otherwise, is ever placed by any author under Vesuvius itself.[27] Particularized in its manifestations in Pindar, Lucretius, Virgil, and the other authors surveyed in Chapter 1, the generalized Idea that Pietro inherited from his Classical forebears presupposes an Etna that (to invoke Charles Martindale's language of reception) is "endlessly *redescribable*," is "constantly being made rereadable in multifarious ways," and hence is continually "in production" in the Greco-Roman tradition and its aftermath.[28] On this approach, the Etna Idea constitutes not a static trope or a collection of stable and staple generic topoi, but an ongoing process of invention and provocation: it amounts to a dynamic catalyst for remakings of the volcano, so that the improvisations of Pindar, say, or Virgil stimulate further rounds of experimentation or adjustment when Etna is revisited and reimagined later in the tradition.

Just as the physical mountain continually undergoes reconfiguration and change through volcanic action, then, so the Etna Idea is an ever-evolving work in progress; in this respect, Chapter 1 is designed in part to offer students of the Classical tradition a selective, stand-alone survey of Etna's literary evolution. A conspicuous feature of this chain of receptions, however, is the phenomenon of doubleness

---

24. See Chapter 2 pp. 95–101.

25. But the problematic dating of the *Sogno* in incunable form complicates matters: Chapter 3 pp. 118–21.

26. Kilpatrick (1986) 332.

27. On these points, Sebesta (2006), esp. 110, and now the searching treatment in C. Connors (2015).

28. Martindale (1993) 13; his emphasis. See now Buxton (2016) for Etna broadly surveyed in the Greco-Roman tradition.

in certain Classical treatments of Etna, by which I mean the tension that a given author may generate by portraying the volcano from different, often directly competing perspectives (e.g., the "scientific" and the "mythic"), or the tension one author may create by explicitly contesting or diverging from another's portrayal of Etna. This phenomenon importantly recurs in *De Aetna*: basic to Pietro's remaking is his appropriation of Etna as a symbolic landscape that, from the different perspectives of father and son, suggestively reflects the differing life outlooks and characterizations of Pietro and Bernardo in *De Aetna.* If for Bernardo, that sober and unexcitable senior statesman, Etna is there to be tamed through the dispassionate, "normalizing" rationalization of its workings, the youthful Pietro perceives it with a freshness of viewpoint, even a passionate sense of thrill in encountering raw nature, that renders his Etna an energizing *locus* of adventure and self-discovery. Through this process of coordinating and yet distinguishing Pietro and Bernardo's different casts of character, *this* Etna serves a symbolic purpose that, in its particular application of the doubleness phenomenon, is unparalleled in the surviving Classical tradition of the Etna Idea. Herein lies much of Pietro's originality of conception in *De Aetna*, a point that I return to in (iii) below and that is taken up at length later in this study, especially in Chapters 1 and 6.

(ii) *De Aetna* and the Aldine Press

After Pietro and Angelo returned to Venice from Sicily in the summer of 1494, their ascent of Etna aroused so much interest, claims Pietro, that he wrote *De Aetna* to stave off yet further enquiries (§3):

> For now, however, since it's already happened that, almost every day after you and I returned from Sicily, we were asked about Etna's fires by people who knew that we'd observed them fairly carefully, I thought it a good idea, so that we could at last be free of this nuisance, to set down in writing the conversation that I had with my father, Bernardo, a few days after our return; henceforth, those who asked anything about Etna were to be referred to that conversation. And so I've written a book for each of us to profit from in common.

Beyond the spectacle described within the work, the published book was itself an impressive spectacle as the first Aldine expression of the roman face prepared by Aldo Manuzio's master type-cutter, Francesco Griffo of Bologna; this, "the face that launched at least a thousand typographic ships,"[29] was revived by the Monotype

29. H. G. Fletcher (1995) 43.

Corporation in 1929 as "the supremely elegant Monotype Bembo"[30] under the guiding influence of the eminent British typographer and historian of printing, Stanley Morison (1889–1967).[31] A central contention of this study is that the materiality of the 1496 Aldine edition—its typeface and page format, to say nothing for now of post-print finery at the stages of binding and cover decoration—is inseparable from the internal, textual meaning of *De Aetna*. Indeed, that materiality contributes crucially to the overall meaning of an edition in which the innovative quality of the printed word matches Pietro's spirit of adventure on Etna's slopes in a symbiotic correlation between type form and book theme. He may hardly have been a pioneer in climbing Etna, as he himself concedes in reporting that he failed to reach the very summit (§28) and that he relies on Urbano Bolzanio (*c.* 1442–1524)[32] for details of conditions at the volcano's topmost crater (cf. §§28, 46). But if he nevertheless resembles a vertical Columbus in his "modern" exploration of the volcano, that analogy is also delicately but tellingly applied to the Aldine *De Aetna* by the distinguished typographer Giovanni Mardersteig (1892–1977):

> For all those who have studied the vast riches of the Italian incunables, *De Aetna* belongs, for the beauty of the type created by Griffo and for the simplicity of the typographic layout, to the most impressive witnesses of the art of printing. The Quattrocento is outmoded, *a new world* ("un nuovo mondo") announces itself.[33]

Beyond this basic correlation between theme and type form, however, or between Pietro's boldness of stride on Etna and Manuzio's enterprising step in applying Griffo's new roman in *De Aetna*, that symbiosis can perhaps be pressed further. Given that *De Aetna* was apparently Pietro's first publication,[34] both author and publisher simultaneously announce themselves in this proto-Aldine production

---

30. H. G. Fletcher (1995) 43.

31. Further, Chapter 5 pp. 201–2, and cf. Crutchley (2011) 46–51 for Morison's own interesting account of the development of the Monotype Bembo (his account is attractively printed in that font), including (p. 50), "[i]n the pages of *De Aetna* the type, then new, looks almost as fresh as if it had come off a present-day type-caster. Manifestly it did come from the hand of a uniquely competent engraver who, perhaps because Aldus had access to some hardening element, encouraged the cutting of serifs finer than had been the custom. The lower case is more brilliant than any of its predecessors, and the design as a whole ranks with the roman of Louis XIV (which brought to a close the two-hundred-year reign of the *Aetna* type) as one of the major typographical 'watersheds.'"

32. For whom Chapter 2 pp. 85–9 and 100–1.

33. Mardersteig (1964) 132 = (1988) 135; my emphasis.

34. But see again p. 7 and n.25.

in Latin: only a few years after his arrival in Venice in the late 1480s, Manuzio's association with the fashionable young Pietro lent a certain prestige and élan to the nascent press, while Bembo stood to gain from this public burnishing of his humanist credentials in the trailblazing Aldine format. But the striking elegance of the new Aldine roman may yet suggest something beyond this aesthetic alliance of sorts between printer and author, Pietro and Aldo: if style is the man, the print style of *De Aetna* offers a tempting typographic portrait of Pietro himself, his face as if pictured in typeface—a dimension of the text that will be explored further in Chapter 5 in particular, with due attention to both Pietro and Bernardo Bembo's demonstrable interest in the interplay of word and image, script and picture, in various artistic media.

The importance that I attach to the materiality of the 1496 Aldine *De Aetna* is usefully illustrated from another angle by glancing at Pietro's text as given at the end of this volume. Reproduced as it is in the modern Monotype Bembo, that text may be "true" to the original font in one way; yet what can never be adequately reproduced in this 2017 setting is the tight synergy in the 1496 original between form and content, between the clean expressiveness of the Aldine typeface and Pietro's unforced ease of expression, or between the spacious elegance of the Aldine page design and Pietro's attractive self-design in words (see Figure Intro.1 for these Aldine features). The same phenomenon of separation applies no less to the second edition of 1530, in which *De Aetna* is not only stripped of its stand-alone singularity by participating in a compendium of Pietro's Latin *Opuscula*; it is also printed in italic, not the distinctive roman font of the 1496 *princeps*.[35] To enlarge on this displacement-effect, Roger Chartier helpfully reflects on "the ways in which transformations of material typography (in the broadest sense of the word) [e.g., in the transition from the codex to the electronic text] have profoundly changed the uses, circulation, and understanding of the 'same' text":[36]

> The significance, or better yet, the historically and socially distinct significations, of a text, whatever they may be, are *inseparable from the material conditions and physical forms that make the text available to readers*.[37]

The lesson, Chartier urges, is that

> the transfer of a written heritage from one medium to another, from the codex to the screen, would create immeasurable possibilities, but it

35. See Chapter 5 pp. 203–5.

36. Chartier (1995) 21.

37. Chartier (1995) 22; my emphasis.

> would also do violence to the texts *by separating them from the original physical forms in which they appeared and which helped to constitute their historical significance.*[38]

Much of the present study aims to counter this distancing effect by highlighting the inseparability of material form and content in *De Aetna*, albeit with ironic consequences for my inclusion of the text in this volume. For all its accessibility between these covers, and even though it is printed in Monotype Bembo, the text as reproduced here merely exposes and incurs the very separation problem that I seek to address in my several chapters: Pietro's written voice is disembodied, so to speak, and the reading experience at least partially distorted, when the text is encountered in anything other than its first, uniquely impactful incarnation on the Aldine page.

(iii) *De Aetna* and Symbolic Etna

After the reawakening of Vesuvius in 1631 and the major eruption of Etna in 1669, the discovery of Herculaneum in 1709 and the beginning of systematic excavations there and at Pompeii in (respectively) 1738 and 1748 gave further impetus to modern volcanology.[39] Beyond their purely scientific interest, however, the powerful mystique exercised by volcanoes widely infiltrated eighteenth-century discourses on sublimity; it spawned multiple forms of entertainment as a branch of the "imaginary of disaster" in novels, plays, operas, and spectacles; and it had far-reaching metaphorical applications, as volcanic eruptions could symbolize (e.g.) the flexing of a ruler's divinely ordained authority, the flaring of the French Revolution, or the seismic transformations brought about by the rise of industrialization.[40] Volcanoes predictably played their part in firework entertainments, adding to the sublime accent of such events.[41] So in 1772, for example, Marylebone Gardens hosted an elaborate staging of *The Forge of Vulcan* on Etna: the fireworks over, a curtain rose, revealing Vulcan and the Cyclops at the forge; Venus entered with Cupid, the plea for new arrows for her son was heeded, and Etna promptly erupted, with the

38. Chartier (1995) 22; my emphasis.

39. In general on these developments, Sigurdsson (1999), esp. 84–111; Young (2003) 9–15; Scarth (2009), esp. 135–244; Darley (2012) 33–95; Cocco (2013).

40. On these points, Daly (2011), esp. 255–61.

41. See Werrett (2010) 212–19 ("Sublime Fireworks") with Salatino (1997) 54–76 ("The Eruptive Sublime"), including (p. 55): "Mount Etna as exemplar of nature and matter's unceasing fluidity and transience is . . . an ideal subject for a festival machine, a device almost as intrinsically ephemeral as the fireworks it houses."

illusion of lava flows streaming down from on high.[42] This spectacle, itself often repeated at Marylebone Gardens, was notably emulated in May 1792 at Ranelagh Gardens in Chelsea, where Vulcan's forge on Etna was featured once more, albeit with the Cyclops now shaping the armor of Mars to the music of Gluck, Haydn, Giardini, and Handel; thick smoke, fiery effusions, and simulated lava flows all added to the heady atmospherics of the occasion.[43] Whether through spectacles such as these or through natural eruptions, volcanoes could acquire lifelike personality, their storied pasts embellished through mythical associations and hyperbolical elaboration; telling in this respect is the personifying implication of the title of Alwyn Scarth's relatively recent *Vesuvius: A Biography*.[44] For present purposes, these early modern examples of volcanoes brought to life, to the stage, or to metaphorical consciousness balance my earlier focus on the Classical tradition of the Etna Idea by illustrating certain post-Bembo applications of the volcano idea. But the personifying tendency conveniently introduces the symbolic identification between man and mountain, Pietro and Etna, that I now posit for *De Aetna*.

If from one perspective in *De Aetna* the imposing *auctoritas* of Bernardo is temptingly figured in Etna's reassuring bulk and majesty, from another perspective the volcano is endlessly temperamental, unpredictable in its fiery energies, passionate and moody, often calm but always potentially explosive; it is also important to stress that Etna's personifying credentials are explicitly stated in the text.[45] On this approach, which is developed in detail in Chapter 6, Etna potentially functions as a symbol of Pietro's own raw energies and spirit of independence at a far remove from the Venetian civic *cursus*. As he embarks on his ascent in *De Aetna*, he carefully describes the lush landscape of the volcano's lower reaches; as he moves higher up the mountain, however, landscape appears to give way to an otherworldly mindscape in his vision of Faunus ranging sportively over an impossibly idyllic *locus amoenus* on a high promontory (*Altissima in specula*, §48). Bernardo reacts to Pietro's claims with a wry skepticism ("Oh how beautiful the delights of nature!," §49), as if firmly grounded even as Pietro rises on the upper slopes to heights of fabulist projection onto the mountain—a solipsistic-like fantasy that is all the more personalized if the Faunus Pietro locates on Etna is identified with the familiar

---

42. See Daly (2011) 260 with Wroth (1896) 105, Werrett (2010) 215–16, and Darley (2012) 132 (in an engaging chapter on "Making Vesuvius"). The Marylebone Gardens extravaganza was the work of the Italian pyrotechnician Giovanni Battista Torré; for the many imitations and elaborations inspired by his shows, Werrett 218.

43. See Daly (2011) 260 with Wroth (1896) 215–16.

44. Scarth (2009), imputing to Vesuvius (p. 1) "a personality that centuries of scrutiny have brought out in all its intimate detail."

45. See Chapter 6 p. 259.

Faunus of Pietro's own juvenile *carmina*.[46] If the Etna analogy at first implies a correlation between the mountain's simmering restlessness and the eruptive energies that Pietro indulges far from the Venetian career path, that correlation is modified as the dialogue progresses: by inscribing his Faunus onto the mountain's distinctly un-menacing slopes, he molds and appropriates the volcano according to his own escapist design—only to be partly indulged, partly brought down to earth, by Bernardo's typically pragmatic warning on the dangers of seduction by Siren songs (§51).

Whereas Bernardo seeks objective report of Etna's landscape, then, Pietro views and interprets that landscape with the dreamer's eye for figurative elaboration. Through these different perceptions of landscape in *De Aetna*, father and son are differentiated in terms of life choice and their relative degrees of devotion to Venetian civic duty; Pietro's ascent may be the central event of the dialogue, but this delineation of character difference between father and son, I argue, is its central theme. Beyond these competing visions of the specifically Etnean landscape, however, my further concern, especially in Chapter 6, is to weigh two competing conceptualizations of nature in *De Aetna*, the one Venice-centered, the other centered on Etna. If in Venice and the Veneto the natural world is susceptible to molding by architectural design (Venice was after all a city "constructed" in the lagoon), by the culture of *villeggiatura,* and by the rise of the manicured garden, Etna towers forth as a symbol of unbridled nature in all its rawness. Bembo's setting of *De Aetna* in the pleasant family villa of Noniano is strategically crucial in this respect: it facilitates the schematic contrast that permeates the dialogue between home and away, Venice and Sicily, with Bernardo associated with the controllable comforts of the villa garden, Pietro with the uncontrolled but enthralling discomforts of Etna.

The Scope of This Book

This book aims above all to synthesize the three signal features of *De Aetna* that have been distinguished thus far, and to stress to the last their interaction in a work that is steeped in the Classical tradition, a landmark in the history of printing, and also a highly inventive form of engagement with the symbolic possibilities of Etna; through the merging of these threads, each with its own complex storyline that will be traced in due order in this study, *De Aetna* elegantly but pointedly expresses Pietro's crisis of conformity to the norms and expectations of patriciate society in late Quattrocento Venice. The seven main chapters that follow are broadly divisible into four movements; the first three movements consist of two chapters each, while the fourth is confined to Chapter 7. Chapters 1 and 2 are coordinated by the

46. For this Faunus, Chapter 6 pp. 266–8.

overarching theme of *De Aetna* as a fusion of literary memory on the one hand, mnemonic topography on the other. As a preface of sorts to our later investigation (especially in Chapter 6) of the symbolic properties of Pietro's Etna, Chapter 1 explores the rich diversity of Classical treatments of the volcano from Pindar onward. In mapping the Classical dimensions and contours of the cumulative Etna Idea, this chapter not only functions as a form of excavation into the literary geology of Pietro's mountain, but also defines the question that much of the rest of this study seeks to address: in what ways, and to what extent, does Pietro challenge, exploit, and depart from (even upstage) the imaginative applications that are already encoded in Etna's literary past? Chapter 2 builds on the mnemonic significance of the Etna Idea as traced in Chapter 1, partly by relating Pietro's activation of literary memory on Etna to the Classical phenomenon of mnemonic topography, or the embedding of the socio-historical, cultural, and literary past into descriptions of material landscape. But *De Aetna* is also viewed in Chapter 2 in relation to the Renaissance tradition of travel writings that combined topographical surveillance with the visitation of antiquity in a merging of past and present, or of place description and antiquarian recovery. Yet while Pietro's ascent of Etna shows important traces of travel through literary time, *De Aetna*'s setting at Noniano proves to be no less mnemonic in its evocations of the Classical Ciceronian dialogue. A further memory function of *De Aetna* lies in its possible dialogue with, and even its direct response to, Petrarch's celebrated account of his ascent of Mont Ventoux in 1336. The Petrarchan account is duly visited in Chapter 2, but as part of a larger attempt to locate Pietro's Etna adventure within the broader history of mountaineering and of the mixed attitudes toward mountains from antiquity down to the sixteenth century: *De Aetna* importantly reflects, I argue, the "fresh view of nature"[47] that dawned in the Renaissance with the rise of a new realism ("landscapes of fact"[48]) and a growing appreciation of raw, unexplored nature in a fast-expanding world. Hence the gradual erosion of the sinister reputation that had long been attached to the mountainous Other in the medieval imagination—an erosion process to which Pietro makes his own limited contribution.

In the second movement, our focus turns to the complex motivations that led Pietro to leave Venice for Messina in 1492, and to the particular individuals who importantly shaped his humanistic formation both before and during his time in Sicily. Four pivotal figures enter our story in Chapter 3, the first of them *Angelo Poliziano* (1454–94; Angelo Ambrogini by birth, Poliziano by nickname after his place of origin, Montepulciano in central Tuscany), that revolutionary figure in the history of philological method. It is surely no coincidence that Pietro departed for

47. Coates (1998) 64.

48. See Clark (1949) 16–35 with Coates (1998) 64–5.

Sicily soon after assisting Poliziano in collating the celebrated Bembine Terence during the great man's visit to Venice in the summer of 1491; beyond Poliziano's guiding example in the techniques of rigorous collation, that encounter would seem to have intensified Pietro's awareness that Greek was as indispensable as Latin in the armory of the truly proficient philologist. But why distant Messina in the first place? *Constantine Lascaris*' reputation as a teacher was far reaching, but we shall see that *Giorgio Valla* (1447–1500), Lascaris' former pupil from his Milan days and later Pietro's teacher in Venice, may well have played an important role in steering Bembo toward Messina. The naturalistic interests displayed in *De Aetna* were perhaps nurtured in part by Lascaris, but they also bear the imprint of another major influence on the young Pietro in Venice: *Ermolao Barbaro* (1454–93), that "*Wunderkind* of late Quattrocento Venetian humanism"[49] who was appointed Venetian ambassador to Rome in 1490, but who became estranged from the Republic in scandalous circumstances in 1491. After our introduction to Barbaro in Chapter 3, the story of his estrangement from Venice is taken up in Chapter 4, but in the context of our larger coverage of the shift that is discernible in Venetian patrician humanism of the late Quattrocento—a shift away from the disciplined devotion to public duty and the common cause that characterizes the distinctly Venetian strain of civic humanism earlier in the century. Whatever the extent to which Barbaro's estrangement from the Republic may have influenced Pietro's ambivalence toward the conventional patrician career path, Bembo's detachment from Venice as portrayed in *De Aetna* is related in the rest of Chapter 4 to these broader currents in the evolution of Quattrocento Venetian humanism.

The third movement begins, in Chapter 5, with the rise of the Aldine Press at Venice in the early 1490s, and with *De Aetna*'s place in relation to Aldo Manuzio's wider innovations and pattern of print experimentation down to the introduction in 1501 of his renowned octavo *libelli portatiles* ("portable little books"). The interaction that I posit between theme and typographic form in *De Aetna*, or between Pietro's adventure on Etna and the novelty of Manuzio's own print venture, unites author and printer in a mode of mutually reinforcing self-display and aesthetic alignment: the dialogue is dignified by Aldo's typographic élan, the Aldine page graced by Bembo's fashionable pen. At the same time, this interactive dynamic between word and type form is also interpretable in terms of Pietro alone, to the effect that the verbal picture of him in *De Aetna* is supplemented by his figurative picturing in and through the physical text: face as typeface. True, Bernardo's presence in *De Aetna* complicates this vision of its type form as a physical picturing of Pietro in particular—unless, that is, we find the stately Bernardo similarly pictured, father like son, in a distinctive familial sharing of print script. At the

49. Ogilvie (2006) 122.

very least, however, Bernardo was demonstrably interested in the kinds of interplay between textual form and content, word and (print)image, that are explored earlier in Chapter 5; that interest is demonstrated in the last part of the chapter, partly by appeal to Petrarch, but especially through our focus on a famous portrait that Bernardo himself very possibly commissioned: Leonardo da Vinci's *Ginevra de' Benci*, which now resides in the National Gallery of Art in Washington, DC. The father-son relationship recurs as the central theme of Chapter 6, albeit with the spotlight now on Etna as a powerful symbolic marker of the generational tensions and the differences of career outlook—Bernardo committed to civic duty in the traditional Venetian patrician way, Pietro far more ambivalent about that calling—that underlie (and gently qualify?) their congenial exchanges in *De Aetna*: whereas Bernardo views Etna with studied detachment, resisting its aura of wonder by systematically explaining its workings in terms of a larger volcanic typology, Pietro's Etna is as much a mountain of the mind as it is a formidable physical challenge; whereas Bernardo objectifies nature, Pietro views Etna with a far more subjective eye for fabulist projection onto its slopes, for engaging with its air of mystery and enchantment,[50] and above all for making the mountain his own as a figurative *locus* of self-expression. To put the point differently, if Bernardo expounds *de Aetna*, Pietro exults *de sua Aetna*; whereas Bernardo deciphers the mountain, Pietro encrypts it in his own code of fantasy.[51]

We progress in the fourth movement, in Chapter 7, to Pietro's renown as a collector of antiquities, books, manuscripts, contemporary art, and scientific instrumentation in accordance with the larger Renaissance appetite for self-fashioning through collecting. *De Aetna*'s relevance to this topic lies partly in its credentials as a work of naturalist collection in itself, recording as it does the physical conditions and topographical features that Pietro encountered on Etna. But my further purpose is to explore the ways in which, far later in his life, the world of *De Aetna*—not just his climb of Etna, but also the *otium*-rich atmospherics of Noniano at a far remove from the Venetian *cursus*—is nostalgically evoked in the material arts. Our main exhibits are the portrait medal that Pietro commissioned in the early 1530s from Valerio Belli, that eminence among Renaissance medalists, and the badly preserved portrait of Cardinal Bembo (*c.* 1546) by Titian that now resides in the Museo di Capodimonte in Naples. But we also consider the controversial case of Giovanni Bellini's *Portrait of a Young Man* of *c.* 1505, not to argue (against the weight of prevailing opinion) that Bellini's sitter in this painting is Pietro himself, but rather to illustrate from a different angle of approach the interplay that I claim for *De Aetna* between its content and form, its typeface and verbal portraiture. Here our journey

50. So well captured by Corti (1999), with pp. 64–9 on *De Aetna*.

51. Cf. Corti (1999) 8 on Etna as "un'opera di fantasia creativa, non un semplice monte."

to Etna reaches its end: the volcano at last returns to dormancy after these seven stages of varied Bembine activity.

De Aetna: *A Brief Synopsis*

De Aetna opens with a prefatory address (§§1–4) to Angelo Gabriele, Pietro's companion in Sicily, explaining the work's ostensible raison d'être as a means of circumventing the many enquiries that their ascent of Etna has aroused since their return to Venice in the summer of 1494. Pietro claims to offer a more or less verbatim account of the proceedings that took place when, at Noniano, the family villa near Padua, he described his activities in Sicily to his father, Bernardo (§4). Beginning in §5, the dialogue proper is conveniently divisible into five main sequences:

1. §§5–10. Comfortably positioned before the house, on the bank of the river Piovego, at around noon, father and son engage good-naturedly in their opening exchanges, with Bernardo's dutiful commitment to the Republic set against the freer spirit of Pietro, fresh as he is from his Sicilian adventure. Bernardo relishes his time at Noniano and craves relaxation there, but his thoughts keep drifting back to the affairs of state (§5), returning him from the serene riverbank (*ripa*) to the "wave" (*unda*) of his civic duties at Venice (§§5–6). In fact, in the years after his service as *podestà* of Bergamo in 1489–90, Bernardo was appointed in October 1492 and then in November 1493 to two *zonte* of the Venetian Council of Ten, or commissions of elected nobles that expanded and supplemented the Council of Ten in matters of special importance or complexity. In 1494 and 1495 he served as public prosecutor (*avogador di comun*), one of the most prestigious positions of state; in October 1496 he was elected to the Council of Ten, a position he held until his appointment as *visdomino* of Ferrara in June 1497.[52] In terms of the larger military-political theater beyond Venice, the summer of 1494 witnessed the beginning of French intervention in the Italian peninsula, and the commencement of the long series of Italian Wars that lasted down to 1559.[53] In early 1495 Charles VIII of France took Naples, but that success was short-lived: Charles withdrew to France after the inconclusive battle of Fornovo in July 1495 against a hastily formed Italian coalition, and Naples was lost by 1496.[54] But the French stirrings coincided with the last

52. Further on these offices, Giannetto (1985) 50–2, 210 with King (1986) 336.

53. Background: Vernon (1909) 1–32 with Norwich (1982) 369–82.

54. Further, Potter (2008) 27–30.

months of Pietro's stay in Sicily; Pietro's allusion to these events in *De Aetna* touches on a matter that is of deep personal, if no immediate political, concern to Bernardo (§8). The conversation turns in due course to Sicily, with Bernardo apparently at ease (§9: ". . . we certainly have time at the moment. What else are we to do at midday in the heat here?") and eager to hear Pietro's account of Etna's fires.

2. §§11–21. Pietro recounts his and Angelo's journey from Messina to Etna, first describing how they had studied Greek with Constantine Lascaris in Messina for fourteen months without a break. Hence their well-earned visit to the volcano (§§11–12). Accompanied by guides, they traveled by horseback along the coastline to the town of Taormina, where they found a wealth of Greco-Roman monuments and antiquities (§13, with allusion to Bernardo's own taste for archeology[55]). After leaving Taormina and the coast, they entered a valley between the foothills of Etna on their left, the mountains of Taormina to their right; by that route they reached the town of Randazzo at the base of Etna after a twenty-four-mile journey from Taormina. The valley was watered by a river shaded by plane trees, and Bernardo reacts with renewed attention when he hears of them (§14): if only the climate were such that he could grow plane trees at his own Noniano! This thought causes Bernardo to reflect on his country estate, and on how he has built it up over the years (§§15–21): had he planted plane trees, he would have carefully nurtured them (§15), but he can yet take real pride in the poplars that he *has* grown at Noniano (§16). After all, everything that he has achieved at Noniano has been not for his personal benefit but for that of his children (§17)—a thought to which Pietro responds by fondly expressing his gratitude to Bernardo for the latter's devotion to Pietro's education and training in "all of the cultured arts," a legacy more valuable than "any magnificent villas that you might have built for me" (§18). Ever the pragmatist, Bernardo returns to the need for a material legacy to underwrite the benefits of a cultured education (§19), only for Pietro to counter by stressing that it was Bernardo who so often impressed upon him that the riches of the mind vastly outweigh material considerations (§20). The conversation has strayed far from Etna at this point, and Pietro eventually steers it back in that direction (§21).

3. §§22–9. Turning to Etna itself, Pietro begins by describing its general topography before dividing it up, Chimaera-like (his own analogy, §26),

55. See Chapters 6 pp. 249–50 and 7 p. 279.

into three parts. First, the natural beauty, fertility, and vegetation of the mountain's lower reaches are briefly surveyed in an idyllic vision that is enhanced by Pietro's exuberant comparison with the orchard garden of Alcinous, king of the Phaeacians, in *Odyssey* 7 (§§22–3). We then rise to Etna's middle region, where woods of pines and beeches coexist with arable land of a legendary bountifulness (§24). Finally, all digressions aside and following a more direct path of narration (§25), Pietro advances to the arid upper reaches, where the sparsely grassed terrain shows outcroppings of tufa, and where whole stretches are covered with lava, others with sand. Pietro reports that there were two craters at the top, but that he and Angelo made it only to the lower of them, edging their way along the stony plateau surrounding it until "we actually touched [the crater] with our hands" (§26). Smoke belched forth; the ground between their feet oozed fire. Bernardo is duly alarmed to hear as much (§27), but youthful exhilaration emboldened Pietro; yet such was the smoke billowing forth from the uppermost crater, such the force of the wind, that he and Angelo could ascend no farther (§28). He relies instead for his account of the upper crater on the eyewitness report that he allegedly received later at Messina from Urbano Bolzanio.[56] Bernardo apparently "knew and esteemed" Urbano (§28), an endorsement that enhances the credibility of Pietro's subsequent account via Urbano of the harsh conditions at the upper crater (§29).

4. §§30–8. Bernardo proves to have been very well informed about volcanic theory all along: after Pietro expresses wonder (*mirum*, §29) about aspects of wind action relative to eruptions from the upper crater, Bernardo counters with a rationalizing discourse on how Etna's exhalations change with the winds: "That shouldn't seem remarkable, son, as it isn't at all extraordinary (*mirum*)" (§30). The tables are now turned: Bernardo has been eager thus far to hear Pietro's firsthand account of Etna's fires (cf. §9), but now it is Pietro who asks his father why the eruptions occur, and how, once started, they continue on (§32). In §§33–8 Bernardo offers a lengthy, essentially Classical theorization of subterranean trauma and volcanic action. The earth, like the human body, he asserts (§33), is permeated by veins and channels. Nowhere are those passages larger than in areas near the sea, because the sea is always eroding the land. Wind enters those openings; hence earthquakes are nowhere more prevalent than in places near the sea. If strong winds come into contact with veins of sulfur, fires break out easily because "sulfur has

56. For whom Chapter 2 pp. 85–9 and 100–1.

a very great capacity for catching fire, and winds too, through their own force, set other substances on fire"; so it is, spectacularly, in the case of Etna (§34). But how do Etna's fires persist when once begun? They presuppose an immense fuel source, but why should that supply be difficult for nature when she is so obviously capable of so many other wonders (§§35–6)? For Bernardo, water and fire clearly provide the volcanic fuel source: through the combinational effect of heat and moisture, the soil exudes substances such as sulfur, pitch, and alum, substances that in turn feed the fires; nor is there anything remarkable about the seemingly endless stream of rocks that the volcano spews forth, given that "the earth is forever pregnant with itself and always self-reproducing" (§§37–8). After completing his theoretical discourse on the origins of Etna's fires, Bernardo turns, with customary directness, to no-nonsense questioning of Pietro: what were the lava flows actually like?

5. §§39–52. In contrast to Bernardo's drier mode of exposition, Pietro sets the tone for his colorful account of the lava flows by beginning with his own Latin rendition of the Hesiodic simile describing Typhoeus' demise in the *Theogony*: much of the earth burns and melts like tin in the furnace, or like iron as it seethes under Vulcan's controlling hand (§39; cf. *Theog.* 861–8). The quotation is diverting, concedes Bernardo, but he still awaits a plain answer to his query about the lava flows (§40). Yet Pietro takes wing at this point, using extravagant imagery (not least the language of birthing from the womb of mother Etna) and vibrant description to dramatize his picture of lava streams teeming forth and hardening into stone. Flow after flow creates the buildup of rock piles that cover much of the mountain, but in time their color fades and they begin to crumble; hence the sandy material around the summit, and also the sloping streams that extend all the way down the mountain to the Catania region and as far as the sea (§§41–3). Given this harsh terrain at the summit, Pietro asserts (§44), the craters can be reached only by crawling uncomfortably for two or so miles. After Bernardo's long-distance explication of Etna's workings, the stress that Pietro places on the practical hazards of the mountain gently presses the point that there is no substitute for direct experience of the volcano. The same point resurfaces in his observation that, in winter, practically the whole of Etna is white with snow, and that at the peak the snow remains throughout the summer (§44). But, objects Bernardo, Strabo mentions snow *only* in winter—only for Pietro to counter both Strabo and Bernardo by asserting the importance of direct, up-to-date experience of Etna over the

Classical word of authority (§§44–5); the unimpeachable Urbano can also attest to snow at the peak in early June (§46).

For all the fearsome explosiveness of Etna, Pietro subsequently lingers on certain charming aspects of the mountain's topography, describing first a sparkling spring named Crana that gushes forth halfway between Catania and the summit (§47), and then a meadow that amounts to a remarkable *locus amoenus* high up on the mountain (§48). It is as if Pietro softened, appropriated, and even in a sense personalized Etna in these sections, projecting onto the landscape an idealized, bucolic vision that appears more literary than real—an impression reinforced when he claims that the god Faunus is said by shepherds to frequent this idyllic place (§49–50). Bernardo reacts with benign forbearance to Pietro's mentioning of Faunus, since "I know that, every so often, you like to amuse yourself by sporting with him in verse" (§49). But Pietro is wary of testing Bernardo's patience further: "these are frivolous matters, and it's not right for me to talk to you without proper consideration" (§50). Yet there is surely a place for diversion from the serious matters of study and life, he continues; Bernardo concurs, provided that the mind is securely fortified against being captivated by Siren-like pleasures (§51). Bernardo has the last word, quoting from Horace's *Epistles* (philosophically a world away from Pietro's ludic Faunus) to support his case for keeping the pleasures in check. Paternal rigor thus counters filial whimsy as evening draws in, the thoughtful Bernardo withdraws all too fittingly to his library, and the dialogue draws to its close in §52.

1

The Etna Idea

EARLY IN *DE AETNA*, before Pietro Bembo recounts to his father, Bernardo, his ascent of Etna, he first describes the largely uneventful progress that he and his companion, Angelo Gabriele, made from Messina to the town of Taormina on the coast, and then on to Randazzo, at the northern foot of the mountain. Soon after they leave Messina, Calabria on the mainland becomes visible to their left; on their right, a chain of hills borders the coastal plain, which is "a rich producer of wine, and famous for its Mamertine vineyards—perhaps less famous than it once was, as if its praises had now been worn out precisely because they're so old, but still famous enough nonetheless" (§12).[1] Then, roughly halfway through their journey to Etna, the fortress of Nisus comes distantly into view on a lofty cliff: it was from this place, says Pietro (§12), that Ovid derived the line "Mothers descended from Nisus, and daughters of Sicily" (*Nisiades matres sicelidesque nurus*) in the fifteenth of his *Heroides* poems, purportedly written by Sappho to her lover, Phaon. Bernardo's interest is immediately piqued by this verse: in the philological controversy that he recalls in §13 ("when I was a boy, if I remember correctly, scholars had yet to agree about this line of the poet"), *Nisiades* as read in the majority of manuscripts came under challenge from *Nasiades/Nesiades*.[2] "But carry on," Bernardo then urges, and Pietro next tells of their arrival at Taormina, of the ancient monuments that could

1. For the renown of Mamertine wine (i.e., produced around Messina [ancient Messana], whose inhabitants were known as *Mamertini*), Plin. *HN* 14.61–6 (there fourth ranked after (1) Caecuban, (2) Falernian, and (3) Alban and Surrentine wines), Mart. 13.117 ("If a jar of Mamertine, as old as Nestor, is given to you, it can have whatever name you please," i.e., it is the equal of any wine whatsoever); Dalby (2003) 206–7, 356–7 with Nesto and Di Savino (2013) 7.

2. *Nas-/Nesiades* to the effect of "'of the island': Sicily may have been so called *par excellence*" (A. Palmer [1898] 429). *Nisiades* might be taken to denote the female descendants of Nisus, king of Megara (and father of Scylla), the Sicilian connection then tenuously supplied by Megara in Sicily being a colony of the Greek Megara. But for (effectively identical) *Nas-/Nesiades* favored, see the interesting expatiations of Ellis (1892) 344–6 and (1901b) 260. Cf. also Knox (1995) 290 on *Her.* 15.54 *Nisiadesque* (in effect "Sicilian"): "One wonders whether the unusual epithet occurred in Sappho."

be seen in the town, and of the Greek coins that could apparently be dug up with ease there, just as they could in Syracuse most of all, "and pretty much throughout the entire island" (§13).

This chapter explores some of the ways in which Etna is imaginatively portrayed in the Greco-Roman literary tradition on which Bembo so conspicuously draws in composing *De Aetna*: just as Pietro gradually progresses from Messina to the foothills from which Etna eventually rises, so our journey through the literary past in this chapter is designed to lead up to, and artistically to contextualize, the highly idiosyncratic version of Etna that he configures in *De Aetna*. Hence the relevance of our initial glances above at the Mamertine vineyards, the fortress of Nisus, and the antiquities of Taormina: from the outset of Bembo's journey from Messina, he not only captures a certain local flavor in the landmarks and curiosities he describes; he also combines topographical description with visitation of the Classical past, be it in the form of the Mamertine wine that was prized in antiquity, the philological problem posed by Ovid's *Heroides* 15.54, or the ancient vestiges of Taormina. As soon as we become attuned to this connectivity with the Classical past as we travel with Bembo over space and time in *De Aetna*, the Etna that we might reasonably expect to encounter in that work is not just the literal mountain that Pietro climbed in the summer of 1493, but also a volcano of a far more flexible meaning and imaginative possibility. Bembo's specific departure point in Messina, it is important to stress, was the learned school of Constantine Lascaris, his teacher of Greek. Pietro apparently ventured to Etna as a respite after more than a year of uninterrupted work at Lascaris' school (§11), but his climb as portrayed in *De Aetna* constitutes the application, I argue, of the Classical learning that he worked to acquire both before and during his stay in Sicily: while he records his direct experience of the mountain in *De Aetna*, this short work is also crucially centered on his literary experience of the storied volcano.

After thus far tracing Bembo's progress from Messina to the foot of the literal volcano, then, we embark in this chapter on a preliminary journey of our own, as if traversing the literary landscape that stands before Bembo's idiosyncratic Etna as drawn in *De Aetna*. A central contention of this study is that he drew from the ancients the stimulus that shapes his own highly imaginative elaboration of what I term the Etna Idea—the generic name that I give to the phenomenon, or rather the dynamic principle, that underlies the diverse, highly inventive portrayals of Mount Etna in the Greco-Roman literary tradition.[3] The Etna Idea constitutes no formal ancient category of definition; rather, it brings to order in this chapter a

3. Vesuvius predictably lends itself to a similar Idea (cf. now C. Connors [2015]), but for present purposes it remains another matter. Etna is now well surveyed in the Greco-Roman tradition by Buxton (2016), but my own approach to the Etna Idea is significantly different, esp. in what I identify below as the "doubleness" phenomenon in certain Roman treatments of it.

collection of treatments that may in many cases be related through allusive contact or thematic overlap, but that nevertheless differ profoundly in their idiosyncratic meaning(s) within their given works or contexts.

To introduce the Etna Idea more fully, and to establish a vantage point from which to observe major developments in its Latin literary evolution in particular, we turn first to the Greek tradition, and specifically to Pindar's first *Pythian* ode—the earliest extant example of Etna's complex elaboration to symbolic effect in Greco-Roman literature. Thereafter we turn to Lucretius, Virgil, Ovid, Seneca and the so-called *Aetna* poem (its author unknown) of the later first century CE. Yet other treatments of Etna could have been chosen for analysis, but my focus on these authors is designed to exploit one particular interpretive opportunity. First, however, an important caveat is to be registered. In surveying modern interpretations of (say) Lucretius, Virgil, and Ovid below, I hardly insist that Bembo himself would necessarily have interpreted the texts in those particular ways, or that he would have applied anything like the same literary-critical apparatus and outlook to those texts. My claim is rather that he was all too alive to the creative impulse that underlay those prior treatments—an impulse that is broadly visible even if the niceties of a particular interpretation of (say) Lucretius on Etna can hardly be straightforwardly attributed to, or intuited in, Bembo's own reading of Lucretius.

But then the opportunity just prefigured: for all the safeguards expressed in my caveat above, this chapter is designed to introduce the feature of Etna's doubleness which, I argue, is basic to *De Aetna*. By that doubleness I mean the different perspectives from which Pietro simultaneously portrays Etna within his text: as we shall see in Chapter 6 in particular, Bernardo's cool, detached, and rationalizing approach to the mountain is set in tension with Pietro's warm vibrancy of expression as he describes his direct engagement with Etna. This doubleness of vision is already encoded, I contend, in the Greco-Roman tradition of Etna treatments, albeit with several variations in how that doubleness is deployed. In Lucretius and Ovid, for example, we shall see that Etna is differently represented at different points within both the former's *De rerum natura* and the latter's *Metamorphoses*, and that each poet enterprisingly exploits the tension that results from that duality of representation in their respective works. Then there is the doubleness that results from one poet asserting a vision of Etna that engages with, challenges, or counters a prior representation of it: our prime illustration in this category will be the "corrective" that Virgil applies in the *Aeneid* to the Lucretian representation of Etna in *De rerum natura*. In turn, the younger Seneca offers a further variation on this doubleness in his *Moral Letters*, or at least in those missives that are addressed to his friend Lucilius after the latter is installed as procurator of Sicily: hovering as it does between its status as so familiar a literary landmark on the one hand, its subjection to Seneca's inquiring, "scientific" eye on the other, his Etna is drawn with a wry ambivalence of tone that is fully in keeping with his larger authorial persona in the *Letters*. But if Seneca already exploits this tension between Etna as a staple literary phenomenon on the one side, Etna as the object of naturalistic inquiry on the other, we shall see that the *Aetna* poet sets these two visions of the volcano against each other in a still more confrontational fashion in his treatment of those twin peaks, the Etna of *fabula* and the Etna of *ratio*.

In touring this chosen landscape of Etna receptions from Lucretius to the *Aetna* poem, then, this chapter aims not just to contextualize Pietro's treatment of the volcano within the Greco-Roman lineage of the Etna Idea, thereby asserting the Classical provocation for his own idiosyncratic development of that Idea. By focusing on the doubleness of Etna's deployment in the Latin tradition in particular, this chapter also seeks to identify an important subcategory within the larger Classical repertoire of the Etna Idea—a subcategory that strikingly anticipates Pietro's own elaboration of Etna's doubleness in *De Aetna*. Hence the structuring principle that coordinates my coverage below of authors such as Lucretius and Virgil is this phenomenon of double vision; but for initial orientation on the Etna Idea we turn to Pindar.

1.1: Pindar, Pythian *1*

The eruption of Etna that Thucydides reports for the year 426/5 BCE occurred, he asserts, fifty years after the last such event (3.116.1–2).[4] No eruption for 475 or so is reported in the Parian Chronicle; but the Chronicle does record one—the same or a different eruption?—under 479–8.[5] If on the basis of these sources we broadly accept that Etna erupted in the 470s BCE, Pindar surely evokes that event[6] when, writing in his first *Pythian* ode, he tells of Typhoeus/Typhon's[7] imprisonment under the volcano:

---

4. Albeit (Gomme [1956] 432) "Thucydides is not vouching for the accuracy of his date."

5. *IG* XII.5 no. 444 fr. A l. 68 = *FGrHist* 239 para. 52; further on the dating problem, Hornblower (2004) 104 and n.74.

6. And perhaps witnessed it? For speculation, Hornblower (2004) 104 and n.72; for the Pindaric account as "our earliest non-fragmentary reference to a volcanic eruption," Hine (2002) 70.

7. Τυφώς-Typhon at *Pyth.* 1.16, 8.16, but Τυφάων-Typhaon at Hes. *Theog.* 306 (Τυφῶν -ῶνος in Pind. *Ol.* 4.7) and then Τυφωεύς-Typhoeus at 821, 869; "The origin of the name and its variant forms are unexplained" (West [1966] 252 on *Theog.* 306). Apart from "Typhon" as given in *Pythian* 1 as quoted below, for standardization I use "Typhoeus" throughout this study. In Hesiod, Typhoeus—half man, half dragon—comes after the Giants, but for his later identification as a Giant, and for the frequent conflation of the Titano- and Gigantomachic legends in the Hellenistic and Roman eras, see Nisbet and Rudd (2004) 72 on Hor. *Carm.* 3.4.53 with Hinds (1987) 165 n.30.

ὅσσα δὲ μὴ πεφίληκε Ζεύς, ἀτύζονται βοὰν
Πιερίδων ἀίοντα, γᾶν τε καὶ πόν-
τον κατ᾽ ἀμαιμάκετον,
ὅς τ᾽ ἐν αἰνᾷ Ταρτάρῳ κεῖται, θεῶν πολέμιος,
Τυφὼς ἑκατοντακάρανος· τόν ποτε
Κιλίκιον θρέψεν πολυώνυμον ἄντρον· νῦν γε μάν
ταί θ᾽ ὑπὲρ Κύμας ἁλιερκέες ὄχθαι
Σικελία τ᾽ αὐτοῦ πιέζει
στέρνα λαχνάεντα· κίων δ᾽ οὐρανία συνέχει,
νιφόεσσ᾽ Αἴτνα, πάνετες χιόνος ὀξείας τιθήνα·

Β΄ τᾶς ἐρεύγονται μὲν ἀπλάτου πυρὸς ἁγνόταται
ἐκ μυχῶν παγαί· ποταμοὶ δ᾽ ἁμέραισιν
μὲν προχέοντι ῥόον καπνοῦ
αἴθων᾽· ἀλλ᾽ ἐν ὄρφναισιν πέτρας
φοίνισσα κυλινδομένα φλὸξ ἐς βαθεῖ-
αν φέρει πόντου πλάκα σὺν πατάγῳ.
κεῖνο δ᾽ Ἁφαίστοιο κρουνοὺς ἑρπετόν
δεινοτάτους ἀναπέμπει· τέρας μὲν
θαυμάσιον προσιδέσθαι,
θαῦμα δὲ καὶ παρεόντων ἀκοῦσαι,

οἷον Αἴτνας ἐν μελαμφύλλοις δέδεται κορυφαῖς
καὶ πέδῳ, στρωμνὰ δὲ χαράσσοισ᾽ ἅπαν νῶ-
τον ποτικεκλιμένον κεντεῖ.
εἴη, Ζεῦ, τὶν εἴη ἁνδάνειν,
ὃς τοῦτ᾽ ἐφέπεις ὄρος, εὐκάρποιο γαί-
ας μέτωπον, τοῦ μὲν ἐπωνυμίαν
κλεινὸς οἰκιστὴρ ἐκύδανεν πόλιν
γείτονα, Πυθιάδος δ᾽ ἐν δρόμῳ κά-
ρυξ ἀνέειπέ νιν ἀγγέλ-
λων Ἱέρωνος ὑπὲρ καλλινίκου
ἅρμασι.

Pythian 1.13–33

But those whom Zeus does not love are stunned
with terror
when they hear the cry of the Pierian Muses, whether
on the earth or on the resistless sea;

among them is he who lies in dread Tartarus, that enemy
of the gods,
Typhon with his hundred heads. He was nurtured of old
by the famed Cilician cave,
but now the steep cliffs above Cumae, and Sicily too,
lie heavy on his shaggy breast.
And the column that soars to heaven
holds him down, snow-covered Aetna, nurse of keen
frost all year round,

from whose inmost caves burst forth the purest streams
of unapproachable fire.
In the daytime her rivers roll forth a fiery flood of smoke,
while in the darkness of night the crimson flame hurls rocks down
with crashing din to the deep plain of the sea below.
And that monster sends forth the most terrible streams of fire;
it is a marvelous wonder to behold, and a wonder even to hear
when men are present.

Such a creature is he that lies bound beneath the dark-leafed
heights of Aetna
and beneath the plain, while his rugged bed goads the whole length
of his back stretched out against it.
Grant, grant that we may please you, Zeus,
you who frequent this mountain, this brow of a fruitful land,
whose namesake city near at hand was glorified
by its renowned founder, when the herald at the Pythian racecourse
proclaimed her by telling of Hiero's triumph with the chariot.

This ode was occasioned by the victory won by Hiero I, tyrant of Syracuse from 478 to 467 BCE, in the chariot race at the Pythian Games at Delphi in 470. He had himself proclaimed there as Hiero of Aetna, in celebration of the city that he had recently established near the volcano (cf. 30–2), and in that same year, 470 BCE, he also installed his son, Deinomenes, as ruler of Aetna. This new city was formerly Catana (modern Catania); as part of his broader resettlement program to consolidate Syracusan control over the northern and eastern coasts of Sicily, Hiero had in 476 transferred the original population of Catana as well as Naxus to Leontini and replaced the people with 10,000 Dorian colonists, renaming the city Aetna.[8] If the

8. Background: Asheri (1992) 149–50.

eruption happened soon after Aetna was founded, Pindar's portrayal of Typhoeus' punishment would be all the more topically relevant, even admonitory, given the ode's complex fusion of athletic celebration, political resonance, and symbolic message through mythological appeal.[9]

Already in his *Theogony* Hesiod had recounted how, after defeating the Titans, Zeus faced a final challenger in the form of monstrous Gaia's last child, Typhoeus (820–80); defeating him in single combat, Zeus "in terrible anger threw him into wide Tartarus" (868). If Αἴτνης is read at *Theogony* 860 ("And flame shot forth from the thunder-stricken lord in the rugged glens of the mountain Etna"), Typhoeus is first associated with Mount Etna in Hesiod—an association perhaps playfully taken up by Pietro Bembo in his suspicion, *à propos* of Hesiod's vivid description of the earth burning after Typhoeus' demise at *Theogony* 861–8, that "that famous shepherd from Ascra had at some point climbed Etna, and that he took from there the lines that he wrote about the entire earth" (*De Aetna* §39). But the reading Αἴτνης is clearly open to serious objection,[10] not least because Hesiod departs from the Etna myth in portraying Typhoeus not as languishing *under* the (unidentified) mountain but as lying aflame on the mountainside before being hurled into Tartarus; Hesiod "seems not to be thinking of a volcano, but of a bare, scorched region."[11] If Αἴτνης is duly rejected, and if we accept that [Aeschylus'] account of Typhoeus' imprisonment under Etna in *Prometheus Bound* 363–72 is later than and closely modeled on *Pythian* 1,[12] then it is Pindar who provides the first attestation of eastern Typhoeus[13] in the Greek west. Moreover, Pindar's departure from the Hesiodic tradition is explicitly signaled by his initial allusion to Tartarus ("he who lies in dread Tartarus," 15; cf. *Theog.* 868) before *his* Typhoeus is emphatically placed under "snow-covered Aetna" (20).[14] By locating Typhoeus in both places, Pindar may partly exploit the belief that Mount Etna was an opening to the underworld;[15] but he also achieves a movement from the general and the eternal to the specific in the here and now, as Kathryn Morgan nicely observes: "An account that started with the monster lying

9. See now Morgan (2015) 300–58, esp. 313–26 on "Typhon and the West," with Hine (2002) 70–2.

10. See West (1966) 393 on *Theog.* 860.

11. West (1966) 393. Cf. also the Homeric simile at *Il.* 2.780–5, where Typhoeus is surely not buried under a volcano (let alone Etna), but the earth groans as when Zeus "scourges it about Typhoeus in Arima," "which probably implies an earthquake" (Kirk [1985] 243; cf. Hine [2002] 59).

12. The chronological relationship of the two works remains a vexed question, but for the anteriority of *Pythian* 1 see Griffith (1983) 149–50 on 351–72 and 152 on 363–72 with Berranger-Auserve (2004) 41 and Billault (2004) 198 and n.12.

13. For this eastern pedigree, West (1966) 379–80 on *Theog.* 820–80.

14. See Morgan (2015) 314–16.

15. See Kingsley (1995) 73–4 and n.10.

Hesiodically in remote Tartaros now has him much closer to the surface, where he can and does affect everyday life."[16]

But the Pindaric Typhoeus' association with Etna as well as with "the steep cliffs above Cumae" (18) is no less topical for political reasons. In answer to a delegation from Cumae (on the Tyrrhenian coast north of the Bay of Naples) for help in its struggles against the Etruscans, Hiero promptly dispatched a fleet that shared in a famous naval victory over a coalition force of Etruscans and Carthaginians off Cumae in 474 BCE.[17] In *Pythian* 1 Pindar alludes directly to this much heralded victory, which contributed to the revival, after the Persian War struggles against Darius and Xerxes, of the Panhellenic myth of heroic Greek resistance to the barbarian Other:[18]

λίσσομαι νεῦσον, Κρονίων, ἥμερον
ὄφρα κατ' οἶκον ὁ Φοίνιξ ὁ Τυρσα-
  νῶν τ' ἀλαλατὸς ἔχῃ, ναυσίστονον
  ὕβριν ἰδὼν τὰν πρὸ Κύμας,
οἷα Συρακοσίων ἀρχῷ δαμασθέντες πάθον,
ὠκυπόρων ἀπὸ ναῶν ὅ σφιν ἐν πόν-
  τῳ βάλεθ' ἁλικίαν,
Ἑλλάδ' ἐξέλκων βαρείας δουλίας.

Pythian 1.71–5

I entreat you, son of Cronus, grant that the war-cry of the Phoenicians
  and Etruscans
may remain at home in peace and quiet, now that they have seen their
  arrogance
bring lamentation to their ships off Cumae. Such were the losses they
  suffered
when conquered by the lord of the Syracusans—a fate that flung
  their young warriors from their swift ships into the sea,
delivering Hellas from oppressive bondage.

"[B]ut now the steep cliffs above Cumae, and Sicily too, lie heavy on [Typhoeus'] shaggy breast" (17–19): beyond the geological linking of Cumae and eastern Sicily here as connected hotbeds of volcanic activity,[19] Hiero's recent naval victory "off

---

16. Morgan (2015) 318.

17. Succinctly on this episode, Asheri (1992) 151–2.

18. On this point Asheri (1992) 152 with Morgan (2015) 25, 40–1, 85, 155–7.

19. For the reference to "steep cliffs above Cumae (ὑπὲρ Κύμας . . . ὄχθαι)" perhaps suggesting "the whole surrounding volcanic region, including Vesuvius" or "possibly referring to the heights

Cumae" (πρὸ Κύμας, 72) aligns the defeated Etruscans and Carthaginians (72) with the vanquished Typhon of lines 15–20.[20] Just as Zeus subdues Typhoeus, so Hiero, by implication Zeus' earthly surrogate, dispenses an equivalent form of justice in thwarting his own eastern challengers.[21] If Hiero is configured as Zeus' regent on earth, then in his different way Pindar functions as Zeus' instrument, channeling the music that is heaven-sent:

> Χρυσέα φόρμιγξ, Ἀπόλλωνος καὶ ἰοπλοκάμων
> σύνδικον Μοισᾶν κτέανον· τᾶς ἀκούει
> μὲν βάσις ἀγλαΐας ἀρχά . . .
> . . . .
> καὶ τὸν αἰχματὰν κεραυνὸν σβεννύεις
> αἰενάου πυρός. εὕδει δ' ἀνὰ σκά-
> πτῳ Διὸς αἰετός, ὠκεῖ-
> αν πτέρυγ' ἀμφοτέρωθεν χαλάξαις,
> ἀρχὸς οἰωνῶν . . .
> . . . .
> ὅσσα δὲ μὴ πεφίληκε Ζεύς, ἀτύζονται βοάν
> Πιερίδων ἀίοντα . . .
>
> *Pythian* 1.1–2, 5–7, 13–14

> Golden lyre, rightful joint possession of Apollo and the violet-tressed Muses,
> lyre, to which the dance-step listens, the beginning of splendid festivity . . .
> . . . .
> You quench even the warlike thunderbolt of everlasting flame;
> and the eagle, king of birds, sleeps on the scepter of Zeus,
> relaxing his swift wings on either side . . .
> . . . .
> But those whom Zeus does not love are stunned with terror
> when they hear the cry of the Pierian Muses . . .

---

of the volcanic island of Ischia, 'opposite' . . . to Cumae," Kirkwood (1982) 132 on 18 with Hine (2002) 70–1 and n.39.

20. The topical importance of the allusion to Cumae in this context is underscored by the fact that (as Hine [2002] 71 points out) when Pindar refers elsewhere to Typhoeus under Etna (*Ol.* 4.6–7), there is no mention of Cumae.

21. On this point, Murgatroyd (1988) 59–60; Lefkowitz (1976) 109 ("Like Typhos, the Etruscans were believed to originate from Asia Minor"); Skulsky (1975) 21–2 (noting that ὁ Φοίνιξ in 72 [=

The lyre's music enchants its hearers as long as they enjoy Zeus' favor: from the outset, the lyre—and, by extension, Pindar's own song—operates within an overarching structure of obedience to Zeus, with both Hiero and the poet aligned as his servants.[22] But while Pindar's Etna imprisons Typhoeus, the recent eruption of *c.* 475 BCE allows no room for complacency: the Etruscan threat may have been thwarted in 474, but Etna's eruption signals the restlessness of an enemy who yet struggles, however intermittently, against his captivity. Hence the further implication for Hiero, perhaps, is that the repression of disorder is no once-and-for-all achievement but an ongoing challenge that tasks the divinely ordained ruler with ceaseless vigilance; from another angle, Typhoeus' fate may also warn of the dangers of misapplying absolute power by failing to heed measurement and (Pindaric) stricture about the art of rule, and thereby failing to stay on the side of Zeus and the lyre.[23]

For all the omissions in this brief overview of a poem as complex as *Pythian* 1, our priority for now is Pindar's treatment of Etna and Typhoeus. Here is the earliest Greco-Roman example of Etna configured not just (or only) as an intimidating physical immensity per se, but also as an *idea* of immense imaginative appeal, a landmark that Pindar molds and exploits as a highly versatile carrier of both symbolic meaning and artistic possibility. Pindar claims the mountain as his own, as if inscribing it with his idiosyncratic design of Typhoeus- and Hiero-centered interpretation. A central claim of this study is that Pietro Bembo, in his *De Aetna*, appropriates Etna as a symbolic landmark in a similar way, albeit with a figurative meaning that is very much his own. He was evidently directly familiar with *Pythian* 1,[24] and his experience of Pindar's creative fashioning of the mountain may well have contributed to his experimentation with the Etna Idea, but only as one of multiple influences. From Pindar, we therefore progress to my promised coverage of the doubleness of viewpoint that characterizes Etna in Lucretius, Virgil, Ovid, Seneca, and the *Aetna* poet. In relating that doubleness to a parallel phenomenon in *De Aetna*, I introduce and illustrate via my ancient *comparanda* the tension that Pietro exploits between

---

Phoenician] "recalls the φοίνισσα φλόξ [24] associated with Typhon"); Berranger-Auserve (2004) 45–7; Morgan (2015) 309, 314, 318.

22. Further, Morgan (2015) 310–11.

23. Cf. Lefkowitz (1976) 109 with Billault (2004) 197–8, setting Typhoeus' fate in lines 13–33 against the protocols of just and measured rule that Pindar urges on Hiero in lines 85–100 (e.g., 86: "Direct the host with the steering oar of justice. Forge the tongue on the anvil of truth"); Segal (1986) 131 for "[b]oth *Pythian* 1 and 4 . . . offer[ing] paradigms of hybristic violence (Typhon, the Aloades) and cruel or illegitimate kingship (Phalaris, Pelias) that might be construed *as a warning to the ruler who commissioned the poems*" (my emphasis).

24. Cf. *De Aetna* §46: "On this matter you can also appreciate Pindar's knowing choice of soubriquet when he called Etna 'nurse of snows.'"

a "scientific," rationalizing approach to volcanic nature on the one hand, and a more fictive, myth-based perception of Etna on the other; a harder formulation of this point would propose that Pietro directly, if differently, applies in *De Aetna* the dynamic of doubleness that he already found embedded in the Classical Etnean intertexts that he knows so well. In mining this tradition, sections 1.2 to 1.4 below amount to a form of literary geology as we probe into the Classical substrata of *De Aetna*: just as the lava effusions from Etna cool to form fresh layers on the mountain, reshaping it in the process (cf. *De Aetna* §§41–2), so the Greco-Roman past supplies its own multiple layers to the evolving literary history of the volcano, all of which give underlying support, substance, and stimulus to Bembo's development of the Etna Idea. Before we ascend Etna with Bembo, then, we first build on our initial sampling of Pindar's *Pythian* 1 by exploring the mountain's literary layers, with Lucretius and Virgil supplying our first accretions.

1.2: Virgil and Lucretius

(i) Virgil

In his hyperbolical description of Etna in *Aeneid* 3, Virgil sought to rival (*aemulari*) Pindar's version in *Pythian* 1—or so thought the Roman sophist, philosopher, and polymath Favorinus of Arelate (modern Arles, *c.* 85–*c.* 165 CE),[25] at least according to his devotee Aulus Gellius in his *Noctes Atticae*, published (internal evidence suggests) *c.* 180 CE. Although no stranger to Latin study,[26] Favorinus, a pupil of Dio Chrysostom and a friend of Plutarch, worked exclusively in Greek throughout his professional career—an orientation that seemingly colors his critique in *Noctes Atticae* 17.10 of what he presents as those parts of the *Aeneid* that lacked finish, the allegedly overblown lines on Etna a special case in point. In the Virgilian description, Aeneas tells Dido and the Carthaginian court of how, voyaging from Troy, he and his men eventually approached the Sicilian coast near Etna (*Aen.* 3.570–82):

> Portus ab accessu ventorum immotus et ingens
> ipse, sed horrificis iuxta tonat Aetna ruinis,
> interdumque atram prorumpit ad aethera nubem,
> turbine fumantem piceo et candente favilla,
> attollitque globos flammarum et sidera lambit;
> interdum scopulos avolsaque viscera montis
> erigit eructans, liquefactaque saxa sub auras

25. In general on Favorinus, Holford-Strevens (1997) and (2003), esp. 98–130, with Beall (2001).

26. See Holford-Strevens (2003) 118–29 on "Favorinus the Latinist."

cum gemitu glomerat, fundoque exaestuat imo.
fama est Enceladi semustum fulmine corpus
urgeri mole hac ingentemque insuper Aetnam
impositam ruptis flammam exspirare caminis,
et fessum quotiens mutet latus, intremere omnem
murmure Trinacriam et caelum subtexere fumo.

There is a haven out of the winds' reach, undisturbed and vast
in itself, but nearby Etna thunders with dreadful eruptions,
and now spews forth a black cloud into the sky,
a cloud smoking with its pitch-black eddy and white-glowing ashes,
and it throws up balls of flame and licks the stars;
and now it hurls high the rocks that it vomits up, and the mountain's
ripped-out entrails, and with a roar it gathers up the molten rocks
in the air and boils up from its furthest depths.
The story goes that Enceladus' body, half-scorched by a lightning bolt,
is buried under this mass, and that, piled on top of him, massive Etna
breathes forth flame from its ruptured furnaces;
and as often as he turns over his weary side, all Sicily moans
and trembles, and veils the sky with smoke.

Just before quoting lines 570–7 in a direct *synkrisis* with *Pythian* 1.21–6,[27] Gellius' Favorinus characterizes the passage as "among those that particularly seem to have needed revision and correction ... For since he wanted to rival the verses that the earlier poet Pindar composed about the nature and burning of [Etna], he has heaped up such expressions and words that in this passage at least he is more abnormal and inflated (*insolentior ... tumidiorque*) even than Pindar himself, who was thought to have too overloaded and rich a style of eloquence (*nimis opima pinguique ... facundia*)" (17.10.8). Whereas Pindar realistically (cf. *veritati magis obsecutus*, §11) distinguishes the sight of smoke by day from that of flame by night, Virgil is taken to task for confusing day and night in a bombastic description (*in strepitu sonituque verborum*, §12) that vastly elaborates on its model, importing emphases and, for Favorinus, excessive infelicities of diction that render the Virgilian passage self-referential, its monstrous theme (cf. already τέρας "monster" at *Pyth.* 1.26) matched by a form of verbal monstrosity: "It is

27. Cf. also Macrob. *Sat.* 5.17.8–14, a passage based on *NA* 17.10.8–19. On the comparative technique as "a critical procedure much favoured by Gellius," see Vardi (1996), esp. 502–4 for his Gellius' partiality to originals (p. 503: "Out of eleven instances of such comparative evaluations only once does he come near to asserting the superiority of an imitation over its model").

the most monstrous of all monstrous descriptions" (*omnium quae monstra dicuntur monstruosissimum est*, §19).[28]

It may be that the contrast drawn by Favorinus here between Pindar's realism and clarity (cf. *luculente*, §13) on the one side, Virgil's overblown grandiosity on the other, is implicated in a strand of ancient literary criticism in which Pindar offered one paradigmatic model of the "high style"; further, that in *Noctes Atticae* 17.10 Gellius reflects the movement of a Greek discourse of stylistic criticism that sets two passages or authors against each other toward a cross-lingual discourse that sets a Latin text against its Greek model.[29] But beyond the fact that Favorinus makes nothing of the seething sound effects that Virgil so powerfully pounds out through assonance and alliteration,[30] his critique is blinkered because of his fixation with Pindar alone: nothing is said of Virgil's likely engagement with [Aeschylus'] *Prometheus Bound* as well as with Lucretius' portrayal of Etna in his *De rerum natura* (cf. 1.722–5, 2.593, 6.639–702), and Richard Thomas duly stresses the Homeric frame that unmistakably surrounds the localized Pindaric presence in *Aen.* 3.570–87 as a whole.[31] From this enlarged perspective, Favorinus' critique is not only one-dimensional; it also gives no hint of how Virgil actively distances himself from his Pindaric model among competing models. Whereas Pindar locates Typhoeus under Etna, Virgil follows the alternative tradition that placed Enceladus under the volcano (578), and he thereby sides with Callimachus on this Alexandrian *zetema*, signaling the arcane literariness of his maneuver through the "Alexandrian footnote" delivered in *fama est Enceladi . . . corpus/ urgeri mole hac* (578–9).[32] Yet still more important as a line of defense against Favorinus' critique are the cosmic implications of Virgil's hyperbole at 3.570–7—implications widely felt throughout the epic, to the effect that the alleged excesses of the Etna hotspot in Book 3 cannot be judged, as they are in *Noctes Atticae* 17.10, purely on their own terms and regardless of the wider poetic context.

Throughout the night Aeneas and his men endure the sound of Etna's monstrous horrors (*immania monstra*, 583), only to encounter a different monstrosity on the next day: already warned of Polyphemus' presence by the

---

28. On the frequency in the *Noctes Atticae* of the theme of Virgil's use and abuse of Greek models, Baldwin (1973) 23.

29. See Hunter (2012) 151–84, esp. 177–8.

30. Duly noted by R. D. Williams (1962) 178 on 576–7 and 179 on 579–80 and 581–2.

31. Thomas (1999) 283–6; further on the allusive texture of 570–87, Horsfall (2006) 394–5.

32. For Callimachus' Enceladus (*Aet.* fr. 1.36 with schol. ad Pind. *Ol.* 4.7 = p. 132.5–7 IIC Drachmann) and for the knowing touch in *fama est* see Hollis (1992) 273–4 with Thomas (1999) 286 and Horsfall (2006) 400–1 on 578.

traumatized Achaemenides, that companion of Ulysses who was left behind on the island (616–18), the Trojans finally witness the Cyclops on the mountain top (*summo . . . monte*, 655), moving his great mass (*vasta . . . mole*, 656) toward the shore, "a terrifying monster, shapeless, massive, robbed of the light" (*monstrum horrendum, informe, ingens, cui lumen ademptum*, 658). The hyperbole and verbal cacophony that erupt in the description of Etna are now suitably matched in Virgil's description of this monstrous man-mountain:[33] already when we first glimpse him on high (*summo . . . monte*) in line 655, his spatial positioning anticipates the assimilation to Etna that is surely irresistible in lines 670–4, where the roar that he unleashes when he cannot catch the fleeing Trojans causes the seas to shudder, Italy to tremble, and Aetna to bellow in its winding caverns (*curvis . . . immugiit Aetna cavernis*, 674). Just as Aeneas and his men cower during the night, hidden in the woods (*silvis*, 583) and assailed by Etna's monstrous noise (cf. *immania monstra*, 583), so the castaway Achaemenides relates how he "drags out his life in the woods" (*vitam in silvis . . . traho*, 646–7), ever trembling at the Cyclopes' "voices and the sound of their feet" (*sonitum . . . pedum vocemque tremesco*, 648). At 3.423 the monstrous Charybdis is said to "lash the stars with her waves" (*sidera verberat unda*), as if in symbolic emulation of the Gigantomachic assault on the heavens. In his different way the towering Polyphemus "strikes against the high stars" (*alta . . . pulsat/ sidera*, 619–20), thereby also emulating Etna, which "licks the stars" through its effusions (*sidera lambit*, 574). Charybdis alternately sucks in the waves and throws them up (*erigit*, 423), an action echoed in Etna's spewing of its innards (*avolsa . . . viscera montis/ erigit eructans*, 575–6); after gorging on his human victims and drowning in wine, Polyphemus completes the chain of eructation when, stretched out on the floor of his cave in his measureless bulk (*immensus*, 632: Etna-like in his massiveness?), he vomits forth his gory feast (*saniem eructans et frusta*, 632).

Through these linkages Virgil's Etna is anthropomorphized (cf. *viscera*, 575; *eructans*, 576; *gemitu*, 577) as a mountain in some ways akin not just to Polyphemus, but also to the Giant Enceladus imprisoned beneath it: as Philip Hardie has shown so well, the Gigantomachic implications of Etna assaulting the heavens by hurling its ash cloud and fire balls to the skies and by "licking the stars" (572–4) align the volcano as one of the forces of disorder, one of the *monstra*, that challenge cosmic stability in the *Aeneid* more generally.[34] Hence Aeneas' experiences in Sicily as described in *Aeneid* 3 can be viewed, as Francis Sullivan well puts it, as "a prelude and preparation for [the Trojans'] future struggles against *monstra* of all kinds, whether embodied in natural forces, such as storms, or in human beings moved

33. On this parallelism see esp. Hardie (1986) 263–5 and (2009a) 91–3 with Scarth (2000) 598–9 and Johnston (1996) 59–60.

34. Hardie (1986), esp. 263–7, and (2009a) 88–92.

by violence and *furor*."[35] Among these *monstra* of all kinds are Charybdis, Etna, and Polyphemus, the three of them so tightly connected by the verbal bindings just sampled above; but the list extends to Cacus in *Aeneid* 8, his cannibalistic cruelty and primitive cave (cf. 8.193–7) so reminiscent of Polyphemus. Etna-like in his great bulk and in vomiting fire (8.198–9), Cacus still more closely resembles the volcano when Hercules, for Virgil that "symbol of the heroic qualities needed to establish Roman power,"[36] leaps down into the cave and throttles the smoke- and fire-spewing monster (cf. *faucibus ingentem fumum ... /evomit*, 8.252–3; *Cacum in tenebris incendia vana vomentem*, 259).[37] Beyond Cacus, Virgil's Allecto, Turnus, and Mezentius all show conspicuously volcanic signs of character,[38] with Turnus and Mezentius in particular applying at the human level the disordering implications of Virgil's Etna description in *Aeneid* 3: in their resistance to Aeneas and, by extension, to Rome's sanctioned destiny, they threaten the order of *fatum*, just as Etna symbolically threatens the sanctity of cosmological and theological order in the epic. On this approach, Favorinus' dismissive quip that Virgil's Etna passage is "the most monstrous (*monstruosissimum*) of all monstrous descriptions" (*NA* 17.10.19) could not be truer, but for a reason absent in his critique. The excessive, monstrous, hyperbolical element is *essential* to Etna's function in the *Aeneid*'s larger symbolic tectonics: rather than describing the volcano simply for itself, as if in an isolated purple passage of set-piece description in Book 3, Virgil applies the Etna Idea to highly creative, connective effect within a network of cross-poem significations.

In contrast to Virgil's seething hot, cosmically threatening Etna in *Aeneid* 3 stands another man-mountain, the personified Atlas: there Mercury briefly pauses at 4.246–51 as he descends to Carthage to remind the tarrying Aeneas of his duty in Italy (cf. 223–37). Aged, weather-beaten, and ice-bound (249–51), Virgil's Atlas is impressively steadfast (cf. *duri*, 247) in his Stoic-like *apatheia*;[39] a giant who has been "immobilized and rendered safe," transformed from "hubristic skyreacher" to "a stable prop of the established order,"[40] he is the upholder of the cosmic firmament

---

35. Sullivan (1972) 189.

36. Hardie (1986) 266; cf. p. 111 on the Hercules-Cacus struggle as "a struggle between the representative of Olympian order ... and the wholly wicked Cacus."

37. On Cacus in relation to Etna and Polyphemus, Hardie (1986) 115, 116–17, 266 and (2009a) 97 with Sullivan (1972) 190, Johnston (1996) 60–1, and Scarth (2000) 601–3. For Hercules' leap into Cacus' cave possibly evoking Empedocles' leap into Etna, Hardie (1986) 116 and (2009a) 172.

38. See Sullivan (1972) 189–91 with Glenn (1971), Hardie (1986) 118–19 and 266–7, and Johnston (1996) 60 and n.13.

39. Cf. Hardie (2009a) 81 for Atlas "allegoriz[ing] easily as Stoic *apatheia*."

40. Hardie (1986) 278.

(*caelum* . . . *vertice fulcit*, 247), and hence symbolic (*contra* Etna) of the containment of Gigantomachic energies.[41] Within Book 4 Atlas is also set in contrast to Virgil's *Fama* (173–88):[42] while Atlas towers to the heavens, his head girded by clouds (248–9), *Fama*, quick and agile (cf. *mobilitate viget*, 175) like an incendiary thunderbolt,[43] spans heaven and earth, walking on the ground but with her head hidden in the clouds (177). Whereas Atlas upholds the cosmic order, *Fama* sows disorder and terror (*territat*, 187) through the facts and falsehoods she spreads as she flits about between heaven and earth (*caeli medio terraeque*, 184); through this disordering effect, this sister of Enceladus (179–80; in retrospect the "Alexandrian footnote" at 3.578, *fama est Enceladi* . . . , takes on added nuance),[44] fully lives up to her heritage as the daughter of Earth, enemy of the gods (cf. *Terra parens, ira inritata deorum*, 178). *Fama*, this *monstrum horrendum, ingens* (181), is also Polyphemus-like in her monstrousness (cf. *monstrum horrendum, informe, ingens*, 3.658), a linkage underscored by the derivation of Polyphemus' name from the Greek φήμη/*fama*.[45] But these points of contact between Etna in *Aeneid* 3 and Atlas and *Fama* in Book 4 are further complicated by Virgil's simultaneous engagement with Lucretius: the latter's portrayal of *religio* in *De rerum natura* 1 has important affinities with Virgil's *Fama*, and his deployment of Etna in connection with the Gigantomachy theme also provides a counterpoise for Virgil's experimentation with the same idea.

(ii) Lucretius

If Virgil re-mythologizes[46] Etna after Lucretius applies a cold dose of *ratio* to explain its workings at *De rerum natura* 6.639–702, Lucretius ironizes the Gigantomachy theme through a technique that appears to be "corrected" in the *Aeneid* through Virgil's starker juxtaposition of the forces of cosmic chaos on the one side (Etna symbolically prominent among them) and those of order on the other (Atlas symbolically prominent among them).[47] Early in *DRN* 5 Lucretius assails belief in the

---

41. Hardie (1986) 281, with implications for Aeneas, who "in his resolution is identified with the universal steadfastness of which Atlas was a general symbol" (p. 280; further, pp. 372–3 on 8.729–31).

42. See Hardie (1986) 278; (2009a) 80–1, 84; (2012) 94, 209–10. More generally on Virgil's *Fama*, Hardie (1986) 273–80, (2009a) 67–135, and (2012) 78–125.

43. Hardie (2009a) 71–2, 73, 86, 88.

44. Hardie (2009a) 91–2 and (2012) 99–100.

45. Hardie (2009a) 92 and (2012) 99 with Bakker (2002), esp. 135–6.

46. Johnston (1996) 58.

47. On this key tension between the Lucretian and Virgilian approaches to the Gigantomachy theme, Hardie (1986) 209–13 with (2009a) 104–5.

divine nature and governance of the world, appropriating for himself the language of oracular authority as he readies to deliver his Epicurean "prophecies" (*fundere fata*, 110) on the mortality of the world "more scrupulously and with much surer reason (*sanctius et multo certa ratione magis*)" even than the Pythian oracle (111–12). In this rebellion against bridled obedience to *religio* (cf. *religione refrenatus*, 114), he in effect aligns himself with the Giants as drawn in lines 117–21:

> . . . propterea que putes ritu par esse Gigantum
> pendere eos poenas immani pro scelere omnis
> qui ratione sua disturbent moenia mundi
> praeclarumque velint caeli restinguere solem,
> immortalia mortali sermone notantes.[48]

> [. . . I shall set out comforts lest you think that the world is immortal,]
> and for that reason you believe it right that, in the manner of the Giants,
> all they should pay the penalty for a monstrous crime
> who shake the walls of the world through their reasoning
> and want to extinguish the radiant sun in heaven,
> branding things immortal with mortal speech.

The association that is all but explicitly drawn here between thrusting Epicurean-Lucretian *ratio* and the Giants' assault on the heavens is suggestively anticipated in Lucretius' eulogy of Epicurus in Book 1:

> Humana ante oculos foede cum vita iaceret
> in terris oppressa gravi sub religione,
> quae caput a caeli regionibus ostendebat
> horribili super aspectu mortalibus instans,
> primum Graius homo mortalis tollere contra
> est oculos ausus primusque obsistere contra,
> quem neque *fama deum* nec *fulmina* nec *minitanti*
> *murmure* compressit caelum, sed eo magis acrem
> irritat animi virtutem, effringere ut arta
> naturae primus portarum claustra cupiret.
> ergo vivida vis animi pervicit, et extra
> processit longe flammantia moenia mundi
> atque omne immensum peragravit mente animoque,
> unde refert nobis victor quid possit oriri,

48. Already well analyzed by Hardie (1986) 209–11.

quid nequeat, finita potestas denique cuique
quanam sit ratione atque alte terminus haerens.
quare religio pedibus subiecta vicissim
obteritur, nos exaequat victoria caelo.

DRN 1.62–79

When human life lay before all eyes groveling on the ground,
miserably crushed beneath the weight of superstition,
which showed its head from the regions of heaven,
pressing upon mortals from above with ghastly aspect,
a Greek man first dared to raise mortal eyes against it,
the first to stand against it. Neither *the renown of the gods*
could suppress him, nor *thunderbolts*, nor the heavens
with their threatening roar, but all the more they stirred up
the fierce courage of his soul, so that he was first of mortals to desire
to shatter the confining barrier of nature's gates.
Therefore, the vigorous force of his mind prevailed, and he proceeded
forth far beyond the flaming ramparts of the world,
and wandered over the universal immensity in mind and thought;
from there he brings back in victory knowledge of what can come
into being and what cannot, and, in sum, by what principle each thing
has its power limited, and its boundary mark set deep.
Hence superstition is in turn cast down and trampled underfoot,
while his victory now makes us stand equal to heaven.

Like those who "shake the walls of the world (*moenia mundi*) through their reasoning" at 5.119, so Epicurus' force of mind reaches dynamically beyond the *flammantia moenia mundi* (1.73), attacking the gods and—unlike the Giants—succeeding in the attempt (cf. *victor*, 75; *victoria*, 79). On the Gigantomachic analogy, Epicurus leads the charge from below (*in terris*, 63) and upward to the celestial heights (*caelum*, 64, 69), freeing human life from oppression beneath the (mountain-like?) weight of *religio*. In this uprising, the truer monsters, perhaps, are *religio* (cf. *horribili . . . aspectu*, 65) and the traditional gods:[49] if the Virgilian portrait of *Fama* is based in part on Lucretius' *religio*, Virgil arguably exploits the correlation drawn between *religio* and *fama deum* at *DRN* 1.63 and 68, fully activating the pejorative shading that is already implicit in Lucretius' use of *fama*; and while the clinical assault of Epicurean *ratio* results in Lucretius' controlled surveillance of the cosmic whole (74), the combination of *fama deum, fulmina,* and *minitanti/ murmure . . . caelum* (68–9) appears

49. Hardie (1986) 210–11.

backward-looking, as if confronting the new pretender with old lore and primeval repression and succeeding only in goading him to greater *virtus* (cf. 70). The reversal of fortunes is complete by the passage's end, with *religio* now cast down (*pedibus subiecta*, 78) as once was human existence (cf. *in terris oppressa* [sc. *vita*], 63); moreover, even though the Gigantomachic analogy is obviously crude in one way (Epicurus is in a class of his own as an intellectual giant), it becomes still more compelling in retrospect when these *laudes Epicuri* are viewed in light of Lucretius' treatment of Empedocles later in Book 1.

Given his atomistic commitment to the perishability of fire, air, earth, and water, Lucretius could hardly endorse Empedocles' pluralistic theory that the world sphere consisted of the four root elements that remained permanent and unchanged, and that formed the world of things by combining with one another in varying proportions under the influence of Love and Strife. Yet Lucretius' admiration for Empedocles is reflected in the profound influence that the latter's own poem on nature, Περὶ φύσεως, exerted on *De rerum natura*; Lucretius was, in David Sedley's neat formulation, "the servant of two masters. Epicurus is the founder of his philosophy; Empedocles is the father of his genre."[50] Already at 1.62–79 Empedocles is an important sub-presence, his own praises of (almost certainly) Pythagoras offering a "clear . . . model" for Lucretius' *laudes Epicuri*.[51] Hence, when Lucretius pays homage to Empedocles at 1.716–33, he balances out his praises of his two masters, with Etna now crucially illuminating the implied volcanic subtext of 1.62–79. Empedocles is introduced as follows:

> quorum Acragantinus cum primis Empedocles est,
> insula quem triquetris *terrarum* gessit in oris,
> quam fluitans circum magnis anfractibus *aequor*
> Ionium glaucis aspargit virus ab undis . . .
>
> 1.716–19

> Foremost among them[52] is Empedocles of Acragas,
> who was born within the three-cornered coasts of that island
> around which the Ionian sea flows with its great windings,
> spraying salt-water from its green waves.

As Sedley points out, *terrarum* here is no "otiose addition" as Cyril Bailey would have it,[53] but a detail that contributes importantly to Lucretius' broader representation

50. Sedley (1998) 34.

51. See Sedley (1998) 29–30 with Graham (2010) 411.192 fr. 137 (= D-K 31B129) and 430 *ad loc.*

52. I.e., pluralists who posited a primary substratum of the four elements: Bailey (1947) 2.722–3.

53. Sedley (1998) 14; Bailey (1947) 2.725 on 1.717.

not just of Sicily itself, but also of why it gave rise to Empedocles' theory of the four elements: earth and water are supplemented later by fire (*ignis*, 724, of Etna) and air (*caelum*, 725)[54] in a symbolic topography that, for Emily Gowers, resembles (via the picture of the sea surrounding the island in 718–21, and then of fiery Etna at the heart of the Empedoclean passage in 722–5) "a larger version of Empedocles' inner bodily landscape of fiery heart surrounded by cooling blood."[55] At 1.722–5 Etna threatens to erupt once more:[56]

> . . . hic *Aetnaea minantur*
> *murmura* flammarum rursum se colligere iras,
> faucibus eruptos iterum vis ut vomat ignis
> ad caelumque ferat *flammai fulgura* rursum.

> . . . here the rumblings of Etna threaten
> that it gathers once more the rage of its flames,
> that again in its might it may vomit forth the fires bursting from
> its throat, and once more carry to the heavens its flashes of flame.

As later in Virgil, Etna is here personified (*minantur*, 722; *faucibus*, 724) to telling effect: in its threatened eruption and assault on the heavens (725) it heaves with seemingly Gigantomachic intent,[57] as if countering the Jovian bolts and threats (cf. 1.68–9: *quem* [sc. *Epicurum*] *neque fama deum nec fulmina nec minitanti/ murmure compressit caelum*) with bolts of its own (*flammai fulgura*, 725). But given Empedocles' elemental inscription within the Lucretian-Sicilian landscape, Etna's effusions offer a tempting analogy for Empedocles' own rationalizing assault on traditional theology, with Etna's roars and Empedocles' god-like vociferations (*carmina . . . divini pectoris eius/ vociferantur*, 731–2) combining in a form of "counter-*fama* to the *fama deum* [cf. 1.68] of the unenlightened."[58] On this approach, Empedocles and Etna,

---

54. Sedley (1998) 14–15; *caelum* justified as "air" because "Empedocles himself uses 'sky' (οὐρανός) as a name for his element air ([D-K 31] B22.2)."

55. Gowers (2007) 23; already on this "pictorial catalogue of Empedocles' four elements," Snyder (1972), and on the treatment of Empedocles in 1.714–41 in general, Garani (2007) 1–5, 136–7. For the sea as "the sweat of the earth" in the Empedoclean system, D-K 31A66 and B55 with Graham (2010) 377.99, 100, and for the physiology of the heart in relation to the surrounding blood, D-K 31B105 with Graham 399.163 and 429 *ad loc.* ("Blood is the medium for thought, and the central processing center is the area around the heart").

56. Possibly with an allusion to the eruption that engulfed Catania in 122 BCE? See Guittard (2004) 261.

57. See Hardie (1986) 211–12 and (2009a) 88–90.

58. Hardie (2009a) 90.

that potent symbol of "an Empedoclean sublimity,"[59] anticipate Epicurus' assault on the heavens at 1.62–79; but whereas Epicurus triumphs (75, 79), Empedocles is ultimately no more successful than any other of Epicurus' philosophical predecessors, all of whom are said to "have come to a crash with regard to the first-beginnings of things: great they were, and great and heavy was their fall in this matter (*graviter magni magno cecidere ibi casu*)" (740–1).[60] Given this stress on ultimate failure, a certain irony may in retrospect color Empedocles' credentials as superhuman (733) and divine (cf. *sanctum*, 730; *divini*, 731); for can the language of falling in line 741 fail to remind us of the legend that Empedocles wanted physically to vanish so that people would think he had become a god, and that he therefore died by hurling himself into Etna's fires?[61] Yet one of his brazen sandals was thrown up in the flames, exposing his mortality: if *casu* (741) gently recalls Empedocles' fate, the divine aspect at *DRN* 1.731–3 is instantly complicated, even compromised, with Lucretius' adoration now in tension with Lucretian irony, and another "god" struck down.

For Lucretius, then, the Gigantomachic associations of Etna emblematize the struggle of philosophical rationalism against monstrous (cf. *horribili*, 1.65) *religio*; and by arraying Empedocles and Epicurus on the rebel side against belief in the gods, he applies the Etna Idea to seemingly paradoxical effect, at least in comparison with Virgil's "corrective" alignment of Etna with the other forces of cosmic disorder in the *Aeneid*. Hence the doubleness that I claim for the Lucretian and Virgilian visions of Etna in combination, the one countering the other; yet within the six-book arc of *De rerum natura* itself, the doubleness phenomenon is no less discernible in Lucretius' own shifting perspectives on Etna in Books 1 and 6. Given the symbolic importance of Etna in Book 1, Epicurus' triumph as portrayed in Lucretius' eulogy of him (cf. *victor*, 1.75) is suitably complemented by Lucretius' treatment of terrestrial phenomena in Book 6 (535–1137), volcanoes prominent among them, Etna his main exhibit in lines 639–702. And if at 1.716–33 Empedocles' four-element theory is itself symbolically inscribed into Lucretius' Sicilian topography, we find a comparable process of meta-inscription at work in 6.639–702. As we saw above, in Book 1 Epicurus' force of mind advances far beyond the "ramparts of the world" (*moenia mundi*, 73) as he "wander[s] over the universal immensity in mind and thought" (74): the controlling perspective that masters the all here (*omne immensum*) is re-applied in Book 6, where the far-reaching effects of Etna's (recent?)[62]

---

59. Hardie (2009a) 90.

60. Cf. Hardie (1986) 212: "Paradoxically, they fail because they do not go far enough in their scientific 'impiety.'"

61. Cf. already Hardie (2009a) 216–17. For the legend cf. D. L. 8.69, Strab. 6.2.8, 10, etc., with (also on its symbolic implications) Chitwood (1986) and Kingsley (1995), esp. 233–56, 272–7, 289–92.

62. See n.56 above.

eruption are at first described in a hyperbolical pitch that relates the perceived scale of the phenomenon ("all the regions of the heavens smoke and sparkle ...," 644) to the degree of panic that it induces in its observers ("they filled their breasts with shuddering distress," 645). But against this vastness of volcanic action and popular reaction Lucretius re-invokes the universal viewpoint as attributed to Epicurus at 1.73–4: "In considering these matters you must look far and deep," the poet asserts at 6.647–8, "surveying widely into all quarters" so as to impose a sublime form of controlling perspective on the particularized phenomenon. Through the technique of *proportion* Etna is re-conceptualized as but an infinitesimal fraction of the universal whole (649–54); through *analogy* Etna becomes explicable by relation to normative human experience, with disease in the body related to disease in the cosmic body (655–72); and through *relativity* the seemingly singular scale of Etna's eruption is recalibrated through a further retraining of perspective, whereby measurement by human standard gives way to measurement by a universal standard (673–9).[63] Through this expansionist repertoire Lucretius re-inscribes Etna in a form of cosmic topography that "normalizes" and reduces its seemingly wondrous dimensions and features; in this way the Epicurean mindset as portrayed at 1.72–4 is itself inscribed or, perhaps better, embedded, as a *modus videndi* of pervasive application not just in Lucretius' coverage of Etna and other terrestrial phenomena in this part of Book 6, but throughout the whole of *De rerum natura*.

A further implication of Lucretius' treatment of Etna in Book 6, and his explanation of its volcanic workings at 6.680–702, leads us back to his highly dramatic, personifying description of the mountain in his eulogy of Empedocles in Book 1. He offers two causes of eruptions, the first (6.680–93) based on the heating and violent agitation of air in caverns under the volcano, the second (694–702) positing that sand and rock are driven by wave action into caves and passages beneath the crater, only then to be violently expelled through wind action.[64] We have seen how, at 1.722–5, Etna symbolically erupts against the heavens, as if a metaphor for Empedocles' own rationalizing assault on the gods. If in Book 1 Lucretius thereby exploits the mythological apparatus of Etna to cast it as a form of Gigantomachic challenger to the divine order, that exuberant yet fictive embellishment is itself reined in and controlled when Lucretian *ratio* takes a different approach to the volcano in Book 6. Hence the doubleness effect as "correction" thus finally qualifies fabulist dalliance: in a revisionist gesture that effects a mini-form of closure to the volcano theme across the span of *De rerum natura*, the imaginative elaboration of

---

63. On these techniques of proportion, analogy, and relativity, Guittard (2004) 263–4 with Garani (2007) 137–9.

64. On these theories, Bailey (1947) 3.1655–7.

Empedocles-Etna as fiery collaborators in Book 1 gives way in Book 6 to Lucretius' cool, methodical decoding of the volcano, that wonder no more.

1.3: Seneca, Ovid, and the Aetna *Poet*

(i) Seneca

Seneca's appropriation of the Etna Idea in his *Moral Letters* conveniently introduces Ovid's earlier experimentation with the Idea, and also the further development that it undergoes in the so-called *Aetna* poem, probably of the later first century CE. Our Senecan focus is mainly on *Letter* 79, written in *c.* 64 CE and addressed, as are all of Seneca's extant *Moral Letters*, to his younger friend, Lucilius Junior. Of humble origin (*Letter* 19.5) in Campania, Pompeii apparently his birthplace (*Letter* 49.1, 70.1), Lucilius rose to equestrian rank (*Letter* 44.2, 6); after varied military service outside Italy (cf. *Letter* 31.9), he eventually rose to become procurator of Sicily in or around 62 CE—in fact, "not a very important post."[65] As Lucilius embarks on his new role in Sicily, however, Seneca, for so long that guiding power behind Nero's throne, is in a very different position. If Tacitus' account in *Annals* 14.52–6 of the deteriorating relations between Nero and Seneca in the early 60s CE is to be credited, Seneca became increasingly detached from the Neronian court in and after 62—a *de facto* withdrawal that culminated in his enforced suicide in 65 CE (cf. *Ann.* 15.60–4). But whatever the precise historical truth of the matter, Seneca's persona as drawn in his *Natural Questions* of *c.* 62–4[66] is that of one at last released in mind and being: announcing, in the preface to *Natural Questions* 3,[67] his ambitious new task of surveying the universe (*mundum circumire*, 3 pref. 1) and enquiring into nature's workings (his special focus in the *Natural Questions* is on meteorological phenomena), he claims to have thrown off all the encumbrances of his formerly preoccupied life in order to devote himself exclusively to his new project, his mind now entirely free for itself (3 pref. 1–3). From this philosophically liberated and cosmically enlightened vantage point, Seneca hopes that Lucilius, again his addressee, can maintain at least a measure of detachment from his task at hand as procurator of Sicily:

> To judge by what you write, my excellent Lucilius, you take delight in Sicily and your office of procurator, with its leisure time (*officium procurationis otiosae*); and you will continue to take delight if you are willing to keep all this

---

65. Griffin (1992) 350 n.2; further on Lucilius in Sicily, Grimal (1980).

66. Dating: G. D. Williams (2012) 10 n.26.

67. Surely the first book in the original ordering of the work, its sequence confused in the medieval manuscript tradition: succinctly on the whole question, Hine (2010) 1–2 and 193 n.2 with G. D. Williams (2012) 13–14.

> within its own bounds, and not treat a procuratorship as supreme power. I know how uninterested you are in ambition, and how at home with leisure and study (*familiaris otio et litteris*).
>
> *QNat.* 4a pref. 1

Lucilius evidently takes pride in his responsibilities as procurator of an island of such historical importance (cf. *QNat.* 4a pref. 21–2). He may have traveled far on his career path to this point; but Seneca has nevertheless traveled further as a cosmic voyager in the *Natural Questions*, with Sicily now but a mere point (cf. *punctum*, 1 pref. 11) in the cosmic mindscape. Hence the change of perspective that he seeks to inculcate in Lucilius by drawing him away from Sicily and its marvels and by introducing him instead to the wonders of Egypt and the Nile later in *Natural Questions* 4a: by this geographical leap Seneca moves to ensure that Lucilius avoids "putting too much confidence in history and beginning to be pleased with himself" whenever he reflects on Sicily's tumultuous past (*QNat.* 4a pref. 21).[68] Just as Seneca qualifies Lucilius' (self-) importance in Sicily by wittily characterizing his office there as a mere *procuratiuncula* (*Letter* 31.9, "a mini-caretakership"), so the wonders of Sicily—and, by silent implication, even the wonder of wonders that is Etna—are subsequently dwarfed by the awesome spectacle of the Nile and its summer flood in the main body of *Natural Questions* 4a: through this change of place Lucilius is gently put in his place.

This tension between Seneca's philosophical release and Lucilius' dutiful persistence *in officio* is no less marked in the contemporaneous *Letters*. In *Letter* 14 Lucilius has apparently already left for Sicily and "crossed the straits" (*traiecisti fretum*, 8): the epistolary relationship between Seneca and Lucilius, friends separated but still very much attached, is symbolically matched by Sicily's closeness to and yet detachment from the Italian peninsula.[69] By *Letter* 49 Seneca is himself on the move, shaking up the coordinates of their epistolary dynamic[70] by writing from Campania (49.1) before he moves on in *Letter* 51 to a one-night stopover in lax and luxurious Baiae, that ultimate test of philosophical resolve. Within the *Moral Letters* Etna first appears in this postcard from Baiae:

> Each man does as best he can, my dear Lucilius. You have Etna there, that lofty and most renowned mountain of Sicily—although I fail to discover why Messal(l)a (or was it Valgius, for I've been reading in both?) called it unique (*unicum*),[71] since very many places belch forth fire, and not just

68. For the general approach, G. D. Williams (2012) 14, 93–135, and see also Chapter 6 pp. 244–5.

69. Further, Gowers (2011) 168–9.

70. Further, Henderson (2003) 32–3.

71. For C. Valgius Rufus, suffect consul in 12 BCE and protégé of M. Valerius Messalla Corvinus, Courtney (1993) 286–90 and Hollis (2007) 290–1 and 298–9 on 171 with Nisbet and Hubbard

> elevated places (where the phenomenon happens more often, no doubt because fire is carried to the greatest possible height) but low-lying places as well. As for myself, insofar as I'm able I'm making do at Baiae . . .
>
> *Letter* 51.1

Etna is symbolically suggestive here on various fronts, such as the inviting contrast to be drawn between the natural volcanic heat in Sicily and the unnatural steaminess (in every sense) of the baths and sweat rooms of Baiae as featured at 51.6; or between the unbridled effusions of Etna and other volcanic phenomena on the one hand (cf. *plurima loca evomant ignem*, 51.1), and the drunken revelries that erupt with their own brand of monstrosity at Baiae (cf. 51.4) on the other. But a further possibility is that Seneca's appeal to Etna is designed once more to check, or at least to ironize, any pretensions to grandeur that Lucilius may harbor as *procurator*: as Emily Gowers puts it, "a posting in the shadow of sublime Mount Etna . . . isn't all it's cracked up to be. Etna is not so unique: plenty of lesser volcanoes belch flames. . . ."[72] In his different way Seneca, too, finds himself in a dangerous hotspot, enduring the seething cauldron that is Baiae; but at least he was able to leave the place after only a day (51.1),[73] while Lucilius continues patiently to work through his tour of duty in Sicily.

If Etna's appearance at the opening of *Letter* 51 offers a wry insinuation about Lucilius' (grand)standing as *procurator*, experience of that earlier missive should perhaps color or qualify our approach to the different Etna configured in *Letter* 79;[74] again, the doubleness effect is operative here. In this case, Seneca has apparently been keenly awaiting a letter from Lucilius, who has been on his travels: Seneca is eager to know "what new information was revealed to you by your tour of the whole of Sicily" (*circuitus Siciliae totius quid tibi novi ostenderit*, 79.1). But true to the naturalistic, cosmic inquirer that he has become in the *Natural Questions*, Seneca immediately thwarts any expectation that he craves political news. Far from it: what he wants far more urgently, he asserts, is a full description of Charybdis,

---

(1978) 134–5. Nisbet and Hubbard 135 speculate on the basis of *Letter* 51.1 that Valgius may have written "a didactic poem" on Etna, but Courtney 290 on fr. 7 has none of it ("no doubt prose"); if both Valgius and Messalla termed Etna *unicus* (whether in prose or verse), the point at issue at 51.1 may amount to (Hollis 299) "which of them wrote first, and which was merely following the other."

72. Gowers (2011) 187.

73. Cf. W. H. Alexander (1951), proposing on the basis of an awkward tense sequence in 51.1 (*contenti sumus Bais; quas postero die quam attigeram reliqui, locum . . . devitandum*) that Seneca interrupted his writing of the letter after *Bais*, to the effect of "'Everyman as best he can. You, down there, have Etna; we, doing our best, get along with Baiae.' [Time gap.] 'I left it the next day after arriving there. It is a place for one to avoid.'"

74. See already the fine treatment in Hine (2002) 60–3.

so that he can assess how the physical reality fits with mythological accounts of the phenomenon (§1). For all his loftiness of position as Rome's representative in Sicily, Lucilius appears recast as Seneca's personal researcher, his time diverted from the practicalities of government to "higher" things, Etna paramount among them: after he has completed his assignment on Charybdis, would Lucilius be kind enough to climb to Etna's summit in order to establish the truth or otherwise of claims that the mountain is growing smaller (§2), and also to ascertain just how near to the crater lies the snow that apparently lingers even in summer (§4)? Not that Seneca need ask Lucilius to do this: the latter's own interest would seemingly take him to Etna unbidden, engaged as he apparently is in a poem on Sicily (§5); the volcano is bound to feature in that work, but, urges Seneca, there is ample scope not merely for an episodic treatment of Etna (as in Ovid, Virgil, and, possibly, Cornelius Severus: §5), but for a whole poem devoted to the subject.[75] Thus far, it is as if literary-philosophical *otium* were, or should have been, Lucilius' priority in his time in Sicily, that rich resource for poetic (let alone political) opportunity; it is as if Seneca, writing in *c.* 64 CE, viewed and shaped Lucilius through his own "retired" eyes. But then the letter takes a new turning. Whatever Etna's changes of size and form over time, towering virtue remains constant:

> I don't know whether this Etna of yours can collapse and fall upon itself, or whether the unceasing power of its fires diminishes this lofty peak, which is visible across great stretches of the vast sea; but virtue will never be brought low by flames or collapse. Hers is the sole greatness that cannot be lowered; for her there can be no further extension or reduction. Her greatness, like that of the stars, is fixed.
>
> *Letter* 79.10

From its beginning in Lucilius' circuit of Sicily, the letter moves outward in this increasingly abstract direction, discoursing at length on the nature of virtue (§§11–18) while Etna recedes ever further from view; the literal climb (*Aetnam . . . ascendas*, §2) gives way to the superior, figurative climb to wisdom (cf. *ascenditur*, §8).[76] On this approach, Seneca draws creatively on the Etna Idea to set a natural wonder against the still greater conceptual wonder that is virtue itself; in relativizing Etna in this way, he varies the tactic by which (as we saw above) the volcano's claim

75. So at least appears to be the drift of 79.5–10, with a full (rather than a merely episodic) treatment perhaps also presupposed in §7: "Now if Etna doesn't make your mouth water, I'm mistaken in you. For some time you've been wanting to write something on a large scale and on the level of your predecessors (*grande aliquid et par prioribus scribere*)"— albeit *grande* here arguably denotes "little more than 'fine writing'" (Summers [1910] 274).

76. On this point, Montiglio (2006) 568–9.

to uniqueness is undermined in *Letter* 51. And if we find that Seneca approaches Lucilius with gentle humor in *Letter* 79, addressing him as if he were first and foremost a devotee of literary *otium* and naturalistic observation and only secondarily the businesslike *procurator* of Sicily,[77] then this playful reshaping of Lucilius' priorities and identity may be compounded by another witty touch. When we observe Lucilius on his *circuitus Siciliae totius* (79.1), the ghost of the satirist Lucilius (*c.* 180–*c.* 102 BCE) hovers enticingly before us, evoking the older Lucilius' own *Iter Siculum*:[78] by association with this shade, perhaps, Seneca reaffirms our Lucilius' credentials as one who is evidently so very literary (cf. *familiaris . . . litteris, QNat.* 4a pref. 1) in name and nature, a *procurator* only by officious title.

(ii) Ovid

In stating that "Ovid could not be prevented from treating this [Etna-]theme just because Virgil had already fully covered it" (*Letter* 79.5), what Ovidian passages does Seneca have in mind?[79] There are two outstanding candidates, both in the *Metamorphoses*, the first in Book 5 when Minerva visits Mount Helicon to see for herself the newly created spring of Hippocrene (250–9). There, one of the Muses goes on to recount to the goddess the story of the singing contest between the upstart Pierids (i.e., the daughters of King Pierus of Emathia) and the Muses. With the nymphs appointed as judges (316–17), a single voice represents each side: first, reports the Muse, one of the Pierids sang of the Gigantomachy (319–20), and of how the gods fled before Typhoeus to Egypt, where they transformed themselves into animals to evade the monster (321–31). In reply, Calliope (her sister, the narrating Muse, recounts) tells the story of Pluto's rape of Persephone, of Ceres' desperate quest for her daughter, and of the final settlement, brokered by Jupiter (564–7), by which Persephone was to spend half the year with her mother, half with her new husband. In setting the scene for her story, Calliope first introduces Ceres (341–5)

---

77. Cf. already Hine (2002) 62–3 for the possible vein of humor: "The lack of specific detail [sc. in the naturalistic inquiries about Etna that Seneca raises with Lucilius] might mean that on this occasion Seneca is, as it were, *just bluffing, going through the motions of scientific curiosity for literary purposes*. Or, more sympathetically, one might suggest that in this highly literary correspondence, written for publication, generic considerations made him disinclined to give precise dates [sc. about Etna's changing height] and distances [sc. about the distance of snow from the craters]. Be that as it may, we do not know whether anything came of his suggestion to Lucilius, *nor indeed how seriously Seneca expected Lucilius or anyone else to take it*" (my emphases).

78. See Mazzoli (1970) 262 and now Gowers (2011), esp. 189–90; for Lucilius' *Iter*, seemingly occupying the whole of his third book of satires, Warmington (1967) 30–48 frr. 94–148.

79. In general on Ovid on Etna, Guzmán Arias (2003).

and then Sicily, pointedly describing how Typhoeus is buried beneath the island as a whole, his head weighed down by Etna in particular:

Vasta Giganteis ingesta est insula membris
Trinacris et magnis subiectum molibus urget
aetherias ausum sperare Typhoea sedes.
nititur ille quidem pugnatque resurgere saepe,
dextra sed Ausonio manus est subiecta Peloro,
laeva, Pachyne, tibi, Lilybaeo crura premuntur;
degravat Aetna caput, sub qua resupinus harenas
eiectat flammamque ferox vomit ore Typhoeus.
saepe remoliri luctatur pondera terrae
oppidaque et magnos devolvere corpore montes;
inde tremit tellus . . .

Met. 5.346–56

The vast island of Sicily is heaped up on the Giant's limbs,
and with its great mass it presses down on the buried Typhoeus,
who dared to aspire to a heavenly abode.
Often that monster struggles and fights to rise again,
but his right hand is held captive by Cape Pelorus, nearest to Italy,
his left hand by you, Pachynos, his legs by Lilybaeum.[80]
Etna weighs down his head; laid out on his back beneath it,
wild Typhoeus belches forth sand[81] and vomits flame from his mouth.
Often he strains to heave back the weight of the earth
and to roll from his body the towns and great mountains.
Hence the earth trembles . . .

For present purposes, the interest of Ovid's exploitation of the Etna Idea here lies above all in his "emphatically mythological description of the volcano," in pointed, "anti-rationalizing" contrast to Lucretius' accounts at *DRN* 1.722–5 and 6.680–702:[82] we shall soon see that this mythological approach is in tension with the seemingly very different, rationalizing perspective on Etna offered in *Metamorphoses* 15—the second passage of major Etna activity within the poem, and one to which

80. Pachynos the southeastern promontory of Sicily, Lilybaeum the island's westernmost promontory; cf. *De Aetna* §22.

81. For the connotation of *harena* in connection with volcanoes, Hine (1981) 336 on Sen. *QNat.* 2.30.1 *ingentem vim harenae urentis effudit* [sc. *Aetna*].

82. Chaudhuri (2014) 100. Cf. Viarre (2001) 25 (at 5.346–58 "une interprétation purement mythologique de l'éruption volcanique").

we shall turn momentarily. But first some implications of Ovid's portrayal of Typhoeus under Etna at 5.346–56: what factors might lead him to begin Calliope's reply to the Pierids with so elaborate a description of the Sicilian and Etnean topography? What agenda, what barbs, might Calliope's portrayal of Typhoeus under Etna barely conceal?

Calliope's reply to the Pierid song competes at the level not just of artistic virtuosity, but also of ideological attitude toward the gods. From the outset the Pierids are cast as brashly confident and aggressive in challenging the Muses (cf. 310–11: "We shall not be outdone in voice or art"). Spoiling for battle (cf. *proelia*, 307), the Pierid who rudely starts the contest without waiting for the drawing of lots to determine which side sings first (*sine sorte*, 318) unsurprisingly "tells of war with the gods (*bella ... superum*), granting false honors to the Giants, and diminishing (*extenuat*) the actions of the mighty deities" (319–20). Given the Augustan implications of the Gigantomachy as a powerful symbol of order triumphing over disorder, and given that the Gigantomachy is so often represented by the Augustan poets as a byword for the ultimate epic task (a task that they routinely reject, renounce, or defer),[83] the Pierid's song is provocative at all levels, as un-Augustan as it is impious in its treatment of the gods. The full extent of this impiety is suggestively revealed by Antoninus Liberalis' second to third century CE summary of the Typhoeus story as recounted in the fourth book of Nicander's lost *Heteroioumena* (second century BCE), also in the context of a Heliconian song competition between the Pierids and the Muses. If the Pierid's song at *Met.* 5.319–31 was directly modelled on the Nicandrian original,[84] Ovid appears to have modified certain details of the storyline, at least as it is preserved in Liberalis' summary:

> He [Typhoeus] desired to have Zeus' rule, and none of the gods could stand up to him as he attacked. They all fled for Egypt out of fear, and *only Athena and Zeus stayed behind.* Typhoeus followed the gods' tracks. They escaped through foresight by changing their appearances into animals. *Apollo became a hawk*; Hermes an ibis; Ares the lepidotus fish; Artemis a cat; Dionysus changed into a goat; Heracles into a fawn; Hephaestus a bull; and Leto a field mouse. Each of the other gods changed his appearance as he could. *But when Zeus hit Typhoeus with a thunderbolt,* Typhoeus, burning, hid himself in the sea and put out the flame. But Zeus did not relent; *no, he threw Etna,*

---

83. On these points, Galasso (2000) 984 with Hinds (1987) 129.

84. See Hinds (1987) 14–15, 54–5. For the sources of this story, including a possible Pindaric allusion to it, Griffiths (1960) with Rosati (2009) 269–70.

the biggest mountain, on top of Typhoeus, and set Hephaestus on its peaks to guard him.[85]

Against this background, Ovid's Pierid indeed "diminishes" (*extenuat*, 320) the achievements of the gods by portraying Zeus/Jupiter disguised as a ram, in craven flight in Egypt (327–8); by making no allusion to Athena's courageous stand alongside Jupiter (the point matters because the Pierid story is of course being reported directly to Athena/Minerva in *Metamorphoses* 5); by demoting Apollo from a hawk in Nicander to a raven (*Delius in corvo*, 329); and, above all, by studiously avoiding any mention of Jupiter's ruthlessly efficient suppression of Typhoeus under Etna. Through these modifications Typhoeus' attack on the gods is matched in its own way by the Pierid's ridicule of them. She also counters the standard portrayal of Typhoeus as a singular monstrosity by saying nothing of his appearance as he mounts his seemingly brave assault on the gods[86]—a silence made still more eloquent if she caricatures the Olympian gods as *monstrum*-like because of their strange animal shapes in lines 327–31.[87]

If the Pierid's song transgresses the limits of theological propriety and generic extremism in its high-epic rerun of the Gigantomachy theme,[88] Calliope more closely resembles "a half-hearted epicist" in her complex, and compromising, generic dialogue with Ovid's elegiac version of the Persephone story in Book 4 of his *Fasti*.[89] But further to distinguish the two sides in point of detail: in contrast to the Pierid's brashness in bullying her way into singing first (318), Calliope's sister is a model of tact in politely seeking Minerva's permission (333–4) before she proceeds to recount Calliope's song. After Typhoeus, child of the Earth, runs riot in the Pierid's song, Calliope offers a far more benign, nurturing vision of the earth by turning to Ceres, "she who first gave to the lands (*terris*) its fruit and wholesome

85. Ant. Lib. 28 = Celoria (1992) 87 (with pp. 178–88 for notes and commentary) = Papathomopoulos (1968) 48 (with pp. 131–4 for notes).

86. Rosati (2009) 270–1.

87. Cf. Rosati (2009) 272–4 on the Pierid's blasphemy (p. 273: "imagining the gods in animal shape is an act of impiety").

88. For the Pierids therefore cast as "rank bad poets," Hinds (1987) 130. A metaliterary reading of *intumuit numero stolidarum turba sororum* (305) may already imply as much (Hinds 131), but for *extenuat* (320) nevertheless perhaps signaling a certain Alexandrian competence (underscored by the Pierid's learned manipulation of Nicander in lines 327–31), Hinds 166–7 n.40; cf. also Chaudhuri (2014) 97 for the Pierid's "iconoclastic art . . . as more intellectually challenging and rich in content than the conventional song of the Muses." If the Pierid has thus found a way of "producing a Gigantomachy with some redeeming features" (Hinds 166 n.40), this positive dimension is of course hardly stressed by the biased Muse-narrator.

89. Hinds (1987) 131.

foods" (342), in the hymn-like opening of her song (341–5).[90] This tactical shrewdness extends much further, not least in the way Calliope controls her storyline so that its content and emphases appeal all too calculatedly to the nymphs who are judging the contest;[91] most important for now, however, is the rebuke she delivers by wasting no time in locating Typhoeus under Etna (346–56), thereby "correcting" the Pierid's song.[92] As if reclaiming the "true" strand of the mythological tradition that the Pierid had apparently edited out of her storyline, namely that Jupiter piled Etna on the vanquished Typhoeus, Calliope ensures that the monster is now duly punished in canonical fashion beneath the volcano; and she perhaps presses the point through her own added hyperbole, crushing the monster under the full weight not just of Etna but of the whole of Sicily as well. Divine order is thus restored, the Pierids are exposed as blasphemous liars, and Calliope delivers a thinly veiled warning of the punishment that awaits them unless they change their ways (cf. 5.664–78 for their transformation into magpies after they gracelessly lose the contest with the Muses).

But the Pierids may yet command a certain sympathy. After all, the silkily skillful Muse, Calliope's sister, surely tailors her entire narrative of the contest to win Minerva's favor: in describing the Pierid's song in only thirteen lines, some of them delivered through the distancing mechanism of indirect discourse (321–6), she passes implicit judgment on the story by telling it, and dismissing it, so briefly.[93] But can we be sure that she delivers the Pierid's song faithfully in the first place, without enhancing or exaggerating its pro-Typhoean bias? Can we avoid the suspicion that she shrewdly offers Minerva a storyline precisely in keeping with the authoritarian vision of the divine establishment that the goddess herself will go on to weave into the tapestry she produces in her contest with Arachne in *Metamorphoses* 6?[94] On this approach, Calliope's portrayal of Typhoeus under Etna at 5.346–56 offers but one version of the mythological "truth"; within its larger context, Ovid's engagement

---

90. For benign Ceres here, Galasso (2000) 987 with Hinds (1987) 128 and Anderson (1996) 533.

91. See Zissos (1999).

92. On this "devastatingly dismissive rejoinder to the Pierid," now Chaudhuri (2014) 99.

93. On the (unfairness of the) vast disproportion between the two songs as told by the Muse, Hinds (1987) 128 and 166 n.40 with Rosati (2002) 299–301 and Chaudhuri (2014) 98; on the Pierid's movement from indirect (321–6) to direct (327–31) speech, Rosati (2002) 300 (it is "as if the narrating Muse wished [in 327–31] to distinguish her own voice, not contaminating it with that of her impious enemy").

94. See now Chaudhuri (2014) 101–3 on "[t]he deliberate emphasis on divine majesty and constancy" in Minerva's tapestry at 6.70–102, and on the comparison of the Pierid's song and Arachne's tapestry, both featuring theriomorphic portrayals of the gods (albeit in Arachne's case with a still more scandalous sexual dimension).

in this "emphatically mythological description"[95] of Etna amounts to an object lesson in how to construct, even invent, a version of reality through the partisan appropriation of inherited storylines—an implication of the singing contest in Book 5 that has troubling reverberations throughout the poem, not least in its effusive (or double edged?) celebration of Julius Caesar and Augustus at the climax of *Metamorphoses* 15 (745–870).[96]

The second Etna passage that concerns us in the *Metamorphoses* occurs in Pythagoras' long, eccentric discourse that dominates the earlier part of Book 15 (75–478). The speech consists of two main movements, the first an impassioned assault on meat eating and animal sacrifice, the second an extended, visionary account of cosmic mutability and imperishability (cf. 165: *omnia mutantur, nihil interit*); the two movements are coordinated by Pythagoras' doctrine of the transmigration of the soul, with its attendant danger that meat eating risks devouring our own familiars (cf. 139–42). This discourse poses major challenges for our understanding of the poem as a whole: beyond the difficulty of gauging its tone (is it a serious didactic experiment, or a spoof?), how, if at all, is its theme of metempsychosis to be reconciled with the metamorphic flux of the previous fourteen books? Does Ovid attempt to offer through Pythagoras some kind of philosophical underpinning for the metamorphic world that he has created? Or does he jeopardize that whole metamorphic framework by propagating, at the very end of the poem, a theory of soul migration that may be couched in the Ovidian language of change (cf. *in varias . . . figuras*, 15.172), but that surely constitutes a process fundamentally at odds with Ovidian metamorphosis?[97] These questions remain very much alive, but my limited focus for now is on Pythagoras' turning to Etna to illustrate his principle of cosmic changefulness at 15.340–55:

nec quae sulphureis ardet fornacibus Aetne
ignea semper erit; neque enim fuit ignea semper.
nam *sive est animal tellus* et vivit habetque
spiramenta locis flammam exhalantia multis,
spirandi mutare vias, quotiensque movetur,
has finire potest, illas aperire cavernas;
sive leves imis venti cohibentur in antris

95. Chaudhuri (2014) 100.

96. See, e.g., Feeney (1991) 210–24.

97. For these issues, Myers (1994) 133–66, esp. 134–5 with bibliography; Hardie (1995) 204 and nn.1, 2, (2009a) 137, and (2015) 487–9. If (e.g.) Niobe is transformed into a rock that endlessly weeps (6.301–12), how to reconcile that unending state (cf. *lacrimas etiamnum marmora manant*, 6.312) with the Pythagorean theory of changeful soul migration/reincarnation?

saxaque cum saxis et habentem semina flammae
materiam iactant, ea concipit ictibus ignem,
antra relinquentur sedatis frigida ventis;
sive bitumineae rapiunt incendia vires
luteave exiguis ardescunt sulphura fumis,
nempe ubi terra cibos alimentaque pinguia flammae
non dabit absumptis per longum viribus aevum
naturaeque suum nutrimen deerit edaci,
non feret illa famem desertaque deseret ignis.

And Etna that gleams with its sulfurous furnaces
will not always have fire; for it never did always have fire.
For [*first theory*] if the earth is an animate creature and lives
and has breathing holes that discharge flame in many different places,
she can alter these breathing channels and, whenever she quakes,
she can close some caverns and open others.
Or [*second theory*] if sprightly winds are confined in deep caves,
throwing rocks against rocks and matter containing the seeds of fire,
and if that matter generates fire through friction,
the caves will grow cold when the winds have abated and left them.
Or [*third theory*] if bitumen has the power quickly to take fire,
or yellowish sulfur burns with small traces of smoke,
then when the earth gives no rich food and nourishment for
the flames,
its strength worn out through the long passage of time,
and when voracious nature[98] is denied the fuel it needs,
she will not endure starvation and, abandoned, she will abandon
the fires.

True to the "scientific" Empedoclean and Lucretian imprint that is conspicuous throughout Pythagoras' discourse,[99] that variation on Lucretius' own *De rerum natura*,[100] his rationalization of Etna's fires here applies the Epicurean-Lucretian technique of multiple explanation in seemingly textbook fashion (*sive . . . sive . . . sive*);[101]

98. I.e., *natura* here as elemental fire (Hardie [2015] 528 *ad loc.*), taken up in *illa* in 355.

99. For the fundamental Empedoclean presence, see esp. Hardie (1995), (2009a) 136–52, and (2015) 489, 491 on 15.60–8, 494 on 15.75–175, etc.

100. His speech is after all delivered in answer to Numa's inquiry as to *quae sit rerum natura* (15.6); cf. also 15.68–9 *rerum causas et quid natura docebat . . . esset* with Myers (1994) 158, and for the didactic dimension, Volk (2002) 64–7.

101. See Hardie (2008), (2009a) 231–63, and (2015) 527 on 15.340– 1 with Myers (1994) 140.

and after Ovid's purely mythological treatment of Etna in Book 5, this natural-philosophical method applies to the volcano a corrective of sorts late in the poem—a contrast arguably designed to burnish Pythagoras' credentials as a hardheaded theorist who is indeed to be taken seriously in *Metamorphoses* 15. The schematic contrast between these two approaches to Etna, mythological on the one side and scrupulously rationalizing on the other, offers an important template for our treatment of the *Aetna* poem in (iii) below, and still more for what we shall see to be a comparable tension in Bembo's *De Aetna*. Before we leave *Metamorphoses* 15, however, can we really be sure of Pythagoras' unqualified commitment to the rationalizing cause? Or could it be that the schematic contrast drawn above between the categories of the mythological and the rationalizing may underestimate Pythagoras' own sense of wonder—his struggle to remain unequivocally "scientific"—as he is transported (cf. 143–52, especially 147–8 *iuvat ire per alta/ astra*) by his trance-like outpourings?

Of the three *causae* of Etna's fires that Pythagoras gives at 15.340–55, only the second of them in fact approximates to the cause of ignition posited by Lucretius,[102] who holds that the flames take their start from the heating and violent friction effect of the air trapped in Etna's underground caverns (6.680–93; for wind-and-water action from the sea as a contributory cause of the eventual eruption by "lifting up the flame," see 6.694–702 and my p. 44); and the first *causa* Pythagoras mentions could not be further from Lucretius' worldview in positing a living, breathing earth in Stoic fashion (342), just as his position that "souls are free from death" (158) is wholly incompatible with Lucretius' insistence that the soul is mortal (cf. *DRN* 3.136–829). This ambiguous relationship to Lucretius is symptomatic of the larger tension that becomes increasingly discernible between Pythagoras' exposition of natural fact on the one hand and, on the other, the rhetoric of wonder that gains impetus as his long discourse takes wing. For all his Lucretius-like impatience with the fictions of poets on such matters as the terrors of death and the myths of the underworld (153–5), he shows a disconcerting nostalgia for that most familiar of poetic topoi—the Golden Age (96–103), here configured as an era lost when appetites were turned to the carnivorous (103–6). Later, in warming to his thesis that nothing retains its original form (*Nec species sua cuique manet*, 252; cf. 259–60), he cites the transformation of places as a case in point (*sic totiens versa est fortuna locorum*, 261), and proceeds to give examples that quickly embrace the outlandish and marvelous. In lines 293–306, for example, he cites the Achaean cities of Buris and Helice, submerged by earthquake in 373 BCE, and then "the tall and treeless mound" (295–7) apparently formed near Troezen on the Greek Argolid through the violence of winds seeking exit from the subterranean caverns that have entrapped

102. On this point, Myers (1994) 154–5 with Hardie (2015) 527 on 15.340–1.

them.[103] By this mound Ovid apparently refers to the event that Strabo records for Methone near Troezen, just after he too mentions Buris and Helice (1.3.18):

> In regard to Boura [= Buris] and Helike, the former disappeared under a chasm, the latter under waves. At Methone in the Hermionic Gulf a mountain seven stadia high was thrown up because of a fiery eruption, and it was inaccessible by day because of the heat and sulphur odor. At night it shone for a great distance, and the sea boiled five stadia away and was disturbed for twenty stadia, heaped with broken-off rocks no smaller than towers.[104]

Significantly, Strabo mentions these cases and others like them to reduce the wonder effect of such events, "normalizing" them through their sheer weight of numbers and their frequency of occurrence (1.3.16):

> In order not to marvel at those changes that we have said are the reason for the inundations and happenings that have been mentioned regarding Sikelia, the islands of Aiolos, and Pithekoussai, it is worthwhile to provide things that do occur, or have occurred, in other places. *A mass of such examples placed before the eyes will cause a stop to consternation*. At present, the unaccustomed troubles the senses and shows ignorance of natural happenings and the conditions of life generally . . .[105]

But whereas Strabo resists the wonder effect, Ovid's Pythagoras seems to want to indulge the marvelous by selecting from his evidently vast stock of wonders (cf. 307–8: "Although many more instances occur to mind that I've heard of or know of, I'll add only a few"). Hence he launches into a lengthy catalogue of wondrous waters in lines 308–34, a passage that shows clear signs of derivation from the paradoxographical tradition;[106] and for the first time in his entire discourse he begins to use the explicit language of wonder (*quodque magis mirum est*, 317; *mirum . . . soporem*, 321). After his allusion to the entrapped winds that gave rise to the mound at Methone (296–306), his account of Etna (340–55) marks a dramatic escalation within his discourse as—in accordance with at least one of his three Etna theories—the trapped air now promises not merely to produce a *tumulus* from below, but to spark a full-blown volcanic eruption (cf. 346–9) as

103. For sources, Hardie (2015) 521–2 on 15.293–5, 296–306.

104. Trans. Roller (2014) 85.

105. Trans. Roller (2014) 84, with slight adaptation; my emphasis.

106. See Hardie (2015) 523–4 on 15.307–36 with Callebat (1988) and Myers (1994) 151 and n.77.

well. But just before he turns to Etna, Pythagoras visits firmly mythico-poetic territory in citing the wondrous cases of Ortygia/Delos, the island that used to float freely, and the Symplegades, or Clashing Rocks, their danger narrowly evaded by Jason and the Argonauts (336–9); then, immediately after his coverage of Etna, he turns abruptly to "two especially miraculous stories,"[107] the first of the Hyperboreans apparently sprouting feathers after bathing nine times in Lake Tritonis (356–8), the second of Scythian witches reportedly acquiring plumage by sprinkling themselves with their poisons (359–60)—another concession to the marvelous after Pythagoras has (amusingly, given his larger interest in wonders) shown due skepticism (*haud equidem credo*, 359) about the mere story (*fama*, 356) of the Hyperboreans' feathers.[108]

In effect, Pythagoras' natural-philosophical disquisition on Etna, that prominent wonder in itself,[109] is incongruously juxtaposed with allusions of a very different register, disconcerting our response to his rationalization of the volcano's workings in between those two bizarre sequences.[110] In turn, the tension in this passage (336–60 as a whole) between the mythological and the "scientific," between *mirum* and *ratio*, exemplifies a far-reaching feature of his entire discourse, and one perhaps with major implications for the interpretation of the *Metamorphoses* more generally: if in Pythagoras' discourse the task of explaining nature struggles to avoid the allure of mythico-metamorphic wonder, the irresistibility of the unpredictable, chaotic, and marvelous in his speech arguably reflects—even sums up—Ovid's own weight of narrative emphasis throughout Books 1 to 14. Pythagoras apparently has no trouble in holding his listeners in silent wonder (cf. *coetus . . . silentum/ dictaque mirantum magni primordia mundi/ . . . docebat*, 66–8), but his overall speech in *Metamorphoses* 15 apparently fails to persuade (*ora/ docta quidem solvit, sed non et credita*, 73–4: "he enunciated a doctrine that was learned but not given credit"). Even before Pythagoras gives voice, it seems, the wonder element (cf. again *mirantum*, 67) takes precedence over the substance of his ensuing argument—a calibration of response that not only conditions our reading of the speech to come, but also suggestively confirms Ovid's own balance of priorities in the poem thus far.

---

107. Myers (1994) 154.

108. The phenomenon is (perhaps all too tellingly) unattested before Ovid here: Hardie (2015) 528 on 15.356–60.

109. For Etna's own place in ancient lists of *mirabilia*, Myers (1994) 154 with Glauthier (2011) 106 and n.43.

110. For the approach, Myers (1994), esp. 147–59 ("*Mirabilia*: Paradoxography vs. Philosophy").

(iii) The *Aetna* Poem[111]

We turn finally to the *Aetna*, that didactic *tour de force* of more than 600 hexameters—on many fronts, "not an easy poem"[112]—whose authorship is unknown, its date of composition far from certain. Given that its author portrays the region between Naples and Cumae as volcanically dormant for many a year (*locus . . . multis iam frigidus annis*, 431), the poem surely predates Vesuvius' eruption in 79 CE; but a *terminus post quem* is far more elusive, and even though the poem is generally thought to be either late or post-Augustan, no narrower time frame for its composition can be reliably established on linguistic, metrical, or stylistic grounds.[113] Allusive contact with other authors is also of limited help in dating the poem: while likely echoes of Virgil and Ovid and possible reminiscence of Manilius suggest at least an early post-Augustan date, the *Aetna*'s precise chronological relationship to Seneca's *Natural Questions* (of *c.* 62–4 CE) in particular remains controversial.[114] The two works show contact, but which of them depends on the other cannot be definitively proven. Hence, even though the *Aetna* may belong to the Vespasianic era before Vesuvius' eruption in 79 CE, that dating is at best provisional; the case for a late-Neronian dating (*c.* 63?) in close proximity to the *Natural Questions* remains open, not least because Seneca's portrayal of Etna in *Letter* 79 as a "ritual topic for all poets" (*sollemnem omnibus poetis locum*, §5) and one that must surely appeal (§§6–7) to the poet in Lucilius Junior, his addressee, has fueled speculation that the *Aetna* was composed by Lucilius himself—an enticing conjecture, perhaps, but it has drawn strong opposition.[115]

Since the extant Greco-Roman tradition offers no parallel for a didactic poem devoted exclusively to volcanology, the *Aetna* appears to be a strikingly original production. Certainly, Lucretius offers a key precedent for the *Aetna*'s rationalizing poetics on a topic that already surfaces in *De rerum natura* 6, as we have seen,[116] and strands of Epicurean influence have been discerned in the *Aetna*; however, our poet

---

111. The text followed below is that of Goodyear (1966), which is almost identical to that in Goodyear (1965) (see on the changes Hine [2012] 317 n.6). The translations below are drawn from Hine (2012), which is itself based on Goodyear (1966).

112. Toohey (1996) 188.

113. See Goodyear (1965) 59 and (1984), esp. 358 ("No evidence excludes composition at about A.D. 70 and much evidence, some strong, some plausible, some tenuous, points in that direction"). Further on date and authorship, De Vivo (1989); Wolff (2004) 79–80; Volk (2005) and (2008) xx–xxi; Taub (2008) 45 and (2009) 125 and n.1.

114. For the bibliography surveyed, Volk (2008) xxi, but on contact with Seneca in particular, De Vivo (1989) with Goodyear (1984) 348–53.

115. For the history of the ascription to Lucilius, and for trenchant dismissal of it ("unsupported by anything which could be called evidence"), Goodyear (1965) 57–8 with (1984) 351; but the theory persists in (e.g.) Paisley and Oldroyd (1979) 6–11.

116. See on 6.639–702 pp. 43–5 above.

hardly operates as a doctrinaire Epicurean in, for notable example, the (Stoically inflected?) ways in which he personifies Etna as a bodily constituent of the living, breathing earth (98–101) and places it under divine protection (*divina . . . rerum/ . . . cura*, 194–6; cf. *divinis . . . rebus*, 370).[117] The nature and extent of the poet's debt to particular scientific authorities are also unclear, although Posidonius and Theophrastus are likely to have been prominent sources.[118] Yet despite these uncertainties about our poet's specific lines of indebtedness, and despite the notoriously corrupt state of the text, there is no mistaking the quasi-Lucretian, missionary-like zeal with which he sets about explaining Etna's workings. After announcing his theme and invoking the aid of Apollo and the Muses (1–8), the poet orientates his scientific agenda by first setting the supposedly hackneyed nature of so much mythological versifying on such themes as (*inter alia*) the Golden Age (9–16), the Argonauts (17), and Troy's fall (18–19) against the daring originality of his own undertaking (24–8); then by rejecting as "the deceit of poets" (*fallacia vatum*, 29) their various mythological explanations of Etna's fires, the first of them that Etna houses Vulcan's forge (30–5), the second that the Cyclopes manufacture Jupiter's bolts at Etna's furnaces (36–40), and the third "the sacrilegious legend" (*impia . . . fabula*, 42) that Enceladus, buried under Etna by Jupiter after being defeated in the Gigantomachy, yet breathes fire as he struggles rebelliously against his confinement (41–73). In all the dramatic detail and dexterity with which he briskly narrates his own mini-Gigantomachy in lines 41–73 in particular, the poet perhaps archly asserts his effortless ability to excel in so hackneyed a genre if he so chose; but not for him the "common license of deceitful rumor" (*mendosae vulgata licentia famae*, 74; cf. *fallacia*, 76) with which poets tell of the torments that await us in the afterlife (76–84), or of the private improprieties committed by the gods (85–90).

For present purposes, the importance of this rejection of the *fallacia vatum* lies in our poet's configuration of two Etnas in the *Aetna*. In contrast to the Etna of mythological fiction, his own pledge of truth (*sed omnis/ in vero mihi cura*, 91–2) ushers in his systematic explication of the "real," scientifically revealed Etna in three main movements.[119] First, lines 94–176 describe the hollows, cracks, and chasms that apparently exist beneath the earth, perforating it throughout (175–6). Secondly, 177–384, on wind as the cause of Etna's volcanic action:[120] when air

117. For the personifying aspect, e.g., *fauces* (319, 374), *corporis* (392), *alimenta* and *nutriat* (386), *evomit* (411), etc., with Wolff (2004) 83–4. For mediation between attempts to show that the poem is Stoic (Sudhaus [1898]) or Epicurean (Rostagni [1933]), De Lacy (1943) remains valuable.

118. See Goodyear (1965) 54–6 and (1984) 352–5, and now Garani (2009) 120–1.

119. For analysis of the structure cf. Ellis (1901a) xcvi–ciii; Goodyear (1984) 345–6; Toohey (1996) 189–90; Hine (2012) 317; and now Welsh (2014) 100–1 with n. 13 for further bibliography.

120. For fine in-depth coverage of this section, Garani (2009).

that has accumulated in the hollows under the mountain is compressed and set violently in motion, the wind that coalesces in the high-pressure form of *spiritus* (324, 343) loosens and breaks through the surrounding matter, thereby causing the volcano to belch forth fire, rocks, and other debris. Thirdly, lines 385–567, on the nature and fuel source of volcanic fire: Etna is composed of various combustible substances, such as sulfur, alum, and bitumen, but when volcanic fire is produced by friction, the chief material that sustains it is lava stone (*molaris . . . lapis*, 399–400), which has the extraordinary property of retaining the flames that it absorbs when it burns;[121] inside the mountain the burning lava stone kindles fire in what surrounds it, thereby fueling and feeding the eventual eruption, and the lava that flows from the erupting volcano subsequently cools and hardens back into rock. After repudiating false assumptions about the nature of this *lapis molaris* (510–64), the poet ends his long scientific disquisition with a brisk, three-line summation of what has preceded (565–7). But then comes an unexpected change of direction: the poem draws to a close on a very different note, first condemning man's appetite for distant travel to visit shrines, famous artifacts, or the sites of legendary events (e.g., Thebes, Sparta, Athens) when none of these sights can rival nature's marvels, Etna chief among them (568–602); and after attributing the *impia fabula* (42) of the Gigantomachy to "the deceit of poets" (*fallacia vatum*, 29), the poet concludes with a *fabula* (603) of a very different stamp: the legend of the pious brothers (cf. *pietas*, 633; *pios iuvenes*, 634) of Catania who rush, during an eruption, to save their aging parents, not their possessions[122]—an act of devotion respected even by the morally sentient lava flows, which gave the brothers free passage as they carried their parents to safety (603–45, esp. 634: *erubuere pios iuvenes attingere flammae*).[123]

How, if at all, is this concluding *fabula* to be reconciled with the *Aetna* poet's rejection of poetic *muthos* in favor of his truth-telling, rationalizing *logos*? How, if at all, are the two Etnas as distinguished above to be reconciled within a coherent conceptual framework that unifies the poem? Or is the *Aetna*'s investigative thrust accompanied, even obstructed, by obligatory genuflection to literary tradition, or by

---

121. I use "lava stone" for convenience, but Hine favors the more literal "mill-stone," pointing out ([2012] 321 n.74) that "Classical Latin has no distinct word for 'lava.'"

122. For the legend and its considerable variations in different sources, Goodyear (1965) 207–8 with Santelia (2012), esp. 24–43 on "Le fonti della *miranda fabula*." Our poet names Amphinomus (625) but not his brother, who is commonly called Anapias; other names are recorded in the tradition.

123. The verb *erubuere* nicely combines the connotations of "red hot" and also "red with shame" (cf. *OLD* 1); line 634 alludes (Santelia [2012] 71) to Prop. 4.1.44 *et verita est umeros urere flamma pios* (of Aeneas carrying Anchises from Troy), but our poet may also have in mind *Aen*. 2.633 *dant tela locum flammaeque recedunt*.

"idle conventions that decorate, rather than enhance, the scientific content?"[124] And if the poet is at pains to assert the primacy of his natural-philosophical approach to the volcano, why dwell at such length—a sixth or so of the entire poem—on the falsities of poetic *muthos*, and why show such "persistent, if sneaking respect for the power of his rejected divine beings?"[125] One partial solution to the problem of reconciling the concluding *fabula* with the poet's unwavering commitment to unveiling the naturalistic truth (cf. *nosse fidem rerum dubiasque exquirere causas*, 226) is to interpret the story of the brothers' piety in light of the earlier praises (219–81) of physical inquiry that seeks to know the earth and its wonders (251–2):[126] whereas greed induces man to mine the earth for gold and silver (277), and whereas gain motivates the farmer to fill his barns and wine casks with his produce (cf. 266–7), the mind's most precious harvest and reward (*fruges, merces*, 271) are the gaining of insight into nature's workings (270–305); just so, as the greedy throng (*avara manus*, 629) rushes to rescue all the valuables that it can from the lava flows in the concluding *fabula*, the only riches that concern the brothers are their parents (*illis divitiae solae materque paterque,/ hanc rapiunt praedam*, 630–1). By extension, the eruption that engulfs Catania symbolically punishes earthly greed, while the flames' reluctance to endanger the brothers (634) signals the natural way of, and nature's reward for, their *pietas*—a vision compounded by the explicit evocations of *pius* Aeneas carrying Anchises to safety from the ruins of Troy in *Aeneid* 2.[127] But the larger problem remains: after railing against the use of legend and myth in naturalistic explanation, why might the poet choose to end with this moralizing *fabula*? "[A] bit of poetic license," perhaps,[128] or possibly a fusing of naturalistic investigation with moral commentary of the sort that we find (albeit on a much more ambitious scale) in Seneca's *Natural Questions*, to the effect that the *Aetna* is didactically engaged in ethical as well as physical instruction.[129] But more relevant for now is a different approach to the problem.

---

124. Welsh (2014) 98, referring to Taub (2008) 55 and (2009) 136 for the line that "[t]he *Aetna* poet is critical of myth and legend as a means to explain natural phenomena, . . . yet he ends his poem with a story about the benevolence of nature, and a god, towards humans. In this way, the *Aetna* poet delineates a boundary for the use of legend and the role of gods."

125. Toohey (1996) 190.

126. See on this line Toohey (1996) 191.

127. For the Virgilian dimension see n.123 above with Volk (2005) 80, Glauthier (2011) 125–6, and now Santelia (2012) 38–40, 68 on 625, 69 on 627–8, etc.; at *Ben.* 3.37.1–2 and 6.36.1, Seneca explicitly sets Aeneas and the two brothers alongside one another. For the poet himself arguably "like the twins who rescue their ageing parents" cf. Toohey (1996) 191: "We [sc. the readers] are rescued from the conflagration of divine displeasure by poet and poem."

128. Taub (2009) 135 after (2008) 55.

129. On this line, Taub (2008) 55 and (2009) 135 with Santelia (2012) 44–5. Cf. also Welsh (2014) 109–13, intriguingly relating the intermittent abating of Etna's volcanic action in the main body

Staple techniques that the *Aetna* poet uses to demystify the volcano's workings are multiple explanations (e.g., 102–17, on the possible causes of the earth's perforation with many channels), careful observation and appeals to common experience (e.g., 135–6, 177–9, 191, 329–31, 448–9), inference from the seen to the unseen (e.g., 117–19, 144–5, 306–10, 546–7), analogy (e.g., 98–101, 320–8, 475–7), and self-conscious reflection on methodological principles (e.g., 247–50).[130] Such techniques are of course hardly unique to our poet, who is doubtless influenced by Lucretius' deployment of them in *De rerum natura*, and possibly also (if the dating controversy allows) by Senecan practice in his *Natural Questions*.[131] But as these techniques take their experimental course through the *Aetna*, our experience of the volcano becomes inseparable from the literary operation that explains it: as Jarrett Welsh well puts it, "the activity of writing and reading [this] poem about science is equivalent to doing science."[132] In this sympathetic correlation between theme and medium, the *opus* of the poet's designing hand is balanced by the physical *opus* that is Etna, with high-pressure wind (*spiritus*, 217) the ultimate agent of its volcanic activity:

> nec tamen est dubium penitus quid torqueat Aetnam,
> aut quis mirandus tantae *faber* imperet *arti*.
>
> 197–8
>
> But there is no doubt about what tortures Etna deep below ground,
> or who the amazing craftsman is who commands such great skill.[133]

The word *opus* is used with striking frequency of Etna's "workings" or "process" through the agency of this artisan-like *spiritus* (so, e.g., 117, 159, 169, 184, 219, 458; cf. also *artificis naturae ingens opus inspice*, 600),[134] and it notably recurs with this sense in the poet's summation of his preceding discourse at 565–7:

---

of the poem to the flames' reluctance to burn the brothers: "That pause in the onslaught of the pyroclastic flow [640], I would propose, is how the poet at last fulfills, albeit in a seemingly altered form, the promise [cf. 221, 281] to discuss the intermission of the volcano's activity" (p. 113).

130. Further on these techniques, Taub (2008) 49–51 and (2009) 133–4 with Garani (2009), esp. 106–8, and Glauthier (2011), esp. 101–5.

131. See now on the Senecan aspect Garani (2009).

132. Welsh (2014) 100.

133. Hine (2012) 320.

134. On the important multivalence of *opus* in the *Aetna*, Wolff (2004) 83 with Glauthier (2011) 108–13 and Welsh (2014) 119–20.

haec *operis* summa est, sic nobilis uritur Aetna:
terra foraminibus vires trahit, urget in artum
spiritus, incendi vis it per maxima saxa.

This is the essence of the process, this is how famous Etna burns: the earth absorbs energy through its pores, wind squeezes it into a restricted space, and a powerful fire moves through the huge rocks.[135]

The poet's own project is enunciated through *opus* in line 188 (*nunc opus artificem incendi causamque reposcit*, "Now my project seeks to know the agent and cause of the fire"[136]), and the word again figures prominently when the action of water and air under Etna is illustrated by two extraordinary mechanical examples:[137]

. . . praecipiti deiecta sono premit unda fugatque
torpentes auras pulsataque corpora denset;
aut, veluti sonat †ora duc† Tritone canoro
(pellit *opus* collectus aquae victusque moveri
spiritus et longas emugit bucina voces)
carmineque irriguo *magnis* cortina *theatris*
imparibus numerosa modis canit *arte regentis*,
quae tenuem impellens animam subremigat unda,
haud aliter summota furens torrentibus aura
pugnat in angusto et magnum commurmurat Aetna.

291–300

. . . the water, streaming down with a rushing noise, presses and drives away the sluggish breezes and condenses the particles (of air) as it dashes against them; for, just as [. . .] sounds with a singing Triton (the reservoir of water and the air that is forced into motion drive *the mechanism*, and the trumpet blares out its long note), and just as *in large theatres*, the organ sings its hydraulic song, playing melodies with its pipes of different length, *through the player's skill*, which makes a rowing movement in the water and thus sets the gentle current of air in motion, in just the same way the wind, displaced by torrents of water, rages and fights in its narrow confines, and Etna roars loudly.[138]

---

135. Hine (2012) 323.

136. Hine (2012) 319.

137. In general on the following passage, now Garani (2009) 112–14 with Glauthier (2011) 108–10.

138. Hine (2012) 320–1; my emphases.

The mechanism described in the first analogy (293–5) is all the harder to define because of the corruption in line 293, but the poet seems to allude to a device shaped as a singing Triton and emitting a musical note.[139] But if Munro's *hora duci* is read in 293, to the effect of "just as the hour of battle is sounded to the general by the trumpeting tones of Triton,"[140] then a suggestive parallel for the device is to be found in Suetonius' account of an extravagant *naumachia* that the Emperor Claudius staged on the Fucine Lake in 52 CE:

> The extravaganza was a clash between the navies of Sicily and Rhodes, twelve triremes on each side. A silver Triton rose up from the middle of lake, hoisted by a mechanical device, and summoned the navies to battle with his trumpet.
>
> *Claud.* 21.6[141]

If, despite the textual crux in line 293, we tentatively accept that the *Aetna* poet means an elaborate mechanical Triton approximating to this Suetonian kind, then the Etna tamed by domesticating analogy here is transformed from an intimidating *monstrum* to a mechanistic marvel[142]—a process underscored by comparison with the water organ, or *hydraulus,* in lines 296–8,[143] where the positive, mechanistic analogy is nevertheless offset by the vast difference of scale and sound effect between organ and mountain, and by the contrast between the *cortina* in the theater (296) and the vast natural theater that is Etna.

But beyond the presentation of Etna as the work (*opus*) crafted or set in motion by the *ars* of its *faber*-like wind agency (cf. again 197–8), Patrick Glauthier usefully presses the insight that Etna as natural *opus* and the *Aetna* as poetic *opus* are one, a unity already encoded in the opening lines, where the poet announces that "Etna . . . will be my song" (*Aetna* [the work's title or the mountain itself?[144]] *mihi . . . carmen erit,* 1–4):

---

139. But for extreme caution in identifying this instrument, Goodyear (1965) 155 n.3 and 157–8 on 293.

140. Munro (1867) 12 and 60 *ad loc.* Cf. Goodyear (1965) 157 on 293: "*duc* may conceivably point to *duci* or *ducis*"; on *ora diu,* "[t]he obvious correction *hora* (perhaps with *die*) may be right."

141. Discussed by Glauthier (2011) 108–9.

142. For further interesting implications of a mechanical Triton horn, see Garani (2009) 113: according to Hyg. *Astr.* 2.23, in the war against the Giants Triton's horn served to frighten them into taking flight; our poet's mechanical Triton horn not only rationalizes Etna as machine-like by analogy, but also symbolically counters the volcano's mythological/Gigantomachic associations.

143. For the *de facto* equivalence of *cortina* (296) and the water organ/*hydraulus*, Ellis (1901a) 142–3.

144. Cf. Welsh (2014) 128–9.

> As a musical Triton or sonorous *cortina*, Mount Aetna is both spectacular and familiar. It constitutes a marvelous wonder that operates according to readily accessible scientific principles and therefore can supplant the falsely constructed and erroneously explained mountain of the literary tradition . . .
>
> *The poem itself becomes the mountain*—its sounds are those of the "sonorous" Triton (*Tritone canoro*, 293), its flowing verses are the "wet song" of the water organ (*carmine . . . irriguo*, 296). At the same time, the poet becomes the skilled worker who actually runs the Triton, the musician whose "art" allows the *cortina* to "sing" (*canit arte regentis*, 297).[145]

On this approach the poet composes or constructs both the *Aetna* and Etna in a fusion of the natural-philosophical and literary operations—a merging process that results, as Jarrett Welsh puts it, in "a volcano that is as textual and poetic as it is scientifically 'real.'"[146] For Welsh, this ability of the poem "to create reality within itself" by fully enacting the investigative experience ("poetry *is* the scientific enquiry")[147] importantly transcends the fictive, mythological poetic mode rejected in lines 9–93: on Welsh's reading, the scientific Etna/*Aetna* is as incompatible with that fictive tradition as the poet's commitment to truth telling (cf. again *sed omnis/ in vero mihi cura*, 91–2) is alien to the *fallacia vatum* impugned in line 29. The dissonance between these two modes as distinguished by Welsh will in due course offer a helpful paradigm (and arguably even a direct model) for the conflicting discourses, fictive and scientific, that Pietro Bembo builds into his portrayal of Etna in *De Aetna*. But whereas the scientific approach clearly wins out in Welsh's vision of the *Aetna* poem, we shall see that Bembo portrays an uneasy tension in *De Aetna* between two versions of Etna itself, the one imaginative, ludic, and rooted in the mythico-poetic tradition, the other far more soberly rationalized in terms of its volcanic workings. Traces of a similar tension, I argue, are already discernible in the *Aetna* poem, but they give way before Welsh's predominant focus on "poetry as science"; hence we turn to Glauthier for guidance on how to relate the different faces of Etna in the *Aetna*.

Central to Glauthier's vision of the *Aetna* is that, for all its ostensible hostility to vatic fictions, the poet ultimately recognizes the irrepressibility of that literary tradition:

---

145. Glauthier (2011) 110, 114; my emphasis.

146. Welsh (2014) 120.

147. (2014) 126, 127.

> I will argue that, even though the poet champions scientific analysis of natural phenomena and sets forth an integrated theory on the nature of Aetna's volcanic activity, he continually encourages the reader to conceive of the mountain as a literary artifact that exists outside the world of scientific analysis. *From the poet's perspective, science cannot suppress the literary history of the natural world, and literature cannot offer causal accounts of nature that satisfy contemporary demands for rationalism.* Despite an ostensible opposition, these are complementary ways of thinking about and giving meaning to the natural world.[148]

For all his efforts methodically to explain the volcano, its vast explosiveness—the kinds of horrors unleashed and hyperbolically magnified in the vatic tradition—continually threatens to disrupt the rationalizing process within the *Aetna* itself. So in lines 199–207, one of what Glauthier characterizes as the poem's "collection of miniature eruptions"[149] by which the legendary Etna sporadically reasserts its wondrous volcanic powers, it is as if the scientific impulse were suddenly distracted, even overwhelmed:

> pellitur exustae glomeratim nimbus harenae,
> flagrantes properant moles, volvuntur ab imo
> fundamenta, fragor tota nunc rumpitur Aetna,
> nunc fusca pallent incendia mixta ruina.
> ipse procul tantos miratur Iuppiter ignes,
> neve sepulta novi surgant in bella gigantes,
> neu Ditem regni pudeat, neu Tartara caelo
> vertat, in occulto tantus fremor omniaque extra
> congeries operit saxorum et putris harenae.

> A cloud of burnt sand is ejected in a mass, blazing lumps fly out, deep below ground the foundations are convulsed, now a crash resounds throughout Etna, now the fires mix with dark debris and give out only a faint light. Jupiter himself, from far away, is astounded at such powerful fires, afraid that new giants are rising up to fight long-buried wars, that Dis is ashamed of his kingdom and is moving from Tartarus to heaven: there is such an uproar hidden within, and outside an accumulation of rocks and crumbling sand covers everything.[150]

---

148. Glauthier (2011) 87; my emphasis.

149. Glauthier (2011) 116.

150. Hine (2012) 320, reading *tantus fremor* (206) for †*tantum tremit* in Goodyear (1965) 73 and (1966) 52.

As Glauthier points out,[151] the order imposed by the scientific treatment of Etna thus far in the poem is challenged by this outbreak of extreme (albeit temporary) disorder; and after the poet's dismissal of the mere *fabula* (42) of the Gigantomachy in lines 41–73, this reversion to the unfettered literary *topos* of the mountain in explosive action is accompanied by a revitalization of the mythological store, with Jupiter a passive onlooker and the Giants seemingly resurgent (203–4). These mini-eruptions reach their climax in the macro-explosion that sets the stage for the pious brothers' rescue of their parents at the poem's close (603–45). But in their lurking threat throughout the poem, they demonstrate above all for Glauthier "the vitality of the literary tradition and scientific inquiry's inability to silence it";[152] to press the analogy between poem and mountain, the *Aetna* itself, like the volcano it represents, might be said to be interpenetrated by conceptual fissures and hollows, and the explosive force that gathers there is capable of sporadic narratival eruptions (such as that at 199–207) that destabilize the work's rationalizing agenda.

The two Etnas that stand in tension in the *Aetna* poem, the one mythologically embellished, the other systematically demystified, merge to form a highly inventive application of our central theme so far in this chapter: the versatility, especially the doubleness, with which the Etna Idea is deployed in the Greco-Roman literary tradition. In the *Aetna* the volcano emerges as a multivalent commodity that receives very different kinds of treatment: while the scientific eye looks to the ordering principles that govern Etna's (and any volcano's) mechanics, to the artistically intuitive gaze the mountain is a *locus* of mythological drama and possibility; at the same time, the legend of filial piety in 603–45 applies the mountain's lava flows to uplifting, moralizing effect. These different perspectives are in tension with one another, but the key point for now is that all are in their diverse ways equally valid, pertinent, and engaging; so much depends on the vantage point from which the mountain is viewed, be it that of the natural scientist, that of the fabulist, or that of the moralist. Similarly, in Pietro Bembo's dialogical exchanges with his father, Bernardo, we shall see in Chapter 6 that each brings his own perspective to bear to Etna, the one youthful, exuberant, and adventurous in his direct engagement with the mountain, the other far more sedate, measured, and scientifically detached in his explanation of its volcanic workings. On this approach, the different Etnas of the *Aetna* poem offer an especially useful paradigm for what I take to be Bembo's differentiation between the competing Etna perspectives of father and son in *De Aetna*: here, perhaps, the *Aetna* poem influences *De Aetna* far more profoundly than (just) through various contact points of volcanic theorizing.[153]

---

151. (2011) 118–19.

152. Glauthier (2011) 116.

153. For those contact points, Chapter 6 pp. 253–5.

1.4: The Open-Ended Etna Idea

The Etna Idea hardly ends here. Further Classical and post-Classical manifestations could be elucidated at length, through coverage of authors as diverse as (e.g.) Callimachus and Claudian, Valerius Flaccus and Nonnus.[154] Beyond the frequency of the Idea, the sheer inventiveness with which it is deployed also hardly lacks for further illustration, as one last example will show. In the fourteenth book of Silius Italicus' *Punica*, that late first-century CE epic on Rome's struggle against Hannibal in the Second Punic War, the action suddenly moves to Sicily, and to the campaign waged there by the consul M. Claudius Marcellus in 214–212 BCE. After the city of Leontini is quickly taken by storm (125–77), Marcellus blockades Syracuse by land and by sea (178–91); but the Syracusan resistance is stubborn and the maneuvering prolonged before the city finally succumbs to Marcellus' forces only at the book's end (618–83). In the larger context of the *Punica*, Silius' Sicily in Book 14 functions as a meta-poetic island of sorts,[155] a mini-epic that stands in microcosmic relation to the entire war and to the entire poem, delivering "a re-run of the epic"[156] with Rome now resurgent. Along the way, Sicily fully lives up to its reputation as a famed *locus* of natural marvels in Silius' introductory description of its geography and the genealogy of its inhabitants (11–78). So, in his account of Etna (14.55–69), the volcano is a wonder not just because of its sustained ragings (cf. 64–5: "Inside it boils with an abundant storm of flames, and the constantly regenerated fire flows forth"), but also—*mirabile dictu* (66)—because the mountaintop is snow covered even as Etna seethes within: it is a paradoxical marvel in terms of both its heat index (red hot yet ice clad, 67–8) and color contrast (white with snow, black with burnt ash, 69).[157]

A wondrous vision, then, but when the name *Aetna/Aetne* recurs later in Book 14, it is in still more astonishing circumstances. In the great sea battle that rages at 14.353–579, the Romans on one side, the Syracusans and Carthaginians under Himilco on the other, the Romans finally prevail, but only after a series of bitter and bizarre encounters. At one point two ships, *Perseus* on the Roman side, *Io* on

---

154. See Callim. *Hymn* 4.141–7; Claud. *De raptu Pros.* 1.153–78 with Moro (1999) and Leroux (2004a); V. Fl. *Argon.* 2.25–33; Nonnus *Dionys.* 1.154–2.649. In the latter case, after being worsted by Zeus in a truly mind-boggling confrontation, Typhoeus is finally buried under Sicily at 2.620–30 in circumstances that depart significantly from the literary tradition (cf. Vian [1976] 32), and Etna is specifically named in association with him only at 13.318–20. For Classical treatments of Etna broadly surveyed see the essays assembled in Foulon (2004) and Bertrand (2004c) with Muecke (2006) and now Buxton (2016).

155. See Stocks (2010) 151.

156. Stocks (2010) 152.

157. On these paradoxes, Spaltenstein (1990) 289 on 14.64, 69 with Leroux (2004b) 65–6.

the Carthaginian, meet in such close proximity that a quasi-land battle (*terrestria proelia*, 521) ensues between the crews. The Romans try to invade the other ship, but on the Carthaginian side a certain Polyphemus, reared in a cave on Etna and suckled by a she-wolf (!), breaks the chains connecting the boats, in an effort to thwart the attack (527–33). He dips his oars so as to maneuver the *Io* away, only suddenly to be transfixed by an enemy shaft; his dying hand still moves the oar, but uselessly, and the *Io* subsequently sinks, albeit not because of any direct Roman action, but because the Carthaginians crowded the part of the ship that was free of the enemy, thereby causing it to give way under the sudden weight (534–41). Here is surely a first in literary history, a Polyphemus of impeccable, Romulus-like[158] credentials who reverses his namesake's *Odyssey* story by trying to effect a ship's (his *own* ship's) deliverance, not its destruction (cf. *Od.* 9.473–542), and who is oar plying, not rock throwing, when we last see him in the Silian (distinctly non-Homeric) saga. After the Carthaginians' defeat, "their captive ships were soon towed to shore in a long procession, while others remained at sea, aflame in their burning" (563–5). Among the burning ships were the *Cyane, Siren, Europa* and *Python*; but among those taken captive was "*Etna* of the rocky peaks" (*ardua rupibus Aetne*, 578). The Syracusan-Carthaginian failure is indeed total: far from blazing forth in a spectacular eruption of fire that would at least be true to its name, the *Etna* limps to shore as if truly a damp squib[159]—surely a knowing touch by which Silius concludes his Etna coverage in *Punica* 14 with a headlong plunge into bathos.

Here we leave our coverage of the Etna Idea, but the Idea itself will remain an immanent presence throughout this study, especially in the form of the doubleness of perspectives on Etna that we have so far witnessed either across works (notably, Lucretius' *De rerum natura* and Virgil's *Aeneid*) or within the same work (notably, *De rerum natura*, Ovid's *Metamorphoses,* and the *Aetna* poem); for that doubleness of viewpoint is fundamental to *De Aetna*, as we shall see in Chapter 6 in particular. Our coverage of the Etna Idea has also amounted to an extended exercise in literary memory thus far, an itinerary that has caused us to visit Pindar, Lucretius, Virgil, Ovid, Seneca, and the *Aetna* poet. But this form of visitation has yet to be related to the full mnemonic properties of *De Aetna* as a textual fusion of landscape and memory. In Chapter 2, therefore, we supplement our treatment of the Etna Idea

---

158. Spaltenstein (1990) 326 on 14.529.

159. At 14.579 this *Aetne* is described as "pyre of the living Enceladus" (*spirantis rogus Enceladi*), but at 14.196 Silius associates Typhoeus with Etna. Perhaps, in combination, a learned nod to a divided tradition (see p. 35 and n.32); or Silius perhaps resorts to Enceladus under Etna after associating Typhoeus with the island of Inarime (now Ischia) at 8.540–1. But if in Book 14 we take it that the "official" Silian line locates Typhoeus under Etna, the failure of the ill-starred Carthaginian *Aetne* is redoubled: a damp squib that is ineptly identified with the "wrong" giant.

by contextualizing it within the larger mnemonic repertoire that Bembo deploys in recalling his ascent of Etna; that memory function will also be related to the forward-looking, "modern" sensibility that *De Aetna* displays in comparison with the earlier, and especially pre-Petrarchan, history of mountaineering in the medieval imagination.

2

From Memory to Modernity

WELL BEFORE PIETRO Bembo finally turns his focus to the volcano in *De Aetna* (cf. §21: "But if you've no objection, let's rather hurry on to Etna, which was our original topic of conversation"), his account of the places and topography that he and Angelo Gabriele had traversed en route to the volcano has already conditioned us to perceive landscape as a storehouse of cultural memory and Classical relic. As we proceed up the volcano with Bembo and observe all the physical features that he details along the way, the Etnean landscape is no less laden, I argue, with the literary-cultural memory of Etna's past in the Greco-Roman tradition. That landscape is palimpsest-like[1] in the mythology and lore that lie buried in it. At the same time, underlying Bembo's own text, and even allusively embedded within that text, are the versions and adaptations of the literary Etna(s) that we have sampled so far in Chapter 1. In probing into these subtexts, we have been engaged in a form of "excavation below our conventional sight-level to recover the veins of myth and memory that lie beneath the surface";[2] however foreign and forbidding the actual volcano must have been to so many of Bembo's readers in his own day, recognition of those subtexts also makes *his* Etna accessible to the initiated reader as a known quantity at least on the bookshelf, or as a force of nature that is at least partially tamed by its history *in litteris*.[3] Bembo's literal experience of the mountain is in these ways inseparable from his, and our, literary experience of the Etna Idea, and travel takes on a mnemonic function in the interplay that I posit between volcanic scree and script, Etna and *De Aetna*.

---

1. Now Spencer (2010) xv, 65 with Larmour and Spencer (2007a) 2–3; see already Bertrand (2004a) for a useful but brief treatment of the mnemonic properties of landscape in *De Aetna* in particular.

2. To borrow the formulation of Schama (1995) 14.

3. For this combination of distance and proximity, of mystery and accessibility, in approaches to the Classical past, cf. on the eighteenth and nineteenth centuries (with a special focus on the Grand Tour) Chard (1997) 101.

This chapter seeks to elaborate on the mnemonic significance of the Etna Idea as traced in Chapter 1, and to do so in seven stages. In section 2.1 below, the congruence that I posit in *De Aetna* between physical movement and the activation of literary memory is related to the Classical phenomenon of mnemonic topography. In 2.2, we turn to the tradition, already well established before Bembo's time, of travel writings that combine topographical description with visitation of antiquity in a fusion of past and present, or of up-to-date reportage and antiquarian (re-)collection. After traveling in 2.2 with such luminaries as Cristoforo Buondelmonti (*c.* 1385–*c.* 1430) and Cyriac of Ancona (1391–*c.* 1452), we encounter in 2.3 a man of the same adventurous mold, but one with whom Pietro Bembo was personally familiar: the Franciscan Urbano Dalle Fosse of Belluno, better known as Urbano Bolzanio (*c.* 1442–1524). In 2.1 to 2.3 as a whole, our focus is primarily on *De Aetna* as a form of antiquarian travel, at least in its mnemonic literary qualities. In 2.4, however, we turn from the mnemonic potential of Etna to that of Noniano, the country-villa setting for the dialogue between father and son in *De Aetna*; we shall see that Noniano too, in its different way, is no less a landscape of literary memory in its evocations of the setting, the sociability, and the literariness of the Classical Ciceronian dialogue. As our vision of mnemonic landscape expands outward from Etna to Noniano, the Etnean dimension is importantly supplemented on a different front in 2.5, where Bembo's climb of the volcano is viewed in relation to Petrarch's celebrated ascent of Mont Ventoux in 1336. Even if it goes too far to hail Petrarch's ascent as a defining moment in the dawning of a "modern" consciousness, a moment when the medieval foreboding aroused by mountains gave way to climbing as an endeavor of choice and (self-)discovery, Bembo emulates, even vies with, the Petrarchan model in *De Aetna*—or so I argue in 2.5. In turn, the Petrarchan comparison raises the question of where *De Aetna* stands in relation to the larger history of medieval and Renaissance (attitudes to) mountaineering. A brief sketch of that history is offered in 2.6, but with the further motive of demonstrating the "modernity" of Bembo's adventurous outlook and (self-)exploratory energies in *De Aetna*; and that "modernity" extends in 2.7 to Bembo's rationalization of Etna's volcanic outbursts as a movement away from medieval myth-based or theocentric explanations of such events. In sum, we progress in this chapter from the mnemonic credentials of *De Aetna* to its forward-looking spirit of endeavor in the transformative 1490s: hence the chapter title "From Memory to Modernity."

2.1: Mnemonic Topography

To the modern observer, the figurative potential of Bembo's climb as a scaling of sorts of the Classical tradition finds many enticing *comparanda*, prominent among them the nineteenth-century phenomenon of Aegean mountaineering as a form of Classical visitation. "In the nineteenth-century eastern Mediterranean," writes Veronica Della Dora,

> high peaks did not serve only as points of juncture between different spatial scales. *These summits were also experienced as temporal links: as links between the present and the Classical past to be activated through the physical act of climbing.*[4]

These Aegean mountains not only exerted a certain exotic appeal, at least in comparison with the more familiar Alps. "Because of their peculiar spatiality and visual connectedness," continues Della Dora,

> those mythical summits came to be experienced as a "memory theatre," as an ordered sequence of sites through which the traveller could at once "live" and "master" ancient history, fulfilling the ideals of physical and moral self-improvement that had long been associated with mountaineering.[5]

For all the physical and technical challenges of Alpine climbing, this Aegean experience was distinguished by the humanistic training that it presupposed in its climbers, for whom the ascent was more than an end in itself; the view from the summit gave a form of topographical control that was also historical and literary in bearing, mapping text on to landscape and thereby confirming or applying the more abstract lessons that the educated climber had already received in the Classical classroom. By analogy, Bembo's climb as recounted in *De Aetna* amounts to a comparable exercise in Classical control, albeit in his case that exercise is focused on redirecting the Etna Idea as received from his Classical forebears: because it is encrusted with so many literary layerings from Pindar onward, his Etna is in its way as much a "memory theater" (in Della Dora's sense) as it is a wonder (cf. *incendiis mirus*, §22) in nature's theatre. But Bembo could also look to influential catalysts of his own, near contemporary as well as Classical in origin, for his fusion of spatial and temporal movement in *De Aetna*, the first of them the phenomenon of what might be termed "mnemonic topography"[6] in Latin literature.

In *Aeneid* 8 Aeneas arrives at Pallanteum, the settlement established by the Greek émigré Evander on what was destined to become the future site of Rome. Aeneas is warmly received by Evander on the strength of their ancestral blood

4. Della Dora (2008) 218–19; my emphasis.

5. Della Dora (2008) 219.

6. See already Larmour and Spencer (2007a) 7 and n.18 for bibliography.

ties (134–51) and Evander's fond recollection of meeting Priam (158, 161–2) and Anchises (155–6, 162–3) in his youth. The language of memory and recognition (*agnosco*, 155; *recordor*, 156; *memini*, 157) in this initial encounter between Aeneas and Evander importantly sets the tone for their subsequent interactions in Book 8,[7] which begin with Evander's explanation of the rites that are being celebrated in honor of Hercules at the very moment when Aeneas arrives at Pallanteum. The notional date is August 12, the day on which Hercules was annually honored in Roman historical times at the Ara Maxima in the Forum Boarium, allegedly the site where the hero slew the monstrous Cacus.[8] As we saw earlier,[9] Cacus is typologically associated with Etna and with the larger grouping of volcanic characters such as Polyphemus, Mezentius, and Turnus who are distributed across the *Aeneid*. In recounting Cacus' demise at Hercules' hands (185–267), Evander anticipates the dynamic of Roman *virtus* triumphing over the enemy Other, a dynamic that recurs later in Book 8 and beyond: literally as well as symbolically central to the shield of Aeneas as ecphrastically pictured at 8.626–728 is Octavian-Augustus' defeat of Antony and Cleopatra at Actium in 31 BCE (675–713), while Aeneas' killing of Turnus at the end of Book 12 notoriously problematizes the distinction that the epic has so far invited between virtuous (proto-)Romans on the one side (Hercules-Aeneas-Augustus), the enemies of that civilizing order (Cacus-Turnus-Antony) on the other. On August 13, 14, and 15 in 29 BCE Augustus commemorated his victories in Illyricum, at Actium, and in Egypt in his famous triple triumph at Rome, an event celebrated on the shield at *Aen*. 8.714–28:[10] through Evander's first meeting with Aeneas on August 12, Virgil connects the Herculean and Augustan celebrations in a form of calendrical alignment that prepares the way for his still more daring manipulations of time later in the book. When Evander takes Aeneas on a tour of Pallanteum (306–69), Virgil offers a "palimpsestic view"[11] of this site of the future Rome: while Evander points out landmarks in the narratival present (*monstrat*, 337, 345), Virgil anachronistically invokes far later ages in using names (e.g., *Romani*, 338; *Romulus*, 342) and alluding to places (e.g., the Romulan asylum, 342; the Tarpeian rock, 347) that Evander cannot of course know. Although he begins in the "now" of Evander's time, that pre-Roman narratival moment vies with the Augustan "now" when, in lines 347–8, Evander "leads Aeneas to the Tarpeian seat (*sedem*) and to the Capitol, golden now (*nunc*), in olden times (*olim*)

---

7. On which now Seider (2013) 52–5 with Edwards (1996) 31–2 and Rea (2007), esp. 91–5.

8. On the site, L. Richardson (1992) 186–7 s.v. *Herculis Invicti Ara Maxima*.

9. Chapter 1 p. 37.

10. On the triumph, Gransden (1976) 16 and n.1 with 182 on 8.714–16.

11. Edwards (1996) 31.

rough with woody thickets": even as Virgil's reference to the Tarpeian rock takes us back to Rome's earliest times, the allusion to the temple of Jupiter Capitolinus—it was traditionally built on the site of Tarpeia's tomb (cf. Plut. *Rom.* 18.1), and restored by Augustus[12]—seamlessly connects the remote past and the Augustan present in the juxtaposition of *nunc* and *olim*. In effect, Aeneas' walk with Evander constitutes an artful movement through time as well as space: Virgil's topographical description desegregates Roman time, merging the ages of Evander, Aeneas, Romulus, and Augustus into an indivisible, kaleidoscopic oneness of cultural memory.

The phenomenon of mnemonic topography finds other important manifestations in Augustan poetry, notably in elegy, and especially (i) in Tibullus' portrayal (2.5.23–38) of the site of Rome as it might have appeared in Aeneas' time (so, e.g., 25–6: "still then the cattle grazed on the grassy Palatine,/ and humble huts stood on the Jovian citadel [sc. the Capitol]");[13] (ii) in Propertius' programmatic survey, addressed to an unnamed visitor (*hospes*, 4.1.1), of the Roman *monumenta* of the Augustan present and their humble pre-state before the felicitous coming of Aeneas (4.1.1–70)—a survey that is darker than the Virgilian and Tibullan iterations, with little or no hint of a primeval Golden Age or *locus amoenus* on the original site of Rome, and a greater accent on the disparity between the moral simplicity of old and the luxurious indulgence of the Propertian present;[14] (iii) in Ovid's *Fasti*, where his aetiological explanation of landmark days in the Roman calendar is so often tied to locations within the city (e.g., 1.463–4, 637–50, 2.67–72, 381–2, etc.), and to his spatial movement through it (e.g., 4.905–9, 6.395–8); and (iv) in the exiled Ovid's depiction of his poetic book traveling back from Tomis to Rome, and thereby enabling the poet to visit his cherished city "at least with what [metrical] foot I may," namely in exilic elegy (*contingam certe quo licet illa* [sc. *loca grata*] *pede*, *Tristia* 1.1.16).[15] Reporting back in its personified voice in *Tristia* 3.1, the book tells of the tour that it makes of Rome's monumental center until it reaches Augustus' house on the Palatine (35), its hope of a reprieve for its master (cf. 49–52) all too ominously offset by the intimidating atmospherics of the place (cf. 53: *vereorque locum vereorque potentem*). From Ovid's authorial perspective, his act of topographic memory is made all the more poignant because he revisits the forbidden city from

---

12. For *sedem* (347) in effect as "temple" see *OLD* 5a with Conington (1883) 120 *ad loc.* ("*Sedem* apparently refers to the temple of Jupiter, not as belonging to Evander's time, but as built afterwards").

13. Further on this aspect of 2.5, Rothwell (1996) 830–2; Papaioannou (2003) 682–6 (682 n.5 on the problem of the relative chronology of 2.5 and *Aeneid* 8); Rea (2007) 95–102.

14. Further, Rothwell (1996), esp. 837–8; Papaioannou (2003) 686; Rea (2007) 106–13.

15. On the familiar metrical pun in *pede*, Hinds (1987) 16–17.

beyond the figurative grave in exile.[16] Whereas Virgil, Tibullus, and Propertius use the device to connect Rome past and present, Ovid's mnemonic tour is predicated on severance despite half-belonging, or on the ambiguity of still inhabiting Rome even as he lives in Tomis and yearns in vain for a return to the lost world: for all the nostalgia with which he recalls the city in his exilic poetry, the Augustan recall never came in reality.

Beyond elegy, a final Classical example of mnemonic topography conveniently leads us back to *Aeneid* 8—an example that blends memory with the still more striking erasure of the past. Late in Book 9 of Lucan's Neronian *Bellum civile*, Julius Caesar, fresh from his defeat of Pompey at Pharsalus in 48 BCE, pursues Pompey by land and then by sea (9.952–3), breaking his journey with a tour of Troy, that "burnt-out city, now only a famous name" (*exustae nomen memorabile Troiae*, 964); no such visit is in fact explicitly attested in the historical record, a point that further complicates the dynamics of literary/topographic memory in this episode. In touring Troy's ruins (cf. *etiam periere ruinae*, 969: "the very ruins have been destroyed"), Caesar is partly modeled on Alexander the Great,[17] that "mad king" (cf. *vaesano ... regi*, 10.42) who made his own visit to the hallowed site, and partly on Virgil's Aeneas as he tours Pallanteum with Evander in *Aeneid* 8. The *Aeneid* passage is itself a part—a key subtext[18]—of the mnemonic topography in play in *BC* 9.964–79 as a whole: Caesar, like Aeneas, knows nothing of the places and palaces over which he wanders, and the narrator describes them with an assurance (e.g., 970–1: "He sees Hesione's rock and the secret marriage chamber of Anchises in the wood, and the cave in which Paris sat as judge ...") by which Lucan would seem to push back at Caesar, asserting his own credentials as an influential shaper and preserver of Roman memory.[19] But whereas Virgil works into his narrative the sites of what, from Aeneas' perspective, is the Rome of the distant future, Lucan's Caesar encounters only the past—a past he cannot read, even though "no rock is nameless/without a story" (*nullum est sine nomine saxum*, 973). Whereas Evander attentively guides and instructs Aeneas on his tour (cf. *monstrat*, *Aen*. 8.337, 345; *testatur* and *docet*, 346; *ducit*, 347), Caesar apparently walks without guidance and knowledge (cf. *inscius*, 974)[20] until "a local Phrygian" (*Phryx incola*) is suddenly introduced in line 976. When that *incola* unceremoniously "bids Caesar not to tread on the shades of

16. Exile as death: G. D. Williams (1994) 12–13.

17. On this association, Zwierlein (1986), esp. 465–9 = (2010), esp. 416–20, with Rossi (2001) 314.

18. Martindale (1993) 49–50; Thompson and Bruère (1968) 16–19 = (2010) 139–45; Zwierlein (1986) 469–72 = (2010) 421–4.

19. See Gowing (2005) 88–92.

20. For bibliography on Caesar's "shortcomings as a tourist," Rossi (2001) 315 and nn.5–7, albeit Rossi argues for Lucan's Caesar as a more knowing observer of the Trojan ruins in Book 9.

Hector" (*manes/ Hectoreos calcare vetat*, 976–7) and asks, "Have you no regard for the altar of Hercean Zeus?" (979), he speaks with a remarkable *libertas*—an unintimidated guide (*monstrator*, 979: Lucan in disguise?[21]) not just to the ruins, but also to Caesar's myopia even as "the venerable past filled his gaze" at Troy (*implevit visus veneranda vetustas*, 987). Caesar vows to restore the city ("the Italians will rebuild the Phrygians' walls in glad return, and a Roman Troy will rise," 998–9), but his random progress over its ruins irresistibly suggests the destructiveness and the disregard for traditional Roman institutions that have characterized him so far in the epic; his inability to read the ruins (mnemonic topography here gives way to topographic illiteracy in a form of generic reversal) is accompanied, perhaps, by his failure to heed their warning of greatness brought low, just as he appears to take inspiration, not cautionary counsel, from his visit to Alexander's tomb early in Book 10.

2.2: *Antiquarian Travel before Bembo*

If this Classical use of mnemonic topography offers one major catalyst for Bembo's experimentation with the phenomenon in his *De Aetna*, the second stimulus to be considered here centers on the rise of antiquarian travel, and the writings that it spawned, in the early fifteenth century. Already in the fourteenth century Petrarch fuses literary excavation with topographical movement in recalling, in a famous letter written between 1337 and 1341[22] to the influential Cardinal Giovanni Colonna (1295–1348; Petrarch had joined Colonna's household as his personal chaplain in 1330), the walks that the two of them had shared in Rome:

> We wandered not only in the city but around it, at every step happening on something to stir our thoughts and words. Here was the residence of Evander, here the house of Carmenta, here the cave of Cacus, here the nursing she-wolf and "ruminalis" fig-tree of Romulus and Remus, which is better called "romularis";[23] here Remus died, here were the games of the circus, the rape of the Sabine women, . . . the place where Romulus disappeared. Here Numa talked with Egeria; here was the Battle of the Triplets, Horatius and his brothers . . .[24]

---

21. Green (1991) 251–2 = (2010) 179–80.

22. *Epistolae familiares* 6.5. Date: Bishop (1966) 63.

23. See, conveniently, L. Richardson (1992) 151 for the *ficus ruminalis*, under which the twins were believed to have been suckled by the she-wolf; for *rumin-* tendentiously linked with *rumis/ruma* ("teat"), Plin. *HN* 15.77 and Fest. p. 266 M. with Hadzsits (1936).

24. Bishop (1966) 63–4.

As the letter proceeds, Petrarch's physical experience of Rome's ruins is inseparable from the literary modeling for his account that he derives most obviously from Virgil and Livy. On the material ruins of the city he imposes a verbal text that follows a chronological course through Roman legend and history down to the age of Christian martyrdom ("And here Christ came to find his fleeing lieutenant; here Peter was crucified, Paul beheaded, Lawrence grilled")[25] and finally to the third/fourth century CE ("here Silvester hid, Constantine was healed of his leprosy . . .").[26] The letter is doubly a reconstruction, first retracing the walkers' steps with a topographical immediacy ("Here . . . here . . . here") that recreates their progress as if in real time within the text; and, secondly, amid Rome's ruins, Petrarch creates the illusion of a seamless and self-evident continuity across time, "looking through," as Leonard Barkan puts it, "Virgil's time telescope [in *Aeneid* 8] the other way, re-creating a physical Rome as Evander pre-created it."[27] In his very different way, I propose, and whether or not he was directly acquainted with this Petrarchan letter, Bembo activates a comparable form of literary-topographic memory on the slopes of his Etna: he imposes on it a textual design that shapes or remakes the volcano in the Petrarchan sense that the literary history of the Etna Idea "thoroughly informs his responses to its material fabric."[28] But a still closer analogy for Bembo's mode of travel writing in *De Aetna*—an analogy that is meant (as in the case of Petrarch above) to illustrate the broad cultural context in which Bembo was writing, rather than to press the case for any direct textual influence—is supplied by the fifteenth-century phenomenon of the *isolario*, or "book of islands."[29] This novel mode of cartographic book combined maps with a chorographic narrative that had a significant historical component. It carried the Petrarchan torch in its archeological dimension, but Cristoforo Buondelmonti (*c.* 1385–*c.* 1430), the progenitor of the form,[30] was a trailblazer in the specifically Greek archeological interests that he indulged during his extensive Aegean travels in the early fifteenth century; he was, as Roberto Weiss puts it, "the first humanist

25. Bishop (1966) 65.

26. Bishop (1966) 65.

27. Barkan (1999) 24.

28. To reapply Edwards (1996) 10: "Petrarch's readings of Livy and Virgil in particular—whose Romes were known to him much earlier than was the physical city—thoroughly inform his responses to its material fabric."

29. On the form in general see Lestringant (2002) with Tolias (2007) and 263 n.1 for bibliography.

30. See Weiss (1964), (1972), and (1988) 135–8; Turner (1987) and (1989); Luzzati Laganà (1987); P. F. Brown (1996) 77–81; Donattini (2000), esp. 167–92; Cachey (2010); Bessi (2012).

who, beyond interesting himself in Greek antiquities, observed them with the eyes and investigative spirit of humanism."[31]

Born into a distinguished Florentine family that had ties with the Greek east through marital connection, Buondelmonti appears to have been introduced to Greek studies at Florence through his involvement in the humanist circle of Niccolò Niccoli (*c.* 1364–1437), and through the influential teaching of the Byzantine scholar Manuel Chrysoloras (*c.* 1355–1415) during the latter's residency in Florence from 1397 to 1400.[32] Among the Greek manuscripts that Chrysoloras brought with him from Constantinople was Claudius Ptolemy's *Geographia*, which radically reshaped perceptions of the known world and the ways in which it was cartographically represented—a more scientific approach far removed from the circular *mappae mundi* that were replete with Biblical references, and from the Greco-Roman tradition of "traveler's tales."[33] Fired by Chrysoloras' teaching and well acquainted with Ptolemy's work, Buondelmonti departed in 1414 for Rhodes, which remained his base during his extensive travels in the next decade and more through the Greek islands and beyond. The first of the two works that resulted from his travels, his Latin *Description of the Island of Crete* (*Descriptio insulae Cretae*), was addressed to Niccoli and dispatched to him in 1417; more ambitious was his *Book of the Islands of the Archipelago* (*Liber insularum Archipelagi*), the original version of which was dedicated to his Roman patron, Cardinal Giordano Orsini, and sent to him in 1420.[34] Buondelmonti went on to produce several further redactions of this work between 1420 and 1422, it was much expanded and supplemented throughout the fifteenth century, and its popularity is reflected in the high circulation of its manuscripts (some sixty-five are known) and by its translation into multiple languages.[35] Influenced in part by the medieval encyclopedic compendia, and seemingly also by the tradition of sailing charts known as portolans, Buondelmonti's combination of map and narrative, text and image, gives the illusion of a visited reality, a "true" picturing of place, that brings the written word to life through graphic accompaniment. But while any pretension to a practical nautical purpose

---

31. Weiss (1964) 116. Cf. (1988) 137: "the first western traveller who looked at Greek antiquities with a really appreciative and sensitive eye."

32. See P. F. Brown (1996) 76–7 for Chrysoloras inculcating "a new way to look at remnants of the past," employing "the ruin to make a full visual reconstruction of Roman culture *without the mediation of a text*" (my emphasis). Further on Chrysoloras, Chapter 3 pp. 130–1.

33. Further, Dilke and Dilke (1994) 118–19.

34. For these works and the circumstances of their production, see, conveniently, Weiss (1964) 107–8 with Turner (1987) 12–13.

35. On these points, Turner (1987) 13.

is misleading (Buondelmonti's maps were hardly reliable guides for navigating such perils as hidden rocks),[36] the *Liber*'s account of Constantinople and of more than sixty Aegean islands or island groups has important ramifications for Venetian interests in the eastern Mediterranean: even though it was not his declared aim to do so, Buondelmonti in effect traces "the corridors of power in Venice's maritime domains, highlighting its piecemeal and interrupted nature";[37] in the face of the rising Turkish threat, he recognized the islands' importance as a Christian outpost in the Levant,[38] and also their centrality within the history of Classical civilization.[39] The past and present are fused in his habit of contextualizing the new places he visits in the framework of Classical antiquity, in a narrative mode that appears to slide between on-scene reportage and bookish commentary. So, for but one example, Delos:

> It remains now to give notice of the island of Delos, about which mention is often made among authors; and in its great fame it stood out in the midst of the Cyclades. Long ago, in olden times, it was said to be capable of moving, and it went by many names: Delos, Asteria, Corana, Midia, Lagia, Cineto, Purpile, and now it is classed Sdiles. The poets tell the following story of it . . . [the myth of Latona's giving birth to Diana and Apollo follows.][40]

Late in his account of Delos he describes his ultimately futile attempt, with no shortage of helping hands, to replace on its original pedestal near an ancient temple a colossal statue (*idolum*) of Apollo—only one of a vast number of such *idola* that he witnessed on the ground.[41] This attempted resurrection of the past is matched in a way by Buondelmonti's closing quotation[42] of Virgil's lines on Delos in *Aeneid* 3, albeit with an intriguing distortion of the Virgilian line ordering. After quoting 3.78–9, he seamlessly adds on 3.84 *templa dei saxo venerabar structa vetusto* ("I [sc. Aeneas] was paying homage to the god's [sc. Apollo's] temple, built of ancient stone"). After his own recent allusion to Apollo's fallen statue near the ancient

36. Donattini (2000) 175.

37. Monique O'Connell (2009) 7.

38. Luzzati Laganà (1987) 74.

39. Donattini (2000) 182.

40. De Sinner (1824) 90 no. 32 (in fact the first printed edition of the *Liber*).

41. Cf. Weiss (1964) 112 and (1988) 136 for Buondelmonti "still medieval enough to refer to the statuary as 'idols.'"

42. De Sinner (1824) 93.

temple (*prope olim templum vetustum*),[43] Buondelmonti's selective quotation of Virgil shows a deft touch: in a merging of the ancient past and the fifteenth-century present, it is as if Buondelmonti conflated his own voice with that of Aeneas, expressing via the first-person verb (*venerabar*) his *own* experience of Apollo's temple.

The first printed *isolario*, also centered on the Aegean and published in *c.* 1485, was that of the Venetian ship captain who took the name Bartolomeo da li Sonetti, in reference to the seventy-one sonnets that accompanied the volume's forty-eight woodcut illustrations.[44] This work was one of many fifteenth-century and later productions that were heavily indebted to Buondelmonti's *Liber*, even though the voyages of discovery extended the scope of the *isolario* form to cover not just the Aegean but the whole of the insular universe as well.[45] In terms of pioneering travel motivated by antiquarian enquiry, however, Buondelmonti's most prominent, and charismatic, successor was Cyriac of Ancona (1391–*c.* 1452).[46] His appetite for travel whetted by his early commercial ventures, this well-connected businessman, diplomat, and man of the world ranged over Italy and the Aegean in the quest for monuments and inscriptions from the ancient world, with Buondelmonti's *Liber* one of his guiding texts. Along the way he compiled a sequence of notebooks that grew to three large volumes by 1441 and had expanded to six by his death;[47] little trace survives of these *commentaria*, almost all of which appear to have been destroyed by fire in 1514,[48] but Cyriac's first forty-five years down to 1435 are covered in the *Vita* compiled by his friend from childhood, Francesco Scalamonti.[49] This *Life* is addressed to the Venetian patrician and humanist, Lauro Quirini (1420–79), apparently as materials for Quirini's own larger project of penning Cyriac's biography. Quirini's undertaking itself reflects Cyriac's close association with Venice throughout his life, not least in his contribution to the Venetian culture of collecting that was gaining impetus by the mid-fifteenth century;[50] and Pietro Bembo's familiarity

---

43. De Sinner (1824) 92.

44. See Donattini (1994–5) and (2000) 193–238.

45. For these works, notable among them Benedetto Bordon's *Libro nel qual si ragiona de tutte l'isole del mondo* (published at Venice in 1528), Donattini (2000) 179–80, 239–64 with Conley (1996).

46. Properly Ciriaco di Filippo de' Pizzicolli, for whom Bodnar (1960) and (2003) ix–xiii; Weiss (1988) 137–42, 169–70; P. F. Brown (1996) 81–91; Ciccuto (1996); Belozerskaya (2009); Mitchell et al. (2015) vii–xviii.

47. Bodnar (1960) 69.

48. On this theory, Bodnar (1960) 70–2; the only surviving autograph portion of the *Commentaria* is now easily accessed in Bodnar (2003) 298–343 (= *Diary* V).

49. See Mitchell and Bodnar (1996) and now Mitchell et al. (2015) 1–171.

50. For Cyriac's Venetian ties, P. F. Brown (1996) 82–3, with the following on Cyriac *qua* collector: "one might say that Cyriacus brought the Greek east into the drawing rooms and *studioli* of the

with Cyriac is signaled by his (or his father's) acquisition of the Strabo codex that Cyriac obtained in Constantinople in 1447, adding to it scholia on geographical, epigraphical, historical, and linguistic matters.[51] Hailed as "the one and only liberator and preserver, patron, and parent of antiquity,"[52] the indefatigable Cyriac recorded and preserved the past as he toured its sites, copying inscriptions and combining textual reportage with illustrations of the monuments he witnessed.[53] He collected manuscripts,[54] but in contrast to the fragilities of manuscript transmission, for Cyriac, as for Petrarch before him, inscriptions gave an unimpeded view of the ancient past:

> It appeared to him, as he looked upon the great remains left behind [sc. at Rome] by so noble a people, cast to the ground throughout the city, that the stones themselves afforded to modern spectators much more trustworthy information about their splendid history than was to be found in books. He accordingly resolved to see for himself and to record whatever other antiquities remained scattered about the world, so that he should not feel that the memorable monuments, which time and the carelessness of men had caused to fall into ruin, should entirely be lost to posterity.[55]

But whereas Petrarch had tended to draw on the material remains to illuminate the text, Cyriac shows the opposite tendency,[56] using the text to shed light on the

---

Latin west, supplying his clients and friends in Italy not only with antiquities, but also—through his inscriptions and excerpts—first-hand eye-witness knowledge of the ancient world. He had been there." Further on the Venetian culture of collecting, Chapter 7, esp. pp. 291–2.

51. This acquisition was limited to the first (containing Books 1–10) of the two volumes into which Cyriac's codex was divided, and which now resides at Eton College: Bodnar (1960) 54 and n.8 and 118–19 with Clough (1984) 315–16 (speculating that, since the codex was used by Guarino da Verona in the early 1450s, it may have been acquired by Bernardo Bembo in Verona, where he was *podestà* in 1502–3; the new acquisition was perhaps meant to complement the text of Strabo, beginning late in the twelfth book, that already belonged to the Bembo library).

52. So Jacopo Zeno (*c.* 1418–81, Bishop of Padua from 1460 onward), as cited in King (1986) 10.

53. See further P. F. Brown (1996) 85–7. For Cyriac's indefatigability cf. Bodnar (1960) 17, citing his friend Francesco Filelfo (*Nunquam quiescit Kyriacus* . . .). For a more humorous assessment of Cyriac's mania for epigraphic travel, see the barb apparently aimed at him in a forged inscription (*CIL* II 149*; now Espluga [2011]), very possibly composed by Francesco da Niccolò Contarini (1424–60), scion of a patrician Venetian family, in which the deceased addresses the reader so: "I, the insane Heliodorus of Carthage, gave orders for me to be buried in this sarcophagus at the far end of the world, to see if anyone more insane than I would make it all the way to this place to visit me."

54. So Scalamonti's *Vita* = Mitchell et. al (2015) 64–5 §71; Bodnar (2003) 124–5 *Diary* II.64–5, 128–31 *Diary* II.72 with (1960) 54.

55. From Scalamonti's *Vita* = Mitchell et al. (2015) 49 §56.

56. P. F. Brown (1996) 85.

material object. For but one example of this phenomenon, consider his account of Samothrace, which he visited in October 1444:

> There [sc. in the old city]. . . we first looked at the ancient walls, built of large stones. Extending from a high, steep hill over a long stretch on a decline that slopes down to the sea, they survive to our day, provided in some part with towers and gates in marvelously diverse architectural styles. Moreover, to add to the island's accumulation of celebrity, it was on it, according to Plutarch, that the young Philip came to know Olympias, the mother of that most noble king Alexander.[57]

Cyriac goes on describe the further antiquities that he found on his Samothracian tour, recording six inscriptions (two of them in Latin) along the way;[58] of special interest, however, is the inference that he appears to have drawn while on Samothrace from his reading of Plutarch's *Life of Alexander* and his familiarity with Aristotle.[59] A sketch that he made of the bust of a bearded man is lost, but it is known from two copies of it, one now in Oxford, the other in Florence.[60] The man is announced as Aristotle; for "[w]hat could be more natural, it must have seemed to Cyriacus, than to find a bust of the great philosopher here in this place where Philip had met Olympias?"[61] The true identity of the figure (Teiresias?)[62] matters less for now than what this episode reveals of Cyriac's procedure in moving from text to object, and in his creative effort not just to document the ruins but also to make sense of them within a constructed narrative of the past: whether or not his rationalizations hit the mark, his aim is commendable.

2.3: *Urbano Bolzanio*

I hardly insist that Pietro Bembo's fusion of spatial movement and Classical visitation in *De Aetna* is directly or specifically influenced by Buondelmonti's or Cyriac's activations of landscape as a repository of Classical memory. But Bembo builds, I argue, on the dynamic approach to landscape that their writings exemplified and

57. As given in the reconstruction of Bodnar (2003) 100–1 *Diary* II.11.

58. Bodnar (2003) 102–5 *Diary* II.15–21.

59. See on what follows Lehmann-Hartleben (1943), esp. 123–8, with Williams-Lehmann and Lehmann (1973) 15–19.

60. Williams-Lehmann and Lehmann (1973) 17.

61. Williams-Lehmann and Lehmann (1973) 16.

62. First proposed by Lehmann-Hartleben (1943) 127–8.

helped to promote—an approach that viewed the ancient remains not as the inert vestiges of a lost past but as a "living" legacy to be reawakened, interpreted, and related to the fifteenth-century present. Bembo was also in a sense following in Cyriac's footsteps, at least as far as Taormina: just as Pietro explored the ruins there (*De Aetna* §13), so Cyriac, on one of his visits to Sicily, had apparently witnessed from afar "the lofty, smoking volcano of Etna [and] arrived at the steep and ancient town of Taormina, where he inspected many large, ancient monuments."[63] But the tradition of travel to seek out antiquities finds still more literal representation in *De Aetna* in the person of Urbano Bolzanio.[64] This interesting figure plays, I propose, an important symbolic role in *De Aetna*, partly because his renown as a traveler in search of Classical inscriptions and manuscripts, his appetite for naturalistic inquiry, and his known association with Constantine Lascaris (Bembo's Greek teacher) in Messina all serve indirectly to endorse the humanistic and naturalistic ambitions of Bembo's own Sicilian/Etnean venture; and partly also because of the suggestive implications of Urbano's presence in *De Aetna* when Bembo's ascent of Etna is compared with Petrarch's famed account of his climb of Mont Ventoux.[65] Bembo tried to emulate Urbano in reaching the higher of the two craters at Etna's summit, but he apparently failed in the attempt:

PIETRO: We were kept from climbing it by the extreme force of the winds and by the billowing clouds of smoke, and so I can't tell you anything else about it unless you want me to recount to you what I subsequently heard from the monk Urbano when he was in Messina. He is indeed someone of the highest integrity, and the most enthusiastic investigator of such matters; for *a few days before us* he'd carefully examined the entire summit during a period of the utmost calm.

BERNARDO: I'd like that very much: I know him and esteem him, as you're aware, and so your whole account will be all the more welcome to me because he's your witness.

De Aetna §28

A pleasing compliment to a figure evidently cherished by both father and son. But then on the question of whether snow persists on Etna throughout the year, and not just in winter:

63. So at least Scalamonti's *Vita* = Mitchell et al. (2015) 26–7 §32.

64. For Bolzanio, Bustico (1905) and (1932); Naselli (1934) 119–22; Beschi (1984); Gualdo Rosa (1986); Rosada (1997) 53–5 and n.68 for bibliography; Gaisser (1999) 270–1; Scapecchi (2001).

65. See pp. 100–1 below.

PIETRO: But, to return to those snows, that same Urbano added that when he was making his ascent on June 1, it snowed plentifully enough and in large quantities; and then a second time, while he was staying at Randazzo a week later, snow fell almost to the depth of a foot over the entire expanse of the mountain.

De Aetna §46

After arriving in Messina on May 4, 1492, Bembo and Angelo worked assiduously on their Greek before, fourteen months later (i.e., late June or July 1493: *De Aetna* §11), they ventured to Etna. In stating that Urbano climbed the volcano "a few days before us" (§28), Bembo presumably means June 1, 1493, in accordance with §46 as given above. But how sure can we be that Urbano was truly in Sicily on or around that date?

According to Urbano's nephew, the humanist Pierio Valeriano Bolzanio (1477–1558), Urbano "did not fail to visit, on foot, either Egypt or Palestine or Arabia or Sinai; he roamed through all of Greece; *he traveled around Sicily; twice he climbed difficult and dangerous Etna to explore the causes of its fire and from the topmost lip of the crater inspected the whole enclosed space of its cavity.* He went to see Constantinople and all of Thrace, accompanying his Maecenas Andrea Gritti, who had been sent as an ambassador for peace by the Venetian Senate."[66] When did Urbano make these travels? Two sequences appear to be distinguishable, the second beginning in 1503: in May of that year Gritti departed on his embassy, returning by early June 1504.[67] As for the first, it is conventionally placed between 1473 and 1484.[68] After traveling around the eastern Mediterranean and collecting inscriptions and manuscripts in the manner of Cyriac,[69] Urbano returned to Italy via Messina, spending time at Lascaris' school. There he apparently worked to perfect his Greek, using Lascaris' library, making copies of grammatical materials, and seemingly working closely with Lascaris himself: of two surviving manuscripts that are attributable to Urbano's hand, one now in Copenhagen, the other in Oxford, the latter shows marginal interventions by Lascaris in a part of the work that renders one of Lascaris' own

---

66. *De litteratorum infelicitate* 2.74 = Gaisser (1999) 243 (with p. 70 for the proposal that Valeriano "conceived and began his work in the spring of 1529"); my emphasis. Apart from Valeriano, Urbano's *vita* is known from a funeral oration delivered by Alberto da Castelfranco and subsequently published as *Oratio habita in funere Urbani bellunensis e minoritana familia unius* (Venice 1524; further, Bustico [1905] 313). The first modern biography is eighteenth century: Doglioni (1784).

67. So on the basis of the available documentation of Urbano's life (but without reference to the complicating factors introduced by *De Aetna*, on which more below) Gualdo Rosa (1986) 89 with Gaisser (1999) 243 n.151.

68. So Gualdo Rosa (1986) 88; Gaisser (1999) 270. Cf. Rosada (1997) 54: Urbano's Sicilian stay cannot be dated with certainty, but "sicuramente prima del 1484," when he moved to Florence.

69. Rollo (2001) 177 with Beschi (1984) 4.

writings, Περὶ ὀνόματος.[70] On his eastern travels Urbano had also compiled, in the tradition of Cyriac, an *Itinerario* in the Venetian dialect; an excerpt of this *Itinerario* survives in the form of the so-called *Anonimo Ambrosiano*.[71] Urbano, it seems, also shared with Lascaris some of the fruits of his labors in collecting inscriptions in the east; for a folio of a manuscript in Lascaris' hand, now housed in Madrid, shows a series of inscriptions that coincide strikingly with the *Anonimo* excerpt, indicating that Lascaris' ultimate source for them was not Cyriac but Urbano.[72] After Messina, the customary *vita* goes, Urbano was in Florence for five years (1484–9) at the invitation of Lorenzo de' Medici, consorting there with the luminaries of the Platonic Academy and tutoring the young Giovanni de' Medici (1475–1521), the future Pope Leo X. When Giovanni was elevated to the cardinalate in 1489, Urbano settled in Venice, and while teaching Greek there (among his pupils were such eminences as Scipione Forteguerri, Niccolò Leonico Tomeo, and Marcantonio Sabellico) he also forged strong links with Aldo Manuzio, the Aldine Press, and the Neoacademic circle around Manuzio. Beyond his editorial collaboration with Manuzio,[73] Urbano was also responsible for the first Greek grammar written in Latin[74]—an act of synthesis and simplification[75] that first saw the light of day in the Aldine *Institutiones graecae grammaticae* of January 1498 (1497 *more veneto*). A second edition, revised and enlarged, was published in two volumes at the Venetian press of Giovanni da Trino in 1512, and in 1523 Urbano prepared a third edition in nine books, only for two decades to pass before its posthumous publication in 1545.

In his 1784 biography, Lucio Doglioni locates Urbano's first travels to the east broadly between 1473 and 1493, thereby positing as a *terminus ante quem* for Urbano's stay in Messina Lascaris' presumed death in 1493.[76] As we saw above, those travels are conventionally dated to between 1473 and 1484; but how then to reconcile that dating with Bembo's claim in *De Aetna* that Urbano was in Messina, and climbing Etna, in June–July 1493? Doglioni's broad time frame offers one convenient way of circumventing the problem, but other possibilities remain: if Urbano visited Messina

---

70. See Rollo (2001) 178 with Martínez Manzano (1994) 289.

71. For this identification with Urbano's *Itinerario*, Beschi (1984) with Weiss (1988) 142–4 and P. F. Brown (1996) 149–50 and 315 n.2.

72. On these points, Beschi (1984) 13–15.

73. For Aldo's high regard for Urbano, Scapecchi (2001) 110 and n.8, 113.

74. See esp. Rollo (2001) with Botley (2010) 36–40.

75. Rollo (2001) 185 with Botley (2010) 36–7, also affirming (p. 37) that "[s]cholars regarded Urbano's grammar highly."

76. Doglioni (1784) 17–18; cf. for the misattribution of Lascaris' death (he died on August 15, 1501) Beschi (1984) 16.

(and first climbed Etna?) before he moved to Florence in 1484, he might conceivably have made a second visit a decade or so later, when Bembo was also there. Alternatively, Piero Scapecchi proposes that Urbano's travels in fact took place in 1488/9–1493, that those five or so years allowed enough time for the collecting of the inscriptions and other materials that were incorporated in his lost *Itinerario*, and that his stay with Lascaris in 1493 marked the consummation of his Greek studies thus far[77]—a reconstruction that fits in nicely with Urbano's presence in *De Aetna*. But the timeline posited by Scapecchi is arguably (far too?) narrow, varied testimony firmly locates Urbano in Venice in the early to mid-1490s, and the harsh practicalities of travel to Sicily surely tell against his making any brief journey to and from Messina in 1493.[78] Hence the suspicion that Bembo may have fabricated his reported meetings with Urbano in Sicily: wanting to fill out his account of his own incomplete ascent of Etna, might he have consulted Urbano only *after* he and Gabriele returned to Venice in 1494?[79] Did he thereby work into *De Aetna* his secondhand description of conditions at the volcanic summit, disguising his sleight of hand and preserving the dramatic and chronological integrity of his dialogue by pretending that Urbano was actually in Sicily in June–July 1493? Of course, the objection goes,[80] any such ruse would have been transparent to Bembo's knowing circle of readers at Venice. But even if we accept that, on balance, Urbano's stay in Messina and his climb(s) of Etna are better located in 1473–84, not 1488/9–93, Bembo's distortion may yet be viewed as a liberty taken, the transparency of his maneuver stark but beside the point: within the tightly woven literary fabric of *De Aetna*, he may displace Urbano's climb of Etna in the chronological sense, but the climb itself remains a documented truth,[81] and one that he seamlessly incorporates into the dialogue so that he can report on the volcanic summit in the written word, if not in person. If, moreover, Bembo fabricates Urbano's presence in Messina in 1493, his stress on Urbano's commitment to the truth (*homo ille quidem verissimus, De Aetna* §28) is wittily ironized. But the larger effect of the distortion is far more profound: by invoking Urbano, that "most enthusiastic investigator of such matters" (*harum rerum cupientissimus sciscitator*, §28), Bembo implicitly inscribes himself into the tradition that Urbano represents not just of naturalistic inquiry, but also, I suggest, of antiquarian travel.

---

77. Scapecchi (2001) 110–11. He posits Urbano's possible departure from Florence as early as late 1488 because, in November of that year, Bolzanio received dispensation from Francesco Sansone da Brescia (general minister of the Franciscan Order from 1475 until his death in 1499) to go to the Holy Land (p. 110, with Beschi [1984] 17).

78. On the latter two points, Naselli (1934) 121.

79. Naselli (1934) 121.

80. Rosada (1997) 54 n.71.

81. So at least Pierio Valeriano on p. 87 above.

2.4: Etna as an Island, Noniano as a Memory Place

Before we leave the theme of antiquarian travel and topographic memory, two further proposals remain to be made. The first concerns the *isolario* tradition as sampled above in the case of Cristoforo Buondelmonti. A striking feature of *De Aetna* is that Bembo's Etna resembles an island within an island,[82] in that "in its overall nature and appearance it draws attention to itself from afar" and "almost forms a circle at its base" (*Ipsa Aetna radices suas fere in orbem deducit*), its circumference at least a hundred miles (§22). Etna appears to dominate Sicily, and even to be hyperbolically co-terminus with it, in the conceptual map that Bembo draws in stating (§22) that

> [o]n the eastern side it drinks from the Ionian Sea and holds Catania on its bottommost foot; to the west it slopes down into the island on the side bordering the Tyrrhenian Sea and what are called the Aeolian Islands; where it slopes down to the north, it meets the promontory of Pelorus on its flank, and there are the straits of Italy; on the other side, the rest of the island lies beneath it, as do all those stretches that join Lilybaeum [sc. modern Marsala, in the westernmost part of Sicily] in extending toward Africa.

Set apart and contained within its own boundaries (*intra suos terminos*, §22), the mountain is nothing short of a *locus amoenus* on its lower slopes, where its fertile microclimate, its beautiful vistas, and its chattering streams form an idyllic picture that is completed when Bembo reapplies to its rich variety of trees Homer's lines on the orchard garden of Alcinous in Phaeacia (§23; cf. *Odyssey* 7.114–21). This luxuriance extends to Etna's middle region, which is extensively wooded (*variis arboribus late sylvescit*, §24) and yet also boasts expanses of arable land that is "so rich in grain that it sometimes brings the farmers a crop yielding a hundredfold return on their investment" (§24). Even though the uppermost part of the volcano is "bare all the way up to the very summit," albeit sparsely grassed in places and interspersed with outcroppings of tufa (§26), Pietro claims to have found "[o]n a very high eminence, where the woods give way and the view is unlimited in its command of the island" (§48), a luscious meadow where, he asserts, the god Faunus is said to roam (§§49–50)—a vision that surely stretches to breaking point the tension that has long existed thus far in *De Aetna* between Bembo's seemingly objective reportage of conditions on the volcano and his highly subjective, fantasy-like projections on to its slopes.[83] To press at this point the island analogy, Bembo's Etna finds

82. Cirelli and Nicosia (2010) 147.

83. See Chapter 6 below, esp. pp. 266–8.

suggestive illumination in Veronica Della Dora's remarks on how "[i]n Renaissance geographical descriptions, the island endured as a principal cognitive form, as well as a practical mnemonic tool. Its self-contained spatiality," she continues,

> allowed the compiler to blend fact and legend, personal observation and hearsay, past and present; it gave textual coherence to the most disparate information. In particular, the Aegean islands offered the perfect chorographic scale, which emphasized the qualitative characteristics of the *locus*. Microcosms to be explored and described, islands in this sense constituted narrative containers and cabinets of wonders. Delimited by their coastline, islands were easy to grasp by the eye and imprint on the memory.[84]

In its own delimited spatiality, Bembo's Etna is itself a narrative container and cabinet of wonders, and through his mixture of scientific exegesis on the one hand, his ludic appeal to Faunus, Typhoeus, and (I argue) the underlying literary apparatus of the Etna Idea on the other, he blends fact and legend, personal observation and hearsay, past and present in the tightly controlled exercise in textual coherence that is *De Aetna*. His portrayal of Etna's bountiful vegetation also invites comparison with Renaissance perceptions of the mountain-island as a natural botanical garden—a theme well explored by Della Dora through the case study of Mount Athos, itself that quasi-island which, like Etna, is easily partitioned into three main vertical regions.[85] Could it be, then, that in so suggestively casting his Etna as an island-like prominence on Sicily, Bembo was consciously reapplying Renaissance geographical attitudes to the island as "a principal cognitive form"? But if, more cautiously, that larger Renaissance attitude is viewed only as a possible ambient influence on *De Aetna* (as opposed to an explicit, textually verifiable reference point), Bembo's Etna nevertheless remains an island of the mind in his shaping of it as a wonder (*mirus*) set apart *intra suos terminos*, a figurative as well as literal singularity (cf. *sibi uni par est*, §22); or so the following chapters will argue in tracing the highly imaginative ways in which Bembo exploits the symbolic possibilities of his Fantasy Island.

Secondly, our predominant focus thus far has been on Bembo's coverage of the Etnean landscape as a form of mnemonic topography. In the dramatic setting of *De Aetna*, however, this mnemonic dimension also extends to Noniano itself, an all too fitting venue for the neo-Ciceronian mode of dialogue that was so fashionable in

---

84. Della Dora (2011) 68.

85. Della Dora (2009) and (2011), esp. 63–7 ("Athos as a *Locus Amoenus*"), 67–71 ("Athos as a Utopia: Athos in Renaissance Island Books"), 218 (on Athos' three main regions, evergreen, wooded, and alpine); cf. also Chapter 6 p. 234 and n.73.

the early Italian Renaissance. In contrast to purely fictional dialogue, the Ciceronian documentary dialogue purports to be a transcription of a real conversation that involves historically identifiable people in a realistic location.[86] Of course, Plato's dialogues are documentary in that they too feature real people in realistic settings, but historical realities impinge far more directly on the Ciceronian dialogue than on Plato; as Virginia Cox puts it, the Roman form is distinguished by its "preoccupation with the individual, the concrete, the historically verifiable."[87] It is the Ciceronian, not the Platonic, documentary mode that prevails in Cox's analysis of the Cinquecento Italian vernacular dialogue—a Ciceronian mode characterized by speakers of relatively high social standing, a concern for historical accuracy, and the closest attention to decorum.[88] We shall soon witness the Ciceronian credentials of *De Aetna*, but Cox also importantly observes that it was only in Italy, not the rest of Europe, that a robust tradition of the Ciceronian documentary dialogue took root. The causes of this phenomenon are importantly sociological, she argues, rather than only philosophical or literary: the elitist overtones of the Ciceronian dialogue gave the form a special appeal in Italian court life.[89] The Cinquecento vernacular form thrived, but far from exclusively so: the neo-Latin tradition continued to prosper well into that century, with certain writers, Bembo prominent among them, authoring dialogues in the vernacular as well as in Latin.[90]

Against this background, the idyllic setting for *De Aetna* may evoke in its shady trees and pleasant stream the *mise en scène* of the Platonic *Phaedrus* (*De Aetna* §5; cf. *Phdr.* 229a–b, 230b); but the Ciceronian accent is far more pronounced. At the beginning of *De legibus* 2, in the general setting of Cicero's family estate near Arpinum, Atticus suggests to Cicero that they continue their conversation from Book 1 while resting, after their walking, on a pleasant island that has just come into view in the river Fibrenus. Cicero enthusiastically agrees (2.1, 3):

> Sane quidem; nam illo loco *libentissime soleo* uti, sive quid mecum ipse cogito sive aut quid scribo aut lego . . . Ego vero, cum licet plures dies abesse, praesertim hoc tempore anni, et *amoenitatem* hanc et salubritatem sequor.
>
> Certainly. I use that spot regularly with great pleasure, whether I am thinking something over or reading or writing something . . . When I have enough

86. For "documentary" as opposed to "fictional" forms of dialogue, Cox (1992) 9–10.

87. Cox (1992) 12; further on the Ciceronian as opposed to the Platonic dialogue, K. J. Wilson (1985) 23–45 with Marsh (1980), esp. 1–23.

88. Cox (1992) 14.

89. Cox (1992) 21.

90. Cox (1992) 23.

> free time, particularly at this season, I seek out the beauty and healthfulness of this place.[91]

Like Cicero, Bernardo Bembo relishes all the precious time that he can afford to spend at his retreat (§5):

> Ego vero, fili, nuspiam esse *libentius soleo* quam in hac cum ripae tum arborum tum etiam fluminis *amoenitate*.
>
> But for my part, son, there's no place where I'm usually happier to be than in this pleasant setting of the bank and the trees and also the river.

Beyond the explicit verbal echoes here, and beyond Pietro's tactful casting of his father in the Cicero role, the Ciceronian presence fundamentally conditions Bembo's entire dialogue, setting the tone for the mixture of urbanity and erudition, of gentle humor and serious-mindedness, of earnestness and conviviality, that characterizes the proceedings that follow. If in this respect we recognize a direct allusion[92] to *De legibus* in Pietro's opening maneuvers, it carries nothing short of programmatic force: from the outset *De Aetna* fashionably bears the hallmark of the neo-Ciceronian dialogue, with "Ciceronian" a marker not merely of style or form, but also of the deeper sociology underlying the humanist dialogical experience.

But the echo chamber resonates yet further: just as the presence of ancestral masks in the Roman house made physical experience of the place inseparable from visitation of the past, so the Ciceronian villa was itself a repository of ancestral memory.[93] To return to *De legibus* 2:

MARCUS: . . . But in fact I have another cause of pleasure here, which is not so relevant to you.

ATTICUS: What is that?

MARCUS: Because, in truth, this is my own and my brother's real fatherland. Here is the most ancient origin of our stock; here are our family rituals and our family; here there are many traces of our ancestors. In brief: you see this house? It was made larger and fancier by our father, who spent most of his life here in study, because of his poor health; but on this very spot, while my grandfather was still alive and it was a small house of the old style, like the house of Curius in the

91. Trans. Zetzel (1999) 129.

92. With Kilpatrick (1986) 333.

93. See O'Sullivan (2011) 104–10 on "Walking in history."

Sabine country, I was born. *And so something abides deep in my mind and feelings which makes me take all the more pleasure in this place . . .* [94]

In a seeming digression from the main Etna theme in *De Aetna*, Bernardo expatiates in comparable terms on how he has built up Noniano as patrimony for his children, but also as a storehouse of memory:

BERNARDO: These acquisitions are for you, sons, for you, I say, not for me. For I know how it's usually more pleasant for sons to receive from their parents what they've sought rather than easily to acquire it for themselves, either because most of us tend to shirk the effort of going after things while all of us enjoy the pleasure of acquisitions; or because the possessions that are left to us by our forebears retain the memory of those who bequeathed them—a memory that may somehow render them more hallowed for us, but certainly also makes them much more pleasurable to receive.

PIETRO: Those words of yours are very precious to me now, father . . . ; and, as long as I live, they will always be implanted in my mind and memory . . . But if we ever outlive you in the natural way of things, I have other reasons, . . . other reasons, I say, why your memory will always be sacrosanct to me, and quite apart from your Noniano.

De Aetna §§17–18

Beyond Noniano as a repository of family memory, however, and beyond *De Aetna*'s own status as a secondary repository in its fond memorialization of Bernardo, the spatial positioning of father and son in relation to each other, their movements, and even their relative postures are reminiscent of how the participants comport themselves in the Ciceronian villa dialogue. When Pietro and Bernardo take to their feet and get into their dialogical stride as they walk along (cf. §10: "let's rather take a walk along the bank near the water, and let's apply ourselves to the rest of our conversation, talking in the river's company"), their gentle progress is set in stark contrast to the rigors of Pietro's climb (cf. §44: "if you want to see any crater you please, you need to crawl for two miles across the shelves I've described"), the manicured charms of Noniano vastly outsized by Etna's raw grandeur. They walk for a time, until Bernardo tires and sits down on the grass while Pietro remains standing (§32): in their balance of walking and sitting they follow in the footsteps of Cicero and his companions,[95] giving a different dimension to "the idea that a stroll through a

94. 2.3 trans. Zetzel (1999) 129–30; my emphasis.

95. Cf. *Div.* 2.8, *Leg.* 1.14, 2.1 with Dyck (2004) 93.

country estate could inspire philosophical reflection about other times and places";[96] for the moving interaction of father and son is itself an act of literary memory, as Bernardo obliquely acknowledges in saying *philosophemur* ("let's be philosophers") just before he sits in §32 and they continue their dialogue in time-honored fashion.

2.5: *Petrarch on Mont Ventoux*

While he converses with his father, Pietro is also in a sense in dialogue with Petrarch, emulating or perhaps rather rivaling the latter's ascent of Mont Ventoux, that "benign 1,910-metre lump in the Vaucluse"[97] in southeastern France, on April 26, 1336;[98] here the mnemonic qualities of *De Aetna* extend to recollection of the Petrarchan mountain-scape and -experience. Petrarch describes that climb in a famous letter (*Epistolae familiares* 4.1)[99] addressed to Dionigi da Borgo San Sepolcro (*c.* 1300–42), his close friend and erstwhile confessor who had joined the Augustinian order at an early age; a student and later a teacher of theology at the Sorbonne in Paris, he went on to teach at Avignon, where he first met Petrarch probably in 1333—the beginning of an association that deeply influenced Petrarch's spiritual and intellectual development.[100] This letter has important implications for *De Aetna* because of the highly creative ways in which Petrarch himself makes symbolic capital of the ascent ofVentoux.

Petrarch was motivated to make the climb, he claims, "solely by the desire of seeing what so great a height had to offer" (*sola videndi insignem loci altitudinem cupiditate ductus*, §1)—a motive that has characterized him by one view (to be contested below) as the first Alpinist on record, and the first to climb a mountain just because it was there.[101] He had apparently long had the ascent in mind, but what finally caused him to take action was his rereading of the Livian episode (40.21–2) in which Philip V of Macedon climbed Mount Haemus in Thrace in 181 BCE.[102] As

---

96. O'Sullivan (2011) 108, citing the case of (e.g.) Seneca's treatment of the villa of Scipio Africanus in *Letter* 86, in which "[t]he modest remains of Scipio's villa transport Seneca (and his readers) to simpler times." See also Spencer (2010) 63–9 on "Philosophical Landscapes: Cicero, *loca* and *imagines.*"

97. Macfarlane (2003) 146.

98. For the Petrarchan challenge,Viallon(-Schoneweld) (2001) 104–5 and (2002) 6; Etna is approximately 3,329 meters in height.

99. Text and subsection numeration below follow Stoppelli (1997).

100. For Dionigi, Moschella (1991).

101. Bishop (1963) 104; cf. along similar lines Burckhardt (2010) 180 with Nicolson (1959) 49–50.

102. On which now Jaeger (2007); through a minor slip Petrarch substitutes Thessaly for Thrace at *Fam.* 4.1.2.

Livy has it, Philip undertook that formidable venture because "he shared the common belief that the Pontus and the Adriatic, the Hister and the Alps could all be seen from that point [sc. the summit of Haemus], and he believed that this prospect before his eyes would in no small measure serve to guide his plans in a war with Rome" (40.21.2); the climb, however, ultimately proved futile because the view at the summit was obscured by cloud (40.22.4; we shall shortly return to Petrarch's use of Livy). Petrarch chose his brother, Gherardo, as his companion for the climb of Ventoux along with two servants (§§3–5), but before they embarked on the ascent they encountered an old shepherd who claimed to have scaled the peak fifty years before. He tried to dissuade them from making the attempt, asserting that all he had received for his pains was nothing "except regret and hardship" (*nihil . . . praeter paenitentiam et laborem*, §7); when they remained undeterred, the shepherd instead turned to admonition (§8). Giving over to him "all such clothes and anything else that might prove burdensome to us" (§8), they started off at a good pace. But while Gherardo took the steeper, more direct route to the top, Petrarch repeatedly sought an easier way, but to no avail: after his futile detours he remained in the valleys (*valles*, §10; *vallibus*, §11; *delusus quadam in valle consedi*, §12), only for his thoughts to shift at this point "from the corporeal to the immaterial" (*a corporeis ad incorporea*, §12), and from the literal climb to its figurative implications: ". . . after long wanderings you must either climb to the summit of the blessed life under the burden of tasks foolishly deferred, or sink sluggishly down in the valley of your sins (*in convallibus peccatorum tuorum*, §14)."

When he finally reached the summit, Petrarch was dazed (*stupendi similis steti*, §17) by the spectacular view, only for him then to turn his gaze within, and to move from the spatial plane to that of time and memory: "Today it is ten years since you completed your youthful studies and left Bologna. Eternal God and immutable Wisdom, how many and how extensive are the changes that this intervening period (*hoc medium tempus*) has seen in your character!" (§19). He had progressed, but it was not yet three years since he had renounced carnal passion (§22), and he foresaw ten more years of struggle before him (§23); he was, as Simon Schama nicely puts it, "at the purgatory summit, residually impure, but at some measurable distance from the base of his original transgression."[103] Then, opening at random the text of the *Confessions* that he apparently always carried with him (§26), a cherished gift from Dionigi, he fell upon a passage from Book 10, at the beginning of Augustine's discussion of the power of the mind discovered in memory (10.8.15):

> And men are moved to wonder by the heights of mountains, by vast waves of the sea, by the widest flowings of rivers, by the ocean's all-embracing

103. Schama (1995) 420.

> expanse, and by the circular motions of the stars; but to themselves they pay no attention.

Stunned (*obstupui*, §28),[104] Petrarch closed the book, angry at himself for still admiring but earthly commodities (*terrestria*) when "nothing is wonderful but the soul" (§28); he had seen enough of the mountain, and instead turned his inward eye on himself (*in me ipsum interiores oculos reflexi*, §29) as he made the descent in silence. Petrarch's account of randomly opening the *Confessions* is itself an act of textual memory, recalling to him (§§30–2) Augustine's chance opening of *Romans* (cf. *Conf.* 8.12.29) just as Augustine himself recalls (*ibid.*) St. Anthony's chance hearing of the admonition in *Matthew* 19.21 "to sell all you have, to give to the poor," and to follow Christ. The mountain's imposing height is now insignificant in comparison with the vast dimensions of human contemplation (*altitudine contemplationis humanae*, §33) that Petrarch perceives; so, in his descent, he has in a way made a secondary ascent toward "trampling on the grandiose peak (*cacumen*) of arrogance and human destiny" (§33). Long after dark (*profunda nocte*) but apparently under a full moon (*luna pernox*)[105] Petrarch and his companions finally reach the inn that they had left before dawn (§35): they had set out in the darkness, but he returns with the inner illumination symbolized by that *luna pernox*.

Did Petrarch truly make it up the mountain, or did he make it up?[106] Even if the climb cannot be dismissed as a complete fiction, an event that he demonstrably never undertook in 1336 or in any other year,[107] his account of it as given in the letter certainly arouses suspicion. Quite apart from the challenge of believing that Petrarch made the climb and the descent in a single day, and that he still had the energy to pen so artfully crafted a letter while the servants prepared supper that night (§35), the symbolic contrast between Gherardo's fast and direct route up the mountain and Petrarch's detour-filled slowness becomes far more pointed if the letter was composed only *after* Gherardo's "lightning conversion"[108] and entry into the Carthusian monastery in Montrieux in 1343. Moreover, the rich texture of literary

104. Surely with an echo of *stupendi similis steti* at §17: there stunned by the (mere) external spectacle, here Petrarch is stunned by the Augustinian call to look within.

105. The full moon in late April is surely a(nother) fabrication. See Billanovich (1947) 197 n.1 and then (1966) 397: "No, non è il plenilunio che illuminò le ultime notti dell'aprile 1336; è un facile chiaroscuro retorico."

106. Zetzel *per iocos*.

107. But Baron (1968) 19 surely goes too far: "For unless this story had some kernel of truth, can we believe that Petrarch would have dared to affirm, 'I invoke God as my witness . . .' [§27]?" Cf. Billanovich (1966) 393 on the scandalizing effects of *Deum testor* . . . only on those "inesperti di retorica."

108. Billanovich (1966) 397.

allusion that belies Petrarch's claim to hasty composition[109] includes references to works that had yet to come to his attention, among them Cicero's letters, that formative model for his own *Epistolae familiares* that he discovered only in 1345 in Verona.[110] Such factors make a compelling case for a date of composition after 1336, and even after Dionigi's death in 1342. Hence Giuseppe Billanovich's influential dating of the work to 1353,[111] a compositional moment when Petrarch's literal and figurative errancy in the letter signaled his slow rate of spiritual progress some ten or so years after the anxieties he had expressed in the *Secretum*.[112]

But even if the 1336 climb is deemed an anachronistic fiction, its symbolic properties may yet give the Petrarchan letter a genuine truth value; or, as Michael O'Connell puts it, in the letter "[f]iction is not . . . given as literal truth, but is used as a means of arriving at a truth about the self otherwise impossible to discover."[113] On this approach, the letter truly captures the struggle toward conversion, and "this intervening period" to which Petrarch refers at the approximate midpoint of the letter (*hoc medium tempus*, §19) itself gestures at the various kinds of mediation that permeate the letter, most obviously between the physical and spiritual worlds, between soul and body, and between time and eternity.[114] Given Petrarch's later renunciation of mere spectacle, his initial motive for climbing Ventoux (his "desire of seeing what so great a height had to offer," §1) appears in retrospect superficial and blinkered, an instance of that "concupiscence of the eyes" condemned by Augustine in Book 10 of his *Confessions*;[115] for all the acclaim that his "joy of seeing" has won him as a proto-Renaissance man,[116] he shows a spiritual blindness that is underscored by the unfortunate example of Philip V of Macedon. It is not just that Petrarch's reading of Livy here (§2) directs him to what is outside the self and appealing to the eyes, and is therefore a negation of the inner turning promoted by his summit meeting with Augustine.[117] Quite apart from the fact that the Livian

---

109. For the wide net of Biblical and Classical allusions, Billanovich (1966) 394–5 with Courcelle (1963) 339–42, Martinelli (1973), and Durling (1977) 305.

110. Succinctly on this "truly revolutionary find in a number of ways," McLaughlin (2015) 26–7.

111. Billanovich (1947) 193–8 with (1966), esp. 399.

112. See Beecher (2004) 56 with Billanovich (1966) 399 for the *Secretum* composed at Avignon between autumn 1342 and winter 1343 and taken up again in Italy between 1353 and 1358.

113. Michael O'Connell (1983) 508.

114. Ascoli (1991) 12–13.

115. On this point, Robbins (1985) 535.

116. Cf. Kirchner (1950) 422: "All the lust for life of the Renaissance man is embodied, like a first blossom, in Petrarch's letter in which he tells of his joy of seeing and observing."

117. Robbins (1985) 535.

Philip never achieves the view he craves at the summit of Haemus (40.22.4), the very idea that the Adriatic and the Black Sea are visible from the peak is itself contested in Petrarch's text: Pomponius Mela affirms as much (2.2.17), but Petrarch interprets the hint of skepticism in Livy[118] as plain fact ("Titus Livius thinks the report is false," §2). In effect, the Petrarchan expedition is motivated by a reading of Livy that itself involves a contested truth—in contrast to the incontestable certainty that Petrarch finds when he randomly opens the *Confessions* at the mountain summit; for "what could I happen upon that would not be righteous and devout (*nisi pium et devotum*)?" (§26).

In vainly seeking a companion for his climb from among his friends, and in finally turning to his brother (§§3–5), Petrarch rehearses a theme—searching far and wide for what is already close at hand—that is brought to fulfillment when, at the summit, he finds in his pocket Augustine, his closest travel companion all along, the imperative to look inward.[119] Augustine remains an influential presence in so many other ways: Petrarch purportedly made his ascent in 1336 at thirty-two, ten years after he completed his youthful studies and left Bologna (§19); Augustine was thirty-two when he read the passage in *Romans* that began his conversion, some twelve years after he read Cicero's *Hortensius* and "was roused with a zeal for wisdom" (*Conf.* 8.7.17).[120] The practical advice tendered by the aged shepherd who tries to dissuade Petrarch from the climb acts as a precursor of sorts for the spiritual rebuke delivered by Augustine, that higher model of pastoral wisdom and authority.[121] When the climbers leave their excess baggage with the shepherd (§8), the pattern is set for Petrarch's higher renunciation of materiality at the summit. While the shepherd found only "regret and hardship" from his exertions (*paenitentiam et laborem*, §7), Petrarch's own toils will lead to *paenitentia* in the purer sense of repentance[122]—and it is surely no coincidence that April 26, 1336 was a Friday, an "indispensable setting" for a story of struggle toward conversion.[123] While Petrarch errs by seeking an easier way through detours that merely confine him to

118. Cf. 40.22.5: "After their descent they said nothing to contradict the popular belief; more, I suspect, to prevent the futility of their march from becoming a subject of ridicule than because the widely separated seas and mountains and rivers could really be seen from one spot." Further on Petrarch's allusions to Mela and Livy, Billanovich (1966) 390–2.

119. Michael O'Connell (1983) 509–10.

120. Billanovich (1966) 394–5 with Michael O'Connell (1983) 513, Robbins (1985) 534, and Ascoli (1991) 11.

121. Michael O'Connell (1983) 514.

122. Michael O'Connell (1983) 514.

123. Billanovich (1966) 396.

a Dante-like locale, a wood in a sinful valley,[124] his brother's fast and direct progress to the summit is cast in the language of straightness and rectitude (*iter rectius*, §9); Gherardo and Franceso are "differentiated as a straight line from a curve"[125] until, the summit attained, the noun *vertex* ("peak," §16) itself suggests by relation to *vertere* that Petrarch has at last reached his turning point.[126]

In addressing this letter to the Augustinian Dionigi, Petrarch all too suitably draws on the Augustinian conversion experience in telling the allegorized story of his own struggle toward conversion. If we accept that Petrarch did indeed climb Mont Ventoux (whether or not in 1336), or at least that the (fiction of the) event was received as true enough, that famous precedent lays down one kind of challenge for Bembo at the foot of Etna. Given all the complexity of the Petrarchan letter, however, and given the powerfully imaginative ways in which Petrarch's ascent is layered in figurative meaning, the literary challenge that confronts Bembo is truly formidable—a challenge that goes beyond merely "renewing a genre opened by Petrarch."[127] The Petrarchan stimulus invites us to anticipate at least the attempt at a similar imaginative elaboration in *De Aetna*, and a similar enterprise in the way Bembo might exploit the symbolic properties of both the mountain and the climb. At the very least, the path to conversion in Petrarch's letter suggestively preconditions *De Aetna* as another story of conversion, albeit of a secular kind: the young Pietro undergoes a rite of passage on Etna, a test of fortitude that quickly grows the man. Moreover, we earlier observed that Urbano Bolzanio reached the higher of the two craters at Etna's summit, on a climb that allegedly took place only a few days before Bembo's own ascent; we also noted that Bembo may have distorted the chronology of Urbano's climb, if not the basic factuality of it.[128] But if we accept that Bembo on Etna consciously vies with Petrarch on Mont Ventoux, could it be that Urbano takes on added significance as a Gherardo-like figure in *De Aetna*? Gherardo's rapid, direct ascent is set in contrast to Petrarch's circuitous, frustrated progress up the mountain; the contrast is still more telling if Petrarch's letter is taken to postdate Gherardo's conversion in 1343. To press the analogy, Gherardo, like the Franciscan Urbano, reaches the summit while Petrarch makes far slower progress to it and Bembo fails to reach the topmost crater on Etna. If the analogy is upheld, Bembo not only emulates (and even outdoes?) Petrarch's climb in the first place; through a convenient historical coincidence—or, just possibly, through

---

124. Ascoli (1991) 22; for the Petrarchan *valles* cf. §§10, 11, 12.

125. Robbins (1985) 536.

126. Further, Ascoli (1991) 23.

127. Viallon(-Schoneweld) (2001) 105.

128. See pp. 85–9.

his own distortion of historical fact (just as Petrarch may have distorted chronological fact)—Pietro also has his own Gherardo near at hand. He thereby replicates the Petrarchan scenario by having his Urbano out-climb him on the mountain in Gherardo-like fashion: in its way, an elegant tribute to Urbano via creative extrapolation from the Petrarchan intertext, and an attractive show of humility if Bembo is seen to give pride of place to the good Bolzanio.

2.6: De Aetna *and the History of Mountaineering*

Bembo's ascent of Etna would seem to claim only a marginal place in the modern history of mountaineering, lacking as it does the extreme vertical challenges and rock-face dangers associated with early Alpine ascents in particular. Yet Bembo's adventure still reflects the larger shift that is evident in Renaissance attitudes to the raw natural world. As we have seen, Petrarch has been hailed as a seminal figure in this respect, "one of the first truly modern men"[129] whose ascent of Mont Ventoux to see "what so great a height had to offer" (*Epistolae familiares* 4.1.1) marks the rise of a new individuality, and of a new engagement with and joy in nature; he has been portrayed as a boundary figure oscillating between the medieval and the modern epochs, or between a newly expressive *curiositas* on the one hand and an entrenched subservience to Christian *humilitas* on the other.[130] But then the turning of the tide: increasing attunement to the layers of allegory and fictionality that complicate the Petrarchan letter has contributed to the critique of the "modern man" interpretation, a nineteenth-century construct whose overly clinical, Western-oriented lines of definition have in any case long been problematized by more nuanced perceptions of modernity-as-process, as opposed to emphasis on the singular Petrarchan moment.[131] For present purposes, however, the Petrarchan ascent, fictional or otherwise, is implicated in the larger story of how attitudes toward mountains shifted from Greco-Roman antiquity to the Renaissance and beyond—a story to which, I argue, *De Aetna* makes its own telling contribution. In what follows Pietro Bembo will emerge as a thoroughly "modern" climber, but not in the radical, epoch-changing sense so controversially claimed for Petrarch; Bembo is "modern" only, for now, in the sense that he bears witness to the intensification of fifteenth-century interest in mountains and mountaineering, and to the (at least partial) erosion of the sinister reputation long associated with the mountainous Other.

---

129. Burckhardt (2010) 179.

130. See, succinctly, Asher (1993) 1050–1 on Cassirer (1972) and Blumenberg (1983).

131. See now Hansen (2013) 9–22.

It is a familiar generalization that the Greeks and Romans by and large shared a deep-seated antipathy to mountains. So writes Marjorie Hope Nicolson:

> The early Greeks had shown some of the awe and aversion of many primitive peoples in the face of a Nature they did not understand, which must be propitiated by sacrifice . . . Yet a people whose life was spent among mountains could hardly have continued this dread indefinitely. In time the earlier attitude gave way to a subconscious feeling of sympathy and kinship . . . The Latin attitude towards mountains, however, at least among classical writers, remained almost consistently adverse.[132]

A more nuanced appraisal of Greek attitudes is offered by Richard Buxton, who surveys the various practical uses that were made of mountains (e.g., for pasturage, raw materials, travel, and warfare) beyond their importance as places where divine sanctuaries were located.[133] For all their wild, mythical, and religious associations, mountains apparently attracted not just detached scientific interest[134] but also touristic and exploratory ascents in the Greek and also the Roman periods:[135] so in Pausanias' time (second century CE) visitors would allegedly throw precious objects into Etna's crater, interpreting it as a good sign if the fire consumed the gift (3.23.9). Quite apart from the Presocratic philosopher Empedocles' famous association with Etna,[136] various other philosophers and inquirers made for the mountains to observe the heavens from high up;[137] Pliny writes of botanical researchers scouring "pathless mountain heights, unexplored deserts and all the bowels of the earth" (*HN* 25.3). Livy's grim account of Hannibal crossing the Alps (21.32.6–37.6) accumulates all the horrors of that storied place, horrors duly echoed by Silius Italicus when the Alps come into view at *Punica* 3.477–95 ("But now all memory of past hardships was dispelled by terror when [the Carthaginians] saw the Alps before them . . ."). Walter Hyde finds in this Livian account an important influence that strengthened Roman distaste for the mountains;[138] however, it is worth noting that,

---

132. Nicolson (1959) 38–9, largely following Hyde (1915); further on the same lines, Malaspina (2007), esp. 41–2 and nn.20, 21 for further bibliography.

133. Buxton (1992) 5 and *passim*; now also Hooley (2012).

134. Notably from the end of the fourth century BCE, when Dicaearchus and others sought to calculate various mountain heights: Hyde (1915) 75 and n.2.

135. In general on esp. Roman attitudes to nature, K. Allen (1899) and Geikie (1912) remain useful repositories.

136. See Chapter 1 pp. 41–3 and n.61.

137. Buxton (1992) 5 and n.39.

138. Hyde (1915) 82.

for all the similarities suggesting that Polybius and Livy used a common source in their accounts of the Carthaginian crossing, Polybius reports that the terrors of the Alps were greatly exaggerated, that Hannibal knew his path and had knowledgeable guides, and that he (Polybius) had visited the Alps to inspect conditions there for himself (3.48).[139] On the more positive side, Livy also portrays the investigative zeal with which Philip V of Macedon scaled Mount Haemus in 181 BCE (40.21–2), while various reports are elsewhere found of the pleasures to be derived from a panoramic view.[140] In his account of the tendency of clouds to accumulate around mountaintops, Lucretius writes of our observations "when we ascend high mountains" (*montis cum ascendimus altos, DRN* 6.469)—one of several clues that cause one commentator to characterize Lucretius as "the only one [sc. of the Classical Roman poets] who appears to have himself climbed mountains and to have taken pleasure in their ascent."[141] As we saw in Chapter 1, Seneca, in his correspondence with Lucilius in the *Moral Letters*, urges his friend, now installed as procurator of Sicily, to climb Etna so as to investigate conditions at the mountaintop on Seneca's behalf (*Letter* 79.2).[142] Strabo describes an ascent of Etna, with a relatively detailed report of conditions at the summit (6.2.8); he elsewhere claims to have ascended Acrocorinth and gives an account of the spectacular panorama that he saw (8.6.21), while at 12.2.7 he mentions infrequent ascents of the formidable Mount Argaeus in Cappadocia. In 126 CE the emperor Hadrian is said to have climbed Etna to observe the sunrise, and also Mount Casius (Jebel Aqra in northern Syria) for the same reason in 130.[143] In sum, if we accept that the Greco-Roman antipathy to mountains is no mere myth, the cases just sampled of visitation, enquiry, and even plain enjoyment at least expose the limitations of the generalization from which we started.

Very few accounts survive of ascents undertaken from Late Antiquity down to the Middle Ages, but mountains appear broadly to have retained a fearsome reputation throughout that period. One possible exception arises in the twelfth-century preface composed by the anonymous translator of Ptolemy's *Almagest* from Greek into Latin (*c.* 1160):[144] laboring over his medical studies in Salerno when he heard of a copy of the *Almagest* that had been sent by the Byzantine Emperor as a gift

---

139. See on these points DeWitt (1943) 30.

140. Hyde (1915) 75; for Philip V on Haemus see already pp. 95–6.

141. Geikie (1912) 287.

142. Chapter 1 pp. 47–8.

143. So at least *Script. Hist. Aug., Hadr.* 13.3, 14.3.

144. For the preface, and for background on it, Haskins (1924) 159–63 and 191–3 with Mallette (2005) 156–8.

to the King of Sicily, the translator voyaged to Sicily in search of the king's emissary who had brought the manuscript from Constantinople; he eventually found his man, the erudite Henry Aristippus (d. 1162; appointed Archbishop of Catania in 1156),[145] "near the spring of Pergusa, *investigating the marvels of Etna, not without some danger*" (*prope Pergusam fontem Ethnea miracula satis cum periculo perscrutantem*).[146] Henry's investigative zeal apart, however, the horrors of mountains remain the more familiar storyline. So Master John de Bremble, a monk of Christ Church, Canterbury, who crossed the Great Saint Bernard Pass in 1188, writes of "shuddering at the hell of the valleys" below him; "'Lord', I said, 'restore me to my brethren, that I may tell them that they come not to this place of torment'. Place of torment, indeed, . . . where, strange to say, although it is so slippery that you cannot stand, the death into which there is every facility for a fall is certain death."[147] Already, in the first half of the eleventh century, an anonymous chronicler of the Monastery of Novalesa, located in the Val di Susa in the Piedmont region of northern Italy, tells of two failed ascents of the so-called Mount Romuleus (*arx Romulea*, later known as the Monte de Roccia Melone or Roche Melon, some 3,538 meters high)—an account that is revealingly dismissive of the climbing theme in the chronicler's closing remarks: "Wherefore, since the opportunity of telling this story has presented itself, and since indiscriminate digression is resulting (*dum circumquaque narratio se extendit*), *let us henceforward devote our pen to the narration of more worthy matters*."[148] The earliest full ascent of Roche Melon that finds mention is that of the knight Bonifacio Rotario d'Asti in 1358; however, his motive was not the climb itself, but apparently his vow to found a chapel at the peak in honor of the Virgin Mary as thanksgiving for his safe return from captivity during the Crusades.[149] Earlier still than Bonifacio's ascent and that of Petrarch on Mont Ventoux was the climb apparently accomplished by King Peter III of Aragon (*c.* 1236–85) on the relatively accessible Pic du Canigou (of some 2,784 meters) in the French Pyrenees.[150] According to his chronicler, Peter made it to the peak alone, there finding a lake that housed a

145. Conveniently on Henry, Dillon (2006).

146. Haskins (1924) 191.28–30; my emphasis. The reference to *Pergusa* remains troubling: the name *Pergus –i* m. is associated with Enna (cf. Ov. *Met.* 5.386, Claud. *De raptu Pros.* 2.112), not Etna, but the phrase *Ethnea miracula* and the stress on danger would seem to point unequivocally to the volcano; hence (Haskins 159 n.11) "[v]ery possibly the author meant some fount in the neighborhood of Etna otherwise unknown to us."

147. As cited in Gribble (1899) 4, but see also Hyde (1917) 107 and Fleming (2004) 51.

148. As quoted in Gribble (1899) 7 and 258 in App. A.; my emphasis.

149. See Gribble (1899) 10–13 with Hyde (1917) 108.

150. For this ascent, Gribble (1899) 14–17 and 262–3 App. C.

monstrous dragon. The chronicler hails the great adventurer with studied hyperbole ("It appears to me that this achievement of Peter of Ar[r]agon may be compared with the achievements of Alexander . . .");[151] but more important for now are the spirit of investigation for its own sake that has been attributed to Peter,[152] and the voice that the chronicler gives to the widespread medieval belief that "mountain regions were haunted by winged dragons, gnomes, goblins, and all kinds of evil spirits."[153]

Again, however, the sinister reputation of mountains that pertained down to the fifteenth century and beyond was not without exception. Already, for notable example, traces of a more measured and sympathetic outlook have been discerned in Dante.[154] From another angle, William Mills usefully cautions against simplistic acceptance of the stereotype that there was a blanket distrust of nature in the Middle Ages,[155] developing his case by exploring the metaphor of nature as text. The Bible is one source of divine revelation, the natural environment another: it was believed, Mills argues, that not one but two books were bequeathed by God to humankind, the first scriptural, the second the book of nature; by the Middle Ages, the book of nature was universally adopted as the image via which the environment was to be read and understood.[156] On this approach, Mills differentiates the medieval and the "modern" by positing a change in metaphorical vision: to the medieval mind that viewed the world as a book, a purely sensual response to nature was to be rejected because nature was set before us for the purposes of instruction.[157] A shift is then discernible in Renaissance attitudes, but not toward a straightforward, unambiguous enthusiasm for nature. Given the legibility of the environment as text, the story of man's fall is impressed in the very fabric of nature:

> For the Renaissance mind, the present form of the earth revealed merely the ruin of its past perfection. Some held that before the Fall and the Flood that

151. As in Gribble (1899) 17.

152. See Kirchner (1950) 422 with Peters (2001) 601, and also Gribble (1899) 262 for the chronicler's portrayal of Peter as *volens exsperiri atque cognoscere quid in montis cacumine haberetur*. But Kirchner's Peter, like his Petrarch, is to be viewed only with caution as a thoroughly "modern" man: "Here is the birth of an attitude which from that time on has possessed the western world, has permeated its thinking, and given direction to its aspirations" (p. 422).

153. Hyde (1917) 108.

154. See Freshfield (1881) with Noyce (1950) 23–33, including, *à propos* of the *Divine Comedy* (pp. 23–4), "By climbing these physical heights we are training ourselves for nothing less than the Purgatorial ascent. Dante is with us. . . "

155. Mills (1982) 238–9.

156. Mills (1982) 239–40.

157. Mills (1982) 240.

> followed it, the earth's surface had been billiard-ball smooth; but this was not universally accepted. What was agreed upon, however, was that just as the faces of old people can become disfigured by wrinkles, warts and wens, so also could the "face" of the earth.[158]

On the microcosmic analogy, mountains are naturalized as a part reflection of the human condition: here was a movement away from the hauntings of medieval superstition, but, in its stress on fallen man, it hardly constituted the assertion of a joyous new immersion in nature. But the "modern" view could yet offer comfort through the objectification of nature: the parallels drawn between the human and the earth's circulatory systems, and also the development of what Mills terms the "machinist metaphor" of world functioning, reinforced the perception that all parts of the natural scheme were implicated in the same overall system.[159] If the world is made for a God-given purpose, no element is without reason or function, mountains included; however inaccessible and threatening they may be, they are there to be understood, not just to be irrationally feared and disowned.

Another factor that complicates tracing the beginnings of the "modern" view of mountains and mountaineering is Columbus' discovery of the New World in 1492 (unsurprisingly, the spirit of the likes of Columbus and Vasco da Gama has been discerned in Bembo's climb of Etna[160]). On a pilgrimage in the Dauphiné region of southeastern France in 1490, Charles VIII first witnessed Mont Inaccessible, whose unremarkable height—only 2,086 meters—is offset by the seeming impregnability of the vertical cliffs that surround the summit. The name itself was perhaps a provocation for the young king, for whom no part of his domain could be beyond access and control. In what amounted to an act of "vertical colonialism,"[161] he ordered the mountain to be climbed by his chamberlain, Antoine de Ville, seigneur of Dompjulien and Beaupré, his "rock-face Columbus."[162] The climb eventually took place on June 26, 1492, a few weeks after Bembo's arrival in Sicily and roughly a month before Columbus set sail on August 3. With seven companions, de Ville had only the equipment of siege warfare to scale the sheer cliffs, but the remarkable feat was achieved. Once at the summit of what was no longer "the inaccessible mountain," the party stayed there for six days, during which it was baptized Mont Aiguille in the name of the Holy

158. Mills (1982) 243.

159. See Mills (1982) 244–8.

160. Alfieri (1981) 32.

161. Schama (1995) 423.

162. Schama (1995) 423.

Trinity as well as (in recognition of de Ville's royal mandate) Saint Charlemagne; mass was said, three crosses erected, and a small hut built, vestiges of which were still visible three centuries later. These details are preserved in the authenticating document that de Ville compiled at the summit and sent down the mountain to the President of the Parliament of Grenoble; that Parliament in turn sent a deputation to investigate de Ville's claims, and the official attestation was duly made.[163] Among the surviving documents is the account offered by François de Bosco, almoner of de Ville, of (*inter alia*) the lush meadow, flowers, birdlife, and even goat-antelopes (chamois) at the summit:[164] de Bosco elegantly configures a vision of "the Alpine purgatory, a.k.a. the terrestrial paradise."[165] A measure of de Ville's achievement is that the mountain was next officially climbed only in 1834 by one Jean Liotard, apparently without equipment for much of the climb, and strategically shoeless for the rock-face portion of the ascent.[166]

Because of the technical difficulty of de Ville's climb, his reliance on equipment to open a way up the cliff face, and the fact that his is the first ascent of which a full and precise account is given,[167] the 1492 achievement has been hailed as *the* modern turning point in the history of mountaineering;[168] the Columbus effect has lent its own momentum to this perception, even though de Ville's was an ordered climb, and no voluntary act of discovery or of immersion in nature. Meanwhile, Renaissance artists such as Leonardo da Vinci were producing unprecedentedly careful studies of rocks and mountains in an era when, as Schama puts it, "something *had* evidently changed in the Western vision of mountains. Apprehension had been overtaken by perception."[169] In *c.* 1511 Leonardo himself climbed what he terms Monboso, which is probably to be identified with Monte Rosa,[170] Switzerland's highest mountain, rising to some 4,600 meters at its main summit. Among his surviving memoranda of the ascent are several observations about ice conditions and cloud conditions, the strength of the sun, and the quality of the light, all of which indicate that he reached considerable altitude, and possibly a height that no one had attained

163. For these various documents, Gribble (1899) 28–34 and 272–5 App. F.

164. For de Bosco's document, Gribble (1899) 32–4 and 274–5 in App. G.; one wonders just how the goats reached the vertical summit in the first place.

165. Schama (1995) 423.

166. For Liotard's ascent, Gribble (1899) 34–7.

167. Gribble (1899) 28.

168. See Hansen (2013) 23.

169. Schama (1995) 426.

170. See Hyde (1917) 108–9 and n.10 with Freshfield (1884) and (1892); Gribble (1899) 25–7 and 271 App. E; McCurdy (2005) 129–32.

before.[171] Other adventurous humanists in this tradition included the Swiss Joachim Vadian (Latinized as Vadianus, 1484–1551), born as Joachim von Watt. In 1518 he and three companions were granted permission by the local authorities to climb Mount Pilatus above Lucerne, in defiance of the superstition that the damned soul of Pontius Pilate, restless in a lake high on the mountain, tormented all who dared set foot on his peak.[172] Vadian returned safely, but without resolutely disavowing the Pilate legend.[173] It was not until 1555 that the famed Swiss naturalist Conrad Gessner (1516–65) climbed Mount Pilatus precisely to challenge both Pilate's wrath and the popular superstition attaching to the place. He emerged unscathed from provocatively hurling stones into the dreaded lake—symbolically an exorcism that is now often interpreted as the starting point for the banishing of superstition from Western attitudes to the mountains.[174]

Reports of other significant climbs survive from the early years of the sixteenth century.[175] Before we revert to Bembo, however, Gessner usefully illustrates the rise not just of a serious scientific interest in mountains, but also of a rapturous sense of engagement with mountain nature that appears proto-Romantic in its release of feeling. So in the famous letter written in 1541 to his friend Jacob Vogel (Latinized as Avienus) on "the love of mountains" (*De montium admiratione*),[176]

> I am resolved henceforth, most learned Avienus, that, as long as it may please God to grant me life, I will ascend several mountains, or at least one, every year, at the season when the flowers are in their glory, partly for the sake of examining them, and partly for the sake of good bodily exercise and of mental delight. For how great a pleasure, think you, is it, how great a delight for a man touched as he ought to be, to wonder at the mass of

171. So at least Shoumatoff and Shoumatoff (2001) 192–3; Freshfield (1892) 346 hazards that Leonardo "may have got as far as the rocks above the Col d'Ollen," at a height of some 2,900 meters.

172. See Gribble (1899) 43–50 with Hyde (1917) 112, Kirchner (1950) 424, and Fleming (2004) 51; in 1387 six clerics were allegedly imprisoned for breaking the official prohibition of climbing the mountain.

173. See Gribble (1899) 49.

174. Macfarlane (2003) 201; for Gessner's climb, Gribble (1899) 51–62 and 280–6 App. H.

175. So, e.g., the Spanish explorer Diego de Ordaz (1480–1532) was the first European to ascend the volcano Popocatépetl in Mexico in 1519; Johann Müller, a Swiss scholar (*c.* 1473–1542, also known as Rhellicanus after his native village of Rhelliken, near Zurich), climbed the Stockhorn above Lake Thun in 1536, celebrating the event in 130 Latin hexameters. For both climbs see Hyde (1917) 109, 112; for Rhellicanus' *Stockhornias* poem, Gribble (1899) 39–42 and 276–9 App. G with Ludwig (1983).

176. For the circumstances of its publication, Hyde (1917) 112 n.18.

> the mountains as one gazes on their vastness, and to lift up one's head as it were amongst the clouds? The understanding is deeply moved, I know not wherefore, by their amazing height, and is driven to think of the Great Architect who made them . . .[177]

True, the voice of Mountain Gloom continues to be heard down to the eighteenth century, a tendency particularly well traced in the English tradition by Nicolson ("Mountains were warts, blisters, imposthumes . . .").[178] But the new appreciation of nature, and especially of wild nature, that prevailed by the late eighteenth century brought the true dawning of Mountain Glory; and the Glory phenomenon gained further impetus with the rise of Romanticism, which found in mountains the allure not just of altitude, but also of exaltation and, above all, individualism.[179] Of course, the mountain rapture of a Gessner and the exaltation of the Romantic spirit, belonging as they do to separate eras and socio-cultural contexts, are hardly identifiable with each other in any simplistic way; but the strain of Mountain Glory that each (differently) manifests offers a loose analogy for, and a useful way of articulating, the spirit of liberated adventure in wild nature that I claim for *De Aetna*. The voicing of that Glory through young Pietro's persona will be documented in detail later in Chapter 6, but my priority for now is to assert *De Aetna*'s underestimated importance in the history of climbing. Antoine de Ville's towering achievement in ascending Mont Aiguille in 1492 obviously surpasses Bembo's relatively undemanding climb of Etna in 1493. But if the former constitutes a—*the*—pivotal modern moment in the annals of mountaineering, *De Aetna* nevertheless delivers something that the surviving documentation of de Ville's climb does not: Bembo offers not just an interesting factual account of his ascent, but also an enactment—even a form of dramatized theorization—of what we might call the modern mountain sensibility in step-by-step, real-time performance.

---

177. Trans. Coolidge (1889) 12–13. Cf. also Benedict Marti, professor of Greek and Hebrew at Bern and a friend of Gessner, writing (in Latin) in either 1558 or 1559 of the view from his native city: "These are the mountains which form our pleasure and delight when we gaze at them from the higher parts of our city and admire their mighty peaks and broken crags that threaten to fall at any moment. . . . Who, then, would not admire, love, willingly visit, explore, and climb places of this sort? I assuredly should call those who are not attracted by them dolts, stupid dull fishes, and slow tortoises . . . In truth, I cannot describe the degree of affection and natural love with which I am drawn to mountains, so that I am never happier than on the mountain crests, and there are no wanderings dearer to me than those on the mountains . . ." (as cited in Freshfield [1904] 449).

178. Nicolson (1959), here at p. 62.

179. Cf. Fleming (2004) 53: "Here was liberty, meditation and a lofty exaltation of body and soul; here was man communing with nature in its most rugged form; here was civilization transported into the realm of noble savagery; and here, above all, here was individualism."

2.7: *Banishing Hellish Myth and Legend*

Finally, Bernardo Bembo's rationalization in *De Aetna* §§33–8 of Etna's volcanic activity as a purely naturalistic phenomenon reflects the larger movement, after the Middle Ages, away from myth-based or theocentric explanations of such occurrences. Given the absence in antiquity and far beyond of sophisticated methodologies and instrumentation for the scientific analysis of volcanoes and other such phenomena, Etna's fearsome aura and intermittent destructiveness naturally lent themselves to myth-based interpretation of the sort rejected out of hand by both Bembos in §31:

PIETRO: So you think that, inside the mountain, the winds are taken in by Etna like breath within the chest? And that through these winds it sometimes breathes gently, and sometimes it's more violently aroused?

BERNARDO: Yes indeed—unless there's more truth in the fabulous inventions that poets concoct about Typhoeus and Enceladus.

PIETRO: Certainly, that's a very true fable. But go on, please, father, and tell me the causes of this fire as well . . .

While the Typhoeus myth accounted for Etna's violence, the mountain also spawned legend of a more positive, comforting kind in the story of the two brothers who risked all to rescue their parents from the lava flows that imperiled Catania.[180] This moralizing thrust is sustained in and after antiquity through the development of "a form of religiosity . . . that does not consider the fire as a purely negative element."[181] Hence the punitive connotation of volcanoes generally as "chimneys of Hell" in which the damned were duly tormented[182]—a belief whose persistence through the ages is well illustrated by the legend, apparently still lingering even in the late eighteenth century, that the ill-fated Anne Boleyn, Henry VIII's second wife, was condemned to burn indefinitely inside Etna for turning Henry into a heretic.[183]

Hampered by scriptural dogma in the Middle Ages, the earth sciences witnessed few advances beyond Classical theories of volcanic and earthquake action; one

---

180. Chapter 1 p. 61 and n.122.

181. Salmeri (1997) 127.

182. On this tradition, Sigurdsson (1999) 71–2.

183. See for the legend Chester et al. (1985) 26 and Sigurdsson (1999) 72, along with the interesting account given by Patrick Brydone (1736–1818), in his *A Tour through Sicily and Malta in a Series of Letters to William Beckford, Esq. of Somerly in Suffolk* (London, 1773, 2 vols.), of visiting Etna and hearing from the locals of one Anne who was said to languish under the mountain: "I could not

factor that contributed to volcanology in particular becoming all but dormant was precisely the linkage often drawn between the horrors of hell and volcanic fire in medieval theology.[184] It was not until the Renaissance that divine science gave way to natural science, and an accelerating economy increased demand for raw materials derived from mining—a development that intensified the study of minerals and geology, and thereby led to new theorizing about the nature of subterranean heat and its accompanying phenomena.[185] As for Etna in particular, its hellish associations and forbidding air of mystery[186] hardly encouraged visitors and explorers in the medieval period, but Bembo's ascent, and that of Urbano Bolzanio before him, amounted to a breakthrough of sorts.[187] The ascent of Tommasso Fazello (1498–1570) followed in 1541, and was briefly described in the fourth chapter (*De Aetna monte et eius ignibus*) of his *De rebus Siculis decades duae*, the first printed history of Sicily, published in Palermo in 1558.[188] In 1591 Anton Giulio Filoteo degli Omodei, himself Etna-born, published at Venice his *Aetnae topographia incendiorumque Aetnaeorum historia*.[189] Scientific in his approach, dismissive of myth-based explanations of Etna's fires, and committed to plotting the historical phases of the mountain's eruptions, its topography, and its vegetation, Filoteo in his book seemingly presupposed that Etna had acquired "una certa popolarità."[190] Bembo perhaps contributed to this familiarization process: the enlightened approach taken by Filoteo is already visible in *De Aetna*, that thoroughly "modern" book in which Bembo shows such a broad attunement to his cultural times.

But despite this cultural attunement, and for all the efforts that have been made in Chapters 1 and 2 to relate *De Aetna* to the traditions of the Etna Idea and of antiquarian travel, to mnemonic topography and to the history of mountaineering,

---

conceive what queen Anne had done to bring her there; and was puzzling myself to find it out, when one of them soon cleared up the matter; he told me she was wife to a king that had been a christian, and that she had made him an Heretic, and was in consequence condemned to burn for ever in mount Aetna. In short, I found it was no other than poor Anne Boloyne [*sic*] . . . I asked, if her husband was there too, for that he deserved it much better than she; *Sicuro*, said he, and all his heretic subjects too; and if you are of that number, you need not be in such a hurry to get thither, you will be sure of it at last. I thanked him, and went to join our company, not a little amused with the conversation" (1.171–2).

184. On this point, Young (2003) 9.

185. On these points, Sigurdsson (1999) 84–6.

186. See esp. Corti (1999) 29–60.

187. Cf. Salmeri (1997) 128.

188. For this ascent, Rodwell (1878) 11 with Salmeri (1997) 127–8.

189. Rodwell (1878) 11–12.

190. Salmeri (1997) 128.

little has been said thus far of the particular circumstances that induced Bembo to leave Venice to study Greek in Messina; of *De Aetna*'s significance within the shifting contours of Quattrocento Venetian humanism; and of the work's importance to the storyline of Pietro's reluctance to embark on the public career that was conventional for one of his Venetian aristocratic class. In short, what of the particular Venetian cultural climate in which *De Aetna* took shape? After lingering on Etna and the Etna Idea in Chapters 1 and 2, then, we travel to Messina and especially to Venice in Chapters 3 and 4 to investigate *De Aetna* from a different angle of approach: to explore the socio-cultural factors that crucially condition the father-son dynamic as portrayed in the dialogue.

3

From Venice to Sicily

BEMBO'S GREEK EDUCATION, HIS TEACHERS, HIS INSPIRERS

WHILE BERNARDO BEMBO strives to find what relaxation he can from his pressing affairs of state when he manages to escape to his beloved Noniano (*De Aetna* §§5–8), Pietro looks back on his time in Sicily with unmitigated pleasure. He may have been relieved to be safely back in Venice ("And I for my part am glad to be here," §9) as the dark clouds of conflict gathered over the peninsula in advance of Charles VIII of France's invasion in the autumn of 1494;[1] however, Bernardo would have been wrong to "imagine that any part of my life has been more enjoyable than those two years in Sicily" (§9). While Bernardo struggles to find time away from his official duties, Pietro struggles to gain a foothold on the career ladder that was the norm for Venetian men of his patriciate class, but partly also with the will to seek that foothold in the first place: in the opening exchanges between father and son in *De Aetna*, their air of affability and mutual affection barely disguises the generational tension between the two over Pietro's reluctance to embark on the patriciate *cursus honorum*. In this respect, the storyline of *De Aetna*—Pietro's actual climb of Etna—is subsidiary to, even fundamentally conditioned by, the larger storyline of shifting Venetian attitudes in and around the 1490s to the particular mode of civic humanism that had long been fundamental to Venetian self-identity in the Quattrocento.

In many ways, of course, *De Aetna*'s relevance to the familiar narrative of Bembo's controversial life choice in favoring an existence devoted to scholarship and social advancement within the world of the secular and papal courts is as self-evident as it is unsurprising. But in this chapter Pietro's complex motivations to leave Venice in order to study Greek in Messina are explored through a lens that focuses on the particular individuals who certainly were, or who may well have

1. For background, Introduction pp. 17–18.

been, major influences on his youthful humanistic development. Our focus in section 3.1 below is on his formative training in Venice before he left for Sicily in the spring of 1492, and especially on his relations with Angelo Poliziano (1454–94). After arriving with Bembo in Messina in 3.2, we renew our acquaintance there with Constantine Lascaris, his distinguished teacher of Greek, and we observe Pietro's rapid advancement in that language during his stay at Lascaris' school. Yet Pietro may in fact already have made substantial progress in Greek before he left for Sicily: we explore that possibility in 3.3, tentatively identifying Giorgio Valla (1447–1500) as (at least one of) his likely Greek instructor(s) in Venice. The spotlight will then turn to Ermolao Barbaro (1454–93), who will soon prove to be something of an absent presence in *De Aetna*, not least because his committed interest in the natural sciences appears to have influenced the young Bembo in the same direction. My treatment in this chapter of Barbaro in particular is preparatory to our continuing focus on him in the earlier part of Chapter 4, and in this respect the two chapters are closely coordinated. Such is our projected path; but first to Venice in the summer of 1491, when an eminent visitor graced the Bembo residence with his presence.

3.1: Poliziano, the Bembine Terence, and Bembo's Sogno

On June 3, 1491 Poliziano and his close friend, the distinguished philosopher Giovanni Pico della Mirandola (1463–94), set out from Florence on a journey that took them to Bologna and then on to Ferrara, Rovigo, and Padua before they eventually reached Venice on or around June 19.[2] There they stayed until July 9, continuing their journey's quest for books and manuscripts for the library of Lorenzo de' Medici, their great patron at Florence. In visiting the Bembo residence, Poliziano resumed the cordial relations that dated back to Bernardo Bembo's service as Venetian ambassador to Florence in two periods, the first from January 1475 to April 1476, the second from July 1478 to May 1480.[3] But beyond the call of friendship,[4] Poliziano's visit is now known principally for his collation of the famous manuscript of the Roman comedy writer Terence (*c.* 195–*c.* 159 BCE), dating to the fourth or fifth century CE, that was acquired by the Bembo family in the

2. On this journey and their route, Pesenti (1916) and Frati (1916–17) with Ribuoli (1981) 19 and Branca (1983) 134–56.

3. On these periods of service, Giannetto (1985) 29–38, 131–52 with della Torre (1900) and Pintor (1911).

4. There is in fact no evidence to show that Bernardo was certainly in Venice during Poliziano's stay there: Giannetto (1985) 202.

fifteenth century and now generally goes by the name of the Codex Bembinus. The first known owner of this manuscript was the larger-than-life Neapolitan humanist Giannantonio de' Pandoni (before 1405–after 1485), Il Porcellio ("the little pig") by nickname; how the Terence came into his possession is far from clear.[5] From Porcellio the manuscript passed in 1457 to Bernardo Bembo, presumably at great expense, at least if his own inscription within it is interpreted to the letter:[6] *codex mihi carior auro* ("A book dearer to me than gold"). After Bernardo's death in 1519 the manuscript passed to Pietro Bembo. Eventually, after protracted negotiations, in May 1579 it was acquired from Torquato Bembo (1525–95), Pietro's son and heir, by the prodigious Roman collector Fulvio Orsini (1529–1600), who in turn bequeathed it in 1600 to the Vatican Library, where it resides today.[7]

Poliziano began work on the manuscript on June 23, 1491, as he himself attests in a marginal annotation in the printed edition of Terence—now housed as Banco Rari 97 in the Biblioteca Nazionale Centrale, Florence—that he appears to have acquired during his Venetian stay specifically for the task of registering the readings of the Bembinus.[8] But more important for now is the acknowledgement of Pietro's help that Poliziano offers in that edition, in the subscription at the end of the *Adelphoe*, and hence at the end of his work of collation:

> Ego Angelus Politianus contuleram codicem hunc Terentianum cum venerandae vetustatis codice, maioribus conscripto litteris, quem mihi utendum commodavit Petrus Bembus, Venetus patricius, Bernardi iurisconsulti et equitis filius, studiosus litterarum adulescens . . . Ipse etiam Petrus operam mihi suam in conferendo commod[avit.[9]

---

5. Prete (1970) 7–8. The soubriquet was allegedly earned because of his sexual *mores*; cf. Frittelli (1900) 14–15 and, engagingly, Aldrich and Wotherspoon (2002) 399–400.

6. Prete (1970) 9.

7. Further on the history of Vat. lat. 3226 and its acquisition by Orsini, Cian (1885) 102–4; Nolhac (1887) 109 and 236–9; Prete (1970) 10, 15–17; Danzi (2005) 213–15.

8. See Ribuoli (1981) 54 no. 2: *Anno 1491, die .23. Iunii, vigilia sancti Iohannis Baptistae, Venetiis conferre coepi cum vetustissimo codice Petri Bembi, Veneti patricii, Bernardi filii, ego Ang. Pol.* (fol. 18*v*, at the end of the *Andria*). For another Terence annotated by Poliziano before 1491, Cesarini Martinelli (1985). Banco Rari 97 is dated July 21, 1475 but gives no indication of where it was printed—perhaps at Venice, possibly at the press of Adam de Ambergau: see Ribuoli 17 and n.7 with J. N. Grant (1988) 214 and n.12; Dane (1999) 99 and n.1; Daneloni (2013b). For Poliziano's acquisition of it only after his arrival in Venice, Ribuoli 20.

9. Fol. 66*v*, Poliziano's words as given in Ribuoli (1981) 64 no. 78. Though last in the ordering of the plays in the Bembinus, the *Adelphoe* is differently positioned in the ordering of Banco Rari 97: see J. N. Grant (1988) 220.

> I, Angelo Poliziano, had collated this codex of Terence against a codex of venerable old age, written in capital letters, that was supplied for my use by Pietro Bembo, a Venetian noble, son of the jurist and knight Bernardus, and an eager young student of letters . . . Pietro himself gave me his assistance in the collating.

Bembo's intimate friend from early youth, Girolamo Savorgnan (1466–1529), was also present at the collation, or so at least Poliziano indicates in the following annotation in Banco Rari 97: *Hieronymus Savornianus, patricius Venetus et primarius Foroiuli, et Petrus Bembo* ("Girolamo Savorgnan, a Venetian noble and leading citizen of Friuli, and Pietro Bembo");[10] we shall return shortly to this association of cultured young minds. Another incunable of Terence, now in the Biblioteca Ambrosiana in Milan (Inc. 1523), is printed in the same type and bears on its identical colophon the same date, July 21, 1475, as Banco Rari 97, but it differs in its preliminaries; given their identical date, the two volumes surely constitute not separate editions but variant versions of the same edition that were issued together, but with some pages reset by the printer during the production process.[11] This second incunable contains notes and corrections on the text that are almost identical to those in Poliziano's version: if we accept the persuasive case made by Riccardo Ribuoli that these notes and corrections are in Bembo's hand,[12] Pietro must have quickly acquired his own Terence to match as closely as possible (despite the different preliminaries in the two versions) that used by Poliziano—a match necessitated in large part because of wide variations in the colometry of incunable printings of Terence. Poliziano's high regard for his collaborator, that "eager young student of letters" (*studiosus litterarum adulescens*), is fully reflected in the care that Pietro took to transcribe faithfully, and in short order during the great man's Venetian sojourn, Poliziano's entire collation in Banco Rari 97 of the Bembinus, his copy of the scholia, and his marginal annotations. Pietro continued to work on the text of Terence after Poliziano's departure from Venice, in part by correcting and supplementing aspects of the latter's collation, and partly also through further inspection of the Bembinus itself;[13] these later interventions are distinguished from the preexisting notations in Inc. 1523 by a mark that he explains thus: *ubi .N. littera, ea glossa a me erit perlecta post discessum Politiani* (fol. 20*v*: "Where the letter N,

10. Fol. 36*r*, Poliziano's words as given in Ribuoli (1981) 59 no. 44.

11. On Inc. 1523 in relation to Banco Rari 97, Ribuoli (1981) 79–82 with J. N. Grant (1988) 218–120, Dane (1999), and Daneloni (2013a).

12. Ribuoli (1981) 80.

13. See Ribuoli (1981) 80 with Campanelli (1997) 304.

that will be a gloss reviewed by me after Poliziano's departure," where *N* = *nova* [sc. *glossa*]).[14]

In combination, the two Terence incunables, Banco Rari 97 in Florence and Inc. 1523 in Milan, bear witness to the profound influence that Poliziano's visit had on Pietro's humanistic development. Here was a revelatory experience in the techniques of collation, in deciphering ancient script, in the correct separation of words and lines of verse, and in the minutiae of the linguistic and orthographical analysis of manuscripts.[15] But the larger lesson was in rigor and system—a methodology that, in the realm of textual criticism, prioritized establishing the complex interrelationship between manuscripts, thereby grounding conjectural emendation not in the vagaries of informed guesswork or the ingenious proposal, but in determining the earliest traceable stage of transmission.[16] Poliziano's stress on the holistic viewpoint in determining the relationships between manuscripts, and in carefully comparing and evaluating his ancient sources in a systematically historical way before drawing any inferences from them, also extended to the comparative study of Latin and Greek: only through a mastery of Greek literature could the critic discern the Latin forms of Greek words, find illumination for Latin texts even when the manuscript evidence was inconclusive or lacking, and begin to understand where and how the Latin writers were following, modifying, or distorting their sources.[17] Against this background, it is surely no coincidence that Bembo left Venice for Sicily to improve his Greek under the tutelage of Constantine Lascaris in Messina less than a year after Poliziano's visit: aside from Ermolao Barbaro, who was himself Poliziano's long-term friend, correspondent, and rival,[18] it was to Poliziano, we might infer, that he largely owed his awareness, or at least the reinforcement of his awareness, that he required a real proficiency in Greek language and culture if his Classical studies were truly to prosper[19]—a proficiency that Bernardo Bembo signally lacked.[20] Pietro's departure from Venice in 1492 also amounted to an emphatic declaration

14. Ribuoli (1981) 80 and n.6; Daneloni (2013a) 99.

15. See Vecce (1998b), esp. 484.

16. See Grafton (1977), esp. 172 = (1991) 64 ("No previous scholar had even come close to formulating the set of critical principles which Politian considered to be generally valid") and (1983), esp. 32–3, with Pozzi (1973–9) 1.cl–cli; Branca (1983), esp. 12–16, 78–83, 134–81, 193–296, and (1998) 89–91; Campanelli (1997) 309.

17. See Grafton (1977) 172–82 = (1991) 64–72 and (1983) 32–8.

18. See Pozzi (1973–9) 1.cxlv–clii; Branca (1983) 13–17, 144–6, (1996) 19–20, and (1998) 87–90; Fera (1996), esp. 193–4.

19. See Branca (1996) 35–6; Vecce (1998b) 482–4; Finotti (2004) 54–5.

20. See Giannetto (1985) 203 n.290.

of independence,[21] at least for now,[22] from the conventional Venetian *cursus*, and of his commitment instead to a life of letters. Again, Poliziano's visit may have brought the young Bembo to a crossroads in this respect, committed as Poliziano was to the belief that the study of Greco-Roman antiquity was "irrelevant to civic life"[23]—a position diametrically opposed to that of a previous Florentine generation whose civic-minded humanism was based on the ancient Roman example.[24] But further light is shed on Pietro's turning, and on both his and Girolamo Savorgnan's association with Poliziano in the summer of 1491, by an early work that Bembo, then around twenty, addressed to Girolamo.

The earliest samples that survive of Bembo's vernacular poetry are preserved in cod. Ital. 1543 of the Bibliothèque Nationale in Paris. Within the larger vernacular miscellany assembled in this manuscript, on fols. 105*r* to 112*v* sixteen pieces are attributed to *M(esser) Piero bembo venetiano*; the twelfth of these, in 193 hendecasyllables and entitled *Sogno* (*Dream*), is preceded by a dedicatory letter to Girolamo, also in the vernacular.[25] In the opening lines of the poem proper, the setting is springtime, the day just dawning. The poet visualizes himself in a cool, flowery cave (19–20), the sun's rays peeking through the narrow opening; naked, he reclines against a large rock (25–6), while the pensive Girolamo sits on the grass at his side. A female figure suddenly appears before them (40–1), slow of step and shrewd of manner (42), noble in bearing yet of humble dress (51) and hence probably an incarnation of philosophy, or perhaps of philology (an incarnation even of the Greek language?[26]); she embarks on a heartfelt exhortation to virtue, exalting human nature and its rational capacities and urging release from all the common muddiness of life (*Uscite fuor del fango de' volgari*, 109). Petrarchan in its language, Dantean in its scene setting, and Platonic in its appeal to the cave, to dream experience and to allegory (with clear resonances of the Florentine Neoplatonic movement),[27] the poem itself enacts the very calling that it exhorts to the cultured life of the mind. But when

21. Cf. Floriani (1966) 41.

22. But for his later efforts to seek election to Venetian office see my Introduction p. 4 and Chapter 4 p. 162.

23. Grafton (1977) 182; (1983) 40; (1991) 72.

24. Further, Grafton (1977) 182; (1983) 40–1; (1991) 72–3; and see Chapter 4 pp. 156–7.

25. In general, Curti (2013a). For the text, Zanato (2002) 208–13 and now Donnini (2008) 1.467–79 no. 205, with the dedicatory letter in both cases; both Zanato (p. 196) and Donnini (esp. 2.947–50) take account not just of the manuscript evidence for the *Sogno*, but also of the extant incunable version of it, for which see below.

26. Baldacchini (1987) 118.

27. Curti (2013a) 96.

precisely did Bembo pen his *Sogno*? On the basis of the chronological markers distributed more widely in Ital. 1543, Tiziano Zanato assigns the miscellany to "*non post* 1493"[28]—a dating that, crucially for our purposes, then indicates that the *Sogno* was composed before Pietro left for Sicily in April 1492. After all, the relentlessness with which Bembo claims to have studied Greek after his arrival in Messina—fourteen months without a break before the expedition to Etna (*De Aetna* §11)—hardly suggests that he had much time to devote to composing in the vernacular; even if he did find time in Sicily to write any or all of the verses of his contained in Ital. 1543, it is hardly likely that they could have been transmitted all the way back to Venice and then circulated quickly enough for the hand of Ital. 1543 to have received and reproduced the text by Zanato's *terminus* of "*non post* 1493." No: surely written before Bembo's departure for Messina, the *Sogno* amounts to an exhortation to himself and Girolamo, even the charter of a *modus vivendi*, that coincides all too tellingly with Poliziano's inspirational visit of the previous summer; and it may even have been intended to persuade Girolamo to join Pietro and Gabriele in their Sicilian venture,[29] with a suggestive allusion to the Greek studies that await in Messina when, at the *Sogno*'s climax, Girolamo, Pietro's faithful Pirithous (187), is summoned to "his high undertaking" (*all'alta impresa*, 187).

If any doubt remains about the pre-Messina dating of the *Sogno*, Bembo's own words would seem to settle the matter once and for all. From Noniano on August 21, 1498 he wrote as follows to his friend Alberto Pio, Prince of Carpi (1475–1531), who as a child had been tutored by Aldo Manuzio (1449–1515), and who later, in the 1490s, became a significant supporter of the nascent Aldine Press at Venice:[30]

> . . . I finally took myself to the library. When I was there yesterday, there came into my hands the vernacular poem of mine (*vernaculum carmen meum*) that I'd composed in this very place before I set out for Sicily, in order to awaken myself and a certain friend of mine, as if we were sleeping, to the duties of the good life and to the pursuit of attaining virtue (*ut me ipsum atque amicum quendam meum ad bene vivendi officia, et capessendarum virtutum studium, quasi dormientes excitarem*). When I'd read through it with a certain curiosity, as tends to happen when we look back over those writings that have lain neglected for a long time, as if we're far distanced from the memory of them, I took more pleasure from reading it than I'd thought

28. Zanato (2002) 147.

29. Baldacchini (1987) 119.

30. Lowry (1979) 52, 58–9; for Pio's possible financial as well as more general encouragement see Chapter 5 p. 187 and n.21.

> I would. And so, since I was not dissatisfied with them, I've decided to send those verses to you, both for you to have as if the first fruits of this estate, and also to show you that I'm in the habit of singing not just love songs (*amatoria*) in poems that are not of this stamp, but also the kind of song that fits your own moral and philosophical interests (*quod ad mores et philosophiam tuam illam faciat*).[31]

The clue in *quasi dormientes* in particular can surely only mean that the vernacular poem Bembo mentions here is the *Sogno*, the friend Savorgnan: the awakening as if from figurative sleep coincides all too neatly with the rousing exhortation to virtue in the *Sogno*, and the latter's moral-philosophical component amply bears out Pietro's insistence in the letter that his poetic repertoire extends beyond erotic verse. But the letter is of interest for two further reasons. First, if we suspect a (not uncharacteristic) element of calculation in Bembo's missive to Pio, that well-known supporter of the Aldine Press, and if the idea that Bembo just happened "yesterday" to stumble on his youthful vernacular poem stretches credulity, was he courting Pio's interest in the *Sogno* with a view to its possible printing? Secondly, and to develop this first point from another angle: we can only speculate on whether or not, given the Aldine publication of *De Aetna* in February 1496, Bembo approached Manuzio about the *Sogno*, but the fact remains that it was indeed printed in incunable form. This incunable, discovered in the Biblioteca Nazionale Braidense of Milan in the 1980s, consists of only four leaves, unnumbered and without a frontispiece or subscription; hence the mystery of its provenance.[32] On the basis of its typeface, Lorenzo Baldacchini favors production by the brothers Giovanni and Gregorio de Gregori at Venice.[33] Positing for technical reasons centered on the character design of the lettering a *terminus ante quem* of 1497, Baldacchini further narrows the date of production to 1492–4, albeit doubting that the work could have been printed during Bembo's absence in Sicily.[34] On Baldacchini's line of argument, then, we are left with the case for production either early in 1492, before Bembo left for Messina,[35] or late in 1494, soon after his return to Venice. Even if the case for 1492 is rejected out of hand,[36] the later dating to 1494 would still distinguish this incunable as the

31. Travi (1987) 25 *Letter* 29.15–26.

32. See Curti (2013a) 94–5 (p. 88 for the incunable pictured) with Baldacchini (1987), esp. 115–19, and Zanato (2002) 148; the printed text is reproduced in its entirety by Baldacchini 123–30.

33. Baldacchini (1987) 117, 119.

34. (1987) 117.

35. Baldacchini's favored option, (1987) 118.

36. See Zanato (2002) 148: differences between the text in Ital. 1543 and that in the incunable make it reasonable to suppose "a certain lapse of time between the initial drafting, prior to the

earliest known imprint of Bembo's, vernacular or otherwise. A further advantage of this early dating is that it circumvents the difficulty posed by the striking discrepancy between the relatively unkempt appearance of the *Sogno* imprint on the one hand, and the clean, handsome finish of *De Aetna* on the other: if the *Sogno* incunable were the later production, how to explain Bembo's readiness to tolerate so inferior a print quality, especially when he is known to have kept so watchful an eye throughout his life on the editorial procedures that his own works underwent?[37] Yet Baldacchini ignores Bembo's letter to Pio of August 21, 1498: if the *Sogno* incunable was printed before that date, we are left to ponder (i) how Pietro could claim any casual rediscovery of his youthful poem just "yesterday," on August 20, 1498, and (ii) how he could earnestly promise to send on to Alberto, for exciting new disclosure, a text that had already circulated in print. Given these considerations, the *terminus post quem* for the *Sogno* imprint is surely more likely to be late August 1498,[38] even though the relative coarseness of appearance in comparison with the 1496 *De Aetna* remains problematic enough to allow no definitive closure to the dating question. For now, however, the importance of the 1498(?) imprint, and indeed of the letter to Pio, lies above all in Bembo's retrospective consciousness—his *published* consciousness—of the life choice and transition moment that confronted his pre-Messina self: if it does indeed postdate *De Aetna*, we might speculate that the *Sogno* incunable was meant as a vernacular complement to that earlier work, differently expressing the anxieties over life direction that had already been voiced in *De Aetna*.

3.2: Bembo's Greek Studies in Messina

Bembo's journey to Sicily brought major challenges and discomfort, as he reports in a letter that he wrote to his father on May 30, 1492, almost four weeks after his and Angelo's arrival in Sicily on May 4.[39] After they sailed from Venice to Chioggia, the original plan had been to make the rest of the journey on horseback,[40] but the scarcity of inns and their poor provisioning caused Pietro and Angelo to change their strategy at Naples; they sailed from there, eventually reaching Sicily after a

---

journey to Sicily, and the *Sogno*'s entry into print-form"—a consideration that renders highly improbable Baldacchini's hypothesis that "the printing could have been completed by the de Gregori brothers in the very first months of 1492" (148 n.20).

37. Curti (2013a) 95.

38. Cf. Vecce (1998b) 483 n.17, inclining to attribute the printing, "in un ambiente molto vicino ad Aldo, *alla fine del 1498*" (my emphasis).

39. Travi (1987) 4–5 *Letter* 2.

40. See Travi (1987) 4 *Letter* 1.51–3 (Pietro to his teacher Giovanni Alessandro Urticio, March 29, 1492).

ten-day voyage blighted by seasickness.[41] That Bernardo consented to the hazardous venture in the first place signals his positive support for Pietro's learning of Greek, and later, in a letter to Piero de' Medici of May 25, 1493, he wrote with pride of his son's great progress "sotto un famoso preceptore e scientissimo de quella lingua, messer Costantin Laschari," whereby Pietro is evidently set to become a "grecolo tuto."[42] As if to reassure Bernardo in his letter to him of May 30, 1492, Pietro offers a pleasing portrait of the fatherly Lascaris:

> But all the nuisance [sc. of the journey to Sicily] was wiped away by our most kindly meeting with Constantine Lascaris, who received us very gladly and graciously gave us assurances. And that holds good in practice: he teaches us with his wonderful attentiveness, and then with a love that is almost fatherly (*tum amore prope paterno*). There is altogether nothing more kindly that that old man, nothing more venerable.[43]

Apparently born in Constantinople in 1434, Lascaris was taken prisoner after the city's fall to the Ottomans in 1453. Gaining his freedom by escape or ransom, he made for Greece, living on Rhodes, in Pherae, and possibly in Crete before finding employment in Milan from 1458 to 1465, first as Greek tutor to Ippolita, the eldest daughter of Francesco I Sforza, Duke of Milan (1401–66); he was then formally appointed to a professorship of Greek in 1463. After leaving Milan in 1465, and after a short and unhappy stay in the court of Ferdinand I, King of Naples (1423–94), Lascaris arrived in Messina in 1466, intending to make for Greece once more. But there he was appointed in 1467 to a professorship at the Greek school attached to the Basilian monastery of San Salvatore in Messina, and there he remained, by no means uniformly content, until his death from the plague in 1501.[44] Before he died he donated his impressive library to the senate and people of Messina. This collection was assembled with great difficulty, partly through his own prodigious efforts

41. Travi (1987) 4–5 *Letter* 2.3–6. For the logistical challenges, and hence the relative scarcity, of travel south of Naples through the sixteenth century, see Jaworska (1992) 162 with Bastiaensen (1996) 366.

42. See Cian (1896) 358–9 with Giannetto (1985) 203–4. Cf. Travi (1987) 4 *Letter* 1.46–50: "after he [sc. Bernardo] learnt of my intention in this matter [sc. of going to Messina], he even praised me, and he overlooked none of the duties of a good father, so that I lacked for nothing, not just for the journey but much more also for my stay, which he didn't doubt would be for less than a year; but I think it will be two years."

43. Travi (1987) 5 *Letter* 2.7–10.

44. For more detail on his life, Rosalia (1957–8); Fernández Pomar (1966) 213–21; Förstel (1992) 1.85–99; N. G. Wilson (1992) 120–3 = (2017) 136–9; Harris (1995) 122–4; Martínez Manzano (1994) 6–32 and (1998) 3–20; Ceresa (2004).

as a copyist on his diverse travels, and partly through purchase or donation. It later found its way into the private library of Juan Francisco Pacheco, the Fourth Consort Duke of Aceda (1649–1718), while he was viceroy in Sicily (1687–96), and it eventually went from there to Madrid, where it now resides in the Biblioteca Nacional; of the eighty-three manuscripts that have survived by this route, twenty-five were copied by Lascaris in their entirety, and forty-three others show restorations by his hand.[45] His library played a key functional role in his teaching.[46] But despite (or beyond) his emergence as a celebrated teacher who drew students not just from Sicily but also from the Iberian and Italian peninsulas,[47] and even though the range of his interests and instruction seems to have extended significantly into the sciences (especially mathematics and astronomy) and philosophy,[48] Lascaris' renown in his own day was due mostly to his authorship of works on Greek grammar. As we shall see in (v) below, Bembo was to play a significant role in the Aldine publication of Lascaris' grammar. But first we survey four other areas that illustrate not just the rapid advances that he made in his Greek studies in Messina, but also the blend of youthful ambition and self-promotion that he was later to show in *De Aetna* as well.

(i) Bembo's letter to Demetrius Moschus

This letter, written in Messina on January 1, 1493 and addressed to Moschus (*c.* 1450–*post* 1519[?]) in Venice, is, significantly, the sole surviving missive in Greek in Bembo's extant correspondence.[49] The learned Demetrius, of Spartan origin, taught Greek at Ferrara, Mirandola, and Venice, and was perhaps Giovanni Pico della Mirandola's instructor in the language;[50] before such an addressee, Pietro's

45. Further, Fernández Pomar (1966), esp. 211–12, 221–2; N. G. Wilson (1992) 122 = (2017) 138; Martínez Manzano (1994) 282 and (1998) 49–53.

46. See Förstel (1992) 1.97 with Vecce (1998b) 484.

47. Förstel (1992) 1.96–7 with Martínez Manzano (1994) 25 and (1998) 21.

48. For Lascaris' scientific interests, Moscheo (1988b), esp. 597–608, and (2001); she detects a revitalization of his teaching in the early 1490s because of the diversified student body (Pietro Bembo and Angelo Gabriele being cases in point) that was gradually drawn to his school from further afield, not least through Lascaris' contacts with northern Italian humanists. Hence from 1492 his school "became comparable to a centre for advanced studies" ([2001] 21; already [1988b] 606), albeit it experienced "a total collapse" (Moscheo [1987] 538) after his death in 1501; for Moscheo (1988b) 608–9, the eminent Sicilian mathematician Francesco Maurolico (1494–1575; see Introduction, p. 2), whose father Antonio was himself Lascaris' pupil and apparently Pietro Bembo's contemporary there, embodied through his cultural formation the last traces of the now defunct Lascaris establishment.

49. Travi (1987) 5–6 *Letter* 3.

50. See Geanakoplos (1962) 124 n.53 with Meschini (1977) 25 n.1 and J. N. Grant (2011) 116–17 (= Lilio Gregorio Giraldi, *Dialogi duo de poetis nostrorum temporum* 2.14–15) and 313.

letter tests and validates his growing proficiency in Greek. Infelicities remain in his use of accents and prepositions and in his control of grammar, indicating that the letter was not overseen by Lascaris before its dispatch; it is unfortunate that the letter's bearer, Paolo Ralis, was charged with reporting in person to Demetrius on the nature of Pietro's studies with Lascaris, and that Bembo therefore reveals nothing in the letter of the operation of Lascaris' school.[51] The letter itself is part apology, part request: after addressing why, before he left for Sicily, he had failed to inform Demetrius of his imminent departure, he gives two motives for writing, the first to stress that he remains fondly mindful of Demetrius, and eager to be of continuing service to him (*Letter* 3.13–16). But then his second motive: would Demetrius be sure to send him the poem that he had composed on the rape of Helen—a favor already much anticipated by Lascaris himself, eager as he reportedly was to know Demetrius' qualities as a poet (*Letter* 3.16–22)? This poem, in some 460 Homeric hexameters, was published with a Latin translation by Demetrius' friend Ponticus Virunius at Reggio Emilia possibly as early as 1497,[52] but its composition was presumably completed only shortly before Bembo's enthusiastic request of January 1, 1493.[53] In his *Dialogi duo de poetis nostrorum temporum*, published in 1551, Lilio Gregorio Giraldi (1479–1552) remarks as follows on Demetrius' accomplishments as a poet, and on the eventual publication of his *Helen*:

> Demetrius composed many poems: epigrams and elegies. As for his comedies, he did not allow them to be performed publicly, limiting acquaintance with them to intimate friends. However, after undertaking a poem on Helen in hexameter verse, he allowed this to be printed for all to read. It shows marvelous fluidity of style (*heroicum vero carmen aggressus de Helena palam omnibus excussum typis legendum tradidit, in quo mira est facilitas*).[54]

The *facilitas* to which Giraldi refers is borne out in the fluency with which Demetrius works into his *Helen* an abundance of Homeric and Apollonian echoes.[55] But why

51. On these points, Piccolomini (1890).

52. For the poem, Meschini (1977). The colophon in the *princeps* lacks a date. For "*ca.* 1497" see Walton (1963) 212, but then apparently second thoughts: cf. (1971) 13 for "not before 1500" in accordance with Goff (1964) 434 M-865; Meschini 9–10 inclines to "not before the start of 1501." For Virunius (sc. Ludovico da Ponte, *c.* 1460–1520), Ricciardi (1986).

53. See Donadi (1983) xiii n. 23.

54. 2.14 J. N. Grant (2011) 116–17.

55. Speake (1974) 117–18, albeit observing that certain errors of prosody occur; on the wider network of influences, Meschini (1977) 15–19.

were Lascaris and Bembo so interested in this *Helen*? It may be that the work sparked curiosity because (as Ponticus Virunius observes in his dedicatory preface to the Reggio Emilia edition) Demetrius, like Helen, was a native Spartan.[56] But Bembo's interest was surely connected with the second of the materials that attest to his progress in Greek in Messina: his Latin translation of Gorgias' *Encomium of Helen*.

(ii) Bembo's Gorgias

This translation of Gorgias was accompanied by a prefatory letter of dedication to Fernando de Acuña, viceroy of Sicily from 1489 until his death in December 1494[57]—a letter indicating that the translation was completed probably no later than the first months of 1493, and certainly well within the first year of Bembo's sojourn in Sicily:

> Since I embarked on the Greek language from its very first principles a few months ago (*paucis abhinc mensibus)* [i.e., from May 1492 onward] in this city of yours, I neither dared nor had the ability to take on a greater task. Please accept, therefore, with that kindness in which you surpass all, the first fruits of my studies: the praise that our Gorgias directed in jest at Helen . . .[58]

The text as it survives is a copy of the original, and is dated to May 1, 1493 in the subscription supplied by Pirro Vizani;[59] hence the case for Bembo's authorship within months of his arrival in Messina. That Bembo never published this translation may well reflect his own view of it as an immature and experimental exercise, an exhibition piece preceded by a dedicatory letter that itself teems showily with allusion to a wide array of influences.[60] But why specifically Gorgias' *Encomium*, a challenging text that presented difficult and unusual features of style? Perhaps Bembo was partly guided by what Francesco Donadi posits as an interest, in the manner of Poliziano, in lesser-known texts that invited rediscovery and appealed to "la curiosità del secolo."[61] Another

56. See, in reproduction of the preface, Meschini (1977) 93–4 (*in eadem civitate natus est* [sc. *Demetrius*] *qua Helena*).

57. For Fernando, Di Blasi (1842) 123–9.

58. Lines 24–8 Donadi (1983) 5; cf. in praise of Fernando Travi (1987) 9 *Letter* 7.40–3.

59. For which Donadi (1975b) 127, (1982) xlviii, and (1983) xii and 18.

60. For which Donadi (1983) 5–8, esp. nn. 3, 6–12, and 14.

61. Donadi (1983) xiii.

topical motive was supplied by Gorgias' origins in the Greek colony of Leontini in Sicily. Lascaris was also engaged in his last years in preparing his *Vitae illustrium philosophorum Siculorum et Calabrorum*; the version finally published in Messina in 1499 after a long gestation consisted of sixty-nine biographies of Sicilian philosophers (Gorgias among them), and thirty-five of Calabrian philosophers.[62] We might suppose that Lascaris solicited the help of his students for this large task; if so, could it be that Bembo's translation arose out of his involvement in Lascaris' project, in which Gorgias was so obviously implicated? Whatever his precise motivation, however, the source of Bembo's translation appears certainly to have been a manuscript in Lascaris' own hand, identified by Donadi as Matritensis gr. 7210 in the Lascaris collection that now resides in the Biblioteca Nacional, Madrid;[63] it is very possible that Lascaris made his copy in Florence after his departure from Milan in 1465, in one stopping point en route to Naples and, ultimately, to Messina.[64] For present purposes, the interest of Bembo's reliance on Lascaris' manuscript lies in the further evidence that it reveals of Pietro's close association with the Aldine Press at Venice. In the 1513 *Rhetorum graecorum orationes*, Manuzio states in the dedicatory preface addressed to Giambattista Egnazio that he owes to his close associate at the press, the eminent scholar-editor Marco Musuro (*c.* 1470–1517),[65] the inclusion of Gorgias' *Encomium*: "To these orations of Isocrates we have added, on the suggestion of our friend Marcus Musurus, Alcidamas' speech against the teachers of rhetoric, Gorgias in praise of Helen, and Aristides in praise of Athens."[66] The Aldine text of the *Encomium* substantially reflects, some modifications apart, that of Lascaris. But why this recourse to Lascaris when the work was readily available in at least three manuscripts at Venice itself?[67] Bembo had evidently brought back with him from Messina a copy of Lascaris' manuscript;[68] the editorial decision, presumably Musuro's decision, to base the 1513 imprint on the version derived from Lascaris offers its own measure of Lascaris' enduring authority—a belated but significant footnote to the story of Bembo's Sicilian venture.

---

62. On this work, which survives in two redactions (the second features the sixty-nine Sicilian and the thirty-five Calabrian lives), Donadi (1975b) 127 and (1983) xiii; Martínez Manzano (1994) 152–5 and (1998) 186–8; Lamers (2015) 195–8.

63. See Donadi (1975a) 174–84; (1975b) 128–33; (1982) xliv–v, xlviii; (1983) xiv.

64. See Donadi (1975a) 181; (1975b) 128; (1982) xlv; (1983) xv and n.30.

65. For whom see esp. Foffano (1892) and Geanakoplos (1962) 111–66 with Lowry (1979) 164–7.

66. Botfield (1861) 301, and now N. G. Wilson (2016) 224–5 (his translation).

67. On this point, Donadi (1975a) 181, 183–4.

68. Further, Donadi (1983) xxii.

(iii) Bembo as Advocate for Greek Letters

Probably in the first months of 1494, while he was still in Messina, Bembo composed an essay in Greek, Περὶ τοῦ βοηθεῖν τοῖς τῶν Ἑλλήνων λόγοις (*On coming to the aid of Greek letters*), which was never published but survives in two copies.[69] This essay, cast in the form of an address to the Venetian senate but replete with formulae suited to the age of Classical Athens,[70] was presumably an imaginary exercise for private circulation among friends. It evidently cannot have been meant for practical delivery, unless it also existed in a vernacular version that would have been intelligible to its intended audience.[71] Bembo is in fact known to have addressed the Senate on a different matter in 1495, but that occasion would seem to be later, at least to judge by his claim in his Greek address that he "had not spoken previously" (p. 58.416–17).[72] Bembo's ostensible, *suasoria*-like goal[73] in this essay is to persuade the government to take steps to ensure the resurgence of Greek studies and to set in place a stable platform for the teaching of Greek language and literature. The innate virtue and wisdom of members of the Venetian government, Bembo argues, could only be fortified by Greek studies, which Venice had in any case long regarded (cf. p. 26.72–4). To the objection that it is quite enough to work for the preservation of Latin, let alone Greek, and that the Greeks themselves should be left to preserve their language and literature (p. 30.107–9), he asserts that the Greeks are in no position to do much on their own behalf (cf. pp. 32.127–34.137); scarcely one percent of Greek literature survives (p. 36.166–7),[74] and that too will be endangered unless action is taken. He then strives to demonstrate that the Greeks were masters of all the sciences and arts; he casts Greek *logos* as fundamental to the development of civilized society, and hence as a tool of vital interest to Venetian rule. Venice is well placed to promote Greek studies, he argues, given its many Greek territorial

69. For these copies, Pertusi (1980) 183 and n.24; N. G. Wilson (1992) 125–6 and 184 n.6 (= [2017] 143 and 214 n.6) and (2003) 13–17. The date 1494: Pertusi (1980) 185–6 n.30 (the speech composed "verso la fine del suo soggiorno a Messina"), rightly rejecting attribution to 1531 (cf. Geanakoplos [1962] 227 n.11 and 279) or to 1539. Bembo surely refers to this speech in a letter of December 23, 1508 to Federico Fregoso, who appears to have asked Pietro for a copy of it, receiving this response: *Orationem meam graece scriptam, et quidem manu mea, habebis cum his litteris* (Travi [1990] 25 *Letter* 283.35–6).

70. See N. G. Wilson (2003) 9.

71. N. G. Wilson (2003) 8.

72. All textual references in this paragraph follow page and line number in N. G. Wilson (2003).

73. Cf. N. G. Wilson (1992) 126 = (2017) 143: "One wonders if the Greek reflects a maiden speech given at an unusually early age or is simply the product of an attempt to revive the ancient educational practice of the imaginary speech (*suasoria*)"; (2003) 8–9.

74. Cf. N. G. Wilson (2003) 36–7 *ad loc.*: "This is the most interesting assertion in the whole essay. I am not aware of any similar calculation by other humanists."

possessions and its riches in books, libraries, and schools (pp. 46.274–48.283); by exploiting those advantages, and by looking to the Greek past, Venice stood to enhance the cultural formation of its leaders in the Republic, not least through nurturing the power of the word (cf. pp. 42.226–44.249, 52.349–54.368). The highest levels of achievement in many branches of knowledge are in any case unattainable without Greek (cf. pp. 60.435–64.494), and reliance on medieval translation and exegesis merely distorts key tenets of Aristotelian and Platonic doctrine (cf. pp. 68.526–70.545); far better to take the direct path to the original texts, integrating our Latinate culture with its Greek counterpart.

"It remains quite unclear," writes Nigel Wilson, "how much effect his views had, even in the circle of his friends."[75] Regardless of any practical consequence, however, Bembo's essay remains symbolically important as a manifesto of sorts, especially in the context of comparable works that sought to protect and promote the transmission of Greek learning from Byzantium to Italy after 1453. Notable in this category are the brief *Oratio in laudem litterarum Graecarum* of the Byzantine émigré Andronicus Contoblachas, addressed probably to a Venetian audience in or around 1458;[76] the double discourses of the distinguished Byzantine humanist from Athens, Demetrius Chalcondyles (1423–1511), who was appointed to the newly established and highly prestigious chair of Greek studies at the University of Padua in 1463, and whose inaugural speech of 1463 and second inaugural at the commencement of his second year in 1464 were recorded in combined form by his pupil, Hartmann Schedel (1440–1514);[77] and the *Oratio de laudibus literarum graecarum* of Scipione Forteguerri (1466–1519), that early collaborator of Aldo Manuzio in Venice who was a major presence in the circle of philhellene scholars around Manuzio that evolved into the so called New Academy by the late summer of 1502.[78] The single printed sheet that survives in the Vatican Library, setting out the rules for meetings of the Academy, was originally composed by Forteguerri, and its margins show heavy annotations in his hand.[79] Under the imposing title of ΝΕΑΚΑΔΗΜΙΑΣ

75. N. G. Wilson (1992) 127 = (2017) 144.

76. For text and background, Schmitt (1971) with Pertusi (1980) 181 and Ciccolella (2008) 76–7 n.4 (Contoblachas taught Greek at Basel from 1473 to 1477). The Venetian audience is signaled by the vocative *viri patritii* (Schmitt 266 and 275 line 8 from the top of the printed text).

77. On these speeches see in general Geanakoplos (1974) with (1962) 92 and 133 and Pertusi (1980) 183 (Chalcondyles held the chair from 1463 to 1471). For the physician, humanist, and book collector Schedel, now best known for authoring the text of the *Nuremberg Chronicle*, see Geanakoplos (1974) 120–2 with n.7 for bibliography.

78. For Forteguerri, Piovan (1997). On the New Academy, Lowry (1976) and (1979) 195–8 with Davies (1995a) 55–8, and see further Chapter 5 p. 186.

79. See Lowry (1979) 196 with Davies (1995a) 55–6 and 60–1 fig. 30; for the text with translation, now N. G. Wilson (2016) 288–93.

NOMOΣ (= *Neakademias Nomos*), this document appears partly lighthearted in tone, as if setting the rules for a dining club, but it also shows serious intellectual ambition.[80] Tensions within the Academy were not slow to emerge, however, and Forteguerri for one was not to stay in Venice for long after 1502, leaving in ill temper in 1504.[81] For present purposes, what matters is that Manuzio published Forteguerri's *Oratio* in May 1504, and that Manuzio benefited from the attention that Forteguerri drew to Aldo's achievement in supplying sounder texts than had been available at any period since the Roman Empire's end.[82] This *Oratio*, Carlo Vecce suggests,[83] was openly derived from Bembo's 1494 Greek essay. That suggestion may be overoptimistic;[84] at the very least, however, in drafting his document in distant Messina, Bembo surely sought to inscribe himself into the larger philhellene movement to which Aldo gave such momentum in Venice of the 1490s: the piece was no mere diversion for itself, but strategically self-serving and prescient.

(iv) Claudian's Greek *Gigantomachia*

The only letter that Bembo addresses to Poliziano in his extant correspondence bears the date November 18, 1493.[85] This letter was prompted by a request from Poliziano that had reached Bembo, Pietro states, only indirectly through Sicilian merchants returning from Florence: the great man sought a copy of Claudian's Greek *Gigantomachia*, which he had heard to be in Lascaris' possession. Anxious to please and suitably deferential, Bembo describes the circumstances in which Lascaris stumbled upon the poem as follows:

> But as for the *Gigantomachia* of Claudian that Lascaris has, that is rather a *Battle of the Bookworms* (*Blattomachia*). In years past, while he himself was diligently inspecting, as is his custom, individual items among certain old and all but lamented books that a certain person of no great learning had gifted to him, he discovered together with the fragments of Hesiod . . . the title of

80. Davies (1995a) 56. Yet for the Academy as but a loose association of like-minded idealists, Lowry (1976) 385: "In plain fact, the Aldine Academy was never more than an undefined company of friends, dreaming of a glorious past and peering hopefully into a golden future which never materialized."

81. On this point, Lowry (1976) 399–400, and cf. p. 414: "After 1506 all references to an Aldine Academy become more scattered, less connected to any one place, and ever more dream-like."

82. Lowry (1979) 198.

83. Vecce (1998b) 491.

84. N. G. Wilson (2003) 13.

85. Travi (1987) 6–7 *Letter* 4.

> Claudian's *Gigantomachia*, and only a very few hexameters—and then again a second page, on which the work ended. As for the rest, the worms had so ravaged it that it was unreadable; and these very parts too are corrupted and suspect enough, like parts transcribed by copyists who lack learning.[86]

The source to which Bembo refers here is now lost, but Lascaris copied the poem, probably in 1465 or soon thereafter,[87] in the manuscript that survives as Matritensis gr. 4691: in his copy he attempted to reproduce the *Gigantomachia* as he apparently found it in his exemplar, transcribing the *vita*, the title and seventeen lines on one folio, sixty lines (twice thirty) on another, and leaving space in between those portions for the remainder of the lines—Bembo asserts a collection of 145 in all (*Letter* 4.26) —that were apparently irrecoverable in the exemplar.[88] In announcing that he has attached to the letter a copy, in his own hand, of the lines as transcribed by Lascaris (*Letter* 4.23), and in sending his and Gabriele's greetings to Giovanni Pico della Mirandola as well (*Letter* 4.31–4), Pietro in Sicily affirms and continues the association with Poliziano that had begun with the latter's visit to Venice in 1491; he writes as if striving to prove himself before an inspiring mentor.

(v) Lascaris' Greek Grammar

In 1476 Lascaris' *Summary of the eight parts of speech* ('Επιτομὴ τῶν ὀκτὼ τοῦ λόγου μερῶν) was published in Milan by Dionysius Paravisinus in partnership with Demetrius Damilas, an outstanding calligrapher who styles himself Demetrius the Cretan in the preface, revealing that he was responsible for the character of the typeface and for the printing—a responsibility that perhaps extended to the actual cutting of the punches.[89] This book is closely modeled on the 'Ερωτήματα (*Questions*) of Manuel Chrysoloras (*c.* 1355–1415): the latter, "the most popular and most frequently printed Greek book of the Renaissance,"[90] was first printed as

86. Travi (1987) 6 *Letter* 4.10–18.

87. See Vecce (1998b) 487, but Hall (1986) 142 remains more circumspect ("between 1465 . . . and 1493").

88. Further on Lascaris' copy, Birt (1892) lxx–lxxi; Zamora (1993); Vecce (1998b) 487–8; Hall (1986) 142–3; Martínez Manzano (1994) 176–8 and (1998) 192–3.

89. See Proctor (1900) 51–8 with Barker (1992) 19, 30–1 and now Speranzi (2015). For the epigram in which Poliziano hailed Dionysius and Demetrius on the 1476 publication of Lascaris' grammar, see Del Lungo (1867) 120–1 no. XXII with Proctor 58; Pontani (2002) 198–9; Finotti (2004) 55 n.166.

90. Layton (1979) 70. Cf. Nuti (2013) 260: "It is likely that, during his early period of private teaching in Milan and before creating his own manual, Lascaris chose Chrysoloras' *Erotemata* as a basic reference manual for his pupils because its theoretical innovation in the noun system was the key

early as *c.* 1471 at Venice by Adam de Ambergau, at least in the form of an abridged version of Guarino da Verona's Latin translation of Chrysoloras.[91] Another bilingual abridged edition of Chrysoloras' 'Ερωτήματα with the Greek text and Guarino's Latin translation was printed in 1475 or the first half of 1476 in Vicenza by Giovanni da Reno.[92] In contrast to these early print editions, however, Lascaris' 1476 *Summary* was a truly pioneering achievement: quite apart from its status as the first Greek book to announce where it was printed, by whom and when,[93] it was the first book to be produced *entirely* in Greek, with the only Latin in it confined to the preface (itself given in both Greek and Latin) and the colophon. By the century's end eight versions of Chrysoloras' 'Ερωτήματα had appeared, and six of Lascaris' work,[94] among them the important Aldine edition of the 'Επιτομή produced at Venice in 1495.[95] This was Aldo Manuzio's first substantial print production, in 166 folios, and the first to bear a date,[96] preceding by only a few months the first volume of his landmark Aristotle (November 1, 1495) and his edition of Theodore Gaza's *Introductivae grammatices libri quatuor* (December 25, 1495), which was itself a typographical landmark.[97] What, then, led Aldo to Lascaris' grammar as his first substantial undertaking?

Bembo's role in the whole matter was apparently pivotal. If in the fifteenth century publishers of school-oriented grammatical manuals felt little obligation to revert to authorial autographs or archetypes, relying instead on the vulgate, the

to success with Western students." Further on Chrysoloras and his work, Geanakoplos (1962) 24–8; N. G. Wilson (1992) 8–12 = (2017) 9–14; Ciccolella (2005) 3–12 and (2008) 118–24; Botley (2010) 7–12; and cf. also Chapter 2 p. 81.

91. See Layton (1979) 74–8 with Pertusi (1962) 323–4; for Guarino (1374–1460), N. G. Wilson (1992) 42–7 = (2017) 49–54, and cf. Chapter 2 p. 84 n.51.

92. But the attribution to da Reno has been challenged; see Layton (1979) 70 with Pertusi (1962) 325.

93. Layton (1979) 72: *Mediolani impressum per Magistrum Dionysium Paravisinum. MCCCCLXXVI. Die xxx Ianuarii.*

94. See Förstel (1992) 1.183 with Pertusi (1962) 326–8.

95. After first writing an essential elementary handbook (the 'Επιτομή), Lascaris composed a more comprehensive version in three books for advanced students (for an overview of the evolution of his grammatical writings, Martínez Manzano [1994] 182–240 and [1998] 133–63). The three-book edition was produced by the Aldine Press (undated, 1501-3; December 1501 with N. G. Wilson [2016] 83?), and was reprinted in 1512 (Martínez Manzano [1994] 226, 228 and [1998] 209); for the December 1501 (?) Latin preface to Angelo Gabriele, now Wilson 82–5.

96. Clough (1998) 57; further Barker (1992) 44 n.9 ("The main text is dated 25 February 1495 [1494 *more veneto*], the additional tracts 8 March 1495").

97. Barker (1992) 58: it "exhibits a number of combinations for complete words commonly used, a triumph of typefounding." Further on Gaza, Förstel (1992) 1.71–84, 183; Ciccolella (2005) 9 and n.25 and (2008) 121–4; Botley (2010) 14–25.

Aldine 'Επιτομή of 1495 showed a certain novelty in its reversion to Lascaris himself.[98] Or so at least Manuzio claims in the preface to the 1495 edition:

> In the meantime, students of literature, accept Constantine Lascaris' elements of grammar in a much more accurate form than in the printed copies available. Constantine himself has corrected the work in about 150 passages, which anyone who compares those copies with these will recognize; he will find some deletions, many corrections, and a great deal added. A copy so corrected by Constantine himself (*emendatum manu ipsius Constantini librum*) was lent to me by Pietro Bembo and Angelo Gabriele, Venetian patricians, young men of great nobility and outstanding talents, who recently learned Greek with Lascaris himself on the island of Sicily and are now studying the liberal arts together in Padua (. . . *Petrus Bembus et Angelus Gabriel, patritii Veneti, adeo nobiles praestantique ingenio iuvenes, qui nuper in insula Sicilia Graecas litteras ab eo ipso Lascari didicerunt et nunc Patavii incumbunt una liberalibus disciplinis*). We have added a Latin version on facing pages on our own initiative, reckoning it would be more convenient and helpful for beginners in Greek. I hope those who prefer these texts without a Latin version will be sparing in their criticism, because we have seen to the printing of Lascaris' textbook for the benefit of novices entirely ignorant of Greek . . .[99]

The source to which Manuzio refers in *emendatum . . . librum* is standardly identified as Vat. gr. 1401; that manuscript is indeed glossed in Lascaris' hand, and a number of those glosses are indeed reflected in the 1495 Aldine version. But Manuzio has surely exaggerated, to say the least. As Martin Lowry points out, it appears that Lascaris worked through the text not so much to make corrections in the Greek but to render it more intelligible for beginning students; clarification, not alteration, characterizes the majority of the 150 interventions claimed by Manuzio.[100] As for the latter's 1495 version, apart from "his inclusion of a few glosses or expansions"[101] from Lascaris' manuscript, he followed the Greek text of Buono Accorsi in his Milan edition of September 1480: "since the manuscript was not used as copy and does not appear to have been taken into the print-shop, we must assume that it served only as a quarry from which occasional alterations could be carried into the

98. For novelty also in its method of indexing *errata* by reference to exact pages and line numbers, Vecce (1998a) 111–12.

99. N. G. Wilson (2016) 5; already in Orlandi (1975) 1.3 no. IA.

100. Lowry (1979) 224–5.

101. Lowry (1979) 225.

Milanese edition which must have served as exemplar."[102] As for Manuzio's Latin translation, it amounted to a lightly modified version of the translation of Giovanni Crastone, which was printed alongside Accorsi's text in the 1480 edition—a retouching that introduced only superficial but sometimes distorting changes. "When the hybridisation, the thinly disguised plagiarism, and Aldus' free adaptations stand revealed," concludes Lowry, "the whole provides an astonishing illustration of the liberties which an editor could safely and respectably take."[103] Moreover, reliance on Accorsi's text may circumvent another difficulty, or perhaps rather raise a suspicion: given that Pietro was back in Venice in the summer of 1494 (as evidenced by his letter to his tutor, Giovanni Alessandro Urticio, dated August 15 at Venice),[104] how to account for the facts that the end page of Vat. gr. 1401 bears the date *1494, 25 Novembris*,[105] and that Lascaris' annotations extend as late in the manuscript as fol. 164? Unless we imagine that Manuzio used either a Lascaris original other than Vat. gr. 1401 or an interim copy of it that Pietro brought back with him from Messina, another scenario suggests itself: Manuzio relied primarily on Accorsi's text, Vat. gr. 1401 became available to him by some means only late in 1494 or soon thereafter (and well after Pietro's return home from Messina), he consulted that manuscript only secondarily, and in the preface to the 1495 edition he in effect constructed a convenient but highly misleading sequence of events.

Whatever the truth of the matter, and even if Lowry is seen to be "anachronistically critical" of Manuzio's "apparently casual treatment" of his Lascaris source,[106] Manuzio had good reason to play up his association with Pietro and Angelo in the preface to his 1495 edition. A novel typographical feature of the nascent Aldine Press was the "set piece," a publication that advertised the equipment newly implemented by the press.[107] Beyond constituting the first of these "publicity" productions,[108] the 1495 edition could also claim a certain freshness of authority and

---

102. Lowry (1979) 225.

103. Lowry (1979) 225. Cf. Clough (1998) 58: "such liberties were typical of editors of the time, and while in no way unique to Aldo, they were consistent features of his publishing."

104. See Travi (1987) 8 *Letter* 6, esp. lines 3–4: *Gratae mihi tuae litterae fuerunt, quibus mihi de reditu e Sicilia meo gratularis.*

105. Two other dates are given, on fol. 50*v* *Messanae 1494. 3 calen. Junii* and fol. 129 *18 Julii 1494. Messanae*: Martínez Manzano (1994) 328 and (1998) 43–4. Vecce (1998b) 491 n. 38 rightly senses the problem posed by the date *1494, 25 Novembris*, which "mi sembra escludere l'identificazione con la copia portata da Bembo e Gabriele."

106. Barker (1992) 45 n. 13.

107. Barker (1992) 45.

108. Barker (1992) 45.

authenticity[109] by recounting Pietro and Angelo's direct experience of Lascaris, and then their return to Venice with Lascaris' autograph corrections in hand. The two young nobles could doubtless also lend a certain prestige to the volume. They too stood to gain, however, from their association with the philhellene Manuzio, not least through the advertisement of their humanist credentials in this public investiture of sorts: here on the printed page, in Aldo's fresh new typeface, was an eye-catching announcement that they were back in Venice after studying Greek with one of the most eminent scholars of the age.[110]

3.3: Absent Presences: Giorgio Valla and Ermolao Barbaro

But why Messina in the first place? After all, Bembo could have easily studied Greek in Venice: the Republic had of course long been a colonial presence in much of the Greek world, a great influx of Greeks had come to this "second Byzantium" (*quasi alterum Byzantium*)[111] both before and especially after Constantinople's fall in 1453, and in the late Quattrocento in particular many Greek intellectuals were drawn to the city by the rise of printing in Greek there.[112] But despite such ripe opportunity for Greek study at home, Bembo's motivation to go elsewhere may have been stimulated in part by his experience of accompanying his father on the latter's diplomatic assignments to such cultural centers as Florence, Rome, and Bergamo. But where specifically to study Greek if not in Venice or nearby, such as in Padua? Further afield, Milan, Rome, and Florence were obvious possibilities, but all posed idiosyncratic difficulties of one kind or another,[113] and in early 1492 Messina may well have appeared a relatively safe option, at least in comparison with the uncertain political climate leading up to Charles VIII of France's invasion of Italy in the autumn of 1494. Another factor was the allure of the illustrious Lascaris

---

109. Or at least the appearance of such freshness, given Aldo's cavalier use of the Lascaris source, as described above.

110. Further, Clough (1998) 58: "One can see why Aldo would want to bolster his edition by associating it with two young Venetian patricians, but why, in particular, did Bembo agree to this? *My supposition is that Bembo, whose actions usually were self-centered and calculated, loaned the manuscript primarily to advertise his own humanistic studies*" (my emphasis). Cf. also Finotti (2004) 56 ("Era quasi un'investitura pubblica per il Bembo").

111. So the eminent Cardinal Basilios Bessarion in a letter to the Doge of Venice in 1468: Omont (1894) 139 with Geanakoplos (1962) 35.

112. On these points, Rosada (1997) 45–6, with bibliography; for the émigré impact on Venice in particular, Geanakoplos (1989) 23–31, noting (p. 23) "a genuine intensification of Venetian humanist interests" after 1453.

113. Rosada (1997), esp. 47–50, with Dionisotti (1966a) 133–4 = Vela (2002) 144.

himself. Perhaps Bembo chose the man, not the place; but just how did he learn of Lascaris? Various clues indicate that Pietro had in fact already gained at least some proficiency in Greek before he left Venice, and also point to the identity of his teacher(s): in his prefatory address to Angelo Gabriele in *De Aetna* §1 he remarks on how, as an adolescent, he "gave [him]self over completely to [his] Greek teachers for instruction" (*nos ... totos tradidimus graecis magistris erudiendos*); even if his remark were taken to extend chronologically to his Greek studies under Lascaris in Messina, his use of the plural in *magistris* implies a teacher or teacher(s) in his pre-Sicilian phase.[114] Lascaris himself now helps with the task of identification: in a letter seemingly penned in June 1492[115] to his former pupil from his Milan days, Giorgio Valla, the distinguished humanist scholar-educator who held the chair of rhetoric at the Scuola di San Marco in Venice from 1485 until his death in 1500,[116] Lascaris writes of his years of teaching in Messina; his Sicilian students are indolent, he claims, but he also draws pupils from the peninsula, among them "*of your pupils* Pietro Bembo and Angelo Michele, Venetian patricians and outstanding in both languages" (*ex discipulis tuis Petrum Bembum et Angelum Michaelem patricios venetos utraque lingua insignes*).[117] If we accept that Valla taught the young Bembo and Angelo the rudiments of Greek in Venice in the later 1480s or so, and that their level of attainment may in fact have been considerable (so at least Lascaris' *utraque lingua insignes* indicates), it was plausibly Valla who first brought Lascaris and his Greek grammar to Pietro's attention; he may also have encouraged the idea of studying under Lascaris in Messina, not least because Lascaris' range of teaching appears to have extended far beyond the purely linguistic and codicological to the sciences and philosophy.[118] Perhaps he wrote a letter of introduction to his former teacher, a letter that Bembo and Gabriele carried with them when they traveled to Sicily; or so we might infer from Lascaris' own letter as sampled above, and from its tone as a reply to a missive received, even if Lascaris' acquaintance with Bembo and Gabriele was still new enough to cause him to misname the latter as *Angelum Michaelem*, not *Chabrielem*.[119]

---

114. Further, Rosada (1997) 52.

115. For the letter, Heiberg (1896) 413–15 and then Rosada (1997) 56; persuasively for the dating, Rosada 56–9.

116. For Valla, Heiberg (1896) and Branca (1981) with King (1986) 439–40; now Raschieri (2012), esp. 127 n.1 for further bibliography. For Smiley (1920) 72, "Valla's period of pupilage under [Lascaris in Milan] must have begun at latest in mid-1462, and probably continued till 1465."

117. Heiberg (1896) 414; also in Rosada (1997) 56, and see further on Lascaris' relations with Valla Martínez Manzano (1994) 261–3 ("Geschichte einer langen Freundschaft") and (1998) 21–8.

118. See p. 123 and n.48 above.

119. On these points, Rosada (1997) 59.

It was possibly through Valla, then, that Bembo first came to know of Lascaris' grammar in Venice. Bembo's familiarity with that grammar is attested in a letter that he wrote to his tutor Urticio on March 29, 1492, just before his departure for Sicily. For all his respectfulness of tone in this letter, he combines a certain distance with a hurried leave-taking:[120]

> I indeed wanted—much as always, but now more than ever—to see you and to talk with you, so as to consult (as I ought) both your wisdom and your love for me concerning my learning Greek (which you often urged on me) and the plan for my departure, which is as yet unknown to you . . . But though I thought that, before I decided anything, there would be no lack of time to visit you, everything changed so suddenly that I was forced to take my departure plan in hand and to hasten my leaving,[121] to the effect that I couldn't visit you . . . But I come to my plan: there is in Sicily, at Messina, Constantine Lascaris, a man who is not only Greek but also from Byzantium. Messina is the only city, from the entirety of Greece, that is assuredly said to retain that Attic purity of the ancient tongue,[122] if indeed any such purity of that language still remains. And in that city he opened a school, and has run it for many years already, with integrity and considerable merit. He wins very great plaudits in the talk of all men. *For the instruction of boys he wrote a book on the first elements of grammar—a book that is both used and read.* I'd decided that he was the one to teach me, if you'd have approved, whether because he himself was easily pre-eminent in that kind of teaching (and every art is to be imbibed from the best teachers), or because he was practicing that art in Sicily, where I would be distracted from my zeal for learning by no private or public responsibilities, by no duties to friends, and by no obligations to my father (*ubi non domesticis curis, non publicis, non amicorum officiis, non paternis ullis muneribus a discendi studio interpellarer*), if I took myself there . . . You have my plan for departure. I wish I'd written to you about it before: I would be getting on the way with more peace of mind.[123]

This letter will soon prove to be important for far more than just its reference to Lascaris, illustrating as it does Pietro's quest for escape in Sicily from the path of

---

120. See Floriani (1966) 38 ("un reale distacco"); Pietro's tone appears warmer in his letter to Urticio of August 15, 1494 (Travi [1987] 8 *Letter* 6), after his return from Sicily.

121. The reason for this hurried departure is unknown.

122. But cf. N. G. Wilson (1992) 126 = (2017) 143 for bewilderment on this point.

123. Travi (1987) 3–4 *Letter* 1.3–6, 11–14, 20–33, 43–4.

aristocratic duty at home.[124] For now, however, if Valla was his esteemed teacher at Venice before Bembo left for Sicily, why no mention of him in this letter? Perhaps the omission is innocent and inconsequential, or tactfully contrived to avoid any hint of offence to Urticio, so long Pietro's apparently beloved "guide and organizer of his studies."[125] But why no mention of Valla in *De Aetna*, especially when Valla's own relationship with Lascaris may well have been instrumental in causing Bembo to head for Messina in the first place? The tempting answer in this case is predicated on an unfortunate confluence of events in February 1496: in the very month when *De Aetna* was published, Valla was imprisoned by the Council of Ten on suspicion of treason in supporting the Milanese faction of Gian Giacomo Trivulzio despite the Venetian preference for Ludovico Sforza. Valla was eventually found innocent, released in October 1496, and reinstated in his position at the Scuola di San Marco.[126] But in February 1496 any mention of Valla in *De Aetna* would surely have been an ill-timed embarrassment; hence, perhaps, Bembo's last-minute intervention (even the suppression of a dedicatory letter?) to avoid all such awkwardness even as the work was going to press.[127]

Beyond the intrigue that surrounds Giorgio Valla as an absent presence in *De Aetna*, however, another such presence may well have influenced or conditioned the work still more profoundly. A Venetian patrician by birth, Ermolao Barbaro (1454–93) embarked upon the civic career expected of one of his class, but he struggled to reconcile those duties and expectations with his devotion to literary study.[128] We shall soon return to Barbaro's life story, and to the possible implications that his example—his submission to state service on the one hand, his aspiration for the life of letters on the other—has for assessing Bembo's own schism of self between the civic and literary callings; first, however, the influential shadow that he seemingly casts on *De Aetna* in other ways. To begin with, Barbaro was instrumental in securing Giorgio Valla's move from Milan to Venice to take up his appointment at the Scuola di San Marco in 1485.[129] If Valla taught Bembo Greek in the later 1480s, it is tempting to speculate that Barbaro had a hand in facilitating that arrangement, or that he himself encouraged Bembo to study Greek;[130]

124. See p. 145.

125. Cf. Travi (1987) 8 *Letter* 6.7: *quorum* [sc. *studiorum*] *mihi et dux et moderator semper fuisti.*

126. On these events, Preto (2010) 58 and 71 n.27 for further bibliography.

127. Rosada (1997) 60.

128. For basic orientation on Barbaro, Branca (1943), (1963a), (1969), (1973), (1980), (1996) and (1998) 51–216; Paschini (1957) 11–42; Pozzi (1973–9), esp. 1.lxi–clxviii; King (1986) 197–205, 322–3; Biow (2002) 104–20; Egerton (1983) 553–68; Ogilvie (2006) 31–3, 122–6.

129. See Branca (1996) 25; (1998) 110–12.

130. For background, Rosada (1997) 53.

Barbaro was evidently on cordial terms with Bernardo Bembo,[131] while Pietro was later to draw an affectionate portrait of him in his *De Virgilii Culice et Terentii fabulis liber*, and also to recall him fondly in a letter that he penned in February 1545 to Daniele Barbaro (1514–1570).[132] But beyond any shared involvement with the Bembos, Valla's activities as a translator and editor of a vast array of texts ranging from the literary to the philosophical and from the theoretical to the applied sciences[133] made him a kindred spirit and loyal disciple of Barbaro, that key architect of the "new philology" in late Quattrocento Venice.[134] We have already observed the profound influence that the experience of collating the Bembine Terence with Poliziano in 1491 appears to have had on the young Pietro.[135] But Barbaro, long Poliziano's correspondent and friendly rival, was no less committed to the reasoned collation of manuscripts;[136] to techniques of linguistic reconstruction that were based not on lockstep principles of grammatical abstraction or schematization, but on rigorous literary-historical documentation; to the careful identification of the sources used by a given author; and to the close scrutiny of direct or indirect testimony in support of a given fact or reading, consensus between authors being the prime criterion for emendation.[137] True to the line of humanist Aristotelianism that sought to combine eloquent Latin versions of the Greek with close philological study of the original texts, Barbaro applied this holistic approach to the task of purging Aristotle of the misunderstandings and confused interpretations that bedeviled the medieval commentary tradition.[138] To that end, between 1474 and 1485 at Padua and Venice, he set out to translate the whole of Aristotle into a precise and clear Latin that applied his belief in the unity of *verbum* and *res*, philosophical knowledge and rhetorical elegance,[139] and he broke

---

131. See Giannetto (1985) 212.

132. See *De Virg.* 1530 ed. fol. b iv (*Nam et ipse Bernardum Bembum amo, et ille me. Eius autem Petrus Bembus filius mihi etiam secundum patrem plurimum tribuit*) with Campanelli (1997) 292–3, and cf. Chapter 4 p. 149; for the 1545 letter, Travi (1993) 519 *Letter* 2466, esp. lines 9–13.

133. Now Raschieri (2012) with Gardenal (1981) and Landucci Ruffo (1981).

134. See esp. Branca (1963a) and (1998) 59–127.

135. See pp. 115–18.

136. Albeit not without differences of strategy and emphasis: see Pozzi (1973–9) 1.cxlix–clii, clxii, and cf. Branca (1996) 20 and then (1998) 93: ". . . il Barbaro basa la sua filologia sul ragionato confronto—seppure non prioritario e non sistematico—dei codici."

137. On these points, Branca (1973) 222–3; (1996) 20–1; (1998) 93–4.

138. Further, Branca (1963a) 200–1; (1996) 25–8; (1998) 70–3.

139. See esp. Branca (1963a) 202–3, (1996) 28–9, and (1998) 73–6; on Barbaro's dispute with Giovanni Pico della Mirandola about the compatibility of eloquence and philosophy, McLaughlin (1995) 228–48.

new ground by producing the first humanist version of any of Aristotle's ancient commentators in his translation of Themistius' paraphrases of Aristotle, published at Treviso in 1481.[140] An important corollary of Barbaro's new Aristotelianism was the inseparability of the human and the natural sciences, *naturalis philosophia* and *studium humanitatis*,[141] an outlook that in turn fundamentally conditioned his most influential work, the *Castigationes Plinianae et in Pomponium Melam*, one part of it published at Rome in 1492, another in 1493.

For present purposes, this extraordinary work, itself consciously Plinian in its bare economy of words,[142] encapsulates several aspects of the late Quattrocento intellectual climate and print culture that are pertinent also to *De Aetna*. If for medieval scholars Pliny's encyclopedic *Natural History* in thirty-seven books was a treasury of useful knowledge, the accuracy of the text a relatively minor concern,[143] critical attitudes were transformed by the rise of the printing press. One of the first books produced in Venice was the edition of the *Natural History* printed by Johannes de Spira in 1469.[144] This book had no preface, no named editor, and little critical ambition; because it also lacked Greek type, blank spaces were left in the text, or Greek words were clumsily rendered in roman letters.[145] In 1470 the edition of Giovanni Andrea Bussi (1417–75) was published by Conrad Sweynheym and Arnold Pannartz at Rome; Bussi made no reference to the 1469 Venetian edition, but he announced his text as a clear improvement on those currently in circulation,[146] and his version indeed appears to have been regarded by contemporaries effectively as the Plinian *princeps*.[147] But Bussi's text found a formidable critic in Niccolò Perotti (1429/30–80), author of the famed *Cornucopiae* that was posthumously published in 1489.[148] Seemingly in late 1470 or 1471, Perotti prepared a long letter to Francesco Guarneri, secretary of the papal nephew, Cardinal

---

140. For this edition and Barbaro's progress on his translation (begun between 1471 and 1473 and finished by 1480), Todd (2003) 72, 74–7.

141. Cf. Branca (1963a) 203, (1996) 30, and (1998) 75 for Barbaro as "nel '400 uno dei più generosi e energici cultori e promotori delle scienze naturali . . . che quale scienziato ebbe fama europea altamente proclamata dal Linacre a Linneo e al Leibniz."

142. Cf. Pozzi (1973–9) 1.clxi on "la volontà di discorrere intorno a Plinio usando uno stile pliniano."

143. On these points, Nauert (1979) 73–4 with (1980) 306–7.

144. For which Nauert (1980) 307.

145. On these points, Davies (1995b) 241–2 with Nauert (1980) 307–8.

146. See Davies (1995b) 245.

147. Monfasani (1988) 4.

148. For the *Cornucopiae*, Chapter 5 p. 188.

Marco Barbo, in which he launched a scathing attack on Bussi's edition.[149] The wide distribution of the printed page, Perotti perceived, meant that the text as circulated in this medium quickly became the standard recension, regardless of its possible inferiority to preexisting manuscript recensions (we might loosely compare the instant legitimacy too often accorded to modern Internet publications). In response, Perotti proposed two safeguards, the first the establishing of a common method for editors, the second the appointment of an accomplished scholar to oversee the publication of all Classical texts. For all his idealism, Perotti appears not to have appreciated the sheer volume of print production that he meant to patrol; and even if papal intervention had indeed been secured, it would have applied only to Roman printing, with no jurisdiction beyond that limited sphere.[150] For now, however, Perotti's harsh critique of Bussi's edition of the *Natural History* has an interesting denouement: Perotti, it appears, was at least partly responsible for the second Sweynheym and Pannartz edition of the *Natural History* that was issued on May 7, 1473.[151] Poliziano, in his own later work on Pliny's text, annotated a copy of this 1473 edition; and Poliziano it was who gave spark to the Plinian controversy that was to flare up in the 1490s.

Here Barbaro enters the story, albeit in connection with the hostile intervention of Niccolò Leoniceno (1428–1524), long distinguished at the University of Ferrara and far beyond as a humanist physician who pioneered the translation of Greek as well as Arabic medical texts.[152] The possessor of a remarkable collection of Greek texts,[153] Leoniceno stood out for his extreme Hellenocentricity even among his Hellenophile contemporaries.[154] For him, the sciences as practiced by his contemporaries were flawed because they were too often based on the faulty

149. For this episode, and for the *Commentariolus in prooemium Plinii* (first published in Venice in *c.* 1482 and afterward often attached to editions of the *Cornucopiae*), see Davies (1995b) 248–9 and n.32 with Monfasani (1988) 4–11; Nauert (1980) 308, 325–9; Grafton (2001) 149–51.

150. Monfasani (1988) 9–13.

151. Davies (1995b) 249–50; Nauert (1980) 308.

152. For Leoniceno, Pellegrini (2013) with Mugnai Carrara (1979) and (1991); Nauert (1979) 81–3 and (1980) 310–11; Nutton (1997b) 3–4; Egerton (1983) 528–43; Ogilvie (2006) 30–4, 126–33; Touwaide (2008), esp. 40–2. Leoniceno became Pietro Bembo's teacher when Bernardo Bembo was appointed *visdomino* of Ferrara in 1497 and Pietro joined his father there in 1497–9 (Kidwell [2004] 18); see also Clough (1998) 62 for Leoniceno's close association with the Aldine Press and with Manuzio himself (in June 1497 Manuzio published his famous work on syphilis, *Libellus de epidemia, quam vulgo morbum Gallicum vocant*, and in 1497 or 1498 his treatise *De tiro seu vipera*: on both works, Arrizabalaga et al. [1997] 65–6).

153. Mugnai Carrara (1991) with Nutton (1997b) 7 ("the largest single collection of Greek scientific, philosophical, and medical writings in western Europe, if not the world").

154. Nutton (1997a) 161.

construal of the sources; only by returning to the Greek originals, he insisted, could authoritative meaning be restored and stabilized.[155] Pliny may have been widely perceived as a good source for the Latin equivalents of Greek naturalistic terminology, not least because Pliny himself was deemed a near-enough contemporary of many of his Greek sources; but Leoniceno was having none of it. In a letter to Poliziano, no longer extant, Leoniceno apparently targeted mainly Avicenna,[156] but he noted in passing that Pliny seemed to have confused the Greek κίσσος (ivy) and κίσθος (rock rose), twice apparently using the Latin *hedera* (= ivy) for the latter.[157] In his reply in January 1491,[158] Poliziano commended the critique of Avicenna but politely took issue with Leoniceno for attacking so noted an author as Pliny on grounds of such relative slightness; whereupon Leoniceno responded with his *De Plinii et aliorum in medicina erroribus* of 1492, in which he defended his original assertions and charged Pliny with many more errors resulting from verbal confusion.[159] Just when Leoniceno was launching his broadside, however, Barbaro's *Castigationes Plinianae* appeared, seemingly a work in progress from February–March 1491 onward,[160] but composed without knowledge of Leoniceno's simultaneous stirrings. Barbaro claims to have corrected some 5,000 textual errors in the *Natural History*,[161] but his special relevance for now lies in (i) his defense of Pliny himself via his attribution of the textual errors that he found to the ignorance and carelessness of copyists, editors, and printers, not to the *auctor ipse*, and (ii) the limited scope of his work as primarily "a humanistic exercise in a purely literary form."[162] But with the quiet collusion of Poliziano and his circle, anxious as they were to protect

155. Further, Nutton (1997b) 6 with Nauert (1980) 310.

156. An attack motivated by his concerns at the influence exercised by Arabic texts in the teaching of medicine at Ferrara: see, conveniently, Ogilvie (2006) 131 with Nardi (1957) 250 and Butler (2006) 102–5 (= *Letter* 2.7.4, Leoniceno to Poliziano).

157. *HN* 12.74, 16.145; but for Pliny's own awareness of the potential for confusion cf. 24.81 with Doody (2011) 116–18.

158. *Angeli Politiani opera quae quidem extitere hactenus omnia* (Basel, 1553) 19–20; with translation in Butler (2006) 92–9.

159. But for Leoniceno's continuing friendly relations with Poliziano, Nardi (1957).

160. Pozzi (1973–9) 1.xxxvii.

161. Pozzi (1973–9) 1.2 lines 3–4 = Branca (1943) 2.79 *Letter* CLVI: *Quinque milia in eo fere vulnera librariorum sanavimus aut certe quemadmodum sanari possent ostendimus* (cf. also Branca 2.71 *Letter* CLIII).

162. Castiglioni (1953) 274, albeit one-sidedly disparaging Barbaro's scientific credentials: "Barbar[o] had no knowledge of medicine or botany. He tries only to clarify the botanical definitions and to identify some plants; and, at the same time, he strongly defends Pliny's name and reputation against all attacks."

the mode of philological humanism that Leoniceno was in effect attacking, a far more strident defender of Pliny emerged in the form of the accomplished diplomat, politician, and jurist Pandolfo Collenuccio (1444–1504). Printed in Ferrara in early 1493, his *Pliniana defensio adversus Nicolai Leoniceni accusationem* provocatively took up the fight at Leoniceno's home base; while it was still in press, Collenuccio read Barbaro's work, and thereafter the two authors jointly added an appendix to the *Defensio*.[163] As for Leoniceno, he sought to justify himself in a letter at least to Barbaro, but the latter died in 1493 before it was completed; that writing became incorporated (with further materials) in the enhanced edition of Leoniceno's *De Plinii . . . erroribus* that appeared in 1509.[164]

Others entered the fray on both sides, but Leoniceno held firm before Collenuccio's assault, compounding his initial charge of 1492 with further demonstrations of apparently Plinian error, as opposed to secondary error on the part of copyists, editors, or printers. For Leoniceno, confusion in Pliny's terminology, especially in botanical matters, had serious implications that reached far beyond the confines of antiquarian controversy: the defects that Leoniceno found in the *Natural History* warned anyone taking or prescribing cures on the basis of the suspect intermediary authority that he discerned in Pliny. In this respect, for all his Hellenocentric focus on the Greek medical writers, he was interested not in textual restoration per se, but in establishing the factual and medical truth;[165] in his stress on applications and outcomes, he was in effect championing one of two competing modes of humanist commentary, one purely philological in focus, the other more practical in orientation.[166] In light of this controversy, consider now an eye-catching moment in *De Aetna* when Bembo refers directly to Pliny (§§44–5), in circumstances that openly question his factual reliability:

PIETRO: Throughout the winter almost the whole mountain is white with snow, and the peak isn't without it even throughout the summer.

BERNARDO: What of the fact that both Pliny and Strabo record that there's snow only in winter? (*Quid, quod hyemare tantum eas* [sc. *nives*] *et Plinius et Strabo meminere?*)

PIETRO: But firsthand inquiry (*experentia*) tells you that it lasts, as does practical experience (*usus*), which is no lesser an authority (if Strabo will pardon me for saying so). And so, father, watch out again and again that you're not upset if I disagree

163. See French (1986) 254.

164. Further, French (1986) 254.

165. On these points, Nauert (1979) 81–3.

166. Pinon (2010) 624.

> with the ancient writers in any aspect of our present discussion of Etna. There's no reason that, at that time, all was not as they recounted it long ago, of which a very great deal has persisted down to our own day, certain things have changed, and even some new features have arisen. To offer but one example, they've repeatedly asserted that the topmost peaks are partly covered with ashes,[167] but there's no trace of this phenomenon now; for on the entire mountain there are no ashes to be seen.

The text as given here is in fact misleading: in the 1496 *princeps* (and in the text as reproduced at the end of this volume) Bembo has Bernardo mention only Strabo, not Pliny, to the effect of "What of the fact that Strabo records that there's snow only in winter?" (*Quid, quod hyemare tantum eas* [sc. *nives*] *meminit Strabo?*, §44.) Pliny officially entered only in the second edition of 1530,[168] and through that supplement Bernardo enhances his case by redoubling his appeal to Classical authority, fortifying Strabo's testimony (6.2.8: "The upper districts are bare and ash-like and *full of snow in winter*") by invoking a weighty second opinion (*HN* 2.236: Etna is "cloaked in winter with snow [*nivalis hibernis temporibus*] and covering its output of ashes with hoar-frost"). In light of the larger Pliny controversy of the 1490s and beyond, Bembo's inserted reference to Pliny in a context that sets the authority of the Classical *datum* against the claims of practical *experientia* and *usus* is surely, at the very least, an intriguing intervention. Of course, it may be that the supplement is as white in its innocence as the snow that Pliny claims only for Etna's winter; but Bembo's slyness of maneuver elsewhere in *De Aetna* should perhaps enjoin caution. Could the insertion function as an Alexandrian footnote of sorts, gently adverting to the Plinian controversy that was still raw when *De Aetna* first appeared? Or are we dealing here not so much with a later addition to the 1496 edition as a deliberate omission from the *princeps* in the name of tact? But to speculate no further, the subtlety of Bembo's maneuver in §§44–5 lies not just in his effortless show of [Plinian and] Strabonic learning, but also in the deftness with which he may evoke, at least for the knowing reader, a whole critical climate and complex storyline through his seemingly minor amendment to *et Plinius et Strabo meminere*.

Given his commitment to the purely philological correction of Pliny's text, and given his haste in completing the project so as to forestall yet more error-strewn

---

167. See p. 347 n.67.

168. With the further modification in §45 of *quod quidem venia illius dixerim* (1496) to *quod quidem venia illorum* [sc. Strabo and Pliny] *dixerim* (1530). For the insertion, Bühler (1951) 137 with Mariano (1991) 442. In Bühler's survey of twenty copies of the 1496 edition (p. 138), the insertion is made in only three of those copies, and so it was presumably introduced not when *De Aetna* was freshly printed, but only after a good number of copies (without the reference to Pliny) had already left the shop.

printings of the *Natural History*, Barbaro had little scope for displaying the fruits of his own naturalistic observations, especially in the botanical realm. More flexible in this respect was his so-called *Corollarium in Dioscoridem*, the appendix that he wrote to accompany his Latin version (before 1489[169]) of the *De materia medica* of the first-century CE physician and botanical pharmacologist, Pedanius Dioscorides; both the *Corollarium* and his translation were published only posthumously, in 1516. The *Corollarium* was not strictly a commentary as such, and no pathbreaking contribution to medical theory, but rather a gathering of all that had been written, before Dioscorides and after, of the plants he mentions. Beyond the extreme learning involved in Barbaro's detection and desegregation of different plant types that went by the same name in the ancient sources, he was also a pioneer in drawing on his own observations to supplement or qualify received knowledge, and in relating past and present by recording fresh facts from his own day about plants known to the ancients. For present purposes, however, the importance of his work on Dioscorides as well as on Aristotle and Pliny lies in what it reveals of the range and depth of his naturalistic interests, and of the influence that he wielded as "a main initiator of interest in science and natural history in the Veneto."[170] Given his personal ties to Bernardo and Pietro Bembo, the naturalist orientation that gave rise to *De Aetna* may well have been at least partly shaped and encouraged by Barbaro,[171] while Pietro's extended account of Etna's vegetation (§§13, 22–4) reflects the botanical interests (again encouraged by Barbaro?) that he shared with his father—interests that made of the villa garden at Noniano nothing less than a sort of "open-air museum."[172] But if we then surmise that Barbaro lurks as another absent presence along with Valla in *De Aetna*, his infamy at Venice in the early 1490s (on which more shortly) readily explains why Bembo should choose not to name him in that youthful work, and why a decade or so was to pass before Pietro revived him in his *De Virgilii Culice et Terentii fabulis liber* of 1503.

---

169. See Riddle (1980) 27 ("The translation was probably made in 1481–82, whereas the commentary may have been added in 1489").

170. Logan (1972) 83; further on the *Corollarium*, Egerton (1983) 561–8 with Reeds (1976) 524–6 and esp. Ramminger (2005) (the *Corollarium* as a philologically oriented supplement to, not strictly a commentary on, Dioscorides).

171. Already Dionisotti (1966b) 12 = Vela (2002) 26 ("La scelta dell'argomento [sc. in *De Aetna*], la descrizione cioè e lo studio del vulcano e della sua attività, studio fondato insieme sulla esperienza diretta e informazione *in loco* e sulla discussione delle testimonianze classiche, *richiama a quell'interesse scientifico che aveva ispirato le Castigationes Plinianae del Barbaro e che non era stato estraneo all'enciclopedismo ultimo del Poliziano*"; my emphasis); Branca (1996) 36 and (1998) 122, 130; Vecce (1998b) 486. But for the young Pietro's scientific orientation very possibly shaped by Constantine Lascaris and Giorgio Valla as well as by Barbaro, see pp. 123 and 138 with Travi (1978), esp. 416–18 on *De Aetna*.

172. Curti (2010) 457.

3.4: The Half-Story so Far

For all the impact that helping Poliziano to collate the Bembine Terence in 1491 appears to have had on the young Bembo, we have seen that Giorgio Valla and Ermolao Barbaro may well have exercised a profound formative influence on Pietro before he left Venice for Sicily, not least in nurturing the naturalistic interests that he indulged by visiting Etna in 1493. In Barbaro's case, however, his story is as yet only half told, his importance in the history of Quattrocento philology only part of his relevance to this study. In Pietro's letter to his tutor Urticio of March 29, 1492, we remember,[173] he looks forward to absorbing himself in his studies in Messina, where he will be distracted "by no private or public responsibilities, by no duties to friends, and by no obligations to my father."[174] This ambition to devote himself to his studies at a far remove from the Venetian *cursus* has to be viewed, as we shall see in Chapter 4, in the context of important developments in the history of late Quattrocento Venetian humanism, a context in which Barbaro figures prominently. In 1491 Ermolao abruptly left the service to the Republic in circumstances that were as dramatic in their happening as they were acrimonious in their aftermath; he did so largely to liberate himself for his beloved *studia*. Pietro's own ambition for *otium in litteris* may have been spurred or emboldened, at least in part, by Ermolao's example; hence we now turn to that other half of Barbaro's story.

173. P. 136.

174. Travi (1987) 4 *Letter* 1.31–2.

4

De Aetna *in the Context of Quattrocento Venetian Humanism*

THE STORY OF Ermolao Barbaro's severance from the Republic in 1491 is in many ways singular, as we shall see in section 4.1. But his ardent devotion to letters, and hence his longstanding ambivalence about serving the Republic in the traditional patrician way, are also symptomatic of a larger shift that is discernible in Venetian humanism of the late Quattrocento—a shift away from the disciplined rigor and absolute devotion to the common cause that are such defining features of the distinctively Venetian strain of Italian humanism earlier in the century. Barbaro's particular case is therefore contextualized in 4.2 within this larger framework of Venetian humanism; so too is Pietro Bembo's diptych-like portrait in *De Aetna* of his own youthful detachment from the Venetian *cursus* on the one hand, and his father's more traditional, unswerving commitment to it on the other. But while *De Aetna* is importantly implicated in the macro-process of Quattrocento humanistic development in Venice, it is also a major component in the ongoing life narrative of Pietro's inability to reconcile himself to the conventional Venetian career path down to 1506, when he decisively departed from the Republic for Urbino. That narrative is selectively surveyed in 4.3, in which we also examine Pietro's relations with certain of his aristocratic peers who were similarly disinclined to follow the conventional Venetian path. But we begin with Barbaro, with Bembo's representation of him in his *De Virgilii Culice et Terentii fabulis liber* of 1503, and with the circumstances of Ermolao's estrangement from the Republic in 1491.

4.1: Ermolao Barbaro, Born for Letters, Bred for State Service

Pietro Bembo's portrayal of Barbaro in his *De Virgilii Culice* is directly relevant to the present study because of the role that the Bembine Terence plays in the dialogue, which is set in Rome in the early 1490s.[1] The work purports to record the discussion that Barbaro shared with that celebrated Roman humanist, Pomponio Leto (1428–98), on the theme of the loss or corruption of so much of the culture of the ancients, literary texts included; Bembo's purported source for the conversation is his friend Phaedrus Volaterranus (i.e., the Volterra-born Tommaso Inghirami, 1470–1516, canon of St. John Lateran and papal librarian under Julius II). The fiction extends to the illusion that Barbaro owns the Bembinus, while Leto is granted that further jewel in the Bembo library, the ninth-century Virgil now housed in the Vatican Library as Vat. lat. 3252;[2] both also show fantastic feats of memory in being able effortlessly to quote so extensively from their respective manuscripts. In the third and last main section of the dialogue, Barbaro draws on the Bembinus to argue that many of the corruptions that blight printed editions of Terence could be removed through close attention to manuscript collation. Those quotations are largely accurate in their correspondence to the actual Bembinus, but in those cases in which there are deviations from it, some can be explained as mere slips (whether on the part of Bembo or the printer), others because Bembo followed the text in the edition—Biblioteca Ambrosiana, Inc. 1523—in which he recorded Poliziano's collation of the Bembinus in 1491;[3] on the assumption that he composed *De Virgilii Culice* while absent from Venice in 1502–3, it is hardly likely that he took the Bembinus, as valuable as it was fragile, with him on his travels. As for those few places where the quotations show readings that are found in neither the Bembinus nor Inc. 1523, most of these aberrations can again be attributed to simple error (whether on Bembo's part or the printer's), while conjecture is possible in two instances, certain in one;[4] but the notorious case of *Andria* 346–8 poses a very different sort of problem. Those lines are not found in the Bembinus as it now survives, and they go unmarked (because uncollated by Bembo and Poliziano in 1491) in Inc. 1523; however, they are claimed for the Bembinus at least as the latter is described in *De Virgilii Culice*. As given in the dialogue, the lines are far superior to any other reading available in printed editions of the period. Hence the suspicion that Bembo cites them not from the actual Bembinus but from a separate manuscript that is known to have been owned by his family (Oxford, Brasenose College

1. In general on the dialogue, its date and dedication to Ercole Strozzi (1473–1508), and the circumstances of its composition, Grafton (1983) 45–6; J. N. Grant (1988) and (1992); Campanelli (1997); Victor (2006).

2. See on this manuscript (which contains several pseudo-Virgilian *opuscula* as well as the *Eclogues* and *Georgics*) Giannetto (1985) 297–8.

3. For detailed analysis, J. N. Grant (1988) with (1992) 264; for the role of Inc. 1523 in the 1491 collation with Poliziano, Chapter 3 pp. 116–17.

4. See J. N. Grant (1988) 232–7.

18)—a distortion by which he shamelessly sought to enhance the perceived quality of the precious Bembinus.[5]

Amid these complexities, Bembo's sleight of hand in placing Barbaro in possession of the Bembinus symbolically conjoins Barbaro with Poliziano: after Poliziano collated the text in 1491, the manuscript soon passes (as if like Hercules' bow) to Barbaro within the dialogue's fictional 1490s chronology, and Barbaro scrupulously follows Polizianic precept by enshrining careful manuscript collation as foundational to textual improvement. By extension, Bembo *qua* author implicitly inscribes himself into this meeting of minds, as if a new standard-bearer for the philological values upheld in *De Virgilii Culice*. Yet his affinity to Barbaro in particular may well be personal in nature as well, in that Pietro projects through Ermolao his own lingering aspiration for the lettered life at a far remove from the Venetian civic *cursus*.[6] Early in the dedicatory preface addressed to Ercole Strozzi (1530 ed. fol. a ii*r*), Bembo touches briefly, and circumspectly, on the essentials of the scandal that quickly transformed Barbaro in 1491 from a distinguished servant of Venice to a disgraced *persona non grata*.[7] Appointed Venetian ambassador to Rome in 1490, Barbaro, though yet a layman, was nominated to the office of Patriarch of Aquileia by Pope Innocent VIII on March 6, 1491 in succession to Marco Barbo, who had died four days earlier. Appointment to the Aquileia position was traditionally from among the Venetian patriciate, in accordance with the Republic's own preference. But Barbaro was appointed without Venetian consultation, and he accepted the position in obedience to the Pope but without Venetian permission.[8] The Republic's displeasure was expressed in several rounds of punitive motion, remonstration, and appeal to the Pope to reverse his decision. Barbaro's patrician friend, Girolamo Donato, was dispatched to Rome to order him back to Venice to account for his actions, and his father, Zaccaria, was pressured to persuade Ermolao to return, but such measures were to no avail: refusing to leave Rome, Barbaro stayed close to the papal court,

5. For this approach, Victor (2006), with 245 n.8 for the history of "the skeptical view" according to which *An.* 346–8 could not have been in the Bembinus in Pietro's time. Hence the presumption at least of Bembo's carelessness in *De Virgilii Culice* (cf. Prete [1970] 15: "si tratta di una svista"), but Grafton (1981) 406–7 yet harbors the possibility that "Bembo had a scrap of Bembinus with all or part of [*An.*] 346–48 on it."

6. On this point, Campanelli (1997) 292.

7. See further on what follows Paschini (1957) 18–42; King (1976) 42–3 = (2005) V 42–3 and (1986) 197–205; Queller (1986) 121–2, 188–9; Figliuolo (1999) 133–42.

8. For his own surprise and prevarication cf. Branca (1943) 2.73 *Ep.* CLIV (to Jacopo Antiquario, for whom see below): "The Pope came at me when I was unknowing and with my thoughts entirely elsewhere; he chided me when, in my astonishment, I was dumbfounded at the unexpectedness of the matter; he turned to intimidation when in my resistance I resorted to delaying tactics; and he applied force when I sought exemption and wrangled as much as possible in the circumstances."

bitter at the Republic's high-handedness and distressed by the disgrace to the family name, but absorbed nonetheless in his work on the Plinian *Castigationes*. Matters remained at an impasse until Barbaro, at the age of only thirty-nine, died of the plague on July 24 or 25, 1493,[9] just around the time when Bembo was climbing Etna; on November 4 Pope Alexander VI named Niccolò Donato, the Republic's nominee, the new Patriarch of Aquileia, thereby finally closing the controversy over Barbaro. When Bembo briefly recounted these events in his role as historian of the Republic some forty years later, his duty to the public record interestingly vies with his stress on Ermolao's purity of character: he writes of Barbaro that he "had attained considerable fame for his great gifts in the study of literature and the liberal arts, both with foreign nations and above all among his own people: to his unique reputation for learning he had joined a life of unbroken innocence [*vitae perpetuam innocentiam*, where *perpetuam* appears especially pointed]."[10] For the official record Bembo was bound to set the civic ideal before the interests of any one individual: "But all that [sc. Barbaro's prestige through his scholarly fame and social standing] was not enough to protect him against every eventuality, since esteem for the law and its majesty in itself counted for more with the senators than the repute and renown of any of its citizens, whatever famous names they boasted."[11] Yet Bembo's admiration remains undimmed in his last, epitaph-like words on the matter, which stress not final disgrace but the achievement of a lifetime: "And so ended the life of Ermolao Barbaro, undoubtedly the greatest scholar of Latin and Greek literature the city had produced to that point."[12]

For all the anguish caused by his sudden elevation, Barbaro could also express elation at his appointment, and at the freedom that it brought him for his beloved studies. So in a letter of April 1491 to his friend, the humanist Jacopo Antiquario of Perugia (1444/5–1512), he writes thus:

> I live in good cheer, I live in freedom, I live for letters (*vivo hilaris, vivo liber, vivo litteris*); the whole of me covets them after many years when not even half of me could pay them attention.[13]

However tragic[14] the circumstances in which Barbaro was alienated from the Republic, the strain of long tension was finally resolved. "A large part of my life, as

---

9. On the date, Figliuolo (1999) 142 and n. 161.

10. *History of Venice* 1.53 = Ulery (2007) 63.

11. 1.53 = Ulery (2007) 63.

12. 1.53 = Ulery (2007) 63.

13. Branca (1943) 2.65 *Ep.* CXLVI.

14. King (1986) 205 and n. 330; Labalme (1996) 341 (cf. p. 333: "We grieve for Ermolao himself . . .").

you know, has always been devoted to letters," he writes in 1491 to the Florentine humanist poet Ugolino Verino (1438–1516); "now it will be the entirety of it."[15] Years before, he had succumbed to the career expectations of one of his class:

> I was born for letters, I was devoted to letters, I cannot be without letters, I can only be without the interferences that hinder, get in the way of, and keep me away from letters. I have held many distinguished offices in the Republic, with what trust, reputation and esteem I wouldn't say. It is satisfying to have spent twelve years altogether, but eight of them continuously, in service to the Republic; yet that whole time was virtually lost to letters. They would call to me, every so often telling me to make amends to them for that lost time; conversely, I thought to put them off to the future, not because my offices and magistracies were enjoyable, but to comply with my father, brothers and friends, who thought that my service in the State would be of benefit, though I myself didn't see it.[16]

Barbaro's craving for release and self-realization through his studies is a recurrent refrain in his extant letters well before the events of 1491. "You ask if I'm married," he writes in February 1486 to the learned Carmelite monk, Arnold de Bost (1445–99), of Ghent:

> I am not, nor do I even think of a wife. It is enough for me to be busily preoccupied with letters; moreover, quarrelsome they are not. Again, nothing is so inimical to letters as the yoke of marriage and caring for children. I don't condemn marriage; without it, not even letters would have existed. But I yearn to be a man of letters, an observer of God, of the stars and of nature, free and released from this shackle.[17]

Arnold's query as to whether Barbaro was married was seemingly prompted by a remark that Ermolao had made in an earlier letter to his friend in distant Ghent. In response to Arnold's request that Ermolao give an account of his studies and his past and projected publications, Barbaro writes, "In my eighteenth year I composed in boyish fashion two books *On celibacy*."[18] This work, addressed to his father, Zaccaria,

---

15. Branca (1943) 2.66 *Ep.* CXLVII.

16. Branca (1943) 2.70 *Ep.* CLII, to Antonio Calvo (on the problem of *which* Antonio Calvo, King [1986] 345–6).

17. Branca (1943) 1.96 *Ep.* LXXVI.

18. Branca (1943) 1.92 *Ep.* LXXII.

and compiled in the early 1470s,[19] is set in obvious counterpoise to his grandfather Francesco Barbaro's *De re uxoria* of 1415, itself a treatise of significant originality that he addressed as a wedding gift to his friend Lorenzo de' Medici the Elder.[20] Although aristocratic families from across the Italian city-states faced the challenge of self-preservation through strategic marriage and the cultural shaping of each next generation, the Venetian patriciate was unusually challenged because of the *Serrata* ("closing") of the Great Council in 1297: after the creation of a uniquely entitled governing elite whose membership was increased only in very exceptional circumstances (thirty families were added in 1381 for distinguished service in the war of Chioggia), strategic marriage played a key role in the safeguarding of family succession and the stability of patriciate participation in government.[21] Hence Francesco Barbaro's *De re uxoria* was vitally concerned with preserving the privileged status and pure lineage of the Venetian nobility—goals that are by no means straightforwardly countered or undermined by Ermolo's *De coelibatu*, which is more of a dyad-like complement than a contrast to his grandfather's work.[22] In *De coelibatu* the conjugal life is rejected not because it is intrinsically intolerable per se, but because the demands that come with it in the way of domestic duties and civic responsibilities are incompatible with the unencumbered life of the mind and of letters. Yet the celibate does not reject the active life for a contemplative existence wholly devoted to either monastic self-sacrifice or lettered self-indulgence; Ermolao forges a vision of an alternative ideal whereby the celibate can proudly renounce civic life in the name of self-discovery and the pursuit of wisdom, his abilities simply unsuited to the rigors of civic life.[23] In sum, as Margaret King puts it, his defense of celibacy is "a plea for individual self-determination in a social context where family and state limited the possibilities for self-determination."[24]

Yet this advocate of the celibate life remained in an uneasy marriage with the Republic, serving her with distinction and yet devoting what time he could to his precious studies until the final separation came in 1491. When he was ambassador

---

19. Text: Branca (1969) 53–156 with (1952). On the work, Branca (1969) 3–8, (1996) 31–4 and (1998) 76–80; King (1976), esp. 35–44 = (2005) V 35–44 and (1986) 197–201; Queller (1986) 121; Rodini (2013), esp. 114–16.

20. On Francesco's *De re uxoria*, King (1976) 31–5 = (2005) V 31–5, (2014) 77–85, and now esp. (2015); Tenenti (1996); Nauert (2006) 64–5.

21. On these points, Rodini (2013) 107; King (1976), esp. 19–21 = (2005) V 19–21; Clough (1998) 57 (for "closure of the patriciate in 1382, when it became virtually a closed caste").

22. See Branca (1952) 85–6 and (1969) 5; King (1986) 197.

23. Branca (1952), esp. 92–6.

24. King (1976) 41 = (2005) V 41 and then (1986) 201 (cf. p. 197: "*On Celibacy* is the quiet but potent manifesto of Venetian humanism's most genuine rebel").

to the Duke of Milan in 1488–9, he wrote to his friend Girolamo Donato of all the *otium* that he had at his disposal there despite his official duties, and of how "nothing more pleasant has befallen me in this legation than the fact that virtually the whole of it is free for reading that is as varied as you like. I believe that the shades of Dioscorides and Aristotle secured this legation for me so that they [sc. his works on both authors] could at some point be finished off."[25] Yet between his return from Milan in April 1489 and his departure for Rome in May 1490 to serve as Venetian ambassador there, he wrote the brief treatise *De officio legati* (*On the duty of the ambassador*), a work in which diligent obedience to the state and to one's masters is all:[26] "The same end applies to the ambassador that applies to all others who serve the Republic: to do, say, deliberate, and reflect upon what, in their judgment, can be relevant to maintaining and augmenting the optimal condition of their state";[27] "The ambassador, unless he believes himself to be far inferior in both judgment and experience to the Fathers, at once falls short of the ambassadorial goal";[28] serving the state before oneself is of key importance, and especially so for a Venetian, "since the greatness of our empire has taken root, grown and lasted for no other reason than the harmonious unity of its citizens (*civium inter se concordia*): the person who hates this unity hates not just the people he hates, but evidently the Republic itself."[29] An impressive codification of ambassadorial conduct, and even, from the Venetian perspective, a blueprint for the fullest self-realization of the individual not (just) through the family but through devotion to the state; yet how to reconcile this uplifting vision with Barbaro's own breach of obedience to the Republic less than two years later? The work was perhaps meant as a mature complement to *De coelibatu*, whereby the celibate ideal at a remove from civic life now gave way to a different vision of self-completion and self-ennoblement through sociopolitical engagement.[30] Alternatively (and short of positing his straightforward insincerity), Barbaro perhaps writes without real conviction, as if trying to persuade himself

---

25. Branca (1943) 2.14 *Ep.* XC.

26. Text: Branca (1969) 157–67; for the dating (April–May 1489?), Figliuolo (1999) 78 with Branca 20. On the work, Branca 17–25; King (1986) 202–4; Figliuolo 77–90 (esp. 78–81 for the treatise as a *de facto* defense of Barbaro's diplomatic activities at the Sforza court in Milan); Biow (2002) 104–5, 108–20; C. Fletcher (2015) 38–42, 54–5.

27. Branca (1969) 159 §7.

28. Branca (1969) 161 §14.

29. Branca (1969) 165 §46.

30. Cf. for this self-realization through state service Branca (1963a) 207: "Come appare chiaramente nell'ultimo trattatello del Barbaro, il *De officio legati*, lo spazio umano in cui la persona poteva realizzarsi era lo stato, non la famiglia: uno stato che con la sua salda e aristocratica costituzione oligarchica e con i suoi alti ideali di libertà *poteva offrire veramente le condizioni per l'armonico sviluppo delle dignità umane*" (my emphasis).

of an ideal that he struggles truly to internalize for himself.[31] Whatever the (now irrecoverable) psychological truth of the matter, the ambiguity that had long characterized Barbaro's relationship to the *vita activa* is captured and compressed all too painfully in the close temporal juxtaposition of *De officio legati* on the one hand, his own renunciation of his *officium legati* on the other.

A final problem brings appropriately ambiguous closure to our mini-portrait of Barbaro. The problem centers on one of the cycle of nine canvases by Vittore Carpaccio (*c.* 1460–*c.* 1525) that portray the life, martyrdom, and apotheosis of St. Ursula.[32] Her legend has many variants, but Carpaccio appears to have relied on the version recounted in the famous *Legenda Aurea* (*Golden Legend*) of Jacopo da Varazze (*c.* 1230–98), an Italian translation of which was published at Venice in 1475. The daughter of the Christian King Nothus of Brittany, Ursula was betrothed to the pagan prince Etherius, but only on condition that Etherius converted to Christianity and allowed his bride to make a pilgrimage to Rome in the company of ten ladies-in-waiting, each attended by a thousand virgin escorts. Ursula, her husband,[33] and her followers traveled across Europe, and on reaching Rome they were received by the Pope. But in a dream soon thereafter Ursula had a premonition that she would suffer martyrdom—a premonition realized when, after arriving at Cologne on her homeward journey in the company of her entourage, she was slain and martyred by the Hun army. The sequence of pictures, which are generally dated to between 1490 and 1500, was produced for the Scuola di Sant'Orsola in Venice; after the Scuola was suppressed in 1806, they were moved in 1810 to the Gallerie dell'Accademia in Venice, where they hang today.[34] As we have seen,[35] the institution of marriage was of central importance to the safeguarding of patriciate self-identity and continuity at Venice, and the St. Ursula sequence is heavily implicated in that larger discourse by "speak[ing] firmly of aristocratic marriage appropriately sanctioned and properly managed."[36] For now, however, the particular canvas that concerns us features Ursula's arrival in Rome (Figure 4.1):[37] as

31. Cf. King (1986) 204: his words in *De officio legati* "are, perhaps, signs of his intention to conform to a patrician norm still inimical to him, or they may be, perhaps, insincere."

32. For the legend and Carpaccio's selectivity of emphasis within it, Rodini (2013).

33. For Etherius' inclusion among the travelers to Rome seemingly as one of Carpaccio's unique additions to the legend, Rodini (2013) 99, 110.

34. See P. F. Brown (1988) 279.

35. P. 152.

36. Rodini (2013) 110.

37. For its dimensions, date, etc., P. F. Brown (1988) 281.

she kneels side by side with her husband to receive the blessing of Pope Ciriaco, there stands prominently behind the Pope a figure clad in the red of the patrician senator, his head turned away from the marrying couple. If this figure is indeed Ermolao Barbaro,[38] the painting poses perplexing challenges of interpretation that begin with its date: the case for a *terminus post quem* of his death in July 1493 rests on the improbability of the disgraced Barbaro being so represented at Venice while he was still alive, but it remains inconclusive.[39] If an early date is entertained (1490–1?), how to interpret Barbaro's averted gaze? In light of his *De coelibatu*, is he set in opposition to Ursula and her husband? Or, if both Barbaro and Ursula are viewed as kindred spirits in their breaking away from the traditional protocols of aristocratic marriage, she through spiritual devotion, he through devotion to the life of the mind, is he in fact drawn in sympathetic relation to her? In effect, as Elizabeth Rodini has it, "[p]erhaps the two figures are paired here as contrasting models of behavior, or perhaps as two sides of the same coin."[40] Whether pictured as an idealist condoned or as a misfit whose turned head connotes his rejection of core Venetian (marriage) values, Barbaro is indeed a striking presence here, and one that "surely drew attention, invited speculation, and gave prominence, in one form or another, to matters of patrician obligation and civic duty":[41] a multi-sided, ambiguous figure to the last.

4.2: The Evolution of Quattrocento Venetian Humanism

However profoundly Ermolao Barbaro may have influenced the young Pietro's naturalistic and philological orientations, and however powerful the example of self-liberation that he set when he dramatically broke with the Republic in 1491, the changing face of Venetian humanism in the Quattrocento importantly contextualizes Barbaro's relevance to our story. For all the exceptionality of Ermolao's case, the tensions of life choice and career trajectory that surface in *De Aetna* are symptomatic of the fading in the late Quattrocento of certain patrician humanist values that were long central to Venetian self-identity. Those values became entrenched

38. See Branca and Weiss (1963); Branca (1963a) 210–11.

39. See P. F. Brown (1988) 281 with Branca and Weiss (1963) 39.

40. Rodini (2013) 115.

41. Rodini (2013) 115. Cf. Labalme (1996) 342 for Barbaro "stand[ing] forever in the senatorial robes from which he was forever banned, almost completely detached from the religious events being enacted behind him, his face averted toward some private vision of his own, perhaps a perfect resolution of those conflicting allegiances whose incompatibility had sundered his life . . ."

from the late Trecento onward through two key factors,[42] the first the formalization of the patriciate as a legally codified elite at the heart of Venetian power, the second Venice's transition from a *stato da mar* to a *stato da terra* through expansion into the Terraferma. As the mainland cities such as Bassano, Vicenza, and especially Padua came under Venetian control, the humanistic habits of thought that had taken root in the mainland began to infiltrate the Republic, adding impetus to the interests that were already incipient there; Petrarch himself was an influential presence in Padua and also Venice itself, where he resided (albeit not continuously) between September 1362 and the spring of 1368, championing the establishing of a public library based on his own collection.[43] The bureaucratic demands of Venice's expanding empire also meant that notaries and scribes were needed in growing numbers to deal with the ever-increasing volume of correspondence (a phenomenon that was hardly confined only to Venice in the Quattrocento).[44] In turn, this demand for notaries presupposed an expanding supply of teachers of Latin who looked to the Classics for models of style and form, but who also fostered a deeper engagement with the social, political, and literary culture represented by those models. But while similar developments were taking place in other Italian cities, the rise of Venetian humanism was distinguished from the first by its commitment to upholding the mythic ideal of Venice as a society predicated on *unanimitas*, or the subordination of individual aspirations and interests to the single, collective will.[45] "The result," in Craig Kallendorf's sharp summation, "was a humanism of moral severity, pronounced piety, and committed republicanism—a humanism, in other words, that privileged certain traditional, fixed beliefs over disciplinary modes of enquiry."[46] Here the term "civic humanism" is relevant, but not with the specifically localized connotations that it carried when it was first introduced by Hans Baron to characterize what he saw as a historic shift at Florence at the dawn of the fifteenth century:[47] from an individualistic literary movement that was disengaged

42. King (1986) 208 with Branca (1996) 12–18 and (1998) 54–60.

43. For Petrarch's influence, Branca (1996) 9–15 and (1998) 51–8 with Lazzarini (1963). He offered his library in 1362 on conditions (including that the collection was to be kept in a protected space and not sold or divided after his death) accepted by the Republic, but how much of his library actually remained in Venice after his death at Arquà in 1374 is far from clear.

44. King (1986) 214 with n.26 for bibliography.

45. See amid the very large bibliography King (1986), esp. 92–203 on *unanimitas*; Branca (1996) 12–17; Kallendorf (1999), esp. 20–4.

46. Kallendorf (1999) 23.

47. The term is esp. associated with Baron (1955) but was already coined (as "Bürgerhumanismus") in 1925; see Fubini (1992), esp. 560. For all its influence, the concept has been much challenged and continues to draw skepticism: see, e.g., Hankins (1995) and (2000a) as well as several of the other essays assembled in Hankins (2000b), and also Nauert (2006), esp. 32–3.

from civic life and medieval in its preference for the *vita contemplativa*, Florentine humanism looked beyond the cultivation of the individual to the active life of civic participation (on the Roman republican model) as the highest secular goal of existence. But whereas Baron's Florentine mode of civic humanism presupposes the formation or awakening of a new consciousness, and whereas it connected the virtuous will for self-fulfillment with engagement in civic action, at Venice the claims of self-realization were entirely subordinate to the collective interest, there was little or no questioning of the Republic's settled institutional structures and their functioning, and there was no dawning of a strikingly new civic awareness to inflect, let alone transform, the course of Venetian humanism.[48]

Half a century or so after the rise of civic humanism at Florence, generational change was a likely catalyst for the further cultural shift that is discernible in the waning of the civic ethic there, and in the surge of interest in more speculative, philosophical, and theological areas of enquiry.[49] This shift has important implications for both Bernardo and Pietro Bembo, in that during his two periods of service as Venetian ambassador to Florence (1475–6 and 1478–80; Pietro accompanied him on the second of these assignments) Bernardo came into close contact with this "new" humanism through his association with the cultural milieu of Lorenzo de' Medici and the Platonic Academy led by Marsilio Ficino.[50] Very young though Pietro was at the time, this exposure to the very different cultural atmospherics of Florence, and his later experience of Rome when he accompanied his father there twice in the mid- to late 1480s, meant that he came of age with at least some familiarity, however immature and incomplete, of a world far removed from the distinctive rigidity of Venetian humanism.[51] The latter did indeed undergo development, but not of the kind that was so conspicuous in Florence after the mid-1400s. According to the tripartite scheme influentially proposed by Margaret King,[52] the first humanist generation, born in the last decades of the Trecento and witness to Venice's early expansion into the Terraferma, consisted mostly of

48. Cf. Kallendorf (1999) 23, citing King (1986) 172 ("The Venetian [humanist] corpus includes, to my knowledge, no works challenging economic or social assumptions . . .") en route to observing that "when compared to, say, the Florentine model, Venetian humanism can appear somewhat truncated."

49. On this phenomenon see, conveniently, Nauert (2006) 66–70, 73–4.

50. See Giannetto (1985) 131–52 with Cian (1896), della Torre (1900), Pintor (1911), and Floriani (1966).

51. Cf. Floriani (1966) 31 for Pietro's time in Florence with his father amounting to "un primo apprendistato culturale," whereby Bernardo aimed to advance his son's education in "un clima di elevata cultura così congeniale a lui stesso."

52. For this schema, King (1986) 219–36, (1988) 213–19 = (2005) II 213–19, and cf. already the four-part schema in Branca (1963b) 193.

nobles who sought to integrate humanist methodologies and values within the traditional *mores* of the patriciate. Educated by professional humanists, many of them transient rather than permanent settlers in Venice, this generation sought relief from the pressures of political duty and the faceless observance of convention through the diverse range, intellectual challenge, and intrinsic appeal of *studia humanitatis*.[53] The second generation delineated by King[54] came of age in the early decades of the Quattrocento, when Venice was engaged in almost unrelenting war to extend and consolidate its mainland acquisitions, and when the Venetian empire *da mar* was coming under increasing threat from the Turks in the Aegean sphere. According to King, in this second generation, humanistic skill was deployed to arm Venice with the word in vigorously pleading its causes and representing its interests before friend and foe; the importance of this civic dimension is further underscored by the establishing in 1446 of the Scuola di San Marco for the training of students for careers in the bureaucratic secretariat—a counterpart of sorts to the philosophical instruction offered at the Scuola di Rialto that was established in 1408.[55] Venetian humanism grew to maturity in this phase, fully maintaining its strong adherence to Aristotelian philosophy and Christianity, both of which offered important paradigms for the Republic's structural stability in their combined appeal to universal systems of order and obedience to an ordaining authority.[56] This generation supported Venice's ideological mission still more committedly than did the first generation, but with restrictive effects for humanism: its potential as a form of spiritual balm or release for the individual was curbed, the "enthusiastic classicism"[57] of the first generation markedly tempered. In the third generation, born after 1430,[58] the task of embedding the humanist cause in Venice was already accomplished, and, for King, this last phase extended the achievements of the earlier phases while also admitting a greater diversity of expression, especially in connection with the rise of printing. Transient foreigners increased in number in this phase, partly as learned companions to the Venetian nobles and partly to instruct their heirs, but also to staff the many presses that sprang up in the last decades of the Quattrocento. Through their patronage, many patricians in this phase were "social" humanists rather than active, "literary" practitioners in the vein

53. King (1986) 219–25, (1988) 213–14 = (2005) II 213–14.

54. (1986) 225–31, (1988) 214–16 = (2005) II 214–16.

55. See Grendler (2002) 138–9.

56. King (1986) 184–5 with Branca (1996) 12–13 and (1998) 54–5.

57. King (1986) 229.

58. King (1986) 231–6, (1988) 216–19 = (2005) II 216–19.

of Ermolao Barbaro or Girolamo Donato.[59] As a result, patrician humanists, often ostentatious in their fashionable collecting and dilettanti in their interests, tended more to a spectator role; because fewer patricians were figures of major political importance, their humanistic activities became more of an adornment to life than an essential means of exercising their citizenship.

The malaise that Margaret King associates with this third phase of Venetian humanism had numerous symptoms and causes. Pietro Bembo came of age in an era when the patrician grip that had controlled Venetian intellectual life for much of the Quattrocento was losing its firmness of hold. While the Turkish threat remained to the east, the uncertain political climate that prevailed in the peninsula before and after Charles VIII invaded in 1494 was inevitably felt in Venice as well. The worst was to come when the League of Cambrai formed against the Republic in 1508, inflicting on it the catastrophic defeat at Agnadello in 1509; but already by the early 1490s Venice, like other city-states, was touched by uncertainty and introspection about what protections and guarantees the state offered in unpredictable times.[60] As for the governance structure of the Republic, the competition for public offices was strong (significantly more so than when Bernardo was a young man[61]), but so was the antagonism between the old (*longhi*) and new (*curti*) nobles of the patriciate, and the strategizing on both sides was as bitter as it was intense.[62] Beyond the possible alienating effects of that strength of competition, however, the myth of civic devotion that Venetian humanism sought to celebrate and perpetuate was in many ways just that: the reality behind the myth was that self-interest hardly wilted before the rhetoric of *unanimitas*; that corruption was widespread among nobles in office (Bernardo Bembo himself was charged in 1487 with financial impropriety connected to his links with the Medici);[63] and that, for all the competition in the final determining of outcomes, many tried to avoid office, whether by (e.g.) resignation, pleading excuse, or striving not to be elected in the first place through such tactics as absenting themselves abroad, claiming some flaw in the election process, or even nullifying their candidacy through breach of the law.[64] And given the centrality of the family and the institution of marriage to patrician ideology, it is striking that

59. "Social" as opposed to "literary" humanists: Maxson (2014) 9–12.

60. Cf. Dionisotti (1966b) 12 = Vela (2002) 25–6.

61. So at least Clough (1998) 56.

62. Further, Clough (1998) 56–7.

63. See Giannetto (1985) 178–86: after initial action, the Republic ultimately resolved not to proceed against Bernardo, a decision that for Giannetto 184 signals that Bembo had committed "una scorrettezza più che un vero e proprio reato."

64. See for dense cataloguing of these abuses Queller (1969) and esp. (1986).

some fifty percent of male nobles who lived into adulthood in the fifteenth century apparently remained bachelors.[65] In the area of philology, despite the methodological rigor pioneered by the likes of Poliziano and Barbaro in the areas of manuscript collation, the careful identification of sources, and the holistic study of Latin texts in relation to the Greek tradition, the late Quattrocento witnessed a certain desiccation of the word. As Anthony Grafton puts it, Poliziano "belonged to a whole generation of humanists who turned—in Rome and Venice as well as in Florence—from the oration to the emendation, from an audience of eager young citizens to a reading public of crabbed, jealous scholars";[66] the concentrated philological focus could often appear anemic and sterile in its remoteness from any broad view of the world and of man's place or purpose within it.[67] This stress on the particular point and on narrow technicality was exacerbated by the rise of print culture in Venice, and by the editorial mission of "fixing" and disseminating standardized texts of the Greek and Latin authors. But the rapid growth of the print industry also challenged the traditional scope and mission of Venetian humanism by competing with print culture elsewhere in Italy and beyond, and by ushering in a new experimentalism unrestricted by any blinkered loyalty to the myth of Venice. The Aldine Press was a key innovator in this respect, as we shall see.[68] But a fitting symbol of the changing times is offered by the 1499 Aldine *Hypnerotomachia Poliphili*, for Margaret King "that disorganized, fanciful, sensuous *pasticcio* of a romance, a shattered mirror of Venetian taboos and verities."[69] Eccentric in its language, content, and print form, this extraordinary work, so idiosyncratic and freewheeling in its creativity, is hard to reconcile with the stern discipline and conformity to type that were fundamental to the Venetian humanistic ideal: in its way, the book is a telling chronicle of its era.

The Bernardo Bembo we witness in *De Aetna*, then, relishing his limited leisure time at Noniano but thoroughly committed to serving the Republic, belongs to King's third generation of Venetian humanists,[70] but before the malaise set in. As for Pietro, his veneration of Petrarch adds nuance to his ambivalence about embarking on the Venetian *cursus*, his uncertainties perhaps informed or affirmed by Petrarch's own ambivalence about the claims of the active as opposed to the contemplative life.[71]

---

65. Chojnacki (1994) 78 = (2000) 249.

66. Grafton (1983) 41; cf. Branca (1963a) 196 ("una situazione stagnante e senza uscite").

67. King (1986) 236.

68. See Chapter 5, esp. pp. 184–99.

69. King (1986) 236, (1988) 218 = (2005) II 218; further on the *Hypnerotomachia*, Chapter 5 pp. 188–91.

70. For Bernardo classed as one of *the* triad (with Girolamo Donato and Ermolao Barbaro) of leading late-century Venetian humanists, Giannetto (1985) 211–12 with King (1986) 337–8.

71. See, e.g., Stephens (1990) 42 for a balanced picture ("Petrarch did not praise the contemplative life and deride the active life. He thought cultured leisure befitting to the philosopher and suited

This Petrarchan dimension apart, however, the Pietro we witness in *De Aetna* captures, even in many ways symbolizes, the fading that King associates with late third-generation Venetian humanism. But it is time to turn the spotlight away from what was lost by this fading process to what was gained by it—to approach *De Aetna*, that is, as something of an anthem for youthful release in its lively sense of self-discovery and adventure in distant Sicily, but an anthem that is not straightforwardly one-sided: conservatively inclined and yet open minded in his benign attitude to Pietro (a benignity that was not always so evident in their real-life relations), Bernardo serves as a trusty foil to Pietro's thrusting rapier in *De Aetna*, the Republic's man to the core while his son goes his own way in Sicily. For all the youthful independence of spirit displayed in *De Aetna*, however, Pietro was hardly a unique trailblazer, but rather one of a coterie of patrician coevals who shared, to a greater or lesser degree, his ambivalence about following the conventional Venetian career path. In briefly surveying below Pietro's relations with such figures as Trifone Gabriele (1470–1549), Vincenzo Quirini (1478–1514), and Tommaso Giustiniani (1476–1528), we shall not only set the liberating credentials of *De Aetna* in the larger context of youthful aversion to conventional service at Venice in the 1490s and beyond; we shall also relate the tensions between father and son in *De Aetna* to Pietro's own continuing alienation from the Venetian *cursus* down to the turning point of 1506, when he decisively left Venice for Urbino.

4.3: Pietro's Peers, Gli Asolani, *and the* Leggi della Compagnia degli Amici

Our treatment of Pietro's youthful circle of associates is tripartite in structure. We turn in (ii) below to Trifone Gabriele in connection with *Gli Asolani*, and in (iii) to the ecclesiastical calling of Vincenzo Quirini and Tommaso Giustiniani. But we begin in (i) with Angelo Gabriele, and, soon after their return from Sicily, with Angelo's divergence from Pietro in following a more conventional career path within the Venetian bureaucracy.

(i) Angelo Gabriele

Three letters to Angelo usefully illustrate his and Pietro's different trajectories in the later 1490s. Loved like a twin brother,[72] Angelo accompanied Pietro to study

---

to himself. The active life was for the statesman and the ruler . . ."); Vickers (1990) 111–17; Nauert (2006) 22–3, 28; Bondanella (2008); Arnold (2011) 30–1; Ruggiero (2015) 235–7.

72. Cf. Travi (1987) 28 *Letter* 33.7–8 (to Domenico Grimani, September 13, 1498), of Gabriele as *hominis mihi coniunctissimi, et quem ego semper in germani fratris habui loco.*

philosophy at Padua after their return from Sicily in 1494: in a letter written to Giovanni Battista Stato in Messina in September 1494, Pietro states their intention to go to Padua, and in another missive to Stato of October 1, he duly announces their arrival there "for the leisurely pursuit of letters, and especially of philosophy" (*ad otia litterarum, praesertimque philosophiae*).[73] By late 1497, however, their paths had begun significantly to diverge. Even though Pietro had entered the Great Council at only twenty in 1490, he was in fact nominated for an office (that of paymaster to the Venetian army) only in July 1499, but his candidacy suffered a heavy defeat—a result repeated when he was nominated as envoy to the king of Hungary in December 1500, and as envoy to the king of Portugal in March 1501. Several further defeats followed down to October 1505, when he apparently last stood, or was last willing to stand, for office.[74] Pietro's close association with the Aldine Press from the mid-1490s onward may have been motivated in large part by his wish to advertise his humanist credentials before Venetian patricians who could advance his career;[75] but his literary pursuits, *Gli Asolani* (*The people of Asolo*) in particular, may ultimately have done more harm than good to his prospects of election,[76] especially in conjunction with his extended voluntary absences from the Republic. After Bernardo Bembo's appointment as *visdomino* of Ferrara in June 1497, Pietro joined his father there before the year's end, and there he stayed until 1499, continuing his philosophical studies[77] and immersing himself in the vibrant artistic life of the Ferrarese court. Under Ercole I d'Este (1431–1505), Duke of Ferrara from 1471 to his death, Ferrara's growth into one of the most important cultural centers of the age witnessed the flowering of long-embedded literary and artistic tendencies: while the claims of Classicism remained undiminished, the Ferrarese court's fostering of vernacular literature was accompanied by a special predilection for the chivalric romance—a predilection famously manifested in the writing at Ferrara of Matteo Maria Boiardo's *Orlando innamorato* (first published in 1482) and its continuation in Ludovico Ariosto's *Orlando furioso* (published in its first version in 1516). It was in Ferrara that Pietro appears to have drafted *Gli Asolani*, his own

73. For the first announcement, Travi (1987) 9 *Letter* 7.22–5; for the second, Travi 10 *Letter* 8.12–14.

74. For these candidacies, Dionisotti (1966a) 135, 138 = Vela (2002) 146, 150 with Giannetto (1985) 241 and Clough (1998) 54.

75. So Clough (1998) 57.

76. Cf. Clough (1998) 66 on *Gli Asolani* "suggest[ing] the contemplative life and literary pursuit rather than commitment to participation in the civic life of Venice . . . It seems to me that *Gli Asolani* was the first step in the author's bid for patronage beyond Venice, and in that sense its publication marked his crossing of the Rubicon."

77. Cf. Travi (1987) 32 *Letter* 36.27–8 (*partim detinent* [sc. *me*] *studia dialecticae disciplinae*) with Floriani (1966) 47.

ambitious experiment in the old Tuscan vernacular; or, more precisely, if the work was planned or begun at Venice before June 1497, the first known references that he makes to it belong to his Ferrarese years.

In the meantime, Angelo was already seeking to make his way in the world in 1496, albeit spending three years in a fruitless quest for ecclesiastical office,[78] struggling with syphilis along the way.[79] By 1499, however, his fortunes were changing: in a letter to him of March 1,[80] Pietro writes of the performances of Plautus' *Trinummus* and *Poenulus* and Terence's *Eunuchus* that he had seen at Ferrara during five days of "the loveliest entertainments" (*pulcherrimorum ludorum*)—entertainments that Angelo had missed because of his involvement in "elections and civic affairs" (*comitiis et foro*) at Venice, where, Pietro has apparently been informed, Angelo had become "a great man" (*omnes mihi respondebant magnum civem te esse factum*). The letter continues in a wittily chiding fashion, taking Angelo to task for his failure to make a promised visit to Ferrara. But Pietro remains expectant: "I eagerly await you; if you come, although the theaters are silent, there'll nevertheless be something for us to laugh at" (*Letter* 37.17–18). In a letter of March 29, 1499 Pietro duly congratulates Angelo on his unanimous election to a civic magistracy.[81]

A different tone is struck in a letter of September 12, 1500,[82] in which Pietro responds to Angelo's criticism of his allegedly abundant *otium*. In reality, Pietro writes, he is hardly at leisure: the task of tending to his ailing mother is such that

> not only am I not in the country [sc. at Noniano], and in my books and letters, for which you take me to task at the moment. On the contrary, I'm preoccupied night and day with very considerable worries that rob me of all my means and feeling for writing.[83]

---

78. See Travi (1987) 33 *Letter* 38.13–17.

79. See Travi (1987) 29–30 *Letter* 34 with Kidwell (2004) 22. Cf. Boehrer (1990) 208–9: "And for Bembo, too, the *Syphilis* [of the distinguished physician and scholar Girolamo Fracastoro, *c.* 1476–1553, who began work on his famous poem in *c.* 1510 and sent a draft of it to Bembo in 1515, eliciting from him precise recommendations on some 111 lines and passages before the published version was eventually dedicated to Bembo in 1530] is not a purely disinterested contribution to literary history; the cardinal, a notorious womanizer who dallied with Lucrezia Borgia and kept a mistress after entering holy orders, would certainly have had a more than intellectual interest in the new disease" (!).

80. Travi (1987) 32 *Letter* 37.

81. Travi (1987) 33 *Letter* 38.2–5.

82. Travi (1987) 101–2 *Letter* 110.

83. Travi (1987) 101 *Letter* 110.7–10.

If his mother recovers and Pietro can revert to Noniano, then he will

> show you, if I can, that my leisurely devotion to letters in villa and country (*villaticum nostrum otium et agreste litterarum*), which you find fault with, is of no less value or less distinguished than that public and civic business of yours (*vestro illo negotio forensi et urbano*) that you so greatly extol.[84]

But then an interesting further development when Pietro laments his inability to enjoy the *otium* that he craves:

> For to be sure I sometimes distance myself as much as I can from all concern for matters of both domestic and public business, and I devote myself to letters. But goodness! By some means, in pursuing it, I've never experienced a wind so favorable that it doesn't immediately blow back on me in the opposite direction, and just as in the Euripus, so in that order of life I've scarcely begun to run nicely when I'm pulled backwards (*nunquam tam secundo vento usus sum, quin is mihi statim reflarit, et tanquam in Euripo, sic in ea ratione vitae vix incepi currere, cum reducor*). But let's set all this aside for another time . . . As for the fact that you've undertaken to come to me, nothing could be more delightful to me.[85]

For all Angelo's alleged criticism, Pietro's affability in his last words here hardly suggests that any real offense has been taken; and, in a maneuver that illustrates their depth and deftness of mutual understanding, the literariness of the letter may itself gently assert the very *otium* that he defends. The allusion in Euripus is to the violent flux and reflux that was associated especially with the eponymous strait separating Euboea from mainland Greece;[86] in using the term here to illustrate his fluctuating efforts to engage in his studies, Pietro perhaps plays on the figurative connotations of Euripus in the Greek tradition.[87] This was not Pietro's first allusion to Euripus in a letter to Angelo. Already in his missive of December 3, 1498 he laments the ebb and flow of his studies: *sed diu est cum tamquam in Euripo: huc illuc mea studia fluctuant.*[88] In his letter of September 12, 1500, then, his allusion to

84. Travi (1987) 101 *Letter* 110.14–17.

85. Travi (1987) 101 *Letter* 110.18–25.

86. On the science of the phenomenon (including ancient observation of it), Eginitis (1929) with, conveniently, Marmer (1931).

87. *LSJ* s.v. εὔριπος I, incl. "prov. of an unstable, weak-minded person."

88. Travi (1987) 29 *Letter* 34.19–20.

Euripus has a backstory of its own, to the effect that Pietro is still, two years after the letter of December 1498, *tamquam in Euripo*. But the allusive memory in play in the letter of September 1500 may extend yet further, in that Pietro's lament that he cannot enjoy the *otium* he craves finds a suggestive precedent in Bernardo's words at *De Aetna* §6:

> . . . as if from the waves (*tanquam a fluctibus*) I retrieve myself from the city and its mass of people to this haven of solitude for the purpose of finding some respite from my cares, relaxing my mind for a time, restoring myself to my proper condition, and fortifying myself for the tasks to come . . . But if those very cares pursue me into the country as well, . . . I undoubtedly achieve nothing. This is precisely what happened to me just now: I sat down alone on this bank to reflect on something worthy of that peaceful tranquility when, lo and behold! that very wave of civic responsibilities sucked me back again (*ecce nos ita etiam unda illa ipsa resorbuit urbanorum negotiorum*), and I gradually sank back (*delapsus sum*) into the cares of my commission.

The Classical pedigree of the nautical/heavy-seas metaphor for immersion in civic affairs[89] invests Bernardo with a suitably Ciceronian tone of voice in the above passage, where the troubled waters are also poignantly set in contrast to the calm flow of the quaint Piovego at Noniano (cf. §5). But to compare Pietro's letter of September 12, 1500, father and son briefly glimpse relaxation in *otium* before, in both cases, the figurative language of wind and waves returns them to the anxieties from which each seeks respite (cf. Pietro's *is* [sc. *ventus*] . . . *reflarit* and Bernardo's *unda* . . . *resorbuit*, the former's *reducor* and the latter's *delapsus sum*). The metaphorical language may be well worn; but if we accept that the flow-and-reflux parallel between father and son nevertheless remains striking, what, perhaps, was Angelo—the addressee of *De Aetna*, we remember—to make of the echo when he read Pietro's letter in September 1500? Briefly to speculate, could it be that Pietro parries Angelo's criticism of his *otium* by quiet appeal to the example of the imposing Bernardo? In his letter Pietro presents Angelo with an ironic modification of the lament that Angelo had already heard from a different Bembo, Bernardo, in *De Aetna*. No one was more committed to serving the Republic than Bernardo, and yet he too craved relaxation: does Pietro in effect justify his *otium* by subtly invoking Bernardo's own quest for leisure time in *De Aetna*, with the further implication that such *otium* is by no means incompatible with loyalty to the state? After all, Pietro ends the letter by protesting that he has hardly abandoned the Republic: "Be sure in the meantime to keep well, and attend to the troubled Republic in the most difficult of times. *I've not*

89. See Zetzel (1995) 97 on Cic. *Rep.* 1.1.3.

deserted it, as you write, and never will desert it, but I nevertheless remain aloof from its duties—duties which are entrusted to you great men—with utter calmness of mind (*plane aequo animo*)."[90] The aloofness he describes represents the degree of difference between father and son: Pietro stands aloof, Bernardo is rarely free of preoccupation, but *otium* is their shared desideratum, generational contrast an important factor in their different approaches to attaining that common goal.

The calmness of mind that Pietro claims for himself late in his letter of September 12, 1500 to Angelo is further displayed in a letter that he addressed on October 31, 1502 to both Angelo and Vincenzo Quirini (1478–1514), Bembo's friend from their student days in Padua in the mid-1490s; [91] the letter was written at the family villa of his friend Ercole Strozzi at Ostellato, some sixteen miles southeast of Ferrara, a pleasant retreat for his continuing work on *Gli Asolani*. While Angelo and Vincenzo are engaged in their civic affairs, Pietro appears to luxuriate in his leisurely routine in this idyllic place, and in his recounting of it: morning hours are spent in reading or writing, but occasionally in the afternoon, when his energies for such studying begin to flag, he takes exercise by joining the hunt; yet he steals away from his companions "more often even than the wild animals they're pursuing," going his own way to "reflect on some light verses even amid the chase" (*Letter* 141.27–9). Then back to the villa and to his studies by lamplight before dinner, where there are no weighty discussions of the sort that Pietro associates with "you who are great philosophers, great advocates of causes," but "some chatter for us sometimes to laugh at" (*Letter* 141.29–34). This contrast between earnestness and levity is nicely elaborated in Pietro's gesture toward enquiry of his busily engaged friends (*Vosne, qui togati in foro deambulatis?*, perhaps with a hint of ironic *gravitas*) before he suddenly lapses back into trivia: "When I was writing this, a servant came to me from the library, reporting that mice had gnawed off the clasps and labels of Aristotle's books about animals"—apparently the only books by Aristotle or any other author that they attacked. Were the mice retaliating for an Aristotelian slight against their kind? Pietro surmises as much; all joking aside (*extra iocum*), however, his tone now (wryly?) serious, Pietro asks Quirini, that statesman so used to dealing with "so many thousands of problems at Rome," if he could supply one of his precious Egyptian cats to deal with the mouse problem at Ostellato (*Letter* 141.40–50). In tenor and content, the entire letter amounts to a written manifestation of, even a manifesto for, villa-*otium*, and in setting his cat-and-mouse story before those *magni viri*, Angelo and Vincenzo, Pietro playfully exploits the yawning distance between their world and his: if we find

---

90. Travi (1987) 102 *Letter* 110.29–33.

91. Travi (1987) 134–5 *Letter* 141, on which see Kidwell (2004) 73–4. For Pietro's relations with Quirini, Jedin (1946).

a certain defensiveness about his *modus vivendi* in his letter to Gabriele of September 12, 1500, this letter of 1502 projects an unabashed ease in villa life.

Finally, a very different document: Angelo's transition to civic life is celebrated in the "Song of congratulation" (*Ad Angelum Gabrielem gratulatio*) in 119 hexameters that was first published by Marco Pecoraro in 1959 as one of "due carmi inediti attribuiti al Bembo."[92] If the poem is indeed accepted as Bembo's work, it was surely composed in the period *c.* 1499 when Angelo was beginning to progress in the Venetian *cursus*:

> Maxima facundae subiit certamina linguae
> iam puer et, patriae caros amplexus honores,
> rite salutavit venientia munera noster
> Angelus et primam gaudet decorare iuventam.
>
> 1–4

> Now the youth has entered the greatest contests of eloquent speech
> and, embracing the precious offices of the fatherland,
> our Angelo has duly welcomed his coming duties
> and rejoices to bring honor to his early manhood.

With its pleasing echo of Venice's name in *venientia* (3), these lines set the tone—playful, hyperbolical from the first (*Maxima*, 1), in every way unrestrained—for Bembo's appeal to Apollo to tune his lyre in readiness for celebrating Angelo, his foster child (*alumnus*, 5). So long "the companion of [Pietro's] ways and studies" (*tu modo iampridem . . . / . . . morum studiique comes*, 12–13), Angelo is set to embark on labors that are epically inflated in the loaded terminology of lines 15–17:

> disce palatinos iuvenis perferre *labores*,
> otiaque in *magnas* mutare Heliconia *curas*
> et Musas vestire toga.

> Learn while young to shoulder the tasks of government,
> and to exchange the leisure of Helicon for great responsibilities,
> and to clothe your Muse in the civic toga.

As if in a revisionist restaging of his mission in *Aeneid* 4 to rouse Aeneas from his tarrying in Carthage, Mercury descends to report to Angelo, who is dearer

92. Pecoraro (1959) 177–80 (albeit taken to task by Dionisotti [1961] 592 = Vela [2002] 203–4 for the bareness of his treatment of the poem); it is now accessible in Sodano (1990) 95–9 and Chatfield (2005) 180–9.

to Jupiter "even than Trojan Iulus" (*nec Iliacus tantum dilectus Iulus*, 72), that he has been granted the Jovian gift of *patria* (74; cf. 97–8); Angelo is an Aeneas remade, his destiny pre-made. From the child's earliest days, Mercury was ordered by Jupiter to stand as guardian over him and to guide his progress: "Let him learn the riches of the mind and master the learned arts (*discat opes animi, doctasque excalleat artes*, 88)"—a variation, perhaps, on Anchises' injunction to Aeneas at *Aeneid* 6.847–53 to practice the Roman art of government (cf. *hae tibi erunt artes*, 852), while shades of the golden child announced to the world in *Eclogue* 4 may also color Bembo's picture of the young Angelo. Mercury has done his duty faithfully, ensuring Angelo's safe return from his travels across the Adriatic and "the western bays" (*Hesperios . . . sinus*) to learn "the habits and customs of other places" (94–6); for all its generality, the itinerary perhaps includes an oblique allusion to Angelo's and Pietro's stay in Sicily. But Angelo might expect from his old friend some stings of wit amidst his (vastly overwrought?) effusions, and they are not hard to find. To cite but one example, Pietro calls on the Naiads to join in the celebrations for Angelo's success (26–30), then proceeding in lines 31–6 with

> insanire lubet, neque non cum Troica castra
> fregerat et praeda spoliisque redibat opimis
> Aeacides, fesso magis applaudebat amico
> Patroclus, nec, post Cretei funera monstri,
> laetior Actaeo venientem in littore Theseum
> Haemonius longis suscepit nexibus Heros.

> It's a delight to revel madly, just as Patroclus more than just cheered
> for his weary friend when Achilles had shattered the Trojan camps
> and returned with booty and rich spoils; and just as the Thessalian hero
> [sc. Pirithous] was more than joyful when, after the death of the Cretan
> minotaur, Theseus returned to the Athenian shore
> and he received him with long embraces.

At a superficial level, Pietro conjoins himself with Angelo here in a glowing tribute to their friendship: he is Patroclus to Angelo's Achilles, Pirithous to Angelo's Theseus, and in his call to mad revels (*insanire lubet*, 31), Pietro-Patroclus-Pirithous faithfully hails his boon companion's ever-so-heroic achievement in setting his foot on the Venetian career ladder. But then the sting in the tail: Achilles was of course soon to know the anguish of losing his beloved Patroclus, and the joyous welcome that Theseus allegedly received from his Pirithous on returning to Athens was of course offset by the suicide of his father, Aegeus, after Theseus forgot to change his ship's sails from black to white and Aegeus wrongly inferred that his son was dead (cf. Catullus 64.207–48). *Insanire lubet*: the truer madness, perhaps, is to take Pietro's surface jollities only at their face value, and not to see that he disarms even as he charms.

(ii) *Gli Asolani*, and Pietro's Correspondence with Trifone Gabriele

The vernacular dialogue *Gli Asolani* is set in the retirement retreat of Caterina Cornaro (1454–1510), the Venice-born former Queen of Cyprus, in the Venetian-controlled fief of Asolo in the foothills of the Alps about fifty kilometers northwest of the city. Married in 1472 to James II ("the Bastard") of Cyprus[93] in a match much favored at Venice because it furthered the commercial interests of the Republic, Caterina was widowed soon after the wedding. Upon her infant son's death in 1474, she became monarch, ruling Cyprus until 1489, when political expediency forced her to cede her kingdom to Venice. In recompense she was awarded Asolo, where for the next two decades she oversaw, as John Julius Norwich puts it, "a cultivated if distinctly vapid court," a "tinkling world of music, dancing and the polite conversation of learned men."[94] The court as portrayed in *Gli Asolani* appears to reflect Bembo's experience of Ferrara, but he also draws on his direct familiarity with Asolo, related as he was to Caterina Cornaro.[95] The conversations on love that Bembo purports to relate in *Gli Asolani* took place, he has it, on the occasion of the marriage of the Queen's favorite maid of honor—an event that appears historically true, and plausibly datable to the autumn of 1494, not long after Bembo's return from Sicily.[96] On each day of the celebrations, the midday dinner is followed by entertainment for the guests. Early in Book 1, after paying due reverence to the Queen, two damsels offer two songs to the accompaniment of the lute, the first a song on love's torments, the second on its joys;[97] when the Queen then summons her principal lady-in-waiting, the latter sings a third song, on this occasion to the viola, on the theme of pure, otherworldly love whose "bountihood is not by world or common folk believed."[98] This triad of songs forms a loose structural paradigm

---

93. The marriage was agreed in 1468, when Caterina was fourteen, but James thereafter considered other possible marital alliances; it was formalized at Famagusta on Cyprus in October or November 1472.

94. Norwich (1982) 367–8. Further on Caterina, Syndikus and Rogge (2013) with Colasanti (1979); Collmer (2003) 155–9; Hurlburt (2009); De Girolami Cheney (2013).

95. The exact relationship is unclear (Kidwell [2004] 425 n.4); a Marco Bembo, seemingly her nephew or cousin, was killed in her palace on Cyprus during an attempted *coup d'état* on the night of November 13–14, 1473.

96. But the dating is far from sure: Dilemmi (1991) xxxviii with Berra (1996) 14–15.

97. 1.3 Dilemmi (1991) 83.12–84.39; trans. Gottfried (1954) 10–11.

98. 1.3 Dilemmi (1991) 84.52–85.62; trans. Gottfried (1954) 11.

for the three discourses on love delivered by three pseudonymous speakers over the three books of the work as a whole.[99] In Book 1 Perottino, who "never spoke other than evil of love's work,"[100] embarks on an invective against love, which is characterized as more *amaro* ("bitter") than *amore*.[101] On the next day, in Book 2, Gismondo counters Perottino by expatiating on the joys of love if it is rightly conceived, rational and temperate as all natural things are, love foremost among them; since love is "the cause of everything," it must also be "the cause of every good thing everywhere,"[102] thereby giving rise to friendship, society, and civilization. By the third day, word of mouth about the discourses has reached the Queen, who chooses to join the proceedings. Her very presence is itself symbolically elevating as Lavinello refutes both Perottino and Gismondo, rising above the sensory captivity of earthly love to the higher desire for true beauty in the divine. In telling of his alleged encounter with a hermit who subjects him to a form of Socratic elenchus akin to that applied by Diotima in the *Symposium*, Lavinello offers a highly Platonizing account (here Bembo was undoubtedly influenced by Ficino's Neoplatonic interpretation, in his *De amore* of 1484, of Diotima's speech) that culminates in love of and in virtue as the ultimate good: "Nay, furthermore, our future state is everlasting, Lavinello," concludes the hermit, "and so we must believe that virtuous love is to be eternally enjoyed and that the other which is evil damns us to eternal grief."[103] After these climactic words, *Gli Asolani* abruptly draws to a close.

Within this tripartite structure the work follows an ascendant path from the agonies of earthly, sensual love as portrayed in Perottino's speech to the rational protocols of love in Gismondo's account, and, finally, to the spiritual elevation of Lavinello's discourse. But this tidy mapping of the work belies the gradual stages of development that *Gli Asolani* underwent through (i) the version of Book 1 preserved in an autograph manuscript now housed in the Biblioteca della Fondazione Querini Stampalia in Venice (henceforth given as Q).[104] This version, which is plausibly datable to before the beginning of Bembo's love affair with Maria Savorgnan in the spring of 1500,[105] itself preserves two stages of redaction,

99. On this paradigm, Bolzoni (2006) 14–15; (2010) xxi, 16; (2013a) 134–5; (2013b) 286–7.

100. 1.7 Dilemmi (1991) 88.9–10; trans. Gottfried (1954) 16.

101. Cf. the wry tone struck by Wind (1968) 92: "Like the 'bitter-sweet' pun of *amare-amaro*, to which Bembo devoted a whole book of the *Asolani*, the threatening equation of *amare-armare* became indispensable to lovesick sonneteers."

102. 2.20 Dilemmi (1991) 154.50–2; trans. Gottfried (1954) 113.

103. 3.22 Dilemmi (1991) 210.43–6; trans. Gottfried (1954) 194–5.

104. See on Q Dilemmi (1991) xli–lxii with Berra (1996) 11–167 and Curti (2006) 23–4.

105. But matters are by no means straightforward: see Dilemmi (1991) xxxvii–lxii with Berra (1996) 23–8.

the first a copy of a lost antegraph, the second a later round of revisions introduced by Pietro, including the excision of whole passages. (ii) The first printed edition of March 1505, at the Aldine Press in Venice. Whereas in the Q version the work is dedicated to an unnamed "madonna," the 1505 edition is prefaced by a dedication letter dated August 1, 1504 and addressed to Lucrezia Borgia.[106] Of the sixty-nine copies of this first printing invoked by Cecil Clough,[107] approximately a third of that number lacks this dedication letter. The tactical suppression of that letter in one of two issues of the 1505 printing has been alleged, but Clough offers a more convincing explanation for the partial omission: Bembo submitted his dedication letter late, falsely backdating it to August 1, 1504, after a third or so of the sheets of the first gathering had already been printed without it.[108] (iii) The second edition printed in Venice at the da Sabio press in 1530. The extensive textual alterations in this reworking aligned *Gli Asolani* with the rules and standardizations set out in Bembo's *Prose della volgar lingua* of 1525.[109] This second edition also excluded the dedication letter to Lucrezia, but the omission appears tactical: it was transferred, as if an authentic letter, to the epistolary collection that Bembo himself was preparing for publication in those years.[110] (iv) The third edition posthumously printed in 1552–3 at the Scotto press in Venice. Since the sixteenth century this edition, which again omits the dedication to Lucrezia, has been recognized as the vulgate of *Gli Asolani*, representing Bembo's ultimate intentions for the work; by Claudia Berra's count, this edition shows only a hundred or so significant variants on the 1530 edition,[111] a number that signals relatively little editorial intervention beyond Bembo's authorial wishes.

Against this background, the evolution of *Gli Asolani*, especially in its transition from the Q version to the first edition of 1505, is rich in biographical suggestion. Pietro's correspondence amounts to an invaluable resource in this respect, even if allowance has to be made for his later editing of his letters for publication, and so for revisionist distortions of the sort that Clough observes in Bembo's love letters to Maria Savorgnan in 1500–1—letters to which he "appears to have added

106. Travi (1987) 177–8 *Letter* 192; Dilemmi (1991) 77–8; trans. Gottfried (1954) 1–3.

107. Clough (1969), esp. 20–1, supplemented by Clough (1972).

108. Clough (1969) 24–6.

109. For these revisions, Berra (1996) 300–19 after Dilemmi (1991) lxvi–cxv; see also Berra 301 and Dilemmi lxxi for the revisions glaringly understated in a letter of June 27, 1530 to Pietro Pamfilio (Travi [1992] 157 *Letter* 1117.6–8: "Averete con questa le mie *Rime* e gli *Asolani* ristampati, e in qualche parte differenti da' primieri").

110. Clough (1969) 25–7.

111. Berra (1996) 323.

... references to work on *Gli Asolani*."[112] Pietro first alludes to *Gli Asolani* in a letter to Trifone Gabriele written at Ferrara on December 11, 1497;[113] the allusion suggests that the undertaking was already well known to Trifone, and that Pietro had been working on it for some time. Most of his morning, Pietro writes, and even the predawn hours are devoted to *Gli Asolani* (*Letter* 22.2–3), but his sleepless lucubration is also caused, we infer, by the lovesickness he describes later in the missive: "As for your advice that I should set a limit to my grief and serve my health and peace of mind, I would indeed be doing so if I could, especially with your encouragement and urging; but assuredly I cannot" (*Letter* 22.20–2), continually drawn back as he is to reflection on what he has lost (*quid amiserim cogito, Letter* 22.23). His suffering appears connected to the hasty and apparently forced separation from the woman to whom he mysteriously refers as "M.G." in a letter to Trifone of January 20, 1498,[114] again penned in Ferrara: he writes of his need "to fulfill a vow that I must fulfill at this time and I do not really know how long I will stay" (*Letter* 23.3–4); in his absence from Venice, he implores Trifone to visit "M.G." on his behalf.

Who was this Madonna G.? She has been plausibly identified as Costanza or Gostanza Fregoso, scion of the noble Fregoso family of Genoa, and sister of the Ottaviano and Federico Fregoso who figure prominently in Baldassare Castiglione's Urbino in *The Book of the Courtier*.[115] Given that Bembo was apparently already working on *Gli Asolani* by late 1497, and given his allusion in his letter to Trifone of January 20, 1498 to his enforced separation from "M.G.," the dedication of the Q version to an unnamed "madonna" from whom Pietro is painfully separated is all too suggestive: if Bembo's "madonna" in the Q version is taken to be Costanza Fregoso, we might then suspect that Perottino's diatribe against love in Book 1 reflects Pietro's tribulations in his affair with Costanza.

112. Clough (1969) 27. For Bembo and Maria's shared correspondence see Dionisotti (1950) with Farnetti (2012).

113. Travi (1987) 20–1 *Letter* 22; but for the possibility of *ex post facto* (re)casting for the purposes of publication, Berra (1996) 16.

114. Travi (1987) 21 *Letter* 23, on which Kidwell (2004) 21 ("Bembo's first recorded love affair").

115. For this identification, Clough (1965b) with Kidwell (2004) 138. Lucco (2000) intriguingly connects what he identifies as an early Raphael portrait (*c.* 1507) of Costanza with that of Pietro Bembo (now lost) that Marcantonio Michiel (for whom Chapter 7 pp. 275–7) claims to have seen in Bembo's Paduan residence. When all three—Costanza, Bembo and Raphael—were present in Urbino in 1506-7, the two pictures were commissioned, Lucco conjectures, as a pendant pair to be exchanged between the two lovers, in keeping with the common practice of the age. Within two or so years, however, Pietro and Costanza had parted ways, and in 1509 she married the Piacentine aristocrat Marcantonio Landi di Bardi. At that point, Lucco surmises (p. 68), the two Raphael portraits would have been returned to their respective sitters; hence the Bembo portrait that Michiel apparently saw in Padua.

After the beginning of his affair with Maria Savorgnan in 1500, her jealousy of "M.G." contributed to the mixture of anguish and ecstasy that is arguably reflected in the contrasting discourses on love in *Gli Asolani* 1 and 2. Beyond the suggestive anagrammatic relation of their names, Pietro explicitly identifies himself with Perottino at one point in his correspondence with Maria,[116] but Gismondo's discourse finds many more resonances in Bembo's letters; this congruency signals that, even if Book 2 was drafted before the affair with Maria started, it underwent significant revision in the course of their liaison.[117] At 2.17 Gismondo declares his age through an elaborate periphrasis (" . . . he [sc. Perottino] is no older than I am; and the number of my years is still two less than there are days within the shortest month");[118] Bembo perhaps alludes obliquely to his age when he first embarked on the work.[119] Another biographical clue surfaces in Pietro's letter to Giovan Giorgio Trissino of March 21, 1505:[120] the reason he is so keen to acquire the gold medal of Berenice (II, wife of Ptolemy III Euergetes?) that had apparently been promised to Trissino by "M. Anton Nicolò" (*Letter* 202.14, 29), he writes, is because the portrait closely resembles a living woman whom he much esteems, and whom he has termed Berenice in *Gli Asolani* (*Letter* 202.29–31).[121] As for Lavinello, a boy of that name, seemingly his nephew, recurs in Pietro's letters to his brother and half-brother, Carlo and Bartolomeo respectively;[122] but the special significance (if such it is) of this coincidence of names remains unclear.

After the fading of Pietro's affair with Maria Savorgnan in 1501[123] and the first stirrings of his love for Lucrezia Borgia in late 1502, he sent Lucrezia the first

116. Travi (1987) 125 *Letter* 131.52 = Dionisotti (1950) 131 *Letter* 76; see further Berra (1996) 61 and n.145, and cf. Kidwell (2004) 102 for Perottino as "almost his namesake."

117. See Berra (1996) 27.

118. Dilemmi (1991) 148.21–5; trans. Gottfried (1954) 105.

119. Dionisotti (1966b) 414 n.4 with Berra (1996) 12.

120. Travi (1987) 189–91 *Letter* 202.

121. For the identification with Ptolemy's Berenice on what he takes to be an ancient coin in the ownership of the Vicentine noble Anton Nicolò Loschi, see Gasparotto (2013c) 483–4, *contra* Bolzoni (2010) 354–5, who holds that the medal is modern and that it is the work of Anton Nicolò Loschi (cf. Travi [1987] 287 for "Nicolò Antonio intagliatore"—a problematic index entry, given that Travi 286 separately lists the "Loschi de' Antonio Nicolò" named in *Letter* 227.4–6 in reference to the same medal and the same business with Trissino); but Bolzoni (2013b) 307 appears to accept Gasparotto's interpretation of the medal. See further on the whole affair Kidwell (2004) 119–21, and cf. on the medal Chapter 7 p. 282.

122. See, e.g., Travi (1987) 131 *Letter* 137.7; 132 *Letter* 138.2; 147 *Letter* 154.32, etc.

123. Attested in Travi (1987) 127–8 *Letter* 132 = Dionisotti (1950) 134–6 *Letter* 77, of September 3, 1501; Kidwell (2004) 67–8.

book of *Gli Asolani* in June 1503.[124] In a letter to her of July 24, 1503 he is rapturous in his envy of *Gli Asolani*: "At the most timely moment it came into your hands. Messer Lodovico[125] writes to me saying that he feels there is no need for it to be brought out and read by all the world in order to gain glory, for more than it enjoys already could never come its way; and he speaks the truth."[126] For her part, Lucrezia was apparently anxious for the work to be published. In a letter of July 25, 1504 Pietro has gone into seclusion "to a little villa of mine for two months so that I may finish those things that I began for you," among them *Gli Asolani* as now dedicated to her; if the work is read a century after they are gone, it will be because of "the high renown of your name which [the books] bear before them, and which of itself is companion to eternity."[127] The final draft was in place two months later: by September 22, 1504 Bembo can report that the finishing touches have been applied, and that "if all were up to me it could come out tomorrow as I have no need to look it over further."[128] Even though Pietro's dedicatory letter of August 1, 1504 implies that Lucrezia had yet to see Book 3,[129] Lavinello's presence in that book is perhaps symbolically charged in light of their affair – or so Carol Kidwell suspects in hazarding that Lavinello "may reflect something of [Pietro's] idealisation" of his relationship with the "fundamentally unobtainable" Lucrezia.[130]

In the prefatory address to "madonna" in the Q version of *Gli Asolani,* Bembo presents the work as the happy outcome of all the literary leisure ("Gli otij, madonna . . . delle lettre")[131] that he has been free to enjoy in his youth. The reality was rather different, however, or so it appears from his correspondence. In a letter to Trifone of February 2, 1498 he laments the burden of his preoccupations

124. Travi (1987) 145 *Letter* 151.32. In general on the affair with Lucrezia, Kidwell (2004) 71–98 with Shankland (1987) and Braden (1996) 404–12.

125. Ariosto, with Shankland (1987) XII and Raboni (1989) 47–8? But Lodovico Tessira is favored by Travi (1987) 286 in index s.v. "Lodovico Messer." For an overview of the controversy, Gnocchi (1999) 290–1.

126. Travi (1987) 153 *Letter* 162 in app. The quoted words do not appear in the 1552 *princeps* of Bembo's published letters; on the implications of that absence, Gnocchi (1999) 290. For the translation as given here, Shankland (1987) XII.

127. Travi (1987) 176–7 *Letter* 191.8–9, 13–14; trans. Shankland (1987) XXVI.

128. Travi (1987) 180–1 *Letter* 194.17–18; trans. Shankland (1987) XXVII.

129. For the letter cited ("If I have not sent you earlier these discussions . . ."), and for the implication that Lucrezia had yet to see Book 3, Kidwell (2004) 89–90 and 422 n.70; but for the possibility that Bembo falsely backdated the dedicatory letter to August 1, 1504 see p. 171.

130. Kidwell (2004) 110.

131. 1.1 Dilemmi (1991) 5.1.

at Ferrara, beset as he is by his studies and by public affairs, the latter perhaps connected to Bernardo Bembo's position as *visdomino*. His studies are making fitful progress, he reports, and *Gli Asolani* is dormant:

> *Nosti rerum nostrarum statum, et tempora. Gli Asolani plane dormiunt*, né penso si possano risvegliare in quest'aria. Ad essi farebbe uopo d'un altro esilio, al primo simile.[132]

Whether or not Pietro is taken to refer in "un altro esilio, al primo simile" to his two-year stay in Messina in 1492–4,[133] *Gli Asolani* is here synonymous with an undistracted *otium* for which he yearns. Matters had improved little by the year's end: in a letter to Angelo Gabriele of December 3,[134] Pietro reports that *Gli Asolani* is far from finished, its progress hampered by his failure to apply himself ("pigrizia del mio ingegno," *Letter* 34.27); it still needs much leisure for revision and polishing ("lungo ozio e lima," *Letter* 34.27–8). Writing once more to Trifone from Ferrara on March 1, 1499, he characterizes *Gli Asolani* as still asleep (*Asulani mei plane dormiunt*), a circumstance "I'd put up with more easily if [the work] were less well regarded by you." Family business (*negocia domestica*) and his specialized studies (*studia dialecticae disciplinae*) apparently deprive him of the leisure he needs for *Gli Asolani*[135]—the kind of *otium* that Pietro imputes to Trifone earlier in the missive, now that he has finished his term of ecclesiastical office and (Pietro anticipates with vicarious glee) he can look forward to a life of unfettered leisure and devotion to study (*Letter* 36.9–10).

It is striking that these various allusions to *Gli Asolani* are all contained in letters to either Trifone or Angelo Gabriele, as if that work and the anxiety for *otium* that Pietro associates with it amounted to a totem-like summation of the values that bound a tight coterie of youthful idealists.[136] Yet while Angelo was making his way in the Venetian *cursus*, Trifone remained closer in spirit to Pietro's aspirations for the literary life, taking holy orders in 1498 but later refusing to accept any preferment or office from the Republic;[137] he continued actively to support Pietro's work on *Gli Asolani*, as a letter of December 24, 1502 (Bembo to Carlo, his brother) attests.[138]

---

132. Travi (1987) 22 *Letter* 24.15–18.

133. Berra (1996) 19 is open minded.

134. Travi (1987) 29–30 *Letter* 34.

135. Travi (1987) 32 *Letter* 36.25–8.

136. On this special *sodalitas*, Berra (1996) 21.

137. On his life choice, Dionisotti (1967) 65 with Bellomo (1997) 61–2 (noting Trifone's immersion "in quell'*otium* vagheggiato da molti e perseguito da pochi").

138. Travi (1987) 137 *Letter* 145.7–9.

Within *Gli Asolani* this same tension between *otium* and *negotium* is expressed in multiple ways, with Asolo and its Boccaccian garden[139] cast as a leisurely *locus amoenus* ideologically distant from the civic milieu and Venetian deontology. But even as the work appears to function as a discreet manifesto for Pietro's preferred *modus vivendi* away from the duties expected of the Venetian patriciate,[140] Venice still looms menacingly; in a system of contrasts akin to that in *De Aetna*, the escapist credentials of *Gli Asolani* are predicated on the juxtaposition of country and city, leisure and duty, courtly decorum and the grind of government. Early in the Q version, Pietro briefly recounts the circumstances in which Caterina Cornaro acquired Asolo after ceding her kingdom of Cyprus to the Republic:[141] for all the charms of Asolo, and for all the official esteem that Caterina won for her sacrifice,[142] her power, such as it was, was all too transparently dependent on the Venetian center. In describing Asolo, Pietro refers more than once to Venice as "Signoria *nostra*,"[143] an inescapable point of reference even in his detachment from the usual career path there. The husbands of the three ladies who consort with Perottino, Gismondo, and Lavinello in *Gli Asolani* are forced to return to Venice on business:[144] it is hard not to discern in this balance of opposites—while three unmarried gentlemen (Perottino, etc.) are playfully at ease at Asolo, the three husbands dutifully hasten back to the city—the challenges of life choice and career expectation that Bembo negotiated in the *Gli Asolani* years.[145] Further illustrations could be offered of this Venetian shadow, but all to the effect of showing that, despite their profound differences of theme, setting, scope, and language (the vernacular as opposed to Latin), *Gli Asolani* in many ways takes up, and updates, the major preoccupations of *De Aetna*: both works are mutually informing when they are read against each other, because both deploy varied techniques of self-portraiture to convey Pietro's deviation from the "true" Venetian path.

---

139. For the Boccaccian dimension, evoking in particular the garden described in the introduction to the third day of the *Decameron*, Bolzoni (2002), esp. 97–9, and (2010) 80–5, esp. 81, with Berra (1996) 55–61.

140. Dionisotti (1966b) 20 = Vela (2002) 33. Cf. Curti (2006) 22: "l'opera comprometteva Bembo non solo come scrittore, ma come patrizio veneziano, *ponendolo definitivamente al di fuori di quell'impegno politico* a cui era stato invano avviato" (my emphasis); also Clough (1998) as cited on p. 162 n.76.

141. 1.2 Dilemmi (1991) 7.1–13.

142. For the sacrificial imagery connected to the fêting of her service to the Republic, Hurlburt (2009), esp. 73–4.

143. Q 1.2 Dilemmi (1991) 7.7, 10.

144. Q 1.2 Dilemmi (1991) 8.39–40.

145. Berra (1996) 51–2.

(iii) Vincenzo Quirini and Tommaso Giustiniani

A different perspective on Pietro's reluctance to embark on a conventional patrician career is offered by his relations with Vincenzo Quirini, who entered our story earlier,[146] and with Tommaso Giustiniani (1476–1528). Quirini had achieved outstanding early success in service to the Republic; remarkably, he was only twenty-six when elected ambassador to Philip, Duke of Burgundy, in December 1504.[147] But already from about 1500 onward he and Giustiniani, his fellow patrician and student-companion at Padua, had resolved to withdraw to the monastic life of contemplation.[148] The personal vow of chastity that each took in 1501 was a measure of their seriousness of purpose, but in the years that followed Giustiniani consistently showed a greater commitment to the monastic ideal, attempting at different times to embrace the solitary life on Murano in the Venetian lagoon and in the Holy Land.[149] Meanwhile, Quirini struggled to reconcile the secular and spiritual callings, and it was not until February 1512 that he finally joined Giustiniani in the eremitical order at Camaldoli in Tuscany, taking the name Fra Pietro to Giustiniani's Fra Paolo. As reformers of the Camaldolese order and agitators for wider Church reform, they are now perhaps best known for their efforts (based on hopes that ultimately proved illusory) to launch major changes at the Fifth Lateran Council convened in 1512. Quirini died in Rome in September 1514, probably of natural causes, but one measure of the political and curial intrigues in which he was involved is that rumors of poisoning circulated soon after his death.[150] For present purposes, Quirini and Giustiniani exemplify the religious calling that drew, late in Margaret King's third generation of Venetian humanists,[151] certain patricians who sought escape in the inner life from the civic expectations incumbent on their class. Pietro showed signs of the same religious calling, but with less strength of commitment,[152] a cause of tension between him and Quirini, as we shall see. But Quirini and Giustiniani are of further relevance to our story because of their involvement, along with Bembo, in the small literary society—a

---

146. See p. 166.

147. On this embassy, Bowd (2002) 46–51.

148. On the sequence of events, Bowd (2002), esp. 27–60, with Leclercq (1951), esp. 17–40.

149. See Bowd (2002) 61–2 with Leclercq (1951) 27–40.

150. Further, Bowd (1999) 44–5 and (2002) 206–7; for these whispers in relation to Bembo's rivalry with Quirini, Kidwell (2004) 184–5.

151. For which see pp. 158–9.

152. Cf. Dionisotti (1966b) 30 = Vela (2002) 42: "Non aveva alcuna vocazione religiosa, ma nelle condizioni di allora il beneficio ecclesiastico senza cura d'anime era via aperta a quanti aborrissero dalla servitù della vita civile."

form of mini-Academy—whose guiding principles are set out in an autograph document in Pietro's hand known as the *Leggi della Compagnia degli Amici*; this document, discovered and published by Carlo Dionisotti, is plausibly datable to the first years of the new century (*c.* 1502–3?).[153] These *Leggi* will in due course inform our approach in Chapter 5 to *De Aetna* as a "candid," living print portrait of Pietro as well as Bernardo Bembo. But for our entrée to the *Leggi* we first turn to the elaborate letter that Pietro, then in Urbino, wrote to Vincenzo in Venice on December 10, 1506.[154]

This lengthy missive was apparently prompted by Vincenzo's disapproval of Pietro's installation in the court of Urbino late in 1506. In a letter of May 3, 1506 to Elisabetta Gonzaga, Duchess of Urbino, and to her devoted lady-in-waiting, Emilia Pia da Montefeltro,[155] Bembo states that he has abandoned his civic ambitions at Venice and, because he lacks the resources to support himself at Rome with adequate leisure for his literary studies, he has resolved to withdraw to the hermitage of the Holy Cross at Fonte Avellana near Urbino. There he means to stay for a year and perhaps more, he claims, enjoying the tranquility of place, mind, and literary *otium* that the abbey affords. Given his ambition to enter that hermitage (cf. "in quel romitaggio," *Letter* 231.119–20), Lavinello's hermit in *Gli Asolani* 3 may well embody the spiritual calling that Pietro appears to have felt as a real life choice in the first years of the new century[156]—a source of unease that still persisted in 1506, when "he seemed to aim to have one foot in Fonte Avellana and the other solidly in the world."[157] But Pietro ultimately gave up his intention of staying at the abbey, instead reverting to the court of Urbino; hence Quirini's disapproving missive. In reply to Quirini, Bembo insists *inter alia* that he has made many efforts to gain office, but without success; now he seeks repose in the life of letters, his own master rather than toiling in public service. He has not changed, he asserts, and would rather remain himself "with the face I have" than don a misleading mask, risking exposure

153. Text, Dionisotti (1966b) 699–703, but not in the first edition, Dionisotti (1960); the manuscript resides in the Biblioteca Ambrosiana, Milan. For the date, Gnocchi (1999) 277 with Dionisotti (1966b) 696: "È certo del periodo veneziano del Bembo, del periodo cioè degli *Asolani*, più vicino al compimento e alla stampa di quest'opera, che non al suo concepimento e prima stesura, *insomma dei primi anni del '500*, subito prima o più probabilmente subito dopo il soggiorno ferrarese del Bembo" (my emphasis). I use the title inferred by Dionisotti from the content of the work: see p. 181.

154. Travi (1987) 234–9 *Letter* 245, on which Bowd (1999) 48 with Kidwell (2004) 124–6.

155. Travi (1987) 216–20 *Letter* 231 with Bowd (1999) 47, Kidwell (2004) 116–19, and esp. Vagni (2010) on Bembo's self-presentation in this missive, which amounts to "una sorta di dichiarazione programmatica, in cui egli volle esplicitare i suoi progetti e le sue ambizioni" (p. 734).

156. Bowd (1999) 47 with Bolzoni (2010) 94–5.

157. Bowd (1999) 47.

and derision for wearing another's clothes (*Letter* 245.202–4). It may be tempting, at least on one reading, to suspect that Pietro answers Vincenzo's criticism with a certain ironic edge, such as in his allusion to Lavinello (*Letter* 245.205): he wishes Quirini every success, whether he is drawn in the direction to which the hermit steers Lavinello in *Gli Asolani* 3, or he persists in public life, on the path to becoming "the greatest, most honored man of our state" (*Letter* 245.213–14). The barb, if such it is, presupposes Pietro's keen awareness that Quirini was powerfully drawn to the contemplative life even as he had just completed one ambassadorial assignment (to Burgundy, whence he returned to Venice in October 1506) and was soon to be elected to another—that of envoy to Maximilian I, Holy Roman Emperor (1459–1519), a still more important and delicate posting to which he was officially appointed in February 1507;[158] Quirini aspires to be a Lavinello, the barbed thought might go, but his (ambition for a glittering) civic career stands in the way.

Or perhaps Pietro writes without irony, simply wishing Vincenzo well on whatever path he chooses. After all, in stating earlier in the letter how much he values Quirini's good opinion of him, he adds his appreciation of the frank directness of speech that his "true and loyal" friend had apparently used in his original letter to Bembo (*Letter* 245.188–91). Pietro, we infer, would seem to employ a similar candor in return, especially given that candor was central to the charter of friendship, the *Leggi* of *c.* 1502–3(?), that bound the intimate circle of Bembo, Quirini, Giustiniani, and Niccolò Tiepolo.[159] The laws, aims and doctrines of this charter are highly idealized, as if generated by the ambition to codify youthful friendship into a lifelong institution based on utopic values.[160] In accordance with the ancient proverb that friends hold all things in common,[161] no affect or passion is to be held in private, but whatever is held *nel cuore* is to be revealed, the wishes and thoughts of each member as visible to the others as their brows and faces are; to lie is equivalent to nothing less than murder. If the group admits other members, women or men, learning and devotion to literature are essential qualifications for entry; when a new member is admitted, all are bound to celebrate for eight consecutive days of merriment and conviviality, and with sonnets or other forms of composition by their own hand; the strong collective ethos is courtly and knightly in aspiration and nostalgia, eschewing a purely philological pedantry. Given this detailed code of

---

158. On this embassy, Bowd (2002) 54–8.

159. For "T.G." Dionisotti (1966b) 699 n.2 infers Trifone Gabriele, but Tommaso Giustiniani is surely more likely, esp. given that the surviving *postille* accompanying the *Leggi* are in his hand: see p. 181 with Gnocchi (1999) 278.

160. Further on their general character, Bolzoni (2010) 89–92.

161. See, conveniently, Dyck (1996) 168–9 on Cic. *Off.* 1.51.

conduct, the *Leggi* offer an important corollary to *Gli Asolani*, in that they set out an ideology of cultured companionship that finds at least a loose approximation in the carefully regulated turn taking, the rarified sociability, and the high literariness of the proceedings at Asolo.

But still more important for now are the emblems of membership that the *Leggi* mandated for each friend. The first was a gold medal with the three Graces depicted on one side, the inscription *amicorum sodalitati* ("for the sodality of friends") on the other.[162] No directives are given as to whether the Graces are to be shown clothed or naked, and in what bodily position in relation to one another—differences that were important in the iconographic history of the Graces from antiquity onward.[163] But Seneca's stoicizing account of the three Graces in *De beneficiis* 1 may well be Pietro's reference point in the *Leggi*, especially given Seneca's special influence on Renaissance representation of the Graces more generally:

> . . . why are the Graces three in number and why are they sisters? Why are they holding hands? . . . What is the point of their holding hands in a dance that goes back on itself? That there is a sequence of kindness, passing from one hand to another, which nevertheless comes back to the giver, and that the beauty of the whole is lost if the sequence is anywhere interrupted, while it is loveliest if it hangs together and maintains its succession.[164]

Beyond evoking this seamless reciprocity, Pietro may also draw on the tradition, extending back at least to Hesiod, of the Graces as the incarnation of beauty, mirth, and prosperity;[165] given the centrality of Cupid and Venus within the Neoplatonic pantheon (Cupid the mediator of communication between mortals and gods, Venus personifying the universal exchange system for the distribution of divine gifts), Bembo perhaps further evokes the Graces' allegorical importance as symbols for the economy of divine gift circulation in Ficino's and Pico della Mirandola's Neoplatonic scheme.[166] Each member is to wear the medal on the left arm above

---

162. Text: Dionisotti (1966b) 700 with (on the Graces) Bolzoni (2010) 359–60.

163. See Wind (1968) 26–35, esp. 28–31 on the distinct typologies represented by Servius (the Graces naked, one pictured from the back, two facing us, "because for one benefit issuing from us two are supposed to return": Serv. *ad Aen.* 1.720 = I p. 200.3–4 Thilo-Hagen) and by Seneca (the three Graces clothed and, in their handholding, intertwined in a three-part sequence of giving, receiving, and returning: *Ben.* 1.3.2–4).

164. *Ben.* 1.3.2, 4. See Wind (1968) 31–2, and cf. now Collareta (2013) 228 n.29 (Bembo "non cita ma ha evidentemente in mente Seneca, *De beneficiis* 1,3,2").

165. See *Theog.* 909 with West (1966) 409; the Graces are there named as Ἀγλαΐα ("Beauty"), Εὐφροσύνη ("Mirth"), and Θάλεια ("Prosperity").

166. Wind (1968) 38–9.

the elbow, where it is to hang from a chain of the purest gold, and never to be removed: while text and image illuminate each other on its two sides, the medal simultaneously reflects both the inner character of each individual bearer and the unity of the group as a whole; that unity is further underscored by each medal's derivation from the same source (*un solo conio e sola stampa*). In a sense this medal functions as a portrait of each as well as a portrait of all, their individual identities merged under a common symbol; but the *Leggi* also allow for a more individualized form of portraiture. In addition to the medal, each member's portrait[167] is to be executed from life by a single artist on a small panel (*una tavoletta*), of the same dimensions and kind in every case; the name is to be rendered in lettering on the portrait side, the family emblem of each on the other side; and the panels are to be compiled in the form of a book (*tutte* [sc. *tavolette*] *insieme poste a guisa di libbro*), its contents memorializing the inner person as well as the external appearance of each member.

For present purposes, the details of these *Leggi* are important for two reasons, both of them contingent on Bembo's authorship, and hence on what they reveal of his aesthetic idealism at a remove from dutiful service to the Republic. First, the tensions that we observed above in his correspondence with Quirini surface once more, albeit on this occasion with Giustiniani to the fore. In the Ambrosian manuscript containing what Dionisotti terms the *Leggi della Compagnia degli Amici*, the work is in fact entitled *Leggi dell'Amicitia*; that title was added by a later hand.[168] After the *Leggi* in Bembo's hand, the manuscript presents a sequence of note-like additions to them, but in a different hand, almost certainly that of Giustiniani.[169] That Giustiniani actively formulated these additions rather than merely drafting them as an appointed scribe is indicated by the strong sense of mission in their content. Whereas Bembo's *Leggi* offer a utopic vision of close companionship in devotion to literature and cultured pleasure, Giustiniani prioritizes *i beni del'animo* and the gaining of wisdom: each member is obliged to share with his companions "all the skills, all the knowledge, every writing and each language that he knows."[170] Resisting the idea of succumbing to enmity in the first place, Giustiniani refutes the call made in the *Leggi* for the enemy of any one member to be the enemy of all; since friendly exhortations and loving reprimands best equip the mind for *la strada de le virtude*, all members are obligated to offer frank encouragement and correction,

167. Text: Dionisotti (1966b) 700; see also Bolzoni (2010) 361.

168. See Dionisotti (1966b) 699 n.1 with Gnocchi (1999) 277 and n.2.

169. Dionisotti (1966b) does not publish this additional text (see 699 n.1). For the text see, conveniently, Gnocchi (1999) 280–1 with Bolzoni (2010) 91–2, 362; for Giustiniani's hand, Gnocchi 278.

170. Gnocchi (1999) 280 [I].

and no major life decisions are to be made without consulting at least two or three companions; all are to undergo every year a form of public confession in which each reviews his undertakings, his loves, and his desires with his companions as he would with himself.[171] Through these and his other proposals (extending to abstention from marriage, from meat eating, and from wine drinking, with the implication of distance from a "normative" mode of worldly sociability),[172] Giustiniani effectively transforms the tenor of the original *Leggi*, applying a rigorous moralizing dimension that coincides with the intensification of his commitment to the contemplative life in the early years of the new century. On this approach, Bembo's *Leggi* and Giustiniani's *postille* serve very different agendas: if the former offers a manifesto for the convivial life of letters in a community of like-minded devotees, the latter freights that manifesto with a heavier moral cargo and a different *gravitas*;[173] it is fitting that Bembo and Giustiniani were both soon to leave Venice on their diverse paths, Pietro making for courtly Urbino in 1506 while Tommaso sought spiritual withdrawal first on Murano in 1506 and then in the Holy Land in 1507 before reverting to Venice by the beginning of 1508.

Secondly, fundamental to the artifacts that Pietro mentions in the *Leggi*—the medal showing the three Graces, and the book-like ensemble of the portraits of each member—is the interplay of text and image, and also the sympathetic correlation between external representation on the one hand, the picturing of inner character on the other. Such interplay between word and image, internal quality and outside appearance, illusion and reality was hardly a new departure for Bembo, whose experimentation in this area has been well documented for *Gli Asolani* in particular.[174] But the verbal-visual dynamic in play in the *Leggi* conveniently introduces the similar phenomenon that I claim for *De Aetna*: beyond the (illusion of) realism that Pietro achieves through the dramatized exchanges of father and son within the dialogue, the printed word in *De Aetna* is itself visually meaningful, I argue, capturing as it does in its novel Aldine type form the sprightly energies that characterize Pietro on Etna. To develop this argument further, we turn in Chapter 5 to the circumstances in which *De Aetna* was produced at the Aldine Press in early 1496, and, not least, to the physiognomic potential of typeface.

---

171. Gnocchi (1999) 280 [II], [III], [IV], [V].

172. Gnocchi (1999) 280 [VI].

173. Cf. Gnocchi (1999) 281: "Le posizioni del Bembo e del Giustiniani sono inconciliabili e le *Leggi della Compagnia degli Amici* sembrano così un tentativo nostalgico di salvare una comunanza di prospettive in realtà avviata al dissolvimento."

174. See esp. Bolzoni (2010) and (2013b).

5

Physical Form and Textual Meaning in the Aldine Book

THE SYMBOLIC SIGNIFICANCE OF TYPEFACE

AFTER THE ETNA Idea and mnemonic topography predominated in Chapters 1 and 2, our focus turned in Chapters 3 and 4 to the Venetian humanist context, as well as the personal circumstances, in which Bembo composed *De Aetna*. But too little has been said thus far of *De Aetna*'s importance in the history of the printed book. Accordingly, this chapter explores the circumstances in which the work was published at the Aldine Press in February 1496, but with particular attention to its originality as the first embodiment of the roman typeface devised by Francesco Griffo for Aldo Manuzio in the early 1490s. That typeface, this chapter argues, gives a highly distinctive print appearance to the dialogical exchanges between Pietro and Bernardo Bembo, complementing through its newness of visual appeal the sociocultural refinement of their neo-Ciceronian interactions and the "modern" cast of their rationalizing conversation about Etna's workings. On this approach, the elegance of the printed page suggestively projects and affirms both the élan of the Aldine Press and the prestige of the *gens Bembina*. But given that *De Aetna* is very much Pietro's text, not his father's, at least in the sense that Pietro's master voice introduces the dialogue proper and narrates it from beginning to end, my further argument is that the type form functions as a reflection of the dynamic, free-spirited Pietro in particular: print adventure coincides with mountain adventure as Pietro's climb is described in this novel Aldine format, where his vibrant energies and countenance are captured or matched by that freshness of typographic face.

The inventiveness of physical form that I attribute to *De Aetna* in this chapter is naturally to be viewed in the larger context of Manuzio's experimentation both typographically and in terms of page size, book format, and the overall elegance of the finished Aldine product. Hence, after surveying the rise of the Aldine Press and its major improvisations in the 1490s in section 5.1, we turn in 5.2 to the form for which the press is perhaps best known today, the octavo handbook, the first instantiation of which was the famous Virgil published in April 1501. Against this background of rich invention, our focus shifts back to *De Aetna* in 5.3, and to the intimate relationship that I posit between the work's typographic form and its textual meaning, to the effect that the typeface itself shows portrait quality not just in what it says (a picture in words), but also in its actual physical appearance (the print face as picture). But while much is made in 5.3 of the type form as a physical "picturing" of Pietro in particular, the father-son balance is restored by our focus on Bernardo in 5.4. While Bernardo too is no less "pictured" in the ennobling Aldine-Bembine typeface, and while section 5.4 duly represents both sides of the father-son diptych (so to speak) that is *De Aetna*, my further objective is to supplement our coverage thus far of Pietro's interest in the interplay of text and/as picture by exploring Bernardo's own inclinations in this same direction. My claim is not, of course, that Bernardo necessarily exerted a direct, decisive, or unilateral influence on Pietro in this respect, but simply that Bernardo was evidently well attuned to the kind of self-conscious verbal portraiture that *De Aetna* enacts. Further, the dialogical interaction between father and son in *De Aetna* is related in 5.4 to another intriguing case, Petrarch central to it, where they are conjoined through Pietro's playful co-ordination of different textual-visual media; the interplay of word and image in *De Aetna* is itself representative, I argue, of Pietro's far wider interest and experimentation in this visual-verbal direction.

The enterprising application of typeface, then, is our predominant theme in this chapter before we move to invention of a different but complementary kind in Chapter 6. There we shall see that the differences of characterization between father and son in *De Aetna* are articulated through their differing perceptions of Mount Etna. The Etna Idea as configured in Chapter 1 will return to the fore at that point: Bembo builds with striking originality, I argue, on the invention that is already richly displayed in Greco-Roman elaborations of the Etna theme. In combination, therefore, Chapters 5 and 6 are tasked with demonstrating two of the most arresting features of *De Aetna*, its typographic novelty and its imaginative deployment of the Etna Idea. To set us on our path, however, we return once more to Venice, and to the rise there of the Aldine Press.

5.1: Venice, the Rise of Printing, and the Aldine Press

Almost a third of all books produced in Europe in the fifteenth century were printed on the Italian peninsula, which boasted in Venice, Rome, and Milan three of the ten main centers of European production.[1] Despite the Turkish challenge to Venetian influence in the eastern Mediterranean, Venice's commercial power remained broadly intact in the second half of the fifteenth century down to the great voyages of discovery. This general prosperity, combined with other factors such as Venice's importance in the history of paper production, its large Greek émigré community, the relatively high rate of literacy,[2] and the presence within its territories of the university towns of Padua and Ferrara, meant that printing developed there with unparalleled rapidity after the German resident and print master, Johannes de Spira (d. 1470), secured in 1469 a five-year monopoly over the craft in Venice and its dominions.[3] When he died within months of securing the monopoly, his activities were taken over by his brother, Wendelin.[4] But because the privilege expired with Johannes, competitors quickly emerged, and in 1470 alone at least four printers were active in Venice, producing twenty-three editions, a number that grew to some eighty-five editions in 1471—a third of all the printed books produced in Europe in that year. Production fell by roughly a half in 1473, a crisis precipitated in part by a glut in the market for printed Classical texts when supply outran demand; humanist criticism of inaccuracies in the printed text, of the often dirty and smudged appearance of the lettering, and of the carelessness or inefficiency of the printers also brought negative comparison with the quality of traditional manuscript production.[5] Nevertheless, despite the commercial risks inherent in an industry of such rapid technological advancement, some four thousand editions were printed in Venice by the century's end.[6] After Johannes de

1. I am much indebted in this paragraph to Pettegree (2010) 49–51, 55–62. Specifically on Venice see Gerulaitis (1976); Lowry (1979), esp. 7–47, and (1991); B. Richardson (1994) 28, 39, 42, 109, and 200 n.44; Fremmer (2001); Nuovo (2013), esp. 21–45; Marzo Magno (2013).

2. See Fremmer (2001) 51–107, esp. 67 (10–20 percent of Venetians "more or less" literate in the fourteenth and fifteenth centuries); for Grendler (1989) 42–7, 78 and (1992) 213, by the late 1500s around 33 percent of adult males and 13 percent of females could read. Cipolla (1969) 57–8 points out that illiteracy was actually an asset (for reasons of guaranteeing confidentiality) in certain branches of the fifteenth-century Venetian administration; yet even though in mid-century "about two thirds of the adult [male] population in Venice was essentially illiterate" (pp. 58–9), literacy "made noticeable progress" (p. 23) thereafter.

3. For the privilege, Kostylo (2008b).

4. Significantly financed by Johannes de Colonia, who married Johannes de Spira's widow, Paola, in 1471, and quickly became one of the leading figures in the Venetian print industry: Nuovo (2013) 21–31.

5. See further on such misgivings B. Richardson (2009) 10–14, pointing to (i) the challenge that "print seemed to demand a greater degree of polish in the use of the Italian language," (ii) "the ambiguous social and cultural status of printing," and (iii) the perceived power of money to buy fame through print publication, thereby potentially compromising the quality of the printed word.

6. Venetian numbers: Pettegree (2010) 52 with Lowry (1979) 7–8.

Spira's untimely death, the French engraver Nicholas Jenson (*c.* 1420–80) emerged as Venice's most celebrated publisher in the 1470s, in robust partnership with two Frankfurt merchants, Johannes Rauchfass and Peter Ugelheimer.[7] Beyond following a sound commercial strategy by focusing on specialist productions in law, medicine, and theology, Jenson gained renown by breaking away from the traditional black-letter or Gothic types (based on written script) and introducing instead the first model roman types. When Venice was stricken with plague in 1478, half of the twenty-two print companies then active either suspended operations or left the city. Two syndicates, one of them French (based on Jenson's firm) and the other deriving from Johannes de Spira's firm, merged to form a single conglomerate at the end of the 1470s, but from the end of 1481 there is no record of its activities.[8] Even as the shadow of past prosperity lingered, new names gave Venice's publishing world a more diffuse character in the 1480s.[9] Yet by that decade major printers had sufficient measure of their markets to be able to focus on particular kinds of publication, with confidence that they could match supply and demand while also guaranteeing a high-quality product.[10]

Such was the general picture when Aldo Manuzio arrived at Venice at the end of the 1480s, already an established humanist scholar and teacher who was then approaching his forties.[11] In Chapter 3 we observed Manuzio's importance in philhellene circles at Venice from the 1490s onward, and his centrality to the developments that gave rise to the so-called New Academy early in the new century.[12] Before his arrival in Venice, little printing of Greek had taken place there, and little elsewhere in Italy or in Europe generally. Demand for Greek books was small, and much of that demand was in any case for elementary grammars and primers; however, most challenging of all to the nascent printing industry was the technical difficulty of rendering Greek script in type form.[13] Hence only Homer, Theocritus, and part of Hesiod had been printed before the emergence of the Aldine Press, and only some sixty Greek editions, bilingual volumes included, were produced by the end of the fifteenth century; this was in fact a respectable number when

7. See Lowry (1991) with Nuovo (2013) 31–4.

8. Concisely on these developments, Nuovo (2013) 28–9 with Lowry (1979) 18–19.

9. Lowry (1979) 19.

10. Davies (1995a) 9.

11. In general on Manuzio, Lowry (1979) with Dionisotti (1963); H. G. Fletcher (1988) and (1995); Barker (1992); Marcon and Zorzi (1994); Davies (1995a); Zeidberg (1998); Marzo Magno (2013) 43–60; for further bibliography, Kallendorf (2010); and now Beltramini and Gasparotto (2016) with Wilson (2016) and Grant (2017).

12. Chapter 3 pp. 128–9.

13. Barker (1992), esp. 21–42, with Davies (1995a) 9–10.

viewed against all the early impediments to the printing of Greek.[14] In this climate Manuzio set himself the daunting task of committing to type the works of Greek antiquity that had yet to be published in the original language. Capital for the new press was supplied by Andrea Torresano (1451–1528), an established publisher in Venice who, in 1493, oversaw the first edition of Manuzio's own Latin grammar, the *Institutiones grammaticae*;[15] another key underwriter in the early days, the highly placed Pierfrancesco Barbarigo,[16] invested heavily in the firm, with a stake that brought him half of the firm's profits while the other half was shared by Torresano and Manuzio, probably jointly.[17] After the appearance of Lascaris' grammar in February–March 1495, Manuzio's first book to bear a date,[18] in the two decades between 1495 and 1515 (albeit with intermissions totaling four or so years) he was remarkably productive, overseeing some thirty-one editions in thirty-eight volumes on the Greek side alone. His Aristotle, initiated by the *Organon* of November 1, 1495[19] and then supplemented by four more volumes in 1497–8, was a landmark event that secured his reputation: "in terms of the labour involved and the magnificence of the result," opines Martin Davies, this Aldine Aristotle constitutes no less than "the greatest publishing venture of the fifteenth century."[20]

By 1499, however, a change of direction is observable at the Aldine Press. For all his pioneering achievements thus far, and for all the romanticized image of Manuzio as "a dedicated humanist sponsored by a dedicated humanist and prince [sc. Alberto Pio of Carpi],"[21] the fact remained that the expensive Greek texts that he produced found a small market, and that he himself inevitably had to defer to his financial backers. Hence came the pressure to adopt a more diverse range of productivity—a development that appears to have fueled complaints early in the

14. Davies (1995a) 10.

15. See Scaccia Scarafoni (1947) with Jensen (1998) and now Grant (2017) 170–9; beyond business partner, Torresano was also Manuzio's father-in-law.

16. The son of Marco Barbarigo, seventy-third Doge of Venice in 1485–6, and nephew of Agostino Barbarigo, Doge from 1486 to 1501.

17. See Davies (1995a) 13 with Lowry (1979) 85.

18. Cf. Chapter 3 p. 131 and n.96.

19. *Organon*/ὄργανον, literally "Instrument," according to Minio-Paluello (1963) 254–5 a title not in fact derived from antiquity but from an epigram prefixed to the 1495 Aldine edition.

20. Davies (1995a) 20.

21. Lowry (1979) 86. For Alberto Pio, Chapter 3 p. 119, but cf. also Davies (1995a) 13: "Whether Albert Pio . . . also contributed capital we do not know for certain: in the many fulsome prefaces addressed to him, it is difficult to disentangle the practical from the moral backing. But it seems beyond doubt from the dedication to Pio of all five parts of the Greek edition of Aristotle that the long years of preparation had some substantial support from him."

new century that Torresano was blocking publication in Greek and that Manuzio had "deserted Greece for Italy."[22] Certainly, production on the Greek side showed a significant decline: according to Martin Lowry, 4,212 leaves were produced up to 1500, a number that fell to 2,235 between 1500 and 1503; in those years, the proportion of Latin (3,839 leaves) to Greek (2,235) amounts to an almost exact reversal of the proportion up to 1500.[23] Yet despite this reduction on the Greek side, the diversity of Manuzio's productivity in the first years of the new century was astonishing, and he was printing in four languages, namely in Hebrew as well as in Greek, Latin, and the Italian vernacular.[24] On the Latin side, this process of diversification is marked by two signal productions of 1499, the first of them the *Cornucopiae, sive linguae latinae commentarii* of Niccolò Perotti (1429/30–80). On one view a "ponderous lexicographic commentary on Martial,"[25] this book in fact amounts to a massive, and massively rich, encyclopedic compendium (just over 700 pages in the Aldine version) on the Latin language, containing as it does Perotti's definitions of Latin words with some twelve thousand illustrative quotations drawn from Latin authors.[26]

The second work is the remarkable *Hypnerotomachia Poliphili* ("Poliphilo's dream of love-struggle"),[27] that famous two-book allegorical prose romance whose dream story of Poliphilo's yearning for and pursuit of his beloved Polia follows a bizarre sequence of events and scene shifts that approaches the absurd even by the forgiving standards of the genre.[28] This work, so different from its scholarly Aldine predecessors in its *prima facie* content and plot line, corresponded to what in modern terms would be called a commissioned book,[29] and Manuzio was evidently hesitant about its prospects.[30] But however "dull" and "unreadable" in terms of its

22. Lowry (1979) 86 with Davies (1995a) 32.

23. Lowry (1979) 141–2.

24. On these points, Lowry (1979) 142. For Hebrew letters pioneered by Manuzio at Venice, Marx (1919) with Lowry 105 n.71 and Campos (1994).

25. Oliver (1947) 376; cf. p. 377 n.1 for "the arrangement of a lexicon in the form of a commentary on Martial" as "perhaps the most unhappy idea ever to be conceived in the history of lexicography."

26. See further Ogilvie (2006) 118; Furno (1995); Stok (2002).

27. So Stewering (2000) 6, but see further on the title's polyphonic suggestiveness P. F. Brown (1996) 208. For the *Hypnerotomachia* see already Chapter 4 p. 160; the standard edition with commentary is Pozzi and Ciapponi (1980).

28. So Lefaivre (1997) 8.

29. See H. G. Fletcher (1995) 48.

30. Lowry (1979) 125.

storyline,[31] from a purely technical standpoint the *Hypnerotomachia* amounts to a singular achievement, an extremely adventurous visual text or textual vision in which some 170 woodcuts, all original in design, picture many of the scenes, architectural settings, and characters that Poliphilo encounters in his dreams; it was the only illustrated book that Manuzio ever produced. Narrative flow is itself aided and figured through pictorial representation (sampled in Figure 5.1): a number of sequential double-page illustrations create the illusion that progress through the storyline is matched by actual physical movement, while the recurrence of images generates visual momentum of its own from one page to the next. The text itself is made mobile and mutable through variations in page layout that reproduce, in the tradition of Greek *technopaignia*, such forms as vases and drinking vessels.[32] Beyond this sympathetic interplay of text and image, however, the printed word is itself visually striking on its own terms, partly because it was the first vernacular work printed by Manuzio. From the linguistic standpoint, the text is perhaps best described as a hybrid production written in "a Latinate Italian or an Italianate Latin,"[33] and teeming with a sort of Joycean invention[34] as its author restlessly "form[s] new words, adding Latin suffixes and prefixes to Italian words, and vice versa, creating adverbs, verbs, adjectives, diminutives, and augmentatives."[35] Cryptic and esoteric terminology, sudden shifts of construction and subject, and smatterings of Greek, Hebrew, Arabic, and even hieroglyphics[36] add to the disconcerting visual-linguistic effect. But this quirkiness is offset by one of the most attractive features of the *Hypnerotomachia*: its Aldine roman font. After Nicholas Jenson's invention of roman, this font was developed and refined by Manuzio's master cutter—Francesco Griffo, a key figure in our story to whom we shall soon return—into the Aldine roman first used in *De Aetna*.[37] Griffo subsequently reapplied the lower case of this font in the *Hypnerotomachia* with light adjustments to it, but he revised the upper case by basing it on inscriptional models and reducing its scale in proportion to the small letters.[38]

31. So at least Ivins (1923) 249, but that assessment is clearly open to challenge. So, e.g., Carver (2007) 184 on the work as "probably the most remarkable piece of prose fiction to emerge in the fifteenth century," providing as it does "a conspectus of ancient, medieval, and Renaissance fiction."

32. Further, Donati (1950) 155–6 with P. F. Brown (1996) 212.

33. H. G. Fletcher (1995) 48; further, P. F. Brown (1996) 211 with Rowland (1998) 64.

34. Lefaivre (1997) 83.

35. Trippe (2002) 1229.

36. On which Millet (2012), esp. 270–1, with Iversen (1958) 19, P. F. Brown (1996) 212–13, and Vercellin (2001) 53–7 (on Arabic).

37. See Mardersteig (1964) = (1988) 107–58 with (1969a) = (1988) 197–215.

38. See Mardersteig (1964) 136–7 = (1988) 139, and also (1969a) 224–5 = (1988) 199, with Berry and Poole (1966) 68: "Griffo's [*De Aetna*] character has the dignity of Jenson's roman, but surpasses

As with so much that is disorienting in the *Hypnerotomachia*, its anonymous author's identity has drawn much conjecture. Amidst other circumstantial evidence, the case for Francesco Colonna (1433–1527, a Dominican monk of Venetian origin) as author is based in large part on an acrostic formed from the initial woodcut capitals that begin each of the thirty-eight chapters, to the effect of *Poliam Frater Franciscus Columna Peramavit* ("Brother Francesco Colonna deeply loved Polia"). But whoever the author was, whether this first Colonna or a namesake who belonged to the powerful Roman Colonna family (born *c.* 1453, from 1484 Lord of Palestrina), whether Leon Battista Alberti (1404–74)[39] or—at the more imaginative end of speculation—Lorenzo de' Medici or even Manuzio himself,[40] there can be no doubt about the depth and breadth of this humanist's learning. Quite apart from the sophistication of its linguistic experimentation and its wealth of allusion to a vast network of source texts and genres,[41] the work shows a striking familiarity with the specialist writings of Vitruvius and Leon Battista Alberti in the myriad descriptions of buildings, gardens and architectural design that occupy more than half the book. But then there is so much more, a cascade of contents well brought out in Liane Lefaivre's breathless description of it:

> Far from being limited to architecture, the astounding level of erudition in the *Hypnerotomachia* extends to other fields. No person, no place, no thing is presented without reference to classical mythology, classical geography, classical art. The story offers its own interpretation on every page by referring to [a] vast amount of scholarly detail. The range of topics is exhaustive: music, musical instruments, *ars topiaria*, statuary, fountains, mosaics, intaglio and intarsio techniques, woven fabrics and cloth, geometry, the effects of distance on the perception of color, epitaphs, furniture, paintings, embroidery, herms, friezes, vases, tripods, trophies, candelabras, lapidary, perfume, food, wine, opera, choreography, ritual processions, and botany.[42]

---

it in vigour. Generously rounded, yet tall and strongly serifed, it has a sparkle and elegance unique in fifteenth century types. The capitals were considered to be too heavy and squat and another version was cut which Aldus first used . . . in a Perottus *Cornucopia* of July 1499 and then in December 1499 in the *Hypnerotomachia* of Francesco Colonna, where the new larger and lighter capitals work splendidly with the original lower case."

39. So Lefaivre (1997).

40. For overviews see Rowland (1998) 272–3 with P. F. Brown (1996) 287–90; on the problem of the illustrator's identity, Painter (1984) 179–83.

41. Conveniently, Lefaivre (1997) 42 with P. F. Brown (1996) 214–16.

42. Lefaivre (1997) 41–2. Alchemy might be added to the list: Blunt (1937) 123–6.

This congested listing of the topics on offer in the *Hypnerotomachia* well captures the crammed storehouse of knowledge that is this extraordinary work. For now, however, the visual and physical properties of the book are paramount: in 1499 it presupposed a reader-viewer who encountered for the first time a multidimensional text that was far ahead of its time; it was, as Lefaivre well puts it, "the first ever experimental montage of fragments of prose, typography, epigrams, and pictures," "an extraordinary visual-typographical-textual 'assemblage' of a type not repeated until the avant-garde books of the 1920s and 1930s in Russia, Italy, and France."[43] It is little wonder that the *Hypnerotomachia* has been heralded as the most glorious of Renaissance books,[44] and as one of the most beautiful books, even the most beautiful, ever produced.[45] And yet another novelty of the *Hypnerotomachia* is that the famous Aldine printer's device of the dolphin-and-anchor emblem appeared first in prototype in this work, albeit in a horizontal configuration that is out of keeping with the predominantly vertical format of the printed page.[46] Thereafter the device was printed with a vertical orientation—a modification that again sets the *Hypnerotomachia* apart as a highly idiosyncratic Aldine production.

As for Griffo, much about the precise identity, origins, and life of this master type cutter remains uncertain, but the case for identifying him with the painter and goldsmith Francesco di Marco di Giacomo Raibolini of Bologna (known as Francesco Francia, *c.* 1450–1517) has long been discredited.[47] Our man, still active after Raibolini's death, is more probably the *Franciscus Griffus de Bononia* [sc. Bologna] *incisor litterarum stampae* mentioned in the Perugian archives for 1512.[48] This Francesco possibly designed the roman types deployed by the brothers Giovanni and Gregorio de Gregori in their productions of the *Decameron* in 1492, a translation of Herodotus in 1494, and Johannes de Ketham's *Fasciculus medicinae* of 1495;[49] and his ownership of the punches—a point that will shortly matter because of Griffo's later wrangling with Manuzio—is signaled by his subsequent use of them at the Aldine Press.[50] Griffo's crucial importance to the Aldine success is

---

43. Lefaivre (1997) 17.

44. Barolini (1992) 91.

45. See Pottinger (1941) 74; Donati (1950) 140.

46. See H. G. Fletcher (1988) 44 with (1995) 26. Much has been made of Bembo's role in Aldo's adoption of the device for his printer's mark: see Chapter 7 p. 281 and n.71.

47. See, decisively, Mardersteig (1964) 121 = (1988) 121 with Orioli (1900) 178–9.

48. Lowry (1979) 87 with Orioli (1900) 179; see further the materials collected by Milroy (1999) with Norton (1958) 8–10 and Barker (1992) 44, 62–3, 102–3.

49. Mardersteig (1964) 118–19 = (1988) 117–19 with Lowry (1979) 88.

50. Mardersteig (1964) 119 = (1988) 119.

touchingly commemorated in the following inscription that Manuzio inserted in the title page verso of the 1501 octavo Virgil:

IN GRAMMATOGLYPTAE LAUDEM:
Qui graiis dedit Aldus, en latinis
Dat nunc grammata scalpta daedaleis
Francisci manibus Bononiensis.[51]

IN PRAISE OF THE LETTER-CARVER:
Look! Aldus, who gave letters for Greek works, now
gives them, engraved by the Daedalian hands
of Francesco da Bologna, for Latin works.

But then came trouble: Manuzio and Griffo fell out early in the new century. Seeking to protect his company's heavy investment in print design, Manuzio sought from the Venetian senate, and on March 23, 1501 was granted, a ten-year privilege[52] that gave him exclusive rights over the use of italic type in the Venetian domains. Three further Venetian privileges, two senatorial and one dogal, were granted on, respectively, October 17 and November 14, 1502 and March 17, 1505; Manuzio also received papal protection by the privileges that were granted by Alexander VI on December 17, 1502, by Julius II on January 27, 1513, and by Leo X on November 28, 1513.[53] For all Manuzio's claims in his petitions to have invented the italic cursive and new methods of printing Greek, Griffo was undeniably responsible for their implementation, as Manuzio himself acknowledged in the 1501 inscription as cited above. In seeking his privileges Manuzio may not have set out maliciously to harm Griffo's interests, but the latter was in effect prevented from selling any of his designs to other printers. Antagonized by this loss of earnings, and perhaps by his place in Manuzio's shadow, Griffo appears to have left Venice in late 1502 to find work elsewhere—a parting of the ways that coincides all too suggestively in date with the privileges granted on October 17 and November 14 of that year.

Griffo is known to have cut several punches for Lyonese firms, which produced some fifty-nine "Aldines" between 1501 and 1526.[54] He also prepared duplicate punches for the Jewish-Italian printer Girolamo Soncino of Fano,[55] who, in the

51. Orlandi (1975) 1.49 no. XXVII B, with reproduction (Tav. V) opposite p. xxxii; now Pagliaroli (2015) 105 and n.14 and Grant (2017) 16–17.

52. Conveniently for which, H. G. Fletcher (1988) 143.

53. For these privileges, H. G. Fletcher (1988) 144–56.

54. Steinberg (1996) 34.

55. For whom Lowry (1979) 88–90 with Amran (1909) 70–145 and Boorman (2006) 232–4.

dedicatory preface to Cesare Borgia in his 1503 printing of the *Opere volgari* of Petrarch, launches the following attack on Manuzio:

> . . . through my persuasion there have come here not only the most notable and capable compositors whom it was possible to bring, but also a most noble cutter of Latin, Greek and Hebrew type, called Messer Francesco da Bologna, whose skill I certainly believe to be unequalled in this work. For he not only knows how to cut fonts most perfectly *but he has invented a new form of letters called cursive or chancery, which neither Aldo Romano nor others who cunningly have tried to adorn themselves with the plumes of others, but this very Messer Francesco first invented and designed*, and it was he who cut all the fonts of letters from which the said Aldo ever printed, as well as the present font with a grace and beauty that speak for themselves.[56]

After serving other printers Griffo eventually returned in 1516 to his native Bologna, where he founded a press of his own; he had ambitious plans, but only six works are known to have appeared from the press.[57] The last echo of his dispute with Manuzio is heard in the preface to his 1516 edition of Petrarch's *Canzoniere*, where Griffo stingingly refers to the types—his own creation—with which Manuzio "had not only come into much wealth, but had assured himself of immortal fame with posterity."[58]

There the written record of the Manuzio-Griffo saga ends, but Griffo's colorful life was to take an extraordinary turn before he vanished from the historical record. From Bolognese archive documents inspected by Emilio Orioli at the end of the nineteenth century,[59] it emerges that Griffo had a single child, Caterina, who married a certain Cristoforo, a merchant; the newlyweds lived with Griffo. For reasons that remain unclear, however, in May 1518 Griffo and Cristoforo came to blows. By one account the two men engaged in a duel with swords, but Cristoforo sought to escape, whether through revulsion at the proceedings or through fear of being bested by the vigorous Griffo. In that moment Griffo seized an iron bar—"perhaps an incomplete type punch?"[60]—and struck his son-in-law on the head with such force that Cristoforo died a few days afterward. Before this final showdown,

56. Trans. Amran (1909) 98; my emphasis.

57. See the detailed listing in Norton (1958) 9.

58. Amran (1909) 102–3.

59. See Orioli (1900) 177–83 for the following narrative of events.

60. Lowry (1979) 88.

Caterina had apparently taken her father's side against Cristoforo, and such was her strength of feeling that, after the young man had fallen, she allegedly wanted to wound him in his side with the very sword that he had let drop. Griffo was accused of murder, his daughter of complicity, but the surviving records make no mention of the judicial outcome. In a contract of October 5, 1519, however, he is referred to as deceased.[61] Hence the distinct possibility that Griffo, that typographical Daedalus, died on the gallows.

5.2: *The Aldine Octavo Handbook*

The Aldine interest in physical form found its most important development in the innovative *libelli portatiles*, or "portable little books,"[62] that Manuzio launched with the publication of his Virgil in April 1501. The novelty of these volumes lay in the newness not just of their handy octavo format but also of their italic typeface, which emulated the humanist cursive form that had become fashionable in the fifteenth century; favored by scribes of the city chancelleries, it came to be known as *cancellaresca* ("chancery") script. Decorous but unencumbered in their binding,[63] these Aldine volumes also offered an edited text unencumbered by the weight of commentary associated with the more traditional, larger-format (folio or quarto) scholastic book that catered more for study and reference than for plain reading. Whereas the realities of keeping the scholastic book secure but accessible meant that it tended to be fixed in place (whether chained to a desk, say, or attached to a cabinet), and so required the user to stand or sit often uncomfortably before it, the octavo was far more convenient because it was physically so easy to use in virtually any position and posture.[64] Despite the "modern" novelty that is often associated with these *libelli portatiles*, however, the portable book was not in fact an Aldine invention, but rather an adaptation of the religious or devotional books, hand-sized in form and of elongated, narrow shape, that were available long before 1501;[65] by committing Classical and Italian literature to print in the octavo format,

---

61. See Orioli (1900) 181 for the wording *Domina Caterina quondam Francisci de Griffis*.

62. Described by Manuzio himself as *Libelli portatiles in formam enchiridii* ("Portable little books in the shape of a handbook") on p. 4 of the catalogue of June 22, 1503 (= Orlandi [1975] Tav. XIII, opposite 1.79); further on the phenomenon, Lowry (1979) 142–7 with H. G. Fletcher (1995) 49–54 and Davies (1995a) 40–50.

63. It is improbable that Manuzio used an in-house bindery: see Quilici (1992), esp. 384–5, with Hobson (1998).

64. H. G. Fletcher (1988) 88; further on the scholastic "libro da banco," Petrucci (1969) 297–8.

65. For a statistical listing of octavo editions printed in Venice and elsewhere in Italy between 1465 and 1500, B. Richardson (1999) 127.

Manuzio introduced what Carlo Dionisotti nicely characterizes as a "prayer book of a lay culture."[66] But in other ways as well the Aldines combined novelty with a retrospective aspect.[67] So in graphic design the octavos applied geometric principles that were long traditional.[68] As for italic type in general (as opposed to its specifically Aldine application), it was based on the script that was first regularly used by the distinguished Florentine humanist Niccolò Niccoli (*c.* 1364–1437)—a form of humanistic cursive sprinkled with gothic, and a precursor of italic type form just as the script of Poggio Bracciolini (1380–1459), Niccoli's friend, provided the prototype for roman fonts.[69] After the rise of chancery, Manuzio and Griffo followed contemporary humanist fashion in adapting the cursive script to their italic type;[70] Aldine italics are first glimpsed, possibly in rough-hewn prototype, in the five words on the woodcut frontispiece of the September 1500 edition of the *Letters* of Catherine of Siena.[71] Various hands have been claimed as models for the Aldine italic, most notably those of Pomponio Leto (1428–98),[72] Bartolomeo Sanvito (1435–1518)[73] and Manuzio himself, none with anything approaching certainty. But whether or not we suspect a particular Aldine source, his key aim was to capture the personal feel of the handwritten book in printed form, perhaps in reaction to what Martin Lowry characterizes as "the stylistic lethargy into which [printing] had fallen since Jenson's death."[74]

It has often been supposed that Manuzio applied the italic as a cost-cutting device that compressed the text laterally across the page, thereby saving paper. Hence Manuzio himself has been viewed in some quarters as a committed social

---

66. Dionisotti (1966b) 14 = Vela (2002) 28. Manuzio's reliance on established precedents is also indicated by his dedicatory letter to Pietro Bembo in the October 1514 Virgil, to the effect that he "took this small format of the hand-book from your library, or rather from that of your most kind father, Bernardo" (Orlandi [1975] 1.152 no. LXXXIX; H. G. Fletcher [1988] 78; Barker [1992] 114; now Grant [2017] 162–3).

67. For this "backward look," Carter (1969) 31.

68. See Montecchi (1992).

69. Ullman (1960) 60.

70. See Barker (1992) 109–16.

71. See H. G. Fletcher (1988) 79. Proof versions of the 1501 Virgil were also in circulation "well in advance of publication, and outside Venice at that" (Fletcher 79, but see also p. 82).

72. See Barker (1992) 113–14 with H. G. Fletcher (1988) 77, 79.

73. See Barker (1992) 114 with H. G. Fletcher (1988) 77–8, and cf. Wardrop (1963) 35: "Did Bartolomeo Sanvito, the friend of the Aldine academicians Fra Giocondo and Bernardo Bembo, . . . the type-founder associate of Aldus, did Sanvito come into the picture? If so, to what extent? His script and Aldus's type are not identical; but I know of no other script which, in form and print, so closely resembles it."

74. Lowry (1979) 141.

liberal, a master designer set on disseminating the good literary word.[75] But space was not necessarily saved by recourse to an italic font;[76] if Manuzio's aim was to reduce the cost of his editions, why did he run to the expense of having 150 separate sorts cut and cast, and why the contemporary criticism of his generous margins?[77] In petitioning the Venetian senate for privileges to protect his italic, he advertises its attractive appearance, not its cost-effectiveness: why this emphasis if cost-cutting was so important?[78] In a surviving copy of the Aldine catalogue of June 22, 1503, Manuzio made handwritten entries that are datable to 1505 on the basis of the titles listed therein: the Latin octavos are priced at three marcelli each (Greek octavos were at least twice as expensive), a sum equivalent to a quarter of a ducat in times when a skilled worker could expect to earn about three ducats a month.[79] Even if we accept the still rosier estimate that the Latin octavos could be bought by their likely market of educated professionals (teachers, civil servants, etc.) for the equivalent of one or two days' salary,[80] and even if they were generally cheaper than books on the market before 1501, the fact remains that they were still expensive in absolute terms. Further evidence to this effect is supplied by the rapidity with which forgers copied the italic type and octavo format, thereby causing Manuzio to seek protection by privilege and to take legal action against rogue competitors.[81] While these forgeries attest to the market impact of the Aldines, they also suggest that the originals quickly faced competition from cheaper imitations: however (relatively) inexpensive they may have been in one way, the Aldines were evidently costly enough to provoke significant price competition. All in all, modern perceptions of Manuzio as a crusading figure who sought to bring high literature to an expanding readership in a convenient, inexpensive format are surely misleading, and Martin Lowry more realistic: "Aldus' ideals were of editorship and design, and the purpose of his octavos was to set standards of scholarship and taste, not to take learning to a wider audience."[82] On this approach, Lowry rightly challenges comparison of the Aldine production of octavos to the rise of

75. Overview in Lowry (1992) 238.

76. Carter (1969) 74.

77. See Lowry (1979) 141.

78. Lowry (1992) 240.

79. See H. G. Fletcher (1988) 90–1 with Lowry (1992) 240–1.

80. H. G. Fletcher (1988) 90.

81. Counterfeit editions of the Virgil began to appear in Lyons by 1502 at the latest: see Shaw (1993) 117 and *passim* with B. Richardson (1999) 42–3 and Kostylo (2008a), and now also Grant (2017) 244–53.

82. Lowry (1992) 251.

the modern paperback:[83] "if the printer knew that he was widely heralded as the originator of some kind of 'paper-back revolution,' he would probably writhe in his unknown grave."[84]

Despite this qualified view of Manuzio's motivation in launching the octavos, they nevertheless played a key role in emancipating learning,[85] at least in the sense that they allowed the Renaissance humanists to encounter the Classical past in a strikingly different and flexible way. These status symbols[86] sold well, finding a strong market among (in Martin Davies' nice formulation) "persons who had education but little leisure, or education and too much leisure"[87]—cultured readers on the move such as prelates, politicians, and diplomats, for whom the more static properties and dense commentary of the traditional scholastic book were inconvenient or unappealing. A fitting spokesperson for this group is an early customer, the Hungarian royal secretary Sigismund Thurzo, who, in a letter to Manuzio of December 20, 1501, writes as follows from Budapest:

> For since my various activities leave me no spare time to spend on the poets and orators in my house, your books—which are so handy that I can use them while walking and even so to speak, while playing the courtier, whenever I find a chance—have become a special delight to me.[88]

To illustrate the point further through a different medium, the handiness about which Thurzo so enthuses here is suggestively emblematized in a famous sixteenth-century portrait whose attribution has been much disputed. This *Portrait of a Young Man with a Green Book* (Figure 5.2), long in the possession of the distinguished Onigo family in Treviso, was acquired by the English art patron and historian Sir Herbert Cook in 1907; it currently resides in the Fine Arts Museums in San Francisco.[89] Because of this association with the Onigo family, the young man has been tentatively identified as either Giovanni Onigo or his

83. See H. G. Fletcher (1995) 49 with (1988) 88 ("a sort of paperback revolution before paperbacks").

84. Lowry (1979) 142. Cf. also Dionisotti (1965) 269 = Vela (2002) 93 for withering remarks on Clough (1965a) 3 on Manuzio's alleged role "in the introduction of cheaply printed books—a revolution comparable in its time to the paperback books of today."

85. Lowry (1979) 147.

86. Beltramini, Gasparotto, and Tura (2013) 128.

87. Davies (1995a) 46.

88. Nolhac (1888) 26 no. 23; trans. Grafton (1999) 186; now also Grant (2017) 242–3. See also John Lascaris' letter to Manuzio of December 24, 1501 (Nolhac 26–8 no. 24) with Lowry (1976) 396 and n.3.

89. Succinctly on its ownership history, Ballarin (2013) 147.

cousin Pileo,[90] but much uncertainty remains. The portrait is acknowledged to show multiple traits of Giorgione (born Giorgio Barbarelli da Castelfranco, *c.* 1477/8–1510), but also discrepancies that enjoin caution; hence the alternative attributions that have been proposed. The details of this controversy are now usefully summarized and updated by Alessandro Ballarin.[91] But Ballarin's own position in the debate is of special interest because, disowning his own former attribution to Giovanni Antonio de' Sacchis (known as Pordenone, *c.* 1484–1539) to around 1515 ("un errore di giovinezza"), he instead attributes the portrait to Giorgione himself in *c.* 1502.[92] If this attribution and dating are provisionally accepted, and if for now we leave aside the problem of the sitter's identity, that sitter is still recognizable as an idealized manifestation of the early-sixteenth-century reader.

Man and book form a tight unity in this picture, but the book compellingly draws the viewer's eye through its placement in the left foreground, and through the decorous combination of its Moroccan green leather cover, the golden corner effects that encase the front cover, and the central stud design that completes what amounts to an inset portrait of the volume itself. Given its physical dimensions and elegant but not overwrought appearance, the book has been interpreted as an example of the new Aldine octavos.[93] It is significant that no table, desk, or bookrest of any kind is shown: supported by the young man's right hand alone, the volume sits comfortably in his fingers, as if light and agile in feel, and as easy on the arm as it is on the eye. The young man's glove, with its protruding finger for the easy turning of the pages, betokens the cultured book lover who appears, from the direction of his gaze, to be reflecting on an idea stirred by his silent reading. In this regard the portrait sees inwardly, capturing the inner stimulus provoked by the book; the contrast between the young man's lightly drawn features and the darkness that prevails at the base of the portrait suggests his rise toward illumination. The experience of reading is itself projected as intensely private and personally meaningful, devotion to literature perhaps implicitly in tension (as in Bembo's case) with dutiful loyalty to the official *cursus*.[94] If we accept that the book is an Aldine octavo, however, the portrait's key significance for now lies in its vision of "modernity" in *c.* 1502—not just the

90. So, e.g., Cook himself (1910) 328.

91. Ballarin (2013).

92. Ballarin (2013) 148.

93. See esp. Macola (2007) 90–6 ("Un lettore aldino") with Ballarin (2013) 148–9.

94. Cf. Beltramini, Gasparotto, and Tura (2013) 128 (the engrossed sitter "rappresenta in tutto una nuova generazione di aristocratici veneziani che sempre più si sentono estranei al tradizionale *cursus honorum* dei padri").

technical modernity of the Aldine product, but also that of its fashionable and sensitive model reader.[95] Given his own affiliations with courtly society, both literal (in his two-year sojourn at Ferrara in 1497–9) and literary (in *Gli Asolani*), and given his closeness to the Aldine Press in the later 1490s, Pietro Bembo himself closely conforms to this Giorgionesque ideal—an affinity felt still more strongly if we suspect that Pietro had a hand in devising the handy Aldine *libelli portatiles* in the first place.[96]

5.3: The Interrelationship of Physical Form and Textual Meaning

This brief sampling of Aldine experimentation at the physical level, whether in typeface design or in overall book format, has focused on two main examples, the 1499 *Hypnerotomachia* and the octavos that flowed forth from 1501 onward—examples that are offered as a prelude of sorts to our examination of the circumstances in which *De Aetna* was published in February 1496. More specifically, I impute to *De Aetna* the first Aldine expression in Latin of a key creative concept that Manuzio was to reapply with great imaginative power in such projects as the *Hypnerotomachia* and the octavos, namely that *the physical and/or typographical form in which a given work is presented is inseparable from its textual meaning.*

To put the point differently, the book historian John Feather comments as follows on the relationship between text and book as physical object:

> The relationship between text and object is a complex one, which has rarely been considered, and yet it could be argued that *our understanding of a text is ultimately influenced by the physical form of its presentation*. . . [Feather's] principal point is . . . that authors can only envisage the dissemination of their works in the physical form that is the normal product of the techniques available at the time of writing. When the techniques or the forms undergo major changes, such as those from the scroll to the codex, or from manuscript to print, or from print to V[isual] D[isplay] U[nit], the text itself may be the same, *but the reader's perception of it is profoundly different*.[97]

95. Cf. Romani (2013) 37 on this "intensa apparizione del lettore ideale delle edizioni aldine."

96. On this last thought, Petrucci (1969) 310.

97. Feather (1986) 13; my emphasis. Cf. for the general point B. Richardson (1999) 122 ("form defines the way in which the text is read"), himself citing McKenzie (1999) 17 ("the particular enquiry I wish to pursue is whether or not the material forms of books, the non-verbal elements of the typographic notations within them, the very disposition of space itself, have an expressive function in conveying meaning") and Chartier (1994) 10 (on "the traditional sort of literary history that thinks of the work as an abstract text whose typographic forms are without importance").

The complex relationship to which Feather refers here between text and book-as-object has an immediate relevance to Manuzio's achievement and legacy. However uninspired the storyline of the *Hypnerotomachia* of 1499 may have been, the work's distinctive visual personality—its combination of linguistic eccentricity, lavish woodcut illustration, and freshness of typeface in the recently devised and revised Aldine roman—is integral to the book's overall meaning not just as an erotic adventure but as a print adventure: the reader's "normative" perception and expectations are meant to be challenged, even transformed, by the novel textual/physical experience offered by this extraordinary production. So in the case of the *libelli portatiles*, the evocations of humanistic cursive script and devotional handbooks are offset by the obvious novelty of format and typeface in the Aldine italic octavo. In, say, the 1501 Virgil, the text may in one sense remain the same (albeit newly edited), but the simple elegance of the work as presented in this format, the ease with which it is carried and used, and the new mobility of the Classical reading experience all contribute to the change of reader perspective that is provoked by the innovative physical object. If we seek a model symbolization of this change, Giorgione's (?) young man is plausibly our guide.

In the case of *De Aetna*, however, Feather's comments take on added interest because of the work's larger print history within Bembo's lifetime. Almost certainly Pietro's first publication and the first Latin book to be published by Manuzio, *De Aetna* broke new ground as a secular production by a living author who had yet to establish his reputation in the world of letters.[98] Given that Pietro sought from the Republic no privilege of protection for the printing of the work, that there was no listing of it in Manuzio's two earliest catalogues of available books, and that Bembo had a strong incentive to distribute complimentary copies to certain Venetian patricians who might influence his advancement, *De Aetna* may well have been published at his own expense at the Aldine Press.[99] If so, the novel print form of the book matched the spirit of adventure on display both in its subject matter—the climb of Etna—and in Pietro's outlay on its production. Of thirty folios in quarto (21.5 by 15.5 centimeters), this relatively slight work nevertheless marked a "watershed"[100] in the history of printing, set as it was in the new Aldine roman typeface. For the eminent incunabulist George Painter, Griffo's achievement in *De Aetna* amounted to "a manifesto":

---

98. Pincus (2008) 101.

99. On these points, Clough (1998) 59–60.

100. Cf. Stanley Morison as given in Crutchley (2011) 50 (already cited in my Introduction p. 9 n.31).

> Since the achievements in the 1470's of the de Spira brothers and Nicholas Jenson, who had introduced roman types of surpassing beauty based on the athletic elegance of manuscript hands, the standards of Venetian roman had declined in the direction of cheapness and nastiness. Aldus's new roman [for *De Aetna*] was a manifesto: rivalling Jenson's in classic dignity, it was for the first time consciously designed according to purely typographic ideals, in liberation from manuscript models. Rounded and strong, tall in uprights and firmly seriphed, both bold and delicate, equally dark and radiant in its blacks and whites, Aldus's Bembo type is the most modern in appearance of fifteenth century types . . .[101]

The Aldine roman quickly became widespread in Italy and far beyond, and it proved hugely influential in typeface design for centuries to come, not least in modern typewriting. A seminal figure in this respect was the eminent English typographer Stanley Morison (1889–1967), whose so-called Aldine hypothesis changed the narrative of typographical history in the 1920s by displacing, in Manuzio's favor, the entrenched scholarly view that Jenson's roman was the key model for French roman types of the early sixteenth century.[102] Morison's long association with the Monotype Corporation had begun in 1922 when, at his instigation, the company had developed the English Monotype Garamond face.[103] By early 1923 that association was formalized by his appointment as typographical advisor to the Corporation, and in that capacity he played a key role in its development of multiple typeface revivals. Among them were two faces based on Aldine romans, the first the so-called Poliphilus of 1923, modeled on the 1499 *Hypnerotomachia*; the second, in 1929, was the so-called Bembo modeled on Griffo's design for the 1496 *De Aetna*[104]—with the ironic consequence that Bembo is today perhaps best known in the popular imagination for a typeface that he himself did not design. In an interesting postscript, Morison went on to acquire the 1496 *De Aetna* for £100 in

101. Painter (1984) 184; see also the elegant summations in Mardersteig (1969a) 225 = (1988) 200 ("il nitidissimo 'Bembo' ha oggi la reputazione di essere il più bel carattere del Rinascimento, l'espressione più perfetta della scrittura umanistica trasformata in caratteri da stampa") and Danforth (2003), esp. 15–16.

102. See Amert (2008) with Danforth (2003) 20–1, and cf. Morison (1949) 26–7: "The type of the *De Aetna* equally marks the new epoch in typography. The fame of the publisher added to the prestige of the new letter. It was copied in France (by Garamond, Colines and others) . . . Thus Italian and French typography merged in the stream of that vigorous 'old-face' tradition *which took its rise from the type of the Aldine De Aetna*" (my emphasis).

103. See Barker (1972) 120.

104. But for problems and slow going in the face's design, Barker (1972) 240–8. For varied illustration of the design see Carter et al. (2002) 7 and 182–7.

April 1940, only for it narrowly to escape the effects of the Blitz.[105] He later donated it to the Monotype Corporation, which subsequently gifted it to the Cambridge University Library in 1974; there it resides today.[106]

A central contention of this study is that Griffo's roman typeface in the 1496 *De Aetna*—so fresh and adventurous in print design, not least in its innovative use of punctuation[107]—is itself symbolically meaningful in a work that tells of youthful adventure and (self-)exploration on Etna's slopes. It is now widely recognized in modern typographical research that typefaces have distinct personas, and that the visual properties of a given text can have a delicate impact that goes beyond legibility and readability; they can have an "atmosphere value" or "typeface personality" that conveys meaning beyond the primary meaning conveyed by the words.[108] Choice of typeface, paper, margin size, paragraph indentation, line length, and so on may all affect readers' reception and response: as Robert Connors puts it, "[b]y presenting the reader with a legible, neat, pleasing manuscript, the writer is creating an image of herself for that reader, an image that can support or sabotage her message."[109] A parallel phenomenon of "messaging" is discernible, I propose, in the novel typeface deployed in *De Aetna*. From one perspective, that face elegantly bears Manuzio's reflection, announcing as it does his manifesto-like attachment to "purely typographic ideals, in liberation from manuscript models";[110] it also conjoins Pietro and Aldo in a mutually affirming showcase for the humanistic credentials and ambition of both the aspiring author and the striving printer. From

105. See the preface to Morison's essay *"Black Letter" Text* (originally published in only 100 copies: Morison [1942] = McKitterick [1981] 1.177–205), also reproduced by Barker (1972) 387: "I managed to rescue some good things, including copies of Yciar, Lucas, and a fine *De Aetna*."

106. Further on this Cambridge copy, and on Bembo's variant readings/corrections within it, see now Nuvoloni (2011).

107. The innovations in *De Aetna* included the semicolon and diacritic accent: see Parkes (1993) 86 and 214–15 with Watson (2012) 651 and B. Richardson (1999) 185 n.133. For innovatory punctuation in the vernacular in Bembo's 1501–2 Aldine octavo editions of Petrarch and Dante see Richardson 153–4 with (1994) 51 and Trovato (1998), esp. 197–205 (in a chapter entitled "Caratteri, formato e sistemi di interpunzione").

108. See on these points, e.g., Lewis and Walker (1989), Brumberger (2003), and Henderson et al. (2004), and cf. Carter et al. (2002) 74–82 (on "The typographic message"), including (p. 74): "The typographic message is verbal, visual, and vocal. While typography is read and interpreted verbally, it may also be viewed and interpreted visually, heard and interpreted audibly. It is a dynamic communication medium. In this sense, early twentieth-century typography became a revolutionary form of communication, bringing *new expressive power to the written word*" (my emphasis). We shall see that, in their different way, Manuzio and Bembo already exploit something akin to this "new expressive power" through *De Aetna*'s verbal-visual interplay.

109. R. J. Connors (1983) 64–5.

110. Painter (1984) 184, as cited on p. 201.

another perspective (one hardly irreconcilable with the first), however, the face is *Pietro's*: from the first, in his introductory preface to Angelo (§§1–4), Pietro's voice is brought to life on the printed page, there to be "heard" in the freshly cut Aldine revivification of the man; even when Bernardo speaks later in the dialogue, still we see and hear that master voice as introduced in the preface, controlling as it does the flow of narration throughout the entire work. On this approach, *De Aetna* is truly stamped with personality, and the typeface functions as one dimension of the overall portrait of the young Bembo, part visual, part verbal, that the text delivers: a picture in words, but with the added nuance of typeface *as* picture. In effect, to glance back at Feather's words as quoted earlier, our understanding of the 1496 edition is indeed "ultimately influenced by the physical form of its presentation" because its publication was truly a unique event: the newness of the typeface, and the convergence with Bembo's authorial face, gave the 1496 imprint a distinctiveness of identity that was necessarily a one-off phenomenon, the freshness of its first instantiation simply unrepeatable in any later reprinting.

At this point our story moves to 1530, when *De Aetna* appeared in its second edition. Pietro's youthful visit to Sicily had taken place nearly four decades before, but his fond memory of it remained undiminished. To return to the letter of June 26, 1536 that he wrote in reply to Francesco Maurolico's report (*inter alia*) of Etna's eruption earlier that year, Pietro casts his mind back to the volcano, recalling how he "wrote a dialogue on that subject when I was very much a young man—a dialogue that is in fact in circulation."[111] As we saw earlier,[112] Pietro surely refers here to the second, revised edition of *De Aetna* published at Venice in 1530 in the da Sabio quarto edition of his Latin *opuscula*.[113] After *De Aetna* came *De Virgilii Culice et Terentii fabulis liber*, at last published some twenty-seven years after it was written;[114] then Bembo's life of Guidobaldo da Montefeltro (1472–1508), Duke of Urbino, and his cultured wife, Elisabetta Gonzaga (*De Guido Ubaldo Feretrio deque Elisabetha Gonzagia Urbini Ducibus liber*, composed in 1509–10);[115] and finally the dyad of Giovanni Francesco Pico della Mirandola's essay on imitation (*De imitatione libellus*, cast in the form of a letter written on September 19, 1512), and then Bembo's epistolary riposte of January 1, 1513—a reply that countered Pico's case for

111. Travi (1992) 649 *Letter* 1759.30–1.

112. Introduction p. 3.

113. For this edition, Adams (1967) 109 no. 584.

114. See already Chapter 4 pp. 147–9.

115. For the date and allusions to the work in Bembo's extant correspondence, Lutz (1980) 15 with Travi (1990) 37 *Letter* 294.8–9; 45 *Letter* 302.2–5; (1992) 157 *Letter* 1117.8–9; the vernacular version penned by Bembo remained unpublished until the edition of Lutz (1980).

the generalized study and emulation of Greco-Roman antiquity by urging special attention to Cicero and Virgil and the imitation of their model styles.[116] Already in 1525 Bembo had published his *Prose della volgar lingua*, and in 1530 appeared his *Rime* and the revised edition of *Gli Asolani*, a phase of activity by which he consolidated his stature as a foundational figure in the development of the Italian language. In this moment, his decision to republish or to publish for the first time four relatively slight Latin works from his past was doubtless calculated to reaffirm his humanist credentials: for all his pioneering endeavors in Italian, the 1530 imprint marked his unstinting commitment to the Classical tradition.[117]

The 1530 text of *De Aetna* departs from that of the 1496 original in more than 150 places. Already, on the basis of his inspection of twenty copies of the first edition, Curt Bühler demonstrated in an important article[118] how, from patterns of correction in those copies, their relative order of distribution from the press could be determined: the more mistakes discovered, and the more corrections manually incorporated over time within those copies, the later the date of their individual distribution. Given that the 1530 text includes almost all of the changes found in the copies of the 1496 edition examined by Bühler, he holds it likely that the 1530 version amounts to a revision authorized by Bembo himself.[119] Bianca Maria Mariano goes further, explicitly attributing the more than 150 adjustments in the 1530 text to Bembo, partly on the basis of the strong circumstantial evidence that she adduces.[120] But decisive for her is the coordinated nature of the variants that he introduces: through the uniformity of editorial choices and the maturity of form (in language, grammar, and style), the revision process presupposes the work of a single consciousness, matured by long experience of Ciceronianism.[121] If, however, we accept that Bembo carefully oversaw the second edition of *De Aetna*, and if we also accept that the fresh new face of the 1496 *princeps* is itself pictorially symbolic ("portrait of a young man"), then two features of the 1530 version are immediately disconcerting: it is printed in italic, not the Griffo roman of the 1496 version, and the stand-alone singularity of the 1496 edition is lost in its new setting within the assembled *opuscula*.

In one way, of course, the revivalist air of the 1530 edition—its (re)printing of works composed decades earlier—cannot avoid being symbolically suggestive. As if

116. On this dispute, McLaughlin (1995) 249–74; this Pico (1470–1533) was nephew of the philosopher Giovanni Pico della Mirandola, for whom Chapter 3 pp. 114, 123, 130 and 138 n.139.

117. See Dionisotti (1966b) 51 = Vela (2002) 61.

118. Bühler (1951).

119. Bühler (1951) 139; cf. also p. 307.

120. Mariano (1991) 445.

121. Mariano (1991) 445.

gathering distinct *membra* of the younger Bembo's formation and development as a Latin philologist into a unified body of materials, the volume collects the man, reasserting his fidelity to the Classical heritage, as we saw above. But in comparison with the visual novelty of its 1496 instantiation, the second edition of *De Aetna* is visually arresting precisely because of the change of font. The effect may simply be coincidental, the da Sabio use of italic a practical measure of no special symbolic consequence. But the result is that *De Aetna* shows its age, so to speak, by departing from its 1496 type form in its 1530 iteration: after the passage of some thirty-five years, the 1530 impression has visibly grown out of and left behind its youthful incarnation, as if a textual acknowledgement that the blossoming flower of 1496 had long lost its freshness.[122]

5.4: Bernardo Bembo, Petrarch's Laura, and Leonardo da Vinci's Ginevra de' Benci

We now turn to the other side of the picture in *De Aetna*, and to Bernardo Bembo's interest in that interplay of word and image that we have so far explored largely through Pietro's eyes. This part of our story begins in Burgundy, where Bernardo served as Venetian ambassador at the court of Charles the Bold between 1471 and 1474. During his time in Burgundy, Bernardo may have commissioned directly from Hans Memling the famous diptych of *Saint John the Baptist* and *Saint Veronica* whose parts are now separated between the Alte Pinakothek, Munich (home to the *John* panel), and the National Gallery of Art, Washington, DC.[123] His acquaintance with Memling is surely confirmed by the

122. A loose but interesting analogy for this change of typeface is supplied by William Wordsworth. When he first published *The River Duddon* series of sonnets in 1820, the last sonnet (*Conclusion*), in keeping with the preceding sonnets in the sequence, was printed in roman typeface. But when he revised *The River Duddon* sequence for the collected works of 1827 (5 vols., London), Wordsworth changed the title of this last sonnet to *After-Thought* and reset it entirely in italics (4.156)—a modification that was far from merely casual or insignificant, but a highly self-conscious maneuver, the italics emphasizing for Robinson (2002) 461 the poem's "corrective difference from not only the conclusion but also the entire sequence." See further Simonsen (2007), esp. 876: "The italics foreground the artificiality of the poem; they make it stand out as an object or indeed a 'picture' surrounded by the white marginal frame of the page. The visual presence of the poem argues against absence and death in the same way that the visual presence of the river belies the unsettling thought of its '*being past away*' [line 2] that sparks the poem."

123. On the diptych see now Lauber (2013a) 456–8 and Hand (2013), esp. 438–9 on its problematic dating. One school of thought dates it to 1471–4, another to *c.* 1480–3; if the latter, Bernardo evidently acquired the diptych only after his period of service in the Low Countries. The diptych is duly included in Marcantonio Michiel's inventory of Pietro Bembo's collection as witnessed in the 1520s/early 1530s (see Chapter 7 p. 276 and n.42), albeit with the bizarre misidentification of Veronica as the Virgin with Child: see Lauber 457 with L. Campbell (1981) 468–71 and Hand 434–5 (the possibility that there were two northern diptychs in the Bembo family's possession, one of St. John and St. Veronica, the other of St. John and the Virgin, is surely doubtful).

latter's *Portrait of a Man with a Roman Coin* in the Royal Museum of Fine Arts, Antwerp (Figure 5.3). True, no other authentic portrait of Bernardo exists for the purposes of comparison, the picture is nowhere mentioned as part of Pietro Bembo's inherited collection, and its provenance before 1807 is undocumented; but Memling's sitter is nevertheless now widely identified as Bernardo Bembo.[124] Beyond the archive evidence of Bernardo's presence in Memling's Bruges in mid-November 1472,[125] this identification is supported by telling visual signs. First, Bernardo's personal emblem, a wreath of laurel and palm, is suggestively echoed in what seems to be a sprig of laurel visible at the panel's lower edge and in the palm tree in the background to the right.[126] Second, the ancient coin (with an image of Nero) held by the sitter appears to be a sestertius, at least to judge by its dimensions relative to the hand showing it;[127] through this gesture the portrait may well reflect the contemporary fashion for coins as a gift-commodity, to the effect that the sestertius represents a token of esteem given to the sitter by a friend or admirer.[128] The coin corresponds to known exemplars,[129] and, if Bernardo is taken to be the sitter, it was perhaps acquired by him during his time in Burgundy; could this be the coin that Pietro Bembo mentions when, in a letter to Valerio Belli many years later, he refers to that "bello Neron grande che io ho?"[130] But the most intriguing clue to identifying the sitter as Bernardo arises from comparison with Giovanni Bellini's *Portrait of a Young Man* of *c.* 1505 (Figure 5.4). That Bellini's sitter in this portrait is Pietro Bembo has drawn strong and serious objection (a controversy to which we shall return),[131] but momentarily to countenance that possibility: the figures portrayed in the two pictures appear to be of roughly the same age and of compatible physiognomy ("note the long pointed nose"),[132] they are clothed in a similar style, each is shown before a blue sky blotted with cloud, and both portraits feature a landscape setting with

124. See D. A. Brown (2013) 321 and n.42 for bibliography.

125. Giannetto (1985) 28–9 with Nalezyty (2013a) 423.

126. On this point, D. A. Brown (2013) 321 with Nalezyty (2013a) 422 n.6.

127. Burns (2013) 115.

128. See Cunnally (1994) 133–4.

129. Burns (2013) 115.

130. Travi (1990) 232 *Letter* 509.6 (January 2, 1525). For the possible link with Memling's picture, Gasparotto (2013c) 484 n.22.

131. See Chapter 7 pp. 302–4.

132. D. A. Brown (2013) 322.

turrets visible in the background;[133] also highly suggestive is the fact that, while the bust-length portrait in three-quarter view in a landscape setting is unique in Bellini's surviving oeuvre, it is widespread in fifteenth-century Flemish art.[134] Again, the case for identifying Pietro Bembo as Bellini's sitter is open to serious doubt, and the two pictures also show significant differences of emphasis and approach that offset their ostensible similarities.[135] But if Bembo is still entertained as Bellini's sitter, it is tempting to speculate that Memling's portrait was a source or model for Bellini, and that the two portraits are more than just casually related: although separated by three or so decades in time, when viewed in combination they enact a form of dialogue between father and son[136]—a coincidental visual variant, we might hazard, on the dialogical form of *De Aetna*.

This mode of visual play appealed to Bernardo—or so we might infer from his wider appetite for games with word and image. As a young student at Padua in the 1450s he was entranced by a certain Magdalena, who became the mother of his illegitimate son Bartolomeo;[137] in a witty play Bernardo casts her as *Magnaleda*, i.e., an *altera Leda*.[138] In the copy of his *Xandra* that Cristoforo Landino had made for Bernardo and which is datable to 1478–81,[139] the manuscript (Vat. lat. 3366) is customized for Bembo not only through an autograph letter of dedication[140] and, on the lower margin of fol. 1*r*, the insertion of Bembo's arms accompanied by the motto-like words *virtus* and *honor*; the first letter of the first word (*Qui*) of *Xandra* 1.1 is also decorated with a tiny Leda with a swan[141]—a tempting allusion to Bembo's Magdalena-Magnaleda. On the title page of his Horace, a copy probably prepared at his order by Bartolomeo Sanvito,[142] the first letter of the first *Ode* (*Maecenas atavis edite regibus* . . .) is elaborately decorated with two mini-images of Pegasus

---

133. On these points, Nalezyty (2013a) 422–3.

134. D. A. Brown (2013) 321.

135. D. A. Brown (2013) 322.

136. On Memling as Bellini's model see, e.g., D. A. Brown (2013) 322 with Marinelli (2013) 465; on the dialogical aspect, Nalezyty (2013a) 423.

137. For whose closeness to Pietro Bembo in later life, Giannetto (1985) 118–19 and n.80.

138. See Giannetto (1985) 103–4 and n.52.

139. Date: Garrard (2006) 55 (3).

140. Now reproduced in Chatfield (2008) 318–21.

141. See Giannetto (1985) 335 with J. M. Fletcher (1989) 812.

142. Ms. 34, King's College Library, Cambridge: see Giannetto (1985) 299–301 with Danzi (2005) 336 no. 38. For Sanvito, p. 195 and n.73 above.

(after whom Bernardo's favored horse was named),[143] while at the bottom of the same page Pegasus recurs together with the Bembo arms and motto.[144] Beyond the marginalia and corrections visible in Bernardo's own hand in this and other texts in his possession, he also makes notable use of the *manicula,* or "pointing hand," to demarcate passages of special importance. He was hardly the first to deploy *maniculae,* which were "increasingly common" in manuscript production and annotation in fourteenth- and fifteenth-century Italy, often in ways "shockingly fanciful and delightfully stylized."[145] But William H. Sherman credits Bernardo in his London *zibaldone* (i.e., the commonplace book that now resides in the British Library)[146] with "[t]he most lifelike manicules I have come across to date";[147] in an interesting postscript to this appraisal of the *zibaldone,* it was the distinctive character of the manicules in a 1483 incunable of Pliny's *Letters* (Treviso: Johannes Vercellius) at Stanford University that first led Sherman to suspect that the volume had once belonged to Bernardo—a suspicion quickly confirmed by the Bembine arms and motto that Sherman found on turning back to the first page.[148] The "whole theatre of gesturing hands and . . . full display of Bernardo's graphic techniques [in this volume]"[149] reflect his deep engagement with a work that evidently struck a chord not least because of Pliny's frequent evocations of villa culture and of restorative *otium* away from the civic arena. Hence Bernardo's use not just of manicules but also of what Sherman terms opticules, or eyes peering into the text from the margins, sometimes competing with a *manicula* in a graphic form of hand-eye coordination,

143. Pegasus neatly relates Bernardo's literary interests to his significant equestrian interests: see J. M. Fletcher (1989) 815 with Cian (1887) 86–7.

144. See Giannetto (1985) 300 with J. M. Fletcher (1989) 812, Clough (1984) 308 and p. 324 pl. 3, and now Garrard (2006) 55 (7). Pegasus recurs in the Harvard Sallust, also prepared by Sanvito, which dates to *c.* 1490 (see Garrard 55 [6] with bibliography). The horse was also to be featured on the reverse of Danese Cattaneo's (?) medal of Pietro Bembo (see Chapter 7 p. 285 and Figure 7.5). In the London *zibaldone* (for which see immediately below), Bernardo repeats no fewer than six times Pietro's Latin epigram on Pegasus, albeit in a form different from its later printed version (Giannetto [1985] 379 and n.23 with W. H. Sherman [2013] 124 and n.13); for the printed version, first published posthumously in the Scotto *Petri Bembi carminum libellus* (Venice, 1552/3, p. 44), see Pecoraro (1959) 159 XII, Sodano (1990) 51 XXIII, and Chatfield (2005) 90–1 XXIII.

145. W. H. Sherman (2008) 35.

146. For concise description of its contents, Neilson (1895) with Levi (1896); it was acquired by Neilson in interesting circumstances (p. 871: "Amidst the wrack stranded on the outside shelf of a bookshop in London, I lately bought a parchment-bound anonymous fifteenth-century MS. folio").

147. W. H. Sherman (2008) 36; in this paragraph I am much indebted to Sherman (2008) and (2013).

148. See W. H. Sherman (2013) 124–5.

149. W. H. Sherman (2013) 125.

and fully bedecked with eyelids, eyelashes, and characterful brows.[150] At *Ep.* 2.2.2, for example, Pliny writes that he "is in the country (*ad villam*), dividing my time between enjoyable reading and relaxation, each of them born of leisure (*utrumque ex otio nascitur*)": at this point in the Stanford Pliny a manicule accompanies the telling words *Sic ego*, an insertion made all the more appealing if we speculate that it was written at Noniano. Many other cases could be cited, but an especially delightful touch is found in Bernardo's text at *Ep.* 4.23, where Pliny expresses his pleasure at his friend Pomponius Bassus' well-earned retirement to a cultured life of *otium* after a commendable career of service: above the elongated finger of an elaborate manicule the words *NOTA BEMBE* thunder forth their witty imperative.[151] By literally drawing attention in these ways, Bernardo "not only *drew* eyes but *developed* an eye, cultivating a visual style";[152] and that visual sensibility extends to his eye for pictorial development in Pliny himself, as when Bernardo writes as follows, in a marginal comment stretched over two pages of text, on Pliny's account in *Ep.* 2.17 of the joys of his villa at Laurentum: *LAURENTUM SUUM GRAFICE PINGIT* ("he depicts his Laurentum *like a painter*").

Virtus et honor, Bembo's motto, also figures conspicuously in his restoration, at his own expense, of Dante's tomb at Ravenna during his term of service as *podestà* there in 1482–3. On the monument executed by Pietro Lombardo[153] and inaugurated on May 27, 1483, an incised wreath of laurel and palm is accompanied by the words *Virtuti et honori* ("to [Dante's] virtue and honor"); the motto is repeated in the form *Virtus et honor* on a plaque that is now set in an exterior wall adjacent to the monument, but which is thought to have stood on an outside arch of Lombardo's original construction.[154] The monument as a whole contributed importantly to tomb typology in the Renaissance:[155] conforming to the type of round-headed wall tomb introduced to 1470s Venice by the workshop of the celebrated sculptor and architect Antonio Rizzo, Lombardo's design replaces the

150. W. H. Sherman (2013) 125.

151. The play on *bene/Bembe* is also exploited by Landino in an elegy to Bernardo (*Carm. var.* 5.14 = Chatfield [2008] 282–3): *horum* [sc. the beauty, *forma*, and mind, *animus*, of Ginevra de' Benci] *utrum superet, non bene, Bembe, vides* (the poem is quoted more fully on p. 213).

152. W. H. Sherman (2013) 125; his emphasis.

153. This after Lombardo had seemingly already executed for Bembo the low-relief sculpture of the Virgin and Child that once graced Noniano: see Callegari (1997a), dating (pp. 865–6) the commissioning of the Noniano relief to the interlude between Bernardo's return from his second ambassadorship to Florence in 1480 and his departure for Ravenna as *podestà*.

154. See Giannetto (1985) 157–8 with Garrard (2006) 40 (with illustration of the plaque now on the exterior wall) and Bolzoni (2010) 345–6.

155. This paragraph draws heavily on Pincus and Shapiro Comte (2006), esp. 736–7.

traditional depiction of a recumbent image of the deceased with a portrait relief of the living Dante at his lectern. The fashion in fifteenth-century manuscript and book production of creating an elaborate frontispiece that enclosed a block of text within a complex architectural formation (a feature well represented in manuscripts commissioned by Bernardo) influences the design of Dante's tomb, as does the phenomenon of the author portrait in medieval and Renaissance manuscripts. But Lombardo breaks from convention by showing Dante not in the act of writing but deep in thought, his left arm propped on a book that stands open on the lectern and his little finger touching his bottom lip as if in pause for thought: the focus is on the mind that composes, not the writing hand, as if capturing the inspiration that precedes the written word—an emphasis that conceivably reflects Bernardo's, not Lombardo's, design preference.[156] By inscribing himself via his motto on the monument, Bernardo fuses word and image not just to proclaim his act of homage to Dante, or to link himself with the master through the shared ideal of *virtus et honor*; as we shall now see, his message also extends to Florence, and to the cultured circles in which he had moved during his two periods of service there as Venetian ambassador in the 1470s.

Already by the end of the fourteenth century there was agitation at Florence to repatriate Dante's remains, a cause taken up enthusiastically by Lorenzo de' Medici with the aim of establishing a sumptuous tomb that would proudly proclaim the master's Florentine identity. Pressured by Lorenzo, Bernardo appears to have tried in 1476 to intervene on his behalf before the Venetian authorities, but without success.[157] Now installed in Ravenna after his Florentine ambassadorships, Bernardo

---

156. On this point, Giannetto (1985) 157–8. It is noteworthy that Landino presented to Bernardo a copy of his 1481 *Comento sopra la Comedia di Danthe Alighieri poeta Fiorentino* (Florence, Niccolò di Lorenzo della Magna); it now resides in the Bibliothèque Nationale in Paris (further, Danzi [2005] 322 no. 1). It was accompanied by a letter of dedication in his own hand when the book was sent as a gift after the restoration of Dante's tomb, and also by a sumptuous drawing of the tomb, very possibly by Lombardo's son, Tullio. Bernardo presumably inserted both letter and drawing as extraneous *addenda* to the book. The drawing may have originally constituted a workshop design object or contract drawing, but when it was incorporated into the Landino Dante, Pincus and Shapiro Comte (2006) argue that it was transformed, in a secondary phase of drawing, into a *de facto* author portrait for the book. In light of Pietro Bembo's 1502 Aldine edition of Dante, however, Pincus and Shapiro Comte 746 further suggest that the idea of converting the workshop piece into an author portrait may in fact have been *Pietro's*, and that the author portrait as it survives (i.e., after the secondary drawing) may even have been executed by Pietro himself (the motto *Virtuti et Honori* in the drawing is "in a sixteenth-century hand that is consonant with Pietro Bembo's formal handwriting"). Pietro's larger motive: "That the portrait in the . . . drawing reverts to the medieval image of Dante, without his laurel crown yet with the hawk-like profile of the sixteenth century, calls to mind that Pietro Bembo's attitude to Dante was quite different from that of Landino's and his father's generation. Landino worked to transform Dante along Neoplatonic lines into the poet of man's higher destiny. *Pietro . . . wanted to overturn such interpretations and see Dante in his fourteenth-century role as an innovator in the development of poetic language*" (p. 746; my emphasis).

157. See for documentation Giannetto (1985) 156 and n.176.

sought to aid the stabilization of Venetian relations with Florence by undertaking the restoration of Dante's tomb at his own initiative; and in this Florentine connection the presence of his motto on the tomb takes on added nuance. This part of our story again concerns Bernardo's interest in the interplay of text and image, and it begins with the young Leonardo da Vinci's famous portrait of Ginevra de' Benci, acquired by the National Gallery of Art, Washington, DC, in 1967 (Figure 5.5; this remains the sole da Vinci portrait on public display in the Americas). Ginevra (1457–*c.* 1520) was the well-connected daughter of Amerigo Benci, a prominent Florentine financier, collector, and patron of the arts who counted Ficino among his friends.[158] The picture as it survives, showing its sitter in a three-quarter view directly engaging our eyes (the pose is itself a new departure for female representation in Italian portraiture),[159] is only part of the original; if Leonardo's drawing of female hands in the Royal Library, Windsor Castle, is taken to be a preparatory study for the Ginevra portrait, the panel appears to have lost about a third of its original height.[160] The sitter's identity is signaled by the juniper tree positioned behind her head:[161] the visual pun on ginepro-Ginevra is repeated on the reverse side (Figure 5.6), where a wreath of laurel and palm encircles a sprig of juniper, and a curling scroll with the inscription *VIRTUTEM FORMA DECORAT* ("She adorns virtue with her beauty [*formā* ablative]," or "Beauty [*formă* nominative] adorns virtue")[162] loosely embraces the laurel and palm branches and also the juniper between them. The portrait on the one side is accompanied on the other by an emblematic image of her inner self, her *virtus*, as if the reverse captures an essence beyond the mere physical impression. But then a further development: infrared reflectography reveals that the motto as given on the reverse, *Virtutem forma decorat*,

---

158. See Giannetto (1985) 137 and n.122 with Walker (1967) 1 and D. A. Brown (1998) 101–22 and (2001) 142.

159. Garrard (2006) 25: "the profile view was still normative for women in the 1470s (though not for men)"; "never before in Italian portraiture had a woman looked at us straight in the eye, dissolving the boundary of the picture plane to connect with the viewer psychologically. In this, Leonardo effected a permanent change."

160. See D. Bull (1992) 72 with D. A. Brown (1998) 202–3 n.37. The history of this modern proposal is conveniently summarized by Clark (1968) 1.104–5 no. 12558. But see now Syson (2011) 214 for "a consensus . . . emerging" that the drawing in fact belongs to the late 1480s and is to be associated instead with the portrait of Cecilia Gallerani (*Lady with an Ermine, c.* 1489–90) of the Czartoryski Museum, Cracow.

161. The identification was established long ago: see von Bode (1903) with Cook (1912), Giannetto (1985) 137–8 n.123, and now Elam (2013) 408–9 and n.8. The Ginevra/juniper linkage is underscored by "the juniper [being] observed and painted with the same interest and intensity as the sitter" (D. A. Brown [2001] 145).

162. On the double translation, Garrard (2006) 26; Bolzoni (2013c) 210.

covers a preexisting motto that reads *Virtus et honor*—Bernardo's motto. And so why was that first motto painted over? By whom was the portrait commissioned, and in what circumstances?

In 1474, at sixteen, Ginevra married Luigi Niccolini, a widower aged thirty-two, not rich but of a respected family. Despite her somewhat doleful countenance,[163] one proposed explanation for Leonardo's portrait is that it commemorated her betrothal or marriage, and that it therefore dates to in or around 1474.[164] But when Jennifer Fletcher, in an important contribution,[165] identified the laurel-and-palm device on the reverse as Bembo's own, she proposed that the portrait was commissioned by Bernardo himself during one of his two ambassadorships to Florence in the 1470s. Whether dated to 1475–6 or to 1478–80, the portrait then becomes implicated in the following storyline. After his arrival in Florence in January 1475, Bernardo soon took his place in courtly events, among the first of them the grand *giostra* that was held on January 29 to mark Florence's new anti-Turkish alliance with Venice. The joust was sponsored by Giuliano de' Medici; following the lead of his brother, Lorenzo, who had dedicated the tournament he held in 1469 to the married Lucrezia Donati, Giuliano dedicated the 1475 joust to his own platonic beloved, the married Simonetta Cattaneo Vespucci.[166] From this beginning, and with his own wife in Venice, in knightly fashion Bernardo took as his platonic love the married Ginevra, who was twenty-six or so years his junior at the time. Bernardo's successful entrée into the Medici circle, Ficino's Academy, and the company of such luminaries as Alessandro Braccesi, Cristoforo Landino, Naldo Naldi, and Poliziano was in a sense completed by his professed love for Ginevra: that relationship fulfilled the Florentine ideal of a higher love, philosophical and pure, platonic rather than sexual, and it was enthusiastically celebrated as such in the sequence of ten Latin elegies that Bernardo

163. Cf. Kent (2001) 43: "a prickly personality, like the leaves of the juniper bush that stands for her name, may be revealed in her poetry [cf. n. 167 below], of which a single telling line survives: "I ask your forgiveness and I am a mountain tiger.'"

164. On the history of the marriage/nuptial theory, and also on another theory that the portrait was commissioned as a gift of friendship for Ginevra's family, Garrard (2006) 26 with Elam (2013) 410. But for Ginevra's lack of jewelry and her plainness of dress as a striking departure from the high adornment to be expected if Leonardo does indeed celebrate the union (a departure precipitated by contemporary sumptuary legislation at Florence?), Woods-Marsden (2001) 72–3. Yet see also Garrard 43–4 for Ginevra's stay as a boarder at the Benedictine convent of Le Murate in Florence prior to her marriage, and for the loss of independence thereafter: "if there is a hint of melancholy, perhaps it is because she faces a world that she already knows will limit her ambitions" (p. 44).

165. J. M. Fletcher (1989).

166. On Simonetta, and on the "cult" of Simonetta as cultivated by Lorenzo's circle, see Schmitter (1995) 40–2.

received from Braccesi and Landino, albeit with some possible sexual innuendo within them.[167] In the context of this love affair, the ribbon that embraces the juniper between the encircling branches of laurel and palm on the portrait's reverse connects Ginevra and Bembo in a pictorial embrace; the fact that the ribbon only loosely encircles the juniper, as if chastely and without physical contact, may signal Bernardo's restraint as her platonic lover.[168] For those who know the intimate secret that his motto underlies hers on the reverse, the two lovers are further connected by the complicity of her *virtutem* and his *virtus*.[169] On this approach, Landino's verses in particular seem all too fortuitously (or knowingly?) insightful about the portrait's inner workings when he remarks that, with but a small change of lettering, Ginevra could be conjoined with Bernardo at least in name: if the combination of *virtus-virtutem* on the portrait's reverse achieved a form of verbal complicity between Ginevra and Bernardo, Landino achieves much the same effect in *Bencia quae fuerat, Bembia nomen erit* (*Carm. var.* 5.115–16: "[by changing only two letters,] she who had been *Bencia*, will be *Bembia* by name."[170] Then 5.11–16:

His flammis Bembus talique accensus amore
  uritur, et *medio corde Ginevra sedet.*
Forma quidem pulchra est, *animus* quoque pulcher in illa:
  horum utrum superet, non bene, Bembe, vides.
Ergo nil mirum est, nam maxima semina flammis
  virtus et dominae dant tibi *forma* tuis.[171]

Bembo is afire and burning with these flames and with a love
  of this sort, and Ginevra sits at the center of his heart.

---

167. For the cultural ambience for this affair within these Florentine circles, Bolzoni (2010) 334–44 and (2013c) 213–15. For the poems conveniently collected see della Torre (1900) 320–33 and, with translation, Walker (1967) 28–37; for Landino's poems only, Chatfield (2008) 276–303 = *Carm. var.* 3–8. The first of Braccesi's four poems is addressed to Ginevra, the other three to Bernardo directly, as are Landino's six elegies. As for innuendo cf. Walker 3–4: ". . . in constantly praising Ginevra's chastity the poets seem to protest too much. To judge from the number of illegitimate children recorded in Florentine chronicles, Renaissance love affairs seldom remained platonic. A less cynical observer would point out that whether Ginevra retained her virtue or committed adultery is something we shall never know. The poems are obscure. . . ." For Ginevra sometimes upheld as a poet in her own right, albeit only a single verse survives, Cox (2008) 45 (cf. also n.163 above).

168. Elam (2013) 413.

169. On this verbal/visual complicity, Bolzoni (2010) 250–1 and (2013c) 213

170. Chatfield (2008) 290–1.

171. Chatfield (2008) 282–5.

Her appearance is indeed beautiful, her mind also beautiful within her:
which of these wins out over the other, Bembo, you don't well see.
It's therefore no surprise; for your lady's virtue and beauty
give the greatest sparks to your flames of passion.

As Lina Bolzoni points out, the phrase *medio corde Ginevra sedet* (12) constitutes "un topos della tradizione lirica."[172] But it could also felicitously describe Leonardo's portrait, in that on the reverse she (via the juniper sprig) sits at the heart (cf. *medio corde*) of his laurel-and-palm device.[173] The dyad of *forma* and *animus* in line 13 also nicely captures the combination of physical beauty and inner virtue that the portrait's front and back cumulatively convey; and if *forma* (13) gently alludes to Ginevra's motto *Virtutem forma decorat*, that allusion is spelled out still more directly in *virtus et . . . forma* in line 16.

If we accept, then, that the front and back of the panel were planned and painted as a unity by the same artist (albeit oil on the obverse, tempera on the reverse),[174] Bernardo's platonic love for Ginevra offers an attractive explanation for the interplay of device and motto on the reverse. Much must of course remain uncertain, and alternative explanations for the one motto being superimposed on the other cannot be ruled out definitively. Yet it is surely improbable that, even if Bernardo took the portrait back to Venice with him after either of his two Florentine ambassadorships, he kept it there on a lasting basis: there is no mention of it in Marcantonio Michiel's inventory of Pietro Bembo's collection[175] or in any other Venetian source, and, tellingly, there is no reflection of it in Venetian portraiture.[176] Hence Caroline Elam conjectures that Bernardo returned to Venice with the portrait in 1476 after his first ambassadorship, and that while he was there he commissioned a local artist (Jacometto Veneziano?)[177] to confirm the panel's precious personal meaning by rendering Bernardo's device and motto on the reverse. But when Bernardo embarked on his second ambassadorship in 1478, he took the portrait back with him to Florence and gave it to Ginevra, a change of ownership that for Elam "prompted, indeed required, a change of motto";[178] hence the

172. Bolzoni (2010) 338 and (2013c) 213.

173. Bolzoni (2010) 338 and (2013c) 213.

174. See against theories that one side of the panel was painted first, the reverse left empty, Garrard (2006) 26–9.

175. For which Chapter 7 pp. 275–7.

176. See J. M. Fletcher (1989) 813 with Garrard (2006) 37 and 50 n.57.

177. Conveniently, D. A. Brown (2001) 145.

178. Elam (2013) 415.

modification into *Virtutem forma decorat*. But Mary Garrard offers a still more radical argument.[179] There is no firm evidence, she asserts, that Bernardo adopted the *Virtus et honor* motto before the early 1480s; she claims that it first appears in deliberate and unequivocal connection with him only on Dante's monument at Ravenna. Inside the mausoleum, the inscription that reads *Virtuti et honori* is framed, as we saw above, by a laurel-and-palm design; on the plaque now set on the exterior wall adjacent to the mausoleum, the laurel and palm recur along with a juniper sprig, and with the motto *Virtus et honor* set on a flowing ribbon that closely resembles the design on the reverse of Leonardo's portrait (which, for other reasons posited by Garrard, was for her by no means certainly commissioned by Bembo). Hence Garrard connects the Dante project with the Ginevra portrait, arguing that the laurel-and-palm emblem and the *Virtus et honor* motto were originally *hers*, and that Bernardo exploited them on the tomb discreetly to assert his own personal ties to Florence. If, then, Bernardo claimed Ginevra's emblem and motto as the platonic lover's prize and appropriated them as his own, she found a measure of restitution at the end of the relationship: the change of motto on the painting's reverse was her, or her family's, way of restoring or reshaping her identity.

But even if Ginevra is seen to reclaim herself through the change of motto, Bernardo's act of appropriation surely remains all too visible in the laurel-and-palm device that accompanies the juniper sprig on the panel's reverse. If he took that device from her and used the laurel-and-palm component freely as his own after *c.* 1481, and if Ginevra sought to counter that "stealing of her very identity,"[180] we might wonder why she changed only the motto, and not the larger image, in her attempt at self-reclamation. Moreover, Petrarch now enters to add a further dimension to Leonardo's portrait; to lend it an erotic charge that emboldens the suspicion that the painting was indeed commissioned by Bernardo; and ultimately to lead us back to Pietro Bembo through his and his father's shared devotion to Petrarchism. If the Florentine "cult of Simonetta" (i.e., Giuliano de' Medici's platonic beloved) amounted to a form of "fetishistic Petrarchan ritual,"[181] emulating Petrarch's devotion to his Laura, it is no surprise to find that Petrarchan accent heavily pronounced on the Ginevra panel. The laurel-and-palm device immediately evokes the "ramoscel di palma/ et un di lauro" that the deceased Laura bears when, coming from "the serene Empyrean," that "kind, faithful comforter of mine/ to give my tired life a little rest/ sits at my bedside there on my left side."[182] "The palm is victory," she later

179. (2006), esp. 34–42.

180. Garrard (2006) 44.

181. Garrard (2006) 37 with Schmitter (1995) 40–2, 45–6.

182. *Canzoniere* 359.1–11; trans. Musa (1996) 493.

explains, "and I still young,/ conquered the world and myself; laurel means/ triumph, of which I'm worthy,/ thanks to that Lord who gave me strength enough."[183] She rebukes the poet for still craving her corporeal beauty, a vision that yet holds him: "Is this the blond hair and the golden knot,"/I say, "that still bind me, and those fair eyes/ that were all mine?"[184] The Laura who appears to him has transcended mere physicality in her post-mortal deliverance—a movement beyond the corporeal realm that finds a suggestive point of comparison in the Leonardo portrait: if on the one side Ginevra is pictured in all her physical beauty, the Petrarchan associations of the laurel-and-palm device on the reverse hint at a transcendent, non-corporeal essence, her virtuous self rather than her mere form. In effect, through this dialectic between front and back Leonardo looks beyond Ginevra's surface appearance to capture an image that outlasts the moment caught on canvas, and which also overcomes temporal-spatial distance; as Elizabeth Cropper well puts it, "the withdrawn presence before us is not Ginevra but her redeeming appearance, more beautiful than ever, a memory image that fills the void of her absence."[185]

On this approach, the Petrarchan associations of the Laura-like Ginevra pictured by Leonardo reflect Bernardo's larger fascination with images of Laura. Bernardo may well have paid homage to Petrarch by visiting Avignon, and perhaps even Petrarch's Vaucluse, on his way either to or from his ambassadorship to Burgundy in 1471–4 or at some point in between. There is no hard evidence to this effect, but in a manuscript (Vat. lat. 3357) containing Petrarch's *De vita solitaria* and *Itinerarium Syriacum,* Bernardo inserts a note to this effect:

> Avignon. On the face of the porch of the cathedral church of St. Mary, young girls from the district exposed to the jaws of the dragon; [one] with the features of Mistress Laura [and] verses of Petrarch entreating the knight St. George.[186]

The oldest testimony for the claims that Bembo makes here—testimony that Bernardo arguably merely echoes rather than drawing on any personal experience of the place—is supplied by Luigi Peruzzi.[187] Between 1436 and 1439, this

183. *Canzoniere* 359.49–52; trans. Musa (1996) 495.

184. *Canzoniere* 359.56–8; trans. Musa (1996) 497.

185. Cropper (1986) 188.

186. *Avinioni. In frontispitio hostii ecclesiae maioris Divae Mariae, e regione puell*[a]*e exposit*[a]*e faucibus draconis, sub facie Do. Laur*[a]*e carmina Petrarcae Divum Georgium equitem deprecantia*: Giannetto (1985) 128 and n.101 with Trapp (2001) 104 and n.145 and Nolhac (1887) 293 (the note was discovered by Nolhac, but he misread *deprecantia* as *celebrantia*).

187. For whom Trapp (2001) 62.

dedicated inquirer into Laura's true identity wrote that among the frescoes that the Sienna-born Simone Martini (*c.* 1283–1344) had painted in the Cathédrale Notre-Dame-des-Doms in Avignon was a scene of St. George and the dragon, and that Martini had portrayed the noblewoman rescued by St. George, the princess of Trebizond, in the likeness of Laura; he adds that Petrarch had celebrated St. George's heroism in the Latin quatrain (visible on the wall below the fresco) to which Bembo also refers.[188] For present purposes, Peruzzi's report and Bembo's note are of special interest for two reasons. The first concerns the allusion that Marcantonio Michiel makes, in his inventory of the treasures of Pietro Bembo's Paduan residence,[189] to a portrait of Laura allegedly copied from a wall painting of St. Margaret in Avignon; the artist is unnamed.[190] Unless we suppose that Laura's image was featured in more than one fresco at Avignon, Michiel presumably means a copy of Laura as portrayed in Martini's *St. George* fresco; his confusion may arise from the separate tradition that associated a dragon with St. Margaret's legend.[191]

Secondly, Peruzzi states that the Avignon fresco occasioned the two famous sonnets (*Canzoniere* 77 and 78) that Petrarch wrote in praise of Simone's portrait of Laura. In the first, not even Polyclitus or any other of the most famous artists of antiquity could capture Laura's beauty even if they studied it for a thousand years; Simone was evidently in Heaven when he created his celestial image of Laura *in carte* ("on paper," 7); for "[t]he work is one that only up in Heaven/ could be imagined, not down here with us."[192] In the second, if only Simone had endowed his portrait with voice and mind as well as likeness, he would have freed Petrarch from so much sighing (78.1–6)! She seems to listen so patiently to the words he addresses to her; how much more fortunate was Pygmalion, for whom the image of his beloved actually came to life (78.12–14)! But the phrase *in carte* in *Canzoniere* 77 surely indicates that the Simone portrait to which Petrarch refers is not the Avignon fresco, but an easily carried picture of the sort described in a telling passage of the Petrarchan *Secretum*. There, Augustine takes Petrarch to task for tormenting himself

188. For the quatrain and its attribution in fact to Cardinal Jacopo Stefaneschi, Giannetto (1985) 127–8 with Bevilacqua (1979) 117 and Trapp (2001) 102–3.

189. See Chapter 7 p. 277.

190. See J. Morelli (1800) 18–19 and 130 n.39 (then Frizzoni [1884] 50) with Giannetto (1985) 128 n.101 and Trapp (2001) 105 and n.155; Jacopo Bellini has been hazarded as the artist (see Dal Pozzolo [1993] 260 with J. M. Fletcher [1989] 815 n.45).

191. See Trapp (2001) 105.

192. *Canzoniere* 77.9–10; trans. Musa (1996) 131.

not just because of his carnal love for Laura, but also because he intensifies his torment by always having her image to hand:

> And furthermore, what greater madness than, not content with looking upon the actual semblance of her from whom come all these ills, to have sought out, from an artist of the highest skill [Simone Martini?], a man-made image of her *and* to carry it with you wherever you go, so as to give yourself further occasion for perpetual tears?[193]

At this point, now that Bernardo's linkage with Petrarch via Avignon has been established, we turn to Pietro Bembo's linkage to Petrarch and Laura before tracing the chain of connection back to Ginevra de' Benci.

In the second, 1568 edition of his *Le Vite de' più eccellenti architetti, pittori, et scultori italiani*, Giorgio Vasari reports that Pietro commissioned from Giovanni Bellini a portrait of his beloved just as Petrarch had from Simone Martini:

> Among the portraits executed by Giovanni Bellini was that of a lady beloved by Messer Pietro Bembo, before the latter went to Rome to Pope Leo X [sc. in 1513], and whom he portrayed with so much truth and animation that as Simone of Siena was celebrated by the first Petrarch the Florentine so was Giovanni by this second Petrarch the Venetian, as may be seen in the sonnet,
>
> *O imagine mia celeste e pura.*
> Wherein he says, in the commencement of the second quatrain,
>
> *Credo che 'l mio Bellin con la figura,*
> with that which follows . . .[194]

No trace of this Bellini portrait survives, and it has been securely identified with no known painting. But the parallel with Simone's portrait of Laura is secured by the *two* sonnets[195] (*Rime* 19 and 20)—not merely the one cited by Vasari—that Pietro composed on the Bellini picture in emulation of the two sonnets with which Petrarch honored Simone Martini. In the first Bembo sonnet, Pietro addresses the Bellini image directly, as if it were alive and not just drawing reaction from Bembo

193. *Secr.* 3.7.4, as rendered by Trapp (2001) 101.

194. Lavin (1967) 1.202. Cf. the briefer statement in the 1550 edition (Bellosi and Rossi [1986] 445): *Ritrasse Giovanni per M<esser> Pietro Bembo, che ancora non stava con Leone X, la sua innamorata, da 'l quale ebbe oltra al pagamento un bellissimo sonetto che comincia "O imagine. . . ."*

195. Dionisotti (1966b) 521–3; for the Petrarchan and Bembine sonnets conveniently assembled with translation, Rogers (1986), esp. 300–1.

but itself seemingly capable of showing reaction. Itself "like a lady" (*come donna*, 9) in its seeming capacities now to show pity for his torment (10) and now to give no reply if he begs for mercy (11), the image is nevertheless more amenable than the real-life lady it represents; "for at least, when I search for you, you do not hide."[196] In the second sonnet, the pictorial image of Bembo's beloved vies with that "imprinted on my soul" (7): the painted vision of her eyes, brow, and tresses fires his imaginative vision of "Love enthroned" on her face, with his "hopes, pleasures, fear and grief" taking wing on one side (10–11), his beloved's "wisdom, courage, beauty, grace, nature and art" scattered forth like stars on the other (12–14). This imaginative elaboration outruns the limits of the painted image; or, as Elizabeth Cropper nicely puts it, "[n]one of the qualities expressed in this *blason* can be encompassed in the silent docility of the painted representation of her face."[197]

Pietro's beloved in these sonnets has been identified as the recently widowed Maria Savorgnan, with whom he embarked on a passionate affair in 1500–1.[198] Yet this identification rests in large part on allusions in their shared correspondence to two portraits of herself that Maria sent on separate occasions to Pietro as keepsakes: if she commissioned those portraits, they would seem to be incompatible with the Bellini portrait featured in the two Bembo sonnets—a picture apparently commissioned by Pietro himself.[199] Much uncertainty remains. But given the absence of all surviving trace or mention of the Bellini portrait, can we be sure that it existed in the first place? After all, the mere phantom of the Bellini picture would add another layer to the complex interplay of "real" image and illusion in the two Bembo sonnets, and their combined focus then turns first and foremost to the interplay with Petrarch: each of the two poets, Petrarch and Pietro, writes two sonnets in praise of an artist (Simone Martini, Giovanni Bellini) for his wondrous depiction of the beloved (Laura, Maria [?]). Hence the suspicion that the portrait of Pietro's beloved may be but a figment of the imagination, and a strategy by which Bembo aligns himself with Petrarch as both poet and lover;[200] and the suspicion can perhaps be pressed further on the basis of both Bernardo and Pietro's shared immersion in "the cult of the Petrarchan mistress image."[201] Given this commonality, the portrait of Ginevra de' Benci that Bernardo apparently commissioned from

196. Trans. Rogers (1986) 301.

197. Cropper (1986) 182.

198. See Dionisotti (1966b) 521 with Kidwell (2004) 24–70 on the affair; further, Chapter 4 pp. 171–3.

199. See on Maria's portraits D. A. Brown (2013) 316 and n.23 for sources.

200. D. A. Brown (2013) 317.

201. J. M. Fletcher (1989) 816.

Leonardo is suggestively matched in the next generation by the Bellini portrait of his beloved that Pietro lauds in his two sonnets—a match all the more playfully contrived if we accept that the Bellini portrait may never have existed in the first place. At the same time, on the poetic front Pietro's Petrarchan credentials are burnished through his emulation of the two Petrarchan sonnets in honor of Simone's portrait of Laura. But then perhaps a sting in the tail: if we suspect that Pietro teases the reader in his allusion to a nonexistent Bellini portrait (and perhaps his allusion even to a nonexistent lover?), he arguably varies an already well-established Petrarchan ambiguity between fiction and reality; for how sure can we be that Petrarch's Laura herself truly existed in the first place?[202]

5.5: *Endpoint, Start Point*

Given these examples of Bernardo's as well as Pietro's engagement with the interplay of text and image, the word-as-portrait phenomenon that I claim for *De Aetna* not only finds helpful *comparanda* in both Bembos' wider appetite for experimentation in this area, but it also underscores the closeness of the father-son relationship in *De Aetna* by activating their shared interest in the textual-visual dynamic. Chapter 5 thus draws to a close by stressing consensus and cooperation between Bernardo and Pietro, but at a cost: given their different commitments to civic duty, what of the frisson of tension that gently qualifies the surface affability of the dialogue? How might that tension reveal itself in Bembo's deployment of the Etna Idea, and especially in Pietro and Bernardo's divergent perceptions of, and different ways of talking about, the volcano in *De Aetna*? We pursue these questions in Chapter 6: after their meeting of minds in Chapter 5, our focus now turns to the contrasting attitudes and aptitudes of father and son that Pietro delineates by drawing on Etna's figurative energies in his (artistic) attempt on the mountain.

202. See Trapp (2001), esp. 59–61.

6

Activations of Landscape in De Aetna

IN VIRGINIA WOOLF'S *To the Lighthouse*, that beacon of high modernism published in 1927, the lighthouse itself functions as a powerful, multivalent symbol,[1] reflecting in different ways the diverse traits and tendencies of the novel's characters, most prominent among them the central pairing of Mr. and Mrs. Ramsay. Mr. Ramsay "had made a definite contribution to philosophy in one little book when he was only five and twenty; what came after was more or less amplification, repetition" (p. 23).[2] If his brightness of intellect is suggestively figured in the lighthouse's beam, the repetition of that pulsing light may also signal the repetition that defines his later career. Now over sixty (p. 70), he is still "a great man in his own way" (p. 21), but this father of eight is in many respects remote from the family that surrounds him, appearing irascible, self-absorbed, and vain,[3] craving recognition[4] but also drawn to distance ("He would like a little solitude," p. 68). Early in the novel he is pictured as impressively, even menacingly, sharp, as "lean as a knife, narrow as the blade of one" (p. 4); late in the book he stands "very straight and tall" (p. 207) as he readies to leap from the boat that has finally brought him to the lighthouse, which stands "stark and straight, glaring white and black" (p. 203). In a sense, Mr. Ramsay *is* the distant lighthouse, at least until he approaches the real thing: there, at the journey's end, his egotistical preoccupations give way to a truth outside himself, the uniqueness of ego succumbing to an impersonal reality.[5] At the same time, however,

1. On this symbolism see, e.g., Beja (1970a); Daiches (1970) 95–7; Hafley (1970) 135–6; Kaehele and German (1970), esp. 189–97; Stewart (1977); Güneş (1999).

2. Cited from the Harvest/HBJ edition (New York, 1989), with a foreword by Eudora Welty.

3. E.g., "All his vanity, all his satisfaction in his own splendor . . ." (p. 30); his son James "hated him . . . for his exactingness and egotism" (p. 36).

4. E.g., "It was sympathy he wanted, to be assured of his genius, first of all, and then to be taken within the circle of life . . ." (p. 37); "he needed always praise" (p. 45); "[h]e asked you quite openly to flatter him, to admire him" (p. 46).

5. On this point, Daiches (1970) 95, 96.

Mrs. Ramsay is no less—perhaps still more—figured in the lighthouse: the sweep of light that it sends forth with fixed regularity suggestively symbolizes the rhythm and harmony that Mrs. Ramsay creates within the household,[6] where she emanates a maternal, sustaining light, even drawing on the lighthouse as "an ultimate source of creative energy"[7] and consciously identifying herself with its beam.[8] If Mr. Ramsay's detached, precise intellect is figured in the black-and-white starkness of the lighthouse, for Mrs. Ramsay the latter radiates imaginative, colorful possibility; it is vital, not sterile, a landmark to be closely embraced rather than distantly perceived. For all Woolf's insistence in a letter to the artist and critic Roger Fry that she "meant *nothing* by The Lighthouse,"[9] it is surely hard to take her at her word:[10] on so many levels the same place, the same symbol, conjoins and separates husband and wife, combining and differentiating their divergent characters and mindsets.

This glance at *To the Lighthouse* usefully introduces a comparable if differently inflected phenomenon that I claim for *De Aetna*, and that is explored in detail in this chapter: Bembo's exploitation of Etna as a symbolic landscape, and of different perceptions of that landscape, to delineate the contrasting outlooks of father and son as portrayed in *De Aetna*. For Bernardo, there is nothing remarkable about Etna's volcanic fires. Their cause and nature are systematically explained in his highly derivative discourse in §§33–8, where all spark of wonder is quickly extinguished (§38):

PIETRO: But the fact that the rocks themselves haven't at some point run out, and that the mountain hasn't collapsed upon itself—isn't that remarkable (*mirum*), father?

BERNARDO: No, son, that's not remarkable (*mirum*) either.

---

6. Lee (1988) 22.

7. Stewart (1977) 379; further on the language of light associated with Mrs. Ramsay, Kaehele and German (1970) 190–1.

8. Kaehele and German (1970) 191, citing p. 63: "She looked up over the knitting and met the third stroke and it seemed to her like her own eyes meeting her own eyes, searching as she alone could search into her mind and her heart, purifying out of existence that lie, any lie. She praised herself in praising the light, without vanity, for she was stern, she was searching, she was beautiful like that light."

9. Nicolson and Trautmann (1977) 3.385; Woolf's emphasis. She continues (with cautionary implications for any attempt to define the lighthouse's meaning): "One has to have a central line down the middle of the book to hold the design together. I saw that all sorts of feelings would accrue to this, but I refused to think them out, and trusted that people would make it the deposit for their own emotions—which they have done, one thinking it means one thing another another. I can't manage Symbolism except in this vague, generalized way. Whether its [*sic*] right or wrong I don't know, but directly I'm told what a thing means, it becomes hateful to me."

10. For "nothing" as loaded and affected by Woolf's broader "poetics of negation," Rubenstein (2008).

True to the statesman that he was, the Bernardo drawn more generally in *De Aetna* shows a judicious measurement and restraint, an easy benevolence but also an unmistakable *gravitas*; it may not be too far-fetched to see in Etna's massive grandeur a reflection of Bernardo's own standing as both *paterfamilias* and pillar of the Venetian establishment. But in contrast to Bernardo's matter of fact rationalization of Etna's workings, for Pietro Etna is a place of wonder and excitement, of mystification and imaginative possibility.[11] Whereas Bernardo sees deep inside the mountain from distant Venice and explains its functioning with an assurance bolstered by the Classical authorities on which he draws, Pietro not only experiences Etna at first hand; in climbing its slopes, he also invests it with personality and color, shaping it through literary elaboration so that its lush tree cover is said to surpass the luxuriance of Alcinous' orchard garden in the Phaeacia of *Odyssey* 7 (112–31; cf. *De Aetna* §23), its lava flows are exuberantly pictured through Hesiodic quotation from the *Theogony* (§39), and Faunus and *fabula* range sportively over the upper slopes (§§48–50). On this approach, the dynamism of Pietro's picture suggestively configures his Etna as a self-projection of sorts, its landscape reflecting the imaginative capacities that he brings to bear as he embarks on his great adventure. Hence the Etna Idea as surveyed in Chapter 1 now gives way to Bembo's idiosyncratic adaptation of it to differentiate father and son throughout *De Aetna*.

But the slopes of Etna constitute only one kind of landscape that is symbolically meaningful in *De Aetna*. In section 6.1 below my starting point for examining the figurative properties of Bembo's Etna is the dialogue's country-villa setting at Noniano: we shall see that the rawness of Etna is set in contrast to the manicured orderliness of Noniano, a juxtaposition that has fundamental implications for the rest of this chapter. Our focus turns in 6.2 to the father-son relationship as portrayed in a revealing set of Latin verses composed by the young Pietro some three or so years before he ventured to Sicily in 1492; the divergent characterizations of father and son in those verses strikingly anticipate not just the differences that are drawn between the two in *De Aetna*, but also certain techniques of literary contrast and of landscape juxtaposition that are redeployed in the dialogue. One of those contrastive techniques is highlighted in 6.3: for all the filial affection and respect that he shows toward Bernardo in *De Aetna*, Pietro also articulates his detachment from the Venetian *cursus*, I argue, by gently subjecting his father's Venice-centered, civic-minded viewpoint to a certain recalibration of perspective that is centered on the Sicilian Other, wild Etna and (self-)exploration far from the aristocratic Venetian career path; in this respect, however informative the dialogue may be about Etna, its still greater importance for now lies in the oblique commentary that it offers on the claims of the late Quattrocento individual in the face of the

11. See in this direction the elusive, mystical Etna well captured by Corti (1999).

traditional Venetian devotion to the common cause that we explored in Chapter 4. Finally, in 6.4, the contrasting characterizations of father and son as delineated thus far in this chapter find their ultimate illustration in the two Etnas that are discernible in *De Aetna*—the rational, mechanistic, and thoroughly explicable Etna that is observed through Bernardo's eyes, and the charismatic, mysterious, and inspiring Etna that is focalized through Pietro's eyes *and* his exuberant imagination.

6.1: Venice, the Veneto, and Villa Culture

After Padua passed under Venetian rule in 1405 and the holdings of the Carraresi dynasty that ruled Padua more or less continuously (1328–37 and 1388–90 apart) from 1318 to 1405 were confiscated by the Serenissima, the extensive agricultural property that included the so called Villa Bozza was acquired at auction in 1406 by Bernardo di Giovanni Bembo, our Pietro's great-grandfather, for the princely sum of 16,000 ducats;[12] the name Villa Bozza was derived from its previous owner,[13] but the name Bembo favors in *De Aetna, Nonianum*, is owed to its location in the village of Santa Maria di Non, at the conjunction of the Piovego and Brenta rivers. At Bernardo's death the property passed to his two sons; the holdings that Nicolò, Pietro's grandfather, acquired through this division included Santa Maria di Non and the Villa Bozza. Perhaps because of his civic burdens, Bernardo, Pietro's father, appears to have had only limited entrepreneurial involvement in the estate that he inherited, but Pietro was more engaged; so at least the surviving documentary evidence suggests, and a further sign to this effect is that a mill that dated back to Nicolò's day but had fallen into disrepair by 1520 was restored in Pietro's time, acquiring a fourth wheel in the process.[14] But if Bernardo was less attentive to other aspects of the estate, the villa was a different matter. While a villa already existed on the lands acquired by the Bembo family in 1406, it was restored or replaced by Bernardo in circumstances importantly shaped, it seems, by his two periods of service as Venetian ambassador to Florence, the first in 1475–6, the second in 1478–80.

After his arrival at Florence in 1475, Bernardo's eloquent and erudite elegance of bearing soon brought him into friendly relations with the luminaries of Florentine humanism, as we have seen.[15] This high esteem is amply reflected in the celebratory Latin poems addressed to him by the likes of Cristoforo Landino, Alessandro

12. On the acquisition of the estate, and on its later history, Puppi (1969) 32–3; Giannetto (1985) 190 and n.299; Callegari (1997b) 41–2; Burns (2013) 113.

13. See Callegari (1997b) 49 n.2 with Kidwell (2004) 205.

14. On these points, Puppi (1969) 33 with Callegari (1997b) 42 and 51 n.20.

15. On his cordial relations with the Medici, Cian (1896) and Pintor (1911) with Giannetto (1985) 143, and cf. Chapter 5 p. 212.

Braccesi, Naldo Naldi, and also Poliziano,[16] whose verses nicely affirm the combination of *gravitas* and good humor that Bernardo also projects in *De Aetna*:

Si causam veneti tutaris, Bembe, senatus,
  mox Pitho in labris stat veneranda tuis.
Seria si tractas, credam tractare Minervam;
  si joca, dat puros Gratia nuda sales.
Carmina seu cantas, tibi Musae in pectore cantant;
  sive taces, tacito ridet in ore lepos.
Si graderis, placido non dura modestia vultu
  est comes et dulcis cum gravitate modus.[17]

If you defend the cause of the Venetian senate, Bembo,
  venerable Persuasion soon stands on your lips.
If you handle serious matters, I'd believe Minerva handles them;
  if jestings, the Grace uncovered gives pure wit.
If you sing songs, the Muses sing in your breast,
  or if you're silent, charm smiles on your silent mouth.
If you walk, an easy restraint accompanies you on your calm face,
  and a pleasant manner combined with dignity.

But while Bernardo impressed, Florence also made a deep impression on him, not least in the "ideal of aristocratic *otium*"[18] that he encountered in rarified circles there—an ideal that extended importantly to the phenomenon of the extra-urban villa as a place of cultured retreat. On a literary front, the humanistic yearning for such escape found powerful expression in the bucolic fashion that is traceable to 1460–70 in particular, and in constructions of Arcadia as a place where the ideals of *otium* found fictional enactment.[19] But the dream of escape was actualized by the Florentine humanists through the specific type of villa—not just a residence but the setting for a particular style of living—that found famous example in the Medici villas at Careggi, Fiesole, Poggio a Caiano, and Cafaggiolo.[20] Location was

16. For these poems, Floriani (1966) 31 and n.2; della Torre (1900) 320–33 (Braccesi and Landino; cf. Chapter 5 pp. 212–13 and n.167); W. L. Grant (1963) 613–14 and n.32 (Naldi); Giannetto (1985) 139–42; see also pp. 262–4 below.

17. Del Lungo (1867) 252 *Eleg.* XI.5–12 (the twenty-line elegy is also printed by Giannetto [1985] 142); on this poem, Cesarini Martinelli (1978) 137–8, and cf. also p. 263 below.

18. Floriani (1966) 32.

19. See Puppi (1969) 47.

20. See Curti (2010) 454 with n.14 for bibliography.

paramount, the garden of central importance to this villa ideology, which was partly Classicizing in its evocations of Ciceronian and Plinian *otium* in rural repose.[21] But another important model, Classical in its own underpinnings, was supplied by the Petrarchan concept of the *vita solitaria*.[22]

In the autumn of 1337, after returning to Avignon from Rome, Petrarch first withdrew to the house that he had acquired at Vaucluse, some fifteen miles from Avignon; down to 1353, he spent nine years there over four periods of seclusion amid the pleasures of study and his garden.[23] In his *De vita solitaria*, begun in 1346, the charms of nature are both soothing and restorative:

> Let provision first be made that, after the prosperous conclusion of his mental toil, one may be enabled to put off the burden of his weariness by having easy access to woods and fields and, what is especially grateful to the Muses, to the bank of a murmuring stream, and at the same time to sow the seeds of new projects in the field of his genius, and in the very interval of rest and recuperation prepare matter for the labor to come.[24]

This alluring vision was seemingly borne out in Petrarch's last years, down to his death in July 1374, at his villa in Arquà in the Euganean Hills near Padua.[25] The comforts he found there are pleasantly pictured in a letter of 1371 or 1372 to his brother, Gherardo:

> Finally, . . . I made up my mind to leave behind all the grand projects, such as everyone would pray for, and limit myself to a modest, solitary life. Therefore, not to go too far from a church, I built a small but decent, delightful house in these Euganean Hills, not more than ten miles from the city of Padua; and I have bought olive groves and some vines, which more than suffice for my modest little household. Though sick in body, here, dear brother, I live with no commotion, no alarms, no anxieties, always reading and writing and praising God . . .[26]

---

21. For the Plinian dimension in particular (cf. *Ep.* 1.9, 5.6) see Curti (2010), esp. 451–2, with Azzi Visentini (1995) 22–6, Callegari (1997b) 45, and McEwen (1995).

22. See Puppi (1972) 88 with Cosgrove (1993) 53–4 and Azzi Visentini (1995) 224.

23. On Vaucluse as place of retreat, Wulff (1904) with Trapp (2006) 1–14; on Petrarch as gardener and horticultural experimenter, Mann (1993).

24. Book 1, 5th Tractate, ch. 2; trans. Zeitlin (1924) 157.

25. On the house in Arquà, Wilkins (1959) 181–3 with Trapp (2006) 14–17 and Azzi Visentini (1995) 224.

26. *Sen.* 15.5; trans. Bernardo et al. (1992) 2.572.

Similarly, in a late letter to the jurist and papal secretary Luca da Penne, Petrarch writes of his retreat to the Euganean hills where "old and infirm, I lead the solitary life I have enjoyed since youth, loving the country, hating the cities (*amator ruris, osor urbium*)."[27] Florentine villa culture consciously drew on the Petrarchan example; and so too did Bernardo Bembo, that devotee of Petrarch, after his return to Venice and his beloved Noniano.

In this Petrarchan connection Giovanni Aurelio Augurello (d. 1524) now enters our story. This humanist, of Rimini by origin, is now perhaps best known for his *Chrysopoeia* (1515), that Latin didactic poem in three books on the topic of alchemy that he dedicated to Pope Leo X.[28] But more important for present purposes is Augurello's significance in the history of Petrarchism: a pioneering humanist in seriously exploring the problems associated with literary applications of the Italian vernacular, he urged a close adherence to rigid rules that were based on the poetic and linguistic model supplied by Petrarch.[29] The biographical tradition has it that Augurello was born in 1440–1, but Roberto Weiss argues strongly for a revisionist date of *c.* 1456;[30] the point matters because of its implications for the chronology of Augurello's friendship with Bernardo Bembo. The majority of biographers locate Augurello in Padua in 1457, studying law; if he was born only in 1456, he can hardly have first met Bernardo in or around 1457, when the latter was also studying at Padua. Hence the case for dating their first meeting to 1475 at Florence, soon after Bernardo's arrival there as ambassador. But the further complications that then arise—among them the difficulty of explaining how Augurello so quickly formed such close relations with Bembo at Florence unless their friendship was already established before 1475—allow no final closure to the chronological problem.[31] What does seem clear, however, is that Bernardo largely owed to Augurello's influence his own devotion to Petrarch on both the vernacular and the Latin fronts.[32] Augurello also became close to Pietro, whose own burgeoning devotion to Petrarch is interestingly evidenced in a witty epigram that he apparently composed when, in 1485, he accompanied his father on a Venetian legation to Rome to congratulate Innocent VIII on his elevation to the papacy:

Surge, pater Francisce, tuos insulsus honores
  dissipat: heu magnae dillacerantur opes!

---

27. *Sen.* 16.1; trans. Bernardo et al. (1992) 2.599.

28. Conveniently on this poem, Y. Haskell (1997) with von Martels (2000). For Augurello's life, Weiss (1962a) and (1962b).

29. See B. Richardson (1994) 48 with Weiss (1962b) 1 and López Suárez (1993).

30. Weiss (1962a) and (1962b) 1 and n.4.

31. See on these points Giannetto (1985) 100–2, 133–5.

32. Giannetto (1985) 102, 174.

haec tua quis credat, profert dum rauce[33] Gerardus
carmina, quae mallem, dum canit, esse sua?

Haec Petrus meus inter equitandum, cum Romam proficisceremur ad Innocentium octavum pontificem, anno salutis 1484, Matheo Gerardo recitante Petrarcae rithmos et vulgaria.[34]

Rise up, father Francesco; a dullard destroys
your marks of honor: alas, great riches are torn to pieces!
Who'd believe these poems are yours while Gerardo gives them raucous delivery?
While he sings them, I'd rather wish they were his.

These by my Pietro during the ride, when we were proceeding to Rome to Pope Innocent VIII, in the year of our salvation [i.e., A.D.] 1484, and Matteo Gerardo was reciting verses and vernacular songs of Petrarch.

For now, the interest of this poem lies partly in its status as Pietro's earliest known composition (he turned fifteen on May 20, 1485), and partly also because of what it reveals of Bernardo's general influence in shaping his son's Petrarchism. But Augurello was also clearly influential: whether or not he became Pietro's teacher after he was taken into the Bembo household by Bernardo down to 1485,[35] his closeness to Pietro is reflected in the latter's affectionate allusions to him in *De Aetna* and elsewhere[36]—a proximity touchingly underscored if Augurello is accepted as the author in *c.* 1479 of a vernacular sonnet that is addressed to the young Pietro and that, in hailing his skills of Petrarchan song, unerringly anticipates Bembo's later renown as a vernacular practitioner.[37]

Given this devotion to Petrarch, the Petrarchan shadow surely lingers when, in his *Carmina*, Augurello praises Bernardo's Noniano as "the most delightful villa" (*amoenissima villa*),[38] and when at *De Aetna* §16 Bernardo himself quotes

33. Adv. *rauce* (albeit -ĕ) probably pointed in its Petrarchan derivation: Giannetto (1985) 174 n.218.

34. The epigram, conveniently printed by Giannetto (1985) 170 and Finotti (2004) 23, was inscribed by Bernardo on fol. 168*r* of what is now Ms. 135, Eton College Library (Seneca, *Epistulae ad Lucilium*): see Danzi (2005) 347–8 with Giannetto 170 and n.210, and then 307–9. For Bernardo's error in ascribing the journey (and the epigram) to 1484, not 1485, Giannetto 170–3. Little or nothing is known of Matteo Gerardo, unless the name hints at Maffeo Gerardo: Giannetto 175.

35. Floriani (1966) 37–8.

36. So *De Aetna* §16; for Augurello as "nostro onoratiss. padre" cf. Travi (1990) 58 *Letter* 315.31 and 107 *Letter* 360.7–8.

37. For this sonnet, Danzi (1990) 226–8.

38. See p. 323 n.28.

Augurello's verses in celebration of Noniano's poplars. Those verses, first published in 1491,[39] may well date back to Augurello's years in Padua in 1477–85, thereby suggestively coinciding with Bernardo's likely construction or renovation of Noniano after he returned from his first ambassadorship to Florence in 1476,[40] or perhaps after his second ambassadorship in 1478–80.[41] Beyond his expressions of fondness for Noniano in *De Aetna* itself, Bernardo's profound interest in villa architecture and culture is attested by the surviving annotations that he made in a copy of Pliny's letters;[42] by his visit late in 1487 to the Villa Adriana at Tivoli;[43] by Benedetto Maffei's dedication to Bernardo, no later than 1494, of his *Breve compendium futurorum eventuum rei rusticae*, in the dedicatory letter of which Maffei highlights Bembo's passion for agriculture and the attractiveness of his Paduan retreat, where he was wont *saepenumero cum Musis rusticari in . . . suburbano agro*;[44] by the later testimony of Bernardino Scardeone (1478–1574), who, in his *Historiae de urbis Patavii antiquitate et claris civibus Patavinis libri tres* of 1560, reports that Bernardo set up Noniano as what would prove to be an *amoena sedes* for the young Pietro's philosophical studies;[45] and, perhaps most strikingly, by the request that Bernardo made directly to Lorenzo de' Medici, in a letter written on April 17, 1479 during his second ambassadorship at Florence, that a retreat be made available to him during his stay as ambassador to facilitate his studies away from all urban nuisance and danger.[46]

---

39. Republished in the Aldine *Carmina* of 1505: Floriani (1966) 37 and n.2.

40. On these points, Puppi (1969) 32. The case for renovation of Noniano in *c.* 1476, as opposed to *ex novo* construction, is based on Bernardo's lament, at *De Aetna* §15, that "ever since I built this villa [presumably adapting or replacing the original Villa Bozza], already from before you were born (*ex quo hanc villam exaedificavimus, iam inde ante quam tu esses natus*), I've never yet been able to spend thirty days here in one stretch": if Bernardo (or Pietro *qua* author) is taken at his word here, Bernardo's Noniano was evidently built before 1470.

41. So at least Curti (2010) 454.

42. See Chapter 5 pp. 208–9 with Burns (2013) 118.

43. For which Giannetto (1985) 191 and n.261.

44. See Giannetto (1985) 189–90 with Cian (1885) 37 n.1; Puppi (1969) 32; Callegari (1997b) 41 and 50 n.9; Burns (2013) 118. For Maffei himself, Giannetto 190 n.258 with Castiglione (2006); 1494, the year of Maffei's death, provides a sure *terminus ante quem*, but Giannetto 190 n.259 inclines to composition when Bernardo was at Rome in 1487–8 or soon thereafter.

45. See Callegari (1997b) 49 n.2, and also 50 n.14 for Scardeone's words cited (= p. 306 in the 1560 Basel edition published by Nicolaus Episcopius the Younger): *Bernardus Bembus patritius venetus . . . in hoc vico agrum habuit, in quo quum Petrus filius philosophiae studiis incumbens, suorum sibi studiorum amoenam sedem delegisset, rus istud Nonianum suis scriptis eleganter celebravit.*

46. On this letter, Pintor (1911) 806 with Giannetto (1985) 35; Callegari (1997b) 41–2; Curti (2010) 454–5.

This letter usefully illustrates the Florentine dialectic between *otium* and *negotium* that Bernardo transposed to his beloved Noniano. Here was arguably one of the first realizations of the Tuscan phenomenon in the Veneto, even if it goes too far to single out Bernardo as a pioneering popularizer of Tuscan *villeggiatura* in the region generally.[47] From the architectural standpoint, the Tuscan estate differed from its emergent counterparts in the Veneto, and not just because of what Lionello Puppi characterizes as the Venetian tendency toward "a colorful distribution, mellow and atmospheric, of constituent elements" in place of the "geometrical and modeled organization of the Tuscan garden."[48] Whereas in Central Italy the villa symbolized individual prestige and wealth and tended to be idiosyncratic in its shaping, the Venetian villa of the Quattrocento and Cinquecento was a more generalized phenomenon, an expression not so much of individual caprice but of the lifestyle and standing of an entire social echelon in Venice and the Terraferma.[49] There were nevertheless sub-variations of villa typology within this larger aristocratic fashion;[50] of those variations, Bembo's Noniano conforms to the model of the Venetian suburban villa transposed to the country[51]—a model well illustrated today in details of the renowned map of Venice, bird's eye in perspective, produced by Jacopo de' Barbari in 1500.[52] Nothing now survives of Noniano itself, and the only remaining image of the villa is an eighteenth-century engraving by Francesco Zucchi (1692–1764), its likeness to the Noniano of Bernardo and Pietro's time now unverifiable, that was reproduced in the 1729 four-volume edition of Pietro Bembo's *Opere* published by Francesco Hertzhauser in Venice (Figure 6.1).[53] But one late Quattrocento villa is cited by Puppi[54] as a suggestive approximation to Noniano in external appearance: the Villa Corner dall'Aglio, in Lughignano, Casale sul Sile, in the province of Treviso,[55]

47. On this point, Puppi (1969) 52.

48. Puppi (1969) 49, citing in turn Panofsky (1939) 148: "Where Florentine art is based on design, plastic firmness and tectonic structure, Venetian art is based on colour and atmosphere, pictorial succulence and musical harmony."

49. On this point, Azzi Visentini (1995) 221.

50. See Azzi Visentini (1995) 224–6.

51. For this category of the "casa di città trapiantata, con pochi aggiustamenti, in campagna," Azzi Visentini (1995) 224 with Puppi (1969) 51.

52. See for illustration Puppi (1969) 45, 46, 49.

53. Vol. 4.153; very possibly "a retrospective fantasy" (W. H. Sherman [2013] 121), but in keeping with the ambience projected in *De Aetna*.

54. (1969) 51.

55. For conveniently assembled images (frontal and bird's eye, and a plan of the ground floor), Kubelik (1986) 94; a photograph also in Puppi (1969) 43.

was by one tradition built by Caterina Cornaro, the Sovereign Lady of Asolo whom we encountered earlier, as a wedding gift for her favorite lady-in-waiting, Fiammetta.[56]

Given the traditional importance of Venice's maritime economy and its lack of subject territories on the mainland, landownership was a relatively insignificant source of wealth creation or mode of investment down to the fifteenth century.[57] The conquests of the Terraferma that took place early in that century generated tensions not only with Venice's neighbors but also within Venice itself, where landed interests potentially threated to encroach upon its traditional mercantile mission. Certain factors nevertheless encouraged land investment in the Terraferma: even though the fall of Constantinople in 1453 and the opening of new trade routes through the Portuguese and Spanish voyages of discovery in the 1490s and beyond were hardly fatal blows to Venice's mercantile economy in the short term, those events contributed to the longer-term weakening of its commercial position even before it became embroiled in the War of the League of Cambrai (1508–16). Advances in maritime technology gradually made the Venetian galley obsolete and exposed the limitations of Venetian shipbuilding techniques; the Terraferma provided a bulwark of land protection for Venice itself; agricultural investment there not only yielded tax revenues to ease Venice's burgeoning public debt, but also offered protection against the Turkish threat to the grain supply in the eastern Mediterranean; and an increasing reluctance to invest in high-risk maritime trading ventures to distant parts was accompanied by a greater capital investment in land, whether in Venetian real estate or in agricultural holdings in the Terraferma.[58] With this transition from a *stato da mar* to a *stato da terra*,[59] a new class of rentier landlord arose in the form of the Venetian city dweller deriving income from the Terraferma estates. But the effect of the transition was also cultural and architectural: Venetian requirements for comfortable living in the country brought modifications to traditional rural architecture, but the rising phenomenon of the country retreat as a place purely of recreation provoked a still more radical departure from the architectural norms of the inherited rural tradition.[60] Hence also the proliferation of Venetian landscape art featuring the

56. See Chapter 4 p. 169 with Gottfried (1954) viii; further on Fiammetta Buc(h)ari in particular, Maltezou (2013) 287–8.

57. Succinctly, Cosgrove (1998) 107.

58. On these points, Bouwsma (1968) 105–6; Puppi (1972) 86–7; Cosgrove (1993) 35, 46–7 and (1998) 107–8, 113, 119; Azzi Visentini (1995) 221–2.

59. See Azzi Visentini (1995) 222.

60. See Puppi (1972) 87.

topography of the Terraferma,[61] and of treatises on villa living that were "as much cultural handbooks as agrarian manuals."[62]

If landscape painting offered one way of controlling visual space,[63] landscape design on the estates of the expanding Terraferma imposed control and form on the natural canvas. The rise of the carefully manicured villa garden in the Terraferma (and by no means exclusively there) coincided with, and was in part shaped by, at least two key developments of the age. The first concerns the movement from urban to extra-urban cultural design. The enlarged world that was revealed by the voyages of discovery required new techniques of cartographical representation and control of perspective in the plotting of terrestrial space—a process of reconceptualizing familiar space perception that was still more radically felt through Copernican heliocentrism. The spatial control that cartography, ordnance surveying, and town planning imposed at a practical level in this era of geographical expansion (whether locally through civic population growth or transnationally through overseas exploration) was matched at an artistic/visual and ideological level in landscape painting and in villa/villa-garden design.[64] Fundamental to artistic landscape technique, as in architecture, was linear perspective, the principles of which were first demonstrated by the artist, engineer, and architect Filippo Brunelleschi (1377–1446) at Florence in a celebrated experiment of *c.* 1420; those principles were subsequently codified by Leon Battista Alberti in his *Della pittura* of 1435. With the movement of landscape design outward from the urban center to the subservient country periphery, so linear perspective was an urban invention that moved outward,[65] a technique of civic spatial representation that was widely reapplied in extra-urban villa construction and garden planning.

Secondly, the villa garden functioned as a symbolic boundary separating, and mediating between, cultivated nature and its untamed or unworked counterpart; for Denis Cosgrove, the Renaissance garden and gardening could serve even as "a trope for Europeans' imaginative domestication of a new, global spatiality that was characterized above all by the disruption of previously established spatial, ethnographic, and conceptual boundaries."[66] In this safe haven the intimidating potential of exotic botanical discoveries could be resisted and redirected through

61. See Cosgrove (1988) 259–62, (1993) 50–2, and (1998) 103–6, 122–6.

62. Cosgrove (1988) 259.

63. Further, Cosgrove (1998) 21.

64. Cosgrove (1985) 46.

65. Cosgrove (1985) 49–50.

66. Cosgrove (2008) 53.

their controlled cultivation, while the romantic sensuousness of this *locus amoenus*, pure and inviolable, was also symbolically a world away from the uglier realities of the voyages of discovery, not least among them the virulent spread of syphilis in the Old World.[67] The charms of this garden-as-boundary are well exemplified by the idyllic scene that Pietro pictures in *Gli Asolani* (1505) of the garden at Caterina Cornaro's Asolo:

> This garden was of surpassing charm and beauty: In addition to a fair pergola of vines whose broad and shady structure divided it in the middle like a cross, a long and spacious walk, which was bestrewed with shining flint and might be entered at various places, ran around the perimeter. Except where there was an opening into the pergola, this alley was fenced on its inner side by a hedge of very thick, green junipers whose tops might have reached the breast of one who had approached them in order to enjoy the scene, which was equally agreeable in every part. Along the outer edge time-honored laurels, standing much taller than the junipers and half-overarching the pathway with their upper boughs, grew so close and neatly pruned that not one leaf appeared to desire any place but that assigned to it; nor did they reveal any part of the wall behind them except, at either end of one side, the milk-white marble of two ample windows. *From these, if one sat within them, as the great thickness of the structure here allowed, he could send his eye far out across the plain, which they commanded from aloft.*[68]

This description, which is itself evocative of the garden scenes and woodcut illustrations of the 1499 *Hypnerotomachia Poliphili*,[69] configures an enclosed sanctum idyllically separated from the outside world that is visible from it: "we gaze out from the centre into spaces of potential exploration"[70]—a perspective relatable, Cosgrove suggests, to that of "Bembo and . . . many of his contemporary Venetians living through years of unprecedented change in Europeans' geographical consciousness and vision, [for whom] the space of wilderness and exploration lay beyond Italy and the Old World: across the wilderness of oceans."[71]

---

67. Cf. on this point Cosgrove (2008) 58; also Battaglia Ricci (1996) 24 for the garden in Boccaccio's *Decameron* as an oasis-like safe haven from the ravages of real-world plague.

68. 1.5 Dilemmi (1991) 86.1–18; trans. Gottfried (1954) 13–14 (my emphasis).

69. On these similarities, Cosgrove (2008) 64.

70. Cosgrove (2008) 56.

71. Cosgrove (2008) 56; cf. (1993) 49–50.

To return at this point to *De Aetna*, Bernardo's Noniano stands as a model of Venetian *villeggiatura*, of villa-*otium* in the Petrarchan-Florentine tradition, within the Terraferma. The villa setting of *De Aetna* now becomes crucially important. For Siegmund Günther, Bernardo's aspiration for plane trees in addition to the splendid poplars that he has long nurtured at Noniano, and his account of his more general efforts to build up the estate for the benefit of his heirs (§§14–21), amount to "endless, tiresome chatterings" that bear little or no relation to the book's main Etna theme.[72] From an alternative perspective, however, Bernardo's fond account of Noniano and its growth constitutes one of at least two competing conceptualizations of space in *De Aetna*, the first of them a vision of nature ordered and modeled into (e.g.) carefully patterned rows of fruit trees (*illas fructiferas arbores, quas in quinquuncem dispositas habemus*, §14) and the choreographed cluster of poplars that adorn the riverbank in §16. Secondly, however, in contrast to this manicured picture of the villa estate stands Etna in all its rawness, as if a macro-botanical wonder in comparison with the boutique garden[73]—a counter-conceptualization of space that functions in *De Aetna* not unlike the plain that is visible from the garden enclave that we visited in *Gli Asolani*. From our comfortable vantage point in the Asolo garden we gaze out toward Cosgrove's "spaces of potential exploration." A similar effect is discernible in *De Aetna*, albeit with much greater menace in the volcano that looms far beyond the horto-haven: in the serene setting of Noniano, Etna is configured as the dangerous but safely distant Other, the antithesis of nature as modeled and controlled in the Terraferma.

If this distancing and controlling perspective is associated with Bernardo in particular, that *auctor Noniani* whose assured explanation of Etna's volcanic workings (§§33–8) may itself be relatable to this pattern of imposing design on nature, then Pietro returns to the villa garden from the outside, as it were. In contrast to the proportioned formalism of the garden, his Etna is in every way a singular model of *dis*proportion and volcanically changeful shape, unique rather than conforming to type: "The mountain itself is remarkable (*mirus*)," he gushes (§22), "in its layout, shape, size, fertility, and its fires; in sum, in its overall nature and appearance it draws attention to itself from afar and is absolutely unique (*sibi uni par est*)." True, Pietro may in some ways envisage Etna through the eyes of what might be termed villa perception, as when he declares that the vegetation on its lower slopes is richer even that that in Alcinous' Homeric orchard garden (§23). But in experiencing the

72. Günther (1904) 63.

73. Cf. Della Dora (2009) for interesting analysis of Mount Athos as resembling a vertical botanical garden: Bembo's luxuriant Etna suggestively conforms to Della Dora's assertion (p. 105) that "[m]ountains can resemble islands and botanical gardens as 'vertical microcosms' characterized by microhabitats at different altitudes" (see also Chapter 2 p. 91).

mountain at first hand, in his risk-taking at the crater's edge (§26–7), in his account of the lava flows and the discomfort of journeying across them when they had cooled into rough, crumbling rock (§§42, 44)—through these features and more, Pietro's recounting of his Sicilian adventure in peaceful Noniano is out of place and even otherworldly, as if an intrusive narratival and thematic rupturing of villa-garden shape, proportion, and risk-free tranquility.

If in at least *De Aetna*, then, the villa garden is the limit of Bernardo's experience of nature, Pietro's climbing of Etna constitutes a far more complete and unrestrained immersion in *natura ipsa*—a superlative leap into the wilderness after the merely comparative degree of rural awakening at Noniano. The one landscape is controlled, measured, and stable, the other more exuberant, dynamic, and far less predictable: the dispositions of father and son are suggestively figured by alignment with these different types of landscape, a contrast that can perhaps be taken still further if the shaping of nature at Noniano[74] is related to the constructedness of Venice itself. The latter was "more than most [cities] a purely human creation,"[75] complex hydrology, drainage, and land reclamation crucial to its growth and well-being,[76] and in this respect the technological, cultural, and economic marvel that Venice represents is implicitly contrasted in *De Aetna* by Etna's rawness: if Sicily offers "un prodige de violence brutale," Venice stands as "un miracle de puissance tranquille."[77] The city was itself a symbolic landscape, its stability founded upon the myth of Venice as a perfectly balanced constitution that incorporated monarchy (in the form of the elected Doge), aristocracy, and popular republicanism.[78] The myth was historical in reach, perpetuating Venice's self-idealization as a unique Republic that was heir to the greatness of Classical Rome,[79] even though its civic past was largely invented;[80] the myth was also geographical in scope, its prosperity, security, and freedom seemingly assured by the lagoon that encircled it, by its favorable position at the crossroads of Europe and Asia, and, especially in sixteenth-century

74. Cf. Puppi (1969) 47 on this vision of "[u]na natura . . . non già spontanea, ma modellata e costruita sull'immagine di un sogno, di un'aspirazione ideale. . . ."

75. Cosgrove (1993) 41.

76. See Crouzet-Pavan (2002) 1–45 with Appuhn (2009) 61–74 and Ciriacono (2006), esp. 19–156.

77. Viallon (2002) 9.

78. Further on the myth, King (1986), esp. xviii–xix, 132–40, 174–5 ("Venetian humanism, in brief, perpetuates the 'myth of Venice'"); P. F. Brown (1996), esp. 11–29; Kallendorf (1999), esp. 14–20; Rosand (2001); Crouzet-Pavan (2002).

79. Cosgrove (1993) 41; (1998) 109.

80. See P. F. Brown (1996), esp. 11 ("A Borrowed Past"), 15 ("A Stolen Past"), 21 ("A Simulated Past"), and 25 ("A Roman Past").

representations, by its status "as a realized perfection, sacred centre or *axis mundi* of its maritime and territorial empires."[81] This self-idealization manifested itself through the grandeur of its civic architecture (itself a complex network of visual allusions to Venice's constructed past),[82] but also through cartography: to return to the famous example supplied by Jacopo de' Barbari, his bird's-eye visualization of 1500 distorts and manipulates spatial emphasis so that Venice floats centrally within the lagoon, the ceremonial, administrative, and commercial heart of the city is given special prominence, and the dolphin as symbol of Venice is itself iconographically rendered through topographical shaping and compression.[83] This myth of Venice was also sustained and propagated through the many public ceremonies, processions, and celebrations extending from the sober to the liberating, from ecclesiastical ritual to popular carnival, that punctuated the calendar: Renaissance Venice was "the paradigm city of spectacular civic ritual,"[84] the entire community bound together through this performative mode of Venetian self-consciousness.

Beyond the landscapes of Etna and Noniano, then, I propose that a third landscape conditions *De Aetna* in significant ways: that of Venice itself. Bernardo finds it so hard at Noniano to prevent his thoughts from returning to Venice and his affairs of state there (§§5–8). Through this intrusiveness of *urbs in Arcadia*, the city functions as a permanent sub-presence in *De Aetna*, with the further implications, at least on one reading, that its cultured splendor is aggrandized through contrast with the wilderness of Etna; that the myth of Venice counters the hellish, gigantomachic associations of the volcano in the mythical imagination; and that, for all Etna's spectacular pyrotechnics, Venice is itself a wonder of civilized spectacle because of its physical setting within the lagoon, the splendors of its civic design and architecture, and its highly performative ceremonial calendar. Thus far the view from Venice; but a very different reading of landscape in *De Aetna* beckons as soon as Pietro's Sicilian adventure is understood as a form of release from the Venetian *cursus*, his climb of Etna an expression of youthful energies that seek challenge, risk, and experimentation far from home. When we look back on Venice from this alternative viewpoint, the unaffected naturalness of the mountain, its vast volcanic energies, the massiveness of its proportions, and the spectacle of its lava flows all give pause for reflection: as we survey Venice's carefully regulated and contrived grandeur from this Sicilian perspective, does the myth of Venice sustain itself, or do we find it qualified, even overwhelmed, by comparison with matchless Etna? If in this way

81. Cosgrove (1993) 36, 41.

82. P. F. Brown (1996) 11.

83. On these points, Schulz (1978); Cosgrove (1985) 51 and (1998) 109–11; Howard (1997).

84. Daniels and Cosgrove (1993) 59, with elaboration on pp. 59–64.

Pietro gently interrogates Venetian self-regard from his external vantage point in *De Aetna*, experience of Venetian spatial design might further sensitize our reading of Bembo's Etna in another way: given the pervasive visual symbolism attaching to Venetian landscape, whether in the form of ritual spectacle in public spaces, architectural messaging, or representation in art or cartography, how likely is it that the hand that penned *De Aetna* was insensitive to the symbolic potential of landscape depiction? Venice's reputation as "a singularly nocturnal city"[85] is also very suggestive in this respect, famous as it was for the illuminations that made light of night, and for the mirror effect of flame and firework reflected in its ubiquitous waters. Quite apart from the hazards involved in Venice's harnessing of fire for its industrial capacity and military needs (its production of pyrotechnic munitions chief among them), Renaissance Venice was in any case "a tinder box" that experienced major conflagrations on a serial basis.[86] Yet from the perspectives of both thrill and danger, of festival display and destructive capability, the Venetian experience of fire is dwarfed in *De Aetna* by the ultimate pyrotechnics that erupt in nature's theater. In sum, Classical treatments of Etna had already teemed with imaginative elaboration, as we saw in Chapter 1; beyond the stimulus supplied by that tradition, however, Bembo's own Venetian milieu easily lent itself to juxtaposition with Etna, fueling yet further the volcano's capacities as a generator of figured meaning.

6.2: Father and Son in Pietro's Early Verses

Before we explore the different perceptions of Etna that set Bernardo and Pietro apart in *De Aetna*, important light on their relationship in general, and on how that relationship is portrayed in the dialogue in particular, is shed by one of the earliest known samples of Pietro's literary activity: a set of forty-eight hexameters contained in Ms. Cicogna 1428 (fols. 32*v*–33*v*) of the Biblioteca del Museo Correr, Venice.[87] Carlo Dionisotti identifies this manuscript as a late copy, probably seventeenth century, of a notebook that belonged to three generations of Bembos; for the Latin and vernacular poetry of varied authorship that it contains shows dedications to Bernardo, Pietro, and Torquato, Pietro's son.[88] The lines in question are introduced as follows: *Ad Patrem Petrus Bembus ex otio Noniano quo secesserat ex praetura Bergomensi qua ego tunc fungebar 1483* ("Pietro Bembo to his father, from

85. Hills (2007) 196.

86. So Hills (2007) 190, citing major incidents in 1509, 1514, and the 1570s.

87. Discovered and published by Dionisotti (1965) 289–90 = Vela (2002) 111–12.

88. Dionisotti (1965) 288–9 = Vela (2002) 110–11.

leisurely retreat at Noniano, to which he had withdrawn from my then period of service, 1483, as governor of Bergamo"). The words *qua ego . . . 1483* clearly signal Bernardo's hand in the archetype, but Dionisotti posits 1483 as a copyist's error for 1489, when Bernardo was appointed *podestà* of Bergamo;[89] hence the inference that Pietro composed these verses at nineteen or so. Elegant and witty in their evocation of familiar Classical tropes, the lines gently take Bernardo to task for summoning his sons to Bergamo and thereby disrupting their pleasant repose at Noniano. Their pertinence for now lies in the complementary systems of contrast—epic versus pastoral, *otium* versus *negotium*—that Pietro works into the passage in two stages. First, lines 1–18:

Cur tua tam subitis anguntur pectora curis
absentesque premis natos, atque otia rumpis
nostra nec optatam pateris durare quietem?
Quid si monstriferi biberentur flumina Nili
ultimus aut Tanais nobis? extremave Tyle
pasceret? aut multa positi sub luce Britanni?
Mitte supervacuos, pater o charissime, questus
et compesce tui largas moeroris habenas.
Non nos per longum ninfis mirantibus aequor
phasiacae dubium petimus certamen harenae,
nec labyrinthei frangenda ad cornua tauri
Aegaeo dedimus nigrantia vela profundo,
sed proprii ruris placidaeque ad munera villae
venimus, albentes nunc cum nec Syrius agros
ardet et afflatu Boreas non saevit acuto,
sed pater autumnus compressis sordidus uvis
pomiferum quatiens circum caput arbore frondes
decutit et solito tellurem spargit honore.

Why is your breast tormented by such sudden cares,
and why do you harass your absent sons, disrupting our leisure
and refusing to let our cherished repose last?
What if the waters of the monster-bearing Nile were drunk by us,
or the far distant Tanais? Or remotest Thule were feeding us?
Or the Britons in their place of long daylight?
Dismiss your needless complaints, o father dearest,

89. Dionisotti (1965) 289 = Vela (2002) 111; Giannetto (1985) 199 n.278 and Finotti (2004) 29 n.84 follow Dionisotti's lead on 1489.

and hold in the generous reins of your sorrowing.
We are not seeking perilous strife on the Colchian shore
as the nymphs look on in wonder throughout the distant sea,
nor have we set dark sail on the Aegean sea
to break the horns of the bull in the labyrinth,
but we've come to the gifts of our own countryside and
of the tranquil villa;
we've come now, and not when the dog star scorches the
pale fields,
and not when the north wind rages with its sharp breath,
but when father autumn, discolored by the squeezing of grapes,
shakes his fruit-bearing head around and dislodges the leaves
from the tree,
scattering the ground with his usual offering.

By invoking the familiar Latin literary roll call of the ends of the earth (such as Thule and Tanais), Pietro nicely qualifies Bernardo's cause for complaint and sorrow (cf. *curis*, 1; *moeroris*, 8): were his sons in one of those dangerous extremities, and not in pleasant Noniano, then, and only then, Bernardo might have reasonable cause for concern. In this adaptation of the well-worn Classical *recusatio* of epic, the high generic overtones of Pietro's allusions to the Argonautic mission to Colchis (9–10) and Theseus' encounter with the Minotaur (11–12) are contrasted by the pastoral evocations of lines 13–14 and 16–18, where Noniano is cast not just as a haven of *otium* but also as a highly stylized literary *locus* in and of itself.[90] This contrast between epic adventure in the wider world and the pastoral charms that captivate Pietro at Noniano recurs in lines 19–48, but with added nuance:

Hic nostri nullo rumpuntur murmure somni,
turbantur nec lite dies: seu fertilis horti
et dulces herbas et dulcia carpere poma,
seu iuvat interdum curvos spectare iuvencos

90. For the epic dimension cf. the poem of Giovanni Aurelio Augurello (for whom pp. 227–9) that is also preserved in Ms. Cicogna 1428 and dedicated *Petro Bembo Bernardi Senatoris Clarissimi Filio: O quam principio indolem/ prae se mirifice tulit/ ille, cum patris optimi/ nuper carmine turbidam/ ausus tangere mentem/ admovit solidam ori/ heroi sonitus tubam* (= Augurello, *Carminum libri* 2.6.14–20, in a poem entitled *Ad Musam: In Petri Bembi patritii Veneti laudem*: "Oh what talent he marvelously exhibited from the outset, when he lately dared to move his excellent father's turbid mind with song, and put to his lips the resolute trumpet of heroic sound"); *nuper* refers "without doubt" (Dionisotti [1965] 289 = Vela [2002] 111) to Pietro's poem *Ad Patrem*.

vomere et in longo terram perscindere sulco,
lanigerumve pecus simasque errare capellas
. . . .

Non hic suppositis desunt quos fallere pisces
retibus aut facili lubeat suspendere canna,
nec quos decipiant varias imitantia voces
sibila pendentes viscataque vimina turdi.
Has quoque venatrix silvas coluisse Diana
fertur olim nostrosque arte[m] docuisse colonos
qua violare feras atque arcu figere cervos
quave queant mediis lepores educere silvis
eductosque sequi
. . . .

Et tamen ut desint haec omnia, sola voluptas
maxima, quod totos datur hic absumere soles
seu veterum libris seu parvae munere musae.
Te quoque nunc cultae qui damnas otia villae
atque tuo nostram minuis moerore quietem
haec memini solitum laudare, et saepe beatos
appellare dies, placidis quos condere in agris
sollicitamque simul licet obliviscere vitam.

Here our sleep is broken by no murmur, and the days
are disturbed by no arguing: whether your pleasure is to pluck
the sweet crops and sweet fruits of the fertile garden,
or sometimes to watch the bullocks bent [under the yoke, and to see them]
split open the earth with the plowshare in a long furrow,
or the fleecy flock and snub-nosed goats roam about.
. . . .

Here there's no lack of fish for you to trick as you please
by laying nets or by dangling them from your easy rod of reed,
and no lack of hovering thrushes to deceive with your whistles
that mimic different bird cries, or with branches smeared with bird lime.
These woods the huntress Diana is said once to have frequented as well,
and to have taught our husbandmen the art of wounding wild animals
and shooting stags with the bow, and how they can draw hares

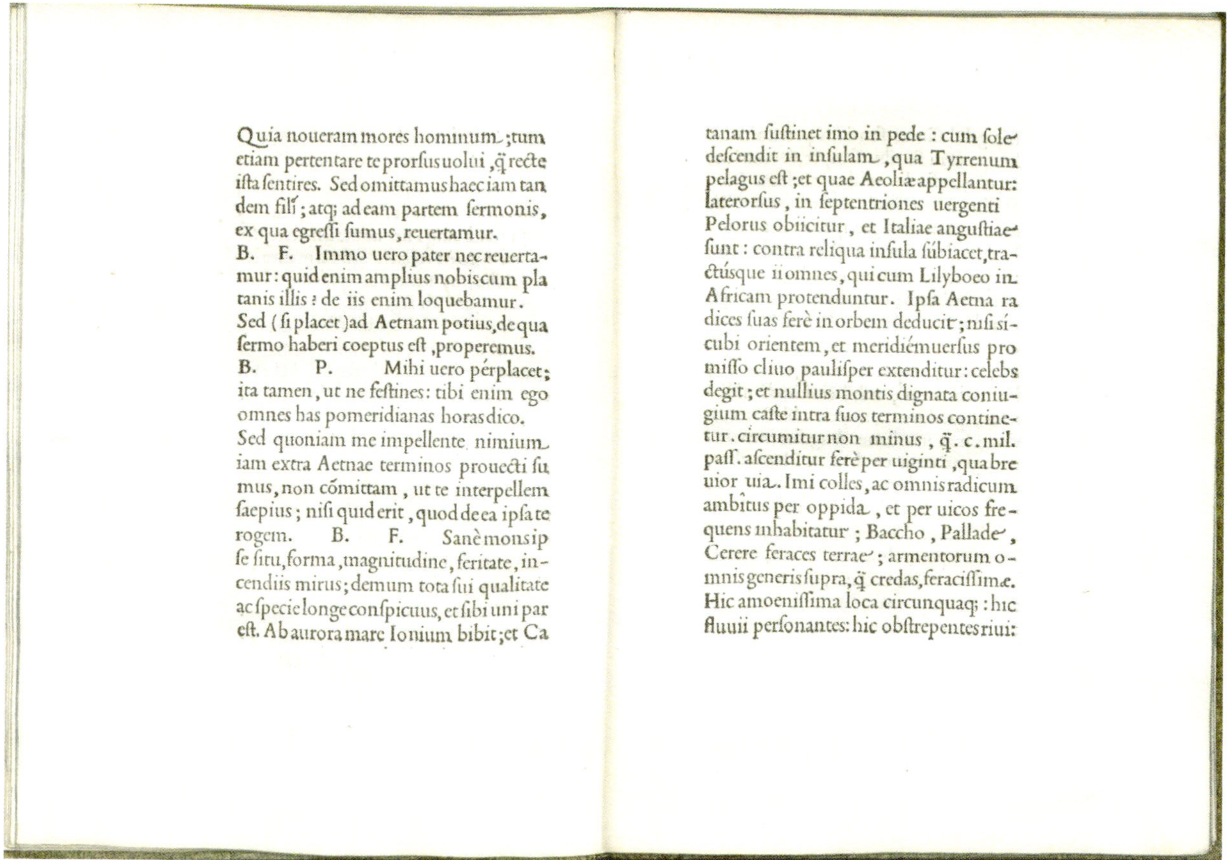

Quia noueram mores hominum ;tum
etiam pertentare te prorſus uolui ,q̃ recte
iſta ſentires. Sed omittamus haec iam tan
dem fili ; atq; ad eam partem ſermonis,
ex qua egreſſi ſumus, reuertamur.
B. F. Immo uero pater nec reuerta-
mur: quid enim amplius nobiſcum pla
tanis illis ? de iis enim loquebamur.
Sed (ſi placet)ad Aetnam potius,de qua
ſermo haberi coeptus eſt ,properemus.
B. P. Mihi uero pérplacet;
ita tamen , ut ne feſtines: tibi enim ego
omnes has pomeridianas horas dico.
Sed quoniam me impellente nimium
iam extra Aetnae terminos prouecti ſu
mus, non cõmittam , ut te interpellem
ſaepius ; niſi quid erit , quod de ea ipſa te
rogem. B. F. Sanè mons ip
ſe ſitu, forma , magnitudine , feritate , in-
cendiis mirus; demum tota ſui qualitate
ac ſpecie longe conſpicuus, et ſibi uni par
eſt. Ab aurora mare Ionium bibit;et Ca

tanam ſuſtinet imo in pede : cum ſole
deſcendit in inſulam ,qua Tyrrenum
pelagus eſt ;et quae Aeoliæ appellantur:
laterorſus , in ſeptentriones uergenti
Pelorus obiicitur , et Italiae anguſtiae
ſunt : contra reliqua inſula ſúbiacet,tra-
ctúsque ii omnes, qui cum Lilyboeo in
Africam protenduntur. Ipſa Aetna ra
dices ſuas ferè in orbem deducit ; niſi ſí-
cubi orientem , et meridiémuerſus pro
miſſo cliuo pauliſper extenditur: celebs
degit ; et nullius montis dignata coniu-
gium caſte intra ſuos terminos contine-
tur. circumitur non minus , q̃. c. mil.
paſſ. aſcenditur ferè per uiginti ,qua bre
uior uia. Imi colles, ac omnis radicum
ambitus per oppida , et per uicos fre-
quens inhabitatur ; Baccho , Pallade ,
Cerere feraces terrae ; armentorum o-
mnis generis ſupra, q̃ credas, feraciſſimæ.
Hic amoeniſſima loca circunquaq; : hic
fluuii perſonantes: hic obſtrepentes riui:

Figure Intro.1 Sample page illustration from the 1496 Aldine *editio princeps* of *De Aetna*.

FIGURE 4.1 Vittore Carpaccio, *St Ursula's arrival in Rome*, part of his *Saint Ursula* cycle, 1488–1495.

Gallerie dell'Accademia, Venice

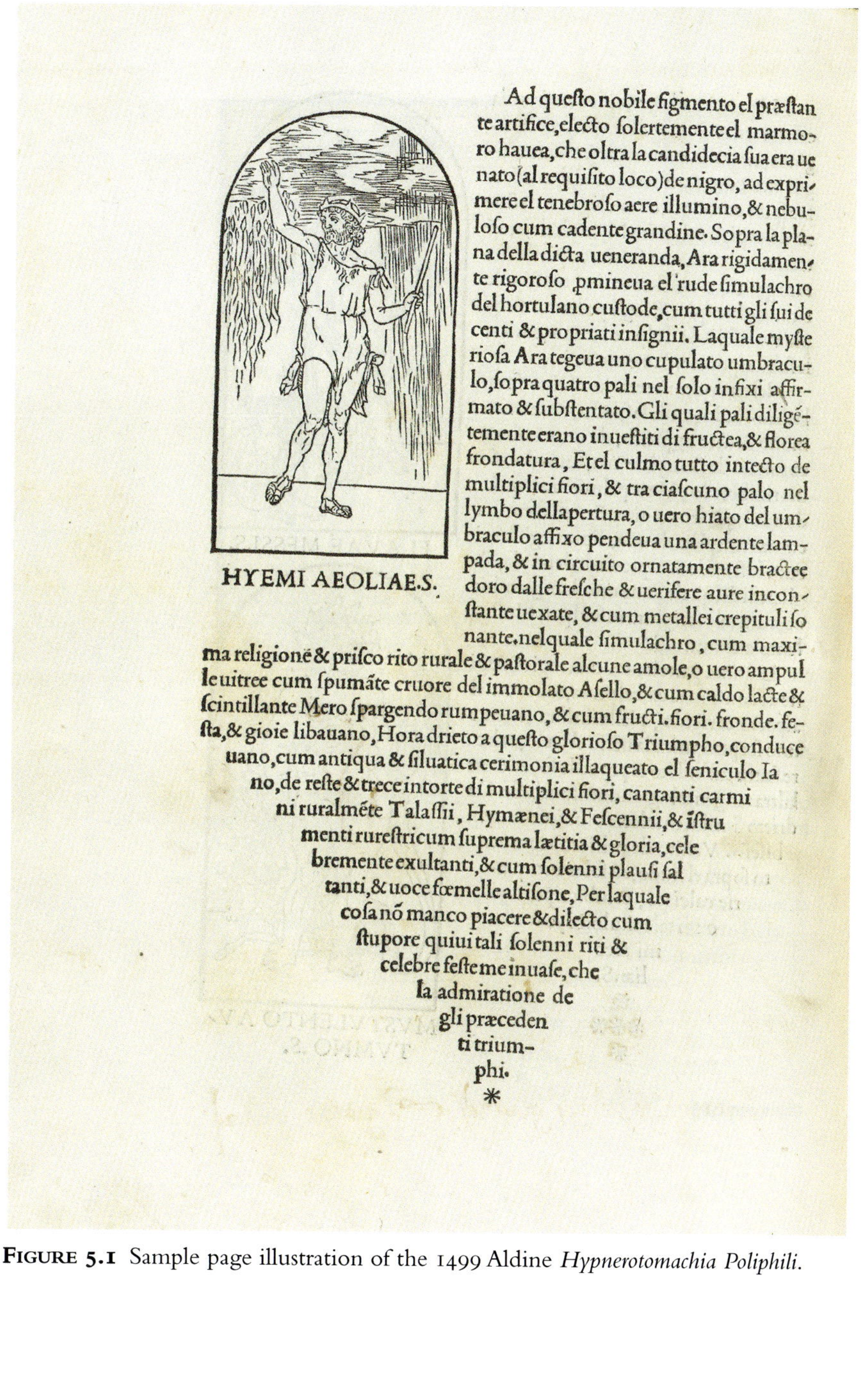

Ad queſto nobile figmento el præſtan
te artifice, electo ſolertemente el marmo-
ro hauea, che oltra la candidecia ſua era ue
nato (al requiſito loco) de nigro, ad expri-
mere el tenebroſo aere illumino, & nebu-
loſo cum cadente grandine. Sopra la pla-
na della dicta ueneranda, Ara rigidamen-
te rigoroſo ꝑmineua el rude ſimulachro
del hortulano cuſtode, cum tutti gli ſui de
centi & propriati inſignii. Laquale myſte
rioſa Ara tegeua uno cupulato umbracu-
lo, ſopra quatro pali nel ſolo infixi affir-
mato & ſubſtentato. Gli quali pali diligē-
temente erano inueſtiti di fructea, & florea
frondatura, Et el culmo tutto intecto de
multiplici fiori, & tra ciaſcuno palo nel
lymbo dellapertura, o uero hiato del um-
braculo affixo pendeua una ardente lam-
pada, & in circuito ornatamente bractee

HYEMI AEOLIAE.S.

doro dalle freſche & uerifere aure incon-
ſtante uexate, & cum metallei crepituli ſo
nante. nelquale ſimulachro, cum maxi-
ma religionē & priſco rito rurale & paſtorale alcune amole, o uero ampul
le uitree cum ſpumāte cruore del immolato Aſello, & cum caldo lacte &
ſcintillante Mero ſpargendo rumpeuano, & cum fructi. fiori. fronde. fe-
ſta, & gioie libauano, Hora drieto a queſto glorioſo Triumpho, conduce
uano, cum antiqua & ſiluatica cerimonia illaqueato el ſeniculo Ia
no, de reſte & trece intorte di multiplici fiori, cantanti carmi
ni ruralmēte Talaſſii, Hymænei, & Feſcennii, & iſtru
menti rureſtricum ſuprema lætitia & gloria, cele
bremente exultanti, & cum ſolenni plauſi ſal
tanti, & uoce fœmelle altiſone, Per laquale
coſa nō manco piacere & dilecto cum
ſtupore quiui tali ſolenni riti &
celebre feſte me inuaſe, che
la admiratione de
gli præceden
ti trium-
phi.
*

Figure 5.1 Sample page illustration of the 1499 Aldine *Hypnerotomachia Poliphili*.

FIGURE 5.2 Giovanni Cariani (?), *Portrait of a Young Man with a Green Book*, undated. Fine Arts Museums of San Francisco

Figure 5.3 Hans Memling, *Portrait of a Man with a Roman Coin*, *c.* 1480. Royal Museum of Fine Arts, Antwerp

Figure 5.4 Giovanni Bellini, *Portrait of a Young Man, c.* 1505.
Royal Collection, Windsor Castle

FIGURE 5.5 Leonardo da Vinci, *Ginevra de' Benci* (obverse), *c.* 1474–1478. National Gallery of Art, Washington, DC

Figure 5.6 Leonardo da Vinci, *Ginevra de' Benci* (reverse), *c.* 1474–1478. National Gallery of Art, Washington, DC

153

PETRI BEMBI
CARDINALIS
EPISTOLARUM FAMILIARIUM.
LIBER PRIMUS.

AD FUNDUM SALETIANUM.

Petrus Bembus Johan. Alexandro Urticio præceptori S. P. D.

OPTABAM equidem, ut semper multum, nunc vero maxime, te videre & colloqui: ut de addiscendis Græcorum literis, quod tu sæpe mihi suasisti, deque profectionis meæ consilio, quod adhuc te latet, & prudentiam, & amorem in me tuum, ut debebam, consulerem. Erat enim æquissimum, ut quem ego unum, secundum Bembum patrem meum, omnium hominum colui maxime, & cujus cum prope in sinu altus, tum consiliis & præceptis semper usus sum, ab eodem etiam sententiam peterem iis in rebus, quæ magnopere ad totius meæ vitæ rationes pertinerent. Sed cum existimarem fore, ut antequam quicquam statuerem, ad te veniendi tempus mihi non deesset, repente omnia ita sunt immutata, ut & consilium profectionis capere, & profectionem maturare coactus sim, sic profecto, te ut convenire non potuerim. Hujus festinationis caussam Carolus frater meus ad te deferet: itaque nihil de ea nunc quidem De meo autem consilio volui ad te ipse perscribere ex Noniani bibliothecula, in qua eram cum has ad te literas dabam: ad quod quidem consilium capiendum, eo solutior fui, quod id abs te probatum iri non dubitavi ex iis sermonibus, quos tu mecum proxime, cum una fuimus, habuisti: eos te memoria tenere arbitror. Sed venio ad consilium meum. Est in Sicilia Messanæ Constantinus Lascaris, vir non modo Græcus, sed etiam Byzantius: quæ quidem urbs sola ex universa Græcia retinere probitatem illam Atticam antiqui sermonis, si qua residet adhuc quidem ejus linguæ probitas plane dicitur. Eaque in urbe ludum aperuit, exercuitque multos jam annos, & caste, nec sine dignitate. Is valde omnium hominum sermone laudatur. Scripsit de primis Grammatices elementis librum ad instituendos pueros, qui habetur & legitur. Hunc ego illum esse statueram, qui me doceret, si tu annuisses, vel propterea quod esset ipse in ejusmodi doctrina facile princeps (est autem ab optimis doctoribus ars omnis haurienda) vel quia in Sicilia eam artem exerceret, ubi non domesticis curis, non publicis, non amicorum officiis, non paternis ullis muneribus a discendi studio interpellarer, eo si me contulissem. Quod cum mihi placuisset, essemque de eo cum Angelo Gabriele meo loquutus, sic ab eo discessi, ut se mecum ad idem muneris venturum esse diceret: ego autem illi etiam gratias agerem, quod se mihi comitem profiteretur. Iis ita constitutis rebus, dies aliquot jam abierant, cum mihi esset persuasissimum nihil aggredi, nisi tu meum consilium probavisses. Nunc autem cum plane cogar te non salutato proficisci, feram animo æquiore, propterea quod

non

FIGURE 6.1 Francesco Zucchi (1692–1764), engraving of the Bembo country retreat, Noniano, near Padua.

As reproduced in the four-volume edition of Pietro Bembo's *Opere* published by Francesco Hertzhauser, Venice: 1729 (vol. 4 p. 153).

Figure 6.2 Thomas Cole, *Mount Etna from Taormina, Sicily*, 1843.
Wadsworth Atheneum Museum of Art, Hartford, CT

Figure 7.1 Valerio Belli, portrait medal of Pietro Bembo, *c.* 1532, first version. National Gallery of Art, Washington, DC; Samuel H. Kress Collection.

FIGURE 7.2 Valerio Belli, portrait medal of Pietro Bembo, *c.* 1532, second version of the reverse.
British Museum

Figure 7.3 Titian, *Cardinal Pietro Bembo, c.* 1540.
National Gallery of Art, Washington, DC; Samuel H. Kress Collection.

FIGURE 7.4 Titian, *Portrait of Cardinal Pietro Bembo, c.* 1545.
Museo Nazionale di Capodimonte, Naples

Figure 7.5 Danese Cattaneo, *Portrait medal of Pietro Bembo.*
Museo Nazionale del Bargello, Florence

FIGURE 7.6 Titian, *Portrait of a Gentleman*.
Musée des Beaux-Arts et d'Archéologie, Besançon

from the midst of the woods and chase them
after they're drawn out.
. . . .
And yet, though all these things be lacking, the single greatest
pleasure lies in spending whole days here
whether with the books of the ancients or in service to
the slender muse.
You, too, you who now censure the leisure of the elegant
country house
and diminish our repose with your sorrowing,
I remember that you too used to praise that leisure,
and often called blessed
those days that you were free to spend in the tranquil
countryside,
and at the same time to forget life's anxieties.

The Argonauts' quest for the golden fleece (9–10) here gives way to Pietro's idyllic vision of the fleecy flock (*lanigerum . . . pecus*, 24), while the horror of the Minotaur (*tauri*, 11) is countered by the pleasure (*iuvat*) of watching the oxen (*iuvencos*) plowing the land in lines 22–3; even as he gently remonstrates with his father, he may also affirm his filial *pietas* by rejecting the Theseus legend, and with it the denouement that Theseus, on his return from Crete to Athens, precipitated his father's death by forgetting to change his sail from black to white (*nec . . . / Aegaeo dedimus nigrantia vela profundo*, 11–12).[91] Beyond the epic-pastoral contrast, however, the pleasures of undisturbed sleep (19), of days without argument (20), of hunting and fishing without any fixed schedule (28–36) and of spending whole days in unfettered study (42–3) generate a secondary tension between *otium* and *negotium*. Pietro surely exaggerates in casting Bernardo as one who was formerly—as if no longer—accustomed to praising and relishing the relaxations of Noniano (44–8). The effect may be amusing caricature; but the Bernardo who now apparently "censures the leisure of the elegant country house" (44; cf. *otia rumpis/ nostra*, 2–3), who is seemingly beset by *cura* (1), *questus* (7), and *moeror* (8, 45), and who is all too familiar with the preoccupied life (cf. *sollicitam vitam*, 48) is drawn as a stern *negotiosus*, a disciplinarian who has to be reminded (cf. *memini*, 46) that he too once enjoyed the recuperative forgetfulness (*obliviscere*, 48) of villa-*otium*. Despite, or perhaps precisely because of, its tone of ironic protest, the poem was evidently well received by Bernardo: so much can

91. Cf. esp. Catullus 64.207–48, and see also Chapter 4 p. 168.

be inferred from the fact that it was apparently integrated in the archetype of Ms. Cicogna 1428 by his own hand.[92]

Some five or so years later, similar tensions surface in Pietro's characterization of Bernardo in *De Aetna*. Scene setting is symbolically important in this respect, as in the early stages of the dialogue proper. "[W]hat can be less conducive to a quiet life than [civic duties]?" Pietro asks pointedly in §8, after Bernardo's expression has already spoken for itself in §6:

> PIETRO: ... your expression wasn't the carefree and relaxed one that you usually have here, but the one we see you wear in the city, every now and then pinched into a frown, and serious.

Beyond the *otium-negotium* contrast, the burdens of Bernardo, that Nestor-like statesman,[93] are projected as epic in scale, partly through Pietro's allusion to martial and political rumblings ("But what manner of problem is it that you'd said was troubling you on the state's behalf? Is it perhaps those reported stirrings among the French, father?," §8),[94] but also through his stress on totality and maximization in §7:

> But all such cares (*curae*), at least those of the most serious kind (*maximae*), have it in their nature not to take flight if you go after them, but also to go after you if you flee them. But that official position of yours is not only extremely demanding in itself (*negotiosissimum per sese*), handling as it does virtually every component part of our Republic (*fere omnes reipublicae nostrae partes*), and managing and maintaining the judicial system of the entire state (*universae civitatis*) and of the other cities under our control; but also, the further fact is that you're one who cherishes peace and ease of mind most of all things (*maxime omnium*), so that you feel more keenly the burdens that weigh on you (*illa ... quae te premunt*).

As Pietro surveys this superlative weight of tasks from his entrenched position *in otio*, the effect is akin to that which the exiled Ovid achieves when, in his appeal to Augustus in the second book of his *Tristia* of *c.* 9 CE, he surveys the emperor's immense responsibilities both at home and abroad. In lines 213–38, Augustus' epic burdens are set against the ludic, elegiac slightness of the *Ars amatoria*: Ovid finds it only too understandable that Augustus has lacked the *otium* actually to read,

92. Dionisotti (1965) 289 = Vela (2002) 111.

93. Nestor: Kilpatrick (1986) 333.

94. For these rumblings, Introduction pp. 17–18 and Chapter 3 p. 113.

and hopefully to reassess, the incriminated *Ars* (cf. 237–8: "Should I wonder, then, that under this weight of affairs you had never unrolled my jestings?").[95] By loose analogy, Bernardo's responsibilities, partly characterized as they are in the generically loaded language of Latin literary tradition (*gravis*, §§6, 8; *non levis*, §7; *durus*, §8),[96] cast an epic shadow over the proceedings at Noniano, darkening Bernardo's thoughts until he finds diversion in Sicily: "But now that our conversation has chanced to pass to Sicily, tell me how it is with what's reported everywhere and what we read about Etna's fires" (§9). The cold that lingered in the scene setting of §5 is left behind as they turn to the fires in §§9–10; and, after his sedentary position in §5 ("You've been sitting here for a long time, father"), Bernardo is suddenly roused to movement, as if symbolically drawn away from the shade of preoccupation that has prevailed thus far:

PIETRO: But on your feet, if you please, and away from this shade (*ab hac umbra*): reclining like this on riverbanks, if it goes on too long, is always apt to be rather oppressive (*gravior*). If you agree, let's make for those box trees of ours, and a seat there.

BERNARDO: You're acting very unfairly: just as you're about to talk about the fires, you think we've got to leave the cool shade (*ab umbra et frigore decedendum*).

§§9–10

Bernardo's witticism here shows a new lightness and looseness (cf. *vultu . . . hilari et soluto*, §6) in this figurative as well as literal progress *ab umbra et frigore* in the dialogue's early stages: after a coldish start, father and son quickly warm to their hot topic.

As the work progresses thereafter, the pressured timetable of civic life gives way to the flexi-time of their conversational drift, with Bernardo for once in no hurry and urging Pietro not to rush, as "I'm devoting all these afternoon hours to you" (§21).[97] Yet for all their cordiality as father and son share the leisurely moment at Noniano, the mode of affectionate protest that we observed in Pietro's poem to Bernardo anticipates what I take to be a comparable feature of *De Aetna*. In the poem to Bernardo, landscape is actively implicated in Pietro's protest, in that the pastoral charms he invokes at such length speak so appealingly for the *otium* that

95. See on the implied epic-elegiac contrast between poet and emperor in 213–38 Ingleheart (2010) 207–8.

96. Concisely on the programmatic charge of these (and other such) terms, Hinds (1987) 21–2 and 141 n.58.

97. Cf. Finotti (2004) 36–7 for the uneven, digressive flow of narrative direction and time in *De Aetna* markedly distancing the dialogue from the disciplined economy of civic rhetoric.

he seeks to vindicate. Through a similar activation of landscape in *De Aetna*, Pietro delicately challenges Bernardo with a recalibration of perspective: to contemplate the vast proportions of Etna's landscape is in so many ways a provocation to reassess our own localized (self-)importance, not least within the Venetian bureaucracy. Some examples will illustrate the range and versatility of this admonitory technique in *De Aetna*; but first, for orientation, a brief turning to the younger Seneca.

6.3: The Recalibration of Perspective through Contrasts of Landscape

We saw in Chapter 1 how, in the preface to Book 4a of his *Natural Questions*, Seneca embarks on a supplement of sorts to his correspondence with Lucilius in his *Moral Letters*.[98] Lucilius is apparently now installed as procurator of Sicily, in or around 62 CE; in his letter-like preface, Seneca elaborates at length on the dangers of flattery that a man of Lucilius' standing faces in Sicily. This theme may at first appear hard to reconcile with Seneca's disquisition on the Nile's summer flooding in the rest of what remains of Book 4a, and with his larger meteorological agenda in the *Natural Questions* as a whole. Or does the preface serve an important contrastive function? After all the entrapments and enticements of flattery as surveyed in the preface, Seneca's expansive account of the Nile in the main body of Book 4a brings welcome diversion from the entanglements of Lucilius' "petty procuratorship" (*procuratiuncula, Letter* 31.9), and a refreshing vision instead of nature's guileless macro-functioning. Lucilius apparently enjoys his new responsibilities, but Seneca urges him "to keep all this within its own bounds, and not [to] treat a procuratorship as supreme power" (4a pref. 1). To that end, Seneca will transport him from Sicily in Book 4a:

> I shall draw you far away from that province of yours, in case you place great confidence in history and begin to be pleased with yourself whenever you think: "I have under my jurisdiction this province, which has both sustained and broken the armies of the greatest cities when it lay as the prize of the vast war between Carthage and Rome. . . ."
>
> *QNat.* 4a pref. 21

So to Egypt:

> So that I can get you completely away from there, even though there are many marvels (*mirabilia*) within Sicily and nearby, for the moment I'll bypass

98. See Chapter 1 pp. 45–6.

> all the questions associated with your province and draw your thoughts elsewhere. For I shall investigate with you . . . why the Nile floods as it does in the summer months.
>
> *QNat.* 4a.1.1

Wondrous as Sicily may be, Egypt's wonders (*miracula*, 4a.2.6) are in a class of their own; important as Lucilius' role may be in the administration of Sicily, the forces that administer the Nile's annual flood merely underscore the smallness of the localized Sicilian perspective, and of its attendant *officia*, within nature's macro-scheme.

In the scene change from Sicily to Egypt in *Natural Questions* 4a, then, Seneca's movement away from the epicenter of Lucilius' official duties and authority in Sicily brings with it a reordering of perspective via a challenge to self-perception.[99] Bembo may not, of course, be drawing explicitly on Seneca, but this recalibration technique nevertheless usefully illuminates a parallel feature in *De Aetna*. There, as Bernardo takes what respite he can at pleasant Noniano from his responsibilities in Venice, Pietro offers diversion by transporting him to Etna: "By all means I'll recount to you, if you like, our entire journey in its exact order of events, and I'll take you from the walls of Messina right up to Etna's summit" (§11). If the majestic Nile has a belittling effect (relative to Lucilius' *procuratiuncula*) in *Natural Questions* 4a, Bernardo's affairs of state, while evidently so urgent and pressing in one way, are similarly relativized in the face of Etna's vast dimensions and energies. The mountain erupts in its own time; it appears timelessly permanent in the massiveness of its physical setting (cf. §§22, 44: ". . . no one who doesn't see Etna can know its dimensions"); it effortlessly spans the epochs of mythical (cf. §31 for Typhoeus and Enceladus under Etna) and historical time; and when Pietro brings it to life as mother-like in its reproductive cycle, the biological analogy merely underscores Etna's superhuman rhythm of time flow and life cycle (§41: "When the time for the birth is fully due, . . . whatever fetus has grown to term in mother Etna's womb is forced out by her straining as she gives birth"). Against this macro-vision of time flow, the pressures that weigh on Bernardo, and his efforts to make time for relaxation at Noniano ("I'm devoting all these afternoon hours to you," §21), appear so confining—evidently an admirable burden and sacrifice in one way, given his devotion to the state (§7), but from the enlarged viewpoint at Etna's summit such demands seem so limiting, so distant, so narrow: in Senecan terms, even though Bernardo moves in high circles and is widely traveled in Venetian diplomacy, he nevertheless still labors *in angusto*.[100]

---

99. Further on this approach to the preface, G. D. Williams (2012) 102–16.

100. For *angustus* and cognates as a key Senecan marker of narrowness, G. D. Williams (2012) 32, 35, 113, 217, and (2015) 176, 180 and n.36, 181.

This recalibration theme has far-reaching ramifications throughout *De Aetna*, especially in connection with landscape description, such as when father and son dwell at length on the subject of plane trees in §§13–21. En route from Taormina to Randazzo, Pietro and Angelo pass through a valley divided by a river, its banks shaded by thick woods of plane trees (§13). Bernardo takes a keen interest in them: how gladly would he exchange all his fruit trees at Noniano for two or three plane trees (§14)! How well would he tend them (§15)! But, replies Pietro, Bernardo must remain content with his poplars, which, as Bernardo himself asserts, have been immortalized in Augurello's verses (§16).[101] Yet still he wishes that he had plane trees, although not primarily for his own sake: all that he has achieved in establishing and improving the estate at Noniano was done to secure his children's future (§§17–19).[102] These exchanges consolidate the larger portrait drawn in *De Aetna* of Bernardo as a diligent provider, so farsighted in his commitment to his family's wellbeing. In Etna's shadow, however, this focus on his cherished Noniano and on his wish list of trees that he would ideally nurture there takes on a more poignant aspect: in contrast to all the effort that Bernardo has invested in building and growing his estate, and in contrast to all the "many rows of the most beautiful trees I've planted for you, whether indigenous or non-native" (§15), Etna effortlessly luxuriates in

> many varied kinds of trees that are strong in shade and fertility. In this respect they so far surpass all other trees that the lines that Homer contrived about the gardens of Alcinous seem to me to be better suited to this place than to Phaeacia itself.
>
> *De Aetna* §23

After Bernardo has quoted the four Latin verses of Augurello in praise of the poplars at Noniano (§16), it is hard not to detect a hint of one-upmanship in Pietro's eight-line Latin rendition of *Odyssey* 7.114–21 later in §23—a passage that is of interest for more than the fertile luxuriance that it projects so lavishly on to Etna's slopes. Pietro's amplification of Homer in point of detail hyperbolically magnifies Etna's superior richness, but the lines show a rich fertility of their own in their allusions to Ovid and Virgil in particular.[103] His turning to the *Odyssey* here may also reflect an important aspect of his Greek studies in Messina under Constantine Lascaris, who evidently made significant use of Homer for teaching purposes.[104] Pietro perhaps

101. For which pp. 228–9 above and 322–3 below.

102. Cf. for this stress on accumulated patrimony Chapter 7 pp. 295–8.

103. See Floriani (1966) 50–1.

104. See now Nicosia (2014), esp. 306–17.

reveals something of the nature and depth of his studies with Lascaris by naming in the last two lines of his Latin translation only two fruits—apples and grapes—of the four that figure in Homer, and by expanding into full verses the two Homeric hemistichs that he chooses to render in his version:

> ὄγχνη ἐπ' ὄγχνῃ γηράσκει, **μῆλον** δ' ἐπὶ **μήλῳ**,
> αὐτὰρ ἐπὶ σταφυλῇ σταφυλή, σῦκον δ' ἐπὶ σύκῳ.
>
> *Od.* 7.120–1

> Pear ripens on pear, apple on apple,
> cluster on cluster of grapes, and fig on fig.

> Et pomo insenuere recentia poma priori
> Et nova iam miti superadvenit uva racemo.
>
> *De Aetna* §23

> . . . and a fresh growth of apples ages on those that precede them,
> and new grapes arrive on top of the cluster that's already ripe.

From the Homeric vulgate as given above, Aristotle (fr. 667 R^3) and later derivative sources omit μῆλον . . . σταφυλή to read ὄγχνη ἐπ' ὄγχνῃ γηράσκει, σῦκον δ' ἐπὶ σύκῳ.[105] Without fanfare, Pietro appears to signal his recognition of this departure from the vulgate, but with a twist: he has wittily reversed the Aristotelian omission, expanding into two lines the Homeric allusions to apple (*pomum*/μῆλον) and grape (*uva*/σταφυλή) but excising the Aristotelian pear and fig. If we accept that this modification is a knowing touch, the care with which Pietro claims to have studied the Homeric lines—"I'll render the lines in Latin if I can, or certainly as I can; for it was with that object in view that, at the time, I paid rather careful attention to that very passage in Homer" (§23)—is borne out in the subtlety of his maneuver in lines 120–1: here, perhaps, is a tacit tribute to the qualities of Lascaris' instruction.[106]

For all the attractiveness of Noniano's poplars, then, Etna's foothills abound in plane trees, to which Bernardo can only aspire; and the middle region too is "partly wooded far and wide with trees of various kinds, and especially with pines and beeches that grow to a very great size in very great numbers" (§24).

105. See Heubeck et al. (1988) 329 with Bolling (1925) 236–7 and Hose (2002) 120–2, 293; now on the whole matter, Nicosia (2014) 317–24.

106. Cf. Nicosia (2014) 323 for the citation arguably amounting to "un 'velato' ed indiretto testimone dell'attività di studio del giovane patrizio veneto a Messina."

Bernardo's Noniano boasts the scenic waters of the Piovego (§14), a channel in fact artificially made to connect Padua with the river Brenta, and so with the Venetian lagoon.[107] But Etna teems effortlessly with "resounding streams, ... clamorous water-courses, ... [and] the coolest springs that flow throughout the year" (§22)—a wealth of scenic waters that makes Noniano appear relatively impoverished by comparison. Yet Bernardo can still set the wonders of the Veneto against those of Etna. So, to press the point that there is nothing unusual or remarkable about Etna's volcanic functioning, he looks to the hot spring of Aponus near Padua, which is known today as Abano Terme and continues to draw visitors who seek relief in its waters (§35).[108] In lauding the healing capacities of this remarkable place, Bernardo applies his learning lightly, nicely quoting in §35 the last four lines (97–100) of Claudian's eulogy of Aponus, written in the late (?) 390s CE (= *Carm. min.* 26).[109] Claudian himself perpetuates the *fama* that had long attached to Aponus in the Latin literary tradition,[110] but *fama* for more than just the healing waters. "Lower than a lofty hill yet higher than the level plain rises [this] gentle eminence, clearly visible from all around" (*alto colle minor, planis erectior arvis/ conspicuo clivus molliter orbe tumet*, 11–12): prolific in its hot waters (13) and its underlying fires (13–18), it is nevertheless drawn by Claudian as a marvel of mixed features, "an oxymoronic landscape"[111] where the smoldering meadow is still verdant with grass (19-20). In alluding briefly to the local legend that Hercules plowed the land of Aponus (25-6), Claudian touches on the tradition that the place had oracular capacities and was associated with Geryon, the triple-bodied giant vanquished by Hercules during his western travels;[112] the plowing was presumably done with Geryon's cattle, given that Hercules' tenth labor was to obtain those cattle for Eurystheus (Hes. *Theog.* 287–94, 979–83, Pl. *Grg.* 484b–c, Apollod. 2.5.10, etc.). Turning his focus to the actual waters of Aponus, Claudian portrays a "living theater" (*viva ... scaena*, 45), a place where nature and artifice are barely distinguishable (cf. *facta manu credas*, 49: "You'd believe it all handmade"), and where a pathway has seemingly been

107. See p. 311 n.8.

108. See Kennell (2001) 197.

109. See the edition with commentary of Fuoco (2008), with pp. 20–2 for judicious discussion of the dating.

110. So, e.g., Luc. *BC* 7.193, Plin. *HN* 2.227, 31.61, Sil. 12.218, Mart. 6.42.4; for analysis, Kennell (2000) 96–8 (on Ennodius *Op.* CCXXIV Vogel) and (2001) with Fuoco (2008) 35–8, and now Mandile (2009).

111. Kennell (2001) 203.

112. On these points, Kennell (2001) 200, 202–4 with Fuoco (2008) 91 on 25.

purpose-built for the nervous walker (47–50). Easy of access and abundant in its waters, this Aponus is a wonder gift of nature, "a source of respite from disease for all, a universal aid to healers, a divine agency propitiously at hand (*praesens numen*), a means of deliverance that costs nothing (*inempta salus*)" (69–70).[113]

Given these broader associations of Aponus as a place of oracular and (via Hercules) mythical significance as well as of thermal wonder, Bernardo's quotation from Claudian's poem in §35 perhaps hints at more than just the remarkable healing properties of the waters. Aponus may be a mere hillock (*colliculus*, §36; cf. *alto colle minor*, Claud. *Carm. min.* 36.11), but the monstrous element in Geryon, its Herculean imprint, its oracular dimension, and, most obviously, its painless healing capacities (that "prerogative of the gods and of nature herself, the ruler and parent of everything," §36) all contribute to a formidable range of attributes that may yet withstand comparison with Etna—or so at least Bernardo teasingly suggests at the end of §36:

> But if you compare the famous depths of your Etna and all its vast floods with the single little spring and channel of Aponus, perhaps I wouldn't be afraid that this little hill of ours is smaller than that mountain of yours.

Whereas Bernardo's Aponus is healthful and restorative, Pietro's Etna is so forbidding and potentially so destructive—surely the most telling point that Bernardo quietly makes in setting landscape against landscape here. But then hesitation: for all Bernardo's aggrandizing efforts, and for all of the volcanic charm and warmth of his Aponus, can those springs *really* bear comparison with Etna, that *naturae miraculum* (§12) without peer (cf. *sibi uni par est*, §22)? Is Etna *really* so easily normalized through association with this wonder place, let alone with the many other *mira loca* whose existence he posits in §35? On this skeptical approach, Bernardo valiantly asserts the localized, Veneto-centered viewpoint by appeal to Aponus, with no shortage of wit and learning along the way; but in this contest of wonders he surely struggles to counter Etna's sheer exceptionality of aura and scale, if not of thermal working.

A variation on this technique of landscape comparison—a technique that has so far worked to Bernardo's disadvantage—centers on Pietro's portrayal of Taormina during his and Angelo's initial journey from Messina to Etna. Pietro's account of this town is nicely shaped to appeal to Bernardo's own antiquarian interests: in surveying Taormina's ancient monuments, Pietro is reminded of the visit to the Roman Colosseum that he made with his father when the latter was serving as ambassador

113. Further on Aponus in relation to the paradoxographical tradition of *mirabilia fontium et fluminum*, Mandile (2009) 350.

at Rome in 1487–8 ("A theater made of brick still remains as well, somewhat smaller than the one we saw in Rome, albeit the latter is an amphitheater," §13);[114] and in mentioning that "Greek coins are often dug up by accident everywhere, all of them skillfully produced and not just stamped on bronze, but also on silver and gold" (§13), Pietro neatly accommodates Bernardo's passion for ancient coins—an interest notably memorialized by Hans Memling if Bernardo is taken to be the sitter in Memling's *Portrait of a Man with a Roman Coin* (Figure 5.3).[115] But more important for now is that, in visualizing Taormina's ancient theater, Pietro presents Taormina itself as a dramatic, theater-like spectacle:

> The city itself is positioned very high up in a prominent place, and, jutting out over the water on a projecting spur of the mountains, it commands a broad view of the Ionian sea from one side to the other. The theater is situated on the outermost crag of the spur . . .
>
> *De Aetna* §13

In his account of Taormina's antiquities, Pietro may seek to magnify Etna's rawness by setting against it the imprint of urban civilization in its periphery, or perhaps to set Etna's timeless majesty against the flux of shifting cultural epochs (Thomas Cole arguably achieves a similar effect in his 1843 rendering of Etna as viewed from Taormina in Figure 6.2). But to focus on the theater's physical setting: the fictions that are staged there are in tension with the natural dramatics played out in the landscape that surrounds it; the theater-goers are spectators not just of the staged spectacle but also of the larger topographical *mise en scène*; and this theatricalizing of nature readies us in turn for the ultimate spectacle of Etna. From one perspective, that spectacle may be partly "staged" and artificial (not unlike the theatrics at Taormina), at least through Pietro's highly literary embellishment of, say, the mountain's vividly drawn richness of quasi-Phaeacian fertility (§§22–3). But for the most part the mountain performs spontaneously, unscripted as it is in its special effects of "sulfurous clouds and scorching smoke, as if from an oven," the fiery streams that spit forth burning rocks, and its glacier-like patinas of lava flow (§§26, 41–2). This high theater is transfixing: "we were gripped by such enjoyment of that spectacle, and we were overcome with such astonishment at the unexpectedness of it all, that none of us paid any attention to himself" (§28). In

114. I take it that the visit took place not in 1485, when Bernardo was in Rome as part of the Venetian legation to Pope Innocent VIII (for which pp. 227–8), but during his second, more prolonged period of service there: see Giannotti (1985) 175–6 and 191–2 with Finotti (2004) 34, and cf. p. 319 n. 17.

115. See Chapter 5 p. 206 and Chapter 7 p. 279.

effect, Taormina functions in *De Aetna* not just as a diverting stopping point on Pietro's route to the volcano, but also as a prelude of sorts for what is to come: his cameo coverage of the place habituates us to the theme of nature-as-spectacle before we progress to Etna, that greatest show on earth.

Important supplementary evidence for Bernardo's archeological interests is supplied by Paolo Marsi (1444–84), that distinguished commentator on Ovid's *Fasti* who was a professor of rhetoric in Rome (1474–84) and a devoted member of Pomponio Leto's Roman Academy.[116] In 1468–9 Marsi accompanied Bernardo when the latter was sent to Spain on his first ambassadorial appointment; Bembo's particular mandate was to oversee the recovery of goods lost when a Venetian galley was shipwrecked on the Spanish coast, and to renew certain commercial privileges that had already been granted to Venice.[117] He was successful on both counts; but what concerns us here is Marsi's poetic account of their journey to Spain in the two books of his so-called *Bembicae peregrinae*, or simply *Bembice*, of eleven and nine poems respectively, all of them elegiac apart from a single piece in sapphics.[118] After setting sail from Chioggia in August 1468, they crossed the Adriatic, reaching Pola on the Croatian peninsula after one day. There, as throughout their voyage, Bembo and his entourage sought out Roman ruins—a form of visitation of the past that is akin to the antiquarian travels sampled in Chapter 2, and by which Marsi continually evokes Rome's former imperial greatness.[119] At Pola they visited the necropolis and "the immense mass of the magnificent theater (*magni moles immensa theatri*)," while later in the voyage, during a visit to Carthage, they see "both the temples of the gods and the high palaces of kings, and fora along with the port and theaters as well as the streets (*et fora cum portu cumque theatra viis*)":[120] when at *De Aetna* §13 Pietro describes his visit to the monuments of Taormina, the theater so prominent among them, the passage caters to an appetite in Bernardo that is amply corroborated by Marsi. But of still greater interest is their itinerary after they left Pola and before they reached the North African coast via Malta. Making their way through "the Ionian or Sicilian sea" (*Ionium Trinacriumve fretum*), they "looked from

116. For Marsi, della Torre (1903). On his commentary, first published in Venice in 1482, now Fritsen (2015), esp. 29–45, 63–87; for his professorial appointment at Rome dating to 1474, not 1480, Fritsen 34 and (2000) 358 n.2.

117. Further, Giannetto (1985) 116 with della Torre (1903) 149–56, Fritsen (2000) 359, and Allés Torrent (2012) 120–1.

118. The work survives in only three manuscripts, at Ferrara, the Vatican, and Eton College: see Giannetto (1985) 116 and n.75 with Allés Torrent (2012) 120 n.32; the text is now most easily accessible via excerpts in della Torre (1903). The route taken by Bembo and Marsi is usefully mapped by Fritsen (2000) 364.

119. On this aspect of the work, Fritsen (2000) with (2015) 170–1.

120. On these lines, Fritsen (2000) 366–8.

a distance on smoking Etna" (*fumantem longe suspeximus Aethnam*).[121] They sought permission to disembark at Syracuse in order to view the city's ancient monuments, but without success: the Syracusan authorities held firm to protect against the risk of disease being carried ashore. Bernardo saw Etna, then, but only at a distance aboard ship, and there is no surviving record of him visiting Sicily at any other point in his life. If we accept that Pietro asserts a gentle one-upmanship through landscape-description and -contrast in *De Aetna*, then Marsi's testimony yields an insight that Pietro surely exploits all too knowingly: Bernardo may have seen Etna, but he has merely sighted the mountain that Pietro has *climbed*.

6.4: Shaping Etna's Landscape through Poetic Inscription

In §29 Pietro expresses surprise that none of the great rumblings from inside Etna that Urbano Bolzanio[122] apparently heard on a calm day was audible to Pietro and Angelo when, during their ascent, the winds were blowing so fiercely. In response, Bernardo is characteristically phlegmatic: "That shouldn't seem remarkable, son, as it isn't at all extraordinary (*mirum*). For it's well established by the written tradition on the subject that Etna's breathing pattern changes along with the winds" (§30). Bernardo holds to the theory that Etna draws in the winds as the lungs take in breath. When Pietro asks for confirmation of his view, his father is typically matter of fact: "Yes indeed—unless there's more truth in the fabulous inventions that poets concoct about Typhoeus and Enceladus" (§31). This rejection of myth and wonder and this reliance on written authority set the tone for Bernardo's subsequent disquisition on the nature and cause of Etna's fires in §§32–8 as a whole. But the spatial positions of father and son as Bernardo embarks on his discourse are also telling:

BERNARDO: . . . let's sit down on this grass for a short time . . . ; . . . I'm tired now from walking about.

PIETRO: You rest as you please, and for as long as you please. But I can still keep standing, and I'd rather it so; in that way I'll hear you better.

BERNARDO: And that too is permitted. But since you now so want to hear me discuss the fires that I'd questioned you about previously, I'll set out what I think in just a few words. . .

De Aetna §32–3

121. On this episode, della Torre (1903) 156–8 with Fritsen (2000) 363.

122. For whom Chapter 2 pp. 85–9, 100–1.

The relative positions of the two here suggestively capture important differences in their larger characterization in *De Aetna*. Now settled on the grass, Bernardo proceeds to a discourse that itself appears settled in the positions that it draws from a range of sources that include Lucretius, Seneca's *Natural Questions*, and, most notably, the *Aetna* poem. But while Bernardo is sedentary in §§32–8, Pietro remains standing to more dynamic effect, as if his uprightness betokens his youthful vitality and inquisitive energies. After all, in contrast to Bernardo's cool reasoning and his largely derivative discourse at such a great distance from the mountain itself, Pietro describes his climb with a conspicuous warmth and enthusiasm, not "normalizing" Etna as his father does in §§32–8, but offering a highly idiosyncratic portrait of it in which the volcano acquires personality and moodiness, the capacity to intimidate but also to fascinate—qualities wholly absent in Bernardo's methodical disquisition.

According to Bernardo, the whole earth, like the human body, is permeated by veins and channels, for which he gives three possible explanations (§33; cf. Sen. *QNat.* 3.15.1, *Aetna* 94–117).[123] Nowhere are those channels larger than near the sea, because water erodes the land (§34; cf. Sen. *QNat.* 6.20.1, *Aetna* 112–13); wind enters those cavities (cf. Lucr. *DRN* 6.684, 697–700, Sen. *QNat.* 6.20.6, *Aetna* 146–9, 301–5, Just. *Epit.* 4.1.2–4), and hence earthquakes are particularly prevalent in places near the sea; if strong winds come into contact with veins of sulfur, volcanic fires break out easily (§34; cf. *QNat.* 5.14.4); and so it is in the case of Etna (§35). Beyond Lucretius, Seneca, and the *Aetna* poet, however, an intriguing additional source here is perhaps supplied by the pseudo-Aristotelian *De causis proprietatum elementorum* (*On the causes of the properties of the elements*), a work now thought likely to be a Latin translation by Gerard of Cremona (d. 1187) of an Arabic treatise of unknown authorship and dating to the ninth century; Gerard himself may have been responsible for the attribution to Aristotle of the urtext supposedly underlying the Arabic version.[124] In the section on hot springs,[125] the theories of a certain Mileus (Thales?), Renufilos (Xenophanes?), and Democritus[126] are rejected in favor of our author's preference for the view that the water is heated by flowing over veins of sulfur—a theory also transmitted

123. Line numbers for the *Aetna* here and below follow Goodyear (1966).

124. For text, translation, and orientation, Vodraska (1969) with Schmitt and Knox (1985) 20, Vermij (1998), esp. 324–5, and Resnick (2010) 17–18. The text is also edited (along with Albert Magnus' commentary on it) by Hossfeld (1980) 49–104.

125. §14 = Vodraska (1969) 192–207.

126. On these identifications, Vodraska (1969) 41–2.

by Seneca (cf. *QNat.* 3.24.4), and possibly ultimately deriving in both cases from Theophrastus.[127] Then Etna:

> And about the volcano which is in the land of Sicily in the Mediterranean Sea, we likewise maintain that the hollows and cracks in which there are fires are due exclusively to the sulfur in the belly of that mountain. When therefore the wind blows and the waves of the sea are roused, *the waves compress the mountain and from this the sulfur heats, and fire is set alight in it and smoke and burnt stones emerge.* The fire, therefore, throws stones in the sea and they float in water . . .[128]

The theory that Etna's eruptions were caused by the compression and ignition of sulfur through the effects of wind and water at the volcano's base hardly lacked for competition in the medieval era; so Albertus Magnus (*c.* 1200–80), in his commentary on the *De causis*, posited sulfurous earth mixed with oily naphtha as the material cause of Etna's fires, and "vapor that is disturbed in the ground and is unable to emerge" as the efficient cause.[129] Bernardo Bembo's explanation is closer to that in the *De causis*, albeit stressing wind pressure rather than water action (§34):

> But if the raging winds also come upon veins of sulfur, then fires are started really quite easily, since sulfur has a very great capacity for catching fire, and winds too, through their own force, set other substances on fire.

For now, the interest of the *De causis* theory lies in its circulation in Venice, where the *princeps* of the treatise was published in 1496 by the de Gregori brothers for Benedictus Fontana under the title *De proprietatibus elementorum* in a folio volume of Aristotle's works in Latin; excerpts from it had in fact already been printed at Venice even before that *princeps*.[130] Bernardo appears to draw on Seneca and the *Aetna* poet for his sulfur theory, but it is nonetheless tempting to speculate that he looks to and yet "corrects" the *De causis* by stressing the ignition effect that wind, not water, has on sulfur. But to proceed with his account: how do the fires, once started, sustain themselves? They require an immense source of fuel, but what is there that nature cannot do (§35)? The fires create their own sustenance out of the products

127. See Vodraska (1969) 38–43.

128. Vodraska (1969) 204–6.

129. Hossfeld (1980) 99 cap. 3 lines 50–3, with translation in Resnick (2010) 115; further, Vermij (1998) 325.

130. See Vodraska (1969) 66, 68–9.

(bitumen, alum) resulting from the erosion-effects that heat and water have on the earth (§37; cf. *Aetna* 385–94);[131] the endless amounts of rock spewed forth from the volcano originate from the earth's endless capacity for self-reproduction (§38).[132] True, Bernardo may be no slavish follower of one or more of his source texts here, and he shows independence in his departures from the *Aetna* in particular, most obviously by making no reference to the liquefying lava stone (*molaris lapis*) that figures so prominently in the *Aetna* poet's treatment (398–564). But despite this freedom of maneuver, his account remains essentially bookish and borrowed, and by asserting general principles to which Etna merely conforms, he fundamentally resists its aura of specialness; true to the high Venetian administrator that he was, systematic rationalization is all.

But then Pietro's turn. As if in the other half of a diptych, he describes, at Bernardo's request, the lava flows that he witnessed on Etna (§§39–44). Just as Bernardo's sedentary positioning in §32 has important symbolic implications for his discourse, so Pietro's initial gambit in §39 is revealing:

> That [sc. describing the lava flows] can easily be achieved right now perhaps through a single simile of Hesiod's by which, in his *Theogony*, he says that the earth melted in just the way you mean, if I'm not mistaken; this when he describes the earth being set on fire after Typhoeus was blasted by a lightning bolt.[133] From this, I'm inclined to suspect even that that famous shepherd from Ascra had at some point climbed Etna, and that he took from there the lines that he wrote about the entire earth:
>
> The vast earth itself is burning, and with the raging heat
> it melts, just as sometimes a strip of tin is melted
> in the hollow furnace by the flames and by the smithies' skill;
> or iron, although the vitals of the rock that mothered it
> have nurtured it to hard strength, when once it has glowed,
> it is tamed by Vulcan's hands, and splits apart on the ground.[134]

---

131. But cf. *Aetna* 399–400: *sed maxima causa molaris/ illius incendi lapis est*; Bernardo makes no mention of this lava stone, focusing only on sulfur, bitumen, and alum.

132. Cf. Lucr. *DRN* 6.694–702 for the supply problem similarly addressed but differently answered: "These [sc. the quantities of flames, ash, rock, etc., emitted from the volcano] may well seem more than can be accounted for by the mere description of the earth beneath the crater unless the supply be kept up from outside, and there is also the presence of sand to be explained" (Bailey [1947] 3.1657); Lucretius' answer is that sand and rocks are driven into the volcano via caves and passages leading from sea to crater.

133. See Chapter 1 p. 29.

134. Hesiod, *Theogony* 861–6.

Pietro's reversion here to Hesiod and to the earthly conflagration *post fulminatum Typhoeum* pointedly counters Bernardo's impatience in §31 with "the fabulous inventions that poets concoct about Typhoeus and Enceladus"; in answer to Bernardo's direct inquiry about the lava flows, Pietro broaches his task indirectly and with dalliance, nonchalantly addressing the fanciful prospect of Hesiod atop Etna before he addresses the volcanic facts. As in the case of his rendering of *Odyssey* 7.114–21 in §23, his rendition of *Theogony* 861–6 here contains subtleties that make it more than a simple reflection of the Greek learning that he had acquired in Messina. Long before the first Greek text of the *Theogony* was printed, it was translated into Latin hexameters by the eminent philologist and humanist Bonino Mombrizio of Milan (1424–*c.* 1480);[135] this translation was first published in 1474 by Andrea Belfort in Ferrara, with a dedicatory preface to Borso d'Este, Duke of Ferrara (d. 1471). Some six years later, the *Works and Days*, edited by the Athenian Demetrius Chalcondyles, was first printed at Milan by Buono Accorsi in *c.* 1480,[136] but the first Greek text of the *Theogony* (along with the Hesiodic *Shield of Heracles* and *Works and Days* as well as Theocritus, Theognis, and other gnomic poets) was produced only in February 1496 (1495 *more veneto*) at the Aldine Press at Venice;[137] interestingly, it coincided almost precisely with the publication of *De Aetna*, so that Pietro's rendering of Hesiod in §39 is strikingly topical and timely from an Aldine perspective. One of the sources postulated by Martin West for the Aldine *Theogony* is the version copied by Constantine Lascaris (Matritensis gr. 4607), or an apograph of that version;[138] Lascaris' manuscript appears to have been compiled in two distinct phases, but the folios containing the *Theogony* and *Scutum* have been dated to *c.* 1462, when he was in Milan.[139] There he evidently came into contact with Mombrizio, as the colophon at the end of the book Περὶ ῥήματος in the December 1501(?) Aldine edition of Lascaris' grammar attests in Greek:

> The tract on the noun (περὶ ὀνόματος) was published in Milan in the reign of Francesco Sforza, at the request of Filippo Ferufino, Bartolomeo Calco and Bonino Mombrizio. With their favor I attached to the *Summary*

---

135. For Mombrizio and this translation, Frazier (2005) 101–67, esp. 127, with West (1966) 61 and Raschieri (2011) 742 and n.6.

136. For this edition, Rogledi Manni (1980) 203 no. 1005; for Chalcondyles, Chapter 3 p. 128.

137. Further on the print history of the *Theogony* in the fifteenth century, West (1966) 61 with Corrales Pérez (1994) 221–2 and Botley (2010) 101–2. At least two distinct impressions of the Aldine edition, the second a corrected supplement of the first, were in fact produced in 1496: see Gow (1950) 1.xlv with Sens (1997) 50–1 (pointing also to a third, intermediate edition).

138. West (1966) 61

139. For the date, Fernández Pomar (1966) 230 with Corrales Pérez (1994) 209–10.

of the eight parts of speech, which has often been printed, also the rules of the verbs . . . in the year 1463.[140]

Mombrizio also translated Lascaris' *Summary* into Latin hexameters,[141] dedicating his version to Ippolita, Francesco I Sforza's daughter, whose Greek tutor was Lascaris.

Given this nexus of associations, Bembo's rendering of the Hesiodic lines is richly suggestive on at least two fronts. First, the *Theogony*, like the *Works and Days*, is cited on numerous occasions in Lascaris' grammatical writings:[142] if we infer that Hesiod figured significantly in Lascaris' teaching at Messina, Pietro's lines in §39 may again, as in the case of his version of *Odyssey* 7.114–21 in §23, obliquely honor the instruction he received in Sicily. Secondly, does Pietro's version gently compete with Mombrizio's? Here is the Hesiodic passage:

αὐτὰρ ἐπεὶ δή μιν δάμασε πληγῇσιν ἱμάσσας,
ἤριπε γυιωθείς, στονάχιζε δὲ γαῖα πελώρη·
φλὸξ δὲ κεραυνωθέντος ἀπέσσυτο τοῖο ἄνακτος
οὔρεος ἐν βήσσῃσιν ἀιδνῆς παιπαλοέσσης
πληγέντος, πολλὴ δὲ πελώρη καίετο γαῖα
αὐτμῇ θεσπεσίῃ, καὶ ἐτήκετο κασσίτερος ὣς
τέχνῃ ὑπ' αἰζηῶν ἐν ἐυτρήτοις χοάνοισι
θαλφθείς, ἠὲ σίδηρος, ὅ περ κρατερώτατός ἐστιν,
οὔρεος ἐν βήσσῃσι δαμαζόμενος πυρὶ κηλέῳ
τήκεται ἐν χθονὶ δίῃ ὑφ' Ἡφαίστου παλάμῃσιν·
ὣς ἄρα τήκετο γαῖα σέλαι πυρὸς αἰθομένοιο.[143]

But when Zeus had conquered him and lashed him with
strokes, Typhoeus was hurled down, a maimed wreck, and
  the huge earth groaned.
And flame shot forth from the thunder-stricken lord
in the dark [?], rugged glens of the mount, when he was smitten.
A great part of huge earth was scorched

---

140. For this text see Legrand (1962) 1.lxxxv with Martínez Manzano (1994) 229–30 and (1998) 142; for the chronology (December 1501?) of this undated edition, Chapter 3 p. 131 n.95.

141. For a sample at least of the dedicatory verse letter to Ippolita, Legrand (1962) 1.lxxiii–v; on the work as a whole, now Raschieri (2011).

142. See Martínez Manzano (1994) 214–22 with Botley (2010) 101–2.

143. Text as in West (1966) 143, albeit ἀιδνῆς παιπαλοέσσης (860) tentatively for West's †ἀιδνῆς παιπαλοέσσης: see West 143 in app. with 393 on 860, and cf. Chapter 1 p. 29.

by the terrible vapor and melted as tin melts
when heated by men's art in channeled crucibles;
or as iron, which is hardest of all things,
is softened by glowing fire in mountain glens
and melts in the divine earth through the strength of Hephaestus.
Even so, then, the earth melted in the glow of the blazing fire.

Here is Mombrizio's 1474 version (A) alongside Bembo's version (B):

A	B
divina Typhoei	*Uritur ipsa ingens tellus* aestuque furente
ora micant: sacrisque iacent exusta favillis.	Liquitur, albentis quondam ceu lamina plumbi
ingemuit nato tellus ardente profundi	*Arte virum*, flammisque cava fornace liquescit,
fulmina senserunt montes: multumque parentis	Seu ferrum, quanquam hoc maternae viscera rupis
iam fuit exustum. seu plumbum saepe frequentes	In duras aluere vires, cum ferbuit olim
aut ferrum candente fabri fornasse minutis	*Vulcani* domitum *manibus*, terraeque fatiscit.[144]
excindunt frust[r]is. ferventi liquitur igni:	
perque solum domitum veluti natat unda metallum.[145]	

In his renderings (italicized in B above) of such phrases as πολλὴ δὲ πελώρη καίετο γαῖα (861), τέχνῃ ὑπ' αἰζηῶν (863), and ὑφ' Ἡφαίστου παλάμῃσιν (866), Bembo achieves a closeness to Hesiod in point of detail that is less evident in Mombrizio's freer version. In rendering Hesiod's κασσίτερος (862) as *albens plumbum*, he also specifies "tin" more stringently than does Mombrizio, whose unaccompanied *plumbum* is used far more rarely than *plumbum album/candidum* to denote the metal;[146] and when Pietro elaborates on the Hesiodic original, he does so with a brio

144. For translation, p. 255 as well as p. 343.

145. "The divine face of Typhoeus flashes/ and lies scorched in the sacred ashes./ The earth groaned at her burning offspring, the depths/ of the mountains felt the bolts, and much of the parent [sc. Earth]/ was now scorched. Or as the thronging craftsmen often tear tin/ or iron away from the white-hot furnace/ in tiny pieces; the metal is melted by the red-hot fire,/ and, now tamed, it floats wave-like across the ground."

146. For bare *plumbum* cf. Mel. 3.47, Plin. *HN* 4.119, but more often with *albus/candidus* at *TLL* 10.1 2457.53–70.

(notably in *seu ferrum . . . vires* for Hesiod's ἠὲ σίδηρος, ὅ περ κρατερώτατός ἐστιν, 864) that surely outdoes Mombrizio's more restrained eye for elaboration in (e.g.) *veluti natat unda metallum*. In effect, in answer to Bernardo's query about Etna's lava flows, Pietro not only departs digressively into verse; if we posit that he was directly familiar with Mombrizio's *Theogony*, he also indulges himself by engaging in a brief but telling test of poetic virtuosity.

Secondarily tested is Bernardo's patience. Even though he apparently enjoys Pietro's rendition of Hesiod ("I take considerable pleasure in the poet's knack—*poetae ingenium*—for describing so adroitly the earth's melting and burning," §40; we might wonder which poet Bernardo means, Pietro or Hesiod, in a witty hedging of his words), he soon grows restive: "But you're giving me far too little in answer to my question, son: I want so very straightforwardly to know from you . . . how those fires flow along" (§40). Pietro complies, as if suddenly reining himself in ("I'll do as you say, father," §41). But the extravagant comparison that immediately follows—Etna nurtures a quasi-fetus in its womb before its birth pangs result in eruption (§41)—betrays his seemingly reflex tendency toward imaginative elaboration; in his own way, he too shows eruptive energies that defy easy quelling by paternal command. It is notable that throughout *De Aetna* Pietro uses superlatives far more frequently than does the measured Bernardo; the exuberance that his superlatives convey is further reflected in the hyperbole with which he likens Etna to the Chimaera in §26, say, or in casting the mountain's lower reaches as a fully perfected *locus amoenus* more bounteous even than Alcinous' Phaeacian orchard garden (§22–3). He takes similar liberties with personification, not merely bringing Etna to life (as when it gives birth in §41) but also commending it for its moral purity: "It leads a celibate existence, disdaining union with any other mountain and chastely confining itself within its own bounds" (§22). Such features of the writing capture, in their flamboyance, something of the risk-taking that Pietro shows on the ascent. So in §27:

BERNARDO: What made you continue on so far beyond recklessness [sc. toward the lower crater's edge]?

PIETRO: We thought we were able to stand there safely; and then we were carried away by our eagerness, or rather our ardent passion, to survey everything.

Both father and son are committed to the naturalistic explication of Etna's fires. But whereas Bernardo resists the rhetoric of *mirum*, Pietro indulges it freely in picturing the wonders of this "natural marvel" (*naturae miraculum*, §12)—a sense of wonderment predicated on his experiencing the pyrotechnics of Etna for the first time.[147] If Bernardo tends to see literally, Pietro sees mythically, as it were, letting his imagination range freely over Etna on the trail of Faunus in §§48–50; and here we find an important corollary to Pietro's use of poetic quotation in *De Aetna*.

Bernardo uses verse quotation sparingly, in §16 (Augurello's lines on Bembo's poplars at Noniano); in §35 (Claudian on Aponus); and, lastly, in §52 when, at the work's end, he invokes Horace, *Epistles* 1.2.27–31:

> Nos numerus sumus et fruges consumere nati,
> Sponsi Penelopes, nebulones, Alcinoique
> In cute curanda plus aequo operata iuventus,
> Quis pulchrum fuit in medios dormire dies et
> Ad strepitum citharae cessantum ducere curam.
>
> We are a mere cipher, born to devour the earth's crops,
> Penelope's suitors, worthless scoundrels, the sons of Alcinous,
> who spent more time than they should in looking after their looks;
> for whom it was a fine thing to sleep to midday, and to rest
> their idlers' cares to the sound of the lyre.

So Bernardo adduces Horace to moralizing effect, warning Pietro against losing self-control and love of virtue (*reiecta continentia atque ipso amore virtutis*, §52) through overindulgence in sensuous pleasure. The quotation builds on Bernardo's allusion to the Sirens in §51:

> Certainly we are [sc. at liberty sometimes to offset our weighty study of philosophy (*gravia illa philosophiae studia*, §50) with lighter tales (*fabellis istis levioribus*), especially at Noniano], provided that it's always held in check, like the Sirens (as they say) checked by the rowers having their ears stopped with wax. And that wisest of poets would undoubtedly never have allowed Ulysses (whom he always portrays as extremely foreseeing) to listen to the Sirens' songs unless respected men of wisdom (*gravibus et sapientibus viris*)—and I don't count myself among them—were at liberty sometimes to attend

147. Cf. Fisher (1998) 17: "For the full experience of wonder there must be no description beforehand that will lead us to compare what we actually experience with what we were told . . . *The object must be unexpectedly, instantaneously seen for the first time*" (my emphasis).

to less serious matters (*minus seriis ... rebus*), and to seek out rather less weighty amusements (*lusus ... non adeo severos*).

The language of generic contrast that we witnessed earlier[148] in distinguishing Bernardo's *gravitas* of demeanor and civic *negotium* from Pietro's immersion in *otium* recurs in the contrast that Bernardo draws here between preoccupation and relaxation, *seria* and *lusus*, philosophical weightiness and the lightness of *fabella*. The passage constitutes an important statement of compromise between "licenza e responsabilità"[149]—a suitably measured compromise on Bernardo's part that is pointedly positioned at the dialogue's climax, where he is significantly given the last word before he retires "to the library, and to his thoughts" (§52). Yet the serious point that Bernardo makes through allusion to Ulysses in §51 is also offset by a ludic lightness of touch, as if that allusion itself achieved its own fine balance between *serium* and *lusus*. To begin with, the Horatian lines as quoted in §52 are immediately preceded at *Epistles* 1.2.23–6 by a reference to the Sirens and Circe:

Sirenum voces et Circae pocula nosti;
quae si cum sociis stultus cupidusque bibisset,
sub domina meretrice fuisset turpis et excors;
vixisset canis immundus vel amica luto sus.

You know the songs of the Sirens and Circe's cups.
If Ulysses had foolishly and greedily drunk them with his companions,
he'd have been a wretched brute under a whore of a mistress;
he'd have lived as a filthy dog, or a pig loving the mire.

Given this fuller context for the Horatian passage as cited in §52, Bernardo's turning to *Epistles* 1.2 there is already, in hindsight, foreshadowed by his earlier allusion to the Sirens and Ulysses: it is as if he already had *Epistles* 1.2 in mind in §51. But his focus on the Homeric Ulysses as so sagacious (*prudentissimum*, §51) in his ability to listen to the Sirens without succumbing to their charms is surely ironized, whether by Bernardo *qua persona* in *De Aetna* or by Pietro *qua* author, when we invoke two *comparanda* deriving from Bernardo's periods of diplomatic service in Florence in the 1470s.

148. P. 243 and n.96.

149. Finotti (2004) 40, in a fine treatment (pp. 37–42) of the Siren theme ("un passo fondamentale," p. 38) in §§50–1.

The first of these *comparanda* is Cristoforo Landino's likening of the much-traveled Bembo to Ulysses in one of the sequence of six elegies that he addressed to Bernardo during the latter's time in Florence:[150]

Es felix igitur, sed non minus illa beata,
  quae quondam tanto vivat amata viro.
Nam quis nobilior Veneto cui prisca Senatu
  progenies multos enumeravit avos?
Est aetas viridis, pulchro est in corpore virtus,
  admixtusque decens cum gravitate iocus.
Smyrnaeo celebrem versu laudamus Ulixem,
  plurima qui magno viderat orbe loca
. . . .
Sirenum fugit cantus, et nota Charybdis
  furta, et Scyllaeos, horrida monstra, canes
. . . .
At si quas terras adiit, quos aequore tractus,
  dum peragit patriae iussa verenda suae,
nunc referam, varias missus legatus in oras,
  Dulichium poterit vincere Bembus iter.[151]

You are fortunate, then, but no less blessed is she[152]
  who may someday live loved by such a man.
For who is nobler than one whose ancient line of descent
  counts so many forebears in the Venetian Senate?
He is robust in age, his handsome body has manly spirit,
  and he mixes a seemly wit with dignity.
In Homeric verse we praise the famous Ulysses,
  who'd seen so many places in the great world. . . .

He fled the Sirens' songs and Charybdis' notorious tricks,
  and those grim monsters, the dogs of Scylla. . . .

But if I should now relate what lands Bembo has visited,
  what regions by sea,
  carrying out his country's venerable commands

150. For these elegies, Chapter 5 pp. 212–13 and n. 167.

151. *Carm. var.* 5.61-8, 77–8, 81–4 = Chatfield (2008) 286–9.

152. Ginevra de' Benci, for whom Chapter 5 pp. 211–20.

after being sent as an ambassador to different shores,
  Bembo could exceed even Ulysses' travels.

So Bernardo as Ulysses; but for an alternative viewpoint we turn to Poliziano's witty portrayal of the Venetian ambassador as Siren- and Circe-like in his attractiveness, to the point of being able to entrance even Ulysses:

Ut miseros quondam nautas acheloia Siren
  in poenam traxit carmine blandisono;
Sic, Bernarde, tuo quemvis succendis amore
. . . .
Sic nos devincis nec vinctos, Bembe, relaxas,
  sic te quisquis adit mox tua philtra bibit.
Frustra ad te florem Cylleni ferret Ulysses,
  sed pro te optasset linquere vel patriam.[153]

Just as the Siren, daughter of Achelous, once drew wretched sailors
  into punishment through her sweet-sounding song,
so, Bernardo, you inflame anyone you please with love for you. . . .

So you hold us fast, Bembo, without releasing us from our fetters;
  so whoever approaches you soon drinks your love potions.
In vain would Ulysses bring Mercury's flower[154] to bear against you,
  but for you he'd have chosen to leave even his homeland.

For all Bernardo's seriousness of point in invoking the example of Ulysses hearing but not being ensnared by the Sirens at *De Aetna* §51, the knowing reader who recalls Poliziano's verses on the Siren-like Bembo[155] can hardly avoid the mischievous implications of Bernardo's mixed history as both a redoubtable Ulysses and an alluring Siren. On one reading, the mature, worldly-wise Bernardo who appeals to Ulysses' example in §51 could not be further removed from the Siren portrayed by Poliziano; or does Pietro ironize Bernardo's demeanor as a time-tested dispenser of life wisdom in §51 by stirring the memory of Bernardo-as-Siren? Or should we rather credit Bernardo himself with a delicate control of irony that nicely illustrates

153. Del Lungo (1867) 251–2 *Eleg.* XI.1–3, 17–20; already on this poem, p. 225 and n.17.

154. I.e., the herb μῶλυ/moly by which Ulysses is protected against Circe's magic in the *Odyssey*: see 10.286–92, 302–6 with Plaitakis and Duvoisin (1983) for the hypothesis (p. 1) that "'moly' might have been the snowdrop, *Galanthus nivalis*, which contains galanthamine, a centrally acting anticholinesterase."

155. Duly noted by Finotti (2004) 39.

the mixture of gravity and wit that Landino and Poliziano apparently found so appealing in him?[156] That is, does his *dramatis persona* in §51 appeal to Ulysses' example in full awareness that his maneuver is saturated with irony, first because of his own Ulyssean credentials as lauded by Landino, and then because of his Siren-like credentials as paraded by Poliziano? On this approach Bernardo nicely lightens his moralizing advice with a touch of humor at his own expense; or so at least Pietro *qua* author presents his father, in what then becomes an affectionate filial nod to Bernardo's subtlety of wit and literary (self-)understanding.

Whereas Bernardo uses verse quotation sparingly, and to moralizing effect in Horace's case in §52, Pietro shows greater adventure and color in his many more forays into verse. So in §12, as we saw in Chapter 1, landscape activates poetic memory when, on the journey between Messina and Taormina, the fortress of Nisus comes into view, a sight that causes Pietro to recall the Ovidian Sappho's line to Phaon, *Nisiades matres sicelidesque nurus* (*Heroides* 15.54). The correctness or otherwise of Pietro's *Nisiades*[157] matters less for now than his fusing of philology and topography at this formative moment in *De Aetna*, where this first sampling of "literary" landscape readies us for his further experimentation with the phenomenon later in the dialogue. So, in §43, he takes issue with Virgil:

> Moreover, that harbor, which Virgil describes as
>
> a haven out of the winds' reach, undisturbed and vast
> in itself (*portus . . . immotus et ingens*), but nearby Etna thunders
> with dreadful eruptions,[158]
>
> was so filled up with Etna's outflows that you'd imagine by now that Virgil was mistaken in calling the harbor there vast, given that it now scarcely exists.

Again, Pietro's experience of the mountain is inseparable from literary experience as he seeks to reconcile the Virgilian past with the topographical present, here with witty diminution of Virgil's *portus . . . ingens*, as if the text is now out of date and in need of footnote-like amendment. As we have seen, Pietro may also advertise his recently burnished credentials in Greek by rendering in Latin passages of the *Odyssey* and *Theogony* (§§23, 39), while in §47 Theocritus enters as well:

---

156. Landino, *Carm. var.* 5.66, as on p. 262; Poliziano in Del Lungo (1867) 252 *Eleg.* XI.7–8, as on p. 225.

157. See Chapter 1 p. 23 and n.2.

158. *Aeneid* 3.570–1.

> Our witness on this point [sc. that above the foothills, Etna's waters are derived from melting snow] is Theocritus, in whom the Cyclops includes the following when he lists his riches to Galatea:
>
> I have a stream of icy water that wooded Etna sets in flow
> from her melting snows for a drink sweet as nectar.[159]

We shall soon see that Pietro's turning to Theocritus here contributes to the idyllic literary landscape that he projects on to Etna's slopes in §§47–8, but first the Aldine significance of Theocritus' presence here. The *editio princeps* of Theocritus (containing *Idylls* 1–18) was published in Milan in *c.* 1480 by Buono Accorsi;[160] this volume also included the *princeps* of the Hesiodic *Works and Days* that was mentioned above.[161] The second, more complete edition of Theocritus to appear was the Aldine impression of February 1496—the same volume that contained (*inter alia*) the *Theogony*, as we saw earlier.[162] Even as Pietro looks to the Classical past in his renderings of Theocritus and Hesiod, his procedure appears strikingly up to date and of the minute as soon as we relate his Latin samplings of each in *De Aetna* to their almost simultaneous incarnations at the Aldine Press. Here is no mere case of ornamentation or showy learning, however. The poetic element is a deeply embedded feature of a text that—not unlike Etna's fissured landscape, where fire-streams intermittently break forth from cracks underfoot (§26)—shows certain fissures of its own: the poetic outpourings and, more generally, Pietro's lively expressions of excitement, hyperbole, and wonder suggestively replicate in their scattered occurrences the sporadic effusions at the summit, while the restlessness of Bembo's lettered *mens* vies analogically with the ever generative and always potentially eruptive *mons*. In this imaginative meeting of mind and mountain, Pietro's Etna is not the objective commodity that it is for Bernardo, to be "normalized" through largely borrowed theorizing from a distance; it is appropriated and personalized, so to speak, and *felt* not just in a physical sense as Pietro exerts himself on the climb and

---

159. Cf. *Id.* 11.47–8: ἔστι ψυχρὸν ὕδωρ, τό μοι ἁ πολυδένδρεος Αἴτνα/ λευκᾶς ἐκ χιόνος ποτὸν ἀμβρόσιον προΐητι. Despite the peculiarity that in *quem* [sc. *rivum*] ... *fluit Aetna* Bembo uses *fluit* with active force for Theocritus' προΐητι, his version is very close to the Theocritean original: for ψυχρὸν ὕδωρ cf. *glacialis aquae*; for ἁ πολυδένδρεος Αἴτνα cf. *sylvosa ... Aetna*; for λευκᾶς ἐκ χιόνος cf. *nivibus ... solutis*; for ποτὸν ἀμβρόσιον cf. *nectareum in potum*, with *nectareum* in nice Ovidian variation (cf. *Met.* 7.707, *nectareus* then at *Culex* 241: further on the Ovidian pedigree, Thomason [1923] 338–9 with Radford [1923] 172) on ἀμβρόσιον/Virgilian *ambrosius* (cf. *Aen.* 1.403).

160. See Gow (1950) 1.xliv.

161. See p. 256.

162. See p. 256.

crawls painfully over the extensive stretches of brittle lava at its upper reaches (§44), but also through a form of self-projection on to the slopes. This aspect of *De Aetna* comes into its own in §48, where Pietro diverts himself to recount a "most beautiful work of nature" that he allegedly witnessed on the mountain's upper reaches, a work that he "especially marveled at."

This *naturae opus* is a grassy plateau sloping down at a gentle gradient and enclosed by a circle of stately, evenly spaced pine trees; the towering beech tree that stands queen-like (*veluti regina*) in the center is divided into four branches of similar shape and size, but, hollow at its base, it collects rainwater to form a reservoir that is cooler than a spring and purer than a well. In describing this idyllic scene, Pietro assembles the staple features of the Classical *locus amoenus* (trees, shade, pure water)[163] into a highly literary mini-*opus* that is surely hard to reconcile with his broader picture of the harsh conditions high on Etna. He may be there on the mountain, but the picture he describes appears to belong elsewhere, as if an idealization by which Pietro moves seamlessly from his exhilarating adventure on the volcano to a fictive supplementation or embellishment of that experience. The literal view from the peak thus begins to compete with the literary vista (§48):

> You'd be unsure there, father, if you had to praise any of these features, which you'd praise above all—the view from the place or the place itself, then the tree itself or its waters. So skillfully have the wood nymph and the river nymph united to beautify both elements, as if their objective were to create uncertainty as to which was the more beautiful.

This fusion of landscapes, real and seemingly imaginary, undergoes further development when Pietro subsequently reports that the water source in this meadow is called the spring of Faunus (§49). At this point Bernardo makes a telling intervention (§49–50):

BERNARDO: I see that you're starting on a tale; but since we've stumbled upon Faunus, do carry on. I can easily put up with being detained by him, since I know that, every so often, *you like to amuse yourself by sporting with him in verse.* But as for what you say of him, how do they know it? Or are they perhaps only inferring as much?

PIETRO: Shepherds say that they see the god himself wandering here and there throughout the woods and pastures . . .

163. For these features, Curtius (1953) 190–3, 195–200.

Already in §15 Bernardo had mentioned Pietro's Faunus, remarking that, had he planted plane trees at Noniano, "you'd now have a place to which you could better entice that Faunus of yours, and he a place where he could more gladly come." In effect, the Faunus who ranges over the grassy plateau in §50 is the Faunus who figures so prominently in the first seven poems of Pietro's *Carminum libellus*, the first edition of which was printed only posthumously, in 1552/3.[164] Bernardo's allusions to "that Faunus of yours" in §§15 and 49 evidently presuppose that Pietro's poetic experimentation with Faunus at least partially predated *De Aetna*.[165] As soon as Faunus is recognized in §49–50 not just as a familiar habitué of Classical pastoral[166] but as a more personalized presence here, as *Pietro's* Faunus, then Bembo inscribes Etna with nothing less than his own signature landscape. Certainly, in §§41–7 Pietro offers at his father's behest an admirably detailed factual account of the lava flows on Etna. By then reverting to ludic *fabella* and to Faunus' presence in the *locus amoenus* of §§48–50, however, he achieves a displacement effect: after Etna has been thoroughly demythologized in Bernardo's disquisition on its volcanic workings (§§33–8), Pietro re-mythologizes it in a different, compensating way, replacing the monstrous, hellish associations of traditional Etnean myth-making with the more benign connotations of his Faunus. Further, the volcano is as if generically alleviated, even temporarily tamed, by the pastoral strains that are evoked in §§48–50, its epically eruptive capacities as if offset by Faunus' wanderings on the smiling slopes; still more important, by locating his Faunus on Etna, Pietro counters its cold and forbidding impersonality with the warmth of proximity and recognition, as if the climax of his ascent as portrayed in *De Aetna* were ultimately to have made the mountain truly his own—a conquest of sorts even though he fails to reach the higher of the volcano's two craters (§28).

Through this activation of landscape Pietro responds to Etna not as a distant Sicilian Other, a world apart from cultured Noniano and Venice, but as a landmark

---

164. Eleven poems had in fact been incorporated in the collection of *Carmina quinque illustrium poetarum* (Venice, 1548): see Pecoraro (1959) 50 with Dionisotti (1961) 589 = Vela (2002) 200–1. The 1552–3 Scotto edition (*Petri Bembi carminum libellus*, Venice) was posthumously prepared in accordance with Bembo's own editorial preferences: so Dionisotti (1961), esp. 588–90 = Vela (2002), esp. 199–202, countering Pecoraro's argument that the authority of a manuscript in Padua (Biblioteca Antoniana, cod. 635) outweighs that of the 1552–3 edition; the controversy is pithily summarized by J. N. Grant (1995) 48–9.

165. *Pace* Salemi (1982) 32, surely erroneously finding in §49–50 "the origin of the Faunus poems." Cf. Pecoraro (1959) 120: "Da questo dialogo [sc. *De Aetna*] . . . si intuisce chiaramente che tutti o quasi tutti i componimenti faunici . . . furono scritti dal Bembo nell'adolescenza, *cioè prima del 1494, data di composizione dell'Aetna*" (my emphasis). Nevertheless, down to 1498 the sole reference to the Faunus poems in Bembo's correspondence is found in a letter to Trifone Gabriele of February 2, 1498 (= Travi [1987] 22 *Letter* 24.18–19).

166. See Nisbet and Hubbard (1970) 218 on Hor. *Carm.* 1.17.2 with Babcock (1961), esp. 15–17.

that he subjectively appropriates and stamps with his idiosyncratic imprint; after the Etna story had been so diversely treated in the Classical tradition, Pietro shows striking novelty, I propose, by effecting this tight identification between person and place. While Bernardo takes pride in his shaping of Noniano's pleasant landscape, and while that estate is a material reflection of a lifetime's effort (cf. §§15–17), in his different way Pietro too is engaged in landscape construction in *De Aetna*, and, like Bernardo's Noniano, his Etna is in a sense a projection of himself. To revert to Woolf's *To the Lighthouse*, we saw earlier[167] that the lighthouse serves as a multivalent symbol of difference between Mr. and Mrs. Ramsay: in one way it is detached and solitary like Mr. Ramsay, but in another way its sustaining light and sweeping range of vision temptingly capture Mrs. Ramsay's life and soul centrality to family functioning. However loose the analogy, the symbolic properties of Woolf's lighthouse help to illuminate the phenomenon of character construction through manipulation of landscape that I claim for *De Aetna*. So it is that Pietro adapts his Etna to a complex story of self, turning landscape into a personalized script; for does he not in a sense violate the Etnean topography by injecting his own dream into what is, simply, there?[168]

---

167. Pp. 221–2.

168. Cf. Tall (1993) 213: "My fear is that I violate topography as I describe it, that I inject my own dream into what is, simply, there . . . Metaphor negates even as it carries us into new understanding. Because every act of depiction is inevitably interpretation, to turn the land into an emblem feels suspiciously like appropriating it."

7

The Bembo Collection, and Evocations of Noniano

TWO THEMES CONVERGE in this final chapter, the first of them Pietro Bembo's famed passion as a collector of antiquities, contemporary art, statuary, scientific instrumentation, and other such treasures, in accordance with the larger Renaissance fashion for collecting, and for establishing and perpetuating an impressive *imago sui* (even a fantasy self) by that means. The second is *De Aetna*'s significance as (i) itself a work of naturalist collection in its showcase-like display of the physical conditions and topographical features that Pietro encountered on Etna; and (ii) a double portrait of Bernardo and Pietro that contributes to the repository of family memory that in many ways was the famed Bembo collection. For present purposes, however, the testimony that bears witness to Pietro's collection in his own lifetime is of interest not just for the treasures that it lists, but also because of what it fails to mention. Notable in the latter category is the commemorative medal (Figure 7.1 and Figure 7.2) that Pietro commissioned in the early 1530s from that eminence among Renaissance medalists, Valerio Belli (*c.* 1468–1546), and also a Titian portrait of Bembo that was allegedly executed in *c.* 1515, during Pietro's period of service as papal secretary to Leo X from 1513 to 1521—a precursor of the "secondo ritratto" that Titian apparently painted after Bembo was elevated to the cardinalate in 1539, and that today resides in the National Gallery of Art in Washington, DC (Figure 7.3).

For now, the Belli medal and at least one of Titian's portraits of Bembo are of special relevance to our study of *De Aetna* because of their nostalgic evocations, direct or indirect, of his youth, of Noniano, and of his devotion to lettered *otium* at a remove from the Venetian *cursus*: the world of *De Aetna*. After the Bembo collection in general is introduced in section 7.1, we turn in 7.2 to the Belli medal, and to the possible allusions that its decorative design makes to the youthful, otiose atmospherics that prevail in the *Sogno, De Aetna,* and *Gli Asolani*—allusions that, in 7.3, are arguably matched by certain landscape features that Titian deploys in the badly preserved portrait of Cardinal Bembo that is now housed in the Museo Nazionale di Capodimonte, Naples (Figure 7.4). In section 7.4 our focus reverts to *De Aetna* as a work implicated in the Renaissance culture of naturalist collecting. But the stress that Bernardo places in the dialogue on the importance of patrimony and the inheritance of intergenerational memory is also relatable, I argue, to the concerns that the aging Pietro was to express about the dispersal of his beloved collection after his own passing. Finally, we turn in section 7.5 to a portrait whose sitter has been identified in certain quarters as Pietro Bembo, an identification that is nevertheless open to serious objection and is now generally rejected: Giovanni Bellini's *Portrait of a Young Man* of *c.* 1505, part of the Royal Collection that was formerly housed in Hampton Court but now resides in Windsor Castle (Figure 5.4). But if the case for identifying Bembo as Bellini's sitter is roundly rejected (and no serious attempt to vindicate the Bembo identification is made in section 7.5), we shall nevertheless see that certain aspects of the portrait, above all the interplay between the italic script of Bellini's signature and the fashionable appearance of the young man he portrays, have an important secondary relevance for our understanding of *De Aetna*; here we shall return to the interaction, already addressed in Chapter 5, between verbal portraiture and print form, face and typeface, in the 1496 *princeps* of the dialogue. Our journey in this chapter thus takes us beyond the confines of the Bembo collection as recorded and memorialized in his own day or soon afterward. But first to the collection itself.

7.1: Pietro Bembo the Collector

Ill health, disillusionment with his duties as papal secretary, and the recent deaths of his father in May 1519 and of his friends Raffaello Sanzio da Urbino (Raphael) and Cardinal Bernardo Dovizi da Bibbiena in, respectively, April and November 1520 all contributed to Bembo's decision to take leave from the service of Pope Leo X in the spring of 1521. He retired at first to Noniano with Morosina, his long-term companion from probably 1513 until her death in 1535, and mother of his three children.[1] But in a letter to Federico Fregoso[2] of July 20, 1522 he enthuses about Padua:

---

1. Retreat to Noniano is signaled by a letter of July 5, 1521 to Pietro's nephew, Gian Matteo Bembo: Travi (1990) 161 *Letter* 417 (Gian Matteo was only loosely Pietro's nephew; see on their precise relationship P. F. Brown [2013] 37–8). For Morosina, probably sixteen in 1513, Kidwell (2004) 174–5.

2. For whom Chapter 4 p. 172.

> I've settled in Padua, a city of most moderate climate and very beautiful in itself and above all convenient and restful and just right for the leisure of writing and for studies, more than any other city that I have ever seen—much more so. And I am sometimes in the city and sometimes in the villa [sc. Noniano], free of all cares.[3]

At first he had no fixed residence in Padua, but relatives of his appear to have had property there, and he may have found at least temporary accommodation through that familial network;[4] social connections also proved helpful.[5] Several years passed before he eventually moved, in 1532, into the property that became his main home down to his departure for Rome as cardinal in 1539. Bembo had in fact acquired this residence in 1527, albeit in convoluted circumstances.[6] Formerly the property of the powerful Borromeo family, it had been confiscated in 1510 by order of the Venetian Council of Ten; this was in retribution for Achilles Borromeo's role in the events that saw Padua briefly go over in 1509 to the Emperor Maximilian I in the War of the League of Cambrai, before Venice recovered it, successfully fending off Maximilian's siege of the city in September of that year.[7] In 1512 the residence was made over in gratitude to Bernardino Fortebracci (1441–1532), for three and a half decades until his retirement in 1515 one of Venice's most distinguished cavalry leaders. But after the Republic took back the property in 1523 (granting Fortebracci grace-and-favor rights to it during his lifetime), it was finally acquired at auction in 1526 by one Maffeo Bernardo. When he learned of this development, the indefatigable Bembo wrote unabashedly to Bernardo on July 18, 1527, approaching him with a mixture of plea ("I will tell you that for two years I had thought of buying it and arranging it for myself as a nest and place of repose for my old age . . ."), puffery ("if through your magnanimity, which I hear is equal to your fortune . . .") and proposal ("I have been emboldened to ask you . . . if . . . you would be kind enough to cede me the house for what you paid for it").[8] Yet Bernardo stood firm, whereupon Bembo appears to have asserted his influence in high places, manipulating the course of events in accordance with the requirement that the conditions of

---

3. Travi (1990) 171 *Letter* 428.39–43, as rendered by Kidwell (2004) 203–4, 238.

4. Puppi (1969) 35.

5. Hence Pietro's stay in the Palazzo Foscari, one of the grand residences encircling the Roman arena: see his letter of October 23, 1526 to Gian Matteo Bembo as in Travi (1990) 385 *Letter* 713, with Kidwell (2004) 238.

6. See Ronchi (1923–4) and Puppi (1969) 35–9 with Kidwell (2004) 239–40 and now Beltramini (2013), esp. 376–7.

7. Background: Norwich (1982) 403–6.

8. Travi (1990) 444 *Letter* 787; here as rendered by Kidwell (2004) 239.

purchase had to be approved by the overseeing *Collegio*—a process that resulted all too conveniently in Bembo getting his way. So it was that by early September 1527 Pietro finally acquired his long-desired property for 1460 ducats, but the grace-and-favor provision for Fortebracci remained in place. Hence it was not until the autumn of 1532 that Bembo was finally installed in his new residence, in what is now known as the Palazzo Camerini in Padua's Via Altinate, today the home of the Museo Storico della Terza Armata.[9]

Further additions were made to the property by Bembo's purchase for 260 ducats in 1535 from Giovanni Benedetto Lampridio of a house with a courtyard, garden, and well, and by his acquisition in late 1527 and again in 1536 of plots of land from the Dal Buò family.[10] Beyond Bembo's long ambition to acquire the place, these augmentations underscore his dynamic ambitions for a residence that amounted to a showcase for a showcase: in the grandeur of its two main buildings, the dimensions of the overall property, and the ornateness of its gardens (which extended to his construction of a botanical garden[11]), his prized collection was housed in a setting that was itself visually and conceptually impressive, and hence suggestively relatable to the phenomenon of the Venetian Renaissance house as a portrait of its owner.[12] Given his serious architectural interests, Bembo may have taken a direct hand in redesigning the interior of the residence and in shaping its garden;[13] but Nicola ("Cola") Bruno, his lifelong friend from his Sicilian days, his private secretary, and general factotum, appears to have presided over the actualities of the building's restoration.[14]

As for the collection itself, no original family catalogue of it survives, and it is hard to tell the extent to which Pietro added to the acquisitions already made by his father. Beyond what his letters and his will reveal of its contents, our primary source of evidence is the eyewitness accounts offered by Bembo's friends and visitors, for whom the collection was nothing short of a "pole of attraction" and "fulcrum of cultural debate."[15] Quite apart from their value as testimony about the collection, these sources

9. For photographs, Puppi (1969) 37, 38, and 42 with Kidwell (2004) 240.

10. For these additions and elaborations, Puppi (1969) 40 and Beltramini (2012), esp. 178–9, and (2013) 377–8 with Piovan (1987) on Lampridio (1478–1540) in particular; the latter was later tutor to Torquato, Bembo's son (see p. 296).

11. See Ronchi (1923–4) 297–8, and cf. p. 294.

12. See Schmitter (2007).

13. Puppi (1969) 40–1.

14. See Nalezyty (2013a) 426 and (2013b) 34 ("Because Bembo was often away, he needed a surrogate curator and exhibition designer. Cola seems to have served in exactly this role"). For the history of the friendship with Cola (1480–1542), Cian (1885) 17 and esp. (1901).

15. Bodon (1993) 168.

amply reflect in their praises the *fama* that Bembo evidently sought through self-display in, as Dora Thornton puts it, "a kind of open house for visiting scholars."[16] According to the Bolognese humanist Ludovico Beccadelli (1501–72), Bembo's friend and biographer who appears to have witnessed the collection in his years in Padua between 1528 and 1534, it drew visitors from far and wide and had few equals in the Italian peninsula for its rich assortment of "Medaglie et Scolture et Pitture antiche et moderne," for its elaborate *tavola* "worked in silver with Egyptian characters" (the piece now conventionally known as the *Mensa Isiaca,* or the Bembine Tablet, for Beccadelli an object "wondrous to behold"), and for its wealth of manuscripts, the famous codices of Terence and Virgil the most precious among them.[17] In an unpublished work on the coinage of the first twelve Caesars,[18] Bembo's friend and pupil, Alessandro Maggi da Bassano (1509–*c.* 1593), digresses as follows on Bembo's collection:

> Pietro Bembo possessed at Padua a library or, to be clearer, a Museum (*cum bibliotecham sive, ut expressius dicam, Musaeum Patavii haberet*) that was crammed not only with books but also with every kind of antiquity; in particular, he possessed the likenesses, or busts, of famous ancients engraved from marble of Paros; and then small images from Corinthian bronze; and, third, coins in an almost incredible quantity, of gold, silver and bronze; and he had all these things for the purpose of relaxing his mind when he would occasionally detach himself from his literary studies, so that he could later return to that same thing with his powers invigorated.[19]

Closely attached to both Pietro and his son, Torquato, the distinguished engraver and printmaker Enea Vico da Parma (1527–67) was a regular visitor to the *Museo,* and his *Discorsi sopra le medaglie de gli antichi* (Venice, 1555) sheds light on multiple aspects of the collection; it was through his friendship with Torquato that he was able to publish, in 1559, his reproduction of the *Mensa Isiaca* in eleven plates

16. Thornton (1997) 114.

17. Further on Beccadelli's account, Danzi (2005) 19, 37–8 with Eiche (1983) 354.

18. On this work and the circumstances of its partial survival, Bodon (2005) 82–4.

19. As cited by Eiche (1983) 354 after J. Morelli (1800) 121 and then Frizzoni (1884) 41; further, Gasparotto (2013d) 58 with Woolfson and Gregory (1995) 256, and more generally on Maggi da Bassano see Zorzi (1962) with Favaretto (2002) 107–8 and Bodon (1991) and (2005) 69–121. For the loaded social and cultural valence of *musaeum* see Findlen (1989), esp. 59 on the sixteenth/seventeenth-century idea of it as "an apt metaphor for the encyclopaedic tendencies of the period. Most compelling about the usage of the term *musaeum* was its ability to be inserted into a wide range of discursive practices. Linguistically, *musaeum* was a bridge between social and intellectual life, moving effortlessly between these two realms, and in fact pointing to the fluidity and instability of categories such as 'social' and 'intellectual', and 'public' and 'private,' as they were defined during the late Renaissance."

of figures and hieroglyphics.[20] Then another interesting figure: in Book 20 of his *Hieroglyphica sive de sacris Aegyptiorum litteris commentarii* (published in Basel, 1556), Pierio Valeriano Bolzanio (1477–1558) records his inspection of the *Mensa* in the company of Bembo himself.[21] Beyond his antiquities and artworks, Bembo's collection also included maps and scientific instrumentation such as globes and astrolabes—a dimension to his *Museo* that is matched by the scientific, astronomical, and geographical interests reflected in his library holdings.[22] All in all, Bembo's collection was such that the colorful playwright, poet, and satirist Pietro Aretino (1492–1556) could assert in a letter to Torquato of September 1549 that Rome had apparently transferred itself to Padua.[23] In his funeral oration for Bembo, the Florentine humanist historian and poet Benedetto Varchi (1503–65) effusively portrays the Paduan residence as a "temple dedicated to Minerva," and he casts Bembo himself "as if a new Apollo," giving oracle-like responses to his visitors.[24] For all his eulogistic exuberance, Varchi consolidates the almost mythical status that these various contemporary attestations conferred on Bembo's *Museo*—a myth founded on a strategy of self-representation through material object,[25] to the effect that to visit the collection was, in a sense, to experience the person behind it, or even to witness a stage-like performance on the part of the collector in his study.[26] To reapply Paula Findlen's remarks on the Venetian patron and collector Giacomo Contarini (1536–95), Bembo's collection was "not simply a product of

---

20. See Westcott (1887) 3; Dannenfeldt (1959) 22; Bodon (1993) 167 and (1997) 168.

21. In the Basel edition (Michael Isengrin, 1556), Book 20 p. 144a; cf. Book 16 p. 124f, Book 23 p. 167f, and Book 33 p. 233c. Further, Danzi (2005) 41–2, and for Valeriano, see also pp. 277–8 and Chapter 2 p. 87.

22. Danzi (2005) 19 (with 123–4 and 141–2), echoed by Gasparotto (2013d) 52. For the astrolabe that Pietro had apparently gifted to Constantine Lascaris in Messina, see Introduction p. 2. For Bembo's ultimately successful efforts to buy a damascened astrolabe, Travi (1992) 243 *Letter* 1227 and 428–9 *Letters* 1476–7 of, respectively, March 10 and 12, 1533. Cf. also a letter written by Girolamo Faletti at Venice (June 3, 1561) to Alfonso II d'Este of Ferrara: "I have bought," writes Faletti, "the globe of Cardinal Bembo for fifteen scudi which is the price of the metal composing it, and I have given it out to be decorated hoping to make of it the most beautiful globe which is possessed by any Prince in the world. It will cost altogether 25 scudi" (as given by Stevenson [1921] 1.120; also noted by Danzi 142).

23. In *Il quinto libro delle lettere di M. Pietro Aretino* (Paris, 1609) p. 159 *Letter* 302 = Pertile and Camesasca (1957) 2.292–3; also cited by Cian (1885) 192, Puppi (1969) 41, and Gasparotto (2013d) 52.

24. As given in Sansovino (1584) 1.55*v*; also cited by Puppi (1969) 41, Nalezyty (2013b) 38–9, and Gasparotto (2013d) 52.

25. Cf. Gasparotto (2013d) 52: "un mito che Bembo stesso—attraverso un'efficacissima 'autorappresentazione' di sé—aveva contribuito a creare e alimentare."

26. For this performative aspect cf. Furlotti (2015).

his desires and interests; in its most essential sense, it was his self";[27] in his Paduan *studio* "the core of his very being was on display,"[28] a being partly defined by family legacy and heirloom exhibit, but also partly invented through his own creativity as a collector.[29]

Other visits to the *Museo* are recorded,[30] but by far the most detailed contemporary account is that now standardly attributed to the Venetian noble Marcantonio Michiel (1484–1552). The handwritten notes preserved in cod. Ital. XI 67 (7351) of the Biblioteca Nazionale Marciana, Venice, were first edited by the Marciana librarian Jacopo Morelli (1745–1819) in 1800 under the title *Notizia d'opere di disegno nella prima metà del secolo XVI esistenti in Padova, Cremona, Milano, Pavia, Bergamo, Crema e Venezia scritta da un Anonimo di quel tempo*; the identification of Morelli's *Anonimo* with Michiel was established in the nineteenth century by Emmanuele Cicogna and Cesare Bernasconi.[31] A collector himself,[32] Michiel assembled in these notes an informal inventory of the artworks, both public and private, that he admired in the various northern cities he visited. The notes were assembled from 1521 to at least 1543, but Michiel gives no date for his visit(s?) to Bembo's Paduan residence, and the chronological question remains vexed. He appears to have known Bembo at least from the time of his stay in Rome from October 1518 to November 1520, and to have been sufficiently well acquainted with him to send Pietro a letter of condolence after Bernardo Bembo died on May 27, 1519.[33] He enjoyed good relations with Pietro thereafter, as Bembo's extant correspondence attests,[34] and in a letter to his nephew Gian Matteo Bembo of May 12, 1529 Pietro asks that Michiel be told that he has free access to the Bembo residence, which he is to regard as his own.[35] For chronological alignment with this letter, Michiel's visit to the Bembo collection has often been dated to after 1529. A *terminus ante quem* has been detected

27. Findlen (1994) 293.

28. Findlen (1994) 293.

29. The collector's creative self-invention: Findlen (1994) 294–5.

30. See Bodon (1993) 166 for the antiquary Costanzo Landi (1521–64) and the French humanist and theologian Gilbert Cousin (1506–72), both of whom visited the collection before 1560; and, with particular attention to Bembo's epigraphic holdings, Bernardino Scardeone (1478–1574) and Carlo Sigonio (*c.* 1524–84).

31. Cicogna (1860) 368–9, already attributing the identification to the eminent professor and librarian of the University of Padua, Daniele Francesconi (1761–1835); Bernasconi (1864) 107–17.

32. J. M. Fletcher (1973) and (1981).

33. See J. M. Fletcher (1981) 461; Lauber (2013b) 344.

34. Samples in Gasparotto (2013a) 326.

35. Travi (1992) 38 *Letter* 966.14–15 ("Dite al Magnifico nostro M. Marcantonio Michele che egli sia il ben venuto ogni volta che vorrà venire, ché questa casa è sua").

in the fact that his entry on Niccolò Leonico Tomeo's house indicates that he was already familiar with the Bembo collection:[36] given that Leonico died in late March 1531, Michiel appears to have visited Bembo before, and perhaps well before, that March.[37] Considerable uncertainty remains, but a much earlier *terminus ante quem* is nevertheless suggested by a point of detail in Michiel's reference to five bronze figurines in Bembo's collection: "Queste *sono*," he concludes, "de M. Bartolomeo insieme con el Mercurio."[38] Michiel's use of the present tense in *sono* suggests that the figurines in question are still, at the time of Michiel's visit, in the ownership of Bartolomeo; if this Bartolomeo is taken to be Bembo's half-brother, the implication is that Michiel's visit took place before Bartolomeo's death on July 12, 1526.[39] But if in general terms we accept that, on the basis of analysis of the inks used by Michiel,[40] the bulk of his entries on Padua was composed between 1525 and 1528, certain additions to his record of the Bembo collection suggest that Michiel in fact visited the *Museo* at least twice, on the first occasion (before July 1526?) very possibly during Bembo's stay in the Palazzo Foscari.[41] In the supplements that he made to his account of the Paduan collection of Marco Mantova Benavides, Michiel used a yellow ink; this account is the sole Paduan entry that is dated, to 1537; since that same ink recurs in his record of two major additions to his Bembo inventory (an ancient sleeping Cupid, and the Memling diptych of the Virgin and St. John the Baptist),[42] another visit to the Bembo collection can be inferred for 1537—on this occasion, of course, to the grand residence in the Via Altinate.

Within his inventory Michiel lists eighteen pictures.[43] Besides the Memling diptych, Jacometto Veneziano is represented by three paintings, including a portrait of the eleven-year-old Pietro and one of his brother Carlo as a newborn in 1472(?);[44] Jacopo Bellini, Andrea Mantegna, and Raphael are each represented by

36. For this entry, J. Morelli (1800) 15; Frizzoni (1884) 38.

37. On the controversy, J. M. Fletcher (1981) 461; Lauber (2013a) 445–6; Gasparotto (2013a) 326.

38. J. Morelli (1800) 22; Frizzoni (1884) 62.

39. See Lauber (2002) 113 n.80 and (2013a) 449–50; Gasparotto (2013d) 53.

40. See Schmitter (2003).

41. See p. 271 n.5.

42. See Schmitter (2003) 566, 571. The Memling in fact appears to have been the diptych of St. John and St. Veronica that was probably acquired by Bernardo Bembo during his time as ambassador to Burgundy in 1471–4: see Chapter 5 p. 205 and n.123.

43. For the inventory see J. Morelli (1800) 17–22; Frizzoni (1884) 40–63; Lauber (2013b) 346–7 with De Benedictis (1991) 217–18. In English translation: Williamson (1903) 21–8; Klein and Zerner (1966) 25–8.

44. See p. 325 n.29.

two paintings; two miniatures by Giulio Campagnola and one of Christ in death by Campagnola's pupil (perhaps Domenico Campagnola, his son)[45] are also listed, as is a portrait of the humanist poet Jacopo Sannazaro (1458–1530) by Sebastiano del Piombo; three portraits of (respectively) Dante, Petrarch, and Boccaccio are assigned to an unspecified hand, as is a portrait of Petrarch's Laura that is drawn, Michiel claims, from a fresco of St. Margaret in Avignon.[46] After the pictures, Michiel lists some twenty items, including bronze sculptures; marble busts of several Roman emperors; earthenware and glass vases; medals of gold, silver, and copper and gems set in rings; all of them are ancient apart from a bronze figurine that served as a candleholder. Beyond the particularities of its content, however, the larger interest of Michiel's account lies in the sub-narratives of social connection and family relationship that inform many of the items that he mentions. Even if more by accident than design, Michiel touches on multiple events and involvements in the lives of Bernardo and Pietro Bembo; beyond this seemingly inadvertent form of biography by allusion,[47] the many "insider" details that he mentions—for example, about the circumstances in which various family portraits were painted; how Bembo's sleeping Cupid differed from the more celebrated version of the legendary collector, Isabella d'Este, Marchesa of Mantua (1474–1539); that Giulio Campagnola helped in his pupil's painting of Christ in death—strongly indicate that Michiel enjoyed a guided tour of the collection.[48] But despite this hint of privileged insight, and even though Michiel well captures the versatility of Bembo's interests, there are conspicuous absences in his account, not least the *Mensa Isiaca* and the portrait medal that Pietro commissioned from Valerio Belli in the early 1530s.

We turn to the Belli medal in section 7.2 below, but the *Mensa* is of interest for now partly because Urbano Bolzanio here briefly reenters our story. The *Mensa*'s absence from Michiel's inventory is of course easily explained if we take it that Bembo acquired it only late in life, perhaps in his last years at Rome after 1539.[49] But how to explain Michiel's silence if the acquisition was in fact made far earlier? A tantalizing clue to early acquisition is offered by Pierio Valeriano Bolzanio[50] in the introduction to Book 33 of his *Hieroglyphica*: there he alludes (p. 233b–c in the Basel edition, Michael Isengrin, 1556) to a visit that he made in the first years of the

45. See Safarik (1974) 320 with Puppi (1974) 312.

46. See Chapter 5 p. 217.

47. Cf. J. M. Fletcher (1981) 455 for only "the tip of the iceberg" visible in Michiel's *Notizia*.

48. J. M. Fletcher (1981) 462.

49. For this possibility, Gasparotto (2013c) 499 and n.81; nothing is known of how, let alone when, Bembo acquired the *Mensa*.

50. For whom see already p. 274 and Chapter 2 p. 87.

century with his friends and associates from the Aldine Academy, Daniele Ranieri, Niccolò Leoniceno,[51] and Niccolò Leonico Tomeo, to his uncle, Urbano Bolzanio, in Venice. When they arrive they find Urbano studying Pindar; the ensuing conversation turns, via Urbano's explication of *Nemean* 8.43–4 ("yet joy is also eager to set before men's eyes a pledge of friendship"), to the hieroglyphic meaning of the eye. Ranieri is all ears: he has already wearied his friends with talk of *Aegyptiaca* because "my friend Bembo has sent me from Rome a copy of a certain table that is remarkable for its antiquity (*tabulae cuiusdam ob antiquitatem admirabilis exemplum*), and also a great number of markings from obelisks" (p. 233c). If this *tabula* is taken to be the *Mensa Isiaca*, and if we take Pierio Valeriano's anecdote at face value, the *Mensa* must have been in Bembo's possession before Urbano's death in April 1524. And so why Michiel's silence in his inventory? He was certainly capable of what may strike the modern reader as extraordinary omissions;[52] but the omission of one of Bembo's centerpieces?[53] In a letter to Gian Matteo Bembo of 1533 Pietro refers to support work done by one Francesco da Brescia at Venice on "i piedi della mia tavola di Bronzo":[54] if this *tavola* is taken to be the *Mensa*, we might speculate that, during Michiel's visit years before, it was temporarily absent because of an earlier stage of restorative or support work on the piece.[55] The matter remains perplexing, but for now the *Mensa Isiaca* usefully illustrates Bembo's interest in, and contribution to, the rising fashion for things Egyptian in the early sixteenth century.[56] Given that the taste for *Aegyptiaca* was at this time a novelty in collecting, the *Mensa* was to have a direct impact on the phenomenon of Egyptomania that took Europe by storm by the century's end—albeit Bembo's studious interest had little in common with the sensationalizing tendencies that later characterized the Egyptomania of the northern European *Wunderkammer*.[57]

---

51. For whom Chapter 3 pp. 140–2.

52. Cf. J. M. Fletcher (1981) 461: "It is admittedly dangerous to date Michiel by such a small scale omission [sc. no reference to Belli's medal of *c.* 1532] when he manages to describe Milan without Leonardo's *Last Supper* and the Carità in Venice without once referring to Rizzo's two tombs of the Doges Barbarigo" (continued in the next note).

53. Cf. J. M. Fletcher (1981) 461 (the δέ to the μέν in the quotation in n. 52): "It is, however, unlikely that Michiel, who had delighted in South American treasures and had a keen appetite for the exotic, would have passed over Bembo's Egyptian *Tavola Isiaca* had it already been installed in his house."

54. Travi (1992) 434 *Letter* 1484.6–8.

55. See further Riccomini (2013) 341.

56. See, conveniently, Curran (2007) 231–7.

57. On these points, Danzi (2005) 44–5.

7.2: Coins, Medals, and Valerio Belli's Bembo

Pietro's lifelong interest in the collecting of ancient coins and portrait medals is already amply reflected in his portrayal in *De Aetna* of the coins that he found amidst the ruins of Taormina when he was en route to Etna.[58] Beyond the relics of "temples, tombs and aqueducts" that he surveyed there, "Greek coins are often dug up by accident everywhere, all of them skillfully produced and not just stamped on bronze, but also on silver and gold" (§13). Although the study of Greek numismatics lagged far behind that of Roman coins at least until the sixteenth century,[59] Pietro was an ardent collector of Greek as well as Roman coins—a passion shared by his father, and nicely memorialized if we identify Bernardo as the sitter of Hans Memling's *Portrait of a Man with a Roman Coin* (Figure 5.3).[60] Pietro's allusion to the coins at Taormina offers its own memorialization of this shared passion, but he also touches on a deeper motivation for such collecting: "I examined all these ruins all the more carefully because I remembered that you always took the greatest pleasure in the statues and monuments of the ancients, *as if witnesses to their virtuous qualities and achievements*" (§13). The instructional benefits that Pietro here associates with examining the antiquarian past lead us back to Petrarch, a transformative figure in the history of numismatics as in so much else.[61]

In contrast to the vulnerabilities of textual transmission, coins seemingly offered a direct window on to the past, allowing Petrarch to set written descriptions of the emperors against their iconographic representation.[62] Beyond this visual aspect, the study of coins brought moral instruction as well as philological insight. When, for example, Petrarch records an audience that he was granted by Emperor Charles IV at Mantua in 1354, he describes how he gave him as a gift

> some gold and silver coins bearing the portraits of our ancient rulers and inscriptions in tiny and ancient lettering, coins that I treasured, and among them was the head of Caesar Augustus, who almost appeared to be breathing. "Here, O Caesar," I said, "are the men whom you have succeeded, here are those whom you must try to imitate and admire, whose ways and character

58. See already Chapter 6 p. 250.

59. Weiss (1968) 186–7.

60. See Chapters 5 p. 206 and 6 p. 250.

61. For Petrarch as collector, Magnaguti (1907) with Weiss (1968) 176–9 and (1988) 37–8.

62. On the complex relationship between early numismatics, history, and portraiture, F. Haskell (1993) 13–79.

> you should emulate: I would have given these coins to no other save yourself. Your prestige has moved me; for although I know their ways and names and deeds, it is up to you not only to know but to follow their example; it was thus fitting that you should have these". . . [D]eeply touched, he appeared to accept my modest gift with the greatest pleasure.[63]

Valuable as historical evidence, ancient coins and medals also served as primary sources for the restoration of Greco-Roman word forms, a practice much extended by the fifteenth-century humanists.[64] Bembo fully reflects these tendencies, as when, in a letter to Bernardino Sandri of June 12, 1529, he applies his numismatic knowledge to elucidating a highly technical, three-way play on the term *Treviri* in a Ciceronian letter to his friend C. Trebatius Testa (*Fam.* 7.13.2).[65] As for the mnemonic aspect, in a letter of November 25, 1505 thanking Giulio Tomarozzo for the gift of ten medals, Pietro asserts that the gift is welcome not just because the medals are "fine enough" in appearance, but also because their images are carriers of ancient memory.[66] Years later, in a letter to Bartolomeo Castellano of October 6, 1532, the habitually acquisitive[67] Bembo acknowledges Bartolomeo's generosity:[68]

> About the ancient coins in your possession, I appreciate your generosity in giving them over to me. For on them I see the likenesses and as if the very faces (*imagines et tamquam vultus ipsos*) of the greatest men of distinction, Greek or Roman. Long habit has made them known to me and recognized, and I relish their near-companionship and intimacy—an intimacy that is wordless and without any show of feeling, but nevertheless both pleasurable and welcome.[69]

---

63. *Epistolae familiares* 19.3; trans. Bernardo (1985) 79–80. For the anecdote, Hill (1911) 259–60 with Weiss (1968) 177 and (1988) 37. For the political background, Petrarch's "boundless egotism," and the "rather naive diplomacy" of his gesture, Bayley (1942), esp. 331, with Thomson (1950).

64. Weiss (1968) 182 and (1988) 174–5.

65. Travi (1992) 55 *Letter* 984, cited by Gasparotto (2013c) 486–7; for elucidation of the wordplay (encasing allusions to a Gaulish tribe, to the magistrates overseeing executions, and to the commissioners of the mint) see Shackleton Bailey (1977) 341–2.

66. Travi (1987) 205 *Letter* 220.15–19, cited by Gasparotto (2013c) 484.

67. Cf. Kidwell (2004) 388 ("Bembo's worst fault was his acquisitiveness"), with examples on pp. 120–1, 187, 288, 322, 331.

68. To be identified with Bartolomeo de' Cordoni da Città di Castello (*c.* 1471–1535), author of *De unione animae cum supereminenti lumine*, posthumously published in 1538? See Zambelli (1964) with Danzi (2005) 313–15 and n.236.

69. Travi (1992) 380 *Letter* 1416.34–9, cited by Gasparotto (2013c) 485.

Evidently well versed in the Renaissance use of coins and medals as gifts of friendship,[70] Pietro presented Aldo Manuzio with a denarius of the Emperor Titus, its reverse showing an anchor entwined by a dolphin. So at least Erasmus asserts of Pietro in his *Adages*, claiming that the device (speed and grace figured in the dolphin, stability in the anchor) denoted one of Augustus' favorite dicta, σπεῦδε βραδέως ("Hasten slowly"); the device soon became an Aldine staple that went through multiple iterations.[71]

The fashion for the Italian portrait medal began only late in the fourteenth century,[72] and Petrarch's influence again looms large in this development: part of his legacy in Padua was that, sixteen years after his death in 1374, the first Renaissance medals were struck in 1390 to mark the success of Francesco Novello da Carrara (1359–1406), Lord of Padua, in retaking the city from the forces of Gian Galeazzo Visconti of Milan in that year.[73] Of the three medals struck, the obverses of two of them showed Francesco in profile, his image resembling that of Vitellius on a bronze sestertius of 69 CE; the third showed his father, Francesco I da Carrara (1325–93), while the reverse of all three bore the Carrara emblem of a four-wheeled *carro*, thereby creating linkage between the Paduan present and the Roman past.[74] In 1393 Marco Sesto, an engraver at the Venetian mint, produced a medal showing an unidentified Roman emperor on the obverse, a female figure representing Venice on the reverse; probably in the same year his brother, Lorenzo, produced a similar but smaller medal, on the obverse of which the portrait-figure (resembling that on Marco's medal, but facing right) is identified as Galba.[75] A medal showing (probably) Alexander the Great on the obverse, a mythological scene of abduction (the rape of Proserpina?) or rescue (Perseus freeing Andromeda?) on the reverse, is signed by Alessandro Sesto, the nephew of Lorenzo and Marco, and dated 1417.[76]

---

70. On which Cunnally (1994).

71. *Adag.* 2.1.1 with Mynors (1991) 3–17, esp. 5–6; for the saying cf. Suet. *Aug.* 25.4, Gell. *NA* 10.11.5. For Bembo's gift dated to 1498–1500, Lowry (1998) 41, and for an illustrated survey of the Aldine device as used in horizontal prototype in the 1499 *Hypnerotomachia* (cf. Chapter 5 p. 191 and n.46) and then in its familiar form from June 1502 onward, see H. G. Fletcher (1988) 43–59 and (1995) 25–34 with Lowry 40–1 and now the illustrated catalogue in Staikos (2009) 8–17.

72. Overview: Scher (2000a).

73. For these medals Hill (1930) nos. 1–4 with Rizzoli (1932) and P. F. Brown (1996) 96; for the Petrarchan dimension, Weiss (1968) 179 and (1988) 53.

74. P. F. Brown (1996) 96.

75. For these medals, Hill (1930) nos. 10–11 with Weiss (1988) 54, Stahl and Waldman (1993–4), and P. F. Brown (1996) 96–7.

76. Hill (1930) no. 12 with Weiss (1988) 54, Stahl and Waldman (1993–4) 183–4, and P. F. Brown (1996) 97.

But despite these pioneering endeavors of the Sesto family, the next example of the Venetian portrait medal is found only in the 1450s.[77] The revival of the ancient medal more generally in Italy was slow to gain momentum until Antonio di Puccio Pisano, called Pisanello (*c.* 1395–*c.* 1455), emerged as the father of the modern form in the d'Este court in Ferrara (he made his first medal in the late 1430s); combining text and image, physically enduring, produced in multiple exemplars, and easily distributed, the portrait medal proved a highly versatile, and quickly prolific, means of immortalizing its honorand.[78] Beyond his collecting, Bembo's interest in medals extended to matters of design and presentation, as none other than Lucrezia Borgia attests in a letter that she wrote to her lover in Spanish in June 1503:

> Trusting in your skill which I appreciated these past days when considering certain designs for medallions, and having decided to have one made according to that most subtle and most apt suggestion you gave me, I thought I would send it to you with this letter, and lest it be mixed with some other element that could detract from its value I thought also to ask you herewith kindly to take the trouble for love of me to think what text should be put upon it . . .[79]

Bembo replied at once in a letter that is itself artfully contrived, obliquely addressing his love for Lucrezia even as he addresses the medal: "As for the fire on the gold medallion which Your Ladyship has sent me with the request that I should devise a motto for inscription, I can think of giving it no nobler location than the soul. Wherefore you might have it thus inscribed: *EST ANIMUM*."[80] If fire "consumes the spirit," the flame of love, we infer, consumes Bembo.

That Bembo was already well acquainted with Valerio Belli by 1505 is signaled in a bumptious letter that he wrote to Giovan Giorgio Trissino on March 21 of that year: much to Bembo's irritation, Trissino had refused to give up a gold medal of Berenice that Pietro longed to acquire for himself;[81] both parties, it transpires, had discussed the medal with a certain Valerio—surely our Valerio, whose expertise as

77. P. F. Brown (1996) 97.

78. Further, Scher (2000a) 5–7.

79. Shankland (1987) II, also cited by Kidwell (2004) 78. On Bembo's relationship with Lucrezia, Chapter 4 pp. 171, 173–4.

80. With nice allusion to Horace *Epist.* 1.2.39. For the letter, Travi (1987) 146 *Letter* 153.7–10, here as rendered by Shankland (1987) III; further, Gasparotto (2013c) 489.

81. For Gasparotto (2013c) 483–4, an ancient gold coin showing Berenice II, the wife of Ptolemy III Euergetes: see Chapter 4 p. 173 and n.121.

a medalist therefore appears already well established by 1505.[82] After his appointment as secretary to Pope Leo X in 1513, Bembo seemingly eased the way for Belli's introduction to the papal court, his gaining of important commissions thereafter, and his movement in rarified circles that included three popes, important cardinals, and artists such as Polidoro da Caravaggio, Raphael, and Michelangelo.[83] There was some friction along the way in Pietro's relations with him,[84] but their long association nevertheless made Belli an obvious choice when Bembo sought to commission his own portrait medal in the early 1530s. Two surviving letters shed important light on what transpired, and also indicate that Bembo was a good deal more informed about the intricacies of the medalist's art than Benvenuto Cellini for one was later to allow in his autobiography.[85] The obverse of the medal (Figure 7.1) shows Bembo in profile facing left, beardless and with his hair reaching to the nape of his neck. As for the figure on the reverse (also Figure 7.1), should he be clothed or nude? In the first, brief letter, of February 28, 1532, Bembo states his preference for "un poco di vestimento."[86] But in the second letter, written some two weeks later on March 12,[87] his pleasure at the plaster-cast version of the reverse (the figure "has seemed to me very fine and excellent, as it indeed is") is tempered by politely stated dissatisfaction at details of the pose: the semi-clad figure who reclines on a smooth rock by a stream under a tree, as if luxuriating in the Classically inspired setting of the poet in an idyllic *otium*, holds a branch in his left hand (Figure 7.1). Bembo goes on to suggest adjustments, and Belli evidently acted on them in his subsequent remodeling of the reverse: in the second version (Figure 7.2),[88] the branch has been removed, the figure reclines on a rock that is now unevenly shaped, not smooth, and a denser, richer variety of greenery supplants the copse in the original.

Of the Classical prototypes to which Belli reverted for this scene of laid-back repose on the reverse, imperial coins frequently featured the typology of the

---

82. See Travi (1987) 189–91 *Letter* 202 with Gasparotto (1996) 185.

83. Gasparotto (1996) 185 with Burns (2000) 22–5.

84. See Travi (1990) 232 *Letter* 509: Bembo had interpreted as a gift an ancient coin with Nero's image on it, but Belli anticipated payment for it.

85. On this point, Gasparotto (2013c) 488. For Cellini's remarks, G. Bull (1996) 172: Bembo was "a very great man of letters and a poet of extraordinary genius, but . . . he was completely ignorant about my own art. . ."

86. Travi (1992) 315 *Letter* 1334.

87. Travi (1992) 320 *Letter* 1339.

88. Attwood (2003) 1.211 no. 325; Burns et al. (2000) 367–8 no. 191; Beltramini, Gasparotto, and Tura (2013) 304; Beltramini, Burns, and Gasparotto (2013) 536.

reclining individual, especially in personifications, as in the cases of a sestertius of Trajan that shows the Genius of the *Aqua Traiana* reclining to the left, the right hand holding a reed and the left arm resting on an urn from which water flows; or a sestertius of Hadrian that shows Hispania reclining to the left on a rock, branch in hand.[89] Belli may also have been influenced by the famous engraving of the reclining Saturn by Giulio Campagnola,[90] whom Bembo knew personally, owning at least two of his works.[91] Despite (or beyond) these possible influences, however, Davide Gasparotto traces the design of the reverse probably to Bembo himself,[92] and in his 1996 interpretation of the scene he finds an idealized vision of Arcadian *otium* inspired by the Augustan poets, especially Virgil and Horace.[93] When he subsequently revisits the scene, however, Gasparotto posits a more exact reference point for the image in Bembo's beloved Noniano as pictured in *De Aetna*.[94] The verdant riverbank, the cool stream, the pleasant trees, and the shade they provide (cf. *De Aetna* §§5, 6) all find alternative expression on the medal, which was commissioned two or so years after the second edition of *De Aetna* appeared in 1530. If we accept that the medal specifically evokes Noniano, the fact that Bembo commissioned it soon after the republication of *De Aetna* suggests the special interplay of text and medal: in his different medium, Belli idealizes what is already a Classically inflected idealization in *De Aetna*. If Bembo did indeed design the medal's reverse, his evocation of that early work underscores the symbolic importance that he continued to attach to *De Aetna*, as if in nostalgic recall of his youthful identity, decades after its first Aldine instantiation.

The story of Belli's medal boasts a colorful postscript. Despite the adjustments that Belli made to the reverse, Bembo remained dissatisfied with the medal, as seems clear from his probable allusion to it in his correspondence from 1532.[95] Some three years later, in a letter of August 10, 1535 to the humanist and Benedictine monk Onorato Fascitelli (1502–64), Bembo possibly refers yet again to this same medal, on this occasion lamenting that he has no better likeness of himself to send as a tribute gift to the Augustinian friar and distinguished

---

89. Mattingly (1936) 184 no. 873; 346 no. 843.

90. Cf. Suida (1936) 281.

91. Rebecchini (2002) 128 with Danzi (2005) 40 and n.95; see also p. 277.

92. See (2013b) 324 and (2013c) 488.

93. Gasparotto (1996) 187, recapitulated in (2000) 366–7 no. 189; cf. Attwood (2003) 1.210 for Horace stressed.

94. Gasparotto (2013b) 325 and (2013c) 488–9.

95. For which see Gasparotto (1996) 188 and (2013b) 324.

theologian (later Cardinal) Girolamo Seripando (1493–1563).[96] He has arranged for another medal to be made, writes Pietro; but if its execution is slow, he will send on the one he has, such as it is. A month before, Bembo had made contact with Benvenuto Cellini via an intermediary, Benedetto Varchi;[97] the celebrated Cellini had agreed to make a medal for Bembo, and it may well be that *this* is the new commission to which Bembo refers in his letter to Fascitelli of August 10. A protracted process of exchange and negotiation with Cellini followed before the latter, en route to the court of Francis I in France, eventually visited Bembo in Padua in the spring of 1537 to make a study for the medal; the final product was apparently to feature Pegasus on the reverse, a wreath of myrtle set around the image.[98] There apparently was a Cellini medal, at least eventually,[99] but few specialists would now identify it with the long-controversial piece that shows the long-bearded Bembo with the inscription *PETRI BEMBI CAR*[*DINALIS*] on the obverse, a winged Pegasus rearing above the spring of Hippocrene on the reverse (Figure 7.5).[100] Already in 1905 Luigi Rizzoli proposed that this latter medal was the work of Danese Cattaneo (*c.* 1512–72);[101] himself part of Bembo's circle, Cattaneo was commissioned by Bembo's executors to sculpt the famous marble bust (1547–8) for the monument to the Cardinal in the Basilica of Saint Anthony, Padua. The similarity to Cattaneo's bust suggests a date of *c.* 1547 for the medal: Rizzoli speculates that the medal was executed by Cattaneo after Pietro's death to commemorate this Paduan monument to Bembo,[102] with possible allusion to Cellini's medal in Cattaneo's own rendering of Pegasus on the reverse. Even if this attribution to Cattaneo lacks definitive proof, the case for Cellini's crafting of the medal is surely unsustainable;[103] however engaging we find Cellini's self-serving version of his encounter with Bembo in his autobiography, his finished medal is as elusive as its author is evasive.

---

96. Travi (1992) 607–8 *Letter* 1707.

97. For Varchi's role, Gasparotto (1996) 188–9.

98. Cellini as in G. Bull (1996) 172–3.

99. See Kidwell (2004) 476 n.10.

100. Attwood (2003) 1.168–70 no. 217; Beltramini, Gasparotto, and Tura (2013) 366.

101. Rizzoli (1905), esp. 279–80. Known medals of Bembo were also made by Alfonso Lombardi and Leone Leoni, but both artists can be discounted as the source of our medal: Attwood (2003) 1.169.

102. Rizzoli (1905) 280.

103. See in summary Gasparotto (1996) 191–5 and (2013e).

7.3: *Titian, Bembo, and Evocation of Sweet Noniano*

Beyond the absence in Michiel's inventory of any reference to Belli's medal, he makes no allusion to any painting of Bembo by Titian, even though a portrait dating to Pietro's years as papal secretary to Leo X from 1513 to 1521 is attested elsewhere. Michiel's silence on the matter is part of a storyline that will ultimately lead us back to *De Aetna*; but first another dimension to the Titian problem. In a letter of May 30, 1540 to Girolamo Quirini (1468–1554, eventually Pietro's literary executor) at Venice,[104] Bembo, newly installed as Cardinal at Rome, expresses grave concern about the illness that apparently continues to afflict Girolamo's cousin, the Venetian patrician Elisabetta Quirini Massolo (d. 1559), Bembo's last great love, his confidant, and his muse.[105] He later goes on to ask Girolamo to thank Titian "for the gift of my second portrait" ("Renderete parimente grazie a M. Tiziano *del dono del mio secondo ritratto*"); he had intended to pay for it, but, since in the event it was gifted to him, he would instead try to offer Titian some service in return.[106] This second portrait has regularly been identified with the celebrated portrait of Cardinal Bembo that now resides in the National Gallery of Art in Washington, DC. But what then of the first portrait? When was it executed, and in what circumstances?

The matter is immediately complicated by Giorgio Vasari's portrayal of Titian in the second edition (1568; there is no independent treatment of Titian in the first edition of 1550) of *Le Vite de' più eccellenti architetti, pittori, et scultori italiani*:

> Now Titian had taken the portrait of Bembo, then secretary to Pope Leo X, and was by him invited to Rome, that he might see the city, with Raphael of Urbino and other distinguished persons. But the artist, having delayed his

---

104. Travi (1993) 307–8 *Letter* 2191.

105. For Elisabetta see Kidwell (2004) 299, 324–33 with Dionisotti (1966b) 614–15 on *Rime* CXXXII and Whistler (2012), esp. 234–6; for her precise relationship to Girolamo (first cousin once removed), A. Sherman (2013) 41 and 50 n.9, with the family tree usefully set out on p. 43. Titian painted her portrait more than once, on the first occasion in 1543: that portrait was apparently commissioned by Elisabetta herself (see Bembo's letter to Girolamo Quirini of December 24, 1543: Travi [1993] 477–8 *Letter* 2403.16–19), and intended as a gift for Bembo in exchange for a Titian portrait of him that Bembo had already given her (further, Whistler 235 with Dionisotti 55 = Vela [2002] 64). The point matters because the Titian portrait that Pietro gave Elisabetta was conceivably the Washington, DC picture (Figure 7.3)—a possibility that has important ramifications for the second-portrait problem: see further p. 288.

106. Travi (1993) 308 *Letter* 2191.16–20.

> journey until 1520, when the Pope and Raphael were both dead, put it off for that time altogether.[107]

Then later,

> Titian made a second portrait of Bembo, when the latter had become a Cardinal, that is.[108]

The first portrait of Bembo to which Vasari refers appears to be separate from, and significantly earlier than, the image of him that Titian apparently included in his large narrative canvas (*ante* 1537)[109] of the *Humiliation of Emperor Frederick Barbarossa before Pope Alexander III* at the Treaty of Venice of 1177. According to the description offered by Francesco Sansovino (1521–86) of the Sala del Maggior Consiglio in the Palazzo Ducale as it was before its devastation by fire in 1577,[110] Titian incorporated in this picture the likenesses not just of Bembo but of several other contemporary luminaries, among them Jacopo Sannazaro (1458–1530), Andrea Navagero (1483–1529, Bembo's predecessor as historian of the Venetian Republic), and Agostino Beazzano (*c.* 1490–1549, effectively secretary to Bembo in his years of service to Leo X); most of the figures he portrays were personally well known to Titian, as his patrons and/or as members of the Aldine circle.[111] As for the putative portrait of *c.* 1515, its existence has been doubted on the grounds not just of Vasari's susceptibility to inaccuracy, but also of Bembo's absence from Venice in the years when it is presumed to have been executed: could Titian have had real opportunity to paint Bembo before the latter's return to Padua in 1521?[112] Were Bembo's relations with Titian in any case strained by the latter's refusal to take up the invitation—apparently engineered by Pietro—to visit Rome in

---

107. Lavin (1967) 2.240. Bembo was appointed Papal secretary in March 1513.

108. Lavin (1967) 2.249 ("Ritrasse Tiziano il Bembo un'altra volta, cioè poi che fu cardinale": Milanesi [1881] 455).

109. For this chronology Gasparotto (1996) 188, but for a much earlier date of completion see, e.g., Wethey (1971) 82 ("completed in 1523") and Joannides (2001) 163, 178 (also citing 1523) with discussion in Coggiola (1914–15) 487–9 and Agosti (1986) 71–2; much rests on how Sansovino's account (for which next n.) of Titian's overall activities and progress in the *Sala* is precisely to be interpreted, but for the *Battle of Cadore* still certainly unfinished in 1537 see, e.g., Coggiola 488 with Tietze-Conrat (1945), esp. 207.

110. Sansovino (1581) 131; cf. also Ridolfi (1648) 1.140 = Bondanella et al. (1996) 64.

111. Further on the full cast of characters, Crowe and Cavalcaselle (1877) 1.167–8 and Coggiola (1914–15) 487 with Marinelli (2013) 473.

112. On this point, Coggiola (1914–15) 486.

1513?[113] And if an early portrait by Titian did indeed exist, Michiel's failure to list it in his inventory would seem remarkable, and hard to explain away on any simple grounds. But if, despite these concerns, we still accept the portrait's existence, it is now seemingly lost—unless, that is, we take up the recent suggestion that the *Portrait of a Gentleman* that resides in the Musée des Beaux-Arts et d'Archéologie, Besançon (Figure 7.6), is an early Titian (as opposed to belonging to the school of Titian), and that its sitter (once improbably identified as Alfonso I d'Este, Duke of Ferrara, or as Francis I of France) is none other than Bembo himself in his early to mid-forties.[114] Certainly, the angular features and sharp nose of the sitter are in keeping with the parallel characteristics on display in the Belli medal of *c.* 1532, and also in Lucas Cranach the Younger's miniature portrait of *c.* 1536; but the temporal distance between the Besançon portrait and those two *comparanda* nevertheless leaves it far from certain that Bembo is Titian's sitter.

Even if Vasari is taken to refer to the Besançon portrait of *c.* 1515, however, Bembo's allusion to Titian's *secondo ritratto* in his letter of May 30, 1540 may yet presuppose something other than a first portrait painted decades earlier. Indeed, whether or not that early portrait ever existed is arguably beside the point; for in mentioning the *secondo ritratto*, Bembo may mean only the second of what he thinks of as a closely related (and recently executed?) dyad of portraits—and Giulio Coggiola is surely right to express at least qualms at the peremptory lack of explanation in the term *secondo*, if the latter presupposes a picture that was completed a quarter of a century or so before Bembo's letter of May 1540.[115] One proposal along these lines concerns the badly preserved portrait that now resides in the Museo Nazionale di Capodimonte, Naples (Figure 7.4). In his letter of May 1540, we remember, Bembo states that he meant to pay for the *secondo ritratto*. The implication is that he actively commissioned it; but why do so if Titian had only recently executed a first portrait? If we accept that the first portrait—that which now resides in the National Gallery of Art, Washington, DC—was sketched from life between March 1539 (when Bembo was created Cardinal) and late September of that year (when he left for Rome), and if it was completed in the months thereafter, one possibility is that Bembo soon gave it away, perhaps to his beloved Elisabetta.[116] If he dispensed in this way with his first "official portrait," Bembo commissioned a second from Titian, and quickly enough for it to be completed before his allusion to the

113. Andrea Navagero was apparently instrumental in persuading Titian to reject the invitation: see Tietze-Conrat (1944) 122 with Kim (2014) 171, 176.

114. See Gasparotto (2013f) 208.

115. Coggiola (1914–15) 493 ("*secondo*, non sufficientemente esplicativo").

116. So speculates Kidwell (2004) 484 n.49; see also now Whistler (2012) 235 and n.67, and cf. my p. 286 and n.105.

finished product in his letter of May 30, 1540. In pursuing this line of argument[117] Coggiola now adds an interesting point of emphasis. The fact that Bembo's beard in the Washington portrait is shorter and more rounded than that in the Naples version clearly suggests at first sight that the former is the earlier picture, but Coggiola takes pains to assert that this difference in beard length is potentially misleading: in the process of all the restorations and retouchings to which the Washington portrait was subjected, the beard could have been cut.[118] If we then infer that the beard was originally of the same length in both the Washington and Naples portraits, the implication is that the two were executed at roughly the same time.

Yet this reconstruction of events is inevitably tentative, and other possible scenarios present themselves, among them the options of positing a now lost precursor (*c.* 1537–9?) that closely resembled the Washington version;[119] or of persisting with the portrait of *c.* 1515 as the *primo ritratto*, the Washington version as the second. In either case, two advantages of taking the Washington version to be the second portrait are (i) that it circumvents the special pleading with which Coggiola tries to explain away the difference in beard length between the Naples and Washington portraits, and (ii) that it allows for a later dating of the Naples portrait, which would then plausibly coincide with the visit that Titian eventually made to Rome with Orazio, his son, between October 1545 and June 1546.[120] For present purposes, and for all the uncertainties that complicate the story and chronology of Titian's various renderings of Bembo, the hypothesis that the Washington portrait predates the Naples version by some six or so years yields telling insights into each. Wearing the scarlet cape and *biretta* that were the uniform of his new office, the Cardinal

---

117. Coggiola (1914–15) 492–4.

118. Coggiola (1914–15) 491–2.

119. Cf. now Nalezyty (2013a) 427–9 on an early-seventeenth-century portrait in the Museo del Prado, Madrid, of Bembo figured as a Knight of St. John of Jerusalem. Already in 1508 Bembo received by papal bull the *commenda* (i.e., the ecclesiastical benefice) of the Knights of St. John of Jerusalem in Bologna; in 1517 he was also made Grand Prior of Hungary in the Order of St. John. This last appointment matters for now because, intriguingly, Carlo Ridolfi reports that Titian painted Bembo's portrait as Prior of Hungary, before he was Cardinal (Ridolfi [1648] 1.140 = Bondanella et al. [1996] 64): given that Ridolfi writes here in the context of Titian's portrayal of the *Humiliation of Emperor Frederick Barbarossa before Pope Alexander III* in the Sala del Maggior Consiglio of the Palazzo Ducale, the first Bembo portrait to which Ridolfi refers would seem naturally to be that in the Sala (but with Bembo there figured as a Knight?). But the Prado portrait bears a striking resemblance to the Washington picture, a coincidence that leads Nalezyty to speculate that the now lost original (*c.* 1538?) of the Prado copy reflected a studio model that also underlies (and may even have become "finished" as?) the Washington picture; the preparation of that model before Bembo left Venice for Rome enabled Titian to portray him despite his absence from the Republic after October 1539.

120. Bembo rapturously reports Titian's arrival at Rome in his letter to Girolamo Quirini of October 10, 1545: see Travi (1993) 544 *Letter* 2500 with Grosso (2013) 369.

shown in the Washington. picture (Figure 7.3) exhibits a *gravitas* of expression and a dignity of manner and mind that befit the responsibility newly conferred upon him. Seemingly younger than his seventy years, he appears as sharp of intellect as he is angular of physique: offset by the hollowness of his cheeks, his aquiline nose outwardly expresses the acuity of mind that is signaled by the bright alertness of his eyes.[121] The beard still grows, as if a symbol of Bembo's destined growth in his new role. Through the alignment of his raised right arm and hand with the bottom of his cape, the picture resembles a sculpted bust, its realism enhanced by Bembo's dynamism of pose as he turns his head to his right while gesturing toward his left. His bearing is that of the idealized Roman orator, his hand exactly as Quintilian recommends in his *Institutio oratoria* (cf. 11.3.142: "The most suitable attitude for the hand is produced by raising the thumb and slightly curving the fingers, unless it holds a document"). In the drama of the moment, Bembo appears to turn his penetrating gaze on his interlocutor or audience, his hand perhaps gesturing to affirm the words that, we imagine, he has just spoken. In sum, this "talking portrait"[122] captures the vitality of a newly appointed Cardinal who is at the height of his powers, his decorum of bearing matched by the characterful intelligence and vigor that Titian captures within the man.

The Naples portrait (Figure 7.4) is a partial repetition of the Washington picture, in that a similarly garbed Bembo again looks to his right while his right arm is similarly angled, albeit resting on the side of the chair in which he now sits. In the seeming dialectic between the two pictures, Bembo retains his *gravitas* of bearing and manner but naturally appears older, his beard now elongated after years as Cardinal. In contrast to the dynamism of his standing pose against the "dark and cold background"[123] of the Washington picture, however, his sedentary position in the Naples portrait is symptomatic of the more leisurely ambience that is evoked partly by the landscape visible in the background, partly by the open book that he holds in his left hand. In contrast to his orator's pose (and pause) in the Washington picture, in the dramatic moment of the Naples portrait Bembo seemingly turns toward an interlocutor who has just interrupted him as he reads in the tranquility of a country haven that is perhaps reminiscent of the green Veneto. The sharply attentive Cardinal of the Washington picture here gives way to a gentler vision of Bembo in repose—a nostalgic vision that may specifically evoke in its landscape background "the delightful

121. Cf. on these and the following points Crowe and Cavalcaselle (1877) 2.28–9; Coggiola (1914–15) 494; Firpo (2013) 24; Collareta (2013) 227; Marinelli (2013) 475; Grosso (2013) 369.

122. Cf. Collareta (2013) 227 ("un ritratto parlante") and Marinelli (2013) 475 ("un ritratto 'eloquente'").

123. Crowe and Cavalcaselle (1877) 2.29.

hills of Asoli" and "sweet Noniano"[124] and his youthful devotion to the Muses in both places. In effect, if the Washington picture is forward looking in its heralding of the new Cardinal, the Naples portrait has a retrospective aspect to it. Even as it pictures Bembo in old age, it deftly bears the memory (the sitter perhaps reflecting on it?) of his younger self in country *otium*: the world of *De Aetna* and *Gli Asolani*.

7.4: De Aetna *and Naturalist Collecting*

Bembo's collection was outstanding even in the context of Padua and Venice as major centers of Renaissance collecting. While Padua in particular shows a fascination with antiquities that extends back at least to the thirteenth century, the earliest known individual in the region who collected in a systematic and voluminous way appears to be Oliviero Forzetta of Treviso (*c.* 1300–73), a contemporary of Petrarch; but whereas the latter's antiquarianism was inseparable from his Classical scholarship, Forzetta, a more committed usurer than scholar, was seemingly guided by no such high-mindedness.[125] The Petrarchan dimension was taken up in the Veneto by a line of antiquarian humanists that included that celebrated pioneer of clock design and Petrarch's friend, Giovanni Dondi dell'Orologio (*c.* 1330–88), Pier Paolo Vergerio the elder (*c.* 1369–1444), Felice Feliciano (1433–79), and Bartolomeo Sanvito (1435–1518).[126] At Venice, meanwhile, humanist collectors were already active in the early fifteenth century, especially in the amassing of Classical texts, and there was a considerable traffic in objects such as coins, seals and gems, as attested by (e.g.) the Florentine humanist and Camaldolese monk Ambrogio Traversari (1386–1439): during his stay in Venice at the monastery of San Michele di Murano, Ambrogio reports his encounters with collectors such as Pietro Tommasi, Francesco Barbaro, and Benedetto Dandolo, but by far the most prominent Venetian collector in this period was Pietro Barbo, later Pope Paul II from 1464 until his death in 1471.[127] Venice's geographical position, mercantile reach and "genius for looting"[128] naturally favored its traffic in collectibles, but collecting was hardly motivated solely or even primarily by commercial ambition. This gentlemanly pastime and badge of civility[129] amounted to a form of material investment that brought social prestige

124. Coggiola (1914–15) 494.

125. See Weiss (1988) 28–9 with Gaffuri (1997) and Favaretto (2002) 33–7.

126. Danzi (2005) 22.

127. On these points see Weiss (1988) 169–70, 185–6 with P. F. Brown (1996) 77, 83; Favaretto (2002) 43–62; and, on Barbo, Salomon (2003).

128. Weiss (1988) 131.

129. Cf. Findlen (1994) 15, 98 ("Civility, in all its forms, shaped the social paradigm of collecting").

and elevation, expressed civic pride, and also implied a correlation between cultural and moral values.[130] At Venice in particular, the presence of an aristocratic patriciate as opposed to a centralized, princely court at the heart of government fostered a competitive culture of display among leading families. While the churches and official buildings of the Republic, most obviously the treasury of St. Mark's Basilica, functioned as public repositories of collectibles, the kinds of artwork they displayed were often dictated by religious, cultic, or civic requirements, and in Bembo's Venice there was no such thing as a secular art gallery open to the public at large.[131] This void was at least partially filled by private collections, access to which was privileged and prized; and the feature of these collections that is most important for now is their cosmopolitan ability to bring the world to the visitor.

Collecting practices were profoundly affected by the radical shifts of self-perception and world understanding brought about in the later fifteenth and early sixteenth centuries by the increasing dissemination of Classical texts in print form, by the expansion of travel and communication networks, and by the voyages of discovery. As experience of the world began to outrun the knowledge stored in ancient texts, and as the idea of a universal, divinely ordained Nature came under challenge from the scientific study of particularized nature, collecting offered one way of controlling the influx of new information about the world at large. The desire to experience nature not just through artistic representation, curio, or relic but through firsthand engagement also had the effect of transforming collectors into travelers; because travel in turn challenged settled perceptions and opened new horizons, it further implied the advancing of self-knowledge.[132] Here *De Aetna* comes into its own as the record of Bembo's rite-of-passage act of naturalist collecting in a region whose topography conformed, as Paula Findlen puts it, to "an imagined moral logic. The path from Rome to Naples to Sicily, as culled from the natural histories of the day, led straight to perdition."[133] Some 150 years after Bembo's ascent of Etna, in 1637 the eminent German Jesuit polymath Athanasius Kircher (1602–80) witnessed Etna in eruption, and in March 1638 he climbed to the crater of Vesuvius, later describing his experience in terms of an awed fascination

130. See Weiss (1988) 180 with De Benedictis (1991) 71 and San Juan (1991) 69 (with reference to "humanist arguments which aligned cultural possession—both physical and intellectual—with moral values"); for civic pride, Findlen (2004) 45–6 and (2005) 55.

131. Further on these points, Pomian (1990) 65–72 with Carrier (2002); but see Stenhouse (2014) for Roman antiquities in particular nevertheless preserved in local collections within the Italian peninsula and southern France—collections designed to promote the Classical pasts, and hence the continuing prestige, of their locales.

132. On these points, Findlen (1994) 3–4, 158–70.

133. (1994) 185.

and a stark reminder of the fragility of human life.[134] Yet he combined this sense of awe with a "modern" scientific commitment to finding order and method in nature: in contrast to earlier naturalists who were concerned primarily with problems of naming, classification, and identification, Kircher sought to engage with the inner processes that underlay the volcanoes' surface phenomena.[135] So in *De Aetna* Bembo captures the awe-inspiring spectacle of Etna's fiery effusions, led as he is by curiosity and daring to the edge of the lower crater where, "as if from a furnace, smoke began to pour forth in a continuous exhalation" and "cracks . . . formed in the mountain's surface through long fires" (§26). Bernardo trembles at Pietro's hair-raising account (§27) and exclaims at his rashness. But the combination of delight in and yet awed astonishment at the spectacle (§28) is Bembo's way of conveying, Kircher-like, the smallness of human existence in the face of nature's vastness of scale and danger.[136] Yet *De Aetna* balances this spectator-like response to the volcano with the "modern" naturalist's keen observation of its topography, vegetation, and lava flows, and in this respect the work is both forward-looking and—in a specific sense—backward glancing in the tension that it generates between passive spectatorship on the one hand, active rationalist inquiry on the other. It is forward looking in its reliance on close observation and the discernment of naturalistic process; to an extent, Bembo may be viewed as Kircher's investigative forerunner on Etna. Yet *De Aetna* is also backward glancing in its evocation—arguably even Bembo's conscious reapplication—of the emboldened approach to nature that is already apparent in Lucretius and Seneca in particular: the work asserts, above all in Bernardo's confident explicatory voice in §§33–8, a reasoned and sublime "superiority" over nature, to the effect that phenomena such as volcanoes and earthquakes are perceived not with a passive, awed helplessness, but with an active, controlling grasp of all such events as but normative processes within the natural macro-scheme.[137]

By bringing back samples from their travels, Renaissance collectors could not only underscore their claims by pointing to empirical evidence for them, but also recapture at least something of the excitement and the memory value of the original experience. Paula Findlen cites the interesting case of Thomas Bartholin (1616–80), the distinguished Danish anatomist and mathematician whose peregrinations across

---

134. On this encounter with "Vulcan's furnace," Findlen (1994) 184–90; in comparison with *De Aetna*, Rowland (2000) 58–60.

135. Findlen (1994) 189–90.

136. In another interesting point of connection with Bembo, Kircher drew centrally on the *Mensa Isiaca* (for which pp. 273 and 277–8) in his attempt to decipher Egyptian hieroglyphics, offering a detailed analysis of it in his four-volume (1, 2.1, 2.2, 3) *Oedipus Aegyptiacus* (Rome, 1652–4): see 3.80–166 with Westcott (1887) 3–10.

137. On this Lucretian/Senecan "superiority" over nature, G. D. Williams (2012) 219–25.

Europe in the late 1630s and early 1640s to establish contact with other physicians and to visit botanical gardens extended to Sicily.[138] There he visited the recently established botanical garden in Messina,[139] but his further aim was to examine the flora of Etna; on that venture he retrieved a piece of the solidified lava flow for the great collection of curiosities (the so-called *Museum Wormianum*) established by his uncle, the physician, antiquary, and polymath Olaus Worm (1588–1654).[140] Some 150 years before, Bembo took his own sample from the mountain: "when they'd cooled down, we carried back to Messina two of the rocks that could be picked up by hand" (§27). He makes no mention of transporting them back to Venice for display, but the amassing of natural objects featured importantly in the collecting culture of the Veneto, and the Republic itself played a prominent role in promoting the study of nature through the close observation of plants, animals, and minerals.[141] Bembo's act of retrieval from Etna thus serves as a useful metaphor for the larger haul of naturalist reportage and evidence that he collects in the entirety of *De Aetna*. The lengthy coverage that he gives to Etna's vegetation in particular reflects the botanical interests that he shared with his father: together with its stone collection and antiquarian ornamentation, the villa garden at Noniano resembled an open-air museum,[142] while the botanical garden that later graced Bembo's Paduan residence belonged fashionably to an age that witnessed the rise of medical botany,[143] the proliferation of botanical field trips to collect samples and to study plants in their natural settings, and the challenge of the new through the importation of exotic flora from the Americas. The Bembo garden was ahead of its time, at least in the sense that it preceded by more than a decade the establishing of the university botanical garden in Padua in July 1545—itself only the second such establishment after the first was created at Pisa in the summer of 1543.[144]

When *De Aetna* is located in this culture of naturalist collecting, then, Pietro's self-presentation in the dialogue not only anticipates the mode of self-fashioning

---

138. Findlen (1994) 159, 187, and esp. 192. Bartholin recorded his travels in his *De peregrinatione medica*: Bartholin (1674), with translation in O'Malley (1961) 43–101. See on his journey Tongiorgi Tomasi (2005) 126–8 with Gabrieli (1938).

139. Bartholin (1674) 39 = O'Malley (1961) 74.

140. Bartholin (1674) 46 = O'Malley (1961) 79; cf. Worm (1655) 47 for his own record of Bartholin bringing this sample from Etna.

141. See Findlen (2005), esp. 56–8.

142. Curti (2010) 457; already Chapter 3 p. 144.

143. See, conveniently, Reeds (1976) with R. Palmer (1985), and cf. Chapter 3 p. 144.

144. On the founding of the Paduan garden, Azzi Visentini (1984) with Rhodes (1984), esp. 327–8, and Minelli (1995); the construction of the Paduan garden was overseen by Daniele Barbaro (1514–70), Ermolao's nephew.

that he later engaged in through his Paduan *Museo*; the dialogue can itself also claim adjunct membership of his collection, partly as an exotic visitation of Sicily and as a volcanological showpiece in its own right, and partly because it projects the *imagines* of father and son in another mini-storehouse of family memory. The work explicitly addresses intergenerational memory function in §§17–18, first in Bernardo's account of how he built up the country estate at Noniano not for himself but for his children (§17):

> For I know how it's usually more pleasant for sons to receive from their parents what they've sought rather than easily to acquire it for themselves, either because most of us tend to shirk the effort of going after things while all of us enjoy the pleasure of acquisitions; *or because the possessions that are left to us by our forebears retain the memory of those who bequeathed them—a memory that may somehow render them more hallowed for us, but certainly also makes them much more pleasurable to receive.*

Then Pietro in §18:

> Those words of yours are very precious to me now, father . . . ; and, as long as I live, they will always be implanted in my mind and memory, and my wish is that you yourself continue to enjoy for a very long time, along with us, all those acquisitions that you've made for me and for my brother.[145]

Pietro goes on later in §18 to contrast Bernardo's material legacy with the still greater gift that his father has already provided through the wealth of education. An apparently heart-felt tribute to Bernardo; but the importance that Pietro attaches to memory here is also reflexive in connotation, drawing attention as it does to the memorializing capacities of *De Aetna* itself. Generational succession, the consolidation and transmission of material property and of the nonmaterial qualities of person, the perpetuation of family character and reputation, and adherence to a form of cultural genealogy:[146] even though the mortal span and the movement of generations are in one way belittled by comparison with timeless Etna, Pietro nevertheless goes out of his way in *De Aetna* to accentuate this familial duty of memory by asserting a strong collective identity that endures through time. Here the work yields an important if unheralded point of comparison with Bembo's collection, especially in his anxiety about the fate of his treasures after his death. This anxiety

---

145. Carlo: see p. 325 n.19.

146. On collecting as creating "una sorta di genealogia culturale," Findlen (2004) 46.

is in turn relatable to the phenomenon widely observed in modern psychology[147] of the collection as an extension of the self, and therefore jealously protected by the collector. The greater or more personally meaningful the collection, the more serious are the pressures and problems surrounding its disposal; hence the attendant anxiety that a collection should not be dispersed, and to that end the collector often attempts to promote in the designated heir a strong sense of attachment to its contents. Many of these characteristics are discernible in Pietro, especially in his relationship with his son Torquato (1525–95).

In addition to Torquato, Bembo was survived by a daughter, Elena (1528–*c.* 1574); an elder son, Lucilio, had died at the age of only eight in 1532. In his will as drafted on November 25, 1535, the year their mother Morosina died, Torquato is left all as Bembo's sole male heir,[148] but tensions soon arose because of Torquato's perceived indifference to the liberal studies that meant so much to his father.[149] In 1537 Bembo entrusted the now twelve-year-old Torquato's education to his scholar friend, Giovanni Benedetto Lampridio,[150] who was by then tutor in Mantua to the son of Duke Federico II Gonzaga. In a letter of November 10, 1538 to Torquato, who is still in Mantua, Bembo expresses the hope that he is applying himself to his studies, and that his work with a teacher of Lampridio's abilities is bearing fruit. But after the injunction that Torquato exert himself fully, a veiled threat:

> And from these efforts the usefulness and the gain will be yours alone. Because no one will be able to take them away from you as they will be able to take away from you all the other things which I have left *or could leave you.*[151]

Bembo expresses his concerns about Torquato's progress in a string of letters to Cola Bruno,[152] but in a missive of September 25, 1540 (he now writes as Cardinal from Rome) his tactic is to ask Cola to show Torquato some of the medals in his *studio* so that he can become better acquainted with, and begin to take pleasure in,

147. See on the following points Pearce (1992), esp. 56, 65; Baekeland (1994), esp. 216–18; Belk (1994), esp. 323–4.

148. For the document, Cian (1885) 201–2 with Eiche (1983) 354.

149. See in general Eiche (1983) 354–6; Findlen (2004), esp. 53–9; Kidwell (2004) 341–2, 355–7; Danzi (2005) 48–53.

150. For whom p. 272.

151. Travi (1993) 142 *Letter* 1968.14–17, here as in Kidwell (2004) 300; my emphasis.

152. Travi (1993) 267 *Letter* 2132; 310–11 *Letter* 2195; 312–15 *Letter* 2199.

the collection that will one day be his.[153] In writing to his son on December 26, 1540, Bembo launches into an impassioned exaltation of liberal studies that ends with another barely veiled threat:

> But letters, once learnt, accompany you all your life and make their possessor dear to every king and every lord, whence the wealth and lofty positions of many learned men . . . If I had not put all my care and effort and thought into this, I would not be able to leave you in that fortune in which I will leave you, if I see that you deserve it (*se vedrò che tu la meriti*).[154]

By July 13, 1542 his patience was wearing thin: unless Torquato makes fine progress in his studies over the next two years, he will enjoy no part of the inheritance.[155] In a letter of July 15, 1544 to Girolamo Quirini, he contemplates leaving his Padua house and his *studio* to Elena.[156] But he never acted on the threat: in his last extant letter to Torquato, of September 25, 1546,[157] he appears resigned to his son's ways, but his decision to retain him as heir was surely designed above all to secure the male line of descent, and hence to preserve the Bembo name.

As did other collectors of the age, Pietro clearly foresaw the danger of his beloved collection being dispersed, and he therefore took steps to safeguard its integrity in his second and last testament, dated September 5, 1544:[158] Torquato is bidden not to sell, pawn, or gift away "any of my ancient items or those of stone or copper or silver or gold," and to preserve his books and pictures in the same way. Despite these measures, this second testament was technically not a *fideicommissum*, or a document that dictated the inalienable transmission of property in a specified order of family succession.[159] No inventory of his *Museo* is known to have been compiled by Pietro himself, and no such inventory is required of Torquato in the surviving versions of the will; because the second version was drawn up at Rome, far from his Paduan collection, it may in any case have been impractical for Pietro to compile or commission anything like a comprehensive inventory at such a distance. Unlike those collectors after him who were careful to prepare such inventories, he may have

---

153. Travi (1993) 324–5 *Letter* 2210 with Danzi (2005) 51.

154. Travi (1993) 337–8 *Letter* 2226, here as in Kidwell (2004) 342; see also Danzi (2005) 51.

155. Travi (1993) 424–5 *Letter* 2339 with Kidwell (2004) 345 and Danzi (2005) 52.

156. Travi (1993) 501 *Letter* 2438 with Kidwell (2004) 356 and Danzi (2005) 53.

157. Travi (1993) 585 *Letter* 2558 with Kidwell (2004) 357 and Danzi (2005) 53.

158. Cian (1885) 203 with Eiche (1983) 355.

159. See Findlen (2004) 55–6.

underestimated the importance of documenting his *studio* in full detail—an unfortunate omission (at least from Pietro's perspective) because it gave Torquato room to maneuver, enabling him to meet the terms of the will as long as he preserved at least some version and proportion of the precious objects as his father had specified.[160] After Pietro died on January 18, 1547, the part of his collection that he had transferred to his Roman residence was reunited with the main body of it in Padua, and for some twenty years Torquato appears to have preserved the whole more or less as it was at his father's death. Already by 1567, however, Jacopo Strada and Niccolò Stoppio, agents for Albert V, Duke of Bavaria, managed to acquire several items. After Elena's death in *c.* 1574 Torquato seems to have shifted to a strategy of selling on a larger scale, so that, as Paula Findlen well puts it, the *studio* of a scholar was transformed into the *museo* of a patrician, its holdings no longer sacrosanct.[161]

Bembo's efforts as witnessed above to encourage Torquato in his studies and to deepen his interest in the family collection are reminiscent of the attentiveness that Pietro praises in his own father in *De Aetna* §18: "When I was a boy you oversaw my education not just carefully but ... even devoutly. ... [Y]ou imbued me with the best moral values, and, to the best of your ability, you always equipped me with all of the cultured arts." For all their differences in characterization in *De Aetna*, Bernardo so attached to public service while Pietro is detached from the Venetian *cursus*, the stress that Bernardo places on cross-generational continuity and material inheritance in that early dialogue was evidently a deeply ingrained habit of thought in his son, at least to judge by the aging Pietro's anxieties about his own legacy: if for Pietro his collection was an extension of himself, a true *imago sui*, so he tried to shape Torquato in his own image as a suitable heir not just to the treasures themselves, but also to all that they represented as a repository of Bembine self-identity and memory.

7.5: *Bembo and Giovanni Bellini*

We turn finally to Giovanni Bellini's *Portrait of a Young Man* (*c.* 1505; Figure 5.4), and to the problem of the sitter's identity—a controversy that has significant implications for the interplay posited in Chapter 5 between verbal portraiture and print form in *De Aetna*. The portrait is nowhere mentioned as part of Bembo's collection, and the details of its history are uncertain before the early eighteenth century,

160. On these points, Findlen (2004) 56.

161. Findlen (2004) 61, and for Pietro's devotion cf. p. 56: "La collezione era la sua seconda progenie e, come spesso accade, la migliore." Further on the disposal of the collection, Findlen 59–67 with Eiche (1983), esp. 355–8, and Danzi (2005) 54–6.

when it is known to have belonged to the collection of the noble Venetian Sagredo family. It was subsequently acquired from that collection in 1752 by Joseph Smith (*c.* 1675–1770).[162] This diplomat, resourceful entrepreneur, and passionate collector settled in Venice soon after 1700, and there he remained for the rest of his life.[163] Appointed British Consul in 1744, he held that post until the accession of George III in 1760, only to revert to it some five years later, at ninety or so, after his successor went bankrupt. In his official capacity Smith became a figure familiar to many English travelers who passed through Venice on the Grand Tour, but his "somewhat ambiguous character"[164] hardly endeared him to all; Horace Walpole for one famously disparaged him as "the merchant of Venice," the owner of a library whose rich holdings he knew only by "the title-page of his understanding."[165] In his epically lengthy will, signed and sealed in Venice in April 1761, he alludes to a "treaty that was commenced on the Part of a Royal Purchaser for my Library," but "nothing was concluded."[166] Hence his wish that

> prior to all others, an offer be humbly made to His Majesty that they [sc. Smith's collection of gems] might be honoured to be in his Cabinet. So likewise if His Majesty should signify his Pleasure to have the drawings also, Books etc., this would be the utmost bound of my ambition, that this whole collection, the work of 40 years uniting together, should be so honourably and advantagiously [*sic*] placed.[167]

In the event, almost everything was acquired for the Royal Collection in 1762, after which the irrepressible Consul seems to have begun buying again.[168] In the surviving manuscript catalogue of the Italian paintings that were acquired by George III in this way (it contains 351 items, about half of which are still traceable in the Royal Collection),[169] no. 285 is given as "Bellino: Portrait of himself with

162. For documentation (a bill discovered by Francis Haskell in a volume in the Biblioteca del Museo Correr, Venice) see Blunt and Croft-Murray (1957) 24 with Pincus (2008) 96 and Whitaker (2013) 330 and n.5.

163. For the remarkable Smith see Cust (1913); Blunt and Croft-Murray (1957), esp. 11; Vivian (1971); F. Haskell (1980) 299–310 and 391–4 Appendix 5.

164. Blunt and Croft-Murray (1957) 11.

165. Walpole in a letter to Sir Horace Mann of June 18, 1744 (= Cunningham [1891] 1.307).

166. Cited by Cust (1913) 152.

167. Cust (1913) 152.

168. See Blunt and Croft-Murray (1957) 11 and n.1.

169. For the catalogue (known as the "Italian List"), Cust (1913) 153–4 and 161.

his name on board."[170] That the picture was a Bellini was in fact long disputed, partly through a cautious suspension of judgment because of the panel's damaged state,[171] but also on the fragile basis of "Morelli's Law,"[172] which held that a portrait that deviated from Bellini's standard signature in Roman capitals (the second L taller) could not possibly be the master's work; by this law, the cursive minuscule signature in the Windsor portrait rules out ascription to Bellini.[173] But some of Bellini's finest late works, notable among them the *Feast of the Gods* (1514) now in the National Gallery of Art in Washington, DC, have a cursive minuscule signature,[174] and the obvious fallacy of the signature test has in any case long been exposed.[175] Today there is no serious disagreement that this portrait was authored by Bellini.

If the dating to *c.* 1505 is accepted, the catalogue claim that the picture is a Bellini self-portrait can safely be ruled out:[176] given that Bellini was seventy-five or so in 1505, the sitter's youthful appearance is evidently ill fitting, and surviving images of Bellini in any case reveal a physiognomy very different from that shown in our portrait.[177] But certain distinctive features of the picture may also have encouraged the idea that this was a Bellini self-portrait. According to Giorgio Vasari, Bellini was responsible for initiating a fashion for portraiture at Venice:

---

170. Cust (1913) 154.

171. Cf. Crowe and Cavalcaselle (1871) 1.182: "the treatment seems hardly equal to that of Giovanni, though it is vain to pretend to a correct opinion when a panel has received so much injury."

172. So Shearman (1983) 43.

173. Cf. G. Morelli (1900) 1.240 and n.7, 264, 269 and n.3: "I have already had occasion to observe . . . that all 'Cartellini' bearing Giovanni Bellini's name in cursive characters are forgeries, and that in his genuine signatures, one L is always taller than the other. In authentic 'Cartellini' which have been touched, we often find that the restorer has tampered with this peculiarity and made the letters of equal height." See on this "nice illustration of the rise and fall of 'Dustbin Art History'" Shearman (1983) 43.

174. See Rubin (2006) 583 with Pincus (2008) 105 ("This [sc. the signature in the *Feast of the Gods*] is the only other Bellini signature in italics that matches the quality" of the Windsor portrait signature).

175. See Shearman (1983) 43 with D. A. Brown (2013) 318 and n.30; brief but trenchant remarks also in Cust (1928).

176. This idea was still current in the nineteenth century, in part because (Whitaker [2013] 330–1) paintings with unknown sitters were regularly interpreted as self-portraits in eighteenth-century inventories, and partly because our portrait's *cartellino* or fictive label (on which see further p. 305) may have been repainted to read *Johanes Bellini ipse*. It was so transcribed by Mrs. Jameson (for Shearman [1983] 42, "generally an accurate observer"), and the picture catalogued as "His own Portrait": Jameson (1842) 2.343 no. 276.

177. See Pincus (2008) 96 and 115 n.35.

> . . . he introduced the custom into Venice that whoever had attained to a certain degree of eminence should cause his likeness to be portrayed either by himself or by some other master. Wherefore, in all Venetian houses, there are numerous portraits, and in many of those belonging to nobles may be seen the fathers and grandfathers of the possessors, up to the fourth generation . . .[178]

Surviving examples of the portraits executed by Bellini and his shop to meet this demand conventionally show the sitter in bust-length and three-quarter pose, behind a parapet that carries the artist's name. The formulaic nature of such pictures was itself visually meaningful: through this standardization of pose, dress, and format, the sitters' individual self-expression was subordinate to their common devotion to the Republic.[179] But the *Portrait of a Young Man* shows an idiosyncratic flair that sets it apart; hence the notion that the picture is a self-portrait. It is significantly larger than Bellini's typical portrait of a private citizen (44 centimeters high and 35.5 wide, as opposed to the norm of a little over 30 centimeters high, 25 wide); it is the sole surviving Bellini portrait to show a landscape in the background; his italic cursive signature is first witnessed in this portrait;[180] and the sitter's look carries a hint of characterful intensity that differs from the greater reserve and neutral expression that are more typical of Bellini's patrician portraits. In contrast to the blank stare that his sitters more usually show as they look out toward the viewer, the gaze is in this case nuanced into a slightly elevated glance to the sitter's right; radiographic analysis indicates that the orientation of the eyes was originally more upward in its cast of vision.[181] The sitter is dressed conventionally enough in the black *biretta* and *mantello* of the Venetian *cittadino*, but his oblique glance suggests an outlook on life, and perhaps an eyeing of objectives, that differ from the Venetian norm of devoted service to the Republic.[182] At the same time, the marble parapet serves as a barrier of sorts, as if separating the world of the portrait from the outer world, and allowing the sitter to luxuriate in the tranquil atmospherics of the landscape background.[183]

---

178. Lavin (1967) 1.201.

179. D. A. Brown (2013) 324.

180. Cf. Pincus (2008) 95: departing from majuscule, this signature is "unique among Bellini portraits to do so." For this last claim defended through the discrediting of several other "[p]roblematic italic signatures in the oeuvre of Giovanni Bellini" see Pincus' appendix (pp. 109–12) with D. A. Brown (2013) 323 n.47.

181. Shearman (1983) 42 with Whitaker (2013) 333.

182. Cf. D. A. Brown (2013) 324 (the sitter's expression "remote, not vacant").

183. See Whitaker and Clayton (2007) 180 with Whitaker (2013) 338.

That this sitter is none other than Pietro Bembo was first proposed by Philip Hendy and Ludwig Goldscheider in 1945,[184] partly on the basis of a resemblance to the Bembo shown on Belli's medal of *c.* 1532,[185] and partly because of Carlo Ridolfi 's allusion, in his *Le maraviglie dell'arte* of 1648, to a Bellini portrait of Bembo "prima che fosse Cardinale."[186] The sitter's appearance seems appropriate for a man of Bembo's thirty-five or so years, the aquiline nose and receding hairline of Bellini's sitter are not inconsistent with the later images of Bembo, and the absence of dark hair and eyebrows is not inexplicable: the eyebrows are absent in the portrait at least as we have it, it is suggestive that most of Bellini's male sitters are shown with blond or light brown hair, and Bembo may conceivably have been pictured in an idealized form.[187] Moreover, Bembo was evidently close to Bellini—an association already anticipated in the previous generation by Bernardo Bembo's connection with Jacopo Bellini (*c.* 1400–*c.* 1470), Giovanni's father.[188] In Pietro's Paduan *Museo,* Marcantonio Michiel claims to have seen two portraits by Jacopo Bellini, the one of Gentile da Fabriano (*c.* 1370–1427, Jacopo's teacher, after whom he named his elder son), the other of Bertoldo d'Este (1434–63), Bernardo's friend who was accidently killed while fighting on Venice's side at the Siege of Corinth in November 1463;[189] the funeral oration that Bernardo delivered for Bertoldo on March 8, 1464 is perhaps his most celebrated speech.[190] Given the sentimental value that the portrait of Gentile da Fabriano must have had for Jacopo, Bernardo's acquisition of it surely indicates his strength of attachment to Jacopo. So too in Pietro's case: after protracted stages of negotiation and stalling on Giovanni Bellini's part, and after the eventual delivery in the summer of 1504 of a Nativity scene for Isabella d'Este, her satisfaction at the finished work led her to desire for her *studiolo* a second, allegorical picture from the artist;[191] Pietro was enlisted to act as an intermediary with Giovanni, a role that figures prominently in his extant correspondence with the Marchesa in 1505–6,[192] and which itself signals his closeness to Bellini. Even

184. Hendy and Goldscheider (1945) 22, 34, then taken up by Pallucchini (1949) 192 and (1959) 100–1, 153.

185. For the medal, pp. 283–4 and Figure 7.1 and Figure 7.2.

186. Ridolfi (1648) 1.56.

187. On these points D. A. Brown (2013) 320.

188. On the linkage between the families, J. M. Fletcher (2004) 30–1.

189. For Michiel's description see J. Morelli (1800) 18; Frizzoni (1884) 49–50.

190. See Giannetto (1985) 26 and 112 with J. M. Fletcher (1989) 816.

191. For the saga of the Nativity picture reconstructed, see J. M. Fletcher (1971) with Cian (1887), esp. 103–9.

192. See Travi (1987) 196, 204, 209–10, and 223 for *Letters* 209, 219, 225, and 234.

though Bembo was some four decades younger than Bellini, their relationship was such that, at least according to Vasari, Pietro entrusted Giovanni with painting the portrait of his lover (Maria Savorgnan?),[193] and, in one of the two sonnets that Pietro composed on the picture, he refers affectionately to "'l mio Bellin."[194] He was no stranger to Bellini's *studio*, as his letter to Isabella of November 20, 1505 attests[195]—an allusion to a visit ("Sono però stato oggi con esso M. Zuan Bellino," *Letter* 219.7–8) during which, Susan Nalezyty suggests, Bembo might possibly have sat for his own portrait.[196]

If Bembo were the sitter, let us briefly pursue the implications of that scenario. Against the background of Pietro's close familiarity with Bellini, the Windsor portrait not only shows a fineness of detail and touch that suggests that it is more than a purely transactional assignment; it also captures aspects of the inner man at a pivotal moment when Bembo was soon to leave for Urbino in 1506, decisively departing from Venice and the Venetian *cursus*. Here the landscape setting, unprecedented in Bellini's portraits, comes into its own, suggestively evoking as it does in the distance, beyond the town, the hilly country of the Veneto that Bembo knew so well. If Bellini depicts a real bridge to the right of the sitter, it has yet to be identified, but the combination of the bridge and the two buildings adjacent to it is also shown on a larger scale in Bellini's *Assassination of St. Peter Martyr* of *c.* 1506–7, now in the National Gallery, London.[197] If, on the other hand, no specific model is assumed or posited for the setting, its ambience is nevertheless in keeping with the tranquil atmospherics of Pietro's Asolo or Noniano; in his upward glance, the sitter appears to avert his gaze from the realities of the world (the Venetian *cursus*?) that lurk beyond the enclosed space of the portrait. Moreover, we saw earlier that a bust-length portrait with a three-quarter pose in a landscape setting is a familiar combination in fifteenth-century Flemish art.[198] If we accept that Bellini deploys a landscape setting in the Windsor portrait after the manner of Hans Memling's *Portrait of a Man with a Roman Coin* (Figure 5.3), we might speculate that Bellini's Pietro Bembo "answers" Memling's Bernardo Bembo by assuming a very different pose in the Bellini picture.[199] Whereas Pietro's head is turned to his right and his eyes glance upward into the visionary distance, Bernardo's head is turned to his

193. But see Chapter 5 pp. 218–20.

194. Dionisotti (1966b) 521 *Rime* XIX 5.

195. Travi (1987) 204 *Letter* 219.

196. Nalezyty (2013a) 422.

197. For this parallel, Mazzotta (2009) 17 with Whitaker (2013) 335.

198. See Chapter 5 p. 207.

199. For the approach cf. Chapter 5 pp. 206–7.

left and his gaze is frontal: the directness of Bernardo's portrait is countered by the softer obliquity of the Bellini picture, to the effect that their respective poses suggest differences of temperament, life outlook, and, by extension, Venetian civic ambition.

For all the attractions of this speculative line of enquiry, however, serious obstacles yet stand in the way of the sitter's identification with Pietro and, at least given the current state of the evidence, the case against it holds the advantage. Take, to begin with, Ridolfi's reference to a Bellini portrait of Bembo "prima che fosse Cardinale." In reporting that, before Bembo became Cardinal, Bellini painted a portrait of his lover (Maria Savorgnan?), Vasari writes as follows: "Giovanni ... ritrasse a messer Pietro Bembo, prima che andasse a star con papa Leone X. . .";[200] it is very possible that Ridolfi has here misinterpreted his source text, failing to register the preposition in Vasari's "a messer Pietro Bembo," and thereby wrongly inferring that Bellini painted Bembo himself;[201] and if Bellini did indeed paint Bembo, whose life and art collection are so well documented, it is surprising (to say the least) that no allusion to the portrait is to be found anywhere before Ridolfi.[202] Quite apart from Ridolfi's problematic testimony, the portrait of *c.* 1505 is separated by a quarter-century and more from the nearest *comparanda* for Bembo's appearance, namely Belli's medal of *c.* 1532 (Figure 7.1) and Cranach's portrait of *c.* 1536; the comparison is hardly aided by so long a time span. Then, even if the fair hair of Bellini's sitter can be explained away despite the fact that Bembo is shown elsewhere with dark hair, the sitter's eyes are set high in the face and his brow is sloping—features that are less apparent in other portrayals of Bembo.[203] All in all, the negative case is well summed up in John Shearman's influential judgment that, even if the case for Bembo faced no objection on biographical grounds,

> the comparison that must, *faute de mieux*, be made with a tiny medallic profile made perhaps thirty years later is not unnaturally fruitless. Like most of Bellini's sitters, this one must remain anonymous.[204]

But even if Bembo is discounted as Bellini's sitter, the portrait is still of relevance to *De Aetna* because of the signature that Bellini chose to deploy in this special case.

---

200. Milanesi (1879) 169, with translation in Chapter 5 p. 218.

201. See von Hadeln (1914–24) 1.73 n.5 ("Offenbar hat Ridolfi die Praeposition a vor messer Pietro Bembo überlesen").

202. So Whitaker (2013) 336.

203. On these points, Whitaker and Clayton (2007) 180; Whitaker (2013) 337.

204. Shearman (1983) 43. For the "chilling effect" that Shearman's doubts have had on later authors, D. A. Brown (2013) 318 and n.33.

Bellini's canonical signature for most of his career was the majuscule IOANNES BELLINUS, with the second L raised higher than the first.[205] By the 1490s, however, Venetian painters were beginning to vary the established signature conventions, a trend that markedly expanded after 1500. True to his larger habit of adaptability to innovative techniques and ideas, Bellini was at the forefront of this new experimentation: from 1500 onward, J begins to appear in his first name, varying the previously standard I; he regularly appended the date in Roman numerals; and a verb such as *pinxit* or *faciebat* sometimes accompanied the name.[206] Whereas before 1500 he had predominantly placed his signature on the traditional engraved ledge, he thereafter began to deploy more widely in his portraits the less impersonal device of the illusionistic *cartellino*, or a slip of paper affixed to an architectural surface but sometimes embedded more imaginatively within the dramatic setting of the picture.[207] In the Windsor portrait the signature is prominently placed on a *cartellino* affixed to the parapet that appears to separate the sitter from the world external to the picture; the signature draws attention to itself not just through its prominent placement, but still more because of its unprecedented italic cursive form. Yet this italic cursive resembles not the surviving samples of Bellini's autograph signature,[208] but rather the Aldine italic that Manuzio used in his Greek, Latin, and vernacular octavo volumes from 1501 onward.

What effect did Bellini perhaps seek to achieve by modifying his signature in this way? By using "the special art of the Aldine italic," with its hint of a Castiglione-like *sprezzatura* or a deceptive ease of flow, argues Debra Pincus,[209] Bellini deliberately modified his standard majuscule signature in the Windsor portrait to inscribe himself in the humanistic movement emblematized by the Aldine cursive. For Pincus, Pietro was indeed Bellini's sitter, and, whether or not Bellini's change of signature was suggested by Bembo (as Pincus speculates), Bellini's turning to italic effected a special form of compact between artist and subject: "Bellini, the craftsman, gains an up-to-date humanist gloss; Bembo, the intellectual, is associated with the crafting of the new fonts of humanism."[210] But this correlation between artist and sitter remains valid even when Bembo is rejected as Bellini's subject: whoever the unknown sitter may be, Bellini's striking departure into italic captures and matches

205. See Matthew (1998) 624, 628–9; Goffen (2001) 315–21; Pincus (2008) 93–4.

206. On these points, Matthew (1998) 629 and 645 n.69.

207. On this shift in Bellini's practice, Matthew (1998) 633 (illusionistic *cartellini* used "almost exclusively to sign portraits dated after 1500") with Goffen (2001) 318–19.

208. See Pincus (2008) 96 (with illustration on p. 97); D. A. Brown (2013) 323 and n.48.

209. (2008) 105; concisely on Castiglione's conception of *sprezzatura*, Louden (1968), esp. 44.

210. Pincus (2008) 107.

(even literally underwrites) the fashionable air and flair of the elusive Young Man. To return at this point to *De Aetna*, this complicity between artist, subject, and script in the Bellini portrait usefully illuminates the parallel phenomenon that I claim for the dialogue: the novel Aldine roman conjoins author and printer, Pietro and Aldo, in a text that reflects fashionably on each, while the correlation that Bellini effects between image and script (the Young Man symbolically "pictured" via the italic signature) matches the interaction of verbal portraiture and print form that we explored in Chapter 5 – Pietro "pictured" in typeface. My claim is not, of course, that Bellini makes any allusion, direct or otherwise, specifically to *De Aetna*, which in any case predates the portrait by a decade or so; if anything, the comparison points to a wider mode of experimentation with the interplay of word and picture, a mode to which Aldo, Pietro, and Bellini all contribute in their different ways and media. It may disappoint, then, not to identify Pietro as Bellini's sitter; but as Anonymous looks distractedly to a world beyond the portrait, and as the charms of countrified ease suggestively beckon in Noniano-like fashion in the background, we surely find in the portrait not just a kindred spirit for the Pietro of *De Aetna*, but also a telling guide to the interaction of verbal and visual meaning in the Aldine *princeps* of the dialogue.

Text and Translation

The text as given here is based on the Aldine *editio princeps* of February 1496 (1495 *more veneto*) as revised by Carlo Dionisotti for publication by Giovanni Mardersteig under the auspices of the Officina Bodoni of Verona in 1969: Mardersteig (1969b) in my bibliography. The Officina Bodoni text and translation were printed in three issues, English, Italian, and German, each of only 125 copies;[1] the Latin text was set in Mardersteig's revivalist Griffo font as prepared by Charles Malin, the renowned French punchcutter, while the translation was set in the Bembo font devised by the Monotype Corporation in 1929 at the instigation of Stanley Morison.[2] In the original Aldine edition certain corrections that are found in multiple extant copies were evidently inserted through stop-press interventions, while other adjustments and additions were made when the printing was completed but before the copies left the shop; hence the number of insertions found in individual copies is variable according to the length of time between a given copy's printing and its departure from the shop.[3] Whether entered by Bembo or by another's hand, these changes were very probably variants introduced by the author himself; this inference is supported by the fact that they recur almost without exception among the more than 150 corrections and additions that were made, apparently with Bembo's authorization,[4] for the second edition printed at Venice by Johannes Antonius da Sabio and brothers in 1530. Given this uneven process of correction and addition to the Aldine *princeps*, the present text anchors itself for convenience in the 1969 version. For present purposes, the section numbers as deployed in M. P. Chatfield's 2005 *I Tatti* edition are here reproduced for easy navigation of the text in the main body of this study; and, in the interests of grammatical orthodoxy and

---

1. Apart from the English translation by Betty Radice (on which see below), the Italian version was by Vittorio Enzo Alfieri (reproduced in Alfieri [1981]), the German version by Kosmas Ziegler. The latter version was in fact published in 1970: Verona, Officina Bodoni, for the Verlag E. Hauswedell, Hamburg.

2. On these developments, and on both the modern Griffo and Bembo fonts as modeled on the 1496 Aldine original, see Mardersteig (1969b) 135–51 = (1988) 217–25 with Chapter 5 p. 201.

3. On the complex evolution of these developments see Bühler (1951); Mariano (1991); Clough (1998) 59–61; Nuvoloni (2011); Curti (2013b) 108–9.

4. See Mariano (1991), esp. 445, with Nuvoloni (2011) 207; further, Chapter 5 p. 204.

syntactical clarity, the 1969 text as reproduced here is modified in the places listed below. These changes do not necessarily correspond in all cases to in-shop modifications attested in extant copies of the Aldine incunable, but most of them (the exceptions are marked with an asterisk below) were ultimately incorporated in the second edition of 1530:

§3 interrogaremus p. 13 Mardersteig: interrogaremur
§15 possuerimus p. 27 M.: posuerimus
§19 in qua depasceres, animum tuum p. 31 M.: in qua depasceres animum tuum
§19 oblectares convivae p. 31 M.: oblectares. Convivae
§22 passuum ascenditur p. 34 M.: passuum, ascenditur*
§28 exemplo p. 42 M.: extemplo
§31 pater huius p. 46 M.: pater, huius*
§45 tradire p. 60 M.: tradidere (tradiderunt 1530)
§48 natura p. 62 M.: naturae

The first published translation of *De Aetna* was claimed for the Officina Bodoni edition of 1969. The 1969 English translation, by Betty Radice, is reproduced in Chatfield (2005), but since 1969 several other translations have appeared in multiple languages: so Alfieri (1981) in Italian, Kilpatrick (1986) in English, Mikołajczyk (1997) in Polish, Viallon (2002) in French, and now von der Gönna (2015) in German. The present translation is informed by its predecessors, but it remains fundamentally my own.

PETRI BEMBI DE AETNA AD ANGELUM CHABRIELEM LIBER

1 Factum a nobis pueris est et quidem sedulo, Angele, quod meminisse te certo scio, ut fructus studiorum nostrorum, quos ferebat illa aetas non tam maturos quam uberes, semper tibi aliquos promeremus. Nam sive dolebas aliquid, sive gaudebas, quae duo sunt tenerorum animorum maxime propriae affectiones, continuo habebas aliquid a me, quod legeres, vel gratulationis, vel consolationis, imbecillum tu quidem illud et tenue, sicuti nascentia omnia et incipientia, sed tamen quod esset satis amplum futurum argumentum amoris summi erga te mei. Verum postea quam annis crescentibus et studia et iudicium increvere, nosque totos tradidimus graecis magistris erudiendos, remissiores paulatim facti sumus ad scribendum ac iam etiam minus quotidie audentiores. Itaque, quas pueri miserimus ad te lucubrationes nostras numerare aliquas possumus, quas adolescentes non possumus. **2** Quo in consilio nobis diutius permanendum esse non puto: nam ut interdum non loqui moderati hominis est, sic semper silere cum eo, quem diligas, perignavi; neque Hercule, si in officio permansimus in prima aetate, debemus nunc, tanquam inexercitati histriones, in secundo aut tertio actu corruisse; praesertim cum aemulatio tuorum studiorum, Angele, nos non excitare modo languentes possit, sed etiam incendere, quippe qui multa et praeclara habuimus a te semper habemusque quotidie et consuetudinis nostrae testimonia et doctrinae tuae. Quare sicuti pueri scriptiunculas nostras, quasi lactentis ingenii acerbitatem, detulimus ad te, sic nunc deinceps etiam ad te adolescentiae nostrae primos foetus deferemus, non quo me ipse plus ames (nam iam id fieri posse vix puto), sed plane quia ita debemus inter nos: neque enim arbitror cariorem fuisse ulli quenquam quam tu sis mihi. **3** Sed de his et diximus alias satis multa, et saepe dicemus. Nunc autem, quoniam iam quotidie fere accidit postea, quam e Sicilia ego, et tu reversi sumus, ut de Aetnae incendiis interrogaremur ab iis, quibus notum est illa nos satis diligenter perspexisse, ut ea tandem molestia careremus, placuit mihi eum sermonem conscribere, quem cum Bernardo parente habui paucis post diebus quam rediissemus, ad quem reiiciendi essent ii, qui nos deinceps quippiam de Aetna postularent. Itaque confeci librum, quo uterque nostrum communiter uteretur. **4** Nam cum essemus in Noniano et pater se, ut solebat, ante atrium in ripa Pluvici contulisset, accessi ad eum progresso iam in meridianas horas die, ubi ea, quae locuti sumus inter nos, fere ista sunt. Tibi vero nunc orationem utriusque nostrum tanquam habeatur explicabo, non tanquam recenseatur. Igitur, cum illum multa in umbra

PIETRO BEMBO'S ON ETNA FOR ANGELO GABRIELE

1 When we were boys, Angelo, it was my diligent practice, as I'm sure you remember, always to present you with a few fruits of my studies, fruits that at that time of life were not as ripe as they were plentiful. For whether you felt pained or joyous about something, two states of feeling that are very much a characteristic of young hearts, you'd immediately receive from me something for you to read, whether to congratulate you or to console you—something feeble and slight, like all things new to life and just beginning, but nevertheless of the sort to offer you proof enough of my utmost affection for you. But later on, as I grew in years and my studies and judgment also grew, I gave myself over completely to my Greek teachers[5] for instruction, and I gradually lost my discipline for writing, even then becoming less adventuresome by the day. And so I can count a fair number of late-night lucubrations that I sent you as a boy, but I can't count any as a young man. **2** I don't think I should persist in this course; for just as the occasional break in speaking marks the man of restraint, so a permanent silence toward one you love can signal only extreme laziness. Goodness me! If I persisted in my proper duty when I was in the first flush of youth, I should at this point hardly have fallen flat like an ill-trained actor in the second or third act, especially when my desire to match your literary pursuits, Angelo, can not just rouse me from my listlessness, but also set me aflame; this because I always had from you, and still have every day, so many very clear demonstrations both of our close companionship and of your learning. And so, just as in boyhood I presented you with my meager writings, as if the sour expression of my suckling talent, so from now on I shall present you with the first fruits of my youth—not so that you love me the more (for I already scarcely think that possible), but simply because that is how it ought to be between us; for no one has ever been dearer to anyone, I believe, than you are to me. **3** But on these matters I've said many enough words on other occasions, and I'll often say them. For now, however, since it's already happened that, almost every day after you and I returned from Sicily,[6] we were asked about Etna's fires by people who knew that we'd observed them fairly carefully, I thought it a good idea, so that we could at last be free of this nuisance, to set down in writing the conversation that I had with my father, Bernardo, a few days after our return; henceforth, those who asked anything about Etna were to be referred to that conversation. And so I've written a book for each of us to profit from in common. **4** When we were at Noniano,[7] and my father had gone off as he usually did to the bank of the Piovego[8] in front of the house, I joined him around noontime, and what we spoke of there is more or less as you have it before you. In fact, I'll set out what each of us said as if it were actually

5. Notably Giorgio Valla: Chapter 3 pp. 135–7.

6. In the summer of 1494.

7. On the history and location of this family villa a few kilometers north of Padua see Puppi (1969) and Callegari (1997b) with Chapter 6 p. 224.

8. The Piovego canal (eleven kilometers long) was excavated in 1209, connecting Padua to the River Brenta and hence to Venice: see Benton (1995) 16 and pl. 13 (the Piovego conveniently mapped within "a plan of water courses in the Veneto").

sedentem comperissem, ita initium interpellandi eum feci:

5 **PETRUS BEMBUS FILIUS**. Diu quidem, pater, hic sedes, et certe ripa haec virens, quam populi tuae istae densissimae inumbrant et fluvius alit, aliquanto frigidior est fortasse quam sit satis.

BERNARDUS BEMBUS PATER. Ego vero, fili, nuspiam esse libentius soleo quam in hac cum ripae tum arborum tum etiam fluminis amoenitate: neque est quod vereare nequid nobis frigus hoc noceat, praesertim in tanto aestatis ardore. Sed fecisti tu quidem perbene, qui me ab iis cogitationibus revocasti, quas et libentissime semper abiicio, cum in Nonianum venitur, et nunc quidem nobis nescio quo pacto furtim irrepserant non modo non vocantibus sed etiam invitis.

BEMBUS FILIUS. De republica scilicet cogitabas aliquid aut certe de triumviratu tuo: saepe enim ex te audivi, si fieri possit, velle te, in agris cum esses, quoniam tibi id cum modice contingeret, tum etiam perraro, de iis, quae in urbe agantur, tanquam lethaeo aliquo sumpto poculo, nihil omnino recordari.

6 **BEMBUS PATER.** Est ita, ut dicis. Nam cum ab urbe propterea me frequentiaque hominum, tanquam a fluctibus, in hunc solitudinis portum recipiam, ut relaxem a curis remittamque paulisper animum meque ipsum restituam mihi atque ad reliquos confirmem labores, ut in ludis athletae solent, qui cum aliquo in cursu desudarint, considunt parumper revocantque sese, ut sint ad reliqua postea certamina valentiores, si tamen illae ipsae me rus etiam prosequuntur, quas fugio curas et sollicitudines, profecto nihil ago. Quod mihi quidem nunc ipsum evenit, qui cum solus in hac ripa consederim, ut dignum aliquid isto silentio meditarer, ecce nos ita etiam unda illa ipsa resorbuit urbanorum negotiorum paulatimque in triumviratus mei curas delapsus sum.

B. F. Ita sane coniectabar: visus es enim mihi iandudum nescio quid multa cogitatione commentari, neque eo vultu, quo esse hic soles, hilari et soluto sed, quo te in urbe conspicimus, contractiore interdum ac gravi.

B. P. Recte coniectabare. Sed ista tandem, quoniam nimis iam molesta sunt, obliviscamur.

taking place, and not recounted in retrospect. Accordingly, when I found him sitting in deep shade, I broke in on him as follows:

5 **PIETRO BEMBO**: You've been sitting here for a long time, father, and surely this verdant riverbank, shaded as it is by those densely thick poplars of yours and fed by the stream, is somewhat cooler, perhaps, than satisfactory.

BERNARDO BEMBO: But for my part, son, there's no place where I'm usually happier to be than in this pleasant setting of the bank and the trees and also the river. There's no reason for you to worry about this cold doing me any harm, especially in such heat of summer. But you've done me a great favor by recalling me from the thoughts that I'm always very glad to cast aside when I come to Noniano; even now they'd somehow crept up on me without my knowing it, not just unbidden but also against my will.

PIETRO BEMBO: I suppose you were reflecting on some matter of state, or at least about the commission to which you belong;[9] for I've often heard you say that, if it were possible, you'd wish, when you were in the country (since that opportunity comes your way not just not very much, but very rarely), to have absolutely no memory of civic affairs, as if you'd drunk down some draught of forgetfulness.

6 **BERNARDO BEMBO**: Yes, it's as you say. For as if from the waves I retrieve myself from the city and its mass of people to this haven of solitude for the purpose of finding some respite from my cares, relaxing my mind for a time, restoring myself to my proper condition, and fortifying myself for the tasks to come—like the practice of athletes in the games who, when they've sweated hard in some race, sit down for a while and restore themselves so that they're stronger for the contests that remain afterwards. But if those very cares pursue me into the country as well, the cares and anxieties from which I'm escaping, I undoubtedly achieve nothing. This is precisely what happened to me just now: I sat down alone on this bank to reflect on something worthy of that peaceful tranquility when, lo and behold! that very wave of civic responsibilities sucked me back again, and I gradually sank back into the cares of my commission.

P. B. I certainly inferred as much; for you seemed to me to have long been reflecting on something with deep thought, and your expression wasn't the carefree and relaxed one that you usually have here, but the one we see you wear in the city, every now and then pinched into a frown, and serious.

B. B. You inferred rightly. But let's finally forget about such matters, as they're now exceedingly tiresome.

---

9. For Pietro's wording in *de triumviratu tuo* cf. Travi (1987) 9 *Letter* 7.13–14, to Giovanni Battista Stato in September 1494: [upon Pietro's return from Sicily] *ego Bernardum patrem meum in amplissimo magistratu triumviratus constitutum . . . repperi*. By *triumviratus* Pietro surely refers in both places to Bernardo's service as *avogador di comun* (public prosecutor) in 1494 and 1495: see Giannetto (1985) 50–1 and 210 and King (1986) 336 with Boerio (1867) 51–2 s.v. *Avogador* (the office was composed of "tre patrizii col titulo di *Avogadori di comun*").

7 **B. F.** Utinam ipse id possis, pater, tibique istud, quando ita te iuvat, tam facile factu esset quam mihi. Sed omnes curae, quae quidem sint maximae, ita se habent, ut, si insequaris, non fugiant, si fugias, etiam insequantur. Munus autem istud tuum cum est ipsum negotiosissimum per sese, quippe a quo fere omnes reipublicae nostrae partes pertractantur quodque universae civitatis caeterarumque urbium nostrarum advocationem agit et sustinet, tum vero illud etiam accedit, quod tu is es, qui maxime omnium tranquillitatem animi requietemque deames, quo fit ut magis etiam illa sentias, quae te premunt.

B. P. Est, fili, est sane causa illa quidem non levis, quae mihi labores adauget meos, sed tamen, ut verum fatear, aliud quiddam maius me movet quod ipsum nuper me in urbem revocaverat, sic dum sederem, revocatque saepissime.

B. F. Quid illud tandem est?

B. P. Quod reipublicae causa non commoveri neque vellem, si possem, neque possem, si velim. Nam cum ab ineunte aetate ita vitam instituerim meam, ut patriae adessem semper, prodessem cum possem; potuerim autem nonnunquam vel iuvenis et domi et foris; illa vero me saepe muneribus reliquis, saepe legationibus honestarit; eam ipse si deseram nunc, cum et experientia et consilio et auctoritate plus valeo, quid sit aliud quam si tu me iuvenis senem destituas, filius patrem?

8 **B. F.** Duas igitur causas praedicas, pater, curarum tuarum, duras tu quidem illas et graves, verum, quia te sciente a te ipso proveniunt, perferendas. Nam qui te idem et actionibus tradidisti, quibus otio inimicius esse quid potest? et rus amas secessusque istos tuos, quae quidem, cum multo diutius ipsis careas quam fruaris, vitam tibi illam efficiunt molestiorem, dolendum tibi non puto, si te vel illis ipsis rebus condemnes, quas fugis, vel fugias omnino, quae te iuvant. Sed illud tamen quale est, quo te dixeras reipublicae causa commoveri? an te fortasse, mi pater, motus ii Galliarum perturbant, qui feruntur?

B. P. Minime illi quidem, verum admodum gaudeo te e Sicilia rediisse. Nam si aliquid evenerit, malo te hic esse, ubi omnes sumus, quam illic, ubi neminem habes tuorum.

9 **B. F.** Equidem adsum ac libens, cum ea de causa tum quia vobis omnibus carebamus iam nimium diu. Cave tamen putes nobis hoc Siciliensi biennio quicquam in vita fuisse iucundius.

7 **P. B.** I just wish you could do so yourself, father, and that it was as easy for you to achieve when you want to as it is for me. But all such cares, at least those of the most serious kind, have it in their nature not to take flight if you go after them, but also to go after you if you flee them. But that official position of yours is not only extremely demanding in itself, handling as it does virtually every component part of our Republic, and managing and maintaining the judicial system of the entire state and of the other cities under our control; but also, the further fact is that you're one who cherishes peace and ease of mind most of all things, so that you feel more keenly the burdens that weigh on you.

B. B. Yes, son, that's certainly the reason, and no slight one, for the increase of my burdens; and yet, to tell the truth, some still greater concern disturbs me, one that had summoned me back to the city just now while I was sitting here, and which does so very frequently.

P. B. What is that, then?

B. B. The fact that I wouldn't want *not* to be troubled on the state's behalf even if I could, and I couldn't [not be troubled] even if I wanted. For from an early age I've made it my rule of life always to be on hand for the state and to be useful to it when I could; and I was able to serve it on various occasions even as a young man, both at home and abroad. The state in turn has frequently honored me with the offices I've held, and frequently with diplomatic missions.[10] Should I abandon it now, when I've become stronger through experience, understanding, and influence, would it be any different from you, a young man, deserting me in my old age, a son a father?

8 **P. B.** Then you state two reasons, father, for your worries—harsh reasons that are not to be taken lightly, but because you know that they originate from yourself, you have to put up with them. For you've devoted yourself to public service; what can be less conducive to a quiet life than that? At the same time you love the country and those places of retreat of yours; but since you do without them for far longer stretches than you enjoy them, they only make your existence more irksome. I don't think you should feel aggrieved if you condemn yourself to punishment from the very things you seek to run from, or if you altogether run from what gives you pleasure. But what manner of problem is it that you'd said was troubling you on the state's behalf? Is it perhaps those reported stirrings among the French, father?[11]

B. B. No, not that at all; but I'm very pleased that you've come back from Sicily. If anything happens, I prefer you to be here with all of us, rather than there, where you have none of your own.

9 **P. B.** And I for my part am glad to be here, not just for that reason, but also because I felt my absence from all of you for far too long now. Yet don't imagine that any part of my life has been more enjoyable than those two years in Sicily.

---

10. For Bernardo's career appointments, Giannetto (1985), esp. 21–76 for a summarized "Cronologia della vita di Bernardo," with King (1986) 335–9.

11. Stirrings in advance of Charles VIII's invasion of Italy in the autumn of 1494: see Introduction pp. 17–18.

B. P. Gaudeo et id quidem, idque ipsum ex eo suspicabamur, quod nondum ad nos cogitabatis. Sed postea quam in eum sermonem incidimus, ut de Sicilia loqueremur, narra mihi quemadmodum ea se habent, quae de Aetnaeis ignibus et feruntur passim et perleguntur: te enim accessisse illuc cum Angelo tuo totumque montem perlustrasse audiebamus; et nobis quidem certe nunc vacat. Quid enim istoc aestu agamus meridiani? neque est, quod ego soleam libentius, quam de naturae miraculis audire.

B. F. Haec vero, ut libet, modo valeam recensere, et quidem eiusmodi sunt, ut tibi audienti afferre vel magnam possint, mihi certe narranti semper aliquam afferant voluptatem; quanquam quidem iam hoc ipsum facimus nimis saepe: quam enim multis nos eadem ipsa censes, postea quam e Sicilia reversi sumus, narravisse? Sed consurge, si placet, ab hac umbra: nam in ripis quidem omnis quae fit accubatio, ea si longior est, esse admodum gravior solet; atque ad illa buxeta nostra, si tibi videtur, sedesque pergamus.

10 **B. P.** Periniquum tu quidem facis, qui de ignibus loquuturus ab umbra et frigore decedendum putas, sed, quando ita vis, propter aquam potius in ripa deambulemus et cum fluvio sermoni reliquo demus operam loquentes: ita mihi videbor melius tuas illas flammas Aetnaeas, si me offenderint, Pluvici mei unda temperaturus.

B. F. Illae vero neque te offendent, cum absint longissime, neque hic si adessent, restinguere illas posset Pluvicus tuus, cum mare ipsum etiam cedat illis volentibus atque earum ardoribus contrahatur.

B. P. Magnum exordium inceptas, fili, ac iam plane vix credenda sunt ista quae dicis; verum, qui ita fiat, explana id etiam mihi.

B. F. Faciam, ut iubes; sed opus est, ante quam illo veniam, ut aliqua te praedoceam deque insulae deque montis natura, quibus cognitis ad ea, quae postulas, recta pergemus via.

B. P. Age, ut libet; modo ad illa etiam aliquando veniamus: quin etiam mihi feceris gratissimum, si ea lege inceperis, ut ne quod pulchrum praetereatur, sive vidisti aliquid, sive audivisti, sive quid es ipse commentatus.

11 **B. F.** Ego vero, si placet, iter tibi nostrum omne ordine ipso, quo factum est, recensebo, teque a Messanae menibus usque in Aetnae cacumen perducam.

B. P. Placet et cupio: incipe igitur viamque ipsam omnem reminiscere et tanquam recurre, si potes.

B. F. Agam sedulo id quidem. Itaque, ne te teneam diutius, quartusdecimus mensis agebatur, ex quo ego et Angelus meus apud Constantinum praeceptorem graecarum litterarum studiis exercebamur, neque sane adhuc vacuum ullum tempus dederamus nobis laboris ac ne unum interea integrum remiseramus diem.

B. B. I'm glad about that, and I suspected as much from the fact that your thoughts had yet to turn to us. But now that our conversation has chanced to pass to Sicily, tell me how it is with what's reported everywhere and what we read about Etna's fires; for we heard that you'd gone there with your friend Angelo, and that you'd explored the entire mountain, and we certainly have time at the moment. What else are we to do at midday in the heat here? And there's usually nothing I enjoy more than hearing about nature's marvels.

P. B. Unquestionably, if only I can recount them as I'd like, they're the sort of thing that can bring you a great deal of pleasure as you hear of them, and certainly the sort always to bring me no little pleasure in telling of them, even though I've already done that much too often: how many people do you think have heard these same things from us since our return from Sicily? But on your feet, if you please, and away from this shade: reclining like this on riverbanks, if it goes on too long, is always apt to be rather oppressive. If you agree, let's make for those box trees of ours, and a seat there.

10 **B. B.** You're acting very unfairly: just as you're about to talk about the fires, you think we've got to leave the cool shade. But since that's your wish, let's rather take a walk along the bank near the water, and let's apply ourselves to the rest of our conversation, talking in the river's company: in that way I'll imagine that, if your flames of Etna give me trouble, I'll have more of a chance to temper them in the waters of my Piovego.

P. B. Certainly, they won't trouble you, since they're very far away; and even if they were near, your Piovego couldn't extinguish them, since even the sea itself submits to their will and is diminished by their heat.

B. B. That's a grand beginning, son, and it's already clear that what you say is scarcely to be believed. But tell me how that happens so.

P. B. I'll do as you bid me; but first, before I get to that point, I need to inform you of a few things about the nature of the island and of the mountain. Those facts established, we'll proceed directly to what you're asking.

B. B. As you wish, provided we get there at some point. But, in fact, you'll oblige me most if you begin on the following terms, that no fine feature is passed over, whether it's something you've seen or heard, or something you've come up with for yourself.

11 **P. B.** By all means I'll recount to you, if you like, our entire journey in its exact order of events, and I'll take you from the walls of Messina right up to Etna's summit.

B. B. Yes, please do: so begin, call to mind every aspect of the route, and as if run back over it, if you can.

P. B. I'll do just that, carefully. And so, to make you wait no longer: it was the fourteenth month since my friend Angelo and I had begun busily studying Greek letters under our tutor, Constantine,[12] and to that point we'd given ourselves absolutely no time away from our work, and along the way we'd allowed ourselves not even a single day off in its entirety.

---

12. Constantine Lascaris (1434–1501), for whom Introduction pp. 1–4; Chapter 2 pp. 87–9; Chapter 3 pp. 121–37.

B. P. Nimium fuistis assidui vestris in studiis adolescentes vel etiam superstitiosi. Annum et menses novae linguae rudimentis incubuisse nullo intermisso die? mirum, si vos vel habitudo illa prior destituit vel color! nos tamen e navigatione traxisse vos pallorem istum et maciem putabamus.

12 **B. F.** Ita evenit; sed en tibi, iam tandem nos ipsos respeximus. Placuit enim ut Aetnam viseremus, atque interea, dum animi relaxarentur, quod efficere vel occupatissimi debeamus, tantum naturae miraculum etiam feriati nosceremus. Ita iocundis aliquot sumptis comitibus, qui nos perductarent, consesso equo Messanam reliquimus; sed iter facientibus nobis Taurominium usque memorabile nihil conspectum est: summa enim littora eraduntur. A leva statim Rhegium et Brutii agri parvo primum, mox latiori maris intervallo aperientibus sese paulatim angustiis prospectantur; a dextra colles continui imminent, Bacchi tota feracissima plaga et Mamertinis vinetis minus fortasse, quam olim fuit, tanquam ab ipsa vetustate contritis iam laudibus, sed tamen satis nunc etiam percelebris. In medio fere itineris vel paulo amplius castellum Nisus ex aeria montis rupe viatoribus late prospicitur, unde illud devectum Ovidianum

Nisiades matres sicelidesque nurus.

Incolae vallem etiam omnem, quae subest, Nisi regionem vocant.

13 **B. P.** Erit isto sane modo etiam aliquid infra Taurominium memorabile. Nam de hoc poetae versu, si recte memini, nobis pueris nondum inter grammaticos conveniebat: qua quidem in re adhuc illi arbitrum si quaerunt, plane video eam controversiam posse dirimi a Niso tuo, a quo nescio quam blande caeteri hospites suscipiantur. Te certe, ut illi dicerent, etiam elegantiorem remisit. Sed sequere.

B. F. Taurominii cum veterum monumentorum reliquiae plures visuntur, templa, sepulchra, aquaeductus, quin saepe temere graeca numismata passim effodiuntur, affabre facta illa quidem, neque in aes modo insculpta, sed in argentum, sed in aurum, quod etiam Syracusis plurimum et fere per totam insulam evenit; tum etiam coctile theatrum adhuc manet paulo, quam id quod Romae vidimus, minus, nisi quod illud amphitheatrum est. Quae quidem omnia eo inspexi diligentius, quod te recordabar plurimum semper veterum hominum imaginibus monumentisque,

B. B. For young men you were much too unremitting in your studies, or else too blinkered in your devotion. To have applied yourself for a year and more to the first elements of a new language without a single day's break? No wonder if you look different from before and have lost your color! Yet we thought your pale complexion and thinness were due to the sea voyage.[13]

12 **P. B.** Well, so it happened. But see! We did eventually look to ourselves. We decided to visit Etna and, while giving our minds a rest (as we should do even when we're at our busiest), to spend our holiday familiarizing ourselves with so great a natural marvel. And so, taking with us a few agreeable companions to guide us, we left Messina on horseback, but as we made our journey we saw nothing worth mentioning as far as Taormina; for the edge of the shoreline is being worn away. On the left, Reggio and the Bruttian region[14] immediately come into view, first across a small stretch of sea and then a wider one as the narrows gradually open themselves out. On the right a chain of hills rises forth, and the entire expanse is a rich producer of wine, and famous for its Mamertine vineyards—perhaps less famous than it once was, as if its praises had now been worn out precisely because they're so old, but still famous enough nonetheless.[15] At roughly the midpoint of the journey or a little beyond it, the fortress of Nisus becomes visible to travelers far and wide from its lofty mountain cliff. From it comes that line of Ovid's,

Mothers descended from Nisus, and daughters of Sicily.[16]

The locals also call the entire valley below it the region of Nisus.

13 **B. B.** In that case there will indeed be something below Taormina that's worth noting. For when I was a boy, if I remember correctly, scholars had yet to agree about this line of the poet. If they're still looking for someone to decide this matter, I quite see that the dispute can be settled by the Nisus you mention. I don't know how pleasantly his other guests are received; but he's certainly sent you back with better taste in your word choice, as those scholars would say. But carry on.

P. B. At Taormina, a good many ruins of ancient monuments are to be seen—temples, tombs, and aqueducts. In fact, Greek coins are often dug up by accident everywhere, all of them skillfully produced and not just stamped on bronze, but also on silver and gold; the same thing very often happens in Syracuse, and pretty much throughout the entire island. A theater made of brick still remains as well, somewhat smaller than the one we saw in Rome,[17] albeit the latter is an amphitheater. I examined all these ruins all the more carefully because I remembered that you

---

13. Does Bernardo wittily recall the letter that Pietro had written to him on May 30, 1492, soon after his arrival in Messina—a letter in which Pietro tells of his and Angelo's sea-sickness en route from Naples: *Itaque naviculam nacti, decimo die Siciliam tetigimus nauseantes* (Travi [1987] 5 *Letter* 2.5–6)?

14. Bruttium is the ancient name of the southernmost region of Italy, roughly corresponding to modern Calabria.

15. See Chapter 1 p. 23 and n. 1.

16. *Heroides* 15.54 (Sappho's letter to Phaon, who "frequents the faraway fields of Typhoean Etna," *arva . . . diversa Typhoidos Aetnae*, 11). Ovidian authorship is in fact hotly disputed: conveniently on the controversy, Knox (1995) 12–14, and see on 15.54 Chapter 1 p. 23 and n. 2.

17. Presumably during the second (?) of Bernardo's two periods of service as Venetian envoy to Rome in 1485 and in 1487–8: see Giannetto (1985) 45, 47–8, 166–77, and 186–95 with Kidwell (2004) 9–10, and cf. also Chapter 6 p. 250 and n. 114.

tanquam virtutum illorum et gestarum rerum testibus, oblectari. Urbs ipsa loco praecelso atque edito sita et montium angulo promissa in pelagus prospectum maris Ionii late hinc inde dominatur: theatrum ultimam anguli rupem insedit, qua collis conspicuus ante omnem urbem in circum planitiem ducens audentior procurrit in mare, atque hinc fluctibus, inde urbe medius ipse terminatur. E Taurominitano demissi iugo et littore paulatim relicto vallemque ingressi, quam a leva Aetnae radices, a dextra Taurominitani montes efficiunt, per eam Randatium usque pervenimus novum oppidum et in Aetnae radicibus, qua parte mediterranea despectat, situm. Iter totum a Taurominio nobis quattuor et viginta milibus passuum confectum est. Vallis sonoro et perpetuo flumine scinditur et irrigatur. Platani numerosa sylva utrasque ripas inumbrantes maximam sibi vallis partem egregiae incolae vendicarunt.

14 **B. P.** Ain, tandem, platanos illae habent ripae?

B. F. Pulcherrimas illas quidem et multissimas, ut non Platonem modo aut Aristotelem, scholasque omnes mitiores suis umbris invitare possint ad philosophandum, sed etiam Gymnosophistas durissimos illos quidem homines et sole admodum delectatos.

B. P. Quam vellem, ut cum earum duabus possem ego vel tribus arboribus etiam omnes illas fructiferas arbores, quas in quinquuncem dispositas habemus, commutare.

B. F. Utinam illae tibi potius, pater, iis stantibus totum Pluvicum obduxissent. Poterant enim vel universum Nonianum; sed nescio an isto sub coelo provenirent.

15 **B. P.** Equidem arbitror: nam illis, posteaquam in Italiam travectae sunt et quidem ab ipsa Sicilia primum, multae urbes abundavere; quanquam posteriorum hominum negligentia deperierint. Nos enim, dum Romae essemus, unam, quae in ima ripa speculi est Dianae Aricinae, pro miraculo vidimus. Sed nihil est profecto, mihi crede, nihil est, fili, ut ego semper dicere soleo, quod effici ab homine cura diligentiaque non possit. Nos enim, ut de me ipso loquar, quibus tamen, ex quo hanc villam exaedificavimus, iam inde ante quam tu esses natus, consumere hic nondum etiam licuit triginta integros dies, neque quando licebit scio, cupiam certe

always took the greatest pleasure in the statues and monuments of the ancients, as if witnesses to their virtuous qualities and achievements. The city itself is positioned very high up in a prominent place, and, jutting out over the water on a projecting spur of the mountains, it commands a broad view of the Ionian sea from one side to the other. The theater is situated on the outermost crag of the spur, where a hill of striking appearance in full view of the entire city forms a circular plateau and runs unflinchingly out into the sea; set in the middle between them, the hill is bounded by the waves on one side, the city on the other. Descending from the ridge of Taormina, we gradually left the coastline behind and entered a valley formed on our left by the foothills of Etna, on our right by the mountains of Taormina. Through this valley we made it all the way to Randazzo, a modern town positioned in Etna's foothills, on the inland side where it surveys the interior. Our entire journey from Taormina covered twenty-four miles. The valley is watered by the resounding, year-round flow of the river that cleaves it, and plane trees shade both banks in an abundance of forest, laying claim to most of the valley as its preeminent inhabitants.

14 **B. B.** What's that? You're really saying that the banks there have plane trees?

P. B. Yes, very beautiful ones, and in very great numbers, so that by their shade they could entice not just Plato or Aristotle[18] and all the softer schools to do some philosophizing, but even the Naked Sages, those hardiest of characters who take such delight in the sun.[19]

B. B. How I wish I could exchange all those fruit trees I have, all carefully arranged in a pattern,[20] for just two or three of them!

P. B. I'd rather wish that they'd formed a covering over the whole of the Piovego, father, with your own trees still standing. They could certainly have shaded even the entirety of Noniano; but I don't know if they'd do well in this climate.

15 **B. B.** Personally, I think they could. After they'd been brought over to Italy, and in fact first from Sicily itself,[21] many cities had plenty of them, but they died away when later generations failed to look after them properly. When I was in Rome,[22] I saw one remarkable example at the foot of the bank of Diana's Mirror at Aricia.[23] But believe me, son, there's absolutely nothing, as I always keep saying, there's nothing that can't be achieved through a person's careful and devoted attention. To speak of my own case: ever since I built this villa, already from before you were born,[24] I've never yet been able to spend thirty days here in one stretch, and I don't know

18. *ut non Platonem modo aut Aristotelem, scholasque* emended by Pietro in the Aldine *princeps* to *ut non Socratem modo, aut Platonem, scholasque* (cf. Pl. *Phdr.* 229a, 230b, Cic. *De or.* 1.28); see Bühler (1951) 137, 139–40.

19. On these Indian philosophers-cum-holy men, known especially for their asceticism, see, e.g., Plin. *HN* 7.22 ("from sunrise to sunset they stare resolutely at the sun with unflinching eyes, standing for the whole day first on one foot and then the other in the burning sand") with Beagon (2005) 151 for further sources.

20. For the five-point pattern of the *quincunx*, "the common Roman arrangement for trees," Powell (1988) 227–8 on Cic. *Sen.* 59.

21. The bookish Bernardo perhaps draws here on Plin. *HN* 12.6: Müller (2002) 294 and n.65.

22. See p. 319 n.17.

23. For the *speculum Dianae*, i.e., Lake Nemi, on whose northern shore the sanctuary of Diana Nemorensis was located, see Green (2007) 3–10.

24. For the vexed chronology of Noniano's construction (and renovation?), Chapter 6 p. 229 and n.40.

semper et peroptabo, vides quam multos tibi posuerimus ordines pulcherrimarum arborum vel nostratium vel advenarum? Quod si etiam platanos habuissem, nunquam illae me vivo periissent, et haberes tu quidem nunc, quo melius invitare posses Faunum tuum, et ille quo libentius accedere.

16 **B. F.** Vellem equidem, mi pater, sed, quando id effici non potest, oblecta te populis tuis; tum etiam, si placet, sicuti matres filiorum nomina, qui desiderantur, in eos saepe transferunt quos habent, ita et nos platanos illas vocemus.

B. P. Mihi vero placet illas populos semper vocari; atque haud scio an etiam cum eas tempestas vetustasve consumpserit, ut ait ille de quercu Mariana, tamen erit in Noniano populus, quam Bembeam populum vocent: ita mihi quidem videtur illas aeternitati commendasse suis carminibus Aurelius noster. Quare

Quae vitreas populus arduo
Bembeas ad aquas vertice tollitur
Vivum cespitem obumbrans
Intonsa bicolor coma

sit semper populus, crescat, surgat altius vel aquula ista, vel poetae versu. **17** Sed, ut ad platanos redeam, non tam mea causa istud ipsum cupiebam, fili, quam tua. Ego enim me oblectavi satis; tum experiendo illud didici, ut nequid admirarer; neque, si quid sero aliquando, quod facio semper, cum licet, sive aedifico aliquid aut paro, propterea id facio, vel quia illis omnibus rebus putem me esse usurum, cui me ipso uti iam meo ipsius iure non licet, vel quia non facile illa possem contemnere, quibus carerem: quid enim mihi potest iam ad eos dies, qui mihi reliqui sunt ad vivendum, esse non satis? Vobis ista parantur, pueri, vobis ista, inquam, non mihi. Scio enim quam a parentibus quaesita ista dulcius accipere soleant filii, quam ipsi facile comparare, sive quod in quaerendis rebus plerique laborem fugimus, in partis omnes voluptatem amamus, sive quod in iis, quae nobis a maioribus nostris relinquuntur, insit etiam memoria illorum, qui tradidere, quae illa nobis nescio quo pacto, cum sanctiora efficiat, tum certe facit multo etiam iucundiora.

18 **B. F.** Mihi quidem, pater, et nunc ista carissima sunt, quae, qua es in nos amoris exuberantia, a te video dici, et erunt semper, dum vivam, fixa animo et memoriae meae, cupioque, ut ex iis ipsis rebus, quae mihi a te quaeque fratri comparantur meo, longissimam ipse nobiscum percipias voluptatem. Sed si tibi nos unquam naturae

when I will be able to, though I'll certainly keep wishing it and desiring it fondly. You see how many rows of the most beautiful trees I've planted for you, whether indigenous or non-native? But if I'd also had plane trees, they would never have died while I still lived, and you'd now have a place to which you could better entice that Faunus of yours,[25] and he a place where he could more gladly come.

16 P. B. I'd like that myself, father; but since it can't happen, take pleasure in your poplars. Besides, if you want, just as mothers often transfer the names of children they've lost to the ones they have, we too could call them plane trees in the same way.

B. B. No, I want them always to be called poplars. I'm inclined to think that, when they've been worn away by the weather and age, there'll nevertheless still be a poplar at Noniano that people may call the Bembine poplar, just as that famous man spoke of Marius' oak.[26] It seems to me that our friend Aurelius[27] has in this way committed them to immortality in his verses. Hence may

> the poplar that rises with its lofty crown
> at the Bembos' glass-like waters,
> shading the lively grass with its unshorn
> leaves, and two-colored,[28]

may it be poplar always, may it grow, and may it rise higher by grace either of those waters or of the poet's verse. **17** But to get back to the plane trees: I had that wish for them not so much for my sake, son, as for yours. For I've had enjoyment enough, and I've learnt by experience not to be carried away by anything. If I ever plant anything, as I always do when I can, or if I build or acquire something, I do so not because I think that I'll profit by all such things myself (since by now I'm not free to profit from myself by my own right), or because I couldn't easily pay no heed to what is not in my possession; for what can now fail to be enough for me for the remaining days of my life? These acquisitions are for you, sons, for you, I say, not for me. For I know how it's usually more pleasant for sons to receive from their parents what they've sought rather than easily to acquire it for themselves, either because most of us tend to shirk the effort of going after things while all of us enjoy the pleasure of acquisitions; or because the possessions that are left to us by our forebears retain the memory of those who bequeathed them—a memory that may somehow render them more hallowed for us, but certainly also makes them much more pleasurable to receive.

18 P. B. Those words of yours are very precious to me now, father, since I see that you speak them with such an abundance of love for me; and, as long as I live, they will always be implanted in my mind and memory, and my wish is that you yourself continue to enjoy for a very long time, along with us, all those acquisitions that you've made

25. For this Faunus in Pietro's youthful poetry cf. §§49–50 below and see Chapter 6 pp. 266–8.

26. The oak tree that Cicero apparently mentioned in his epic poem on the Roman general and statesman Gaius Marius (*c.* 157–86 BCE): see *Leg.* 1.1–2 with Dyck (2004) 54–9.

27. Giovanni Aurelio Augurello, for whom Chapter 6 pp. 227–9.

28. From the opening of *Carmina* 1.5, entitled *Optat Iulium Alexandrum Capellam sub populo in amoenissima villa Bernardi Bembi Veneti senatoris clarissimi sita amoris cura solari* ("He wishes to console Giulio Alessandro Capella for his cares of love under a poplar situated in the most delightful villa of Bernardo Bembo, the distinguished Venetian senator"): see further Chapter 6 pp. 228–9. In his citation Pietro naturally omits the original vocatival address to Capella in line 1 (*Quae, Iuli, uitreas*...).

lege supervivemus, habeo alia ego (ut de me tantum loquar: nam de fratre, quanquam multa possent dici, malo illi integram causam relinquere respondendi tibi), habeo alia, inquam, quae mihi sanctissimam tui memoriam semper efficient etiam absque Noniano tuo, quippe qui me puerum educaveris non diligenter modo, sed plane, quod vere mihi videor esse dicturus, etiam religiose; habueris tecum in legationibus tuis; imbueris optimis moribus omnibusque bonis artibus, quod in te esset, ita semper institueris, ut verear, ne sim prorsus ingratissimus, ultra haec mihi a te si quid unquam relictum optavero, tum si de iis ipsis tibi non ego semper maiores gratias habuero, quam si mihi magnificas villas construxisses. Quare ista quidem de causa nihil est sane quod labores.

19 **B. P.** Ego vero ac multum: nam qui tibi illa praeparaverim, quae sunt longe potiora meo quidem iudicio et, ut video, etiam tuo, curandum est etiam mihi, ista tibi ut ne desint, quae cum minora quidem sint, valde tamen sunt necessaria. Quemadmodum si te quis ad coenam vocet, ferculaque afferat cum varia tum sumptuosa, vina multifariam apponat, ministros adhibeat, calices quaerat et vasa vel aurea vel gemmata, nisi statuerit triclinium, aut mensas in hortulo disposuerit, ut tibi stanti coenandum sit, certe tu illum nihilo probes magis, quam si tam multa omnino non paravisset. Ita mihi eveniet patri: nam quod te recte instituerim a puero, mecum habuerim semper, utramque linguam te docendum curarim, id est ad coenam vocasse te satis dubiam et sumptuosam, in qua depasceres animum tuum, teque ipsum conviva elegans oblectares. Convivae nanque sumus omnes, dum vivimus, neque aliud est omnis vita nostra, qua sub ista mundi luce fruimur, quam longa concoenatio, aut, ut iam verius dicam, convictio; quod si nec sedem ullam tibi nec umbram aliquam praebuero coenanti, hoc est nisi viventi diversorium secessumque gratum aliquem paravero studiis et camenis tuis, profecto non tam in illis laudabis diligentiam meam, quam in his etiam culpabis negligentiam, neque tam pulchra ea tibi esse videbuntur, quibus abundaveris, quam fuisse illa, quibus carebis, necessaria. Ita fiet ut, cum semel abiero, tu me saepius accuses, quam probes.

for me and for my brother.[29] But if we ever outlive you in the natural way of things, I have other reasons (to speak only for myself: much could be said on my brother's behalf, but I prefer to leave entirely to him the opportunity to answer you)—other reasons, I say, why your memory will always be sacrosanct to me, and quite apart from your Noniano. When I was a boy you oversaw my education not just carefully but in plain fact—I feel I'll be saying this truly—even devoutly. You took me with you on your diplomatic missions;[30] you imbued me with the best moral values, and, to the best of your ability, you always equipped me with all of the cultured arts; so that I fear I'd be utterly ungrateful if I ever wanted you to leave me anything further, and if I didn't always show you greater gratitude for these very things than for any magnificent villas that you might have built for me. Hence there's certainly no reason for you to exert yourself on that score.

19 **B. B.** But I do, and very much so. For though I've provided you with what is far more important in my judgment and, as I see, in yours as well, I also have to see to it that you don't lack the things that may be less important but are still very necessary. Suppose someone invites you to dinner and sets before you a variety of extravagant courses, lays on every kind of wine, has servants on hand, and asks for cups and vessels of gold or set with precious stones: if he's not organized a dining room or at least arranged tables in the garden and you have to dine standing up, you'd certainly think no more highly of him than if he'd made absolutely none of his so many preparations. So it will turn out for me as your father: the fact that I trained you properly from boyhood, that I always had you with me, and that I saw to it that you were taught Latin and Greek—that all amounts to your invitation to a dinner that is multifarious enough[31] in its extravagance, a dinner at which to feed your mind, and to entertain yourself as a cultured guest; for we're all dinner guests while we're alive, and this entire life of ours that we enjoy beneath the heavenly light is but an extended common banquet[32] or (to be more accurate) a form of companionship. But if I've made no seat or shade available for you as you dine—that is, unless I've provided for your life some pleasant place of diversion and retreat for your studies and your poetry, you'll undoubtedly praise my carefulness in the one direction less than you'll fault my indifference in the other direction; and the blessings you possess in abundance will seem to you less pleasing in comparison with the vital importance you'll have attached to the things you'll lack. The outcome will be that, when I'm dead and gone, you'd more often blame me than commend me.

---

29. Carlo, Pietro's younger brother, born December 10, 1471 (or possibly 1472: see Giannetto [1985] 119–20); Pietro was deeply affected by Carlo's early death on December 30, 1503 (see Kidwell [2004] 86–7). Apart from Antonia, Pietro's sister (who was the older remains unclear: Giannetto 119), he also had an elder half-brother, Bartolomeo, born probably in the later 1450s (Giannetto 118; see also Chapter 6 p. 207 and Chapter 7 p. 276).

30. E.g., to Florence in 1478–80 and to Rome in 1485 and 1487–8.

31. *coenam . . . dubiam* lit. "a doubtful repast," i.e., one that perplexes the diner with choice; cf. Ter. *Phorm.* 342–3, Hor. *Sat.* 2.2.77.

32. For the familiar banquet-of-life motif see, e.g., *SVF* 3.768, Lucr. *DRN* 3.938–9, Cic. *Tusc.* 5.118, and Sen. *Ep.* 77.8 with P. J. Alexander (1976), esp. 59–61.

20 **B. F.** O mi pater, mene tam impium unquam futurum, ut te audeam accusare? ego te unquam accusem, pater? quid si non tu me saepe monuisses, et ego aliquando scriptum legissem a summis ac sapientissimis viris, animi bona esse, quae beatos homines facerent sola ipsa per sese quaeque opis externae non egerent? ea neque eripi posse cuiquam nec aetate senescere nec morte interire? caetera omnia manca esse, labilia, momentanea, quae quoniam fortuna et casu regerentur, tanto esse magis quenquam, quantum illa contemneret, vel divitem vel etiam sapientem? animos nostros ex aetherea sede in hanc corporis labem profectos ea lege, ut ad illam ipsam purgati aliquando reverterentur, quae hic essent despicere, ad illa se intendere quo properarent? me vero, quem ista quandoque docuisses, nisi mihi villam reliqueris sylvamque platanorum, putas tibi esse succensurum? Non est ita, mi pater, ne putes.

21 **B. P.** Non puto.

B. F. Neque me tam dementem existimes velim.

B. P. Non existimo.

B. F. Quid ita igitur loquebare?

B. P. Quia noveram mores hominum, tum etiam pertentare te prorsus volui, quam recte ista sentires. Sed omittamus haec iam tandem, fili, atque ad eam partem sermonis, ex qua egressi sumus, revertamur.

B. F. Immo vero, pater, nec revertamur: quid enim amplius nobis cum platanis illis? de iis enim loquebamur. Sed, si placet, ad Aetnam potius, de qua sermo haberi coeptus est, properemus.

B. P. Mihi vero perplacet, ita tamen, ut ne festines: tibi enim ego omnes has pomeridianas horas dico. Sed quoniam me impellente nimium iam extra Aetnae terminos provecti sumus, non committam, ut te interpellem saepius, nisi quid erit, quod de ea ipsa te rogem.

22 **B. F.** Sane mons ipse situ, forma, magnitudine, fertilitate, incendiis mirus, demum tota sui qualitate ac specie longe conspicuus et sibi uni par est. Ab aurora mare Ionium bibit et Catanam sustinet imo in pede; cum sole descendit in insulam, qua Tyrrenum pelagus est, et quae Aeoliae appellantur; laterorsus, in septentriones vergenti, Pelorus obiicitur et Italiae angustiae sunt; contra reliqua insula subiacet tractusque ii omnes, qui cum Lilyboeo in African protenduntur. Ipsa Aetna radices suas fere in orbem deducit, nisi sicubi orientem et meridiem versus promisso clivo paulisper extenditur: celebs degit et nullius montis dignata coniugium caste intra suos terminos continetur.

20 P. B. Father! Could I ever be so disloyal as to dare to blame you? Would I ever blame you, father? Hadn't you often reminded me, and hadn't I every so often read in the writings of the wisest and most distinguished men, that wealth of mind is the sole means in and of itself of making people happy, and that it needs no help from without? That it can't be taken away from anyone or deteriorate with age or perish in death? That all other goods are maimed, fleeting, and of short duration and, since they're governed by chance and fortune, any man is all the wealthier and even wiser to the extent that he despises them? That since our souls have left their heavenly abode for this bodily corruption on the principle that they're at some point to return to that abode in a cleansed condition, they despise their existence here and exert themselves toward the goal to which they're hurrying?[33] Given that you've taught me such lessons over time, do you really think I'm going to be angry with you if you don't leave me a country retreat and a wood of plane trees? It's not so, father, don't think it.

21 B. B. I don't.

P. B. I wouldn't want you to think me so mad.

B. B. I don't.

P. B. Then why were you talking in that way?

B. B. Because I've come to know the ways of people; then too I wanted to give you a thorough test of your soundness of thinking on that subject. But let's at last put all this to one side now, son, and let's return to the point where we digressed in our conversation.

P. B. Please, no, father, not there. What more business do we have with those plane trees? For that's what we were talking about. But if you've no objection, let's rather hurry on to Etna, which was our original topic of conversation.

B. B. I'd like that very much, provided that you don't rush: I'm devoting all these afternoon hours to you. But since it was at my instigation that we just moved too far beyond the bounds of Etna, I'll avoid interrupting you too often, unless there's anything for me to ask you about Etna itself.

22 P. B. The mountain itself is remarkable in its layout, shape, size, fertility, and its fires; in sum, in its overall nature and appearance it draws attention to itself from afar and is absolutely unique. On the eastern side it drinks from the Ionian Sea and holds Catania on its bottommost foot; to the west it slopes down into the island on the side bordering the Tyrrhenian Sea and what are called the Aeolian Islands;[34] where it slopes down to the north, it meets the promontory of Pelorus[35] on its flank, and there are the straits of Italy; on the other side, the rest of the island lies beneath it, as do all those stretches that join Lilybaeum[36] in extending toward Africa. Etna itself almost forms a circle at its base, except for where it briefly stretches outwards by extending its incline toward the east and south. It leads a celibate existence, disdaining union with any other mountain

33. A strongly Neoplatonic vision of the soul, suggestively with the imprint of Marsilio Ficino (cf. Kristeller [1943] 214–19), whom Bernardo befriended while serving as Venetian ambassador to Florence in the 1470s (Giannetto [1985] 135–6).

34. The volcanic archipelago to the north of Sicily, now also known (after the name of the largest island) as the Lipari Islands.

35. The northeastern extremity of Sicily, now known as Punta del Faro.

36. In fact, the westernmost extremity of Sicily, the modern Marsala.

Circumitur non minus quam centum milibus passuum, ascenditur fere per viginti, qua brevior via. Imi colles ac omnis radicum ambitus per oppida, et per vicos frequens inhabitatur; Baccho, Pallade, Cerere feraces terrae, armentorum omnis generis supra quam credas feracissimae. Hic amoenissima loca circunquaque, hic fluvii personantes, hic obstrepentes rivi, hic gelidissimae fontium perennitates, hic parata in floribus semper et omni verna die, ut facile quilibet puellam Proserpinam hinc fuisse raptam putet. **23** Hic arborum multiiugae species et ad umbram valentium et ad foecunditatem, in qua etiam tantum excellunt caeteras omnes arbores, ut mihi quidem magis huic loco convenire videantur ea, quae de Alcinoi hortis finxit Homerus, quam ipsi Phaeaciae; in qua certe nos, cum e Sicilia rediremus, nihil eiusmodi vidimus, quod nos tantopere oblectaret; ut etiam non inurbane Angelus meus interroganti eum cuidam ex Phaeacibus, qui nobis urbem omnem ostentarant, quidnam illi videretur, ita responderit: "Ego, Phaeaces, debere vos quidem—inquit—Homero permultum existimo, qui vobis plura etiam tribuit quam ipsa natura." Referam, si potero, latine; vel certe ut potero: nam adverti propterea tum etiam diligentius illum ipsum Homeri locum.

Hic nemora in coelum late crescentia surgunt
Punicei pomum grani malumque pirumque
Et dulces ficus et magnae Palladis arbor
Non illis borealis hyems, non officit aestas
Torrida, sed placidas zephyris spirantibus auras
Arboribus totum superat foetura per annum
Et pomo insenuere recentia poma priori
Et nova iam miti superadvenit uva racemo.

24 Medius mons nunc variis arboribus late sylvescit, et praecipue pinis et fagis maximam in magnitudinem multitudinemque crescentibus, quarum illae inferius, hae sublimiores sunt; nunc nudo latere arabiles in plagas extenditur, et saepe usque ad imum descendit frumentis adeo foecundus, ut credita nonnunquam in centuplam segetem cultoribus ferat. Itaque prudenter, ut multa, illud etiam prisci viri, quod nobilissimum templum Cereris in Aetna constituere: ubi enim potius dea

and chastely confining itself within its own bounds. It is no less than a hundred miles in circumference, and, by the shorter route, the journey to the top is about twenty miles. The lowest slopes and the entire circumference of its base are thickly peopled through towns and villages; the land is fertile in vines, olive trees, and corn, and incredibly productive of every kind of cattle. Here on every side are the most scenic places, here are resounding streams, here clamorous water courses, here the coolest springs that flow throughout the year; here it is springtime every day, with flowers always in bloom, so that anyone would easily think that it was from here that Proserpina was snatched as a girl.[37] **23** Here there are many varied kinds of trees that are strong in shade and fertility. In this respect they so far surpass all other trees that the lines that Homer contrived about the gardens of Alcinous[38] seem to me to be better suited to this place than to Phaeacia itself. Certainly, when we were in Phaeacia on our way back from Sicily,[39] we saw nothing of that kind that was as delightful, so that when one of the Phaeacians who had shown us their entire city asked my friend Angelo what his impressions of it were, he replied rather wittily, "I think, Phaeacians," he said, "that you owe a very great deal to Homer, who has bestowed even more on you than has nature herself." I'll render the lines in Latin if I can, or certainly as I can; for it was with that object in view that, at the time, I paid rather careful attention to that very passage in Homer:

Here the woods grow far and wide and rise skyward,
with pomegranates, apples and pears
and sweet figs and mighty Pallas' olive tree.
The northern blast of winter does not impede them, nor does
the scorching summer, but the west winds breathe their gentle breezes,
and the trees prevail in bearing fruit throughout the whole year;
and a fresh growth of apples ages on those that precede them,
and new grapes arrive on top of the cluster that's already ripe.[40]

24 The middle part of the mountain is partly wooded far and wide with trees of various kinds, and especially with pines and beeches that grow to a very great size in very great numbers; of these, the pines are lower down the mountain, the beeches higher up. Where the slope is devoid of vegetation, this middle part opens out into arable tracts, and often in its downward run all the way to its base it is so rich in grain that it sometimes brings the farmers a crop yielding a hundredfold return on their investment. And so the ancients acted wisely (as so often) in establishing their very famous temple of Ceres on Etna;[41] for where could the goddess of crops better

---

37. Proserpina = Gk. Persephone; the myth of her abduction by Pluto is diversely treated in, e.g., the *Homeric Hymn to Demeter*, Ovid (*Met.* 5.341–661, *Fast.* 4.417–620), and Claudian's *De raptu Proserpinae.*

38. *Odyssey* 7.114–21, rendered below.

39. By Phaeacia Pietro here means the Venetian colony of Corfu, much prized as a bulwark against the Ottomans; for his return voyage from Sicily, Travi (1987) 9 *Letter* 7.15–19 with Kidwell (2004) 11.

40. See on these lines Chapter 6 pp. 246–7.

41. Diod. Sic. 11.26.7 states that the tyrant Gelon (*c.* 540–478) "planned to build a temple to Demeter at Aetna, since she had none in that place; but he did not complete it, his life having been cut short by fate." But no town of Aetna existed until 476 (see Chapter 1 p. 28), and Diodorus may instead have Catania in mind; further, White (1964) 266 and n.18.

segetum coleretur, quam ubi fruges optimae provenirent? Atque id quidem tantum de segetibus, verum ab universa Aetnae fertilitate, ut opinor fabula etiam emanavit, Aristeum giganta eo in monte ita salvum esse atque vivere, ut neque ab Aetna prematur unquam, neque flammis coelestibus inuratur, quod optimi et uberrimi essent fructus, qui per Aetnae loca nascerentur, nullo telluris vitio, nulla aeris offensi malignitate. Nam et Aristeos Graeci quidem illos vocabant, qui vicissent in certaminibus; quod verbum ab optimo deductum esse credo, quia nisi optimi non vincerent; et gigantas scimus esse filios telluris appellatos. Ita, quoniam fructus universos tellus quasi mater parit, cum fructus Aetnaeos esse optimos atque uberrimos vellent dicere, tanquam caeteros superarent, fabulae datus est locus non invenuste quidem, si tibi ita videtur. Expecto enim etiam, quid tu sentias, scire abs te.

25 **B. P.** Mihi sane videtur: itaque redde caetera.

B. F. Reddam, pater, atque illa ipsa quidem, quae a principio postularas et quorum causa ista omnia dicta sunt: ventum est enim ad id, ut iam de ignibus loqueremur.

B. P. Verebar sane tu ne me longius provectares; quanquam quid longum mihi esse hac in re, qua de nunc agimus, atque isto in otio potest?

B. F. Curabo id quidem, ne fiat, si potero, quam potero, diligenter.

B. P. Immo Hercle fiat potius, etiam id si facere ipse, ne fiat, potes: non enim impedio. Illud autem ideo dixeram, quia te putabam ante, quam istuc accessisses, aliquandiutius erraturum.

B. F. Ego vero existimabam, pater, erravisse me sic etiam nimis diu.

B. P. Non est ita, sed, ne nunc tandem erremus, perge de ignibus, ut proposuisti: verum autem, quid tu haeres?

B. F. Pergam equidem, ut iubes: sed scin, quam in salebram inciderim?

B. P. Nihil profecto minus.

26 **B. F.** Dum tibi ad ignes festino, eam Aetnae partem, quae nobis una restabat de tribus (sic enim partiri soleo), et qua sine ad ignes ipsos perveniri non potest, pene omiseram suboblitus: ita Aetnam, quasi Chimaeram, caecideramus et tanquam ream capite mulctaveramus imprudentes. Sed agam nunc tutius ac de utroque

be worshipped than where the best corn yields were being produced? That much only of arable crops. But Etna's general fertility has given rise, I think, to the story that the giant Aristeus leads so secure an existence within the mountain that he is never crushed by Etna and never scorched by heaven-sent fire; this story arose from the fact that the crops produced throughout the region of Etna were of the highest quality and very plentiful because the soil was unblemished and the air untainted by any contamination.[42] For the Greeks used to call those who'd won in the games Aristei, a word I believe to be derived from their word for "best," since only the best would win; and we know that the giants were called sons of the earth. Therefore, since the earth is mother-like in producing crops of any and all kinds, when they wanted to say that Etna's crops were the very best and most plentiful, as if surpassing all the rest, the story was located there—and not without a certain charm, if you agree. For I'm eager to know from you what you think.

25 B. B. Yes, I certainly agree; and so tell me the rest.

P. B. I shall, father, including the matters that you'd asked about at the outset—matters that prompted this whole discussion. For we've reached the stage for me now to talk about the fires.

B. B. I was really afraid that you were taking me by too long a path; albeit what can be long for me in the subject that we're now discussing, and in these leisurely circumstances?

P. B. I'll see to it that that doesn't happen, if I can, as carefully as I can.

B. B. Good heavens, no! Let it happen, even if you can stop it from happening; I'm not preventing you. I'd said that because I thought you were going to go off on a digression for some considerable time more before you reached your goal.

P. B. In truth, father, I was thinking that I'd already been digressing in this way for too long.

B. B. No, not so; but, so that we don't digress after all, do proceed about the fires, as you proposed. But why your perplexity?

P. B. I'll proceed, just as you bid me; but you know the rough patch of road I've come upon?

B. B. Not in the least.

26 P. B. While I was hurrying on to the fires for you, I almost forgot and left out the one part of Etna that was left of the three (I usually divide it in this way), and we can't get to the fires themselves without it. Accordingly, I'd cut up Etna like the Chimaera,[43] unintentionally beheading it as if guilty as charged! But I'll now proceed more

---

42. Pietro appears to conflate different Aristei/Aristaioi, at least four of whom are distinguished in the Greco-Roman mythological tradition (see Fontenrose [1981] 181–8 with *RE* 3.2 852–9 and Roscher 1.547–51). The Aristaios born to Uranus and Ge was the only one of the Gigantes to survive the Gigantomachy; hidden by his mother on Etna in the guise of a dung beetle, he was left unscathed by Jupiter's bolts (Fontenrose 182; for the Etnean associations of the dung beetle, Davies and Kathirithamby [1986] 86–8). But this Aristaios is here apparently conflated with the figure born, at least by the most prevalent tradition, to Apollo and Cyrene (so, e.g., Hes. fr. 216 Merkelbach-West, Pind. *Pyth.* 9.39–65, Ap. Rh. 2.500–27, Virg. *G.* 4.317, 321–4, etc.), his name derived from the Greek ἄριστος (= "greatest"; cf. Pietro's allusion to the derivation below). His credentials as beekeeper, herdsman and cultivator (Fontenrose 182–3) are ideally suited to the luxuriant Etna configured by Bembo; for this Aristaios' particular association with, and benefactions to, Sicily see esp. Diod. Sic. 4.82.5.

43. Perhaps here with a knowing allusion (i) to the monstrous, tripartite hybrid Chimaera as *Typhoeus*' child (cf. Hes. *Theog.* 304–7 and 319–22 with West [1966] 254–5), and hence with topical

simul loquar. Superior itaque montis pars (nam iam de iis, quae infra sunt, diximus) usque ad summum cacumen nuda variam faciem praeostendit. Nam alibi semiherbosi tractus sunt intersurgentibus tophis, qui etiam in pedemontana regione passim visuntur; alibi per summa ora exundans incendium saxis fluentibus totas plagas inoccupavit; alibi arenarum campi magnam in longitudinem et latitudinem extenduntur. In supremo crateres duo sunt, quorum alterum, qui minus altissimus est, ipsi vidimus in putei rotunditatem angustum, emissis veluti gemina sponda hinc inde saxis sulfureo virore fumigantibus. Hunc lapidea planities ambitu angusto circuntenet, quo ut primum inscendimus, sulfureis statim nebulis et suburenti fumo, veluti e fornace percussi ora paene retulimus gradum; mox increscente audacia, qua ventus perflabat, paulatim ingressi craterem ipsum tetigimus manu. Effundebatur inde, sicuti ex camino, fumus non intermissa exhalatione. Is tamen etiam scissa per longa incendia montis cute, ventis intus furentibus, qui eo die imperiosius bacchabantur, multis in locis sibi faciebat exeundi viam; interdum quoque de repente ipsis sub pedibus exiliens manere nos uno in loco non permittebat. Quin etiam illud accidit, ut quem locum maxime contemplabamur, quod erat saxis nuper effusis et adhuc ignem et sulfur retinentibus incrustatus, per hunc, qua parte concesserat in rimam, interflueret igneus rivus ac pedes ipsos inter emissa ex rivo saxa urentia prosilirent.

27 **B. P.** Quid ais? peream, ni me totum commoves, fili, atque etiam perterrefacis tua ista oratione. Quid autem saxa illa? an etiam quenquam vestrum interlaesere?

B. F. Neminem profecto, pater: quin etiam eorum duo, cum refrixissent, quae manu capi poterant, Messanam deportavimus sulfuris partem servantia, caetera subnigra.

B. P. Quid enim vos tam ultra temere procedebatis?

B. F. Quia cum licere illic nobis tuto consistere putabamus, tum etiam perlustrandi studio vel potius aviditate ferebamur.

B. P. An nesciebatis Plinium illum maiorem ita occidisse, dum nimium diligenter, ne dicam inconsulte, Veseviana incendia pertentaret?

28 **B. F.** Quid ni sciremus, pater? verum tanta nos delectatio illius spectaculi detinebat, tanta rei novitas, tantus invaserat stupor, ut sui ipsius iam nemo satis nostrum recordaretur. Sed missa haec faciamus, atque ad illam planitiem, de qua modo dixeram, revertamur, quae quidem ita tamen perurebat ipsa, ut manus, nisi extemplo retulisses, offenderentur: pedes duplici calciamento ita propter ascensus difficultatem comparato tuebamur. Ab eo cratere, quem dixi, mons per fundae iactum

cautiously, and talk about both topics together. The higher part of the mountain, then (for we've already spoken of the lower parts), is bare all the way up to the very summit, but it shows a varied complexion. In some places there are stretches that are sparsely covered in grass, with occasional outgrowths of tufa that are also visible everywhere at the foot of the mountain; elsewhere, the fire that gushes forth through the surface openings has taken over whole expanses with molten rock; in other places, large areas of sand stretch forth very far and wide. At the top there are two craters. Of these, we saw for ourselves the one that is lower but still very high up: it is narrow and rounded like a well, and on either side of it, as if forming a double frame, are rocks that have been belched forth and smoke with the powerful stench of sulfur. A stony plateau encircles this crater with a narrow periphery. When we first climbed up to this periphery, we were immediately struck in the face by the sulfurous clouds and scorching smoke, as if from an oven, and we almost withdrew; but we soon grew in boldness, and, gradually moving toward the crater on the side where the wind was sweeping through, we actually touched it with our hands. From there, as if from a furnace, smoke began to pour forth in a continuous exhalation. Since cracks had formed in the mountain's surface through long fires, and because the winds were raging inside (on that day they were quite tyrannical in their fury), the smoke was forcing an outlet for itself in many places; because it sometimes even burst out without warning right beneath our feet, it wouldn't let us stay in one place. Furthermore, it happened that when we were very closely examining a given spot because it was encrusted with stones that had just been belched forth and were still burning and sulfurous, a stream of fire began to flow through that spot just where it had given way to a fissure, and the burning rocks that were shot out from this stream sprang up right between our feet!

27 B. B. What! I swear you're making me shake all over, son; you're scaring me to death with this story of yours. But what about those rocks? Did they harm any of you?

P. B. No one at all, father. In fact, when they'd cooled down, we carried back to Messina two of the rocks that could be picked up by hand; they still had some of their sulfur, but they were otherwise blackish in color.

B. B. What made you continue on so far beyond recklessness?

P. B. We thought we were able to stand there safely; and then we were carried away by our eagerness, or rather our ardent passion, to survey everything.

B. B. Weren't you aware that the elder Pliny died in just that way, when he was far too assiduous, not to say rash, in investigating Vesuvius' fires?[44]

28 P. B. Of course we were, father. But we were gripped by such enjoyment of that spectacle, and we were overcome with such astonishment at the unexpectedness of it all, that none of us paid any attention to himself. But let's put this aside and return to the plateau that I'd just mentioned: it was burning with such heat that, unless you pulled your hands away at once, they would suffer injury, and we protected our feet with the double layer of sole that we'd obtained precisely because of the difficulty

---

relevance to Etna; and (ii) to the volcanic Mt. Chimaera in Phaselis (now Turkey), which Pliny lists alongside Etna at *HN* 2.236.

44. The younger Pliny famously describes in two letters to Tacitus (*Ep.* 6.16 and 20) the events surrounding his uncle's death when Vesuvius exploded in August 79 CE; further, Sigurdsson (1999) 51–70 with Scarth (2009), esp. 39–85.

insurgit ascensu difficillimo partim salebris impedientibus, partim tardantibus arenis, et clivus statim etiam quoquoversus impendebat. Is universi corporis vertex summus est, et tanquam in urbem arx domina, sic ille in montem prominatur. Ab eius inscensu detinuere nos potentissima vis ventorum et exhalantes fumi. Itaque tibi de illo referre quidem aliud nihil possum, nisi tibi ea vis recenseri, quae ab Urbano monacho accepimus postea, Messanae cum esset, homo ille quidem verissimus atque harum rerum cupientissimus sciscitator: is enim paucos ante nos dies per summam tranquillitatem totum verticem perlustraverat.

B. P. Immo vero cupio: novi enim ego illum atque amo, quod te non latet; quo mihi futura sunt haec omnia illius etiam testimonio gratiora.

29 B. F. Aiebat ille igitur (quando ea tibi narrari postulas, quibus tamen ego tam accedo ut credam, quam omnino si perspexissem) verticem illum esse ab ingenti cratere occupatum ambitu circiter quatuor stadiorum, eumque non usque in imum descendere eodem hiatu, sed alvum sibi intus paulatim astringere eatenus, quoad in medio centro ad evomenda montis incrementa satis amplo ore foraminatur; tum esse in summa montis corona parvum tramitem, ubi pedes firmentur; ex eo si quis declinaverit, aut in craterem obrui, aut e monte deturbari; stetisse tamen se ibi tam diu, quo barathrum exploraret; eructasse tum montem magno strepore incendia caliginosa et perurentes petras supra os, quantum sagitta quis mitteret, vel eo amplius, insurgentes; atque eum, veluti corpus vivens, non perflasse semper, sed emissa semel anima cessasse diutule, dum respiraret; tum se copiam intuendi habuisse quae vellet; mox eiectasse iterum atque iterum pari intervallo usquequaque; interea ingemere intus cavernas auditas, intremere etiam tonitruis montem sub pedibus magno et formidoloso iis, qui aderant, horrore; ex quo illud mirum videtur, quod qui tum strepitus per tranquillitatem sentiebantur, eorum a nobis nihil auditum sit in tanta ferocia ventorum.

30 B. P. Illud vero nec videatur, fili, neque plane ipsum est mirum. Constat enim, quemadmodum scriptores tradidere, simul cum ventis Aetnae animam immutari; et quo flante fumos tantum et caligines exhalet, eo ponente modo puras modo crassiores flammas emittere pro surgentium ventorum qualitate; aliquando etiam effundi torrentes ignium varia exundatione, prout intra montis viscera pinguia vel exilia incrementa sunt. Quae cum ita se habeant, illud etiam posse fieri quis est qui neget, lenissima unius venti aura eos strepitus intra montem excitari, qui vel furente altero non queant? non enim quam perflet quis, sed quam intret in montem quamque

of the ascent. From the crater I've mentioned, the mountain rises a slingshot further in height, and the climb is very challenging, partly because of the rough patches that stand in the way, and partly because the sands slow you down; right from the outset, the incline was also menacingly steep in every direction. That is the highest point of Etna's entire mass, and it stands out over the mountain like an all-controlling citadel over its city. We were kept from climbing it by the extreme force of the winds and by the billowing clouds of smoke, and so I can't tell you anything else about it unless you want me to recount to you what I subsequently heard from the monk Urbano when he was in Messina.[45] He is indeed someone of the highest integrity, and the most enthusiastic investigator of such matters; for a few days before us[46] he'd carefully examined the entire summit during a period of the utmost calm.

B. B. I'd like that very much: I know him and esteem him, as you're aware, and so your whole account will be all the more welcome to me because he's your witness.

29 **P. B.** In that case, then (since you ask for this narrative of events, which I'm as ready to believe as if I'd seen it in all respects for myself), he said that that peak consisted of a vast crater that was about half a mile in circumference, but that it didn't have the same aperture all the way down to the bottom: it gradually narrowed its innards to the extent that, right at its center, it had a cavity with an opening wide enough to spew forth the mountain's accumulated substance. Then, at the topmost rim of the mountain, there was a narrow path that afforded a firm footing; but anyone who deviated from it would either be thrown down into the crater or be sent tumbling from the mountain. However, he stood there long enough to inspect the inner chamber. Then with a great roar the mountain belched forth dark-hued flames and red-hot rocks that soared above his head as far as an archer's arrow-shot or even further. As if a living body, the mountain didn't always blow continuously but, after it let out a breath at any one time, it rested for a short while until it regained its wind. At that point he had the opportunity to look at what he wanted; but the mountain later erupted again and again with regular intermissions, on and on. Meanwhile the caverns were heard groaning within, and the mountain trembled with thunderings under foot, to the great alarm and consternation of those present. Hence it seems remarkable that none of the loud crashings that were noticed in the calm conditions on that occasion was heard by us when the winds were blowing so fiercely.

30 **B. B.** That shouldn't seem remarkable, son, as it isn't at all extraordinary. For it's well established by the written tradition on the subject that Etna's breathing pattern changes along with the winds. When a given wind blows, Etna may breathe out only clouds of smoke and dark vapor, but when that wind subsides, it gives off flames that are sometimes clear, sometimes a bit murky, depending on the nature of the freshening winds. Occasionally also streams of fire gush forth in floods of varying kinds, according to whether the material accumulated within the mountain's innards is rich or meager. This being so, who would reject the possibility that those thunderings inside the mountain are stirred by the mildest breeze of a single wind, though they couldn't be stirred by another wind even it were raging? What needs to be considered isn't how a

45. See on Urbano (*c.* 1442–1524) Chapter 2 pp. 85–9, 100–1 and Chapter 7 pp. 277–8.

46. Presumably on June 1, 1493: cf. §46 below, and see Chapter 2 pp. 86–7.

se in cavernas illius inque viscera insinuet, est spectandum.

31 **B. F.** Intra montem igitur tu, tanquam intra pectus animam, sic accipi ab Aetna ventos putas, quibus illa modo spirat leniter, modo vehementius incitatur?

B. P. Sane quidem, nisi tamen veriora illa sunt, quae de Typhoeo, deque Encelado poetarum fabulositas concinnavit.

B. F. Verissima illa quidem fabella est; sed perge tu mihi atque etiam, pater, huius incendii causas redde, si placet: nam ex incolis quidem inventus est nemo, qui ea nobis paulo verius explicaret.

B. P. Pergam, ut libet; sed non prius id faciam, quam mihi dixeris, quomodo illud sit, quod tu verissimam fabellam dixisti.

B. F. Quia sane ea demum verissima fabula est, quae nihil habet veritatis.

B. P. Pulchre nimirum; atque isto modo ego etiam dicere historiam falsissimam possum, ut ea sit demum falsissime historia, quae falsi habeat nihil.

32 **B. F.** Non sequitur istud, pater; sed nos dialecticen e captiosis sophistarum circulis coronisque ne avocemus: satis enim habet illic negotii. Quare age, mi pater; explana potius illa nobis, quae petimus: ea incendia unde oriantur et orta quomodo perdurent.

B. P. Tu vero postulas etiam sine dialecticis philosophari; quod quidem ipsum fieri quam possit, vel alio tempore ex te ipso cognosces vel cum voles audies de me. Nunc vero age, philosophemur. Interea tamen paulisper hoc in cespite considamus. Neque enim ullis adhuc Nonianis legibus cautum est, ne quis temere quoquo in cespite considat, quemadmodum olim urbanis ne quoquo in solio; et ego iam deambulando defessus sum.

B. F. Tu vero quiesce, ut libet et quandiu libet; ego autem et stare adhuc possum libentius et te ita melius auscultabo.

33 **B. P.** Et quidem hoc etiam licet; sed quoniam ita vis ut, quibus de ignibus ego te antea interrogaram, de iis tu me nunc audias disserentem, brevi expediam quae sentio; neque enim nimis multa sunt. Tellus quidem omnis, Bembe fili, sicuti nostra corpora, foraminibus canalibusque distincta est et tanquam venis internotata; sive quod omnino coire non potest, quae specie quidem multum sibimet differat intra sese; sive quod aut gignit ipsa semper aliquid aut interimit et immutat, neque unum idem omnis atque eodem permanet; sive ut alii tradidere, et quidem principes in philosophia viri, quia plane vivit ipsa atque a mundi anima vitam trahens ab eadem

given wind blows across Etna, but how it enters the mountain and works its way into its hollows and innermost parts.[47]

31 **P. B.** So you think that, inside the mountain, the winds are taken in by Etna like breath within the chest? And that through these winds it sometimes breathes gently, and sometimes it's more violently aroused?

B. B. Yes indeed—unless there's more truth in the fabulous inventions that poets concoct about Typhoeus and Enceladus.[48]

P. B. Certainly, that's a very true fable. But go on, please, father, and tell me the causes of this fire as well; for I found no one among the locals who could give us a somewhat more reliable explanation.

B. B. I shall, as you wish, but not before you've told me what you meant by your words "a very true fable."

P. B. That which is doubtless ultimately a very true fable is that which contains no truth.

B.B. Neatly put, to be sure; and in the same way I can also speak of "very false history," to the effect that history is ultimately at its most false when it contains no falsehood.

32 **P. B.** That doesn't follow, father. But let's not divert logic away from the captious rings and circles of sophist types; she has enough to keep her busy there. Come on, then, father, explain to me rather what I'm after: where do these fires come from, and, once they've come into being, how do they keep going?

B. B. In truth you're asking me to philosophize, but without dialectical techniques. How that could happen you'll either learn for yourself at some point or you'll hear from me when you're prepared to listen. But as it is, come, let's be philosophers. While we do so, however, let's sit down on this grass for a short time. There's nothing yet in any laws of Noniano stipulating that you can't casually sit where you like on the grass, as was once the case with city laws against sitting in just any seat; and I'm tired now from walking about.

P. B. You rest as you please, and for as long as you please. But I can still keep standing, and I'd rather it so; in that way I'll hear you better.

33 **B. B.** And that too is permitted. But since you now so want to hear me discuss the fires that I'd questioned you about previously, I'll set out what I think in just a few words, as I've not too much to say.[49] The entire earth, son, like our bodies, is partitioned by cavities and channels, and as if marked out by veins, whether because it has a great diversity of form within itself and it cannot therefore altogether coalesce as a whole; or because the earth by itself is always generating something, or destroying and changing it, so that in its entirety it never persists as one and the same thing, or to the same end; or, as others have related, indeed among them the leading figures in philosophy, because it is clearly alive itself and, drawing its existence from the World

---

47. In terms of "the written tradition" to which Bernardo alludes early in §30, see on this last point esp. Lucr. *DRN* 6.682–93, *Aetna* 282–384.

48. For the divergent Greco-Roman traditions locating either Typhoeus or Enceladus under Etna, Chapter 1 p. 35 and n.32.

49. On the sources informing Bernardo's ensuing discourse, Chapter 6 pp. 253–5.

mundi anima extra intraque perlustratur. **34** Sed in omni tellure nuspiam maiores fistulae aut meatus ampliores sunt, quam iis in locis, quae vel mari vicina sunt vel a mari protenus alluuntur. Nam cum exedit semper mare consumitque suopte contactu suaque natura omnia, tum autem, si partem est nactum aliquam debiliorem membraque non adeo robusta telluris, erodit illa multo facillime pergitque in viscera ipsa, quam potest. Itaque cum in aliena regna sibi viam faciat, ventis etiam facit: ex quo fit, ut loca quaeque maritima maxime terraemotibus subiecta sint, parum mediterranea. Quod si etiam in sulfuris venas venti furentes inciderint, tum incendia suscitantur sane non difficulter, quoniam et in sulfure concipiendi permagna ignis vis inest et venti etiam aliena succendunt vi sua. Haec autem tu ut in Aetna accidant omnia, vide, quippe, ut modo tute dixisti, quae mare in radicibus habeat, quae sulfurea sit, quae cavernosa, seu quod natura ita fuerit semper ipsa, seu quod salo aliquando subexesa ventos admiserit aestuantes, per quos idonea flammae materies incenderetur. **35** Habes, unde incendia oriantur Aetnae tuae; habe nunc quomodo etiam orta perdurent. In quo quidem nolo ego te illud admirari, quod vulgus solet: magnum esse scilicet tantas flammas, tam immensos ignes post hominum memoriam semper habuisse, quo alerentur. Quid est enim magnum ipsi magistrae rerum omnium et parenti naturae? quid arduum? quid illa tandem non potest? Qui stellas, qui solem, qui coeli convexa, qui terras omnes ac maria, qui mundum denique ipsum, quo nihil est admirabilius, vel potius extra quem nihil est quod admireris, saepe sine admiratione intuemur, iisdem nobis esse Aetna miraculum potest? Cave sis iam imprudens, fili, ut tu id putes. Nam si naturam respicimus, nihil in Aetna est, quod mirum voces. Si rem consideramus ipsam, nonne tibi etiam mira videantur cum alia loca permulta, tum vel Aponi nostri fontes calidaeque illae purissimae, quibus natura non tantum ut calefacerent dedit, quod erat tamen ab aquis alienum, sed multum de iure quoque rerum omnium concessit, multum de nostro, tum aliquid de deorum etiam et suo, ut morbis scilicet mederentur non modo sine ullo aegri dolore, qua de causa graeco verbo Aponus nomen invenit, sed etiam cum voluptate? Itaque qui curantur,

Non venas reserant, (ut ait ille), nec vulnere vulnera sanant
Pocula nec tristi gramine mista bibunt:
Amissum lymphis reparant impune vigorem
Pacaturque aegro luxuriante dolor.

Soul, it is permeated both within and without by this same World Soul.[50] **34** But nowhere in the entire earth are the cavities or channels larger than in those places that are either near the sea or continuously washed by it. For through the contact it makes, and by its very nature, the sea always erodes and devours everything; if, moreover, it comes across some weaker section where the earth's body isn't so durable, it eats away at it with the greatest of ease and moves on to its innermost parts as it can. And so when it makes a path for itself into foreign territory, it does so for the winds as well; as a result, all places near the sea are especially prone to earthquakes, but inland places not particularly so. But if the raging winds also come upon veins of sulfur, then fires are started really quite easily, since sulfur has a very great capacity for catching fire, and winds too, through their own force, set other substances on fire. Observe for yourself how all this happens in Etna's case: as you said just now, it has the sea at its base, it is sulfurous, and it is full of hollows, whether because it was always naturally like that, or because it was periodically eroded by the sea and gave access to the raging winds so that flammable matter was set on fire. **35** There you have how the fires of your Etna come into being; now for how they persist once they've started. On this matter I don't want you to marvel at what usually amazes most people—that it's astonishing that flames of such dimensions and such boundless fires have always had, from the dawning of human memory, a source of supply to feed them. For what is challenging, what difficult, for nature herself, the ruler and parent of everything? What, after all, is she incapable of? We often look without wonder at the stars, the sun, the vault of the heavens, all the lands and seas—in short, at the world itself, which is more wondrous than anything, or, rather, leaves nothing apart from it for you to wonder at: can Etna possibly be an object of wonder to us, those same people? Mind you don't be so foolish, son, as to believe so; for if we look carefully at nature, there's nothing in Etna for you to call wonderful. If we consider the essence of the matter, wouldn't very many other places also seem wondrous to you, and in particular the hot, exceptionally pure springs of our own Aponus?[51] Nature not only bestowed on those springs the capacity to generate heat (a capacity foreign to water), but granted much in the way of power over all things as well—much in the way of our human power, but something of the power of the gods also, and of its own power: to the effect, I of course mean, that they cure diseases, and not only without any pain for the person afflicted (Aponus took its name from a Greek word for that reason),[52] but even with enjoyment. And so, as the poet says, those who are treated there

> open not their veins nor heal their wounds with wounds,
> nor do they drink down draughts mixed with bitter herbs;
> through the waters, they restore their lost strength with no harm done,
> and the patient flourishes as the pain is quelled.[53]

---

50. Platonic in character (cf. *Tim.* 34b–37c with Guthrie [1978] 292–9 on "the soul of the cosmos"), albeit presumably mediated here through Ficino, who (like the Neoplatonists) interpreted the World-Soul of the *Timaeus* as the soul of the all: see, conveniently, M. J. B. Allen (2002) 172 with Hirai (2002) 266–76.

51. Now the spa resort of Abano Terme, near Padua: Chapter 6 pp. 248–9.

52. Aponus from ἄπονος, lit. "without toil or pain"; an alluring etymology already attested by Cassiodorus (*Var.* 2.39.4), but the truer derivation appears to be from the Indo-European root *ap-*, indicating water (Fuoco [2008] 124 on Claud. *Carm. min.* 26.90).

53. Claudian, *Carm. min.* 26.97–100.

36 Nam morbos quidem expellere hominum plane est rerum usum multarum recte callentium; hoc autem, vel sine dolore id efficere, vel, quod multo est maximum, etiam cum voluptate, deorum mihi quidem videtur esse proprium ipsiusque principis omnium et parentis naturae. Quod si cum uno Aponi fonticulo et canali profunda illa comparaveris inundationesque omnes Aetnae tuae, fortasse non verear, ne noster hic colliculus tuo illo monte sit minor. **37** Sed faciam, ut tibi pollicitus sum, et Aetnae incendia, quomodo alantur, docebo. Quoniam igitur, ut scis, humore et calore omnia concipiuntur, cum et semper ardeat mons et semper a mari perlustretur, habes iam duobus istis verbis, quod petis. Ignis enim, qui detrahit semper aliquid atque consumit, gignit etiam semper aliquid sibi, quod consumat, suo ipsius calore humectantibus undis tellurem semperque igni materiam sufficientibus, quo alatur. Nam et bitumen maxime, quod sulfuri simillimum est, fit ex terra et limo exudante tellure: tum et eiusdem fere generis halumen, quod, quia ex salo et terra conficitur, ita vocatur.

38 **B. F.** Unde autem saxa et pumices, pater, et eiectamenta illa, quae vomit? Quid illa tandem sunt? an sulfur tantum, bitumen, halumen omnia?

B. P. Nequaquam, fili, sed tanta est vis ignium, praesertim inclusorum, et ventis intus furentibus, ut non viscera imbecilla modo, sed plane nervi etiam fortiores corripiantur telluris et saxa ipsa durissima liquefiant.

B. F. At ea ipsa saxa non aliquando defecisse, montemque sibi non subsedisse, nonne illud est mirum, pater?

B. P. Neque id, fili, quidem mirum. Tellus enim semper foecunda est sui ipsius semperque semet ipsa parturit; nisi tamen malis tu cum Pythagora sentire, qui quidem apud Ovidium ita praecipiens inducitur, ut audeat affirmare Aetnae incendia non esse usquequaque duratura.

B. F. Ego vero, quid sentiam, non sat scio; quanquam equidem mallem Pythagoram quam Empedoclem imitari: ille enim quae naturae consentanea videbantur, credebat asserens mutari quidem omnia, nihil tamen omnino interire; hic, dum curiosius naturae causas perscrutatur, etiam se ipsum imperscrutabilem facit.

B. P. Sed valere nos illos sinamus, fili, et quoniam nos tibi Aetnae incendia unde fiant, diximus, id velim ego scire item ex te, ipsa ista quomodo fluant.

39 **B. F.** Iam istud quidem fieri sine ullo negotio potest vel una Hesiodi comparatione, qua ille in sua Theogonia fluxisse ait tellurem, ubi eam post fulminatum Typhoeum igne correptam describit isto, ni fallor modo. Ex quo sane libet mihi suspicari etiam pastorem illum Ascraeum aliquando Aetnam conscendisse atque inde sibi

36 It's certainly the role of people who are properly skilled in the application of many resources to banish disease; but to do so either painlessly or (by far the greatest achievement) even with enjoyment is in my view the prerogative of the gods and of nature herself, the ruler and parent of everything. But if you compare the famous depths of your Etna and all its vast floods with the single little spring and channel of Aponus, perhaps I wouldn't be afraid that this little hill of ours is smaller than that mountain of yours. **37** But I'll do as I promised you, and demonstrate how Etna's fires are fed. So then, since, as you know, everything is produced from water and heat, and since the mountain is always burning and is always being washed by the sea, you already have your answer in those two words. Fire, which is always doing away with something and devouring it, is also always creating for itself something for it to devour; it does so by its own heat, with the waters moistening the earth and forever providing fuel for the fire so that it is fed. For bitumen in particular, which very closely resembles sulfur, is created from earth and from slime that oozes out of the ground; and then alum is of a very similar nature, and is so called because it's formed from sea water and earth.

38 P. B. But where do the rocks and pumice stones come from, father, and all the spewings that the mountain vomits forth? What are they really? Or are they all just sulfur, bitumen, alum?

B. B. Not at all, son. No, such is the strength of the fires, especially when they are confined and the winds are raging within, that it's not just the earth's weak innermost parts that are overcome, but evidently the stronger sinews as well, and the hardest rocks are themselves melted.

P. B. But the fact that the rocks themselves haven't at some point run out, and that the mountain hasn't collapsed upon itself—isn't that remarkable, father?

B. B. No, son, that's not remarkable either. For the earth is forever pregnant with itself and always self-reproducing—unless you prefer to agree with Pythagoras. According to Ovid, he was moved in his teaching to dare claim that Etna's fires wouldn't always keep going.[54]

P. B. I'm really not sure what I think, though I for one would rather imitate Pythagoras than Empedocles. For Pythagoras asserted the belief that everything that appeared to be in accordance with nature was subject to change, but that nothing would completely perish; whereas in investigating the causes of natural phenomena more diligently, Empedocles makes himself impenetrable as well.[55]

B. B. Let's take our leave of them, son. Since we've said where your fires of Etna come from, I'd like to know in turn from you just how those outpourings you mentioned flow along.

39 P. B. That can easily be achieved right now perhaps through a single simile of Hesiod's by which, in his *Theogony*, he says that the earth melted in just the way you mean, if I'm not mistaken; this when he describes the earth being set on fire after Typhoeus was blasted by a lightning-bolt.[56] From this, I'm inclined to suspect even that that famous shepherd from Ascra had at some point climbed Etna,

---

54. Ovid, *Met.* 15.340–55, on which Chapter 1 pp. 54–8.

55. For Empedocles (*c.* 490–30), his Sicilian origins, his presence in Lucretius' *De rerum natura*, and his alleged death by leaping into Etna, Chapter 1 pp. 41–3. For his reputation as a philosopher-poet of a taxing, near mystical opacity, see, e.g., Aristot. *Gen. corr.* 315a3–4, *Mete.* 357a24–32, *Eth. Nic.* 1147a19–22, *Rh.* 1407a31–7 with Guthrie (1965) 135–7 and Kingsley (1995) 43 and n.26.

56. See Chapter 1 p. 29.

sumpsisse, quod de universa tellure scriptum reliquit,

Uritur ipsa ingens tellus aestuque furente
Liquitur, albentis quondam ceu lamina plumbi
Arte virum, flammisque cava fornace liquescit,
Seu ferrum, quanquam hoc maternae viscera rupis
In duras aluere vires, cum ferbuit olim
Vulcani domitum manibus, terraeque fatiscit.

40 Et quidem propterea illum ego plumbi et ferri exempla posuisse crediderim, ut alteri ea compararet, quae igne facilius corripiuntur et fluunt, ut sulfurea tellus omnis et eae telluris partes quae tenuiores sunt, alteri autem cum saxa omnia, tum ea quae flammae resistunt magis et sunt suapte natura duriora.

B. P. Mihi haec quidem certe non displicent ipsa per se, atque etiam delectavit me non nihil poetae ingenium, qui tam apte descripserit fluentem et ardentem tellurem; sed tamen tu, fili, nimium perparce respondes ad illa quae peto: non modo enim istud ita simpliciter cupio, ea incendia quomodo fluant, scire abs te, sed etiam, ubi descenderint, quam faciem capiant: tum si perdurant eadem semper an aliquando immutentur, audire.

41 **B. F.** Geram tibi morem, pater, et ea quae postulas, ut potero, explicabo. Pleno iam partu, ut maturior est omnis foetus, quicunque in Aetnae matris utero coalescit, nisu parientis expellitur et eiectatur quacunque prius rimam invenerit aut viam sibi paraverit vi sua: saepe tamen exit ex cratere, quem ipsi vidimus; nunquam ex superiore, quod vel eo inscendere gravis materia non queat, vel, quia inferius alia spiramenta sunt, non sit opus. Despumant igitur flammis urgentibus ignei rivi pigro fluxu totas delambentes plagas; ii paulatim recedente calore priorem sibi naturam reposcentes, in lapidem indurescunt fragilem sane flammis enervantibus et, si complectas, putrem. Stat ea confluvies veluti glacies concreta, usque ut alteri descendant rivi. Ii nanque non suprafluunt, sed inter montis arenosam cutem et priora concreta fluenta insinuantes sese cursum sibi medium quaerunt. **42** Sic quae prius induruerant, quia friabilia sunt, ut dixi, novis incendiis cedentia crepant et in partes disiecta prosiliunt quacunque unda deurgens interfluit; deinde conglaciantem eam altera subiit illuvies, atque ipsa tantundem facit, tum altera item et altera. Non enim continuato fluore mons, sed per intermissos spiritus, ut supra commemoravimus, eructatur; atque ita novissimis semper vincentibus multiplicatoque in immensum incendio ex igneis fluminibus fracti lapides altissimo congestu magnam partem

and that he took from there the lines that he wrote about the entire earth:

> The vast earth itself is burning, and with the raging heat
> it melts, just as sometimes a strip of tin is melted
> in the hollow furnace by the flames and by the smithies' skill;
> or iron, although the vitals of the rock that mothered it
> have nurtured it to hard strength, when once it has glowed,
> it is tamed by Vulcan's hands, and splits apart on the ground.[57]

40 Moreover, I'd have thought that he cited the examples of tin and iron so that he could compare to the former those substances that are more easily set on fire and melted, such as all of the earth that is sulfurous and those parts of it that are rather weak; and compare to the latter all rocks, and also those elements that are more resistant to fire and naturally more robust.

B. B. I certainly don't find those lines unpleasing in and of themselves, and I take considerable pleasure in the poet's knack for describing so adroitly the earth's melting and burning. But you're giving me far too little in answer to my question, son: I want so very straightforwardly to know from you not just how those fires flow along, but also what appearance they take on when they've flowed down the mountain; and then to hear if they always persist in the same way or at some point undergo change.

41 P. B. I'll do as you say, father, and set out what you want to know as best I can. When the time for the birth is fully due, and just as every fetus is more than ready to be born, whatever fetus has grown to term in mother Etna's womb is forced out by her straining as she gives birth, and it's pushed out wherever it has first found a fissure or made a passage for itself by its own effort. It often emerges from the crater that we saw for ourselves,[58] but never from the upper crater, either because heavy matter can't rise to that point or because it doesn't have to, since there are other vents lower down. Driven on by the flames, then, streams of fire leave foam-like deposits as they lick whole areas all over with their sluggish flow. But as their heat gradually dwindles, they seek to reclaim their former nature and harden into a rock that's really quite brittle because the flames have weakened it; it crumbles if you hold it. That flood stands hardened like ice, to the extent that another series of streams runs down [past it]. For in fact the latter don't flow over [the previous flood], but they seek an in-between course for themselves as they make their way amidst the sandy crust of the mountain and the hardened floods from before. **42** In this way, because (as I've said) they easily crumble, the floods that have hardened before give way to the new fires with a sharp crack, and they're split apart and driven in all directions, wherever the wave exerts its pressure as it flows in between them. Then, as that fresh inundation hardens, another succeeds it and does the same thing itself, and then another likewise, and another; for (as I mentioned previously)[59] the mountain doesn't belch forth in a continuous stream, but with pauses for breath. And so the latest floods always prevail in this way, and as the flames expand over

---

57. Hes. *Theog.* 861–6; on Pietro's rendition, Chapter 6 pp. 257–9.

58. See §26 above.

59. §29 above.

montis inoccuparunt; atque ii, quo recentius fluxere, eo et nigriores sunt et firmiores, aetate et pallescunt et resolvuntur. Inde ego esse arenarum plagas omnis, quae circa cacumen visuntur, existimo. Materies omnis aridissima est, atque ideo minus multo, quam vivi lapides, ponderosa: scabra adeo, ut brevi mora, tanquam a lima, inscendentibus calcei exedantur.

B. P. Atqui ego sane in eo mallem Empedoclem imitari, qui ascensurus amyclis aereis utebatur; sed sequere.

43 **B. F.** Ea infra parvum craterem circumversus totum montem complexa est, et cumulum eum, in quo maior crater est, sustinet; demittitur inde alicubi per intervalla imum in montem obliquis fluxibus, quaque Catana iacet, usque in mare, lata saepe qua visus patet, horrendum sane spectaculum modo alveis hiantibus modo impendentibus ripis. Inter maxima profluvia longe memorabile illud est, quod paulo ante nostram aetatem usque intra Catanam decurrens non parvam urbis partem incendio depopulavit: neque sane descensus is minus quam per ducenta stadia conficitur. Quin etiam portum eum de quo ait Virgilius:

> Portus ab accessu ventorum immotus et ingens
> Ipse, sed horrificis iuxta tonat Aetna ruinis,

ita implevere fluenta Aetnaea, ut iam errasse Virgilium putes, quod portum ibi esse ingentem dixerit, qui pene nullus siet.

B. P. Istud nimirum est, quod a principio dixeras cedere illis volentibus atque eorum contrahi ardoribus ipsum mare.

44 **B. F.** Est ita quidem, ut dicis; sed, ut ad propositum revertamur, reptare per eas crepidines, quas dixi, duobus milibus passuum necesse est quemvis craterem visuros: reliquum iter in equis conficitur. Reptationis eius labor haud facile credas quam durus est quamque indigens virentis genu; quippe quia degravante viatore temere ingesti lapides concedunt et in ascensu raptissimo, ni probe posueris pedem, dimoto uno tota congeries devolvitur et in te ipsum ruit. Adde quod etiam, si in plano cecideris, laedunt scabritie sua, et manus crebro contactu, nisi contexeris, offenduntur. Magna haec fortasse videbuntur, pater, audienti tibi; magna enim sunt, ut mihi quidem videri solet, verum nusquam adeo ac nobis videntibus fuere: nam Aetna quanta est, nemo quidem scit, qui non videt. Ex summo vertice contemplari totam insulam licet: termini eius longe esse multo minus videntur quam sunt. Brutia ora ita tibi sub oculis iacet, ut eo posse traiicere pene quidem iactu lapidis putes;

a vast area, the shattered stones from the streams of fire are heaped into piles of very great height that cover a large part of the mountain. The more recent their flow, the stones are both blacker and more robust, but in time they lose their color and start to crumble; this explains, I think, all the stretches of sand that are to be seen around the summit. The basic substance is very dry in its entirety, and for that reason it's much less weighty than stones in their natural state; and it's so rough that the climbers' shoes are soon worn away as if by a file.

B. B. Well then, in that respect I'd certainly prefer to emulate Empedocles, who wore boots of bronze to make his climb.[60] But go on.

43 P. B. This sandy material has covered the whole mountain all around below the small crater, and it supports the mound that houses the larger crater. From here, in some places, it descends at intervals in zigzag flows to the foot of the mountain and, in the vicinity of Catania, all the way to the sea; it is often carried as far as the eye can see, and it's truly an awesome sight, now with its gaping hollows, now with its towering banks. Among its greatest flowings, especially noteworthy is the one shortly before our time[61] that ran all the way down into Catania and devastated a considerable part of the city by fire; indeed, its downward movement covered no less than twenty-five miles. Moreover, that harbor, which Virgil describes as

> a haven out of the winds' reach, undisturbed and vast
> in itself, but nearby Etna thunders with dreadful eruptions,[62]

was so filled up with Etna's outflows that you'd imagine by now that Virgil was mistaken in calling the harbor there vast, given that it now scarcely exists.

B. B. I suppose that's what you meant when you'd said from the outset[63] that the sea itself had to yield to the will of the flows and was diminished by their heat.

44 P. B. Yes, it's just as you say. But, to return to the subject,[64] if you want to see any crater you please, you need to crawl for two miles across the shelves I've described; the rest of the journey is made on horseback. It's hard to believe just how taxing is the effort of making that crawl, and how wanting your knees are even if you're fit. This is because the stones are heaped up haphazardly and give way when the traveler weighs down on them; and, during a very hurried ascent, if you haven't positioned your foot correctly, the dislodging of a single stone means that the entire mass rolls down and descends on top of you. Moreover, if you fall over on level ground, the stones hurt you because of their roughness of texture, and, unless you cover your hands, their repeated contact with the rock injures them. All this will perhaps seem impressive as you hear tell of it, father; for it is impressive, and I'm used to thinking it so, but it's nowhere near as impressive as when I saw it in person, as no one who doesn't see Etna can know its dimensions. From the very top of the mountain you can look upon the whole island, and its furthest points seem much less distant than they really are. The Bruttian coast[65] lies before your

60. For the legend of the brazen sandals, Chapter 1 p. 43 and n.61.

61. For the dating of this eruption (1444, 1408, even 1381?), Introduction p. 6 and n.21.

62. *Aeneid* 3.570–1, on which Chapter 6 p. 264.

63. In §10 above.

64. In §42 above.

65. See p. 319 n.14.

serena tempestate Neapolitani etiam tractus extimantur. Nivibus per hyemem fere totus mons canet: cacumen neque per aestatem viduatur.

B. P. Quid, quod hyemare tantum eas meminit Strabo?

45 **B. F.** At experientia ita te docet, ususque ipse auctor, quod quidem venia illius dixerim, non deterior. Quare illud, mi pater, etiam atque etiam vide, ne quid te moveat, si aliqua ex parte huius nostri de Aetna sermonis cum vetustis scriptoribus dissentimus. Nihil enim impedit fuisse tum ea omnia, quae ipsi olim tradidere, quorum permanserint plurima in nostram diem, quaedam se immutaverint, aliqua etiam surrexerint nova. Nam, ut caetera omittam, quod cinerosa partim esse summa cacumina dictavere, eius rei nunc vestigium nullum apparet. Cinis enim, qui queat conspici, toto monte nullus est. Neque id tamen omnibus annis fuit: nam multorum testimonio accepimus, qui videre, annos ab hinc quadraginta tantos ex Aetna cineres evolasse, ut per totam eam insulae partem, quae versus Pelorum iacet, universam oleam abstulerint, eos etiam in Italiam ventis ferentibus latos. **46** Sed, ut ad nives illas redeamus, addebat idem Urbanus kalendis iuniis ascendente se satis largiter abundeque ninxisse; tum iterum, qui septimus fuerit post eum diem, dum ipse Randatii moraretur, in universam montanam plagam nives fere in pedis altitudinem descendisse: in quo ipso licet et Pindarum suspicere, scite cognomento usum, qui Aetnam nivium nutricem appellarit. **47** Quo latere subest Catana, media fere inter ipsam et cacumen regione purissimus et perennis fons erumpit dorico vocabulo Crana ab incolis appellata. Caeterum toto monte supra radices nullae aquae sunt, nisi quae vel ex nivibus emanant, cuius quidem rei etiam Theocritum testem habemus, in quo dum Galateae Cyclops enumerat divitias suas haec etiam interserit:

Est glacialis aquae rivus mihi quem sylvosa
Nectareum in potum nivibus fluit Aetna solutis

eyes, so near that you'd think it could be reached almost by a stone's throw; in clear weather even the region around Naples is thought visible. Throughout the winter almost the whole mountain is white with snow, and the peak isn't without it even throughout the summer.

B. B. What of the fact that Strabo records that there's snow only in winter?[66]

45 P. B. But firsthand inquiry tells you that it lasts, as does practical experience, which is no lesser an authority (if Strabo will pardon me for saying so). And so, father, watch out again and again that you're not upset if I disagree with the ancient writers in any aspect of our present discussion of Etna. There's no reason that, at that time, all was not as they recounted it long ago, of which a very great deal has persisted down to our own day, certain things have changed, and even some new features have arisen. To offer but one example, they've repeatedly asserted that the topmost peaks are partly covered with ashes,[67] but there's no trace of this phenomenon now; for on the entire mountain there are no ashes to be seen. But this has not always been the case through the years: we've learnt from the evidence of many eyewitnesses that, forty years ago,[68] so much ash was discharged from Etna that it destroyed the entire olive crop throughout the whole part of the island extending toward Pelorus, and that it was carried along by the winds to Italy as well. **46** But, to return to those snows, that same Urbano[69] added that when he was making his ascent on June 1,[70] it snowed plentifully enough and in large quantities; and then a second time, while he was staying at Randazzo a week later, snow fell almost to the depth of a foot over the entire expanse of the mountain. On this matter you can also appreciate Pindar's knowing choice of soubriquet when he called Etna "nurse of snows."[71] **47** On the side above Catania, roughly at the midpoint between the town and the summit, a spring gushes forth that is exceptionally clear and flows throughout the year; the locals call it by its Doric name, Crana.[72] Otherwise, nowhere on the whole mountain is there any water above the foothills, apart from that derived from the snows. Our witness on this point is Theocritus, in whom the Cyclops includes the following when he lists his riches to Galatea:

> I have a stream of icy water that wooded Etna sets in flow
> from her melting snows for a drink sweet as nectar.[73]

---

66. Str. 6.2.8; but for Pietro's allusion to the elder Pliny (cf. *HN* 2.236 for Etna snow covered in winter) as well as Strabo in the second edition of 1530, Chapter 3 p. 143.

67. Cf. Str. 6.2.3 (= Posid. fr. 234 E-K), 6.2.8 ("The upper districts are bare and ash-like"; those who recently made the climb "found at the top a level plain . . . enclosed by an embankment of ashes to the height of a house-wall . . .").

68. Presumably (Viallon [2002] 57 n.67) the major event of 1444, some *fifty* years before Pietro's climb.

69. See §28 above.

70. I.e., "a few days before" Pietro's ascent: see §28 above and n.46.

71. *Pyth.* 1.20: νιφόεσσ' Αἴτνα, πάνετες χιόνος ὀξείας τιθήνα.

72. I.e., Κράνα (*LSJ* s.v. κρήνη).

73. *Idyll* 11.47–8; on Pietro's rendering, Chapter 6 p. 265 and n.159.

aut si quae intra fagorum truncos pluviis descendentibus relinquuntur. **48** Atqui res et locus me monuere ut quod ibi vidimus pulcherrimum naturae opus et mirati fuimus maxime, non praeterirem. Altissima in specula, qua sylva deficiente liberior prospectus in insulam et Tyrrhena fluenta dominatur, herbidus campus leni decumbit clivo: hunc pini procerae pari distantes intervallo ducta corona circunsepiunt. In medio fagus densissima quadrifido robore se subiiciens celsior quam caeterae veluti regina ipsa consurgit. Ea non statim ex imo discriminatur, sed a tellure per spatium cubitalem [*sic*] uno trunco contenta est: inde se in ramos consimiles aequalibus intervallis dispartitur. Interne usque ad imas radices arbor deficiens undis pluvialibus urnam ex sese facit: illae montano purgante aere ac umbris solem arcentibus et fontanis gelidiores sunt et putealibus puriores. Ambigeres ibi tu quidem, pater, si quid eorum tibi laudandum esset, quidnam potissimum laudares, an prospectum eius loci an locum, tum an arborem an undas: ita scite in alteris decorandis, quasi quidem id agerent, ut quid magis pulchrum esset ambigeretur, et Hamadryas et Nais convenere. In honestandis vero alteris admirabile quidem est, quantum gratiae venustatisque sibi invicem afferant Iupiter Genio et Genius Iovi: quo fit ut in utrisque multum Venus etiam permista sentiatur.

49 B. P. O pulchras naturae delicias vel etiam Deorum, ut poetis placet, si qui sunt qui eum montem colant.

B. F. Sunt, pater, ut aiunt, atque incolunt illo ipso quidem in loco.

B. P. Mirabar, si haec temere dicerentur provenire, praesertim a Siculis, quos quidem constat propter sermonis impunitatem et licentiam etiam trilingues vocatos. Sed quis inhabitat Deus?

B. F. Fauni esse fontem illum dicunt.

B. P. Fabellam te video inchoare; sed quoniam in Faunum incidimus, sequere: detineri enim me ab illo facile patior, cum quo te scio libenter etiam carminibus ludere interdum solere. Istud autem qui sciunt? an ita fortasse coniectantur?

There may also be some water left within the trunks of beech trees when the rains descend. **48** But I'm reminded by this topic and place not to pass over the most beautiful work of nature that I saw there and especially marveled at.[74] On a very high eminence, where the woods give way and the view is unlimited in its command of the island and the Tyrrhenian sea, a grassy expanse slopes downward with a gentle incline; this area is enclosed by tall pine trees that are the same distance apart, forming a circle. In the center, a beech tree that is very thick with foliage rises higher than the other trees, as if their queen; at its base, it rises from a trunk that is split in four, but it is not divided right away from its very lowest point. From the ground, it rises for about a foot and a half in a single trunk, and from that point it is divided up into branches that are of similar dimensions and even in their spacing. Inside it, and all the way down to its deepest roots, the tree is hollow, and forms a vessel for rainwater; because the mountain air cleanses it and the shade wards off the sun, that water is both colder than spring water and cleaner than water drawn from a well. You'd be unsure there, father, if you had to praise any of these features, which you'd praise above all—the view from the place or the place itself, then the tree itself or its waters. So skillfully have the wood nymph and the river nymph united to beautify both elements, as if their objective were to create uncertainty as to which was the more beautiful. In fact, in honoring both elements, it is indeed astonishing how much loveliness and charm they mutually offer each other, Jupiter to the spirit of the place, and the spirit of the place to Jupiter; hence Venus too is very much felt as an influence closely associated with both.

49 B. B. Oh how beautiful the delights of nature! Or even of the gods, as the poets have it—if there are gods who frequent that mountain.

P. B. There are, father, as people say, and they dwell in that very place.

B. B. I'd be surprised if such things were said to be happening just by accident, especially when it's said by the Sicilians; it's well known that they're also called triple tongued because of their unrestrained boldness of speech.[75] But what god lives there?

P. B. They say that it's the spring of Faunus.

B. B. I see that you're starting on a tale; but since we've stumbled upon Faunus, do carry on. I can easily put up with being detained by him, since I know that, every so often, you like to amuse yourself by sporting with him in verse.[76] But as for what you say of him, how do they know it? Or are they perhaps only inferring as much?

---

74. On this *locus amoenus* and its association with Classical pastoral, Chapter 6 pp. 266–7.

75. For triple-tongued Sicilians, Apul. *Met.* 11.5.2 (Isis termed "Stygian Proserpina" by the *Siculi trilingues*, i.e., speaking Greek, Latin, and Punic: *LS* 1899 s.v. *trilinguis* III). But in associating their trilingualism with "unrestrained boldness of speech," Bernardo perhaps wittily uses *trilingues* with a knowing allusion to Horace's monstrous Cerberus (*Carm.* 2.19.31–2, 3.11.20; cf. of Hecate at V. Fl. *Argon.* 7.184).

76. See §15 above and n.25; Chapter 6 pp. 266–8.

50 **B. F.** Videre se aiunt pastores ipsum Deum passim errantem per sylvas et pascua; tum etiam sedentem sub illis arboribus coronatum pinu et tacentem saepius, interdum tamen etiam fistula solantem amores. Sed continebo potius me hic, pater: levia enim ista sunt, et mihi loqui tecum, nisi reverenter, non licet. Quanquam quidem, si pergerem, faceremus ipsi hac in re, quod facere etiam reges in coenis solent, qui quidem inter apros et pavones, quibus abundant quotidie, interdum tamen et allium poscunt et betas. Neque sane animus noster vacare semper rebus severioribus potest, neque si vacet, tamen ex illis tam plenam capit iucunditatem, quam si ea ipsa remitteret interdum et mox non longo intervallo intermissa revocaret. Ita nos quidem nunc gravia illa philosophiae studia, quibus quidem certe id omne tempus soles, quod tibi per rempublicam licet, impertire, melius etiam fabellis istis levioribus condiremus, et quidem licet maxime vel in Noniano fabulari.

51 **B. P.** Sane quidem licet, dum illud tamen semper teneatur, ut cerato remige Sirenas, quod aiunt. Et profecto poeta ille sapientissimus nunquam Ulissi concessisset, quem prudentissimum semper facit, ut Sirenarum cantus audiret, nisi liceret etiam gravibus et sapientibus viris, quorum tamen in numero me non pono, minus seriis adesse interdum rebus et lusus captare non adeo severos; modo ne remiges audiant, hoc est ne sensus pateant voluptatibus, quibus et demulcentur ipsi semper et, nisi ratione occlusi sint, saepe etiam facillime capiuntur. Quod tibi esse faciundum in vita maxime semper censeo, Bembe fili: nam nisi te ita informaris, ut voluptatum illecebris animum impervium geras, non possum dicere quam multae tibi occurrent species earum, quae te non adolescentem modo, ut es nunc, demulcere possint et delinire ac iam etiam debellare et devincere, sed plane etiam virum. **52** Itaque illis aut magnanimiter imperandum est, quod fecerunt viri omnes magni et boni et ii, quos propterea deos etiam appellavere, vel omnino turpiter deserviendum; in quo quidem tu, si me audies, non committes ut reiecta continentia atque ipso amore virtutis ex illorum sis grege, de quibus praeclare Horatius

Nos numerus sumus et fruges consumere nati,
Sponsi Penelopes, nebulones, Alcinoique
In cute curanda plus aequo operata iuventus,
Quis pulchrum fuit in medios dormire dies et
Ad strepitum citharae cessantum ducere curam.

50 P. B. Shepherds say that they see the god himself wandering here and there throughout the woods and pastures; at other times he sits under those trees, garlanded with pine, more often in silence, but sometimes also seeking solace for his loves on his pipes. But I'd prefer to stop here, father; for these are frivolous matters, and it's not right for me to talk to you without proper consideration. However, if I were to carry on, we'd be doing in this situation what kings tend to do at banquets: amidst the boars and peacocks that are served in abundance every day, they sometimes nevertheless call for garlic and beets. To be sure, our minds cannot always apply themselves to more serious matters; and if they do apply themselves, they don't take from those matters such full enjoyment as they would if they occasionally rested from them, and later resumed them after they've been left for a short interval. Just so, we might do better at the moment to flavor those serious philosophical studies, to which I know you usually devote all the time that your state affairs allow you, with these lighter sorts of tale; and we're especially at liberty to indulge in such tales when we're at Noniano.

51 B. B. Certainly we are, provided that it's always held in check, like the Sirens (as they say) checked by the rowers having their ears stopped with wax.[77] And that wisest of poets would undoubtedly never have allowed Ulysses (whom he always portrays as extremely foreseeing) to listen to the Sirens' songs unless respected men of wisdom—and I don't count myself among them—were at liberty sometimes to attend to less serious matters, and to seek out rather less weighty amusements. Only let the oarsmen not hear; that is, let their faculties of perception not be exposed to the pleasures that are nevertheless always luring them, and by which they're often very easily won over unless they're restrained by reason. I think that this is what you've always got to do to the fullest degree in life, son; for unless you train yourself in such a way that your mind is rendered impervious to the charms of pleasures, you'll be assailed by countless forms of pleasure that can entrance and bewitch you, and in fact subdue and completely overcome you, not just as a young man, as you are now, but assuredly also when you're a grown man. **52** And so we either have to exercise control over them through our strength of will, as all great and good men have done, and also those who have been called "gods" for that very reason; or we must submit to the shame of being completely in thrall to them. If you'll heed my words on this matter, you won't make the mistake of casting off your self-control and your very love of virtue to join the herd of those whom Horace famously characterized:

> We are a mere cipher, born to devour the earth's crops,
> Penelope's suitors, worthless scoundrels, the sons of Alcinous,
> who spent more time than they should in looking after their looks;
> for whom it was a fine thing to sleep to midday, and to rest
> their idlers' cares to the sound of the lyre.[78]

---

77. See Homer, *Od.* 12.142–200.

78. Horace, *Epist.* 1.2.27–31.

Sed quoniam iam advesperascit, procedamus in atrium: nugae autem pastorales istae tuae sub umbris sunt potius et inter arbores, quam intra penates recensendae.

Quae cum dixisset et iam in atrium pervenissemus, ego finem loquendi feci, ille cogitabundus in bibliothecam perrexit.

But since evening is now approaching, let's move into the house—though those pastoral trifles of yours are better recounted in the shade amidst the trees than indoors.

When he'd said as much and we'd now reached the house, I brought our conversation to a close while he made his way to the library, and to his thoughts.

Bibliography

Adams, H. W. 1967. *Catalogue of Books Printed on the Continent of Europe, 1501–1600, in Cambridge Libraries*. 2 vols. Cambridge.

Agosti, G. 1986. 'Sui teleri perduti del Maggior Consiglio nel Palazzo Ducale di Venezia." *Ricerche di storia dell'arte* 30: 61–87.

Agostini, T. and Lippi, E. eds. 1997. *Tra commediografi e letterati: Rinascimento e Settecento veneziano. Studi per Giorgio Padoan*. Ravenna.

Aikema, B., Lauber, R., and Seidel, M. eds. 2005. *Il collezionismo a Venezia e nel Veneto ai tempi della Serenissima*. Venice.

Aldrich, R. and Wotherspoon, G. eds. 2002. *Who's Who in Gay and Lesbian History: From Antiquity to World War II*. 2nd ed. London.

Alexander, P. J. 1976. "Gregory of Nyssa and the Simile of the Banquet of Life." *Vigiliae Christianae* 30.1: 55–62.

Alexander, W. H. 1951. "An Interrupted Letter." *Classical Philology* 46.4: 240.

Alfieri, V. E. 1981. *De Aetna: Il testo di Pietro Bembo tradotto e presentato da Vittorio Enzo Alfieri; Note di Marcello Carapezza e Leonardo Sciascia; Iconografia*. Palermo.

Allen, K. 1899. *The Treatment of Nature in the Poetry of the Roman Republic (Exclusive of Comedy). Bulletin of the University of Wisconsin, Philology and Literature Series* 1.2: 89–219.

Allen, M. J. B. 2002. "Life as a Dead Platonist." In Allen and Rees. 159–78.

Allen, M. J. B. and Rees, V. eds. 2002. *Marsilio Ficino: His Theology, His Philosophy, His Legacy*. With Davies, M. Brill's Studies in Intellectual History 108. Leiden.

Allés Torrent, S. 2012. "Alfonso de Palencia y el humanismo italiano." *Cuadernos de Filologia Italiana* 19: 107–30.

Altman, W. H. F. ed. 2015. *Brill's Companion to the Reception of Cicero*. Leiden.

Amert, K. 2008. "Stanley Morison's Aldine Hypothesis Revisited." *Design Issues* 24.2: 53–71.

Amran, D. W. 1909. *The Makers of Hebrew Books in Italy: Being Chapters in the History of the Hebrew Printing Press*. Philadelphia.

Anderson, W. S. ed. 1996. *Ovid's Metamorphoses: Books 1–5*. Norman, OK.

Appuhn, K. R. 2009. *A Forest on the Sea: Environmental Expertise in Renaissance Venice*. Baltimore.

Arnaldi, G. and Pastore Stocchi, M. eds. 1980. *Storia della cultura veneta. Vol. 3.1: Dal primo Quattrocento al Concilio di Trento*. Vicenza.

Arnold, J. 2011. *The Great Humanists: An Introduction*. London.

Arrizabalaga, J., Henderson, J., and French, R. K. 1997. *The Great Pox: The French Disease in Renaissance Europe*. New Haven.

Ascoli, A. R. 1991. "Petrarch's Middle Age: Memory, Imagination, History, and the 'Ascent of Mount Ventoux.'" *Stanford Italian Review* 10: 5–43.

Asher, L. 1993. "Petrarch at the Peak of Fame." *Publications of the Modern Language Association* 108.5: 1050–63.

Asheri, D. 1992. "Sicily, 478–431 B.C." In Lewis et al. 147–70.

Attwood, P. 2003. *Italian Medals c. 1530–1600 in British Public Collections*. 2 vols. London.

Avezzù, G. and Pianezzola, E. eds. 1999. *Sicilia e Magna Grecia: Spazio reale e spazio immaginario nella letteratura greca e latina*. Padua.

Azzi Visentini, M. 1984. *L'orto botanico di Padova e il giardino del Rinascimento*. Milan.

———. 1995. *La villa in Italia: Quattrocento e Cinquecento*. Milan.

Babcock, C. L. 1961. "The Role of Faunus in Horace, *Carmina* 1.4." *Transactions and Proceedings of the American Philological Association* 92: 13–19.

Baekeland, F. 1994. "Psychological Aspects of Art Collecting." In Pearce 1994: 205–19.

Bailey, C. ed. 1947. *Lucretius: De rerum natura*. 3 vols. Oxford.

Bakker, E. 2002. "Polyphemos." *Colby Quarterly* 38.2: 135–50.

Balbo, A., Bessone, F., and Malaspina, E. eds. 2011. *"Tanti affetti in tal momento": Studi in onore di Giovanna Garbarino*. Alessandria.

Baldacchini, L. 1987. "Il letterato in tipografia: Il *Sogno* di Pietro Bembo in un incunabolo veneziano sconosciuto." *Schifanoia* 4: 115–30.

Baldwin, B. 1973. "Aulus Gellius on Vergil." *Vergilius* 19: 22–7.

Ballarin, A. 2013. "2.8: Giorgio da Castelfranco, detto Giorgione, *Ritratto di giovane con il libro verde*." In Beltramini, Gasparotto, and Tura. 147–50.

Balmuth, M. S., Chester, D. K., and Johnston, P. A. eds. 2005. *Cultural Responses to the Volcanic Landscape: The Mediterranean and Beyond*. Boston.

Barkan, L. 1999. *Unearthing the Past: Archaeology and Aesthetics in the Making of Renaissance Culture*. New Haven.

Barker, N. 1972. *Stanley Morison*. Cambridge, MA.

———. 1992. *Aldus Manutius and the Development of Greek Script and Type in the Fifteenth Century*. 2nd ed. Oxford.

Barnes, J. and Griffin, M. eds. 1997. *Philosophia Togata II: Plato and Aristotle at Rome*. Oxford.

Barolini, H. 1992. *Aldus and His Dream Book: An Illustrated Essay*. New York.

Baron, H. 1955. *The Crisis of the Early Italian Renaissance: Civic Humanism and Republican Liberty in an Age of Classicism and Tyranny*. 2 vols. Princeton.

———. 1968. *From Petrarch to Leonardo Bruni: Studies in Humanistic and Political Literature*. Chicago.

Barrett-Graves, D. ed. 2013. *The Emblematic Queen: Extra-Literary Representations of Early Modern Queenship*. New York.

Bartholin, T. 1674. *De peregrinatione medica*. Copenhagen.

Bastiaensen, M. 1996. "Voyageurs de la Renaissance et phénomènes volcaniques en Italie." *Annali d'Italianistica* 14: 363–97.

Battaglia Ricci, L. 1996. "Gardens in Italian Literature during the Thirteenth and Fourteenth Centuries." In Hunt. 6–33.

Bayley, C. C. 1942. "Petrarch, Charles IV, and the *renovatio imperii*." *Speculum* 17.3: 323–41.

Beagon, M. 2005. *The Elder Pliny on the Human Animal: Natural History, Book 7*. Oxford.

Beall, S. M. 2001. "*Homo fandi dulcissimus*: The Role of Favorinus in the *Attic Nights* of Aulus Gellius." *American Journal of Philology* 122.1: 87–106.

Beecher, D. 2004. "Petrarch's 'Conversion' on Mont Ventoux and the Patterns of Religious Experience." *Renaissance and Reformation/Renaissance et Réforme* 28.3: 55–75.

Beja, M. 1970a. "Introduction." In Beja 1970b: 11–31.

———. ed. 1970b. *Virginia Woolf, To the Lighthouse: A Casebook*. London.

Belk, R. W. 1994. "Collectors and Collecting." In Pearce 1994: 317–26.

Bellomo, S. 1997. "Lettura delle *Annotationi nel Dante* di Trifon Gabriele." In Agostini and Lippi. 61–81.

Bellosi, L. and Rossi, A. eds. 1986. *Le vite de' più eccellenti architetti, pittori, et scultori italiani, da Cimabue insino a' tempi nostri*. Turin.

Belozerskaya, M. 2009. *To Wake the Dead: A Renaissance Merchant and the Birth of Archaeology*. New York.

Beltramini, G. 2012. "Spaces for Music in Sixteenth-Century Paduan Courts." In Howard and Moretti. 177–94.

———. 2013. "La residenza di Pietro Bembo in contrada di San Bartolomeo a Padova." In Beltramini, Burns, and Gasparotto. 375–406.

Beltramini, G. and Gasparotto, D. eds. 2016. *Aldo Manuzio: Il rinascimento di Venezia*. Venice.

Beltramini, G., Burns, H., and Gasparotto, D. eds. 2013. *Pietro Bembo e le arti*. Padua.

Beltramini, G., Gasparotto, D., and Tura, A. eds. 2013. *Pietro Bembo e l'invenzione del Rinascimento*. Padua.

Benton, T. 1995. "The Three Cities Compared: Urbanism." In Norman. 2.7–27.

Beretta, M. and Citti, F. eds. 2008. *Lucrezio, la natura e la scienza*. Florence.

Bernardo, A. S. 1985. *Franceso Petrarca, Letters on Familiar Matters: Rerum familiarium libri XVII–XXIV*. Baltimore.

Bernardo, A. S., Levin, S., and Bernardo, R. A. 1992. *Francis Petrarch, Letters of Old Age: Rerum senilium libri I–XVIII*. 2 vols. Baltimore.

Bernasconi, C. 1864. *Studi sopra la storia della pittura italiana dei secoli xiv e xv e della scuola pittorica veronese dai medi tempi fino a tutto il secolo xviii*. Verona.

Berra, C. 1996. *La scrittura degli Asolani di Pietro Bembo*. Florence.

Berranger-Auserve, D. 2004. "Pindare et Eschyle, deux visions d'une même éruption de l'Etna." In Foulon. 39–48.

Berry, W. T. and Poole, H. E. eds. 1966. *Annals of Printing: A Chronological Encyclopaedia from the Earliest Times to 1950*. London.

Bertrand, D. ed. 2001. *Figurations du volcan à la Renaissance: Actes du Colloque du C.E.R.H.A.C. (Centre d'Études sur les Réformes, l'Humanisme et l'Âge Classique) de l'Université Blaise Pascal, 8–9 Octobre 1999*. Paris.

———. 2004a. "Décrire l'Etna à la Renaissance: Entre mémoire culturelle et autopsie." In Bertrand 2004b: 39–50.

———. ed. 2004b. *L'invention du paysage volcanique.* Collection Volcaniques. Clermont-Ferrand.

———. ed. 2004c. *Mythologies de l'Etna.* Collection Volcaniques. Clermont-Ferrand.

Beschi, L. 1984. "L'Anonimo Ambrosiano: un itinerario in Grecia di Urbano Bolzanio." *Atti della Accademia nazionale dei Lincei (Rendiconti, Classe di Scienze morali, storiche e filologiche)* 39: 3–22.

Bessi, B. 2012. "Cristoforo Buondelmonti: Greek Antiquities in Florentine Humanism." *Historical Review* 9: 63–76.

Bevilacqua, A. 1979. "Simone Martini, Petrarca, i ritratti di Laura e del poeta." *Bollettino del Museo civico di Padova* 68: 107–50.

Billanovich, G. 1947. *Petrarca letterato, 1. Lo scrittoio del Petrarca.* Rome.

———. 1966. "Petrarca e il Ventoso." *Italia medioevale e umanistica* 9: 389–401.

Billault, A. 2004. "Volcanisme et esthétique: À propos du traité *Du sublime* 35,4." In Foulon. 193–203.

Biow, D. 2002. *Doctors, Ambassadors, Secretaries: Humanism and Professions in Renaissance Italy.* Chicago.

Birt, T. ed. 1892. *Monumenta Germaniae Historica, Auctores Antiquissimi 10: Claudii Claudiani Carmina.* Berlin.

Bishop, M. 1963. *Petrarch and His World.* Bloomington.

———. 1966. *Letters from Petrarch.* Bloomington.

Bloom, H. ed. 1988. *Virginia Woolf's To the Lighthouse.* New York.

Blumenberg, H. 1983. *The Legitimacy of the Modern Age.* Trans. R. M. Wallace. Cambridge, MA.

Blunt, A. 1937. "The *Hypnerotomachia Poliphili* in 17th century France." *Journal of the Warburg Institute* 1.2: 117–37.

Blunt, A. and Croft-Murray, E. 1957. *Venetian Drawings of the XVII and XVIII Centuries in the Collection of Her Majesty the Queen at Windsor Castle.* London.

Bodnar, E. W. 1960. *Cyriacus of Ancona and Athens.* Collection Latomus 43. Brussels.

———. ed. 2003. *Cyriac of Ancona: Later Travels.* I Tatti Renaissance Library 10. Cambridge, MA.

Bodon, G. 1991. "Studi antiquari tra XV e XVII secolo: La famiglia Maggi da Bassano e la sua collezione di antichità." *Bollettino del Museo civico di Padova* 80: 23–172.

———. 1993. "Un approccio metodologico allo studio del collezionismo di antichità: Analisi delle fonti e proposte di ricerca sul Museo Bembo di Padova." *Quaderni di Archeologia del Veneto* 9: 165–70.

———. 1997. *Enea Vico fra memoria e miraggio della classicità.* Rome.

———. 2005. *Veneranda antiquitas: Studi sull'eredità dell'antico nella Rinascenza veneta.* Bern.

Boehrer, B. T. 1990. "Early Modern Syphilis." *Journal of the History of Sexuality* 1.2: 197–214.

Boerio, G. 1867. *Dizionario del dialetto veneziano.* 3rd ed. Venice.

Bolling, G. M. 1925. *The External Evidence for Interpolation in Homer.* Oxford.

Bolzoni, L. 2002. "Il giardino e il bosco, ovvero il 'ritratto doppio' della campagna negli *Asolani*." In Isotti Rosowsky. 81–104.

———. 2006. "Les *Asolani* de Pietro Bembo, ou le double portrait de l'amour." *Italique: Poésie italienne de la Renaissance* 9: 9–27.

———. 2010. *Il cuore di cristallo: Ragionamenti d'amore, poesia e ritratto nel Rinascimento*. Turin.

———. 2013a. "Gli *Asolani* di Pietro Bembo: Un ritratto doppio della corte, dell'amore, della poesia." In Syndikus and Rogge. 133–45.

———. 2013b. "Gli *Asolani* e il fascino del ritratto." In Beltramini, Burns, and Gasparotto. 285–308.

———. 2013c. "I ritratti e la comunità degli amici fra Venezia, Firenze e Roma." In Beltramini, Gasparotto, and Tura. 210–17.

Bondanella, J. C. 2008. "Petrarch's Rereading of *otium* in *De vita solitaria*." *Comparative Literature* 60.1: 14–28.

Bondanella, J. C., Bondanella, P., Cole, B., and Shiffman, J. R. eds. 1996. *The Life of Titian by Carlo Ridolfi*. University Park, PA.

Boorman, S. 2006. *Ottaviano Petrucci: Catalogue Raisonné*. Oxford.

Botfield, B. ed. 1861. *Prefaces to the First Editions of the Greek and Roman Classics and of the Sacred Scriptures*. London.

Botley, P. 2010. "Learning Greek in Western Europe, 1396–1529: Grammars, Lexica, and Classroom Texts." *Transactions of the American Philosophical Society* 100.2: 1–270.

Bouwsma, W. 1968. *Venice and the Defence of Republican Liberty: Renaissance Values in the Age of the Counter-Reformation*. Berkeley.

Bowd, S. D. 1999. "Pietro Bembo and the 'Monster' of Bologna (1514)." *Renaissance Studies* 13.1: 40–54.

———. 2002. *Reform before the Reformation: Vincenzo Querini and the Religious Renaissance in Italy*. Leiden.

Boyd, B. W. ed. 2002. *Brill's Companion to Ovid*. Leiden.

Braden, G. 1996. "Applied Petrarchism: The Loves of Pietro Bembo." *Modern Language Quarterly* 57.3: 397–423.

Branca, V. ed. 1943. *Ermolao Barbaro: Epistolae, orationes et carmina*. 2 vols. Florence.

———. 1952. "Un trattato inedito di Ermolao Barbaro: Il *De coelibatu libri*." *Bibliothèque d'Humanisme et Renaissance* 14.1: 83–98.

———. 1963a. "Ermolao Barbaro e l'umanesimo veneziano." In Branca 1963b: 193–212.

———. ed. 1963b. *Umanesimo europeo e umanesimo veneziano*. Venice.

———. ed. 1969. *Ermolao Barbaro, De coelibatu, De officio legati*. Florence.

———. 1973. "Ermolao Barbaro and Late Quattrocento Venetian Humanism." In Hale. 218–43.

———. 1980. "L'umanesimo veneziano alla fine del Quattrocento: Ermolao Barbaro e il suo circulo." In Arnaldi and Pastore Stocchi. 123–75.

———. ed. 1981. *Giorgio Valla tra scienza e sapienza*. Florence.

———. 1983. *Poliziano e l'umanesimo della parola*. Turin.

———. 1996. "Umanesimo veneziano fra Barbaro e Bembo." In Marangoni and Pastore Stocchi. 9–42.

———. 1998. *La sapienza civile: Studi sull'umanesimo a Venezia*. Florence.

Branca, V. et al. eds. 1978. *Letteratura e scienza nella storia della cultura italiana: Atti del IX congresso AISLLI, Palermo-Messina-Catania, 21–25 aprile 1976.* Palermo.

Branca, V. and Weiss, R. 1963. "Carpaccio e l'iconografia del più grande umanista veneziano (Ermolao Barbaro)." *Arte veneta* 17: 35–40.

Brown, D. A. 1998. *Leonardo da Vinci: Origins of a Genius.* New Haven.

———. ed. 2001. *Virtue and Beauty: Leonardo's Ginevra de' Benci and Renaissance Portraits of Women.* Princeton.

———. 2013. "Bembo and Bellini." In Beltramini, Burns, and Gasparotto. 309–27.

Brown, P. F. 1988. *Venetian Narrative Painting in the Age of Carpaccio.* New Haven.

———. 1996. *Venice and Antiquity: The Venetian Sense of the Past.* New Haven.

———. 2013. "Pietro Bembo e l'arte della diplomazia." In Beltramini, Burns, and Gasparotto. 37–47.

Brown, V. ed. 2003. *Catalogus Translationum et Commentariorum* VIII. Washington, DC.

Brumberger, E. R. 2003. "The Rhetoric of Typography: The Persona of Typeface and Text." *Technical Communication* 50.2: 206–23.

Bühler, C. F. 1951. "Manuscript Corrections in the Aldine Edition of Bembo's *De Aetna*." *Papers of the Bibliographical Society of America* 45: 136–42.

Bull, D. 1992. "Two Portraits by Leonardo: *Ginevra de' Benci* and the *Lady with an Ermine*." *Artibus et Historiae* 13.25: 67–83.

Bull, G. 1996. *The Autobiography of Benvenuto Cellini.* London.

Burckhardt, J. 2010. *The Civilization of the Renaissance in Italy.* Mineola, NY. First published as *Die Cultur der Renaissance in Italien: Ein Versuch* (Basel, 1860).

Burns, H. 2000. "Valerio Belli Vicentino, scultore di luce." In Burns et al. 2000: 17–51.

———. 2013. "Bernardo Bembo, padre di Pietro." In Beltramini, Gasparotto, and Tura. 112–25.

Burns, H., Collareta, M., and Gasparotto, D. eds. 2000. *Valerio Belli Vicentino, 1468c.–1546.* Vicenza.

Bustico, G. 1905. "Un ellenista bellunese del secolo xv: Urbano Bolzanio." *La Rassegna nazionale* 145: 297–313.

———. 1932. "Due umanisti veneti: Urbano Bolzanio e Pierio Valeriano." *Civiltà moderna* 6: 86–103, 344–78.

Butler, S. ed. 2006. *Angelo Poliziano, Letters. Volume I: Books I–IV.* I Tatti Renaissance Library 21. Cambridge, MA.

Buxton, R. 1992. "Imaginary Greek Mountains." *Journal of Hellenic Studies* 112: 1–15.

———. 2016. "Mount Etna in the Greco-Roman *Imaginaire*: Culture and Liquid Fire." In McInerney and Sluiter. 25–45.

Cachey, T. J. 2010. "From the Mediterranean to the World: A Note on the Italian 'Book of Islands' (*isolario*)." *California Italian Studies* 1.1: 1–13.

Callebat, L. 1988. "Science et irrationnel: Les *mirabilia aquarum*." *Euphrosyne* 16: 155–67.

Callegari, R. 1997a. "Bernardo Bembo and Pietro Lombardo: News from the 'Nonianum.'" *Burlington Magazine* 139.1137: 862–6.

———. 1997b. "Sculture *in horto Bembi*." *Nuovi studi: Rivista di arte antica e moderna* 2.4: 41–62.

Campanelli, M. 1997. "Pietro Bembo, Roma e la filologia del tardo Quattrocento: Per una lettura del dialogo *De Virgilii Culice et Terentii fabulis*." *Rinascimento* 37: 283–319.

Campbell, E. J., Miller, S. R., and Carroll Consavari, E. eds. 2013. *The Early Modern Italian Domestic Interior, 1400–1700: Objects, Spaces, Domesticities*. Farnham, UK.

Campbell, L. 1981. "Notes on Netherlandish Pictures in the Veneto in the Fifteenth and Sixteenth Centuries." *Burlington Magazine* 123.941: 467–73.

Campos, A. 1994. "La grammatica ebraica di Aldo Manuzio." In Marcon and Zorzi. 103–6.

Carrier, D. 2002. "Why Were There No Public Art Museums in Renaissance Italy?" *Notes in the History of Art* 22.1: 44–50.

Carter, H. 1969. *A View of Early Typography up to about 1600*. Oxford.

Carter, R., Day, B., and Meggs, P. 2002. *Typographic Design: Form and Communication*. 3rd ed. Hoboken, NJ.

Carver, R. H. F. 2007. *The Protean Ass: The Metamorphoses of Apuleius from Antiquity to the Renaissance*. Oxford.

Cassirer, E. 1972. *The Individual and the Cosmos in Renaissance Philosophy*. Trans. M. Domandi. Philadelphia.

Castiglione, G. 2006. "Maffei, Benedetto." *Dizionario biografico degli italiani* 67: 221–3.

Castiglioni, A. 1953. "The School of Ferrara and the Controversy on Pliny." In Underwood. 1.269–79.

Cavallo, G. and Chartier, R. eds. 1999. *A History of Reading in the West*. Trans. L. G. Cochrane. Amherst, MA.

Celoria, F. 1992. *The Metamorphoses of Antoninus Liberalis: A Translation with a Commentary*. London.

Ceresa, M. 2004. "Lascaris, Costantino." *Dizionario biografico degli italiani* 63: 781–5.

Cesarini Martinelli, L. 1978. "In margine al commento di Angelo Poliziano alle *Selve* di Stazio." *Interpres* 1: 96–145.

———. 1985. "Uno sconosciuto incunabolo di Terenzio postillato dal Poliziano." *Rinascimento* 25: 239–46.

Chard, C. 1997. "Grand and Ghostly Tours: The Topography of Memory." *Eighteenth-Century Studies* 31.1: 101–8.

Chartier, R. 1994. *The Order of Books: Readers, Authors, and Libraries in Europe between the Fourteenth and Eighteenth Centuries*. Trans. L. G. Cochrane. Stanford, CA.

———. 1995. *Forms and Meanings: Texts, Performances, and Audiences from Codex to Computer*. Philadelphia.

Chatfield, M. P. ed. 2005. *Pietro Bembo: Lyric Poetry, Etna*. I Tatti Renaissance Library 18. Cambridge, MA.

———. ed. 2008. *Cristoforo Landino: Poems*. I Tatti Renaissance Library 35. Cambridge, MA.

Chaudhuri, P. 2014. *The War with God: Theomachy in Roman Imperial Poetry*. Oxford.

Chester, D. K. et al. eds. 1985. *Mount Etna: The Anatomy of a Volcano*. London.

Chester, D. K. et al. 2000. "Human Response to Etna Volcano during the Classical Period." In McGuire et al. 179–88.

Chitwood, A. 1986. "The Death of Empedocles." *American Journal of Philology* 107.2: 175–91.

Chojnacki, S. 1994. "Subaltern Patriarchs: Patrician Bachelors in Renaissance Venice." In Lees. 73–90.

———. 2000. *Women and Men in Renaissance Venice: Twelve Essays on Patrician Society.* Baltimore.

Cian, V. 1885. *Un decennio della vita di M. Pietro Bembo (1521–1531): Appunti biografici e saggio di studi sul Bembo.* Turin.

———. 1887. "Pietro Bembo e Isabella d'Este Gonzaga: Note e documenti." *Giornale storico della letteratura italiana* 9: 81–136.

———. 1896. "Per Bernardo Bembo: Le sue relazioni coi Medici." *Giornale storico della letteratura italiana* 28: 348–64.

———. 1897. *L'estetica della storia, considerata specialmente nelle sue manifestazioni letterarie.* Messina.

———. 1901. *Un medaglione del Rinascimento. Cola Bruno messinese e le sue relazioni con Pietro Bembo (1480 c. –1542).* Florence.

Ciccolella, F. 2005. "The Greek Donatus and the Study of Greek in the Renaissance." *International Journal of the Classical Tradition* 12.1: 1–24.

———. 2008. *Donati Graeci: Learning Greek in the Renaissance.* Leiden.

Ciccuto, M. 1996. "L'odeporica di Ciriaco d'Ancona fra testi e immagini." *Annali d'Italianistica* 14: 177–82.

Cicogna, E. A. 1860. "Intorno la vita e le opere di Marcantonio Michiel, patrizio veneto della prima metà del secolo xvi." *Memorie dell'Istituto veneto di scienze, lettere ed arti* 9: 359–425.

Cipolla, C. M. 1969. *Literacy and Development in the West.* Harmondsworth, UK.

Cirelli, C. and Nicosia, E. 2010. "The Myth of Mount Etna: Between Literature and Cinematography." *Studi e Ricerche Socio-Territoriali* 0 [*sic*]: 147–62.

Ciriacono, S. 2006. *Building on Water: Venice, Holland, and the Construction of the European Landscape in Early Modern Times.* Trans. J. Scott. New York.

Clark, K. 1949. *Landscape into Art.* Harmondsworth, UK.

———. 1968. *The Drawings of Leonardo da Vinci in the Collection of Her Majesty the Queen at Windsor Castle.* 2nd ed. 3 vols. London.

Clausen, W. V. et al. eds. 1966. *Appendix Vergiliana.* Oxford Classical Texts. Oxford.

Clough, C. H. 1965a. "Pietro Bembo's Library Represented in the British Museum." *British Museum Quarterly* 30: 3–17.

———. 1965b. "Pietro Bembo, Madonna G., Berenice and Veronica Gambara." *Commentari dell'Ateneo di Brescia per l'anno 1963*, 162: 209–27.

———. 1969. "Pietro Bembo's *Gli Asolani* of 1505." *Modern Language Notes* 84.1: 16–45.

———. 1972. "The Printings of the First Edition of Pietro Bembo's *Gli Asolani*." *Modern Language Notes* 87.1: 134–9.

———. 1984. "The Library of Bernardo and of Pietro Bembo." *Book Collector* 33: 305–31.

———. 1998. "Pietro Bembo's Edition of Petrarch and His Association with the Aldine Press." In Zeidberg. 47–80.

Coates, P. 1998. *Nature: Western Attitudes Since Ancient Times*. Berkeley.

Cocco, S. 2013. *Watching Vesuvius: A History of Science and Culture in Early Modern Italy*. Chicago.

Coffin, D. ed. 1972. *The Italian Garden. Colloquium on the History of Landscape Architecture* I. Dumbarton Oaks: Washington, DC.

Coggiola, G. 1914–15. "Per l'iconografia di Pietro Bembo." *Atti del Reale Istituto veneto di scienze, lettere ed arti* 74: 473–515.

Colasanti, F. 1979. "Caterina Corner, regina di Cipro." *Dizionario biografico degli italiani* 22: 335–42.

Collareta, M. 2013. "Pietro Bembo e la nozione di arte classica." In Beltramini, Burns, and Gasparotto. 223–32.

Collmer, R. G. 2003. "Three Women of Asolo: Caterina Cornaro, Katherine de Kay Bronson, and Eleonora Duse." *Mediterranean Studies* 12: 155–67.

Conan, M. ed. 2005. *Baroque Garden Cultures: Emulation, Sublimation, Subversion*. Dumbarton Oaks Colloquium on the History of Landscape Architecture 25. Washington, DC.

Conington, J. 1883. *P. Vergili Maronis Opera. Volume III: Aeneid VII–XII*. 3rd ed. Revised by H. Nettleship. London.

Conley, T. 1996. "Virtual Reality and the *Isolario*." *Annali d'Italianistica* 14: 121–30.

Connors, C. 2015. "In the Land of the Giants: Greek and Roman Discourses on Vesuvius and the Phlegraean Fields." *Illinois Classical Studies* 40: 121–37.

Connors, R. J. 1983. "*Actio*: A Rhetoric of Manuscripts." *Rhetoric Review* 2.1: 64–73.

Cook, H. 1910. "Venetian Portraits, and Some Problems." *Burlington Magazine* 16.84: 328–9, 332–4.

———. 1912. "The Portrait of Ginevra de' Benci by Leonardo da Vinci." *Burlington Magazine* 20.108: 345–7.

Coolidge, W. A. B. 1889. *Swiss Travel and Swiss Guide-Books*. London.

Corrales Pérez, Y. 1994. *Die Überlieferungsgeschichte des pseudo-hesiodischen Scutum Herculis*. Diss. Hamburg.

Corti, M. 1999. *Catasto magico*. Turin.

Cosentini, G. G. ed. 2007. *Scritti in onore di Quintino Cataudella*. Ragusa.

Cosgrove, D. E. 1985. "Prospect, Perspective and the Evolution of the Landscape Idea." *Transactions of the Institute of British Geographers* 10.1: 45–62.

———. 1988. "The Geometry of Landscape: Practical and Speculative Arts in Sixteenth-Century Venetian Land Territories." In Cosgrove and Daniels. 254–76.

———. 1993. *The Palladian Landscape: Geographical Change and Its Cultural Representations in Sixteenth-Century Italy*. University Park, PA.

———. 1998. *Social Formation and Symbolic Landscape*. Madison, WI.

———. 2008. *Geography and Vision: Seeing, Imagining and Representing the World*. London.

Cosgrove, D. E. and Daniels, S. eds. 1988. *The Iconography of Landscape*. Cambridge Studies in Historical Geography 9. Cambridge.

Cosgrove, D. E. and Della Dora, V. eds. 2009. *High Places: Cultural Geographies of Mountains, Ice and Science*. London.

Courcelle, P. 1963. *Les Confessions de Saint Augustin dans la tradition littéraire. Antécédents et postérité*. Paris.

Courtney, E. ed. 1993. *The Fragmentary Latin Poets*. Oxford.

Cox, V. 1992. *The Renaissance Dialogue: Literary Dialogue in Its Social and Political Contexts, Castiglione to Galileo*. Cambridge Studies in Renaissance Literature and Culture 2. Cambridge.

———. 2008. *Women's Writing in Italy, 1400–1650*. Baltimore.

Cranz, F. E. ed. 1980. *Catalogus Translationum et Commentariorum* IV. Washington, DC.

Cropper, E. 1986. "The Beauty of Woman: Problems in the Rhetoric of Renaissance Portraiture." In Ferguson et al. 175–90.

Crouzet-Pavan, E. 2002. *Venice Triumphant: The Horizons of a Myth*. Trans. L. G. Cochrane. Baltimore.

Crowe, J. A. and Cavalcaselle, G. B. 1871. *A History of Painting in North Italy, Venice, Padua, Vicenza, Verona, Ferrara, Milan, Friuli, Brescia, from the Fourteenth to the Sixteenth Century*. 2 vols. London.

———. 1877. *Titian: His Life and Times; With Some Account of His Family, Chiefly from New and Unpublished Records*. 2 vols. London.

Crutchley, B. ed. 2011. *Stanley Morison: A Tally of Types*. With additions by several hands. Cambridge.

Cunnally, J. 1994. "Ancient Coins as Gifts and Tokens of Friendship during the Renaissance." *Journal of the History of Collections* 6.2: 129–43.

Cunningham, P. ed. 1891. *The Letters of Horace Walpole, Fourth Earl of Orford*. 9 vols. London.

Curran, B. A. 2007. *The Egyptian Renaissance: The Afterlife of Ancient Egypt in Early Modern Italy*. Chicago.

Curti, E. 2006. *Tra due secoli: Per il tirocinio letterario di Pietro Bembo*. Bologna.

———. 2010. "Gli ozi di Pietro Bembo: Echi letterari e passione antiquaria nella *descriptio horti* bembesca." *Lettere italiane* 62: 450–63.

———. 2013a. "1.1: Pietro Bembo, *Sogno*." In Beltramini, Gasparotto, and Tura. 94–6.

———. 2013b. "1.12: Pietro Bembo, *De Aetna*." In Beltramini, Gasparotto, and Tura. 106–9.

Curtius, E. R. 1953. *European Literature and the Latin Middle Ages*. Trans. W. R. Trask. New York.

Cust, L. 1913. "Notes on Pictures in the Royal Collections, XXV: The Paintings Bought for George III in Italy, Consul Smith, and Antonio Canale, I." *Burlington Magazine* 23.123: 150–4, 161–2.

———. 1928. "A Portrait by Giovanni Bellini at Hampton Court Palace." *Apollo* 7.42: 247.

Daiches, D. 1970. "The Semi-Transparent Envelope." In Beja 1970b: 90–104.

Dal Borgo, M. 1998. "Gabriel, Angelo." *Dizionario biografico degli italiani* 51: 32–4.

Dal Pozzolo, E. M. 1993. "Il lauro di Laura e delle 'maritate venetiane.'" *Mitteilungen des Kunsthistorischen Institutes in Florenz* 37.2–3: 257–92.

Dalby, A. 2003. *Food in the Ancient World from A to Z*. London.

Daly, N. 2011. "The Volcanic Disaster Narrative: From Pleasure Garden to Canvas, Page, and Stage." *Victorian Studies* 53.2: 255–85.

Dane, J. A. 1999. "A Ghostly Twin Terence (Venice, 21 July 1475; IGI 9422, 9423)." *Library* 21.2: 99–107.

Daneloni, A. 2013a. "1.4: Publius Terentius Afer, *Comoediae*.' In Beltramini, Gasparotto, and Tura. 99–100.

———. 2013b. "1.3: Publius Terentius Afer, *Comoediae*." In Beltramini, Gasparotto, and Tura. 98–9.

Danforth, T., Jr. 2003. *Pietro Bembo, "Foster Father" of the Modern Book.* Typophile Monograph. New York.

Daniels, S. and Cosgrove, D. E. 1993. "Spectacle and Text: Landscape Metaphors in Cultural Geography." In Duncan and Ley. 57–77.

Dannenfeldt, K. H. 1959. "Egypt and Egyptian Antiquities in the Renaissance." *Studies in the Renaissance* 6: 7–27.

Danzi, M. 1990. "Novità su Michele Marullo e Pietro Bembo." *Rinascimento* 30: 205–33.

———. 2005. *La biblioteca del Cardinal Pietro Bembo*. Geneva.

Darley, G. 2012. *Vesuvius*. Cambridge, MA.

Davies, M. 1995a. *Aldus Manutius: Printer and Publisher of Renaissance Venice*. Malibu, CA.

———. 1995b. "Making Sense of Pliny in the Quattrocento." *Renaissance Studies* 9.2: 240–57.

Davies, M. and Kathirithamby, J. 1986. *Greek Insects*. New York.

De Benedictis, C. 1991. *Per la storia del collezionismo italiano: fonti e documenti*. Florence.

De Girolami Cheney, L. 2013. "Caterina Cornaro, Queen of Cyprus." In Barrett-Graves. 11–33.

De Lacy, P. 1943. "The Philosophy of the *Aetna*." *Transactions and Proceedings of the American Philological Association* 74: 169–78.

De Sinner, G. R. L. ed. 1824. *Christoph. Buondelmontii, Florentini, Liber insularum archipelagi*. Leipzig.

De Vivo, A. 1989. "Considerazioni sull'*Aetna*: Rapporti con Seneca, epoca della composizione." *Vichiana* 18: 63–85.

Del Lungo, I. ed. 1867. *Prose volgari inedite e poesie latine e greche edite e inedite di Angelo Ambrogini Poliziano*. Florence.

Della Dora, V. 2008. "Mountains and Memory: Embodied Visions of Ancient Peaks in the Nineteenth-Century Aegean." *Transactions of the Institute of British Geographers* 33: 217–32.

———. 2009. "Domesticating High Places. Mount Athos: Botanical 'Garden of the Virgin.'" In Cosgrove and Della Dora. 105–25.

———. 2011. *Imagining Mount Athos: Visions of a Holy Place from Homer to World War II*. Charlottesville.

della Torre, A. 1900. "La prima ambasceria di Bernardo Bembo a Firenze." *Giornale storico della letteratura italiana* 35: 258–333.

———. 1903. *Paolo Marsi da Pescina: Contributo alla storia dell'Accademia Pomponiana*. Rocca San Casciano.

DeWitt, N. J. 1943. "Polybius, Livy and the Alps." *Classical Weekly* 37.3: 29–31.

Di Blasi, G. E. 1842. *Storia cronologica dei vicerè, luogotenenti e presidenti del Regno di Sicilia.* Palermo.

Dilemmi, G. ed. 1991. *Pietro Bembo,* Gli Asolani. Florence.

Dilke, O. A. W. and Dilke, M. S. 1994. "The Adjustment of Ptolemaic Atlases to Feature the New World." In Haase and Reinhold. 117–34.

Dillon, J. B. 2006. "Aristippus, Henry (d. 1162)." In Emmerson. 45–46.

Dionisotti, C. ed. 1950. *Maria Savorgnan – Pietro Bembo: Carteggio d'amore (1500–1501).* Florence.

———. ed. 1960. *Prose e Rime di Pietro Bembo.* Turin.

———. 1961. Review of Pecoraro 1959. *Giornale storico della letteratura italiana* 138: 573–92.

———. 1963. "Aldo Manuzio umanista." In Branca 1963b: 213–43; first published in *Lettere italiane* 12.4 (1960): 375–400.

———. 1965. "Appunti sul Bembo." *Italia medioevale e umanistica* 8: 269–91.

———. 1966a. "Bembo, Pietro." *Dizionario biografico degli italiani* 8: 133–51.

———. ed. 1966b. *Prose e Rime di Pietro Bembo.* 2nd ed. Turin.

———. 1967. *Geografia e storia della letteratura italiana.* Turin.

Doglioni, L. 1784. *Memorie di Urbano Bolzanio bellunese dell'ordine dei minori conventuali.* Belluno.

Donadi, F. 1975a. "Esplorazioni alla tradizione manoscritta dell'*Encomio di Elena* gorgiano." *Bollettino dell'Istituto di filologia greca* 2: 170–84.

———. 1975b. "Note preparatorie all'edizione dell'*Encomio di Elena* gorgiano nella traduzione latina inedita di Pietro Bembo." In *Scritti in onore di Carlo Diano.* 121–33. Bologna.

———. ed. 1982. *Gorgia, Encomio di Elena.* Rome.

———. ed. 1983. *Pietro Bembo, Gorgiae Leontini in Helenam laudatio.* Rome.

Donadi, F., Pagliaroli, S., and Tessier, A. eds. 2015. *Manuciana Tergestina et Veronensia.* Trieste.

Donati, L. ed. 1947. *Miscellanea bibliografica in memoria di Don Tommaso Accurti.* Rome.

———. 1950. "Studio esegetico sul Polifilo." *La Bibliofilia* 52: 128–62.

Donattini, M. 1994–5. "Bartolomeo da li Sonetti, il suo *Isolario* e un viaggio di Giovanni Bembo (1525–1530)." *Geographia Antiqua* 3–4: 211–36.

———. 2000. *Spazio e modernità: Libri, carte, isolari nell'età delle scoperte.* Bologna.

Donnini, A. ed. 2008. *Pietro Bembo: Le Rime.* 2 vols. Rome.

Doody, A. 2011. "The Science and Aesthetics of Names in the *Natural History.*" In Gibson and Morello. 113–29.

Duncan, A. M. et al. 2005. "Eruptive Activity of Etna before A.D. 1600, with Particular Reference to the Classical Period." In Balmuth et al. 57–69.

Duncan, J. and Ley, D. eds. 1993. *Place/Culture/Representation.* Abingdon, UK.

Durling, R. M. 1977. "Il Petrarca, il Ventoso e la possibilità dell'allegoria." *Revue des Études Augustiniennes* 23: 304–23.

Dyck, A. R. 1996. *A Commentary on Cicero, De Officiis.* Ann Arbor.

———. 2004. *A Commentary on Cicero, De Legibus.* Ann Arbor.

Edwards, C. 1996. *Writing Rome: Textual Approaches to the City*. Cambridge.

Egerton, F. N. ed. 1983. *Edward Lee Greene: Landmarks of Botanical History, Part II*. Stanford, CA.

Eginitis, D. 1929. "The Problem of the Tide of Euripus." *Astronomische Nachrichten* 236: 321–8.

Eiche, S. 1983. "On the Dispersal of Cardinal Bembo's Collections." *Mitteilungen des Kunsthistorischen Institutes in Florenz* 27.3: 353–9.

Elam, C. 2013. "Bernardo Bembo and Leonardo's *Ginevra de' Benci*: A Further Suggestion." In Beltramini, Burns, and Gasparotto. 407–20.

Ellis, R. 1892. "*Ovidiana*." *American Journal of Philology* 13.3: 343–8.

———. ed. 1901a. *Aetna*. Oxford.

———. 1901b. "On the *Epistola Sapphus*." *Classical Review* 15.5: 258–63.

———. ed. 2008. *Aetna*. With a new introduction and bibliography by Volk, K. Exeter.

Emmerson, R. K. ed. 2006. *Key Figures in Medieval Europe: An Encyclopedia*. New York.

Espluga, X. 2011. "First History of a Forged Inscription (*CIL* II 149*): A Joke about Cyriacus of Ancona by Francesco Contarini (1450 *circa*)." *Zeitschrift für Papyrologie und Epigraphik* 176: 295–300.

Farnetti, M. ed. 2012. *Maria Savorgnan: "Se mai fui vostra"; Lettere d'amore a Pietro Bembo*. Ferrara.

Favaretto, I. 2002. *Arte antica e cultura antiquaria nelle collezioni venete al tempo della Serenissima*. 2nd ed. Rome.

Feather, J. P. 1986. "The Book in History and the History of the Book." *Journal of Library History* 21.1: 12–26.

Feeney, D. C. 1991. *The Gods in Epic: Poets and Critics of the Classical Tradition*. Oxford.

Fera, V. 1996. "Poliziano, Ermolao Barbaro e Plinio." In Marangoni and Pastore Stocchi. 193–234.

Fera, V. and Martelli, M. eds. 1998. *Agnolo Poliziano poeta, scrittore, filologo: Atti del Convegno internazionale di studi, Montepulciano, 3–6 novembre 1994*. Florence.

Ferguson, M. W., Quilligan, M., and Vickers, N. J. eds. 1986. *Rewriting the Renaissance: The Discourses of Sexual Difference in Early Modern Europe*. Chicago.

Fernández Pomar, J. M. 1966. "La colección de Uceda y los manuscritos griegos de Constantino Láscaris." *Emerita* 34: 211–88.

Figliuolo, B. 1999. *Il diplomatico e il trattatista: Ermolao Barbaro ambasciatore della Serenissima e il* De officio legati. Naples.

Findlen, P. 1989. "The Museum: Its Classical Etymology and Renaissance Genealogy." *Journal of the History of Collections* 1.1: 59–78.

———. 1994. *Possessing Nature: Museums, Collecting, and Scientific Culture in Early Modern Italy*. Berkeley.

———. 2004. "Ereditare un museo: Collezionismo, strategie familiari e pratiche culturali nell'Italia del xvi secolo." *Quaderni storici* 39.1: 45–81.

———. 2005. "The Market and the World: Science, Culture, and Collecting in the Venetian Republic." In Aikema et al. 55–68.

Finotti, F. 2004. *Retorica della diffrazione. Bembo, Aretino, Giulio Romano e Tasso: letteratura e scena cortigiana*. Florence.

Firpo, M. 2013. "Il cardinale Pietro Bembo." In Beltramini, Burns, and Gasparotto. 23–36.

Fisher, P. 1998. *Wonder, the Rainbow, and the Aesthetics of Rare Experiences*. Cambridge, MA.

Fitzgerald, W. and Gowers, E. eds. 2007. *Ennius Perennis: The Annals and Beyond. Proceedings of the Cambridge Philological Society* Supplementary Volume 31. Cambridge.

Fleming, F. 2004. "The Alps and the Imagination." *Ambio* Special Report 13: 51–5.

Fletcher, C. 2015. *Diplomacy in Renaissance Rome: The Rise of the Resident Ambassador*. Cambridge.

Fletcher, H. G. 1988. *New Aldine Studies: Documentary Essays on the Life and Work of Aldus Manutius*. San Francisco.

———. 1995. *In Praise of Aldus Manutius: A Quincentenary Exhibition*. Pierpont Morgan Library, New York.

Fletcher, J. M. 1971. "Isabella d'Este and Giovanni Bellini's *Presepio*." *Burlington Magazine* 113.825: 703–13.

———. 1973. "Marcantonio Michiel's Collection." *Journal of the Warburg and Courtauld Institutes* 36: 382–5.

———. 1981. "Marcantonio Michiel: His Friends and Collection." *Burlington Magazine* 123.941: 452–67.

———. 1989. "Bernardo Bembo and Leonardo's Portrait of Ginevra de' Benci." *Burlington Magazine* 131.1041: 811–16.

———. 2004. "Bellini's Social World." In Humfrey. 13–47.

Floriani, P. 1966. "La giovinezza umanistica di Pietro Bembo fino al periodo ferrarese." *Giornale storico della letteratura italiana* 143: 25–71.

Foffano, F. 1892. "Marco Musuro, professore di greco a Padova ed a Venezia." *Nuovo archivio veneto* 3: 453–73.

Fontana, M. J., Piraino, M. T., and Rizzo, F. P. eds. 1980. Φιλίας χάριν*: Miscellanea di studi classici in onore di Eugenio Manni*. 6 vols. Rome.

Fontenrose, J. E. 1981. *Orion: The Myth of the Hunter and the Huntress*. University of California Publications in Classical Studies 23. Berkeley.

Förstel, C. 1992. *Les grammaires grecques du XVème siècle: Étude sur les ouvrages de Manuel Chrysoloras, Théodore Gaza et Constantin Lascaris*. 2 vols. Diss. École des Chartes.

Foulon, É. ed. 2004. *Connaissance et représentations des volcans dans l'Antiquité. Actes du colloque de Clermont-Ferrand, Université Blaise Pascal, 19-20 septembre 2002*. Clermont-Ferrand.

Frati, C. 1916–17. "Un *iter literarium* di A. Poliziano nel 1491." *La Bibliofilia* 18: 289–91.

Frazier, A. K. 2005. *Possible Lives: Authors and Saints in Renaissance Italy*. New York.

Fremmer, A. 2001. *Venezianische Buchkultur: Bücher, Buchhändler und Leser in der Frührenaissance*. Cologne.

French, R. K. 1986. "Pliny and Renaissance Medicine." In French and Greenaway. 252–81.

French, R. K and Greenaway, F. eds. 1986. *Science in the Early Roman Empire: Pliny the Elder, His Sources and Influence*. London.

Freshfield, D. W. 1881. "Notes on Old Tracts, IV: The Mountains of Dante." *Alpine Journal* 10: 400–5.

———. 1884. "The Alpine Notes of Leonardo da Vinci." *Proceedings of the Royal Geographical Society* 6.6: 335–40.

———. 1892. Review of Uzielli 1890. *Proceedings of the Royal Geographical Society* 14.5: 345–7.

———. 1904. "On Mountains and Mankind." *The Geographical Journal* 24.4: 443–60.

Fritsen, A. M. V. 2000. "Testing *auctoritas*: The Travels of Paolo Marsi, 1468–69." *International Journal of the Classical Tradition* 6.3: 356–82.

———. 2015. *Antiquarian Voices: The Roman Academy and the Commentary Tradition on Ovid's Fasti*. Columbus, OH.

Frittelli, U. 1900. *Giannantonio de' Pandoni detto il "Porcellio": studio critico*. Florence.

Frizzoni, G. ed. 1884. *Notizia d'opere di disegno pubblicata e illustrata da D. Jacopo Morelli*. 2nd ed. Bologna.

Fubini, R. 1992. "Renaissance Historian: The Career of Hans Baron." *Journal of Modern History* 64.3: 541–74.

Fuoco, O. ed. 2008. *Claudio Claudiano: Aponus (carm. min. 26)*. Naples.

Furlotti, B. 2015. "The Performance of Displaying: Gesture, Behavior and Art in Early Modern Italy." *Journal of the History of Collections* 27.1: 1–13.

Furno, M. 1995. *Le Cornu copiae de Niccolò Perotti: Culture et méthode d'un humaniste qui aimait les mots*. Geneva.

Gabrieli, G. 1938. "Un medico svedese viaggiatore ed osservatore in Italia nel secolo XVII." *Rendiconti della Reale Accademia nazionale dei Lincei, Classe de scienze morali, storiche e filologiche* 6.14: 909–18.

Gaffuri, L. 1997. "Forzetta, Oliviero." *Dizionario biografico degli italiani* 49: 271–3.

Gaisser, J. H. 1999. *Pierio Valeriano on the Ill Fortune of Learned Men: A Renaissance Humanist and His World*. Ann Arbor.

Galasso, L. ed. 2000. *Ovidio, Opere II: Le metamorfosi*. Turin.

Garani, M. 2007. *Empedocles Redivivus: Poetry and Analogy in Lucretius*. New York.

———. 2009. "Going with the Wind: Visualizing Volcanic Eruptions in the Pseudo-Vergilian *Aetna*." *Bulletin of the Institute of Classical Studies* 52: 103–21.

García Martín et al. eds. 1993. *Estado actual de los estudios sobre el Siglo de Oro. Actas del II congreso internacional de Hispanistas del Siglo de Oro. Volumen II*. Salamanca.

Gardenal, G. 1981. "Giorgio Valla e le scienze esatte." In Branca 1981: 9–54.

Garrard, M. D. 2006. "Who was Ginevra de' Benci? Leonardo's Portrait and its Sitter Recontextualized." *Artibus et Historiae* 27.53: 23–56.

Gasparotto, D. 1996. "La barba di Pietro Bembo." *Annali della Scuola normale superiore di Pisa, Classe di lettere e filosofia*. Serie 4, Quaderni 1–2: 183–206.

———. 2000. "Catalogo delle opere." In Burns, Collareta, and Gasparotto. 303–87.

———. 2013a. "5.5: Marcantonio Michiel." In Beltramini, Gasparotto, and Tura. 326–7.

———. 2013b. "5.1, 5.2, 5.3: Valerio Belli." In Beltramini, Gasparotto, and Tura. 324–5.

———. 2013c. "Medaglie, iscrizioni, marmi e bronzi: Bembo collezionista di antichità." In Beltramini, Burns, and Gasparotto. 479–504.

———. 2013d. "Il mito della collezione." In Beltramini, Gasparotto, and Tura. 48–65.

———. 2013e. "6.13: Danese Cattaneo (attr.), *Medaglia ritratto di Pietro Bembo* 1547–1548." In Beltramini, Gasparotto, and Tura. 378–9.

———. 2013f. "3.19: Tiziano Vecellio, *Ritratto di gentiluomo (Pietro Bembo?)*." In Beltramini, Gasparotto, and Tura. 208–9.

Geanakoplos, D. J. 1962. *Greek Scholars in Venice: Studies in the Dissemination of Greek Learning from Byzantium to Western Europe*. Cambridge, MA.

———. 1974. "The Discourse of Demetrius Chalcondyles on the Inauguration of Greek Studies at the University of Padua in 1463." *Studies in the Renaissance* 21: 118–44.

———. 1989. *Constantinople and the West: Essays on the Late Byzantine (Palaeologan) and Italian Renaissances and the Byzantine and Roman Churches*. Madison, WI.

Geikie, A. 1912. *The Love of Nature among the Romans during the Later Decades of the Republic and the First Century of the Empire*. London.

Gerulaitis, L.V. 1976. *Printing and Publishing in Fifteenth-Century Venice*. Chicago.

Giannetto, N. 1985. *Bernardo Bembo, umanista e politico veneziano*. Florence.

Gibson, R. K. and Morello, R. eds. 2011. *Pliny the Elder: Themes and Contexts*. Leiden.

Glauthier, P. 2011. *Science and Poetry in Imperial Rome: Manilius, Lucan, and the Aetna*. Diss. Columbia.

Glenn, J. 1971. "Mezentius and Polyphemus." *American Journal of Philology* 92.2: 129–55.

Gnocchi, A. 1999. "Tommaso Giustiniani, Ludovico Ariosto e la Compagnia degli Amici." *Studi di filologia italiana* 57: 277–93.

Goff, F. R. 1964. *Incunabula in American Libraries: A Third Census of Fifteenth-Century Books Recorded in North American Collections*. New York.

Goffen, R. 2001. "Signatures: Inscribing Identity in Italian Renaissance Art." *Viator* 32: 303–70.

Gomme, A. W. 1956. *A Historical Commentary on Thucydides: The Ten Years' War. Volume II: Books 2–3*. Oxford.

Goodyear, F. R. D. ed. 1965. *Incerti Auctoris Aetna*. Cambridge Classical Texts and Commentaries 2. Cambridge.

———. 1966. "*Aetna*." In Clausen et al. 37–76.

———. 1984. "The *Aetna*: Thought, Antecedents, and Style." *Aufstieg und Niedergang der römischen Welt* II.32.1: 344–63.

Gottfried, R. B. 1954. *Pietro Bembo's* Gli Asolani. Bloomington, IN.

Gow, A. S. F. ed. 1950. *Theocritus*. 2 vols. Cambridge.

Gowers, E. 2007. "The *cor* of Ennius." In Fitzgerald and Gowers. 17–37.

———. 2011. "The Road to Sicily: Lucilius to Seneca." *Ramus* 40: 168–97.

Gowing, A. M. 2005. *Empire and Memory: The Representation of the Roman Republic in Imperial Culture*. Cambridge.

Grafton, A. 1977. "On the Scholarship of Politian and Its Context." *Journal of the Warburg and Courtauld Institutes* 40: 150–88.

———. 1981. "Pietro Bembo and the 'Scholia Bembina.'" *Italia medioevale e umanistica* 24: 405–7.

———. 1983. *Joseph Scaliger: A Study in the History of Classical Scholarship*. 2 vols. *I: Textual Criticism and Exegesis*. Oxford.

———. 1991. *Defenders of the Text: The Traditions of Scholarship in an Age of Science, 1450–1800.* Cambridge, MA.

———. 1999. "The Humanist as Reader." In Cavallo and Chartier. 179–212.

———. 2001. *Bring Out Your Dead: The Past as Revelation.* Cambridge, MA.

Grafton, A., Most, G. W., and Settis, S. eds. 2010. *The Classical Tradition.* Cambridge, MA.

Graham, D. W. ed. 2010. *The Texts of Early Greek Philosophy: The Complete Fragments and Selected Testimonies of the Major Presocratics.* 2 vols. Cambridge.

Grande, S. 1905. "Le relazioni geografiche fra P. Bembo, G. Fracastoro, G. B. Ramusio, G. Gastaldi." *Memorie delle società geografica italiana* 12: 93–197.

Gransden, K. W. ed. 1976. *Virgil: Aeneid VIII.* Cambridge Greek and Latin Classics. Cambridge.

Grant, J. N. 1988. "Pietro Bembo and Vat. lat. 3226." *Humanistica Lovaniensia* 37: 211–43.

———. 1992. "Pietro Bembo as a Textual Critic of Classical Latin Poetry: *Variae lectiones* and the Text of the *Culex*." *Italia medioevale e umanistica* 35: 253–303.

———. 1995. "Propertius, Ovid and Two Latin Poems of Pietro Bembo." *International Journal of the Classical Tradition* 1.4: 48–62.

———. ed. 2011. *Lilio Gregorio Giraldi: Modern Poets.* I Tatti Renaissance Library 48. Cambridge, MA.

———. ed. 2017. *Aldus Manutius: Humanism and the Latin Classics.* I Tatti Renaissance Library 78. Cambridge, MA.

Grant, W. L. 1963. "The Life of Naldo Naldi." *Studies in Philology* 60.4: 606–17.

Green, C. M. C. 1991. "*Stimulos dedit aemula virtus*: Lucan and Homer Reconsidered." *Phoenix* 45.3: 230–54. Reprinted in Tesoriero. 149–83.

———. 2007. *Roman Religion and the Cult of Diana at Aricia.* Cambridge.

Grendler, P. F. 1989. *Schooling in Renaissance Italy: Literacy and Learning, 1300–1600.* Baltimore.

———. 1992. "Il libro popolare nel Cinquecento." In Santoro. 1.211–36.

———. 2002. *The Universities of the Italian Renaissance.* Baltimore.

Gribble, F. 1899. *The Early Mountaineers.* London.

Griffin, M. T. 1992 [1976]. *Seneca: A Philosopher in Politics.* Repr. with postscript. Oxford.

Griffith, M. ed. 1983. *Aeschylus: Prometheus Bound.* Cambridge Greek and Latin Classics. Cambridge.

Griffiths, J. G. 1960. "The Flight of the Gods before Typhon: An Unrecognized Myth." *Hermes* 88.3: 374–6.

Grimal, P. 1980. "Lucilius en Sicile." In Fontana et al. 1173–87.

Grosso, M. 2013. "6.1: Tiziano Vecellio, *Ritratto del cardinale Pietro Bembo*." In Beltramini, Gasparotto, and Tura. 368–9.

Gualdo Rosa, L. 1986. "Dalle Fosse (Bolzanio), Urbano." *Dizionario biografico degli italiani* 32: 88–92.

Guidoboni, E. and Ciuccarelli, C. 2008. "First Historical Evidence of a Significant Mt. Etna Eruption in 1224." *Journal of Volcanology and Geothermal Research* 178: 693–700.

Guittard, C. 2004. "La représentation des volcans chez Lucrèce." In Foulon. 259–69.

Güneş, A. 1999. "Symbolism in Virginia Woolf's *To the Lighthouse*." *Hacettepe University Journal of Faculty of Letters* 16.2: 173–88.

Günther, S. 1904. "Il Cardinale Pietro Bembo e la geografia." *Atti del congresso internazionale di scienze storiche (Roma, 1–9 Aprile 1903)* 10: 55–68.

Guthrie, W. K. C. 1965. *A History of Greek Philosophy. Volume II: The Presocratic Tradition from Parmenides to Democritus*. Cambridge.

———. 1978. *A History of Greek Philosophy. Volume V: The Later Plato and the Academy*. Cambridge.

Guzmán Arias, C. 2003. "Ovidio e el Etna." *Quaderni urbinati di cultura classica* 74.2: 137–45.

Haase, W. and Reinhold, M. eds. 1994. *The Classical Tradition and the Americas. Volume I: European Images of the Americas and the Classical Tradition. Part 1*. Berlin.

Hadzsits, G. D. 1936. "The *vera historia* of the Palatine *ficus ruminalis*." *Classical Philology* 31.4: 305–19.

Hafley, J. 1970. "The Creative Modulation of Perspective." In Beja 1970b: 133–48.

Hale, J. R. ed. 1973. *Renaissance Venice*. London.

Hall, J. B. 1986. *Prolegomena to Claudian*. *Bulletin of the Institute of Classical Studies* Supplement 45. London.

Hand, J. O. 2013. "The *Saint John the Baptist* and *Saint Veronica* Diptych by Hans Memling." In Beltramini, Burns, and Gasparotto. 433–40.

Hankins, J. 1995. "The 'Baron Thesis' after Forty Years and Some Recent Studies of Leonardo Bruni." *Journal of the History of Ideas* 56.2: 309–38.

———. 2000a. "Introduction." In Hankins 2000b: 1–13

———. ed. 2000b. *Renaissance Civic Humanism: Reappraisals and Reflections*. Cambridge.

Hansen, P. H. 2013. *The Summits of Modern Man: Mountaineering after the Enlightenment*. Cambridge, MA.

Hardie, P. 1986. *Virgil's Aeneid: Cosmos and Imperium*. Oxford.

———. 1995. "The Speech of Pythagoras in Ovid *Metamorphoses* 15: Empedoclean *epos*." *Classical Quarterly* 45.1: 204–14.

———. 2008. "Lucretian Multiple Explanations and Their Reception in Latin Didactic and Epic." In Beretta and Citti. 69–96.

———. 2009a. *Lucretian Receptions: History, the Sublime, Knowledge*. Cambridge.

———. ed. 2009b. *Paradox and the Marvellous in Augustan Literature and Culture*. Oxford.

———. 2012. *Rumour and Renown: Representations of Fama in Western Literature*. Cambridge.

———. ed. 2015. *Ovidio, Metamorfosi. Volume VI: Libri XIII–XV*. Milan.

Harris, J. 1995. *Greek Emigres in the West 1400–1520*. Camberley, UK.

Haskell, F. 1980. *Patrons and Painters: A Study in the Relations between Italian Art and Society in the Age of the Baroque*. New Haven.

———. 1993. *History and Its Images: Art and the Interpretation of the Past*. New Haven.

Haskell, Y. 1997. "Round and Round We Go: The Alchemical *opus circulatorium* of Giovanni Aurelio Augurello." *Bibliothèque d'Humanisme et Renaissance* 59.3: 583–606.

Haskins, C. H. 1924. *Studies in the History of Mediaeval Science*. Cambridge, MA.

Heiberg, J. L. 1896. *Beiträge zur Geschichte Georg Valla's und seiner Bibliothek*. Centralblatt für Bibliothekswesen, Beiheft XVI. 353–481. Leipzig.

Hempfer, K. W. ed. 2002. *Möglichkeiten des Dialogs: Struktur und Funktion einer literarischen Gattung zwischen Mittelalter und Renaissance in Italien*. Stuttgart.

Henderson, J. 2003. *Morals and Villas in Seneca's Letters: Places to Dwell.* Cambridge.

Henderson, P. W., Giese, J. L., and Cote, J. A. 2004. "Impression Management Using Typeface Design." *Journal of Marketing* 68.4: 60–72.

Hendy, P. and Goldscheider, L. 1945. *Giovanni Bellini.* Oxford.

Herlihy, D., Lopez, R. S., and Slessarev, V. eds. 1969. *Economy, Society, and Government in Medieval Italy: Essays in Memory of Robert L. Reynolds.* Kent, OH.

Heubeck, A., West, S., and Hainsworth, J. B. 1988. *A Commentary on Homer's Odyssey. Volume I: Introduction and Books I–VIII.* Oxford.

Hill, G. F. 1911. "Classical Influence on the Italian medal." *Burlington Magazine* 18.95: 259–63, 266–8.

———. 1930. *Corpus of the Italian Medals of the Renaissance before Cellini.* 2 vols. London.

Hills, P. 2007. "Titian's Fire: Pyrotechnics and Representations in Sixteenth-Century Venice." *Oxford Art Journal* 30.2: 187–204.

Hinds, S. E. 1987. *The Metamorphosis of Persephone: Ovid and the Self-Conscious Muse.* Cambridge.

Hine, H. M. ed. 1981. *An Edition with Commentary of Seneca, Natural Questions, Book 2.* New York, 1981.

———. 2002. "Seismology and Vulcanology in Antiquity?" In Tuplin and Rihll. 56–75.

———. 2010. *Lucius Annaeus Seneca: Natural Questions.* Chicago.

———. 2012. "*Aetna*: A New Translation Based on the Text of F. R. D. Goodyear." *Studies in History and Philosophy of Science* 43: 316–25.

Hirai, H. 2002. "Concepts of Seeds and Nature in the Work of Marsilio Ficino." In Allen and Rees. 257–84.

Hobson, A. 1998. "Was There an Aldine Bindery?" In Zeidberg. 237–45.

Holford-Strevens, L. 1997. "Favorinus: The Man of Paradoxes." In Barnes and Griffin. 188–217.

———. 2003. *Aulus Gellius: An Antonine Scholar and His Achievement.* Oxford.

Hollis, A. S. 1992. "Hellenistic Colouring in Virgil's *Aeneid*." *Harvard Studies in Classical Philology* 94: 269–85.

———. ed. 2007. *Fragments of Roman Poetry, c. 60 BC–AD 20.* Oxford.

Holzberg, N. ed. 2005. *Die Appendix Vergiliana: Pseudepigraphen im literarischen Kontext.* Tübingen.

Hooley, D. 2012. "Prelude: Classical Mountain Landscapes and the Language of Ascent." In Ireton and Schaumann. 20–32.

Hornblower, S. 2004. *Thucydides and Pindar: Historical Narrative and the World of Epinikian Poetry.* Oxford.

Horsfall, N. 2006. *Virgil, Aeneid 3: A Commentary.* Leiden.

Hose, M. 2002. *Aristoteles: Die historischen Fragmente.* In H. Flashar ed. *Aristoteles, Werke in deutscher Übersetzung, Band 20: Fragmente, Teil III.* Berlin.

Hossfeld, P. ed. 1980. *Alberti Magni Liber de causis proprietatum et elementorum.* In *Alberti Magni opera omnia* 5.2: 49–104. Münster.

Howard, D. 1997. "Venice as a Dolphin: Further Investigations into Jacopo de' Barbari's View." *Artibus et Historiae* 18.35: 101–11.

Howard, D. and Moretti, L. eds. 2012. *The Music Room in Early Modern France and Italy: Sound, Space, and Object. Proceedings of the British Academy* 176. Oxford.

Humfrey, P. ed. 2004. *The Cambridge Companion to Giovanni Bellini.* Cambridge.

Hunt, J. D. ed. 1996. *The Italian Garden: Art, Design and Culture.* Cambridge.

Hunter, R. L. 2012. *Plato and the Traditions of Ancient Literature: The Silent Stream.* Cambridge.

Hurlburt, H. 2009. "Body of Empire: Caterina Corner in Venetian History and Iconography." *Early Modern Women* 4: 61–99.

Hyde, W. W. 1915. "The Ancient Appreciation of Mountain Scenery." *Classical Journal* 11.2: 70–84.

———. 1916. "The Volcanic History of Etna." *Geographical Review* 1.6: 401–18.

———. 1917. "The Development of the Appreciation of Mountain Scenery in Modern Times." *Geographical Review* 3.2: 107–18.

Ingleheart, J. 2010. *A Commentary on Ovid, Tristia, Book 2.* Oxford.

Ireton, S. and Schaumann, C. eds. 2012. *Heights of Reflection: Mountains in the German Imagination from the Middle Ages to the Twenty-First Century.* Rochester, NY.

Isotti Rosowsky, G. ed. 2002. *La campagna in città: Letteratura e ideologia nel Rinascimento. Scritti in onore di Michel Plaisance.* Florence.

Iversen, E. 1958. "Hieroglyphic Studies of the Renaissance." *Burlington Magazine* 100.658: 15–21.

Ivins, W. M. 1923. "The Aldine *Hypnerotomachia Poliphili* of 1499." *The Metropolitan Museum of Art Bulletin* 18.11: 249–52.

Jaeger, M. 2007. "Fog on the Mountain: Philip and Mt. Haemus in Livy 40.21–22." In Marincola. 397–403.

Jameson, A. 1842. *A Handbook to the Public Galleries of Art In and Near London.* 2 vols. London.

Jaworska, K. 1992. "Appunti sui viaggiatori polacchi in Sicilia dal XVI al XIX secolo." In Kanceff and Rampone. 161–85.

Jedin, H. 1946. "Vincenzo Querini und Pietro Bembo." *Miscellanea Giovanni Mercati* 4: 407–24. Reprinted in *Kirche des Glaubens, Kirche der Geschichte: Ausgewählte Aufsätze und Vorträge* (Freiburg im Breisgau, 1966: 2 vols.): 1.153–66.

Jensen, K. 1998. "The Latin Grammar of Aldus Manutius and Its *fortuna*." In Zeidberg. 247–78.

Joannides, P. 2001. *Titian to 1518: The Assumption of Genius.* New Haven.

Johnston, P. A. 1996. "Under the Volcano: Volcanic Myth and Metaphor in Vergil's *Aeneid*." *Vergilius* 42: 55–65.

Joyal, M. ed. 2001. *In Altum: Seventy-Five Years of Classical Studies in Newfoundland.* St. John's, Newfoundland.

Kaehele, S. and German, H. 1970. "*To the Lighthouse*: Symbol and Vision." In Beja 1970b: 189–209.

Kallendorf, C. 1999. *Virgil and the Myth of Venice: Books and Readers in the Italian Renaissance.* Oxford.

———. 2010. *Aldo Manuzio (Aldus Manutius)*. Oxford Bibliographies Online Research Guide. Oxford.

Kanceff, E. and Rampone, R. eds. 1992. *Viaggio nel Sud, I: Viaggiatori stranieri in Sicilia*. Biblioteca del viaggio in Italia 36. Geneva.

Kennell, S. A. H. 2000. *Magnus Felix Ennodius: A Gentleman of the Church*. Ann Arbor.

———. 2001. "Aponus' Admirers: Omens and Abdomens from Tiberius to Theoderic." In Joyal. 197–216.

Kent, D. 2001. "Women in Renaissance Florence." In D. A. Brown 2001: 25–47.

Kidwell, C. 2004. *Pietro Bembo: Lover, Linguist, Cardinal*. Montreal.

Kilpatrick, R. 1986. "The *De Aetna* of Pietro Bembo: A Translation." *Studies in Philology* 83.3: 330–58.

Kim, D. Y. 2014. *The Traveling Artist in the Italian Renaissance: Geography, Mobility, and Style*. New Haven.

King, M. L. 1976. "Caldiera and the Barbaros on Marriage and the Family: Humanist Reflections of Venetian Realities." *Journal of Medieval and Renaissance Studies* 6: 19–50.

———. 1986. *Venetian Humanism in an Age of Patrician Dominance*. Princeton.

———. 1988. "Humanism in Venice." In Rabil. 1.209–34.

———. 2005. *Humanism, Venice, and Women: Essays on the Italian Renaissance*. Aldershot, UK.

———. ed. 2014. *Renaissance Humanism: An Anthology of Sources*. Indianapolis.

———. ed. 2015. *Francesco Barbaro, The Wealth of Wives: A Fifteenth-Century Marriage Manual*. The Other Voice in Early Modern Europe: The Toronto Series, 42; Medieval and Renaissance Texts and Studies 485. Toronto and Tempe, AZ.

Kingsley, P. 1995. *Ancient Philosophy, Mystery, and Magic: Empedocles and Pythagorean Tradition*. Oxford.

Kirchner, W. 1950. "Mind, Mountain, and History." *Journal of the History of Ideas* 11.4: 412–47.

Kirk, G. S. 1985. *The Iliad: A Commentary. Volume I: Books 1–4*. Cambridge.

Kirkwood, G. ed. 1982. *Selections from Pindar*. Chico, CA.

Klein, R. and Zerner, H. 1966. *Italian Art 1500–1600: Sources and Documents*. Evanston, IL.

Knox, P. E. ed. 1995. *Ovid, Heroides: Select Epistles*. Cambridge Greek and Latin Classics. Cambridge.

Kostylo, J. 2008a. "Commentary on Aldus Manutius's Warning against the Printers of Lyon (1503)." In Bently, L. and Kretschmer, M. eds. *Primary Sources on Copyright (1450–1900)*: www.copyrighthistory.org.

———. 2008b. "Commentary on Johannes of Speyer's Venetian Monopoly (1469)." In Bently, L. and Kretschmer, M. eds. *Primary Sources on Copyright (1450–1900)*: www.copyrighthistory.org.

Kristeller, P. O. 1943. *The Philosophy of Marsilio Ficino*. Trans. V. Conant. New York.

Kubelik, M. 1986. "Palladio's Villas in the Tradition of the Veneto Farm." *Assemblage* 1: 90–115.

Labalme, P. H. 1996. "Secular and Sacred Heroes: Ermolao Barbaro on Worldly Honor." In Marangoni and Pastore Stocchi. 331–44.

Lamers, H. 2015. *Greece Reinvented: Transformations of Byzantine Hellenism in Renaissance Italy*. Leiden.

Landucci Ruffo, P. 1981. "Le fonti della 'medicina' nell'enciclopedia di Giorgio Valla." In Branca 1981: 55–68.

Larmour, D. H. J. and Spencer, D. 2007a. "Introduction. *Roma, recepta*: A Topography of the Imagination." In Larmour and Spencer 2007b: 1–60.

———. eds. 2007b. *The Sites of Rome: Time, Space, Memory*. Oxford.

Lauber, R. 2002. "'Et è il nudo che ho io in pittura de l'istesso Zorzi': Per Giorgione e Marcantonio Michiel." *Arte veneta* 59: 98–115.

———. 2013a. "'In casa di Messer Pietro Bembo': Riflessioni su Pietro Bembo e Marcantonio Michiel." In Beltramini, Burns, and Gasparotto. 441–64.

———. 2013b. "Note per Marcantonio Michiel e Pietro Bembo." In Beltramini, Gasparotto, and Tura. 344–7.

Lavin, M. A. ed. 1967. *Giorgio Vasari: Lives of the Most Eminent Painters*. 2 vols. New York.

Layton, E. 1979. "The First Printed Greek Book." *Journal of the Hellenic Diaspora* 5.4: 63–79.

Lazzarini, L. 1963. "Francesco Petrarca e il primo umanesimo a Venezia." In Branca 1963b: 63–92.

Leclercq, J. 1951. *Un humaniste ermite: Le bienheureux Paul Giustiniani (1476–1528)*. Rome.

Lee, H. 1988. "*To the Lighthouse:* Completed Forms." In Bloom. 9–26.

Lees, C. A. ed. 1994. *Medieval Masculinities: Regarding Men in the Middle Ages*. Minneapolis.

Lefaivre, L. 1997. *Leon Battista Alberti's Hypnerotomachia Poliphili: Re-Cognizing the Architectural Body in the Early Italian Renaissance*. Cambridge, MA.

Lefkowitz, M. R. 1976. *The Victory Ode: An Introduction*. Park Ridge, NJ.

Legrand, É. 1962. *Bibliographie hellénique des XVe et XVIe siècles, ou description raisonnée des ouvrages publiés en grec ou par des Grecs aux XVe et XVIe siècles*. 4 vols. Paris; first published 1885–1906.

Lehmann-Hartleben, K. 1943. "Cyriacus of Ancona, Aristotle, and Teiresias in Samothrace." *Hesperia* 12.2: 115–34.

Leroux, V. 2004a. "L'Etna dans les récits antiques du rapt de Proserpine." In Bertrand 2004c: 33–56.

———. 2004b. "La représentation de l'Etna dans l'épopée latine." In Foulon. 57–78.

Lestringant, F. 2002. *Le livre des îles: Atlas et récits insulaires de la Genèse à Jules Verne*. Geneva.

Levi, E. 1896. "Lo zibaldone di Bernardo Bembo." *Rassegna della letteratura italiana* 4: 46–50.

Lewis, C. and Walker, P. 1989. "Typographic Influences on Reading." *British Journal of Psychology* 80: 241–57.

Lewis, D. M. et al. eds. 1992. *Cambridge Ancient History. Volume V: The Fifth Century B.C.* 2nd ed. Cambridge.

Logan, O. 1972. *Culture and Society in Venice, 1470–1790: The Renaissance and Its Heritage*. London.

López Suárez, M. 1993. "G. A. Augurello: La formulación previa del código petrarquista." In García Martín et al. 579–87.

Louden, L. M. 1968. "*Sprezzatura* in Raphael and Castiglione." *Art Journal* 28.1: 43–9 and 53.

Lowry, M. 1976. "The 'New Academy' of Aldus Manutius: A Renaissance Dream." *Bulletin of the John Rylands University Library of Manchester* 58: 378–420.

———. 1979. *The World of Aldus Manutius: Business and Scholarship in Renaissance Venice.* Oxford.

———. 1991. *Nicholas Jenson and the Rise of Venetian Publishing in Renaissance Europe.* Oxford.

———. 1992. "*Magni nominis umbra*? L'editoria classica da Aldo Manuzio vecchio ad Aldo giovane." In Santoro. 1.237–53.

———. 1998. "The Manutius Publicity Campaign.' In Zeidberg 1998: 31–46.

Lucco, M. 2000. "A New Portrait by Raphael and Its Historical Context." *Artibus et Historiae* 21.41: 49–73.

Ludwig, W. 1983. "Die *Stockhornias* des Joannes Rhellicanus." *Humanistica Lovaniensia* 32: 218–24.

Lutz, M. ed. 1980. *Pietro Bembo: Volgarizzamento des Dialogs "De Guido Ubaldo Feretrio deque Elisabetha Gonzagia Urbini ducibus". Kölner romanistische Arbeiten*, Neue Folge 57. Geneva.

Luzzati Laganà, F. 1987. "Sur les mers grecques: Un voyageur florentin du XVe siècle, Cristoforo Buondelmonti." *Médiévales* 12: 67–77.

Macfarlane, R. 2003. *Mountains of the Mind*. New York.

Macola, N. 2007. *Sguardi e scritture: Figure con libro nella ritrattistica italiana della prima metà del Cinquecento*. Venice.

Magnaguti, A. 1907. "Il Petrarca numismatico." *Rivista italiana di numismatica e scienze affini* 20: 155–7.

Malaspina, E. 2007. "Il paesaggio nel mondo antico (dalle Alpi a Capo Passero). II parte: le Alpi, ovvero dei luoghi inameni." In Cosentini. 34–50.

Mallette, K. 2005. *The Kingdom of Sicily, 1100–1250: A Literary History*. Philadelphia.

Maltezou, C. 2013. "Le donzelle cipriote di Caterina Cornaro dopo il ritorno della regina a Venezia." In Syndikus and Rogge. 279–91.

Mandile, R. 2009. "Note sull'*Aponus* di Claudiano." *Acme* 62.3: 345–59.

Mann, N. 1993. "Il Petrarca giardiniere (a proposito del sonetto CCXXVIII)." *Atti e memorie dell'Accademia Patavina di scienze, lettere ed arti, 104 (1991–2).* Parte III: 235–56.

Marangoni, M. and Pastore Stocchi, M. eds. 1996. *Una famiglia veneziana nella storia: I Barbaro. Atti del Convegno di studi in occasione del quinto centenario della morte dell'umanista Ermolao, Venezia, 4–6 Novembre 1993.* Venice.

Marcon, S. and Zorzi, M. eds. 1994. *Aldo Manuzio e l'ambiente veneziano, 1494–1515.* Venice.

Mardersteig, G. 1964. "Aldo Manuzio e i caratteri di Francesco Griffo da Bologna." In *Studi di bibliografia e di storia in onore di Tammaro de Marinis. Volume III*: 105–47. Verona.

———. 1969a. "Osservazioni tipografiche sul *Polifilo* nelle edizioni del 1499 e 1545." In *Contributi alla storia del libro italiano. Miscellanea in onore di Lamberto Donati*. 221–42. Florence.

———. 1969b. *Petri Bembi* De Aetna *liber, Pietro Bembo on Etna*. Postscript by Giovanni Mardersteig. Verona.

———. 1988. *Scritti di Giovanni Mardersteig sulla storia dei caratteri e della tipografia*. Milan.

Mariano, B. M. 1991. "Il *De Aetna* di P. Bembo e le varianti dell'edizione 1530." *Aevum* 65: 441–52.

Marincola, J. ed. 2007. *A Companion to Greek and Roman Historiography*. Malden, MA.

Marinelli, S. 2013. "Pietro Bembo nella storia della pittura." In Beltramini, Burns, and Gasparotto. 465–78.

Marmer, H. A. 1931. "The Tidal Problem of Euripus." *Geographical Review* 21.4: 678–9.

Marsh, D. 1980. *The Quattrocento Dialogue: Classical Tradition and Humanist Innovation*. Cambridge, MA.

Martindale, C. 1993. *Redeeming the Text: Latin Poetry and the Hermeneutics of Reception*. Cambridge.

Martinelli, B. 1973. "Del Petrarca e il Ventoso." In *Studi in onore di Alberto Chiari*. 2 vols. 2.767–834. Brescia.

Martínez Manzano, T. 1994. *Konstantinos Laskaris: Humanist, Philologe, Lehrer, Kopist*. Meletemata 4. Hamburg.

———. 1998. *Constantino Láscaris, semblanza de un humanista bizantino*. Madrid.

Marx, A. 1919. "Aldus and the First Use of Hebrew Type in Venice." *Papers of the Bibliographical Society of America* 13: 64–7.

Marzo Magno, A. 2013. *Bound in Venice: The Serene Republic and the Dawn of the Book*. Trans. G. Conti. New York.

Matthew, L. C. 1998. "The Painter's Presence: Signatures in Venetian Renaissance Pictures." *Art Bulletin* 80: 616–48.

Mattingly, H. 1936. *Coins of the Roman Empire in the British Museum. Volume III: Nero to Hadrian*. London.

Maxson, B. J. 2014. *The Humanist World of Renaissance Florence*. Cambridge.

Mazzoli, G. 1970. *Seneca e la poesia*. Milan.

Mazzotta, A. 2009. "Gabriele Veneto e un ritratto dimenticato di Giovanni Bellini." *Prospettiva* 134–5: 2–24.

McCurdy, E. 2005. *The Mind of Leonardo da Vinci*. Mineola, NY; first published in New York, 1928.

McEwen, I. K. 1995. "Housing Fame: In the Tuscan Villa of Pliny the Younger." *Res* 27: 11–24.

McGuire, W. J. et al. eds. 2000. *The Archaeology of Geological Catastrophes*. Geological Society Special Publication 171. London.

McInerney, J. and Sluiter, I. eds. 2016. *Valuing Landscape in Classical Antiquity: Natural Environment and Cultural Imagination*. Leiden.

McKenzie, D. F. 1999. *Bibliography and the Sociology of Texts*. Cambridge. (Panizzi Lectures, 1985; first published by British Library, 1986.)

McKitterick, D. ed. 1981. *Stanley Morison: Selected Essays on the History of Letter-Forms in Manuscript and Print*. 2 vols. Cambridge.

McLaughlin, M. L. 1995. *Literary Imitation in the Italian Renaissance: The Theory and Practice of Literary Imitation in Italy from Dante to Bembo*. Oxford.

———. 2015. "Petrarch and Cicero: Adulation and Critical Distance." In Altman. 19–38.

Meschini, A. ed. 1977. *Demetrio Mosco: La storia di Elena e Alessandro*. Padua.

Mikołajczyk, I. 1997. *Pietro Bembo, O Etnie*. Toruń.

Milanesi, G. 1879. *Le Opere di Giorgio Vasari. Tomo III: Le Vite de' più eccellenti pittori, scultori ed architettori scritte da Giorgio Vasari*. Florence.

———. 1881. *Le Opere di Giorgio Vasari. Tomo VII: Le Vite de' più eccellenti pittori, scultori ed architettori scritte da Giorgio Vasari*. Florence.

Millet, O. 2012. "Hiéroglyphes et allégorie dans la première moitié du XVIe siècle: De la reconfiguration humaniste de l'allégorisme." *Revue d'histoire littéraire de la France* 112.2: 263–76.

Mills, W. J. 1982. "Metaphorical Vision: Changes in Western Attitudes to the Environment." *Annals of the Association of American Geographers* 72.2: 237–53.

Milroy, R. 1999. *Franceso Griffo da Bologna: Fragments and Glimpses. A Compendium of Information and Opinions about His Life and Work*. Vancouver.

Minelli, A. ed. 1995. *The Botanical Garden of Padua, 1545–1995*. Venice.

Minio-Paluello, L. 1963. "Attività filosofico-editoriale aristotelica dell'umanesimo." In Branca 1963b: 245–62.

Mitchell, C. and Bodnar, E. W. eds. 1996. *Vita viri clarissimi et famosissimi Kyriaci Anconitani by Francesco Scalamonti*. Philadelphia.

Mitchell, C., Bodnar, E. W., and Foss, C. eds. 2015. *Cyriac of Ancona: Life and Early Travels*. I Tatti Renaissance Library 65. Cambridge, MA.

Monfasani, J. 1988. "The First Call for Press Censorship: Niccolò Perotti, Giovanni Andrea Bussi, Antonio Moreto, and the Editing of Pliny's *Natural History*." *Renaissance Quarterly* 41.1: 1–31.

Montecchi, G. 1992. "L'imposizione nei libri in ottavo di Aldo Manuzio." In Santoro. 1.355–76.

Montiglio, S. 2006. "Should the Aspiring Wise Man Travel? A Conflict in Seneca's Thought." *American Journal of Philology* 127.4: 553–86.

Morelli, G. 1900. *Italian Painters: Critical Studies of their Works*. 2nd impression. 2 vols. Trans. C. J. Ffoulkes. London.

Morelli, J. 1800. *Notizia d'opere di disegno nella prima metà del secolo XVI esistenti in Padova, Cremona, Milano, Pavia, Bergamo, Crema e Venezia*. Bassano.

Morgan, K. A. 2015. *Pindar and the Construction of Syracusan Monarchy in the Fifth Century B.C.* Oxford.

Morison, S. 1942. *"Black Letter" Text*. Cambridge.

———. 1949. *Four Centuries of Fine Printing: Two Hundred and Seventy-Two Examples of the Work of Presses Established between 1465 and 1924*. 2nd ed. New York.

Moro, C. 1999. "Il vulcano degli dei: Geografia del mito, tradizione poetica e tecnica compositiva nel *De raptu Proserpinae* di Claudiano." In Avezzù and Pianezzola. 171–226.

Moschella, M. 1991. "Dionigi da Borgo Sansepolcro." *Dizionario biografico degli italiani* 40: 194–7.

Moscheo, R. 1987. "L'insegnamento del greco a Messina 'dopo' Costantino Lascaris (note in margine ad una pergamena inedita)." *Nuovi annali della Facoltà di magistero dell'Università di Messina* 5: 537–50.

———. 1988a. *Francesco Maurolico tra Rinascimento e scienza galileiana: Materiali e ricerche.* Messina.

———. 1988b. "Scienza e cultura a Messina tra '400 e '500: Eredità del Lascaris e 'filologia' mauroliciana." *Nuovi annali della Facoltà di magistero dell'Università di Messina* 6: 595–632.

———. 2001. "Greek Heritage and the Scientific Work of Francesco Maurolico." In Napolitani and Souffrin. 15–22.

Muecke, F. 2006. "A (Literary) Voyage round Mt. Etna." *Classicum* 32.1: 13–23.

Mugnai Carrara, D. 1979. "Profilo di Nicolò Leoniceno." *Interpres* 2: 169–212.

———. 1991. *La biblioteca di Nicolò Leoniceno. Tra Aristotele e Galeno: Cultura e libri di un medico umanista.* Florence.

Müller, G. M. 2002. "Zur Signatur frühneuzeitlicher Naturwahrnehmung und deren Inszenierung in Pietro Bembos Dialog *De Aetna*." In Hempfer. 279–312.

Munro, H. A. J. ed. 1867. *Aetna.* Cambridge.

Murgatroyd, P. 1988. "Pindar *Pythian* I." *Literator* 9.2: 48–66.

Musa, M. 1996. *Petrarch: The Canzoniere, or Rerum Vulgarium Fragmenta.* Bloomington.

Myers. K. S. 1994. *Ovid's Causes: Cosmogony and Aetiology in the Metamorphoses.* Ann Arbor.

Mynors, R. A. B. 1991. *Collected Works of Erasmus, Volume 3: Adages II i 1 to II vi 100.* Toronto.

Nalezyty, S. 2013a. "'Fortunato è il figlio per avere un tal padre ed il padre un tal figlio.' Continuità e differenze nelle collezioni di Bernardo e Pietro Bembo." In Beltramini, Burns, and Gasparotto. 421–31.

———. 2013b. "From Padua to Rome: Pietro Bembo's Mobile Objects and Convivial Interiors." In Campbell et al. 33–46.

Napolitani, P. D. and Souffrin, P. eds. 2001. *Medieval and Classical Traditions and the Renaissance of Physico-Mathematical Sciences in the 16th Century: Proceedings of the XXth International Congress of History of Science (Liège, 20–26 July 1997).* Turnhout.

Nardi, M. G. 1957. "Niccolò Leoniceno e A. Poliziano." In *Il Poliziano e il suo tempo: Atti del IV Convegno internazionale di studi sul Rinascimento, Firenze, Palazzo Strozzi, 23–26 settembre 1954.* 247–51. Florence.

Naselli, M. 1934. "L'eruzione etnea descritta dal Bembo." *Archivio storico per la Sicilia orientale* 30: 116–23.

Nauert, C. G. 1979. "Humanists, Scientists, and Pliny: Changing Approaches to a Classical Author." *American Historical Review* 84.1: 72–85.

———. 1980. "Caius Plinius Secundus." In Cranz. 297–422.

———. 2006. *Humanism and the Culture of Renaissance Europe.* 2nd ed. Cambridge.

Neilson, G. 1895. "A Venetian's Commonplaces." *The Athenaeum* 3556 (December 21, 1895): 871–2.

Nesto, B. and Di Savino, F. 2013. *The World of Sicilian Wine.* Berkeley.

Nicolson, M. H. 1959. *Mountain Gloom and Mountain Glory: The Development of the Aesthetics of the Infinite*. Ithaca, NY.

Nicolson, N. and Trautmann, J. eds. 1977. *The Letters of Virginia Woolf. Vol. III: 1923–1928*. New York.

Nicosia, R. 2014. "Alla scuola di Omero: Costantino Lascaris e la traduzione latina dell'*Odissea* nel *De Aetna* di Pietro Bembo." *I Tatti Studies in the Italian Renaissance* 17.2: 303–24.

Nisbet, R. G. M. and Hubbard, M. 1970. *A Commentary on Horace: Odes, Book I*. Oxford.

———. 1978. *A Commentary on Horace: Odes, Book II*. Oxford.

Nisbet, R. G. M. and Rudd, N. 2004. *A Commentary on Horace: Odes, Book III*. Oxford.

Nolhac, P., de. 1887. *La bibliothèque de Fulvio Orsini: contributions à l'histoire des collections d'Italie et à l'étude de la Renaissance*. Paris.

———. 1888. *Les correspondants d'Alde Manuce: matériaux nouveaux d'histoire littéraire*. Rome.

Norman, D. ed. 1995. *Siena, Florence and Padua: Art, Society and Religion 1280–1460*. 2 vols. New Haven.

Norton, F. 1958. *Italian Printers 1501–20: An Annotated List, with an Introduction*. London.

Norwich, J. J. 1982. *A History of Venice*. New York.

Noyce, W. 1950. *Scholar Mountaineers: Pioneers of Parnassus*. London.

Nuovo, A. 2013. *The Book Trade in the Italian Renaissance*. Trans. L. G. Cochrane. Leiden.

Nuti, E. 2013. "Reconsidering Renaissance Greek Grammars through the Case of Chrysoloras' *Erotemata*." *Greek, Roman, and Byzantine Studies* 53.1: 240–68.

Nutton, V. 1997a. "Hellenism Postponed: Some Aspects of Renaissance Medicine, 1490–1530." *Sudhoffs Archiv* 81.2: 158–70

———. 1997b. "The Rise of Medical Humanism: Ferrara, 1464–1555." *Renaissance Studies* 11.1: 2–19.

Nuvoloni, L. 2011. "Bembo ritrovato: Varianti e correzioni d'autore nel *De Aetna* aldino della University Library di Cambridge." *L'Ellisse: Studi storici di letteratura italiana* 6: 205–10.

O'Connell, Michael 1983. "Authority and the Truth of Experience in Petrarch's 'Ascent of Mount Ventoux.'" *Philological Quarterly* 62.4: 507–20.

O'Connell, Monique 2009. *Men of Empire: Power and Negotiation in Venice's Maritime State*. Baltimore.

O'Malley, C. D. 1961. *Thomas Bartholin: On the Burning of his Library, and On Medical Travel*. Lawrence, KS.

O'Sullivan, T. M. 2011. *Walking in Roman Culture*. Cambridge.

Ogilvie, B. W. 2006. *The Science of Describing: Natural History in Renaissance Europe*. Chicago.

Oliver, R. P. 1947. "'New Fragments' of Latin Authors in Perotti's *Cornucopiae*." *Transactions and Proceedings of the American Philological Association* 78: 376–424.

Olmos, P. ed. 2012. *Greek Science in the Long Run: Essays on the Greek Scientific Tradition (4th c. BCE–17th c. CE)*. Newcastle upon Tyne, UK.

Omont, H. 1894. "Inventaire des manuscrits grecs et latins donnés à Saint-Marc de Venise par le Cardinal Bessarion en 1468." *Revue des bibliothèques* 4: 129–87.

Orioli, E. 1900. "Contributo alla storia della stampa in Bologna." In *Atti e memorie della R. deputazione di storia patria per le provincie di Romagna: Terza serie, Vol. XVII (anno accademico 1898–99)*. 162–83. Bologna.

Orlandi, G. ed. 1975. *Aldo Manuzio editore. Dediche, prefazioni, note ai testi*. Introduction by C. Dionisotti; Latin text with translation and notes edited by Giovanni Orlandi. 2 vols. Milan.

Pade, M. ed. 2005. *On Renaissance Commentaries*. Hildesheim, Zürich, and New York.

Pagliaroli, S. 2015. "L'ultimo carattere greco di Aldo Manuzio." In Donadi et al. 97–141.

Painter, G. D. 1984. *Studies in Fifteenth Century Printing*. London.

Paisley, P. B. and Oldroyd, D. R. 1979. "Science in the Silver Age: *Aetna*, a Classical Theory of Volcanic Activity." *Centaurus* 23: 1–20.

Pallucchini, R. 1949. *Giovanni Bellini: Catalogo illustrato della mostra, Palazzo Ducale, Venezia, 12 giugno–5 ottobre 1949*. Venice.

———. 1959. *Giovanni Bellini*. Milan.

Palmer, A. ed. 1898. *P. Ovidi Nasonis Heroides*. Oxford.

Palmer, R. 1985. "Medical Botany in Northern Italy in the Renaissance." *Journal of the Royal Society of Medicine* 78.2: 149–57.

Panessa, G. 1991. *Fonti greche e latine per la storia dell'ambiente e del clima nel mondo greco*. 2 vols. Pisa.

Panofsky, E. 1939. *Studies in Iconology: Humanistic Themes in the Art of the Renaissance*. New York.

Papaioannou, S. 2003. "Founder, Civilizer and Leader: Vergil's Evander and His Role in the Origins of Rome." *Mnemosyne* 56.6: 680–702.

Papathomopoulos, M. ed. 1968. *Antoninus Liberalis: Les Métamorphoses*. Paris.

Parkes, M. B. 1993. *Pause and Effect: An Introduction to the History of Punctuation in the West*. Berkeley.

Paschini, P. 1957. *Tre illustri prelati del Rinascimento: Ermolao Barbaro, Adriano Castellesi, Giovanni Grimani*. Rome.

Pearce, S. M. 1992. *Museums, Objects, and Collections: A Cultural Study*. Leicester, UK.

———. ed. 1994. *Interpreting Objects and Collections*. London.

Pecoraro, M. 1959. *Per la storia dei carmi del Bembo: Una redazione non vulgata*. Venice.

Pellegrini, P. ed. 2001. *Umanisti Bellunesi fra quattro e cinquecento: Atti del Convegno di Belluno, 5 novembre 1999*. Florence.

———. 2013. "Niccolò da Lonigo (Niccolò Leoniceno)." *Dizionario biografico degli italiani* 78: 409–14.

Pelletier, M. ed. 1989. *Géographie du monde au Moyen Age et à la Renaissance*. Paris.

Pertile, F. and Camesasca, E. eds. 1957–60, *Lettere sull'arte di Pietro Aretino*. 3 vols. Milan.

Pertusi, A. 1962. "ΕΡΩΤΗΜΑΤΑ: Per la storia e le fonti delle prime grammatiche greche a stampa." *Italia medioevale e umanistica* 5: 321–51.

———. 1980. "L'umanesimo greco dalla fine del secolo XIV agli inizi del secolo XVI." In Arnaldi and Pastore Stocchi. 177–264.

Pesenti, G. 1916. "Diario odeporico-bibliografico inedito del Poliziano." *Memorie del R. Istituto Lombardo di Scienze e Lettere, Classe di lettere, scienze morali e storiche* 23: 229–39.

Peters, E. 2001. "The Desire to Know the Secrets of the World." *Journal of the History of Ideas* 62.4: 593–610.

Petrucci, A. 1969. "Alle origini del libro moderno. Libri da banco, libri da bisaccia, libretti da mano." *Italia medioevale e umanistica* 12: 295–313.

Pettegree, A. 2010. *The Book in the Renaissance*. New Haven.

Piccolomini, E. 1890. "Una lettera greca di Pietro Bembo a Demetrio Mosco." *Archivio storico italiano* 5.6: 307–9.

Pincus, D. 2008. "Giovanni Bellini's Humanist Signature: Pietro Bembo, Aldus Manutius and Humanism in Early Sixteenth-Century Venice." *Artibus et Historiae* 29.58: 89–119.

Pincus, D. and Shapiro Comte, B. 2006. "A Drawing for the Tomb of Dante Attributed to Tullio Lombardo." *Burlington Magazine* 148.1244: 734–46.

Pinon, L. 2010. "Natural History." In Grafton et al. 2010: 621–7.

Pintor, F. 1911. "Le due ambascerie di Bernardo Bembo a Firenze e le sue relazioni coi Medici." In *Studi letterari e linguistici dedicati a Pio Rajna*. 785–813. Florence.

Piovan, F. 1987. "Lampridio, Bembo e altri (schede d'archivio)." *Italia medioevale e umanistica* 30: 179–97.

———. 1997. "Forteguerri, Scipione." *Dizionario biografico degli italiani* 49: 163–7.

Plaitakis, A. and Duvoisin, R. C. 1983. "Homer's Moly Identified as *Galanthus nivalis* L.: Physiologic Antidote to Stramonium Poisoning." *Clinical Neuropharmacology* 6.1: 1–5.

Pomian, K. 1990. *Collectors and Curiosities: Paris and Venice, 1500–1800*. Trans. E. Wiles-Portier. Cambridge.

Pontani, F. ed. 2002. *Angeli Politiani Liber epigrammatum graecorum*. Rome.

Potter, D. 2008. *Renaissance France at War: Armies, Culture and Society, c. 1480–1560*. Woodbridge, UK.

Pottinger, D. 1941. *Printers and Printing*. Cambridge, MA.

Powell, J. G. F. ed. 1988. *Cicero: Cato Maior de Senectute*. Cambridge Classical Texts and Commentaries 28. Cambridge.

Pozzi, G. ed. 1973–9. *Hermolai Barbari Castigationes Plinianae et in Pomponium Melam*. 4 vols. Padua.

Pozzi, G. and Ciapponi, L. A. eds. 1980. *Francesco Colonna: Hypnerotomachia Poliphili*. 2 vols. Padua.

Prete, S. 1970. *Il codice di Terenzio Vaticano latino 3226. Saggio critico e riproduzione del manoscritto*. Vatican City.

Preto, P. 2010. *I servizi segreti di Venezia. Spionaggio e controspionaggio ai tempi della Serenissima*. Milan.

Proctor, R. 1900. *The Printing of Greek in the Fifteenth Century*. Oxford.

Puppi, L. 1969. "Le residenze di Pietro Bembo 'in padoana.'" *L'Arte* 7–8: 30–65.

———. 1972. "The Villa Garden of the Veneto from the Fifteenth to the Eighteenth Century." In Coffin. 81–114.

———. 1974. "Campagnola, Domenico." *Dizionario biografico degli italiani* 17: 312–17.

Queller, D. E. 1969. "The Civic Irresponsibility of the Venetian Nobility." In Herlihy et al. 223–35.

———. 1986. *The Venetian Patriciate: Reality versus Myth*. Urbana.

Quilici, P. 1992. "La legatura aldina." In Santoro. 1.377–400.

Rabil, A. ed. 1988. *Renaissance Humanism: Foundations, Forms, and Legacy*. 3 vols. Philadelphia.

Raboni, G. ed. 1989. *Pietro Bembo, Lucrezia Borgia, La grande fiamma. Lettere 1503–1517*. Milan.

Radford, R. S. 1923. "The Language of the Pseudo-Vergilian *Catalepton* with Especial Reference to Its Ovidian Characteristics." *Transactions and Proceedings of the American Philological Association* 54: 168–86.

Ramminger, J. 2005. "A Commentary? Ermolao Barbaro's Supplement to Dioscorides." In Pade. 65–85.

Raschieri, A. A. 2011. "Bonino Mombrizio traduttore dell'*Epitome* grammaticale di Costantino Lascaris." In Balbo et al. 741–53.

———. 2012. "Giorgio Valla, Editor and Translator of Ancient Scientific Texts." In Olmos. 127–49.

Rea, J. A. 2007. *Legendary Rome: Myth, Monuments, and Memory on the Palatine and Capitoline*. London.

Rebecchini, G. 2002. *Private Collectors in Mantua, 1500–1630*. Rome.

Reeds, K. M. 1976. "Renaissance Humanism and Botany." *Annals of Science* 33: 519–42.

Reidy, D.V. ed. 1993. *The Italian Book 1465–1800: Studies Presented to Dennis E. Rhodes on his 70th Birthday*. The British Library. London.

Resnick, I. M. 2010. *Albert the Great: On the Causes of the Properties of the Elements (Liber de causis proprietatum elementorum)*. Mediaeval Philosophical Texts in Translation 46. Milwaukee, WI.

Rhodes, D. E. 1984. "The Botanical Garden of Padua: The First Hundred Years." *Journal of Garden History* 4.4: 327–31.

Ribuoli, R. 1981. *La collazione polizianea del codice Bembino di Terenzio: con le postille inedite del Poliziano e note su Pietro Bembo*. Rome.

Ricciardi, R. 1986. "Da Ponte, Ludovico (Ponticus Virunius)." *Dizionario biografico degli italiani* 32: 720–3.

Riccomini, A. M. 2013. "5.31: Arte romana; *Tavola bronzea con scene egittizzanti ('Mensa Isiaca' o 'Tabula Bembina')*." In Beltramini, Gasparotto, and Tura. 340–2.

Richardson, B. 1994. *Print Culture in Renaissance Italy: The Editor and the Vernacular Text, 1470–1600*. Cambridge.

———. 1999. *Printing, Writers and Readers in Renaissance Italy*. Cambridge.

———. 2009. *Manuscript Culture in Renaissance Italy*. Cambridge.

Richardson, L. 1992. *A New Topographical Dictionary of Ancient Rome*. Baltimore.

Riddle, J. M. 1980. "Dioscorides." In Cranz. 1–143.

Ridolfi, C. 1648. *Le maraviglie dell'arte, overo Le vite de gl'illustri pittori veneti, e dello stato*. 2 vols. Venice.

Rizzoli, L. 1905. "Una medaglia del Bembo che non è opera di Benvenuto Cellini." *L'Arte* 7: 276–80.

———. 1932. "Ritratti di Francesco il Vecchio e di Francesco Novello da Carrara in medaglie ed affreschi padovani nel secolo XIV." *Bollettino del Museo civico di Padova* 25: 104–14.

Robbins, J. 1985. "Petrarch Reading Augustine: 'The Ascent of Mont Ventoux.'" *Philological Quarterly* 64.4: 533–53.

Robinson, D. 2002. "'Still Glides the Stream': Form and Function in Wordsworth's *River Duddon* Sonnets." *European Romantic Review* 13: 449–64.

Rodini, E. 2013. "The Politics of Marriage in Carpaccio's St. Ursula Cycle." *Early Modern Women* 8: 85–117.

Rodwell, G. F. 1878. *Etna: A History of the Mountain and Its Eruptions*. Cambridge.

Rogers, M. 1986. "Sonnets on Female Portraits from Renaissance North Italy." *Word & Image* 2.4: 291–305.

Rogledi Manni, T. 1980. *La tipografia a Milano nel XV secolo*. Florence.

Roller, D. W. 2014. *The Geography of Strabo*. Cambridge.

Rollo, A. 2001. "La grammatica greca di Urbano Bolzanio." In Pellegrini 2001: 177–209.

Romani, V. 2013. "Pietro Bembo tra cultura figurativa cortigiana e 'maniera moderna.'" In Beltramini, Gasparotto, and Tura. 32–47.

Romano, R. and Sturiale, C. 1982. "The Historical Eruptions of Mt. Etna (Volcanological Data)." *Memorie della Società geologica italiana* 23: 75–97.

Ronchi, O. 1923–4. "La casa di Pietro Bembo a Padova (da documenti inediti)." *Atti e memorie della R. Accademia di Scienze, Lettere ed Arti in Padova* 40: 285–329.

Rosada, R. A. 1997. "'Grecolo tuto.' Appunti sulla formazione umanistica greca del giovane Pietro Bembo." In Agostini and Lippi. 43–60.

Rosalia, A., de. 1957–8. "La vita di Costantino Lascari." *Archivio storico Siciliano* 9: 21–70.

Rosand, D. 2001. *Myths of Venice: The Figuration of a State*. Chapel Hill.

Rosati, G. 2002. "Narrative Techniques and Narrative Structures in the *Metamorphoses*." In Boyd. 271–304.

———. 2009. "*Latrator Anubis*: Alien Divinities in Augustan Rome, and How to Tame Monsters through Aetiology." In Hardie 2009b: 268–87.

Rossi, A. 2001. "Remapping the Past: Caesar's Tale of Troy (Lucan *BC* 9.964–999)." *Phoenix* 55.3–4: 313–26.

Rostagni, A. 1933. *Virgilio minore. Saggio sullo svolgimento della poesia virgiliana*. Turin.

Rothwell, K. S. 1996. "Propertius on the Site of Rome." *Latomus* 55.4: 829–54.

Rowland, I. D. 1998. *The Culture of the High Renaissance: Ancients and Moderns in Sixteenth-Century Rome*. Cambridge.

———. 2000. *The Ecstatic Journey: Athanasius Kircher in Baroque Rome*. Chicago.

Rubenstein, R. 2008. "'I Meant *Nothing* by *The Lighthouse*': Virginia Woolf's Poetics of Negation." *Journal of Modern Literature* 31.4: 36–53.

Rubin, P. 2006. "Signposts of Invention: Artists' Signatures in Italian Renaissance Art." *Art History* 29.4: 563–99.

Ruggiero, G. 2015. *The Renaissance in Italy: A Social and Cultural History of the Rinascimento.* Cambridge.

Safarik, E. 1974. "Campagnola, Giulio." *Dizionario biografico degli italiani* 17: 318–21.

Salatino, K. 1997. *Incendiary Art: The Representation of Fireworks in Early Modern Europe.* Los Angeles.

Salemi, J. S. 1982. "The Faunus Poems of Pietro Bembo." *Allegorica* 7.2: 31–57.

Salmeri, G. 1997. "L'Etna del viaggio e della scienza." In *Etna, mito d'Europa.* 124–35. Catania.

Salomon, X. F. 2003. "Cardinal Pietro Barbo's Collection and Its Inventory Reconsidered." *Journal of the History of Collections* 15.1: 1–18.

San Juan, R. M. 1991. "The Court Lady's Dilemma: Isabella d'Este and Art Collecting in the Renaissance." *Oxford Art Journal* 14.1: 67–78.

Sansovino, F. 1581. *Venetia, città nobilissima, et singolare, descritta in XIIII libri.* Venice.

———. 1584. *Delle orationi volgarmente scritte da diversi huomini illustri.* 2 vols. Venice.

Santelia, S. 2012. *La miranda fabula dei pii fratres in Aetna 603–645.* Bari.

Santoro, M. ed. 1992. *La stampa in Italia nel Cinquecento. Atti del Convegno, Roma, 17–21 ottobre 1989.* 2 vols. Rome.

Scaccia Scarafoni, C. 1947. "La più antica edizione della grammatica latina di Aldo Manuzio finora sconosciuta ai bibliografi." In Donati 1947: 193–203.

Scapecchi, P. 2001. "Vecchi e nuovi appunti su frate Urbano." In Pellegrini 2001: 107–18.

Scarth, A. 2000. "The Volcanic Inspiration of Some Images in the *Aeneid*." *Classical World* 93.6: 591–605.

———. 2009. *Vesuvius: A Biography.* Princeton.

Schaffenrath, F. ed. 2010. *Silius Italicus: Akten der Innsbrucker Tagung vom 19.–21. Juni 2008.* Frankfurt am Main.

Schama, S. 1995. *Landscape and Memory.* New York.

Scher, S. K. 2000a. "An Introduction to the Renaissance Portrait Medal." In Scher 2000b: 1–9.

———. ed. 2000b. *Perspectives on the Renaissance Medal.* American Numismatic Society Numismatic Studies Volume 23. New York.

Schmitt, C. B. and Knox, D. 1985. *Pseudo-Aristoteles Latinus: A Guide to Latin Works Falsely Attributed to Aristotle before 1500.* London.

Schmitt, W. O. 1971. "Eine unbekannte Rede zum Lob der griechischen Sprache und Literatur. Zur literarischen Biographie des Humanisten Andronikos Kontoblakes." *Philologus* 115.1: 264–77.

Schmitter, M. A. 1995. "Botticelli's Images of Simonetta Vespucci: Between Portrait and Ideal." *Rutgers Art Review* 15: 33–57.

———. 2003. "The Dating of Marcantonio Michiel's *Notizia* on Works of Art in Padua." *Burlington Magazine* 145.1205: 564–71.

———. 2007. "Odoni's Façade: The House as Portrait in Renaissance Venice." *Journal of the Society of Architectural Historians* 66.3: 294–315.

Schulz, J. 1978. "Jacopo de' Barbari's View of Venice: Map Making, City Views, and Moralized Geography before the Year 1500." *Art Bulletin* 60.3: 425–74.

Sebesta, J. L. 2006. "Vesuvius in Classical Literature." *New England Classical Journal* 33.2: 99–111.

Sedley, D. 1998. *Lucretius and the Transformation of Greek Wisdom*. Cambridge.

Segal, C. 1986. *Pindar's Mythmaking: The Fourth Pythian Ode*. Princeton.

Seider, A. M. 2013. *Memory in Vergil's Aeneid: Creating the Past*. Cambridge.

Sens, A. ed. 1997. *Theocritus: Dioscuri (Idyll 22). Introduction, Text, and Commentary. Hypomnemata* 114. Göttingen.

Shackleton Bailey, D. R. ed. 1977. *Cicero: Epistulae ad Familiares. Vol. I: 62-47 B.C.* Cambridge Classical Texts and Commentaries 16. Cambridge.

Shankland, H. 1987. *The Prettiest Love Letters in the World: Letters between Lucrezia Borgia and Pietro Bembo 1503 to 1519*. Boston.

Shaw, D. J. 1993. "The Lyons Counterfeit of Aldus's Italic Type. A New Chronology." In Reidy. 117–33.

Shearman, J. K. G. 1983. *The Early Italian Pictures in the Collection of Her Majesty the Queen*. Cambridge.

Sherman, A. 2013. "Murder and Martyrdom: Titian's Gesuiti *Saint Lawrence* as a Family Peace Offering." *Artibus et Historiae* 68.34: 39–54.

Sherman, W. H. 2008. *Used Books: Marking Readers in Renaissance England*. Philadelphia.

———. 2013. "*Nota Bembe*: How Bembo the Elder Read His Pliny the Younger." In Beltramini, Burns, and Gasparotto. 119–33.

Shoumatoff, N. and Shoumatoff, N. 2001. *The Alps: Europe's Mountain Heart*. Ann Arbor.

Sigurdsson, H. 1999. *Melting the Earth: The History of Ideas on Volcanic Eruptions*. Oxford.

Simonsen, P. 2007. "Italic Typography and Wordsworth's Later Sonnets as Visual Poetry." *Studies in English Literature, 1500–1900* 47.4: 863–80.

Skulsky, S. D. 1975. "ΠΟΛΛΩΝ ΠΕΙΡΑΤΑ ΣΥΝΤΑΝΥΣΑΙΣ: Language and Meaning in *Pythian* 1." *Classical Philology* 70.1: 8–31.

Smiley, M. T. 1920. "The Mss. of Callimachus' *Hymns* (Continued)." *Classical Quarterly* 14.2: 57–77.

Snyder, J. M. 1972. "Lucretius' Empedoclean Sicily." *Classical World* 65.7: 217–18.

Sodano, R. ed. 1990. *Pietro Bembo: Carmina*. Turin.

Spaltenstein, F. 1990. *Commentaire des Punica de Silius Italicus (livres 9 à 17)*. Geneva.

Speake, G. 1974. "The Scribal Habits of Demetrius Moschus." *Greek, Roman and Byzantine Studies* 15: 113–33.

Spencer, D. 2010. *Roman Landscape: Culture and Identity*. Greece and Rome New Surveys in the Classics 39. Cambridge.

Speranzi, D. 2015. "Prima di Aldo. Demetrio Damilas disegnatore di caratteri." In Donadi et al. 143–61.

Spezi, G. 1862. *Lettere inedite del Card. Pietro Bembo e di altri scrittori del secolo XVI*. Rome.

Stahl, A. M. and Waldman, L. 1993–4. "The Earliest Known Medalists: The Sesto Brothers of Venice." *American Journal of Numismatics* 5–6: 167–88.

Staikos, K. Sp. 2009. *Printers' and Publishers' Marks in Books for the Greek World (1494-1821)*. Trans. T. Cullen. New Castle, DE.

Steinberg, S. H. 1996. *Five Hundred Years of Printing*. 4th ed., revised by John Trevitt. New Castle, DE.

Stenhouse, W. 2014. "Roman Antiquities and the Emergence of Renaissance Civic Collections." *Journal of the History of Collections* 26.2: 131–44.

Stephens, J. N. 1990. *The Italian Renaissance: The Origins of Intellectual and Artistic Change before the Reformation*. London.

Stevenson, E. L. 1921. *Terrestrial and Celestial Globes: Their History and Construction, Including a Consideration of Their Value as Aids in the Study of Geography and Astronomy*. 2 vols. Publications of the Hispanic Society of America 86. New Haven.

Stewart, J. F. 1977. "Light in *To the Lighthouse*." *Twentieth Century Literature* 23.3: 377–89.

Stewering, R. 2000. "Architectural Representations in the *Hypnerotomachia Poliphili* (Aldus Manutius, 1499)." *Journal of the Society of Architectural Historians* 59.1: 6–25.

Stocks, C. A. 2010. "[Re]constructing Epic: Sicily and the *Punica* in Miniature." In Schaffenrath. 151–66.

Stok, F. 2002. *Studi sul Cornu copiae di Niccolò Perotti*. Pisa.

Stoppelli, P. ed. 1997. *Francesco Petrarca, Opera omnia*. CD ROM: Lexis Progetti Editoriali. Rome.

Stothers, R. B. and Rampino, M. R. 1983. "Volcanic Eruptions in the Mediterranean before A.D. 630 from Written and Archaeological Sources." *Journal of Geophysical Research* 88.B8: 6357–71.

Sudhaus, S. ed. 1898. *Aetna*. Leipzig.

Suida, W. 1936. "New Light on Titian's Portraits, II." *Burlington Magazine* 68.399: 281–2.

Sullivan, F. A. 1972. "Volcanoes and Volcanic Characters in Virgil." *Classical Philology* 67.3: 186–91.

Summers, W. C. ed. 1910. *Select Letters of Seneca*. London.

Syndikus, C. and Rogge, S. eds. 2013. *Caterina Cornaro: Last Queen of Cyprus and Daughter of Venice. International Conference, Venice 16–18 September 2010*. Münster.

Syson, L. 2011. *Leonardo da Vinci: Painter at the Court of Milan*. With Keith, L. et al. Exhibition Catalogue (London, National Gallery). London.

Tall, D. 1993. *From Where We Stand: Recovering a Sense of Place*. New York.

Tanguy, J.-C. 1981. "Les éruptions historiques de l'Etna: Chronologie et localisation." *Bulletin of Volcanology* 44.3: 585–640.

Tanguy, J.-C. et al. 2007. "Mount Etna Eruptions of the Last 2,750 Years: Revised Chronology and Location through Archeomagnetic and ^{226}Ra-^{230}Th Dating." *Bulletin of Volcanology* 70.1: 55–83.

Taub, L. 2008. *Aetna and the Moon: Explaining Nature in Ancient Greece and Rome*. Corvallis, OR.

———. 2009. "Explaining a Volcano Naturally: Aetna and the Choice of Poetry." In Taub and Doody. 125–41.

Taub, L. and Doody, A. eds. 2009. *Authorial Voices in Greco-Roman Technical Writing*. Trier.

Tenenti, A. 1996. "La *res uxoria* tra Francesco Barbaro e Leon Battista Alberti." In Marangoni and Pastore Stocchi. 43–66.

Tesoriero, C. ed. 2010. *Oxford Readings in Classical Studies: Lucan*. Oxford.

Thomas, R. F. 1999. *Reading Virgil and His Texts: Studies in Intertextuality*. Ann Arbor.

Thomason, R. F. 1923. "The *Ciris* and Ovid: A Study of the Language of the Poem, II." *Classical Philology* 18.4: 334–44.

Thompson, L. and Bruère, R. T. 1968. "Lucan's Use of Virgilian Reminiscence." *Classical Philology* 63.1: 1–21. Reprinted in Tesoriero. 107–48.

Thomson, S. H. 1950. "Learning at the Court of Charles IV." *Speculum* 25.1: 1–20.

Thornton, D. 1997. *The Scholar in His Study: Ownership and Experience in Renaissance Italy*. New Haven.

Tietze-Conrat, E. 1944. "Titian as a Letter Writer." *Art Bulletin* 26.2: 117–23.

———. 1945. "Titian's *Battle of Cadore*." *Art Bulletin* 27.3: 205–8.

Todd, R. B. 2003. "Themistius." In V. Brown 2003: 57–102.

Tolias, G. 2007. "*Isolarii*, Fifteenth to Seventeenth Century." In Woodward. 263–84.

Tongiorgi Tomasi, L. 2005. "Gardens of Knowledge and the *République des Gens de Sciences*." In Conan. 85–129.

Toohey, P. 1996. *Epic Lessons: An Introduction to Ancient Didactic Poetry*. London.

Touwaide, A. 2008. "Botany and Humanism in the Renaissance: Background, Interaction, Contradictions." *Studies in the History of Art* 69: 32–61.

Trapp, J. B. 2001. "Petrarch's Laura: The Portraiture of an Imaginary Beloved." *Journal of the Warburg and Courtauld Institutes* 64: 55–192.

———. 2006. "Petrarchan Places: An Essay in the Iconography of Commemoration." *Journal of the Warburg and Courtauld Institutes* 69: 1–50.

Travi, E. 1978. "Pietro Bembo tra letteratura e scienze." In Branca et al. 1978: 414–29.

———. ed. 1987. *Pietro Bembo, Lettere. Vol. I (1492–1507)*. Bologna.

———. ed. 1990. *Pietro Bembo, Lettere. Vol. II (1508–1528)*. Bologna.

———. ed. 1992. *Pietro Bembo, Lettere. Vol. III (1529–1536)*. Bologna.

———. ed. 1993. *Pietro Bembo, Lettere. Vol. IV (1537–1546)*. Bologna.

Trippe, R. 2002. "The *Hypnerotomachia Poliphili*, Image, Text, and Vernacular Poetics." *Renaissance Quarterly* 55.4: 1222–58.

Trovato, P. 1998. *L'ordine dei tipografi. Lettori, stampatori, correttori tra Quattro e Cinquecento*. Rome.

Tuplin, C. J. and Rihll, T. E. eds. 2002. *Science and Mathematics in Ancient Greek Culture*. Oxford.

Turner, H. L. 1987. "Cristopher Buondelmonti and the *Isolario*." *Terrae Incognitae* 19: 11–28.

———. 1989. "Christopher Buondelmonti: Adventurer, Explorer, and Cartographer. In Pelletier. 207–16.

Ulery, R. W. ed. 2007. *Pietro Bembo: History of Venice. Volume I: Books I–IV*. I Tatti Renaissance Library 28. Cambridge, MA.

Ullman, B. L. 1960. *The Origin and Development of Humanistic Script*. Rome.

Underwood, E. A. ed. 1953. *Science, Medicine and History: Essays on the Evolution of Scientific Thought and Medical Practice Written in Honour of Charles Singer*. 2 vols. Oxford.

Uzielli, G. 1890. *Leonardo da Vinci e le Alpi*. Turin.

Vagni, G. 2010. "Da Venezia a Urbino. Ideali e valori del giovane Bembo." *Aevum* 84.3: 733–59.

Vardi, A. D. 1996. "*Diiudicatio locorum*: Gellius and the History of a Mode in Ancient Comparative Criticism." *Classical Quarterly* 46.2: 492–514.

Vecce, C. 1998a. "Aldo e l'invenzione dell'indice." In Zeidberg. 109–41.

———. 1998b. "Bembo e Poliziano." In Fera and Martelli. 477–503.

Vela, C. ed. 2002. *Carlo Dionisotti: Scritti sul Bembo*. Turin.

Vercellin, G. 2001. *Venezia e l'origine della stampa in caratteri arabi*. Padua.

Vermij, R. 1998. "Subterranean Fire: Changing Theories of the Earth during the Renaissance." *Early Science and Medicine* 3.4: 323–47.

Vernon, H. M. 1909. *Italy from 1494 to 1790*. Cambridge.

Viallon(-Schoneweld), M. 2001. "Le *De Aetna* de Pietro Bembo." In Bertrand 2001: 101–18.

———. ed. 2002. *Pietro Bembo: De l'Etna*. Clermont-Ferrand.

Vian, F. ed. 1976. *Nonnos de Panopolis, Les Dionysiaques. Tome I: Chants I–II*. Paris.

Viarre, S. 2001. "Mythologie et philosophie à propos de l'Etna dans les *Métamorphoses* d'Ovide." In Bertrand 2001: 25–34.

Vickers, B. 1990. "Leisure and Idleness in the Renaissance: The Ambivalence of *otium*." *Renaissance Studies* 4.1–2: 1–37 and 107–54.

Victor, B. A. 2006. "Pietro Bembo, Politian and the State of Vat. lat. 3226 at the End of the Middle Ages." *Italia medioevale e umanistica* 47: 243–53.

Vivian, F. 1971. *Il Console Smith, mercante e collezionista*. Vicenza.

Vodraska, S. L. 1969. *Pseudo-Aristotle, De causis proprietatum et elementorum: Critical Study and Edition*. Diss. London.

Volk, K. 2002. *The Poetics of Latin Didactic: Lucretius, Vergil, Ovid, Manilius*. Oxford.

———. 2005. "*Aetna* oder Wie man ein Lehrgedicht schreibt." In Holzberg. 68–90.

———. 2008. "Introduction." In Ellis 2008: vii–xxx.

von Bode, W. 1903. "Leonardos Bildnis der Ginevra dei Benci." *Zeitschrift für bildende Kunst* 14: 274–6.

von der Gönna, G. 2015. *Pietro Bembo,* De Aetna *liber*–Der Ätna. Würzburg.

von Hadeln, D. ed. 1914–24. *Le maraviglie dell'arte, ovvero Le vite degli illustri pittori veneti e dello stato, descritte da Carlo Ridolfi*. 2 vols. Berlin.

von Martels, Z. 2000. "Augurello's *Chrysopoeia* (1515): A Turning Point in the Literary Tradition of Alchemical Texts." *Early Science and Medicine* 5: 178–95.

Walker, J. 1967. "Ginevra de' Benci by Leonardo da Vinci." In *National Gallery of Art: Report and Studies in the History of Art 1967*: 1–37.

Walton, F. R. 1963. "Gennadeion Notes, II: Incunabula in the Gennadius Library." *Hesperia* 32.2: 209–12.

———. 1971. "Incunabula in the Gennadius Library." *Medievalia et Humanistica* 2: 7–20.

Wardrop, J. 1963. *The Script of Humanism: Some Aspects of Humanistic Script, 1460–1560.* Oxford.

Warmington, E. H. ed. 1967. *Remains of Old Latin: Lucilius; The Twelve Tables.* Cambridge, MA.

Watson, C. 2012. "Points of Contention: Rethinking the Past, Present, and Future of Punctuation." *Critical Inquiry* 38.3: 649–72.

Weiss, R. 1962a. "Augurelli, Giovanni Aurelio." *Dizionario biografico degli italiani* 4: 578–81.

———. 1962b. "Giovanni Aurelio Augurello, Girolamo Avogadro, and Isabella d'Este." *Italian Studies* 17: 1–11.

———. 1964. "Un umanista antiquario: Cristoforo Buondelmonti." *Lettere italiane* 16.2: 105–16.

———. 1968. "The Study of Ancient Numismatics during the Renaissance (1313–1517)." *Numismatic Chronicle* 8: 177–87.

———. 1972. "Buondelmonti, Cristoforo." *Dizionario biografico degli italiani* 15: 198–200.

———. 1988. *The Renaissance Discovery of Classical Antiquity*. 2nd ed. Oxford.

Welsh, J. T. 2014. "How to Read a Volcano." *Transactions of the American Philological Association* 144: 97–132.

Werrett, S. 2010. *Fireworks: Pyrotechnic Arts and Sciences in European History*. Chicago.

West, M. L. ed. 1966. *Hesiod: Theogony*. Oxford.

Westcott, W. W. 1887. *Tabula Bembina sive Mensa Isiaca: The Isiac Tablet of Cardinal Bembo. Its History and Occult Significance*. Bath.

Wethey, H. E. 1971. *The Paintings of Titian. II: The Portraits*. London.

Whistler, C. 2012. "Uncovering Beauty: Titian's *Triumph of Love* in the Vendramin Collection." *Renaissance Studies* 26.2: 218–42.

Whitaker, L. 2013. "Bembo in Focus: A Fair Conclusion?" In Beltramini, Burns, and Gasparotto. 329–38.

Whitaker, L. and Clayton, M. 2007. *The Art of Italy in the Royal Collection: Renaissance and Baroque*. With contributions by Loconte, A. London.

White, D. 1964. "Demeter's Sicilian Cult as a Political Instrument." *Greek, Roman, and Byzantine Studies* 5.4: 261–79.

Wilkins, E. H. 1959. *Petrarch's Later Years*. Cambridge, MA.

Williams, G. D. 1994. *Banished Voices: Readings in Ovid's Exile Poetry*. Cambridge.

———. 2012. *The Cosmic Viewpoint: A Study of Seneca's Natural Questions*. Oxford.

———. 2015. "Minding the Gap: Seneca, the Self, and the Sublime." In Williams and Volk. 172–91.

Williams, G. D. and Volk, K. eds. 2015. *Roman Reflections: Studies in Latin Philosophy*. Oxford.

Williams, R. D. ed. 1962. *P. Vergili Maronis Aeneidos Liber Tertius*. Oxford.

Williams-Lehmann, P. and Lehmann, K. 1973. *Samothracian Reflections: Aspects of the Revival of the Antique*. Bollingen Series XCII. Princeton.

Williamson, G. C. ed. 1903. *The Anonimo: Notes on Pictures and Works of Art in Italy Made by an Anonymous Writer in the Sixteenth Century*. Trans. Paolo Mussi. London.

Wilson, K. J. 1985. *Incomplete Fictions: The Formation of English Renaissance Dialogue*. Washington, DC.

Wilson, N. G. 1992. *From Byzantium to Italy: Greek Studies in the Italian Renaissance.* Baltimore.

———. ed. 2003. *Pietro Bembo, Oratio pro litteris graecis.* Quaderni di filologia medievale e umanistica 5. Messina.

———. ed. 2016. *Aldus Manutius: The Greek Classics.* I Tatti Renaissance Library 70. Cambridge, MA.

———. 2017. *From Byzantium to Italy: Greek Studies in the Italian Renaissance.* 2nd ed. London.

Wind, E. 1968. *Pagan Mysteries in the Renaissance.* New York.

Wolff, É. 2004. "L'image de l'Etna dans l'anonyme *Aetna.*" In Foulon. 79–84.

Woods-Marsden, J. 2001. "Portrait of a Lady, 1430–1520." In D. A. Brown 2001: 63–87.

Woodward, D. ed. 2007. *The History of Cartography, Volume 3. Cartography in the European Renaissance: Part 1.* Chicago.

Woolfson, J. and Gregory, A. 1995. "Aspects of Collecting in Renaissance Padua: A Bust of Socrates for Niccolò Leonico Tomeo." *Journal of the Warburg and Courtauld Institutes* 58: 252–65.

Worm, O. 1655. *Museum Wormianum, seu, Historia rerum rariorum, tam naturalium, quam artificialium, tam domesticarum, quam exoticarum, quae Hafniae Danorum in aedibus authoris servantur.* Amsterdam.

Wroth, W. 1896. *The London Pleasure Gardens of the Eighteenth Century.* Assisted by Wroth, A. E. London.

Wulff, F. 1904. *Petrarch at Vaucluse, 1337–1353, with Plates and a Map.* Lund.

Young, D. A. 2003. *Mind over Magma: The Story of Igneous Petrology.* Princeton.

Zaggia, M. 2003. *Tra Mantova e la Sicilia nel Cinquecento.* 3 vols. Florence.

Zambelli, P. 1964. "Bartolomeo di Castello." *Dizionario biografico degli italiani* 6: 707–8.

Zamora, M. J. 1993. "La *Gigantomaquia* griega de Claudiano. Manuscritos, transmisión textual, atribución de autor y fecha de composición." *Cuadernos de filología clásica (Estudios griegos e indoeuropeos)* 3: 347–75.

Zanato, T. 2002. "Indagini sulle rime di Pietro Bembo." *Studi di filologia italiana* 60: 141–216.

Zeidberg, D. S. ed. 1998. *Aldus Manutius and Renaissance Culture: Essays in Memory of Franklin D. Murphy. Acts of an International Conference, Venice and Florence, 14–17 June 1994.* With the assistance of Gioffredi Superbi, F. Florence.

Zeitlin, J. 1924. *The Life of Solitude by Francis Petrarch.* Urbana, IL.

Zetzel, J. E. G. ed. 1995. *Cicero, De Re Publica: Selections.* Cambridge Greek and Latin Classics. Cambridge.

———. ed. 1999. *Cicero: On the Commonwealth and On the Laws.* Cambridge Texts in the History of Political Thought. Cambridge.

Zissos, A. 1999. "The Rape of Proserpina in Ovid *Met.* 5.341–661: Internal Audience and Narrative Distortion." *Phoenix* 53: 97–113.

Zorzi, E. 1962. "Un antiquario padovano del secolo XVI: Alessandro Maggi da Bassano." *Bollettino del Museo civico di Padova* 51: 41–98.

Zwierlein, O. 1986. "Lucans Caesar in Troja." *Hermes* 114.4: 460–78. Reprinted as "Lucan's Caesar at Troy" in Tesoriero. 411–32.

Index of Passages

General Index

Index of Latin Words

Index of Greek Words

About the Type

The text of this book is set in the modern font known as Bembo. This font is based directly on that devised by Francesco Griffo, Aldo Manuzio's master type cutter, for the 1496 edition of Pietro Bembo's *De Aetna*. At the instigation of the distinguished English typographer and historian of printing Stanley Morison (1889–1967), the original Aldine font was revived by the Monotype Corporation in 1929. It remains an irony that the name Bembo is perhaps best known today for Pietro's association with a typeface that he himself did not design.